Study Guide

for use with

Fundamentals of Financial Accounting

Second Edition

Fred Phillips
University of Saskatchewan

Robert Libby
Cornell University - Ithaca

Patricia Libby
Ithaca College

Prepared by
Cheryl Bartlett
Albuquerque Technical Vocational Institute

Mc Graw Hill **McGraw-Hill Irwin**

Boston   Burr Ridge, IL   Dubuque, IA   Madison, WI   New York   San Francisco   St. Louis
Bangkok   Bogotá   Caracas   Kuala Lumpur   Lisbon   London   Madrid   Mexico City
Milan   Montreal   New Delhi   Santiago   Seoul   Singapore   Sydney   Taipei   Toronto

Study Guide for use with
FUNDAMENTALS OF FINANCIAL ACCOUNTING
Fred Phillips, Robert Libby, and Patricia Libby

Published by McGraw-Hill/Irwin, an imprint of The McGraw-Hill Companies, Inc., 1221 Avenue of the Americas, New York, NY 10020. Copyright © 2008 by The McGraw-Hill Companies, Inc. All rights reserved.

1 2 3 4 5 6 7 8 9 0 BKM/BKM 0 9 8 7

ISBN   978-0-07-313658-5
MHID   0-07-313658-1

www.mhhe.com

Contents

CHAPTER 1
BUSINESS DECISIONSAND FINANCIAL ACCOUNTING

ORGANIZATION OF THE CHAPTER

Understand the business	**Study the accounting methods**	**Evaluate the results**	**Review the chapter**

- Organizational forms
- Accounting for business
  decisions
	- The basic accounting equation
	- Financial statements
		- Relevance to financial
		  statement users
		- Reliability of results
			- Demonstration case
			- Chapter summary
			- Key terms
			- Practice material

CHAPTER FOCUS SUGGESTIONS

Introduction

The most common question asked by students taking an introductory accounting class is: "Why do I have to take an accounting class? It's just like algebra...I'll never use it real-life." Followed by something like, "Besides, I'm going to be a video-game programmer...I don't need to know accounting to do that." (Note that 'video-game programmer' can be easily replaced with any of the following: rock star, fashion model, etc.)

The truth is that the people who *don't* understand accounting and *don't* think they need to learn accounting are the people who need it most! The prospective loan officer mentioned earlier probably sees at least *some* benefit in taking this class. But, it's the video-game programmer, rock star, etc. who would benefit most from an accounting class. For example, the rock star will need someone to keep track of the money while he/she tours the country. But, what happens when the rock star comes back from the tour and discovers that the bookkeeper flew off to the Bahamas with all the cash?

Or maybe you'd like to know how it was possible for Enron and Arthur Andersen to mislead millions of investors without anybody suspecting a thing...especially if *you* ever considered investing in the stock market. You wouldn't want that rock star scenario replayed with *your money*, would you? This course will show you what allowed these types of events to occur and the controls that might have prevented them.

Need a more personal example? Ok. You get paychecks from your employer, right? What a bummer it would be if you went to pick up your paycheck one day and discover that the entire company has closed its doors and filed for bankruptcy protection. It sure would have been nice if you could *understand* those financial reports your company gave you every year....you know...the ones you always threw out? You might have been able to anticipate the company's dire situation BEFORE it declared bankruptcy and secured a new job elsewhere before everything hit the fan. You can pretty much kiss that last paycheck goodbye. So, you see, there are many reasons for having a basic understanding of accounting, financial statements, and the rules that are followed in preparing these statements.

Review

Before getting into chapter specifics, let's take a quick peek at some important information in your text. When you read a chapter in a new text, it's easy to be so overwhelmed with the information it contains that you fail to focus on the key information. So, here are a few things for you to focus on throughout the text. First, you probably noticed that there is information shown in the margins of the text. These are very important in helping you understand the material and reinforcing important concepts in each chapter. A brief explanation of each follows:

1) LEARNING OBJECTIVES: These let you know where each Learning Objective is introduced. This can be especially useful when working the exercises and problems at the end of the chapter since they are linked to the corresponding Learning Objective covered in that exercise or problem. Look for the LO1, LO2, etc. next to each exercise/problem indicating the Learning Objective(s) covered.

2) COACH'S TIP: These should never be omitted when you read the chapter. They contain critical, helpful information and should be read after the related paragraph. They provide exactly what you think they do: coaching—that is, guidance on the particular topic presented in the reading. Skipping this icon could create holes in your understanding of the material.

3) **YOU SHOULD KNOW**: These provide quick, understandable definitions of new vocabulary words presented in the chapter. These definitions are more in-depth than those presented in the reading. The vocabulary words defined are easy to identify in the text because they are **bolded.** Definitions of these terms are provided in the margin next to the line where the word is first used. These are great to review for an exam.

4) **TOPIC TACKLER PLUS**: For a fresh, animated tour of various topics throughout the text numerous tutorials are provided in the CD that accompanies your text. These animated tutorials help make learning fun, and provide you with active participation in your learning. It gets your nose out of the book and gives you something visual to enhance your understanding of particularly difficult concepts.

6) **HOW'S IT GOING? A Self-Study Quiz**: These short self-study quizzes are placed strategically throughout each chapter immediately following important concepts or calculations. Take a few minutes to work *every* one of these. They will provide you with immediate feedback about your understanding of the concept.

7) **REVIEW THE CHAPTER/Demonstration Case**: These are important learning tools that will help you immensely in understanding the material. At the end of every chapter there is a problem that is cumulative in nature, along with a step-by-step demonstration of how to approach solving it. Attempt to solve the problem yourself first, and then look at the suggested solution to see if you have the mastered the concepts it covers.

Next, we come to the information that will make your study of accounting more interesting, informative, and fun! These are meant to bring a bit of the 'real-world' into the course because sometimes it's easy to get so immersed in the details of financial statement preparation that you forget this information has *real* value to you and impacts nearly every aspect of your life. Failure to read these items will not impede your learning, but you will miss out on the interesting, enlightening, and humorous *real-life* aspects of accounting you probably never knew existed.

8) **ETHICAL INSIGHTS**: Reading these will help you understand *why* all of these accounting rules exist in the first place! Unethical and downright fraudulent behavior in the business world has made ethics a critical part of accounting programs across the country. All business students should be keenly aware of how ethics (or the lack of it) impacts businesses.

Now, you're ready to embark on the journey to learn financial accounting. While financial accounting can be challenging, it is also incredibly interesting and will provide you a better understanding of many events occurring in the business world today. You are fortunate to be taking a course like this now because you will see that nearly all the scandals you've heard about in business world today involve accounting!

Specifically, they involve the manipulation of the basic *financial statements* by unethical persons. These financial shenanigans can impact the lives of numerous people and businesses. This is especially true for the individual *financial statement users* who rely on the information presented to them on the income statement, retained earnings statement, balance sheet, and statement of cash flows. Heck, this course has all the elements of a great murder mystery!

UNDERSTAND THE BUSINESS

> **Learning Objective 1**
> Describe various organizational forms and business decision-makers

Organizational Forms
When Mauricio Rosa wanted to open his gourmet pizza restaurant in New York, his certified public accountant, Laurie Hensley, described the three most common forms of business:

1. Sole Proprietorship
This is the most common form of business. It is owned and usually managed by one individual. Since it typically requires nothing more than a business license to begin, it is the easiest form of business. The owner reports all profits and/or losses and is personally liable for the debts of the business.

2. Partnership
This form of business is exactly what it appears to be: simply two or more people who go into business together with the intention of making a profit. In a Partnership, the profits, losses, and debts of the business are shared by two or more owners. Formation usually includes the development of a partnership agreement, often drawn up by a

lawyer, that specifically addresses how all profits, losses, etc. are split among the partners; how new partners are added; and what is required when existing partners leave the partnership. The biggest advantage gained from this form of business is that there are more financial resources and business knowledge available to the partnership because there are more individuals involved.

3. *Corporation*

A corporation is recognized as an entity separate from its owners from both a legal and an accounting perspective. As such, the corporation (rather than the individuals who own it) is responsible for its profits, losses, and debts. This is a major advantage to owners. On the downside, the costs of setting up a corporation can be substantial.

A corporation essentially sells chunks of itself to many, many individuals. These chunks of ownership are represented by a legal document called a stock certificate. Owners of stock in a company are called stockholders. Companies whose stock is bought and sold (traded) on public stock exchanges are called *public companies,* while companies whose stock is owned and traded among only a few individuals are called *private companies.* Most companies you are familiar with are public companies.

Accounting for Business Decisions

Regardless of the *form* that a business chooses to operate, *all* businesses must gather and report the results of their business activities on financial statements. This process of analyzing, recording, and summarizing the results of a business's activities is called ***accounting.*** Accounting is often referred to as the 'language of business' because it is such an important facet of every business.

An accountant who is hired as an employee of a business is called a 'private accountant', while someone who provides advice on key business decisions, like Laurie, is a 'public accountant'.

The accounting system generates two types of reports:
1) Financial accounting reports (called *financial statements*) provided to external users such as
   a) Creditors
      a) Banks use the information to determine repayment risk for loans taken out by a business
      b) Suppliers evaluate whether a business can pay for goods or services provided.
   b) Investors
      a) Stockholders evaluate whether a business is financially stable and profitable
   c) Other external users
      a) Customers need to know if future services can be provided on its products and if warranties can be honored
      b) Various local, state, and federal governments collect taxes on the basis of financial statements
2) Managerial accounting reports provided only to internal users such as managers. These reports include detailed financial plans and continually updated reports about the financial performance of the company.

STUDY THE ACCOUNTING METHODS

> **Learning Objective 2**
> Describe the purpose, structure, and content of the four basic financial statements

The Basic Accounting Equation

One of the most important concepts to understanding financial reports is that **what a company owns must equal what a company owes to its creditors and stockholders.** This concept is illustrated below:

Resources Owned..... By the company are called	=	Resources Owed.... To creditors are called	+	To stockholders are called
ASSETS	**=**	**LIABILITIES**	**+**	**STOCKHOLDERS' EQUITY**

This relationship between assets (A), liabilities (L), and stockholders' equity (SE) is called the **basic accounting equation**. It is the business itself that is recognized as the *owning the assets and owing the liabilities of the business*...not the owners of the stock. This is called the **separate entity assumption**.

1. *Assets*

An **asset** is any resource controlled by the company that has measurable value and is expected to provide future benefits for the company.

2. *Liabilities*

A **liability** is a measurable amount owed to a creditor. Common liabilities include (but are not limited to):

(a) Accounts Payable – when a company buys goods from another company on credit (a promise to pay the amount due at a later date)

(b) Notes Payable – a legal document that banks require borrowers to sign which describes details about he company's promise to repay the bank.

(c) Wages Payable – amounts still owed to employees for services performed for the business.

(d) Any account with the word 'payable' in its name is considered a liability.

3. Stockholders' Equity

Stockholders' equity represents the owners' claims to the business. Owners' claims result in two ways:

(a) Contributed Capital – Owners have a claim because of direct investments they have made into the business

(b) Retained Earnings – Owners have a claim on amounts the company has earned through profitable business operations.

(i) Net Income – the profits of a business are the difference between revenues and expenses.

REVENUES	–	EXPENSES	=	NET INCOME

4. Revenues

Revenues are the sales of goods and services to customers.

5. Expenses

Expenses are all of the costs of doing business necessary to earn revenues. Expenses are 'incurred' in order to generate revenues. That is, the activities giving rise to a cost (using electricity or running an ad) have occurred.

6. Net Income

As shown earlier, Net Income is generated when a business earns more revenues than it incurs expenses. A 'Net Loss' occurs when the Revenues generated are *less* than the expenses incurred – a situation that no business likes to find itself in. A portion of the net income is left in the business to accumulate (retained earnings), and some is given out to its owners for their personal use (dividends).

7. Dividends

Dividends are distributions of a company's earnings to its stockholders. Dividends are paid to stockholders periodically as a return on their investment. The most common and simplest form of dividend is paid in cash. **Dividends are not an expense of the company** because they are given at the discretion of the stockholders…not as a necessary cost of doing business.

Financial Statements

The term *financial statements* usually refers to the following four basic financial reports:

1) Income Statement – Net income is a measure of financial performance over a period of time – like a feature film, accumulating events that occur over a period of time.

2) Statement of Retained Earnings – reports the amount of net income and the distribution of dividends over a period of time for a particular business.

3) Balance Sheet – the basic accounting equation is the structure for the balance sheet. Its purpose is to report a company's financial position at a specific point in time – like a snapshot of the company.

4) Statement of Cash Flows – none of the statements described above indicates how a business gets and spends its money. The statement of cash flows provides this information in some detail.

Financial statements can be prepared at any time, but the most common reporting periods are:

a) Monthly Reports – every month

b) Quarterly Reports – every three months

c) Annual Reports – every year

A business may choose any date for the end of their accounting (or fiscal year). Many choose December 31 (called a calendar-year end), but some have chosen January 31, March 31, or June 30 for their fiscal year-end.

1. The Income Statement

- Also called the statement of operations
- Usually the first statement prepared.
- The heading identifies who (the name of the business), what (the name of the report), and when (the time period covered by the report). A fourth line may be included to report amounts rounded to the nearest thousand or million.

- The unit-of-measure assumption says that reports of all U.S. based companies are reported in U.S. dollars. The financial reports of companies based in foreign countries will be shown in the currency used in that country.

The income statement has three major sections reported in this order:

Revenues:
1) Individual types of revenues earned by the business are reported in this section. Usually the largest, most relevant revenue is listed first.
2) Note that goods and services can be provided to a customer in one month...but the business may collect the money from the customer until a later month. So, total revenues earned by a business do not necessarily equal total cash collections from its customers.
3) After all revenue account balances have been listed, the amounts are subtotaled.
4) A dollar sign appears at the top and bottom of a column of numbers.

Expenses:
1) Individual types of expenses incurred by the business are reported in this section. Again, the largest, most relevant expense is usually listed first.
2) Note that a business may incur expenses in one month...but, may not pay for those expenses until a later month. So, total expenses incurred by a business do not necessarily equal total cash payments to its vendors.
3) After all expense account balances have been listed, the amounts are subtotaled.
4) A dollar sign appears at the top and bottom of a column of numbers.

Net income: T
1) Net Income is now calculated using the formulas presented earlier. Total expenses are subtracted from total revenues.

REVENUES	–	EXPENSES	=	NET INCOME

2) The net income amount is double-underlined to emphasize the importance of this figure on the report. The amount will also have a dollar sign.
3) The following is a sample income statement:

Jane's Janitorial Income Statement For the Month Ended June 30, 2008				Who: Name of the business What: Title of the statement When: Accounting period
Revenues:				
Sales Revenue		$ 7,000		Revenue earned from providing services to customers
Total Revenue		7,000		**Total amount earned during June**
Expenses:				
Wages Expense	$ 3,000			Cost of employee wages for work done in June
Rent Expense	1,200			Cost of rent for the month of June
Insurance Expense	400			Cost of insurance coverage for June
Advertising Expense	200			Cost of advertising done in June
Utilities Expense	700			Cost of utilities used in June
Supplies Expense	500			Cost of supplies used in providing janitorial services
Total Expenses		6,000		**Total amount incurred in June to generate revenues**
Net Income		$ 1,000		**Difference between total revenues and total expenses**

2. **The Statement of Retained Earnings**
- This statement tells how much of the earnings generated by a business have been accumulated by the business and how much has been given to owners in the form of dividends. (Note: a brand new company will have no beginning retained earnings since it has not had the opportunity to accumulate any earnings yet.)
- The heading identifies who (the name of the business), what (the name of the report), and when (the time period covered by the report). As with the Income Statement, a fourth line may be presented for large companies.

- The presentation on the statement of retained earnings is shown below:

Beginning Retained Earnings	+	Net Income	-	Dividends Declared	=	Ending Retained Earnings

- If a net loss (expenses exceed revenues) had occurred, the net loss would be subtracted on the statement of retained earnings in place of adding the net income. The Net Income (or Net Loss) amount is taken directly from the Income Statement.
- The ending retained earnings balance is double-underlined and has a dollar sign.
- The following is a sample Statement of Retained Earnings:

Jane's Janitorial Statement of Retained Earnings For the Month Ended June 30, 2008		Who: Name of the business What: Title of the statement When: Accounting period
Retained earnings, June 1, 2008	$ 400	**Last period's ending retained earnings balance**
Add: Net Income	1,000	As reported on the Income Statement
Subtract: Dividends	500	Distributions to stockholders in the period
Retained earnings, June 30, 2008	$ 900	**This period's ending retained earnings balance**

3. The Balance Sheet

- Also called the statement of financial position
- Reports the amounts of the company's Assets, Liabilities, and Stockholders' Equity at a particular point in time.
- The heading identifies who (the name of the business), what (the name of the report), and when. Unlike the previous reports, the balance sheet has is dated at a specific point in time.
- The Balance Sheet is based on the basic accounting equation, so it includes three sections:

ASSETS	=	LIABILITIES	+	STOCKHOLDERS' EQUITY

- In the first section, assets are listed in order of how soon they are to be used or turned into cash. The total of this section MUST EQAUL the combined totals of the remaining two sections.
- In the second section, liabilities are listed in order of how soon each is to be paid or settled.
- The third section completes the equality of the basic accounting equation.

Assets:
1) Cash is reported first.
2) Accounts Receivable represents the amount that the business has the right to collect from customers for prior sales made on credit.
3) Supplies reported indicates the cost of supplies that remain on hand (unused) on the last day of the accounting period.
4) Assets are reported on the balance sheet based on their original cost to the company.

Liabilities:
1) Accounts Payable represents amounts still owed to suppliers for purchases made by the business, on account.
2) Notes Payable represents any written promise to repay loans from the bank.
3) Liabilities are financial obligations of the business arising from past business activities.
4) Assets are reported on the balance sheet based on their original cost to the company.

Stockholders' Equity:
1) Contributed capital reflects all contributions made by the stockholders.
2) Retained Earnings includes all earnings still remaining in the business as of the date of the report.
3) The Retained Earnings figure on the balance sheet MUST equal the double-underlined amount reported on the statement of retained earnings.

- A sample Balance Sheet is shown on the following page:

Jane's Janitorial Balance Sheet June 30, 2008		Who: Name of the business What: Title of the statement When: Point in time
Assets		
Cash	$15,000	Amount of cash in the business bank account
Accounts Receivable	3,000	Amount owed to Jane's for prior work performed
Supplies	2,000	Amount of janitorial supplies on hand
Equipment	10,000	Cost of janitorial equipment used in business
Total Assets	$30,000	**Total amount of the business's resources**
Liabilities		
Accounts Payable	$ 2,000	Amt. due to suppliers for prior purchases on credit
Notes Payable	18,000	Amount of loan owed to the bank
Total Liabilities	20,000	**Total claims on the resources by creditors**
Stockholders' Equity		
Contributed Capital	$ 9,100	Amt. contributed to the company by stockholders
Retained Earnings	900	Amt. kept in business from Stmt of Ret. Earnings
Total Stockholders' Equity	10,000	Total claims on the resources by stockholders
Total Liabilities and Stockholders' equity	$30,000	**Total claims on the business's resources**

4. The Statement of Cash Flows

- Includes only those activities that result in cash changing hands during a specified period of time.

The statement of cash flows is divided into three categories of business activities:

❖ *Operating*: these are activities that are directly related to running the business to earn a profit.

❖ *Investing*: these are activities that involve buying and selling productive resources. These items have long lives…such as buildings, land, and equipment.

❖ *Financing:* these activities include any borrowing from banks, repayment of bank loans, contributions from stockholders, and payment of dividends to stockholders.

- The following is a sample Statement of Cash Flows:

Jane's Janitorial Statement of Cash Flows For the Month Ended June 30, 2008		Who: Name of the business What: Title of the statement When: Accounting Period
Cash Flows from Operating Activities		**Directly related to earning income**
Cash from customers	$6,000	Amount of cash received from customers
Cash to suppliers and employees	(2,500)	Amt. of cash paid to suppliers and employees
Cash provided by operating activities	3,500	Cash inflow minus outflow ($6,000 – 2,500)
Cash Flows from Investing Activities		Related to the sale/purchase of productive assets
Cash to buy equipment	(10,000)	Amount of cash spend on equipment
Cash used in investing activities	(10,000)	
Cash Flows from Financing Activities		Activities with investors and banks
Capital contributed by stockholders	$ 2,900	Amount of cash received from owners
Cash dividends paid to stockholders	(900)	Amount of cash paid to owners
Cash borrowed from the bank	18,000	Amount of cash received from the bank
Cash provided by financing activities	$20,000	
Change in cash	13,500	Sum of three flows [$3,500+ ($10,000) +$20,000]
Cash balance, June 1, 2008	1,500	Cash at beginning of June
Cash balance, June 30, 2008	$15,000	Amount reported on the balance sheet for June

5. Notes to the Financial Statements

- The notes are an important part of the financial statements and provide additional information about the company that the user would not know otherwise. Notes are covered later in the text.

6. Relationships among the Financial Statements

- Net income is used to determine ending retained earnings on the statement of retained earnings.
- The figure derived on the statement of retained earnings is reported on the balance sheet at the end of the period.

EVALUATE THE RESULTS
Relevance to Financial Statement Users

Learning Objective 3
Explain how financial statements are relevant to others.

External users rely on financial statements to provide key information like the following:

1. *Creditors are mainly interested in assessing two things:*
   - Is the company generating enough cash to make payments on its loan? This answer to this question can be obtained from the statement of cash flows. Specifically, creditors would look at the Cash Flows from Operating Activities section to see if positive cash flows are being produced. Jane's operating activities are contributing $3,500 to its cash account. This is a good sign.

   - Does the company have enough assets to cover its liabilities? The answer to this question comes from comparing the levels of assets and liabilities on the balance sheet. Jane's assets of $30,000 are enough to pay off its debt of $20,000. But, the fact that there's not much leeway here, might concern a creditor.

2. *Investors are primarily interested in one of two things:*
   - Earning an immediate return on their contributions to a company (through dividends) or
   - Earning a long-term return (by selling stock certificates at a price higher than what they were bought for).

Dividend payments to owners and higher stock prices are more likely if a company is profitable. So, investors are most interested in the Income Statement (and statement of retained earnings) for this type of information.

Reliability of Financial Statements

1. *Generally Accepted Accounting Principles*

Learning Objective 4
Describe factors that enhance the reliability of financial reporting

   - The primary responsibility for setting the underlying rules of accounting lays with the **Financial Accounting Standards Board (FASB).**
   - The FASB (and its predecessors) publish a group of statements that are the primary source of accounting rules, called **generally accepted accounting principles** or **GAAP** for short.
   - These rules state that financial accounting information should be useful to managers, creditors, stockholders, and others that require confidence in the financial statements presented. Usefulness has been defined as information that is:

     1. Relevant – helpful in making decisions.
     2. Reliable – unbiased and verifiable.
     3. Comparable – can be compared to other companies.
     4. Consistent – follows the same rules over time.

Key Concepts for External Financial Reporting	
Objectives:	To provide useful financial information to external users for decision making
Characteristics of Useful Information:	Relevance, reliability, comparability, consistency
Elements:	Assets, liabilities, stockholders' equity, revenues, expenses
Assumptions:	Unit of measure, separate entity, going concern, time period
Principles:	Cost, revenue recognition, matching, full disclosure
Constraints:	Cost-benefit, materiality, industry practices, conservatism

   - The managers of a company have the primary responsibility for ensuring that GAAP is followed. For greater assurance, public companies (and some private companies) hire independent auditors to scrutinize their financial records.
   - These auditors follow rules approved by the **Public Company Accounting Oversight Board (PCAOB).** They provide their opinion on whether or not the financial statements of the company represent (in most important aspects) what they claim to represent, *and* whether they follow GAAP.
   - The **Securities and Exchange Commission (SEC)** is the governmental agency that oversees the work of the FASB and the PCAOB.

2. *Accounting Ethics*

- The CEO (chief executive officer) and the CFO (chief financial officer) lead management.
- Since management is responsible for following GAAP, problems can arise of members of management are unethical.
- Management of *Enron, WorldCom, Global Crossing,* and *Xerox* were found to have misrepresented the financial results of their respective companies. Top executives in these companies were convicted of fraud and sentenced to lengthy prison terms.
- As a result, the U.S. Congress created the **Sarbanes-Oxley Act of 2002 (SOX)** impacting managers and auditors of public companies. Some highlights of the act are:
  - ❖ Top managers are required to sign a report certifying their responsibilities for the financial statements
  - ❖ An audited system of internal controls must be maintained by the company to help ensure the accuracy of information contained in accounting reports
  - ❖ Maintain an independent committee that ensures managers cooperate with auditors
- Consequences for failure to adhere to SOX, if corporate executives are found guilty of accounting fraud are:
  - ❖ Up to 20 years in prison, and
  - ❖ Up to $5,000,000 in fines
- The American Institute of Certified Public Accountants (AICPA) requires all of its members to adhere to a professional code of ethics and professional auditing standards.
- Intentional financial misrepresentation is unethical and illegal. The impacts of fraud are not limited to management of a company. Consider the following:
  - ❖ Stock prices of a company drop dramatically when fraud is discovered
  - ❖ Creditors often receive much less on amounts owed to them than they are entitled to
  - ❖ Employees not only lose their jobs, but may also lose any/all retirement savings
  - ❖ Customers bear the brunt of the fraud because the costs associated with fraudulent activity must be passed on in the form of higher prices to consumers
- When faced with an ethical dilemma, follow this three-step process:
  - ❖ Identify who will benefit from the situation and who will be harmed by it
  - ❖ Identify the alternative courses of action
  - ❖ Choose the alternative that is the most ethical – an action that you would be proud to report to anyone. Often, there is no one right answer and hard choices will need to be made.

Epilogue

Mauricio Rosa's dream has become reality and **Pizza Aroma** has been voted the "Best Pizza" by the *Ithaca Times* readers' poll several years in a row.

CHAPTER 1 SUPPLEMENT: ACCOUNTING CAREERS

Accounting is one of the fastest growing fields according the government's labor department.

- Private Accounting. Accountants employed by a single organization.
- Public Accounting. Accountants who charge fees for service performed to a variety of organizations.
- Jobs available to new accountants include CPA – Certified public accountant. Many new graduates begin their careers in CPA firms; the Internal Revenue Service (IRS); Federal Bureau of Investigation (FBI), not-for-profit organizations (NPOs)

Certifications available to accountants include:
- CPA (Certified Public Accountant), CFE (Certified Fraud Examiner), CMA (Certified Management Accountant), CIA (Certified Internal Auditor), CFM (Certified Financial Manager), Cr. FA (Certified Forensic Accountant), and CFA (Chartered Financial Analyst)

REVIEW THE CHAPTER

Chapter Summary
LO1. Describe various organizational forms and business decision-makers.
  ❖ Sole proprietorships are owned by one individual, are relatively inexpensive to form, and are not treated legally as separate from their owners. Thus, all profits or losses become part of the taxable income to the owner who is also responsible personally for all debts of the business.
  ❖ Partnerships are businesses similar legally to proprietorships, but with two or more owners.
  ❖ Corporations are separate legal entities (thus, corporations pay taxes) that sell shares of stock to investors (stockholders) and are more costly to establish. Stockholders cannot be held liable for more than their investment in the corporation. Private corporations sell stock to a few individual s while public corporations sell stock in the stock market.
  ❖ Business decision makers include creditors (banks, suppliers), investors (stockholders), customers, governments, and other external users.

LO2. Describe the purpose, structure, and content of the four basic financial statements.
  ❖ The *income statement* reports the net amount that business earned (net income) over a period of time by subtracting the costs of running the business (expenses) from the total amount earned (revenues).
  ❖ The *statement of retained earnings* explains changes in the retained earnings account over a period of time y considering increases (from net income) and decreases (from dividends to stockholders).
  ❖ The *balance sheet* reports, what the business owns (reported as assets) at a particular point in time and whether the financing for these assets came from creditors (reported as liabilities) or stockholders (reported as stockholders' equity).
  ❖ The *statement of cash flows* explains changes in the cash account over a period of time by reporting inflows and outflows of cash from the business's operating, investing, and fiancing activities.

LO3. Explain how financial statements are relevant to users.
  ❖ Creditors are mainly interested in assessing whether the company: (1) is generating enough cash to make payments on its loan, and (2) has enough assets to cover its liabilities. Answers to these questions are indicated by the statement of cash flows and the balance sheet.
  ❖ Investors look closely at the income statement for information about a company's ability to generate profits, and at the statement of retained earnings for information about a company's dividend distributions.

LO4. Describe factors that enhance the reliability of financial reporting.
  ❖ Reliable financial reporting is enhanced by applying generally accepted accounting principles in an ethical business environment.
  ❖ Reliable financial reporting is further enhanced through the involvement of regulators, like the Public Company Accounting Oversight Board (PCAOB) and the Securities and Exchange Commission (SEC), and regulations like the Sarbanes-Oxley Act of 2002.

READ AND RECALL QUESTIONS
After you read each section of the chapter, answer the related Read and Recall Questions below.

LEARNING OBJECTIVE
After studying this section of the chapter, you should be able to:
1. Describe various organizational forms and business decision makers.

Organizational Forms
Define the three main ways a business can be organized.

What is a sole proprietorship? What is a partnership? What is the biggest difference between these two forms of business organizations?

What is a corporation? In what important way does a corporation differ from either a sole proprietorship or a partnership?

Explain the difference between a public company and a private company.

Accounting for Business Decisions
Define accounting.

Who are the primary users of Financial accounting reports? Who are the primary users of Managerial accounting reports?

Define a creditor.

Define an investor.

LEARNING OBJECTIVE
After studying this section of the chapter, you should be able to:
2. Describe the purpose, structure, and content of the four basic financial statements.

The Basic Accounting Equation
What is the basic accounting equation?

Define the separate-entity assumption. Why is it important in accounting?

What are assets, liabilities, and stockholders' equity?

What is an Account Receivable?

What is an Account Payable?

Name the two components in Stockholders' equity. What do they represent? What are dividends?

Define Revenues.

Define Expenses.

What is Net income? What is Net Loss?

Define Dividends.

Financial Statements
What is another name for the Income Statement?

Define the unit-of-measure assumption.

Give an example of an account for each of the following. (1) revenue, (2) expense.

What percentage of new businesses will fail or close within the first six years of opening? Why?

What information does a statement of retained earnings provide to users?

What is the equation for the Statement of Retained Earnings?   Besides Retained Earnings itself, what two items are contained on the statement of retained earnings?

What is another name for the Balance Sheet?

How does the heading of the balance sheet from the other financial statements? Why?

What order are assets listed on the balance sheet? What order are liabilities listed on the balance sheet?

Define a Note Payable. What distinguishes it from an account payable?

List the three main sections of a statement of cash flows.   Briefly describe each one.

What are financial statement notes?

LEARNING OBJECTIVE
After studying the section of the chapter, you should be able to:
3. Explain how financial statements are relevant to users.

Relevance to Financial Statement Users
What are the two primary things creditors are interested in assessing? Which financial statement is best for evaluating each?

What are two things that investors are looking for information on? Which financial statement is best for evaluating each?

LEARNING OBJECTIVE
After studying the section of the chapter, you should be able to:
4. Describe factors that enhance the reliability of financial reporting.

Reliability of Financial Statements
Define generally accepted accounting principles.

What is the FASB? What is its purpose?

What are the four criteria used to determine if financial information is useful to managers, creditors, stockholders, and others?

What is the PCAOB? What is its purpose?

What is the SEC? What is its purpose?

Describe the purpose of the Sarbanes-Oxley Act of 2002. What events led to its enactment?

What are the possible consequences to corporate executives found guilty of committing accounting fraud?

Who, besides corporate executives, suffer as the result of accounting fraud? How are they affected?

What is the three-step process that should be followed when you are faced with an ethical dilemma?

Chapter 1 Supplement: Accounting Careers
What types of jobs can new graduates in accounting look for?

What types of certifications are available to accounting professionals?

FINANCIAL ANALYSIS TOOLS

1. **Financial Statement Headings:** Use the table below to identify the appropriate heading for each of the four basic financial statements.

	Balance Sheet	**Income Statement**	**Statement of Retained Earnings**	**Statement of Cash Flows**
Who	XYZ Corporation	XYZ Corporation	XYZ Corporation	XYZ Corporation
What	Balance Sheet	Income Statement	Statement of Retained Earnings	Statement of Cash Flows
When	December 31, 20XX	For the Year Ended December 31, 20XX	For the Year Ended December 31, 20XX	For the Year Ended December 31, 20XX

2. The following table summarizes the main points for each of the four basic financial statements.

Financial Statement	*Purpose:* **To report**	*Structure*	*Examples of Content*
1. Income Statement	The financial performance of the business *during the current accounting period.*	+ Revenues − Expenses = Net Income	*Sales Revenue* *Expenses* include wages expense, supplies expense, interest expense
2. Statement of Retained Earnings	The accumulation of earnings retained in the business *during the current accounting period* with that of prior periods.	+Beginning Retained Earnings +Net Income (this period) − Dividends (this period) =Ending Retained Earnings	*Net Income* is from the income statement. *Dividends* are amounts distributed this period to the owners.

3. Balance Sheet	The financial position of a business *at a point in time.*	Assets = Liabilities + Stockholders' Equity	*Assets* include Cash, receivables, supplies, equipment. *Liabilities* include accounts payable, notes payable. *Stockholders' Equity* includes contributed capital and retained earnings.
4. Statement of Cash Flows	Inflows (receipts) and outflows (payments) of cash *during the current accounting period.*	+/- Cash flows from operating activities +/- Cash flows from investing activities +/- Cash flows from financing activities =Change in cash +Beginning cash balance =Ending cash balance	*Operating Activities* include cash collected from customers and cash paid to suppliers *Investing Activities* include cash paid for equipment *Financing Activities* include cash borrowed from banks, cash from selling stock.

3. Here is a summary of the relations among financial statements

Statement	Item from Statement	→	Is also on this Statement
Income Statement	Net Income	→	Retained Earnings Statement
Retained Earnings Statement	Ending Retained Earnings	→	Balance Sheet
Statement of Cash Flows	Ending Cash	→	Balance Sheet

HELPFUL STUDY TIP

It's a bit of a challenge trying to remember which accounts go on which statements, what is presented on which statements, etc. So, this section is devoted to helping you learn to distinguish one statement from another, the items reported on the statements, and tricks to remember it all!!! The statements will be covered here in a slightly different order than the text.

1. INCOME STATEMENT-the only reason we're beginning with this statement is because it is the easiest to remember....there are only **TWO** types of items that go on this statement, they are:
- Revenues-Contain one or more of the following words in its account name: Sales, Earned, or Revenues
- Expenses-Nearly always have the word "Expense" in its account name.

Here's an easy way to remember them the items that go on the income statement, just remember the word **IRE**:

IRE	I	R	E
	Income Statement	Revenues	Expenses

2. STATEMENT OF RETAINED EARNINGS
This statement has two items on it that are obvious…Beginning and Ending retained earnings, so we won't worry about those too much. But it also has two more items. Just remember **RE-BEND**

RE-BEND	REBE	N	D
	Retained Earnings Beginning/Ending	Net Income	Dividends

3. BALANCE SHEET-for starters, just remember that the balance is simply the basic accounting equation.
Balance Sheet = Basic Accounting Equation

Then, write down the Basic Accounting Equation:
Assets = Liabilities + Stockholders' Equity
All that's left is a way to identify the types of items that belong in each of these three categories.
Assets are (1) usually (but not always) something you could actually touch; and (2) they are good things! Assets should meet both of these criteria (with a few exceptions). Here's another little hint. If you have absolutely no clue what something is….it's probably an asset.
☺ Remember assets are GOOD and make you HAPPY! ☺

Liabilities usually contain one of the following words in the account name: *payable* or *debt*. These are things we do not like: things we need to pay off, still owe money on, etc. Liabilities are pretty easy to identify because they are things we still owe or still have to pay. So, you will frequently see the word *payable* in the name of a liability, such as Accounts payable, Notes Payable, Mortgage Payable, Taxes Payable…you get the idea. This is the easiest way to identify *most* liabilities

☹ Remember, debt is BAD and makes you UNHAPPY! ☹

Stockholders' Equity only has two items and here's how you can remember them. These make a corporation feel very "**SECURE**" or **SECRE**

SE C RE	SE	C	RE
	Stockholders' Equity	Common Stock	Retained Earnings

4. STATEMENT OF CASH FLOWS

This statement has three categories that are shown in a specific order. To remember the order, just remember **OIF**. After that just add the beginning cash to come up with the ending cash.

OIF	O	I	F
	Operating	Investing	Financing

SELF-TEST QUESTIONS AND EXERCISES

MATCHING
1. *Match each of the key terms listed below with the appropriate textbook definition on the following page.*

_____ Accounting	_____ Net Income
_____ Accounts	_____ Partnership
_____ Assets	_____ Private companies
_____ Balance Sheet	_____ Public companies
_____ Basic Accounting Equation	_____ Revenues
_____ Corporation	_____ Separate Entity Assumption
_____ Dividends	_____ Sole proprietorship
_____ Expenses	_____ Statement of Cash Flows
_____ Financial Statements	_____ Statement of Retained Earnings
_____ Generally Accepted Accounting Principles (GAAP)	_____ Stockholders' Equity
_____ Income Statement	_____ Unit of Measure Assumption
_____ Liabilities	

A. The financial reports of a business are assumed to include the results of only that business's activities.
B. Periodic payments made by a company to its stockholders as a return on their investment??
C. Business organization owned by one person who is liable for debts that the business cannot pay.
D. Equal to revenues minus expenses
E. The results of a business's activities should be reported in an appropriate monetary unit
F. Have their stock bought and sold privately
G. Accounting reports that summarize the results of business activities
H. Sales of goods or services to customers
I. Business organizations owned by two or more people, who often are personally liable for the debts of the business
J. Also called the statement of operations
K. The main source of accounting rules
L. Operate as businesses separate from their owners.
M. Have their stock bought and sold on stock exchanges
N. Accumulate and report the effects of each different business activity
O. Summarizes how a business's operating, investing, and financing activities caused its cash balance to change over a particular period of time??
P. A system of analyzing, recording, and summarizing the results of a business's activities
Q. Reports the way that net income and the distribution of dividends affected the financial position of the company during the period
R. The amount invested and reinvested in the business by its owners
S. Assets are equal to liabilities plus stockholders' equity
T. Costs of the business that are necessary to earn revenues
U. Reports the amount of a business's assets, liabilities, and stockholders' equity at a particular point in time
V. Resources owned by a business
W. Amounts owed by the business

TRUE-FALSE QUESTIONS
For each of the following, enter a T or F in the blank to indicate whether the statement is true or false.

_____1. (LO1) The partners in a partnership are not personally liable for any debts that the partnership is unable to pay.

_____2. (LO1) A private accountant is one who works as an employee of his business.

_____3. (LO1) Financial accounting reports include detailed financial plans and continually updated reports about the financial performance of the company.

_____4. (LO1) Creditors are various local, state, and federal governments who collect taxes based on the financial statements of a business.

_____5. (LO2) The separate entity assumption does not allow a business to include the stockholders' personal transactions on its financial statements.

_____6. (LO2) An account payable is created when a company buys goods from another company by promising to pay for them at a later date.

_____7. (LO2) Retained earnings represent a claim on amounts that owners invested in the business by making direct contributions to the company.

_____8. (LO2) The income statement summarizes the financial results of business activities over a particular period of time.

_____9. (LO2) Companies are allowed to choose any date for the end of the accounting (or fiscal) year.

_____10. (LO2) A fourth line (under the date) in the heading of a financial statement indicates if the numbers reported are rounded to the nearest thousand or million.

_____11. (LO2) It is very uncommon for a business to provide goods or services to customers in one month, but not collect cash from them until a later month.

_____12. (LO2) The balance sheet provides a snapshot of resources (what the company owns) and claims to those resources at the end of that day.

_____13. (LO2) The statement of cash flows is divided into three categories of business activities: Operating, Accounting, and Financing.

_____14. (LO3) Creditors are particularly interested in the operating activities section of the statement of cash flows in assessing whether a company has enough assets to cover its liabilities.

_____15. (LO3) Investors look for either an immediate return on their contributions (by selling stock at a price higher than what they paid) or a long-term return (through dividends).

_____16. (LO3) Generally Accepted Accounting Principles are primarily created and published by the Securities and Exchange Commission (SEC).

_____17. (LO3) In order for financial information to be useful, users need to have confidence that the information is relevant, reliable, comfortable, and consistent.

_____18. (LO3) The Public Company Accounting Oversight Board (PCAOB) makes the rules used by auditors of public companies.

_____19. (LO3) The Sarbanes-Oxley Act of 2002 is a set of laws established to weaken corporate reporting in the United States.

_____20. (LO3) When faced with an ethical dilemma, an employee should identify who will benefit from the situation, identify the alternative courses of action, and choose the alternative that is most ethical.

MULTIPLE CHOICE QUESTIONS
Choose the best answer or response by placing the identifying letter in the space provided.

_____1. (LO1) Which of the following is *not* considered one of the three most common forms of business organization?
   a. Corporation
   b. Limited liability Company
   c. Sole proprietorship
   d. Partnership

_____2. (LO1) Companies that have their stock bought and sold on stock exchanges are referred to as
   a. Private company
   b. Internal company
   c. External company
   d. public company

_____3. (LO1) Which of the following is considered an external user of basic financial accounting reports?
   a. Managers
   b. Supervisors
   c. Employees
   d. Creditors

_____4. (LO1) All of the following are true statements regarding the use of financial statements by external users *except*:
a. Various local, state, and federal governments pay taxes based on them
b. Banks use them to evaluate the risk that they will not be repaid the money they loan out
c. Certain customers use them to judge the company's ability to provide future service on its products and honor warranties
d. Stockholders use them to evaluate whether the business is financially secure and likely to be a profitable investment

_____5. (LO2) All of the following are part of the basic accounting equation, *except*:
a. expenses
b. liabilities
c. assets
d. equity

_____6. (LO2) Which of the following accounts is an asset account?
a. Contributed capital
b. Accounts payable
c. Accounts receivable
d. Pizza Revenue

_____7. (LO2) Which of the following are true statements regarding notes payable?
a. They are amounts owed to investors
b. They are documented using a legal document
c. The amounts owed cannot be measured
d. They are forms of equity

_____8. (LO2) All of the following are true about stockholders' claims *except*:
a. Owners have a claim on amounts the company has earned through profitable business operations
b. Stockholders' claims represent the total amount after liabilities are added to assets
c. Owners will get more money back from the company than what they put in if the company generates income
d. owners have a claim on amounts they directly contributed to the company

_____9. (LO2) All of the following represent the frequency with which financial statements can be prepared *except*:
a. Monthly
b. Quarterly
c. Annually
d. All of these are valid periods that financial statements can be prepared

_____10. (LO2) Which of the following would *not* be found on an income statement?
a. Rent expense
b. Dividends
c. Revenues
d. Net income

_____11. (LO2) Which of the following is *not* a true statement regarding the income statement?
a. The equation for the income statement is Revenues + Expenses = Net Income
b. It is usually the first statement prepared
c. Usually the larges, most relevant revenue is listed first
d. It is common for a business to provide goods and services in one month and collect the cash in a later month

Copyright © 2008, The McGraw-Hill Companies, Inc.

Study Guide, Chapter 1

_____12. (LO2) The statement that shows the profits that have been accumulated in the business over time is:
   a.   income statement
   b.   statement of cash flows
   c.   statement of retained earnings
   d.   balance sheet

_____13. (LO2) Which of the following financial statements covers a specific point in time?
   a.   balance sheet
   b.   income statement
   c.   statement of retained earnings
   d.   statement of cash flows

_____14. (LO2) All of the following are categories found on the statement of cash flows *except*:
   a.   Financing activities
   b.   Operating activities
   c.   Debt activities
   d.   Investing activities

_____15. (LO3) Which of the following is *not* true regarding the relevance of financial information?
   a.   Investors look a delayed return on their contributions to a company through dividends
   b.   Creditors are interested in whether the company is generating enough cash to make payments on its loan
   c.   Investors are looking for a long-term return by selling stock at a price higher than what was paid by the investor
   d.   Creditors are interested in whether the company has enough assets to cover its liabilities

_____16. (LO4) Which of the following is not required in order for financial information to be considered useful?
   a.   The users need to have confidence that the information is relevant
   b.   The users need to have confidence that the information is profitable
   c.   The users need to have confidence that the information is comparable against other companies
   d.   The users need to have confidence that the information is consistent over time

_____17. (LO4) In determining whether, beyond a reasonable doubt, the financial statements represent what they claim to represent, auditors follow rules approved by which of the following?
   a.   PCAOB
   b.   AICPA
   c.   SEC
   d.   CEO

_____18. (LO4) In response to recent cases involving fraud and the misrepresentation of financial results of some companies, which of the following was created by the U.S. Congress in 2002?
   a.   SEC
   b.   SOX
   c.   GAAP
   d.   AICPA

_____19. (LO4) Which of the following is *not* an appropriate step for an employee to take when faced with an ethical dilemma?
   a.   Call the police
   b.   Identify who will benefit
   c.   Identify the alternative choice of action
   d.   Choose the alternative that is the most ethical

_____20. (LO4) All of the following are career choices for private accountants *except*
  a. Internal auditing
  b. budgeting
  c. cost accounting
  d. forensic accounting

EXERCISES
Record your answer to each exercise in the space provided. Show your work.

Exercise 1-1. Identify Important Accounting and Business Entities (LO1, LO2, LO3)
The following is a list of important individuals and entities in accounting and business. Match each with its corresponding definition on the following page (NOTE: Some entities may have more than one definition.)

_____ Auditors	_____ Internal Revenue Service
_____ Certified Public Accountants	_____ Partnership
_____ Corporation	_____ Private company
_____ Creditors	_____ Public company
_____ Financial Accounting Standards Board	_____ Public Company Accounting Oversight Board
_____ Financial Statement Users	_____ Securities and Exchange Commission

A. The individuals who follow the prescribed rules when evaluating a company's financials for compliance with GAAP
B. A business owes debt to these entities
C. A government agency with the power to establish accounting rules that public companies must follow
D. A business organization owned by two or more persons
E. Owners of this type of business are not personally liable for the debts of the business
F. A business whose stock is not traded on stock exchanges
G. Responsible for ensuring that businesses comply with federal tax laws
H. Owners of this type of business are called Stockholders or Shareholders
I. Currently recognizes the FASB as the authority in the United States for establishing accounting rules
J. These individuals are hired by public companies to provide an independent evaluation of their compliance with accounting rules
K. Those who, in part, base their business decisions on information reported in a company's financial statements
L. Establishes the rules used by auditors in determining whether a company's financials are in accordance with GAAP
M. Businesses that *operate* separately from their owners
N. Many accounting graduates begin their careers in a firm of these, oftentimes as auditors
O. A business whose stock is traded on stock exchanges
P. This type of business can issue stock to the greatest number of investors
Q. Establishes the underlying rules for financial reporting
R. Owners of this type of business are personally liable for debts that the business cannot pay

Exercise 1-2. Calculate missing amounts in the Basic Accounting Equation (LO2)
Use the balance sheet equation to calculate the missing item in each of the following six independent situations:

(NOTE: Each *column* is a separate case. The first one has been done for you)

Item	Case A	Case B	Case C	Case D	Case E	Case F
Assets	$16,000	(B)	$50,000	$4,000	(E)	$100,000
Liabilities	5,000	$22,000	18,000	(D)	$500	(F)
Stockholder's Equity	(A)	38,000	(C)	3,000	5,500	24,000

Case A: Case B:
16,000 –   5,000 = 11,000
Case C: Case D:

Case E: Case F:

Exercise 1-3. Balance Sheet Tasks (LO2)
Part A. Mark each item in the following list to indicate whether it would be reported as an Asset (A), Liability (L), or Stockholders' Equity (SE) account on the balance sheet, or NOT (N) on the balance sheet, for Steerz Corporation as of July 31, 20XX. (The first one has been done for you)

A	1. Cash	$640		9. Investments	370
	2. Contributed Capital	950		10. Notes Payable	250
	3. Cost of Goods Sold	230		11. Supplies	100
	4. Retained Earnings	?		12. Buildings	790
	5. Inventory	130		13. Dividends	110
	6. Revenues	930		14. Long-term debt	260
	7. Accounts Receivable	210		15. Income Tax Expense	50
	8. Land	840		16. Accounts Payable	540

Part B Using the information from Part A, determine the balance in Retained Earnings at July 31, 20XX for Steerz Corporation.

HINT: 1) Find all of the "A" items from **Part A** and total them up. 2) Do the same for the "L" and "SE" items. 3) Place each total into the accounting equation. 4) Find the amount that will make the equation equal on both sides.

Part C. Using **Part A** and **Part B**, prepare a Balance Sheet for Steerz Corporation as of July 31, 20XX.

Assets		**Liabilities**	
Cash	$ _____	Accounts Payable	$ _____
Accounts Receivable	_____	Notes Payable	_____
Inventory	_____	Long-term debt	_____
Supplies	_____	Total Liabilities	$ _____
Investments	_____	**Stockholders' Equity**	
Buildings	_____	Contributed Capital	$ _____
Land	_____	Retained Earnings	_____
		Total Stockholders' Equity	_____
Total Assets	$ _____	Total Liabilities and Stockholders' equity	$ _____

Exercise 1-4. Income Statement and Retained Earnings Statement Tasks (LO2)

Part A. Mark each item in the following list to indicate whether it would be reported as a Revenue (R), or an Expense (E) on the Income Statement, an item on the Statement of Retained Earnings (SR), or NOT (N) reported on either statement, for Steerz Corporation as of July 31, 20XX.

_____	1. Accounts Receivable	210	_____	7. Inventory	130
_____	2. General and Administrative	73	_____	8. Marketing and Other Operating Costs	94
_____	3. Retained Earnings, End	?	_____	9. Retained Earnings, Beginning	?
_____	4. Sales Revenue	1,085	_____	10. Cost of Goods Sold	425
_____	5. Dividends	110	_____	11. Interest Charges	104
_____	6. Income Taxes	50	_____	12. Advertising	81

Part B. Using information from Part A, prepare an Income Statement for Steerz Corporation as of July 31, 20XX.

Revenues:		
Sales Revenue		$ _____
Total Revenue		_____
Expenses:		
Cost of Goods Sold	$ _____	
Marketing and Other Operating Expenses	_____	
Advertising Expense	_____	
General and Administrative Expenses	_____	
Interest Expense	_____	
Income Tax Expense	_____	
Total Expenses		_____
Net Income		$ _____

Part C. Using the information from Part A, Part B and the retained earnings equation, compute the amount of beginning retained earnings.

> Hint: Use the Balance Sheet in **Exercise 1-3** to find some of the missing information. Remember that ALL Balance Sheet amounts are as of July 31, 20XX (i.e. they are ending amounts)

Exercise 1-5. Identify Cash Flow Statement Items to Business Activity Categories (LO2)

Mark each item in the list below with a letter to indicate whether it is a cash flow from Operating (O), Investing (I), or Financing (F) activities. Also place parenthesis ( ) around the letter if it is a cash outflow; if it is a cash inflow do not place parenthesis around the letter.

_____ 1. Cash received from selling land   _____ 6. Payments for inventory

_____ 2. Cash paid to suppliers   _____ 7. Expenditures to purchase equipment

_____ 3. Dividend payments to owners   _____ 8. Cash paid for principal on note payable

_____ 4. Cash paid to employees   _____ 9. Proceeds from selling our own stock

_____ 5. Cash collected from customers   _____ 10. Cash received from long-term borrowing

Exercise 1-6. Reporting Amounts on the Four Basic Financial Statements (LO2)

Using the figures listed in the table below and the equations underlying each of the four basic financial statements, show (a) that the balance sheet is in balance, (b) that net income is properly calculated, (c) what caused changes in the retained earnings account, and (d) what caused changes in the cash account. Use the space provided for calculations.

Assets	$ 54,600	Beginning Retained Earnings	$ 25,820
Liabilities	21,250	Ending Retained Earnings	28,220
Stockholders' Equity	33,350	Cash Flows from Operating Activities	15,710
Revenue	31,500	Cash Flows from Investing Activities	(5,430)
Expenses	27,600	Cash Flows from Financing Activities	(6,512)
Net Income	3,900	Beginning Cash	12,456
Dividends	1,500	Ending Cash	16,224

a)

b)

c)

d)

Exercise 1-7. Inferring Values Using the Income Statement and Balance Sheet Equations (LO2)
Apply the income statement and balance sheet equations to each of the following independent cases. Compute the two missing amounts for each case (each row is a separate case.) Assume that it is the end of 2008, the first full year of operations for the company.

Independent Cases	Total Revenues	Total Expenses	Net Income (Loss)	Total Assets	Total Liabilities	Stockholders' Equity
A	$?	63,000	15,000	?	120,000	450,000
B	$156,000	184,000	?	478,000	?	387,000
C	$79,000	?	23,000	?	58,000	95,000
D	?	47,000	(4,000)	142,000	?	105,000
E	296,000	331,500	?	756,000	941,000	?
F	48,500	?	5,500	98,000	36,200	?

Exercise 1-8. Preparing and Analyzing the Income Statement and Balance Sheet (LO2, LO3)
Lo-Main Incorporated began operations on January 1, 2006 and provides landscape services to individuals and businesses. At the end of 2006, the following information was available for Lo-Main.

Total Revenues	$ 120,000	Accounts receivable	12,000
Lawn Maintenance Equipment	65,000	Contributed Capital	50,000
Accounts Payable	24,000	Income Tax Expense	14,000
Other expenses (excluding income taxes)	80,000	Supplies	4,000
Cash Balance, December 31, 2006	19,000	Retained Earnings, December 31, 2006	26,000

There were no dividends declared or paid for 2006.
Part A. Complete the following Income Statement and Balance Sheet for Lo-Main for 2006.

_____
_____
_____

Revenues:
Total Revenue $_____
Expenses:
   Other Expenses $_____
   Income Tax Expense   _____
Total Expenses
Net Income $_____

_____
_____
_____

Assets		**Liabilities**	
Cash	$_____	Accounts Payable	$_____
Accounts Receivable	_____	Total Liabilities	$_____
Supplies	_____	**Stockholders' Equity**	
Lawn Maintenance Equipment	_____	Contributed Capital	$_____
		Retained Earnings	_____
		Total Stockholders' Equity	_____
Total Assets	$_____	Total Liabilities and Stockholders' equity	$_____

Part B. Answer the following questions about Lo-Main's income statement for 2006.
1. What was Lo-Main's average monthly revenue?

2. How much of Lo-Main's revenue was uncollected? Collected? How do you know?

3. Did Lo-Main have good or bad results for its first year of operations? Explain.

Part C. Answer the following questions about Lo-Main's Balance Sheet as of December 31, 2006.
1. How was the December 31, 2006 Retained Earnings figure determined? Is it correct?

2. Why are Supplies listed before Lawn Maintenance Equipment? What is this ordering called?

3. Why is the date in the heading different for each statement? Explain.

SOLUTIONS TO SELF-TEST QUESTIONS AND EXERCISES
MATCHING

P	Accounting	D	Net Income
N	Accounts	I	Partnership
V	Assets	F	Private companies
U	Balance Sheet	M	Public companies
S	Basic Accounting Equation	H	Revenues
L	Corporation	A	Separate Entity Assumption
B	Dividends	C	Sole proprietorship
T	Expenses	O	Statement of Cash Flows
G	Financial Statements	Q	Statement of Retained Earnings
K	Generally Accepted Accounting Principles (GAAP)	R	Stockholders' Equity
J	Income Statement	E	Unit of Measure Assumption
W	Liabilities		

TRUE-FALSE QUESTIONS
1. F – Each partner is personally liable for debts that the partnership cannot pay.
2. T
3. F – External financial statement users aren't given access to detailed internal records of the company.
4. F – This describes one of the Other External Users.
5. T
6. T

Copyright © 2008 The McGraw-Hill Companies, Inc.

7. F – Retained earnings represent a claim the owners have from what the company has earned through profitable business operations.
8. T
9. T
10. T
11. F – This type of event is very common in business.
12. T
13. F – The categories are Operating, Investing, and Financing.
14. F – This section of the statement of cash flows allows the creditors to determine whether the company has enough cash to pay its debts.
15. F – An immediate return on contributions is gained through dividends and a long-term return is gained by selling stock at a price higher tan what they paid.
16. F – Generally accepted accounting principles are created and published by the Financial Accounting Standards Board (FASB).
17. F – The information should be relevant, reliable, comparable, and consistent.
18. T
19. F – This set of laws was established to strengthen corporate reporting in the United States.
20. T

MULTIPLE CHOICE QUESTIONS

1. B	6. A	11. C	16. C
2. D	7. C	12. B	17. D
3. D	8. B	13. A	18. A
4. A	9. B	14. C	19. B
5. D	10. D	15. A	20. B

EXERCISES

Exercise 1-1. Identify Important Accounting and Business Entities (LO1, LO2, LO3)

A, J	Auditors	G	Internal Revenue Service
N	Certified Public Accountants	D, R	Partnership
E, H, M	Corporation	F	Private company
B	Creditors	O, P	Public company
Q	Financial Accounting Standards Board	L	Public Company Accounting Oversight Board
K	Financial Statement Users	C, I	Securities and Exchange Commission

Exercise 1-2. Calculate missing amounts in the Basic Accounting Equation (LO2)

Item	Case A	Case B	Case C	Case D	Case E	Case F
Assets	$16,000	(B) $60,000	$50,000	$4,000	(E) $6,000	$100,000
Liabilities	5,000	$22,000	18,000	(D) $1,000	$500	(F) $76,000
Stockholder's Equity	(A) $11,000	38,000	(C) $32,000	3,000	5,500	24,000

6

Case A: 16,000 – 5,000 = 11,000
Case B: 22,000 + 38,000 = 60,000
Case C: 50,000 – 18,000 = 32,000

Case D: 4,000 – 3,000 = 1,000
Case E: 500 + 5,500 = 6,000
Case F: 100,000 – 24,000 = 76,000

Exercise 1-3. Balance Sheet Tasks (LO2)

Part A

A	1. Cash	$640		A	9. Investments	370
SE	2. Contributed Capital	950		L	10. Notes Payable	250
N	3. Cost of Goods Sold	230		A	11. Supplies	100
SE	4. Retained Earnings	?		A	12. Buildings	790
A	5. Inventory	130		N	13. Dividends	110
N	6. Revenues	930		L	14. Long-term debt	260
A	7. Accounts Receivable	210		N	15. Income Tax Expense	50
A	8. Land	840		L	16. Accounts Payable	540

Part B

1) Total "A" $640 + 130 + 210 + 840 + 370 + 100 + 790 = 3{,}080$

2) Total "L" $250 + 260 + 540 = 1{,}050$
   Total "SE" $950 + ?$

3) $3{,}080 = 1{,}050 + 950 + ?$
   $3{,}080 = 2{,}000 + ?$
   $3{,}080 - 2{,}000 = 1{,}080$ Therefore, Retained Earnings as of July 31, 20XX is \$1,080.
       Proof: $,3080 = 1{,}050 + 950 + 1{,}080$
                  $3{,}080 = 3{,}080$

Part C

Steerz Corporation
Balance Sheet
July 31, 20XX

Assets		Liabilities		
Cash	$ 640	Accounts Payable	$ 540	
Accounts Receivable	210	Income Taxes Payable	250	
Inventory	130	Long-term debt	260	
Supplies	100	Total Liabilities		$ 1,050
Investments	370	**Stockholders' Equity**		
Buildings	790	Contributed Capital	$ 950	
Land	840	Retained Earnings	1,080	
		Total Stockholders' Equity		2,030
Total Assets	$ 3,080	Total Liabilities and Stockholders' equity		$ 3,080

Exercise 1-4. Income Statement and Retained Earnings Statement Tasks (LO2)

Part A

N	1. Accounts Receivable	210	N	7. Inventory	130
E	2. General and Administrative	73	E	8. Marketing and Other Operating Costs	94
SR	3. Retained Earnings, End	?	SR	9. Retained Earnings, Beginning	?
R	4. Sales Revenue	1,085	E	10. Cost of Goods Sold	425
SR	5. Dividends	110	E	11. Interest Charges	104
E	6. Income Taxes	50	E	12. Advertising	81

Part B.

Steerz Corporation
Income Statement
For the Year Ended July 31, 20XX

Revenues:		
Sales Revenue		$ 1,085
Total Revenue		1,085
Expenses:		
Cost of Goods Sold	$ 425	
Marketing and Other Operating Expenses	94	
Advertising Expense	81	
General and Administrative Expenses	73	
Interest Expense	104	
Income Tax Expense	50	
Total Expenses		827
Net Income		$258

Part C

Beginning Retained Earnings + Net Income – Dividends = Ending Retained Earnings
The ending retained earnings is the amount calculated in **Exercise 1-3, Part B**.

Step 1) ? + 258 – 110 = 1,080   Step 3) ? = 1,080 – 148
Step 2) ? + 148 = 1,080   Step 4) 1,080 – 148 = 932

Therefore, the Beginning Retained Earnings amount was $932.

Exercise 1-5. Identify Cash Flow Statement Items to Business Activity Categories (LO2)

I	1. Cash received from selling land		(O)	6. Payments for inventory	
(O)	2. Cash paid to suppliers		(I)	7. Expenditures to purchase equipment	
(F)	3. Dividend payments to owners		(F)	8. Cash paid on note payable	
(O)	4. Cash paid to employees		F	9. Proceeds from selling our own stock	
O	5. Cash collected from customers		F	10. Cash received from long-term borrowing	

Exercise 1-6. Reporting Amounts on the Four Basic Financial Statements (LO2)

(a) 54,600 = 21,250 + 33,350   (b) 31,500 – 27,600 = 3,900   (c) 25,820 + 3,900 – 1,500 = 28,220
(d) 12,456 + 15,710 – 5,430 – 6,512 = 16,224

Exercise 1-7. Inferring Values Using the Income Statement and Balance Sheet Equations (LO2)

Case A: Total Revenues: 63,000 + 15,000 = 78,000   Total Assets: 120,000 + 450,000 = 570,000
Case B: Net Loss: 156,000-184,000 = (28,000)   Total Liabilities: 478,000 – 387,000 = 91,000
Case C: Total Expenses: 79,000 – 23,000 = 56,000   Total Assets: 58,000 + 95,000 = 153,000
Case D: Total Revenues: 47,000 + (4,000) = 43,000 Total Liabilities: 142,000 – 105,000 = 37,000
Case E: Net Loss: 296,000 – 331,500 = (35,500)   Stockholders' Equity: 756,000–941,000 = (185,000)
Case F: Total Expenses: 48,500 – 5,500 = 43,000   Stockholders' Equity: 98,000 – 36,200 = 61,800

Exercise 1-8. Preparing and Analyzing the Income Statement and Balance Sheet (LO2, LO3)
Part A.

Lo-Main, Incorporated
Income Statement
For the Year Ended December 31, 2006

Revenues:		
Total Revenue		$ 120,000
Expenses:		
Other Expenses	$ 80,000	
Income Tax Expense	14,000	
Total Expenses		94,000
Net Income		$ 26,000

Lo-Main, Incorporated
Balance Sheet
December 31, 2006

Assets		**Liabilities**	
Cash	$ 19,000	Accounts Payable	$ 24,000
Accounts Receivable	12,000	Total Liabilities	$ 24,000
Supplies	4,000	**Stockholders' Equity**	
Lawn Maintenance Equipment	65,000	Contributed Capital	$ 50,000
		Retained Earnings	26,000
		Total Stockholders' Equity	76,000
Total Assets	$100,000	Total Liabilities and Stockholders' equity	$100,000

Part B. Answer the following questions about Lo-Main's income statement for 2006.

1. What was Lo-Main's average monthly revenue? $120,000 / 12 = $10,000 average revenue per month

2. How much of Lo-Main's revenue was uncollected? Collected? How do you know?
Total Revenue – Amount uncollected = Amount collected $120,000 – $12,000 = $108,000.
Accounts receivable represent the amount of revenues the business has not yet received from its customers. Since this is the first year of operations, either the revenues were collected or they weren't. If $12,000 of the revenues *weren't* collected…we can assume all the rest of the revenues *were* collected.

3. Did Lo-Main have a good or bad result for its first year of operations? Explain.
Lo-Main had a good result for its first year of operations. It had a profit of $26,000 which is great! Plus it has an adequate supply of cash, a good amount of equipment and, a relatively small amount of debt.

Part C. Answer the following questions about Lo-Main's Balance Sheet as of December 31, 2006.
1. How was the December 31, 2006 Retained Earnings figure determined? Is it correct?
It may appear as if it is simply the net income for the year. But, appearances can be deceiving. You **must** go through the ENTIRE calculation for the statement of retained earnings to determine the ending balance of retained earnings. The calculation is
Beginning retained earnings + net income – dividends declared = ending retained earnings *or*
$$0 + 26,000 - 0 = 26,000$$
Had you failed to do this entire calculation and one of the zero balance items above actually *had* a balance, you would have calculated the wrong amount for the ending retained earnings.

2. Why are Supplies listed before Lawn Maintenance Equipment? What is this ordering called?
The assets on a balance sheet are listed from the item that will be used up or converted into cash the most quickly to the item that will be used up or converted into cash the least quickly. In accounting, this is referred to as the order of liquidity.

3. Why is the date in the heading different for each statement? Explain.
The Income Statements covers a *period of time* (in this case one year) and it represents the income earned from the period January 1, 2006 through December 31, 2006, therefore it is dated *for the year ended*...to inform the user the span of time it covers. The balance sheet represents a specific *point in time* (in this case the day of December 31, 2006) and it is dated *December 31*...to inform the user that the amounts on this statement are true for that one day in time only.

CHAPTER 2
REPORTING INVESTING AND FINANCING
RESULTS ON THE BALANCE SHEET

ORGANIZATION OF THE CHAPTER

Understand the business	**Study the accounting methods**	**Evaluate the results**	**Review the chapter**
- Business activities and balance sheet accounts	- The accounting cycle - The debit/credit framework - Preparing a balance sheet	- Balance sheet concepts and values	- Demonstration case - Chapter summary - Key terms - Practice material

CHAPTER FOCUS SUGGESTIONS

Review

In Chapter 1 you learned about the three basic activities of a business (operating, investing, and financing), and were introduced to the four basic financial statements (income statement, statement of retained earnings, balance sheet, and statement of cash flows) that report the financial results of a business. You know that outside users analyze the information in these statements to (1) better understand the current state of the business and (2) try to 'guess' how the business might perform in the future. Finally, you discovered that all of this information is completely worthless unless the user believes that the statements were prepared and audited by ethical and competent individuals.

Introduction

Now that you know the basic activities of a business and the financial statements created from these activities, chapters 2 and 3 look at how some of these activities are presented on two of these financial statements. Chapter 2 focuses on how investing and financing decisions affect the balance sheet, while chapter 3 deals with how the income statement is impacted by operating activities. In reality, *all* of these activities affect *both* statements but, let's not bite off more than we can chew! We'll deal with additional situations later.

You've probably heard somewhere that to make it through college classes, all you have to do is memorize stuff from the chapters for each test. Then, you can just 'erase' all of that information from your brain and start memorizing stuff for the next exam. Well, in accounting this won't work (trust me…I tried it.) The key to doing well in accounting isn't *memorizing* information in the chapter, it's *understanding* the information in the chapter. If you really *understand* the information being presented, you won't need to memorize as much because it will all make sense to you. So, the key to learning accounting is: work on *understanding* the information and keep the memorization to a minimum.

The focal point of this chapter is the Balance Sheet. Recall that the balance sheet is nothing more than a fancy-looking accounting equation. Keep the accounting equation in mind as you go through this chapter and it will make more sense. The accounting equation is:

ASSETS = LIABILITIES + STOCKHOLDERS' EQUITY

  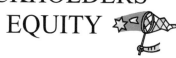

The balance sheet is simply a detailed listing of every item in each of these three categories along with its dollar amount. In other words, it lists all of the assets and their balances, and then adds up the balances. Next, it lists all of the liability and equity accounts and their balances, and then adds those up. The total for the assets balances should be the same as the total for liabilities and stockholders' equity balances combined. Thus the name BALANCE sheet—the left side of the equation must equal or BALANCE with the right side of the equation!

UNDERSTAND THE BUSINESS
Business Activities and Balance Sheet Accounts

Learning Objective 1
Explain and select common
balance sheet account titles.

1. Assets

Assets are, simply put, anything that the business OWNS. They are listed on the balance sheet in order of how quickly they will be used up or turned into cash. Assets also have each of the following three features:

- They will likely generate future economic benefits for the business
- The business obtains these benefits and can control any access to them by others
- The benefits arise because the asset was acquired in the past.

2. Liabilities

Liabilities are amounts that the business still OWES on the assets and they are listed on the balance sheet in the order of how son they will be paid, satisfied, or fulfilled. Liabilities have the following features:

- They are unavoidable obligations
- They require a future sacrifice of resources arising from past transactions

3. Stockholders' Equity

Finally, we come to stockholders' equity. **Stockholders' equity** is made up of two things:

- Contributed Capital – this accounts shows the amount of financing that was contributed to the business by its stockholders
- Retained Earnings - the total earnings of the business that has been retained in the company as of the date of the balance sheet.

Most companies keep a summary of account names and numbers called a **chart of accounts** to ensure consistency in reporting its financial results in the accounting system. A sample Chart of Accounts is shown below. Do not attempt to memorize this chart and don't try to 'force' this chart of accounts onto all of the assignments. It is meant to be a resource, not a complete, comprehensive listing.

Account # and **Name**	Description
Assets	
Cash	Includes cash in the bank and in the cash register
Accounts Receivable	Amounts owed to your business by customers for sales on credit
Interest Receivable	Interest owed to your business by others
Inventories	Goods on hand that are being held for resale
Supplies	Items on hand that will be used to make goods or provide services
Prepaid Expenses	Rent, insurance, and other expenses paid for future services
Notes Receivable	Amounts loaned to others under a formal agreement ("note")
Land	Cost of land to be used by the business
Buildings	Cost of buildings the business will use for operations
Equipment	Cost of equipment used to produce goods or provide services
Intangible Assets	Trademarks, brand names, goodwill, and other assets that lack a physical presence
Other Assets	A variety of assets with smaller balances
Liabilities	
Accounts Payable	Amounts owed to suppliers for goods or services bought on credit
Wages Payable	Amounts owed to employees for salaries, wages, and bonuses
Accrued Liabilities	Amounts owed to others for advertising, utilities, interest, etc.
Unearned Revenues	Amounts (customer deposits) received in advance of providing goods or services to customers
Notes Payable	Amounts borrowed from lenders; involves signing a promissory note
Bonds Payable	Amounts borrowed from lenders; involves issuance of bonds
Other Liabilities	A variety of liabilities with smaller balances
Stockholders' Equity	
Contributed Capital	Amount of cash (or other property) received for stock issued
Retained Earnings	Amount of accumulated earnings not distributed as dividends

STUDY THE ACCOUNTING METHODS
The Accounting Cycle
The accounting cycle is a systematic process for recording the results of a company's business activities. This process has three primary steps:

1. Analyze ➡ 2. Record ➡ 3. Summarize

Step 1: Analyze
Accounting Transactions

A transaction is any event affecting assets, liabilities, or stockholders' equity that can be measured in dollars and cents. Only transactions can be recorded (Step 2) and summarized (Step 3.) A business activity that does not have a direct and measurable financial effect on the business is not recorded in the accounting system.

To determine whether a business activity is considered an accounting transaction, decide whether either one of the following events has occurred. If EITHER event has occurred, there is a recordable transaction:

- *External Exchanges:* Exchanges involving assets, liabilities, or stockholders' equity that takes place between the business and someone outside of the business.
- *Internal Events:* Exchanges, taking place within the business itself, that involve business assets, liabilities, or stockholders' equity.

Note that every internal and/or external exchange is not necessarily considered an accounting transaction, primarily because of the lack of a direct financial impact. In other words, an exchange of 'promises' is not a recordable accounting event. The most common examples of non-accounting transactions are:

- Hiring a new employee. The act of 'hiring' the employee is not an accounting transaction. The direct financial impact of the hiring occurs when the new employee receives their first paycheck.
- Placing an order for goods and/or services. Since the goods and/or services will be received in the future and no economic impact has occurred to the business yet.

Transaction Analysis

After determining that an event is a recordable accounting transaction, it must be analyzed to determine the financial effects it has on the business. This **Transaction Analysis** involves two concepts:

(1) *Duality of Effects.* Every transaction will have at least two effects on the accounting equation. There is always some sort of 'giving something' and 'receiving something' involved in transaction analysis.

(2) **Assets = Liabilities + Stockholders' Equity**. This 'equal sign' is important in transaction analysis. The dollar amount for assets must always equal the total of liabilities plus stockholders' equity for each and every accounting transaction. If you can find only ONE effect on the equation in an event you are evaluating, then you are missing something <u>or</u> the event you are evaluating *isn't* a recordable event.

Two examples of transaction analysis are presented:

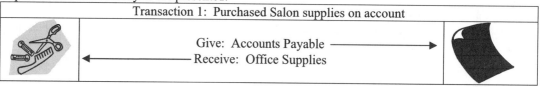

Transaction 1: Purchased Salon supplies on account		
	Give: Accounts Payable ⟶	
	⟵ Receive: Office Supplies	

After determining what's been given and what's been received, the effects on the accounting equation must be examined. Because of this transaction, Office Supplies have increased, and Accounts Payable has increased. Stockholders' equity is not affected. An increase to assets and a corresponding increase in liabilities keep the accounting equation in balance as shown in the following:

	Assets	=	Liabilities	+	Stockholders' Equity
Accounting Equation	⇧ Salon Supplies	=	⇧ Accounts Payable	+	No Change

The next example shows the cash payment for the supplies purchased previously.

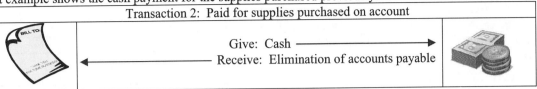

	Transaction 2: Paid for supplies purchased on account
	Give: Cash ⟶
	⟵ Receive: Elimination of accounts payable

In this example, cash is reduced because we have paid off a debt. So, there is a decrease to assets and a corresponding decrease in the amount of money we owe to our suppliers.

Accounting Equation	**Assets**	**=**	**Liabilities**	**+**	**Stockholders' Equity**
	⇩ Cash	=	⇩ Accounts Payable	+	No Change

This concept of 'exchanges' that has been illustrated here brings up an important accounting principle called the **cost principle.** Essentially, this principle requires that transactions be recorded at the amount paid for the original exchange. This is true regardless of what *would have been paid* had the exchange occurred with another company.

DECIDE: An Approach to Transaction Analysis
Follow these steps for every transaction you analyze.
1. **D**etect transactions. Go to the next step **ONLY** if a transaction exists.
2. **E**xamine it for the accounts affected (make sure there are *always* two or more.) Put account names to what was given and what was received.
3. **C**lassify each account named as an asset (A), liability (L), or stockholders' equity (SE).
4. **ID**entify the financial effects on each account. In other words, *how much* does each asset, liability, and stockholders' equity account increase (+) or decrease (-)
5. **E**nd with the effects on the basic accounting equation (A = L + SE).

It may seem like it takes too much time to go through every one of these steps, so you'll be tempted to skip some of them. Don't do it!! **Learning this process is the most important goal in this chapter.** If you try to memorize the different kinds of transactions presented in this chapter, you will not be able to apply the *process* to the more difficult transactions that come up later in the text. It may initially take you a little longer to analyze each transaction by using the **DECIDE** approach, but you will gain speed as you become more comfortable with it and you will discover that you are able to apply it easily to new and unfamiliar transactions as well!

Let's go through a couple of examples:
(a) Purchased Equipment by financing. The business purchased $30,000 of Equipment by paying $5,000 in cash and signing a formal agreement with the bank to pay the remaining balance in one year.

Detect Transactions	The business receives equipment and gives cash and a formal promise to pay.
Examine Accounts	Cash is cash, Equipment is equipment, and the formal promise to pay is a Note Payable.
Classify accounts	Cash is an asset (A), Equipment is an asset (A), and Notes Payable is a liability (L).
IDentify $ effects.	Equipment (A) + $30,000, Cash (A) – $5,000, and Notes Payable (L) + $25,000
End with A = L + SE	

Accounting Equation	**Assets**		**=**	**Liabilities**	**+**	**Stockholders' Equity**
	Equipment	+ 30,000	=	Notes Payable + 25,000	+	No Change
	Cash	– 5,000				

Notice that even though TWO assets were affected, one was increased and one was decreased. The net amount is + 25,000 (+30,000 – 5,000). On the other side of the equal sign, under liabilities, there is ALSO a +25,000. Therefore, the equation is in balance. An important point to see here is that no effect on stockholders' equity was required to make the entry balance. Oftentimes, one or two sections of the accounting equation will be unaffected, but the equation remains in balance.

(b) Purchased beauty products of $600 for cash

Detect Transactions	The business receives Salon Supplies and gives cash.
Examine Accounts	Cash is cash, Beauty products are Salon Supplies.
Classify accounts	Cash is an asset (A), Salon Supplies is an asset (A).
IDentify $ effects.	Salon Supplies (A) + $600, Cash (A) – $600
End with A = L + SE	

	Assets	=	Liabilities	+	Stockholders' Equity
Accounting Equation	Salon Supplies + 600 Cash – 600	=	No Change	+	No Change

In this case, neither liabilities nor stockholders' equity was affected, yet the accounting equation remains in balance because assets increased by $600 and decreased by $600. These have a $0 net effect on assets ($600 - $600) and no effect on liabilities and stockholders' equity. So, the equation remains in balance.

Steps 2 and 3: Record and Summarize
Now that the Analysis phase of the accounting cycle has been examined, we can now look at Steps 2 and 3. Daily transactions in a business are recorded in a **journal.** These daily transactions are periodically summarized in **ledger accounts.** A separate ledger exists for each account (i.e. Cash, Salon Supplies, etc.)

The Debit/Credit Framework
While much of the recording and summarizing of accounting transactions is now performed using computers, an understanding of exactly *what* the computer is *doing* is critical to understanding the accounting cycle. So, this presentation will focus on completing this process manually. The basis for the Debit/Credit Framework is shown below:

> **Learning Objective 3**
> Use journal entries and T-accounts to show how business transactions affect the balance sheet.

ASSETS	=	LIABILITIES	+	STOCKHOLDERS' EQUITY

+ ASSETS –		– LIABILITIES +		– STOCKHOLDERS' EQUITY +	
Increase using Debit	Decrease using Credit	Decrease using Debit	Increase using Credit	Decrease using Debit	Increase using Credit

These are the rules related to this framework:
1. Accounts increase on the same side as they appear in the A = L + SE equation. Accounts on the left side of the accounting equation increase on the left side of the account and accounts on the right side of the equation increase on the right side of the account. Therefore,
    - Assets increase on the left side of the account.
    - Liabilities increase on the right side of the account.
    - Stockholders' Equity accounts increase on the right side of the account.
2. The Left side of an account is the debit (*dr.*) side, the Right side of the account is the credit (*cr.*) side. Therefore,
    - Placing a number on the left side of *any* account is referred to as crediting the account, and placing a number on the right side of *any* account is referred to as crediting the account.
    - Use debits to increase asset accounts (and decrease liability and stockholder equity accounts).
    - Use credits to increase liability and stockholder equity accounts (and decrease asset accounts).

Now that the Debit/Credit framework has been introduced into the accounting cycle, let's see how it has affected the steps:

> **Step 1: *Analyze Transactions:*** The Debit/Credit framework does not affect this step. You will still be using the DECIDE approach to determine whether or not an event is considered an accounting transaction that can be recorded by the business.
> **Step 2: *Recording Journal Entries:*** The debit/credit framework affects how transactions are recorded by the business. Journal Entries are used for this step in the accounting cycle. An example of a formal journal follows:

General Journal				Page G1
Date 2008	Account title and Explanations	Ref.	Debit	Credit
Aug. 2	Equipment	210/✓	42,000	
	Cash	650		42,000
	(Bought equipment using cash)			

Use the previous example to verify each of the following comments:
- Every transaction is dated.
- The Debit is presented first (on top).
- Credits are listed below the debits and are indented to the right (both the words and amounts).
- The order of the debited amounts and/or credited amounts doesn't matter, as long as all the debits are on top (and on the left) and all the credits are on the bottom (and indented)
- Total debits equal total credits for each transaction.
- Dollar signs are not used because the journal is understood to be a record of dollar amounts.
- The reference column (Ref.) will be used in *Step 3* to indicate when the journal entry has been summarized in the ledger account.
- A brief explanation of the transaction is written below the entry.
- The line beneath the explanation is left blank before writing the next journal entry.

Oftentimes, we will be using a simplified format for recording journal entries because of space and time limitations and/or to help you learn the debit/credit framework more quickly. The same 'formal' entry example will be shown here using the simplified format.

(b)	*dr* Equipment (+A)………………………………....	42,000	
	cr Cash (-A)……………………………….		42,000

Note these differences between the 'formal' process and the simplified format are:
- o When no date is provided in the text, use some form of reference for each transaction, such as *(a), (b), (c)*, if the problem provides a lettering sequence or *(1), (2), (3)* if the problem provides a numbering sequence.
- o Do not include the reference column and the transaction explanation column.
- o Indicate that you are debiting or crediting an account by placing a *dr* or *cr* before the account name. (This is primarily to help reinforce the concept of debit and credit.)
- o Include the account type (A, L, or SE) along with the direction of the effect on the account (+ for increases, and – for decreases.

Step 3: Summarizing in Ledger Account: After transactions have been recorded in the journal (called **journalizing**), they must be recorded and summarized in the ledger accounts. This process is referred to **posting.** The dollar amounts of transactions in the journal are posted to the appropriate ledger account, and the new resulting balance of the account is computed. Again, we will be using a simplified version of the ledger account.

Cash					Acct # 101
Date 2008	Account Title	Ref	Debit	Credit	Balance
Aug 1		G1	50,000		50,000
Aug 2		G1		42,000	8,000

Equipment					Acct # 205
Date 2008	Account Title	Ref	Debit	Credit	Balance
Aug 2		G1	42,000		42,000

Again, a simplified format of the ledger account will be used throughout this text. The same 'formal' ledger accounts will be shown here using the simplified format.

dr +	Cash		cr –		dr +	Equipment		cr –
Beg.	0				Beg.	0		
(a)	50,000	(b)	42,000		(b)	42,000		

- The simplified version of the ledger account is called a T-Account. It is called this because it looks like a capital letter "T".
- The Name of the account (i.e. Cash, Equipment, etc.) is written on the line at the top of the "T".
- The area beneath this line is nicely divided into two sides: a left side (used to record debit amounts) and a right side (used to record credit amounts).
- Accounts often have a beginning balance (normally on the increase side of that account.)
- Dollar signs are not used in ledger accounts.
- A reference is shown to indicate the page number of the journal (letters or numbers) of the original transaction.
- The ending balance in the T-account (after posting all transactions to the accounts), is double-underlined and is shown on the side of the T that has the greater total dollar amount (ending balances not shown in these examples).
- Normally, Assets will end up with a Debit balance, while Liabilities and Stockholder Equity accounts will end up with a Credit balance.

A Review of the Accounting Cycle
In an effort to keep this review concise, Step 1 will not be shown again. The assumption will be made that all business events have been properly analyzed and have been determined to be recordable accounting transactions. The focus of this review will be to provide examples of recording and summarizing various transactions.

Four transactions will be presented and each transaction will be presented in a format similar to the one shown below.

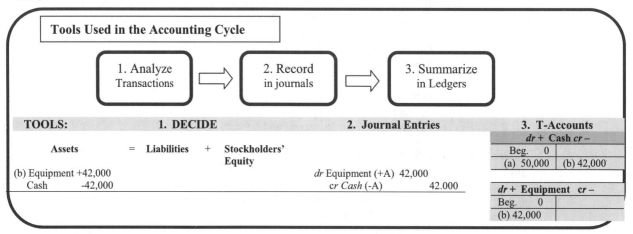

The DECIDE model will be presented, along with the corresponding journal entry, and the resulting postings to the affected T-Accounts. We will assume it is a brand, new business with no activity yet. Ready? Let's go!!

                                                                                    Study Guide, Chapter 2

Example a: The owner contributed Equipment valued at $20,000 to the business in exchange for ownership in the business.

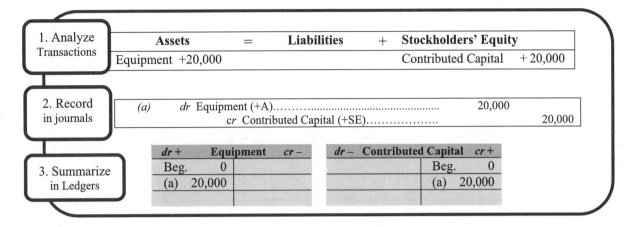

Example b: Financing from Lender – Your company borrows $30,000 from the bank, deposits the entire amount in its bank account, and signs a formal agreement to repay the loan in three years.

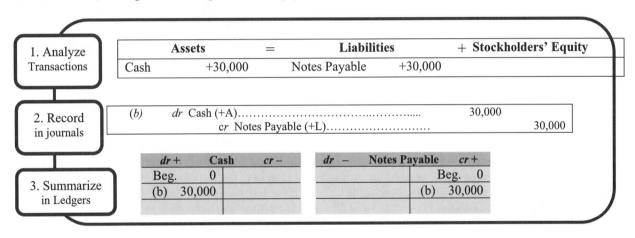

Example c: Purchased supplies on account $500.

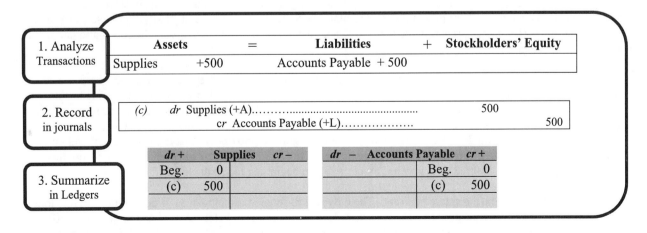

Example d: Paid $200 of the amount owed for the supplies purchased in *Example c.*
Note that since this is the last transaction, the accounts have been totaled.

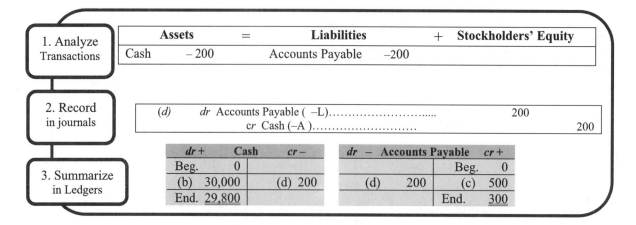

The following is a summary presentation of the journal entries and postings to the corresponding T-accounts for the previous four transactions:

(a)	dr Equipment (+A)......................	20,000	
	cr Contributed Capital (+SE)......		20,000
(b)	dr Cash (+A).............................	30,000	
	cr Notes Payable (+L)..............		30,000
©	dr Supplies (+A)...........................	500	
	cr Accounts Payable (+L).........		500
(d)	dr Accounts Payable (–L)..............	500	
	cr Cash (–A).......................		500

dr +	Cash	cr –
Beg.	0	
(b)	30,000	(d) 200
End. 29,800		

dr –Accounts Payable cr +		
	Beg.	0
(d) 500	(c)	200
	End.	300

dr –	Supplies	cr +
Beg.	0	
(c)	500	
End. 500		

dr –	Notes Payable	cr +
	Beg.	0
	(b)	30,000
	End. ,30,000	

dr +	Equipment	cr –
Beg.	0	
(a) 20,000		
End. 20,000		

dr– Contributed Capital cr +		
	Beg.	0
	(a)	20,000
	End. 20,000	

Preparing a Balance Sheet

The balance sheet is prepared on the basis of the ending balances in the T-accounts after all the journal entries have been posted. Take the ending balances

<table>
<tr><td>Learning Objective 4
Prepare a classified balance sheet</td></tr>
</table>

of each T-account, group these balances so that all of the Assets are together, Liabilities are together, and Stockholders' Equity accounts are together. Then, list the name and corresponding balance of each T-account under the proper category. Add up the total for each category and verify that the total for Assets is the same as the total for Liabilities and Stockholders' equity!

The greatest thing about the Balance Sheet preparing it is simply a matter of copying!!! The balance sheet is nothing more than a fancy way of presenting the accounting equation: A = L + SE. List all of the assets (A) first, then the liabilities (L). When preparing the balance sheet, businesses often separate divide the assets and liabilities into useful sub-categories.

A balance sheet in this format is called a **Classified Balance Sheet.** An asset classified as a *current asset* means that you believe it will be gone or used-up within a year. All the other assets will probably still be in the business after a year, so they will not be classified as current assets. For example, pretend your home is a business and that everything in your home is an asset of this business. Which of the items of the 'business' will be gone within a year? The $10.00 sitting on the kitchen table will probably be gone in one <u>day</u> so, that cash would definitely be considered a 'current' asset. On the other hand, the living room furniture will probably be around for more than a year so it would not be classified as a 'current' asset. Are you beginning to see the logic of it all?

Some liabilities can also be considered current. The only real difference is that instead of determining, "How long will it take before they're gone or used-up?" we ask, "How long will it take before they're completely paid-off or no longer owed?" The electric bill you got yesterday in the mail will certainly be paid off before the end of the year, so it would be classified as a **current liability**. But, your car loan will probably take a few years to pay off and so it would not be classified as a current liability.

Stockholders' equity can easily be calculated as Assets – Liabilities = Stockholders' Equity. This difference or 'net' amount is the reason why Stockholders' Equity is frequently referred to as "Net Assets" or "Net Worth." However, don't make the common error of assuming that this amount represents what the business is actually 'worth.' The riveting tale about why this is true will be told later.

Armed with this information, here is the classified balance sheet for previous example. Verify each of the account balances shown here by looking back at the set of summarized T-accounts for the example.

Jane's Janitorial Balance Sheet June 30, 2008		Explanation of Classification
Assets		
Current Assets:		
Cash	$29,800	Cash will be spent within one year of June 30
Supplies	500	Supplies will be used up within one year
Total Current Assets	30,300	
Equipment	20,000	The equipment will be used for many years
Total Assets	$50,300	
Liabilities		
Current Liabilities		
Accounts Payable	$ 300	The $300 will be paid off within one year.
Total Current Liabilities	300	
Notes Payable	30,000	Bank loan will not be paid for three years.
Total Liabilities	30,300	
Stockholders' Equity		
Contributed Capital	$ 20,000	Stockholder equity accounts are not classified
Retained Earnings	0	Stockholder equity accounts are not classified
Total Stockholders' Equity	20,000	
Total Liabilities and Stockholders' equity	$50,300	

EVALUATE THE RESULTS
Balance Sheet Concepts and Values

This is where the spell-binding story referred to earlier is disclosed. Recall that the stockholders' equity figure on the balance sheet does NOT indicate

> **Learning Objective 5**
> Explain the concepts that determine whether an item is reported on the balance sheet and at what amount

what a business is actually worth. Now that you have completed this chapter, you are better able to understand why this statement is true. Users rely on the financial statements to help them make informed economic decisions about a company. As you learned from the transaction analysis in the chapter, financial statements (the balance sheet in this chapter) are the result of recording and reporting many transactions. Because recording these transactions is *how* the numbers get on the financial statements, the balance sheet figures are primarily based on:

1. *What is (and is not) recorded?* The biggie here is that: only items arising from an 'identifiable' transaction can be recorded. Even though the item(s) may have a great deal of value to the company, the impact of this requirement on the balance sheet is that many items are never recorded because there is no identifiable transaction that can be recorded. Assume that there is a gas station in town that is on a fabulously busy corner. It is easy for people to get to this gas station no matter where they are in town. Half the town uses this gas station instead of any of the others because it is so convenient. In this example, there is no identifiable transaction that the gas station can record to get the value of its LOCATION on the balance sheet. I guarantee you'll never see a balance sheet with an asset called "Fifth and Elm." The location clearly has a great deal of value to the station owners, but they cannot record it as a transaction, and therefore, it will not be recognized because there is no identifiable event.

2. ***Amounts assigned to recorded items.*** Initial transactions are recorded using amounts that were 'identifiable' **at the time the transaction occurred** (cost principle). But, values may have changed drastically since the time a transaction was originally recorded. Oftentimes, things we purchased long ago have become much more valuable since the day they were purchased. For example, if a small business bought a piece of land out in the boonies 40 years ago for $5,000 it was recorded at $5,000 on that day. That land may be prime real estate in the middle of a thriving city now worth millions of dollars. But alas, the cost principle requires that the land must remain on the books when the last identifiable transaction occurred…40 years ago. So, the property's value on the balance sheet will remain the amount of the initial cost – $5,000. Now, you know why Net worth/equity is NOT a good indicator of a company's value. Every number on the balance sheet is based on an amount that could be measured *when the ORIGINAL transaction occurred*, and its value today could be significantly higher or lower!

This possibility of a 'lower' value brings up one exception to the cost principle/measurement rule. A concept called **conservatism**. Basically, this simply means "don't count your chickens until they hatch." Assume you have twelve eggs from the finest stock of roosters and hens ever to inhabit the earth. You suspect that only 8 of the 12 eggs will actually hatch. If you tell everyone that you will have 12 prize chicks available and all 12 have been 'promised' to people in town before the eggs actually hatch, you'll be in BIG trouble if only 8 chicks hatch. Conservatism simply states that it is easier to guess wrong on the low end…than it is to guess wrong on the high end. If you tell everyone that 8 eggs will hatch and you get nine…WOW!!! You're invited to the best hay rides in town! But, if you tell everyone that 12 eggs will hatch and you only get nine, it's shoveling manure for you. Hmmmm…Conservatism sounds pretty good.

REVIEW THE CHAPTER

Chapter Summary

LO1. Explain and select common balance sheet account titles
  ❖ Typical balance sheet account titles include the following:
      o Assets: Cash, Accounts Receivable, Inventories, Supplies, Property and Equipment
      o Liabilities: Accounts Payable, Notes Payable, Bonds Payable
      o Stockholders' Equity: Contributed Capital, Retained Earnings

LO2. Apply transaction analysis to business transactions
  ❖ Transactions include external changes and internal events:
  ❖ Transaction analysis is based on the duality of effects and the basic accounting equation
      o *Duality of Effects* means that every transaction affects at least two accounts
  ❖ Transaction analysis follows a systematic approach of:
      o **D**etermining whether a transaction exists
      o **E**xamining the transaction for the accounts affected
      o **C**lassifying the accounts as assets, liabilities, or stockholders' equity
      o **ID**entifying the direction and amount of the effects
      o **E**valuating whether the accounting equation remains in balance

LO3. Use journal entries and T-accounts to show how business transactions affect the balance sheet.
  ❖ Debit means left and Credit means right
  ❖ Debits
      o increase Assets
      o decrease Liabilities and Stockholders' Equity
  ❖ Credits
      o decrease Assets
      o increase Liabilities and Stockholders' Equity
  ❖ Journal entries:
      o express in debit-equals-credit form, the effects of a transaction on various asset, liability, and stockholder equity accounts
      o are used to enter financial information into the accounting system, which is later summarized in the ledger (T-accounts)

- ❖ T-Accounts:
    - o Are a simplified version of the ledger which summarizes transaction effects for each account
    - o Show increases on the left (debit) side for assets, which are on the left side of the accounting equation
    - o Show increases on the right (credit) side for liabilities and stockholders' equity, which are on the right side of the accounting equation

LO4. Prepare a classified balance sheet.
- ❖ Classified balance sheets are structured with
    - o Assets categorized as:
        - ▪ Current Assets: those to be used or turned into cash within one year
        - ▪ Long-term Assets: those to be used or turned into cash in more than one year
            - • Property and equipment
            - • Intangible assets
    - o Liabilities categorized as:
        - ▪ Current liabilities: those that will be paid, settled, or fulfilled within one year
        - ▪ Long-term liabilities: those that will be paid, settled, or fulfilled after one year
    - o Stockholders' Equity:
        - ▪ Contributed Capital (which is ALWAYS listed before retained earnings)
        - ▪ Retained Earnings

LO5. Explain the concepts that determine whether an item is reported on the balance sheet and at what amount.
- ❖ Because accounting is transaction-based, the balance sheet does not necessarily represent the current value of a business
- ❖ Some assets are not recognized because they do not arise from transactions
- ❖ The amounts recorded for assets and liabilities may not represent current market values because they generally are measured using the exchange amounts established at the time of the initial transaction
- ❖ The concept of conservatism states that when uncertainty exists about the value of an asset or liability, care should be taken to not overstate the reported value of assets or understate the reported value of liabilities

READ AND RECALL QUESTIONS
After you read each section of the chapter, answer the related Read and Recall Questions below.

LEARNING OBJECTIVE
After studying the section of the chapter, you should be able to:
1. Explain and select common balance sheet account titles.

Business Activities and Common Balance Sheet Accounts
What are the three features of Assets?

What are two features of liabilities?

Name and define the two components of stockholders' equity.

What is the Chart of Accounts and why is it used by businesses?

LEARNING OBJECTIVE
After studying the section of the chapter, you should be able to:
2. Apply transaction analysis to business transactions.

The Accounting Cycle
List the three steps in the accounting cycle.

Explain the difference between external exchanges and internal events.

Give an example of a non-recordable business event.

Transaction Analysis
What is transaction analysis? Identify and describe the two elements of transaction analysis.

Describe the **Duality of Effects** concept that underlies transaction analysis. Why is this concept important when analyzing transactions?

Define the **accounting equation** and explain why it is important in analyzing transactions.

A business purchases supplies on account. Explain what the business is Giving and Receiving in this exchange.

Define the cost principle.

DECIDE: A Systematic Approach to Transaction Analysis
What are the five steps for analyzing transactions using **DECIDE**? Don't copy the steps from the text. Try to remember them (as best you can) from memory. It's okay if you don't get it exactly the same as the text. The point of this exercise is to see if you can remember the process using the **DECIDE** method.

Explain the purpose of a journal.

Explain the purpose of a ledger account.

LEARNING OBJECTIVE
After studying the section of the chapter, you should be able to:
3. Use journal entries and T-accounts to show how business transactions affect the balance sheet.

The Debit/Credit Framework
In the following Transaction Analysis Model, write the word Debit on the debit side of each T-account and write the word Credit on the credit side of each T-account. Then, in the T-account for each category, indicate the increase side by writing the word Increase on that side in the space provided. Indicate the decrease side by writing the word Decrease on that side in the space provided.

Define each of the following terms: (1) Debit; (2) Credit and show how each is abbreviated.

At what step in the accounting cycle is a journal used?

At what step in the accounting cycle are ledger accounts used?

List at least three characteristics of the formal journal entry format.

List at least one difference noted when the simplified format for recording journal entries is used instead of the formal process.

Define posting. Why must a journal entry be posted?

List at least three characteristics of a T-account.

A Review of the Accounting Cycle
Assume you are given the following analysis of a transaction:

Assets		=	Liabilities		+ Stockholders' Equity
Cash	+30,000		Notes Payable	+30,000	

(continued)

Show the journal entry for the previous transaction.

Post the journal entry you just made.

dr +	Cash	cr –		dr –	Notes Payable	cr +
Beg.	0				Beg.	0

LEARNING OBJECTIVE
After studying the section of the chapter, you should be able to:
4. Prepare a classified balance sheet.

Preparing a Balance Sheet
What is needed in order to prepare a balance sheet?

Describe a classified balance sheet.

Define a current asset.

Define a current liability.

Do you agree with the following statement? Why or why not?
Stockholders' equity (net worth) provides a dollar amount of what a business is worth.

LEARNING OBJECTIVE
After studying the section of the chapter, you should be able to:
5. Explain the concepts that determine whether an item is reported on the balance sheet and at what amount.

The Effect of a Transaction Focus
Briefly define an 'identifiable transaction'.

Explain the term 'conservatism.' Why is adherence to the conservatism concept important in reporting transactions?

FINANCIAL ANALYSIS TOOLS

1. Classified Balance Sheet: Here is a quick and dirty snapshot of a classified balance sheet. Note that a brief description of some accounts is included in parenthesis. This description should not actually be put on the Balance Sheet. This is **not intended** to be an all-inclusive example. It is merely a guide.

<table>
<tr><td colspan="4" align="center">Company Name
Balance Sheet
Date</td></tr>
<tr><td colspan="2">Assets</td><td colspan="2">Liabilities</td></tr>
<tr><td colspan="2">Current Assets:</td><td colspan="2">Current Liabilities:</td></tr>
<tr><td>Cash</td><td>$ xxx</td><td>Accounts Payable</td><td>$ xxx</td></tr>
<tr><td>Accounts Receivable</td><td>xxx</td><td>Notes Payable (1 yr or less)</td><td>xxx</td></tr>
<tr><td>Notes Receivable (1 yr or less)</td><td>xxx</td><td>Accrued Liabilities</td><td><u>xxx</u></td></tr>
<tr><td>Short-term Investments</td><td>xxx</td><td>Total current liabilities</td><td>xxx</td></tr>
<tr><td>Inventories</td><td>xxx</td><td></td><td></td></tr>
<tr><td>Prepaid Expenses</td><td><u>xxx</u></td><td>Notes Payable (more than 1 year)</td><td>xxx</td></tr>
<tr><td>Total current assets</td><td>xxx</td><td>Mortgage Payable</td><td>xxx</td></tr>
<tr><td></td><td></td><td>Other liabilities</td><td><u>xxx</u></td></tr>
<tr><td>Property and Equipment</td><td>xxx</td><td>Total Liabilities</td><td>xxx</td></tr>
<tr><td>Intangible assets</td><td>xxx</td><td></td><td></td></tr>
<tr><td>Other assets</td><td><u>xxx</u></td><td colspan="2">Stockholders' Equity</td></tr>
<tr><td>Total</td><td>xxx</td><td>Contributed Capital</td><td>xxx</td></tr>
<tr><td></td><td></td><td>Retained Earnings</td><td>xxx</td></tr>
<tr><td></td><td></td><td>Total Stockholders' Equity</td><td><u>xxx</u></td></tr>
<tr><td>Total Assets</td><td><u>$ xxx</u></td><td>Total Liabilities and Stockholders' Equity</td><td><u>$ xxx</u></td></tr>
</table>

HELPFUL STUDY TIP

1. Many students taking an introductory accounting course have difficulty with debit and credit. When do you debit and when do you credit? The study tip in this chapter focuses on a tool that can help you more easily remember this potentially frustrating topic. If you go back over the examples in the text and this study guide using the debit/credit framework, notice that the vast majority of all the transactions involve the Cash account. Therefore, if you can just figure out when to debit or credit this heavily-used account, you have half of the transaction in the bag!!! The Duality of Effects helps explain why this is useful. Because every transaction affects two or more accounts, if you can figure out what to do with *one* of these accounts (debit or credit), you immediately know that the OPPOSITE must be done to the other account. For example, if you know you are going to debit cash….then the other account affected by the transaction MUST be a Credit. You only have to figure out the name of the other account that is affected.

Then how can you determine when to debit or credit the Cash account? It's easy. When you receive cash from somebody you usually take it to the bank and make a deposit, right? So,

DEPOSIT = DEBIT

Similarly, when you pay money out of your bank account you usually write them a check, right? So,

CHECK = CREDIT

That means…Deposit Debit….Check Credit…DD….CC. This makes it easy to remember when you debit cash (when you make a deposit) and when you credit cash (when you write a check). You only make a deposit when you RECEIVE money and you only write a check when you GIVE (pay) money.

If cash is involved in the transaction, you can figure out what half of the transaction is so, all you have to do is figure out the other half. Let's go through an example. Assume you borrow money from the bank in exchange for a promissory note.

When you borrow money from someone, are you RECEIVING money or are you GIVING them money? That's right!!!! You're RECEIVING money and you are going to deposit it in the bank. Using the rule above, that means DD. Deposit=Debit to the cash account.

Now that you know you will be debiting cash, all you have to do is figure out the account you have to credit. (Since you debited cash, the Duality of Effects requires that the other account must be credited.) If you know the other account affected by this transaction is Notes Payable, that's all you need to know!!! You already know the account must be credited.

SELF-TEST QUESTIONS AND EXERCISES

MATCHING

1. *Match each of the key terms listed below with the appropriate textbook definition.*

_____	Chart of Accounts	_____	Journal
_____	Classified Balance Sheet	_____	Journal Entry
_____	Conservatism	_____	Ledger
_____	Contributed Capital	_____	Post
_____	Cost principle	_____	Retained Earnings
_____	Current Assets	_____	Stockholders' Equity
_____	Current Liabilities	_____	T-account
_____	Debits and Credits	_____	Transaction

A. To copy the debit and credit amounts from a journal entry into the corresponding T-Accounts
B. Terms that refer to the "left" and "right" sides of a T-Account
C. Used up or converted into cash within twelve months of the balance sheet date
D. A summary of all account names and corresponding account numbers used to record financial results in the accounting system
E. Indicates the effects of each day's transactions in a debits-and-credits format
F. Organized by date and used to record the effects of each day's transactions
G. The amount remaining on the books when liabilities are subtracted from assets
H. The amount used to record an asset or liability, when in doubt, should be the least optimistic measurement
I. Debts and obligations that will be paid, settled, or fulfilled within twelve months of the balance sheet date
J. Organized by account and used to summarize the effects of transactions on each account
K. Has a direct and measurable financial effect on the assets, liabilities, or equity of a business
L. A simplified version of a ledger account used for summarizing the effects of journal entries
M. Shows a subtotal for current assets and current liabilities
N. The amount used to recorded an asset or liability is based on its original cost at the time the transaction is made
O. Total earnings of the business that have been kept in the company as of the balance sheet date
P. The financing provided to the business by the stockholders

TRUE-FALSE QUESTIONS

For each of the following, enter a T or F in the blank to indicate whether the statement is true or false.

_____1. (LO1) Assets are listed in order of how slowly they will be used up or can be turned into cash.

_____2. (LO1) One feature of assets is that it is probable that they will generate future economic benefits for the company.

_____3. (LO1) All liabilities require a future sacrifice of resources.

_____4. (LO1) Contributed capital refers to the earnings that have been retained by the company.

_____5.   (LO1) To ensure consistency, all companies use the same account names and numbers in the Chart of Accounts

_____6.   (LO2) Transactions are the only activities that are recorded and summarized as part of the accounting cycle.

_____7.   (LO2) When Starbucks sells you an iced coffee, it is considered an internal event because it takes place inside of the business.

_____8.   (LO2) The duality of effects described in the chapter means that every transaction has at least two effects on the basic accounting equation.

_____9.   (LO2) Determining the effects of "give and receive" on the accounting equation occurs during the 'record' step of the accounting cycle.

_____10. (LO2) The cost principle states that the appropriate price to record a piece of machinery (purchased for $5,000 and sold elsewhere at $7,000) is $5,000—the original cost to the company.

_____11. (LO3) A T-account is a simplified version of a formal accounting record called a ledger.

_____12. (LO3) Debit means to increase and credit means to decrease.

_____13. (LO3) When preparing journal entries, credits appear first (on top) and debits are written below and indented to the right (both the words and the amounts)

_____14. (LO3) When writing journal entries and a date is not given, use some form of reference for each transaction, such as a letter to identify the event.

_____15. (LO3) Post means to determine the proper classification of an account as an Asset, Liability, or Stockholders' Equity.

_____16. (LO3) An event that involves the exchange of only promises is considered a transaction and a journal entry is needed.

_____17. (LO4) Long-term assets and liabilities are those that do not meet the definition of current.

_____18. (LO5) The balance sheet reports what a business is actually worth.

_____19. (LO5) An item can only be recorded by a business if it comes from an identifiable transaction.

_____20. (LO5) Because of the cost principle, accounting rules do not allow decreases in asset values to be recorded.

MULTIPLE CHOICE QUESTIONS
Choose the best answer or response by placing the identifying letter in the space provided.

_____1.   (LO1) Assets share all of the following features *except*:
   a.   benefits arise from having acquired assets in the past
   b.   they are unavoidable obligations
   c.   it is probable they will generate future economic benefits
   d.   the company can obtain these benefits and control others' access to them

_____2.   (LO1) Liabilities are defined as
   a.   amounts owed by a business
   b.   amounts invested and reinvested in a company by its stockholders
   c.   resources owned by a business that generate future economic benefits
   d.   none of these define liabilities

_____3.   (LO1) Stockholders' Equity consists of
   a.   contributed capital, liabilities
   b.   contributed capital, retained earnings
   c.   assets, retained earnings
   d.   assets, contributed capital

_____4.   (LO1) Which of the following is **not** an account name you would see used by a company to report a liability for a bank loan?
   a.   account payable
   b.   note payable
   c.   loan payable
   d.   all of these are accounts names used to report a liability for a bank loan.

_____5.   (LO1) The Chart of Accounts is
   a.   a summary of all the account names (and corresponding account numbers) used to record financial results in the accounting system
   b.   must be identical for all businesses in order to maintain consistency
   c.   is seldom ever used by businesses in real life, it is primarily used for learning purposes only
   d.   all of the above are true statements regarding the chart of accounts

_____6.   (LO2) Which of the following is the proper sequence of steps in the accounting cycle?
   a.   record, summarize, analyze
   b.   summarize, analyze, record
   c.   analyze, record, summarize
   d.   analyze, summarize, record

_____7.   (LO2) A transaction can best be described as
   a.   any internal or external event taking place in a business
   b.   an event that impacts the accountant personally
   c.   an event that involves the IRS
   d.   an event that effects assets liabilities, or stockholders' equity and its effects are direct and measurable

_____8.   (LO2) The Duality of Effects concept means that
   a.   each transaction must be recorded two times—in the T-account and in the journal
   b.   two people are involved in each accounting transaction
   c.   each event can be approached from two points of view
   d.   each transaction has at least two effects on the assets, liabilities, or stockholders' equity of a business

_____9.   (LO2) When applied, the Duality of Effects uses which of the following ideas?
   a.   give and take
   b.   push and pull
   c.   open and shut
   d.   all of the above are used when applying the Duality of Effects concept

_____10. (LO2) Which of the following is correct regarding the accounting equation?
   a.   SE = A + L
   b.   L = A + SE
   c.   A = L + SE
   d.   none of these is correct

_____11. (LO2) How would the purchase of supplies with an informal promise to pay it at the end of the month affect Assets, Liabilities, and Stockholders' Equity?
   a.   + assets; + stockholders' equity
   b.   + assets; + liabilities
   c.   − assets; − liabilities
   d.   There is no effect on the accounting equation because this is not considered a recordable transaction

_____12. (LO2) Which of the following describes the effect on the accounting equation when a company issues stock certificates for $5,000 in cash?
   a.   + assets $5,000; + stockholders' equity $5,000
   b.   − assets $5,000; − stockholders' equity $5,000
   c.   + assets $5,000; + liabilities $5,000
   d.   − assets $5,000; + stockholders' equity $5,000

_____13. (LO2) Examine the accounts affected and classify each account of the following transaction: the business borrowed $20,000 from the bank due in 4 years with a formal promise to pay
   a.   Cash (+A) and Accounts Payable (+L)
   b.   Cash (+A) and Notes Payable (+L)
   c.   Accounts Payable (+L) and Contributed Capital (+SE)
   d.   Notes Payable (+L) and Contributed Capital (+SE)

_____14. (LO3) Which of the following are *not* true statements regarding T-accounts, and increase/decrease of account balances?
   a.   assets are increased by debits, and decreased by credits
   b.   liabilities are increased by credits, and decreased by debits
   c.   retained earnings is increased by credits, and decreased by debits
   d.   all of the above are true statements

_____15. (LO3) Which of the following are true statements regarding journal entries?
   a.   they are recorded in the journal using account number order
   b.   total debits must equal total credits for each transaction
   c.   credits are written first (at the top); debits are written below the credits and are indented to the right (both the words and the amounts)
   d.   all of these are true statements regarding journal entries

_____16. (LO3) Which of the following is *not* true regarding the simplified format for journal entries?
   a.   the account type (A, L, or SE) and the direction of the effect (+ or −) is shown next to each account title
   b.   indicate whether you are debiting (*dr*) and crediting (*cr*) each account
   c.   when a date is not given, use today's date for all transactions
   d.   all of these are true statements regarding journal entries

_____17. (LO3) The correct balance for the following T-account is:

Notes Payable			
(b)	3,500	Beg. Bal.	25,000
(d)	4,000	(a)	5,000
(e)	6,500	(c)	3,500

   a. $19,500 debit
   b. $19,500 credit
   c. $30,500 debit
   d. $30,500 credit

_____18. (LO2) After adding transaction analysis, the accounting cycle is expanded to which of the following:
   a.   analyze transactions, record in ledgers, summarize in journals
   b.   analyze ledgers, record in ledgers, summarize in journals
   c.   analyze transactions, record in journals, summarize in ledgers
   d.   analyze in journals, record in ledgers, summarize transactions

_____19. (LO4) A Classified Balance Sheet
   a.   classifies assets and liabilities based on whether they are internal events or external exchanges
   b.   classifies assets and liabilities into current and long-term categories
   c.   classifies assets and liabilities based on whether they are real or fraudulent
   d.   all of the above are true statements about a classified balance sheet

_____20. (LO5) Which of the following would *not* be considered an identifiable transaction and thus would *not* be reported on the balance sheet?
  a. purchase of supplies with an informal promise to pay in one month
  b. assets that are actually bought and recorded by the business
  c. cash received from a customer for providing a service
  d. the value of the name of a business

EXERCISES
Record your answer to each exercise in the space provided. Show your work.

Exercise 2-1. Classifying Balance Sheet Accounts (LO1, LO4)
An alphabetical listing of accounts for the Troy Company are listed below. In the space provided classify each as it should be reported on the balance sheet. Use the following codes:

CA = current asset CL = current liability SE = stockholders' equity
NCA = non-current asset NCL = non-current liability

_____ 1. Accounts Payable   _____ 7. Notes payable (due in 2 years)

_____ 2. Accounts Receivable   _____ 8. Land

_____ 3. Automobile   _____ 9. Wages payable

_____ 4. Building   _____ 10. Office supplies

_____ 5. Cash   _____ 11. Retained earnings

_____ 6. Contributed capital   _____ 12. Notes payable (due in 10 months)

Exercise 2-2. Identifying Events as Accounting Transactions (LO1, LO2)
Are the following events recordable transactions for *Jane's Janitorial*? Answer yes or no in the space provided.

	Event	Yes/No
1.	Jane's sold janitorial supplies to an employee.	
2.	Jane's ordered janitorial supplies from Janitorial Warehouse to be delivered in two weeks.	
3.	Jane's clean a building for a client and the client gave an informal promise to pay for the work at the end of the month.	
4.	Jane's purchases janitorial supplies with an informal promise to pay the amount due in two weeks.	
5.	Jane's hired a new secretary on January 1 who will be paid $900 on the last day of each month.	
6.	Jane purchased a heavy duty vacuum for her home.	

Exercise 2-3. Determining Financial Statement Effects of Several Transactions. (LO2)
For each of the following transactions for Trevor Corporation, indicate the accounts, amounts, and direction of the effects on the accounting equation. The first one has been done for you.

(a) Trevor Corporation issues 6,000 shares of its common stock to new investors for $60,000 cash.

ASSETS	=	LIABILITIES	+	STOCKHOLDERS' EQUITY
Cash +60,000				Contributed Capital +60,000

(b) Trevor Corporation purchases a machine for $20,000, paying $9,000 in cash and issuing a promissory note for the balance. The promissory note is due in 4 years.

ASSETS	=	LIABILITIES	+	STOCKHOLDERS' EQUITY

(c) A customer enters the establishment and wants to use Trevor's services next week. Trevor agrees to do the job next week for $4,000. An appointment is set up for the customer who agrees to pay Trevor when the job is completed.

ASSETS	=	LIABILITIES	+	STOCKHOLDERS' EQUITY

(d) Trevor Corporation lends $3,000 to Joseph Critchter, Inc. in exchange for a promissory note that is to be paid-off within 5 months.

ASSETS	=	LIABILITIES	+	STOCKHOLDERS' EQUITY

(e) Trevor Corporation paid $2,000 of the promissory note for the machines purchased in transaction (b).

ASSETS	=	LIABILITIES	+	STOCKHOLDERS' EQUITY

(f) Joseph Critchter, Inc. pays Trevor Corporation $500 of the promissory note in transaction (d).

ASSETS	=	LIABILITIES	+	STOCKHOLDERS' EQUITY

Exercise 2-4. Identify Increase, Decrease, & Normal Balance of Balance Sheet Elements (LO3)

Complete the table on the following page by placing an **X** in the correct "Type of Account" (only one **X** per line). Then enter the word **debit** or **credit** for the normal balance, increase, and decrease columns of the item. The first one has been done for you as an example.

Account	Type of Account (select ONE)			Debit or Credit Balance	Increase	Decrease
	Asset	Liability	Stockholders' Equity			
Cash	X			debit	debit	credit
Accounts payable						
Accounts receivable						
Automobile						
Building						
Contributed capital						
Land						
Inventory						
Office supplies						
Notes payable						
Retained earnings						

Exercise 2-5. Account Analysis (LO3)

a. Orange Uglad, Inc. borrows cash from the bank on an on-going basis. At the beginning of the year, they owed $25,000 to the bank. During the year they borrowed an additional $63,000 by signing additional notes with the bank. Payments to the bank throughout the year totaled $75,000. What is the balance in Orange Uglad, Inc.'s notes payable account at the end of the year? (Hint: use a T-account)

b. Orange Uglad, Inc. consistently lends cash to customers on a short-term basis. When the year started, customers owed them $4,000. Throughout the year, customers borrowed an additional $34,000 and repaid Orange Uglad, Inc. $27,000 on these loans. What is the balance in Orange Uglad, Inc.'s notes receivable account at the end of the year? (Hint: use a T-account)

c. During the year, Orange Uglad, Inc. collected $139,000 in cash and paid $75,800. At the end of the year, the cash account had a balance of $92,200. What was the amount of cash in Orange Uglad, Inc.'s cash account at the beginning of the year? Hint: Use a T-account.)

Exercise 2-6. Identifying Account Titles (LO1, 2)
Note: Exercises 2-6, 2-7, 2-8, and 2-9 are sequential problems and should be done in order.

In the space provided, write the names of the accounts affected by each of the following events. If the event is not a transaction, write "Not a transaction"

	Event	Account Titles
a.	A new company called Cody Company is created and sells 1,000 shares of stock to investors for $30 per share in cash.	Cash Contributed Capital
b.	Cody Company borrows $12,000 from a local bank and signed a four-month promissory note for the loan.	
c.	Cody Company lent $1,000 to a customer on a six-month note.	
d.	One of the stockholders in Cody Company sells 100 shares of their Cody Company stock for $30 per share to a neighbor down the street.	
e.	The company president purchases a $50,000 Lexus for personal use.	
f.	Cody Company purchased equipment costing $12,000 by paying $4,000 cash and the balance on two-year note.	
g.	Cody Company purchased plumbing supplies with an informal promise to pay $1,000.	
h.	A new Treasurer is hired for Cody Company at an annual salary of $125,000. The treasurer will report to work at the beginning of next month.	
i.	Cody Company received land valued at $20,000 from an investor in exchange for stock.	
j.	The customer from transaction (c) paid Cody Company the amount due (ignore interest)	
k.	Cody Company paid the bank the full amount owed in transaction (b) (ignore interest)	
l.	Cody Company sold some extra supplies they had, to another business in the strip mall, for the same amount they paid for it $100 cash.	
m.	Cody Company bought an automobile with a NADA Blue Book Value of $6,000 for $4,500 cash.	

Required:
a. Indicate the titles of the appropriate accounts, if any, affected in each of the preceding event. Consider what the company gives and receives.) The first one has been done for you.

b. What dollar amount would you use for the purchase price of the automobile in transaction (m)? What measurement principle are you applying?

        Dollar amount: $_____

        Measurement principle applied: _____

c. What reasoning did you apply in answering letters (d) and (h)?

        Reasoning for (d) _____

        Reasoning for (h) _____

Exercise 2-7. Preparing Journal Entries (LO3)

Note: Exercises 2-6, 2-7, 2-8, and 2-9 are sequential problems and should be done in order.

For each of the transactions in Exercise 2-6, write the journal entry using the format shown in the chapter. The sample has been done for you.   (Explanations may be omitted)

	Account	Debit	Credit
(a)	*dr* Cash (+A)....(1,000 * $30)...	30,000	
	cr Contributed Capital (+SE)…....…..................................…………		30,000

Exercise 2-8. Posting to T-Accounts (LO3)
Note: Exercises 2-6, 2-7, 2-8, and 2-9 are sequential problems and should be done in order.

For each of the journal entries prepared in Exercise 2-7, post the effects to the appropriate T-accounts and determine ending account balances. The sample has been done for you.

+ Cash (A) –		+ Notes Receivable (A) –		+ Plumbing Supplies (A) –	
beg bal	0	beg bal	0	beg bal	0
(a)	30,000				
		end bal		end bal	
end bal					

+ Land (A) –		+ Automobile (A) –		+ Equipment (A) –	
beg bal	0	beg bal	0	beg bal	0
end bal		end bal		end bal	

– Accounts Payable (L) +		– Notes Payable (L) +		– Contributed Capital (SE) +	
	beg bal 0		beg bal 0		beg bal 0
					(a) 30,000
	end bal				
			end bal		end bal

Exercise 2-9. Preparing a Classified Balance Sheet (LO4)
Note: Exercises 2-6, 2-7, 2-8, and 2-9 are sequential problems and should be done in order.

Given the transactions in results in Exercise 2-8, prepare a classified balance sheet for Cody Company. Assume it is prepared on December 31, 2008.

SOLUTIONS TO SELF-TEST QUESTIONS AND EXERCISES

MATCHING

D	Chart of Accounts		F	Journal
M	Classified Balance Sheet		E	Journal Entry
H	Conservatism		J	Ledger
P	Contributed Capital		A	Post
N	Cost principle		O	Retained Earnings
C	Current Assets		G	Stockholders' Equity
I	Current Liabilities		L	T-account
B	Debits and Credits		K	Transaction

TRUE-FALSE QUESTIONS

1. F – Assets are listed in order of how quickly they will be used up or can be turned into cash.
2. T
3. T
4. F – Contributed Capital includes the amount of financing contributed by the owners of the business.
5. F – Though companies tend to use similar account names, designated account numbers vary greatly depending on each company's accounting system.
6. T
7. F – Exchanges of assets between the company and someone else (you) are considered external exchanges.
8. T
9. F – The effects of "give and receive" on the accounting equation occur during the 'analyze' step of the accounting cycle.
10. T
11. T
12. F – The term debit means "left" and the term "credit" means right. For some accounts a debit is an increase and for others it's a decrease. For some accounts a credit is an increase and for others it's a decrease.
13. F – Debits appear first and credits are written below and indented to the right.
14. T
15. F – Post means to copy the debit and credit amounts from a journal entry in the corresponding T-Accounts.
16. F – An exchange of only promises is not considered a transaction. No journal entry is needed.
17. T
18. F – While Assets – Liabilities is often referred to as Net Worth, it is not a true indicator of company value.
19. T
20. F – A special concept called conservatism requires that special care be taken to avoid reporting assets at too high an amount or reporting liabilities at too low an amount.

MULTIPLE CHOICE QUESTIONS

1. B	6. C	11. B	16. C
2. A	7. D	12. A	17. B
3. B	8. D	13. B	18. C
4. A	9. A	14. D	19. B
5. A	10. C	15. B	20. D

EXERCISES

Exercise 2-1. Classifying Balance Sheet Accounts (LO1, LO4)

__CL__	1. Accounts Payable		__NCL__	7. Notes payable (due in 2 years)
__CA__	2. Accounts Receivable		__NCA__	8. Land
__NCA__	3. Automobile		__CL__	9. Wages payable
__NCA__	4. Building		__CA__	10. Office supplies
__CA__	5. Cash		__SE__	11. Retained earnings
__SE__	6. Contributed capital		__CL__	12. Notes payable (due in 10 months)

Exercise 2-2. Identifying Events as Accounting Transactions (LO1, LO2)

Event	Yes/No		Event	Yes/No
1.	Yes		4.	Yes
2.	No		5.	No
3.	Yes		6.	No

Exercise 2-3. Determining Financial Statement Effects of Several Transactions. (LO2)

(a)

ASSETS	=	LIABILITIES	+	STOCKHOLDERS' EQUITY
Cash +60,000				Contributed Capital +60,000

(b)

ASSETS	=	LIABILITIES	+	STOCKHOLDERS' EQUITY
Machines +20,000		Notes payable +11,000		
Cash − 9,000				

(c)

ASSETS	=	LIABILITIES	+	STOCKHOLDERS' EQUITY
Not a transaction				

(d)

ASSETS	=	LIABILITIES	+	STOCKHOLDERS' EQUITY
Cash −3,000				
Notes Receivable +3,000				

(e)

ASSETS	=	LIABILITIES	+	STOCKHOLDERS' EQUITY
Cash −2,000		Notes Payable −2,000		

(f)

ASSETS	=	LIABILITIES	+	STOCKHOLDERS' EQUITY
Cash +500				
Notes Receivable -500				

Exercise 2-4. Identify Increase, Decrease, & Normal Balance of Balance Sheet Elements (LO3)

Account	Type of Account (select ONE)			Debit or Credit Balance	Increase	Decrease
	Asset	Liability	Stockholders' Equity			
Cash	X			debit	debit	credit
Accounts payable		X		credit	credit	debit
Accounts receivable	X			debit	debit	credit
Automobile	X			debit	debit	credit
						(continued)
Building	X			debit	debit	credit
Contributed capital			X	credit	credit	debit
Land	X			debit	debit	credit
Inventory	X			debit	debit	credit
Office supplies	X			debit	debit	credit
Notes payable		X		credit	credit	debit
Retained earnings			X	credit	credit	debit

Exercise 2-5. Account Analysis (LO3)

Note: two alternative solutions are shown for each situation

a.
25,000	
+63,000	
88,000	
-75,000	
13,000	

For a Credit Balance Account:
(1) Add the two numbers on the credit side together
(2) Subtract the number on the debit side
(3) To get the ending balance in the account

Notes Payable

75,000	25,000
	63,000
	13,000

b.
4,000	
+34,000	
38,000	
- 27,000	
11,000	

For a Debit Balance Account:
(1) Add the two numbers on the debit side together
(2) Subtract the number on the credit side
(3) To get the ending balance in the account

Notes Receivable

4,000	27,000
34,000	
11,000	

c.
139,000	
-75,800	
63,200	
92,200	
-63,200	
29,000	

For a Debit Balance Account:
(1) Using the two numbers above the subtotal line, subtract the smaller number from the larger number
(2) Now subtract the number you just figured out from the total below the line.
(3) To get what the beginning amount must have been.

Cash

29,000	
139,000	75,800
92,200	

Exercise 2-6. Identifying Account Titles (LO1, 2)

	Event	Account Titles
a.	A new company called Cody Company is created and sells 1,000 shares of stock to investors for $30 per share in cash.	Cash Contributed Capital
b.	Cody Company borrows $12,000 from a local bank and signed a four-month promissory note for the loan.	Cash Notes Payable
c.	Cody Company lent $1,000 to a customer on a six-month note.	Notes Receivable Cash
d.	One of the stockholders in …per share to a neighbor down the street.	Not a transaction
e.	The company president purchases a $50,000 Lexus for personal use.	Not a transaction
f.	Cody Company purchased equipment costing $12,000 by paying $4,000 cash and the balance on two-year note.	Equipment Cash Notes Payable
g.	Cody Company purchased plumbing supplies with an informal promise to pay $800.	Plumbing Supplies Accounts Payable
h.	A new Treasurer is hired ….report to work at the beginning of next month.	Not a transaction
i.	Cody Company received land valued at $20,000 from an investor in exchange for stock.	Land Contributed Capital

j.	The customer from transaction (c) paid Cody Company the amount due (ignore interest)	Cash Notes Receivable
k.	Cody Company paid the bank the full amount owed in transaction (b) (ignore interest)	Notes Payable Cash
l.	Cody Company sold some extra supplies they had, to another business in the strip mall, for the same amount they paid for it $100 cash.	Cash Plumbing Supplies
m.	Cody Company bought an automobile with a NADA Blue Book Value of $6,000 for $4,500 cash	Automobile Cash

a.   See previous table.

b.   Dollar Amount: $ 4,500

              Measurement principle applied: cost principle

c.   Reasoning for (d): nothing is received or given up by the company, so there is no transaction

            Reasoning for (h): thus far, no recordable exchange has taken place. This is an exchange of a promise for a promise

Exercise 2-7. Preparing Journal Entries. (LO3)

(a)   *dr* Cash (+A)....(1,000 * $30)..   30,000

        cr Contributed Capital (+SE)..   30,000

(b)   *dr* Cash (+A)..   12,000

        cr Notes Payable (+L)...   12,000

(c)   *dr* Notes Receivable (+A)...   1,000

        cr Cash (–A)...   1,000

(d)   Not a transaction

(e)   Not a transaction

(f)   *dr* Equipment (+A)..   12,000

        cr Cash (–A)...   4,000

        cr Notes Payable (+L)......($12,000 – 4,000)...........................   8,000

(g)   *dr* Plumbing Supplies (+L)...   1,000

        cr Accounts Payable (+L)...   1,000

(h)   Not a transaction.

(i)   *dr* Land (+A)...   20,000

        cr Contributed Capital (+L)...   20,000

(j)   *dr* Cash (+A)..   1,000

        cr Notes Receivable (–A)...   1,000

(k)   *dr* Notes Payable (–L)...   12,000

        cr Cash (–A)...   12,000

(l)   *dr* Cash (+A)..   100

        cr Plumbing Supplies (–A)...   100

(m)   *dr* Automobile (+A)...   4,500

        cr Cash (–A)...   4,500

Exercise 2-8. Posting to T-accounts. (LO3)

+ Cash (A) –			
beg bal	0	(c)	1,000
(a)	30,000	(f)	4,000
(b)	12,000	(k)	12,000
(j)	1,000	(m)	4,500
(l)	100		
end bal	21,600		

+ Notes Receivable (A) –			
beg bal	0		
(c)	1,000	(j)	1,000
end bal	0		

+ Plumbing Supplies (A) –			
beg bal	0		
(g)	1,000	(l)	100
end bal	900		

+ Land (A) –		
beg bal	0	
(i)	20,000	
end bal	20,000	

+ Automobile (A) –		
beg bal	0	
(m)	4,500	
end bal	4,500	

+ Equipment (A) –		
beg bal	0	
(f)	12,000	
end bal	12,000	

(Continued)

– Accounts Payable (L) +		
	beg bal	0
	(g)	1,000
	end bal	1,000

– Notes Payable (L) +			
(k)	12,000	beg bal	0
		(b)	12,000
		(f)	8,000
		end bal	8,000

– Contributed Capital (SE) +		
	beg bal	0
	(a)	30,000
	(i)	20,000
	end bal	50,000

Exercise 2-9. Prepare a Balance Sheet. (LO4)

Cody Company
Balance Sheet

Assets

Current assets:

Cash		$ 21,600
Plumbing Supplies		900
Total current assets		22,500
Plant & Equipment:		
Land	$ 20,000	
Automobile	4,500	
Equipment	12,000	36,500
Total Assets		$ 59,000

Liabilities and Stockholders' Equity

Current liabilities:

Accounts Payable	$ 1,000	
Total current liabilities		1,000
Notes payable		8,000
Total liabilities		9,000
Stockholders' equity:		
Contributed Capital	50,000	
Retained Earnings	0	
Total stockholders' equity		50,000
Total liabilities and stockholders' equity		$59,000

ORGANIZATION OF THE CHAPTER

Understand the business	**Study the accounting methods**	**Evaluate the results**	**Review the chapter**
- Operating transactions and income statement accounts	- Cash basis accounting - Accrual basis accounting - The expanded accounting equation - Unadjusted trial balance - Review of revenues and expenses	- Income statement limitations	- Demonstration case - Chapter summary - Key terms -Practice material

CHAPTER FOCUS SUGGESTIONS

Review
In Chapter 2 you were introduced to the balance sheet which is merely an expanded version of the basic accounting equation. You learned about the accounting cycle and how to apply transaction analysis to a variety of business transactions. This analysis of the balance sheet was further expanded to include journal entries and T-accounts culminating in the preparation of a balance sheet. Finally, you were presented with a method to determine (1) what items are recorded and (2) the amounts that are assigned to these recorded items, and how the violation of these 'rules' can have huge consequences.

Introduction
Now, you are ready to focus your attention on the operating aspects of the company. This requires a deeper look at the income statement which focuses primarily on the day-to-day operations of a business. The primary purpose of the income statement is to show whether the company enjoyed a profit or suffered a loss as a result of these activities for a period of time. You'll again be applying the DECIDES transaction analysis approach to these operating activities. Lastly, you'll learn the key accounting concepts that determine income statement reporting.

UNDERSTAND THE BUSINESS
Operating Transactions and Income Statement Accounts

Learning Objective 1
Describe common operating transactions and select appropriate income statement account titles.

The great thing about the income statement is that only TWO primary types of items are reported on it (so, it's easy to remember): Revenues and Expenses.
In the immortal words of Porky Pig…."Tha Tha Tha That's all Folks!!" If it isn't a revenue or expense, it belongs on another statement.

Revenues are what the company earns in running its day-to-day operations. Basically, it is what the company does to 'earn a living' much like what you do to earn your living. In accounting lingo, Revenues are sales of goods or services to customers.

The most important thing to remember about revenues is that it doesn't matter whether you RECEIVED the money for any of this stuff yet. If your customers received the goods or were provided the services, the company is entitled to report them as Revenues or Earnings (these two terms are essentially interchangeable). So, if someone tells you that a business 'earned' a certain amount or it had a certain amount of 'revenues,' they are saying the exact same thing. Don't let the terminology confuse you. The accounting period, by the way, is always stated in the heading of the income statement.

Now, ready for the easy stuff? **Expenses** are all the day-to-day costs of the business incurs in providing customers with these sales and services. In other words, the costs a business incurs in order to earn its revenues.

The most important thing to remember about expenses is that they cannot be reported on the income statement as an expense unless and until they have been 'used' up by the business. With most expenses, you can determine this 'usage' easily. For example, salaries and/or wages aren't paid until a company has 'used' the services of its employees. Rent is typically paid at the beginning of each month. The assumption is that you will 'use' the rent for the current month since you've paid for it. The 'usage' of some other items is a bit more difficult to determine. For example, a company doesn't 'use-up' the inventories that it has purchased until the inventories have been 'used' for their intended purpose (i.e. until a company has *sold* them to a customer). So, inventory usage doesn't occur until a sale has taken place.

After all revenues and expenses have been listed on the income statement, the expenses are subtracted from the revenues (revenues – expenses) and this difference, or the net amount, is reported as **Net Income** (often referred to as Net Profit, 'in the Black', or the Bottom Line.) In the event that the expenses are greater than the revenues, the difference is referred to as a Net Loss (or 'in the Red.') It is Net Income that is being referred to in News Reports when you hear things like, "X Company failed to meet its 4th quarter profit expectations", or "Y Company profits exceeded market expectations by 10%". Net income is the figure that drives the stock market and ultimately determines the price that companies can get when they sell their stock! So, this number is of MAJOR importance in accounting.

Every business plans to be in existence for many, many years. But, in order to make investment and credit decisions, financial statement users need information about the company's profits (or losses) in a timely manner. So, the long life of a company can be divided up into shorter periods of time by preparing financial statements annually, quarterly, or even monthly in order to meet these needs. In accounting, this is referred to as the **time period assumption.**

STUDY THE ACCOUNTING METHODS

Cash-Basis Accounting
You may think that determining the revenues and expenses of a business is easy. When money is received by the business – it must be the revenue…and when money is paid by the business – it must be expenses, right? Well, not exactly. The accounting method just described is called **cash basis accounting.** Cash basis accounting probably makes sense to you because if you *get* money, you must have *earned* it; and if you *paid* money, must have *used* something, right? Well, in a word, no. Why not? Let's look at two scenarios: (1) assume you pay your son $10 to mow the lawn, but you give the $10 to him BEFORE he has mowed anything! Should the child be allowed to say he 'earned' that money? No! He hasn't done a thing! No services were rendered (never mind that you're a fool for paying him before he mowed the lawn.) (2) Then again, what if your daughter mows the lawn and you don't have any cash, so you promise to pay her next week. Has she earned the $10 even though you haven't paid her yet? YES! She's done the services and is due the money. These two examples indicate why it is inappropriate to report earnings at the time the cash changes hands rather than when the work was actually performed.

Generally, cash basis accounting doesn't measure financial performance very well when transactions are conducted using credit rather than cash. This is because credit transactions often have a significant delay between the time the activity occurs and the time when the cash account is impacted by the activity.

Accrual-Basis Accounting
The scenario just described is the basis for accrual-basis accounting. **Accrual-basis accounting** reports revenues when they are earned and expenses when they are incurred, regardless of the timing of the corresponding cash receipts or

Learning Objective 2
Explain and apply the revenue and matching principles.

payments. This is the *only* method allowed for external reporting purposes according to generally accepted accounting principles (GAAP). The *rule of accrual* requires that financial effects of business activities be measured and reported when the activities *actually occur* not when the cash related to them is received or paid.

1. Revenue Principle – Revenue Recognition
The *revenue principle* requires that revenues be recognized when they are earned. *Recognized* refers to actually measuring and reporting the revenue in the accounting system. *Earned* means that the company has actually performed the acts promised to the customer. The key factor in determining when to recognize revenue is whether or not the company has performed the promised acts for the customer. Unfortunately, *when* the company receives

the cash and *when* the company performs the promised acts may differ. Three possibilities exist: cash maybe received at the same time the promised acts are performed, cash may be received before the promised acts are performed, or cash may be received after the promised acts are performed. Let's take a look at each of these situations individually:

(1) Cash is received in the **same** *period as the promised acts are performed.*
In this situation, the cash is received in the same period as the promised act or service is performed. The company has more earnings (Revenues) because the act was performed and it also has more money (cash) because the customer paid for the service as soon as it was performed. For example, this is what *should* have happened with the lawn scenario. Your child mows the lawn and you pay him. He has revenue (earned through performance of the act) and cash!

(2) Cash is received in the period **before** *the promised acts are performed.*
This is the situation that occurs when you pay your child *before* he mows the lawn. He has money in his pocket, but hasn't performed the promised act. In accounting, this 'unperformed act' is called *unearned revenue*. He OWES you a lawn-mowing. When someone *owes* something (even if it isn't money that is owed) they have a liability. So, your son has more liabilities (unearned revenue) as well as more assets (cash.) It may seem odd that he has an *increase* in a liability but, consider that he owes MORE 'debt' than he did before (because he owes you a lawn-mowing) so he now has increased his debt. At this time, he cannot report this as income. He must wait until he fulfills his lawn mowing at some point in the future – when he has actually 'earned' it. Then, he can also remove the liability since he will have fulfilled the promise and owes nothing more.

(3) Cash is to be received in the period **after** *the promised acts are performed.*
This is the situation that occurred when your daughter mowed the lawn and therefore earned the $10, but you haven't paid her yet. She has the 'right to collect' the $10 from you (this right is called an Account Receivable in accounting). This Account Receivable has value to her ($10 bucks). So, it is reported as an increase in assets on the balance sheet (Accounts Receivable) and an increase in an income statement account called Lawn Mowing Revenue (revenue). Notice that revenue is recorded in this situation because she has *earned* it (by performing the act), even if she hasn't *received* cash yet.

A company's *revenue recognition policy* is usually reported in the notes to the financial statements.

2.   The Matching Principle – Expense Recognition
The matching principle goes hand-in-hand with the revenue principle. Essentially, it states that expenses must be recorded in the *same period* that the revenues they helped create were reported. For example, if an employee works on December 30 and 31 of 2007, these wages must be *expensed* by the business in 2007…even though they won't be paid until 2008. Why? Because these employees helped to bring in revenues for the business in 2007 (when they worked)…not in 2008 (when they were *paid* for the work), the reporting period of the expense must be *matched* with the period in which the corresponding revenues were earned. The revenue and the employee work both occurred in 2007…so, the wages expense will be reported in 2007. If an expense cannot be directly associated with revenues, we record it in the period that the underlying business activity occurs. It is the *timing* of the underlying business activity that determines expense recognition, not necessarily when the cash is paid out.

Much like revenues, the incurrence of the expenses and the related payment of those expenses may not happen at the same time. There are three possibilities regarding when the cash is paid versus when the expense is incurred: cash may be paid at the same time that the cost is incurred, cash may be paid before the cost is incurred, or cash may be paid after the cost is incurred. Once again, we'll look at each of situations these individually:

(1) Cash is paid in the **same** *period as the cost is incurred.*
Once more, this is the easiest scenario and the only one in which the cash-basis of accounting and the accrual-basis of accounting will result in identical amounts. In this case, the cash is paid in the same period in which the cost was incurred. A good example of this is if the company had a temporary worker come in for one day. At the end of the day, the temporary worker would be paid. The company has less money (Cash) and more expenses (worker's wages). This transaction will decrease both the income statement (because of the additional expense) and the balance sheet (Cash).

(2) Cash is paid in the period before *the cost is incurred.*

The most common example of this type of cost is automobile insurance. Oftentimes, automobile insurance is paid every six months. That is, you are paying for the insurance *before* you actually receive the benefit of it (through the passage of the six months.) The insurance company owes you the six months worth of insurance coverage that you paid for *before* the insurance is used. This creates an increase in assets (Prepaid Insurance) and a decrease in assets (Cash.) The 'unused' insurance remains in the prepaid insurance account the six months have elapsed.

(3) Cash is to be paid in the period after *the cost is incurred.*

A good example of this is your utility bill. You use utilities all month long, but don't pay for them until you get the bill the *following* month (after you've *already* used the gas, electric, etc.) In this situation you actually incur the costs (receive the benefits) before you pay for them. This transaction causes a decrease in the income statement (because you have additional expenses due to the utilities you've used) and an increase in liabilities (balance sheet) because you still owe the utility company for the utilities.

The Expanded Accounting Equation

Chapter 2 focused on the investing and financing activities (balance sheet) of a business. Now, we need to expand the focus to include the operating activities (income statement) presented in this chapter.

> **Learning Objective 3**
> Analyze, record, and summarize the effects of operating transactions, using the accounting equation, journal entries, and T-accounts.

Before getting into the nitty-gritty, a quick review of chapter 2 is in order, starting with the very basics: $A = L + SE$. In dealing with operating activities, we need to focus on the SE chunk of the equation. Remember that stockholders' equity deals with stockholders' investment in the business. This can be provided one to two ways: (1) *Contributed Capital* – the stockholder giving cash to the business in exchange for ownership in the company (shares of stock.); (2) *Retained Earnings* – generated by the company itself through profitable operations.

This chapter has added revenues and expenses into the mix. From the following diagram, you can see that *Retained Earnings* is created from net income, which in turn is determined by revenues minus expenses. Since Retained Earnings is created from revenues and expenses, any increases to retained earnings (revenues) and decreases to retained earnings (expenses) must behave in the same way. That is, retained earnings is increased with credits (revenues) and decreased with debits (expenses). It follows, then that *revenues are recorded on the right* and *expenses are recorded on the left!!*

Now that you understand the debit and credit effects on revenues and expenses, you're ready to add them into the **DECIDES** model from chapter 2 as shown in the following illustration:

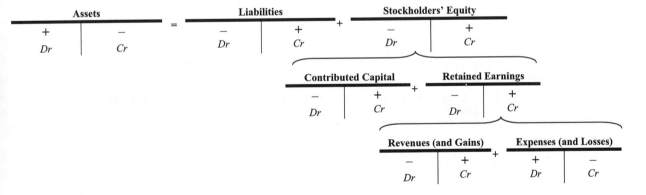

Transaction Analysis, Recording, and Summarizing

Now, it's time to apply transactions analysis to the revenue recognition principle and the matching principle described earlier. An example of each will be provided so that you can expand your understanding of the accounting cycle and learn to apply transaction analysis to operating activities within a business. The best way to learn how this is simply to practice, practice, practice!! Detailed explanations of the transactions will not be presented here. The primary focus will be proper recording of the transactions. Refer to your text for detailed analysis of operating activity transactions. Ready? Here we go!

Assume you own a company that provides landscaping services to a wide variety of residential and commercial customers throughout the city. The name of the business is LandShapes Unlimited. Assume that a $5,000 investment of cash was made by owners in exchange for stock prior to any of the following transactions. (Note: this transaction is not be illustrated due to space considerations)

Example (a) Cash is received in the same period as the promised acts are performed.
A customer asks you to come out and perform a variety of services for $200 cash.

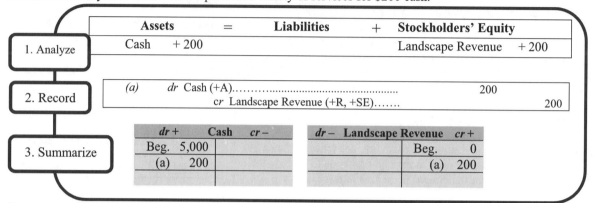

It is important to note that because Landscape Revenue is a subaccount of Stockholders' Equity, both are increase as a result of this transaction (as shown in Step 2.)

Example (b) Cash is received in the period before the promised acts are performed.
One of your biggest customers will be out of the country for six months and has paid you $1,200 to cover the monthly landscape maintenance you will be performing on his estate.

	1. Analyze	Assets	=	Liabilities	+	Stockholders' Equity
		Cash + 1,200		Unearned Revenue +1,200		

	2. Record				
	(b)	dr Cash (+A)...		1,200	
		cr Unearned Revenue (+L)..................			1,200

3. Summarize		dr +	Cash	cr –		dr –	Unearned Revenues	cr +
		Beg. 5,000					Beg.	0
		(a) 200					(b)	1,200
		(b) 1,200						

Recall that a liability exists when money is received for services that have not yet been performed. The $1,200 cannot be reported as income until the monthly landscape maintenance is performed.

Example (c) Cash is to be received in the period after the promised acts are performed. You performed $3,000 of landscaping for a regular customer. She requested that you bill her for the services rendered.

1. Analyze	Assets	=	Liabilities	+	Stockholders' Equity
	Accounts Receivable +3,000				Landscape Revenue + 3,000

2. Record	(c)	dr Accounts Receivable (+A).......................................	3,000	
		cr Landscape Revenue (+R, +SE)............		3,000

3. Summarize					

dr+ Accounts Receivable *cr –*			*dr –* Landscape Revenue *cr +*	
Beg.	0		Beg.	0
(c)	3,000		(a)	200
			(c)	3,000

In this situation, revenue must be recognized since the promised act has been performed. The accounts receivable account serves as an indication that collection has not yet occurred for this transaction.

Example (d) Cash is received for transaction *(c)*.
Although this particular situation was not addressed earlier in the discussion, at some point you will collect the money that the customer owes you in transaction *(c)*. This is the entry that is made when collection occurs.

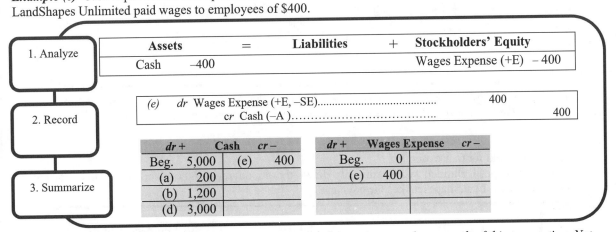

1. Analyze					

	Assets	**=**	**Liabilities**	**+**	**Stockholders' Equity**
Cash	+ 3,000				
Accounts Receivable	–3,000				

2. Record				
(d)	*dr* Cash (+A)..		3,000	
	cr Accounts Receivable (–A)...........			3,000

dr +	Cash	*cr –*		*dr +* Accounts Receivable *cr –*	
Beg.	5,000			Beg.	0
(a)	200			(c) 3,000	(d) 3,000
(b)	1,200				
(d)	3,000				

3. Summarize					

*Note that this entry does not affect revenue. The customer simply paid the **bill** that you mailed to her. When the money is collected, the amount she owes you is eliminated. This is shown in the accounts receivable account because the account has a zero balance after this transaction is posted.*

Example (e) Cash is paid in the same period as the cost is incurred.
LandShapes Unlimited paid wages to employees of $400.

1. Analyze					

	Assets	**=**	**Liabilities**	**+**	**Stockholders' Equity**
Cash	–400				Wages Expense (+E) – 400

2. Record				
(e)	*dr* Wages Expense (+E, –SE)..		400	
	cr Cash (–A)......................................			400

dr +	Cash	*cr –*		*dr +*	Wages Expense	*cr –*
Beg.	5,000	(e) 400		Beg.	0	
(a)	200			(e)	400	
(b)	1,200					
(d)	3,000					

3. Summarize						

*While the expenses of LandShapes Unlimited (costs incurred) have increased as a result of this transaction, Net Income has actually **decreased**. Recall that expenses are **subtracted** from revenues in determining net income. Since expenses are a subaccount of stockholders' equity, this increase in expenses results in decreases to both the net income and the stockholders' equity.*

Example (f) Cash is paid in the period before the cost is incurred.
LandShapes Unlimited purchased a one year insurance policy for the business $2,400.

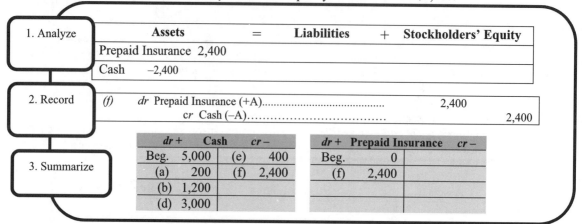

1. Analyze	**Assets**	**= Liabilities**	**+ Stockholders' Equity**
	Prepaid Insurance 2,400		
	Cash −2,400		

2. Record	(f)	*dr* Prepaid Insurance (+A).................................	2,400	
		cr Cash (−A)..................................		2,400

dr +	Cash	*cr −*		*dr +*	Prepaid Insurance	*cr −*
Beg.	5,000	(e) 400		Beg.	0	
(a)	200	(f) 2,400		(f)	2,400	
(b)	1,200					
(d)	3,000					

*This is a payment **now** for services in the future. There is future value here because LandShapes has insurance coverage for an entire year. This is prepayment of services is an asset. Until the year's worth of coverage has expired, this has future value to the company.*

Example (g) Cash is to be paid in the period after the cost is incurred.
LandShapes Unlimited called the City Herald to place an advertisement in the newspaper. The City Herald has agreed to send a bill for the amount due, $500.

1. Analyze	**Assets**	**= Liabilities**	**+ Stockholders' Equity**
		Accounts Payable +500	Advertising Expense (+E), (−SE) − 500

2. Record	(g)	*dr* Advertising Expense(+E, −SE).................................	500	
		cr Accounts Payable (+L)......................		500

dr −	Accounts Payable	*cr +*		*dr +*	Advertising Expense	*cr −*
	Beg.	0			Beg.	0	
	(a)	500			(a)	500	

*In this case, LandShapes has received the benefits of the advertising, but have not yet paid for these benefits. Therefore, they **owe** the City Herald $500. This is considered a liability called Accounts Payable.*

Example (h) Cash is paid for transaction (g).
At some point, LandShapes Unlimited will pay the City Herald the amount due for the advertising. This is the entry that would be made when LandShapes makes the payment.

1. Analyze	**Assets**	**= Liabilities**	**+ Stockholders' Equity**
	Cash − 500	Accounts Payable −500	

2. Record	(h)	*dr* Accounts Payable (−L)......................................	500	
		cr Cash (−A)......................................		500

Study Guide, Chapter 3

3. Summarize in Ledgers	dr +	Cash	cr –		dr –	Accounts Payable	cr +
	Beg.	5,000	(e)	400	(h) 500	Beg.	0
	(a)	200	(f)	2,400		(a)	500
	(b)	1,200	(h)	500			
	(d)	3,000					

Note that this entry does not affect expenses. *LandShapes Unlimited* simply paid the **bill** that they received from the City Herald. When the money is paid, the amount owed is eliminated. This is shown in the accounts payable account because the account has a zero balance after this transaction is posted.

Calculating Account Balances
When all of the transactions have been entered (posted) into the T-accounts, you can calculate the ending balances. As discussed in Chapter 2, the ending balance in each account can be determined by adding the amounts on the "+" side and subtracting the amounts on the "–" side.

Unadjusted Trial Balance

Learning Objective 4
Prepare an unadjusted trial balance.

The possibility of making a mistake when you transfer information from the journal to the T-accounts is very high. We all make errors. The most common types of recording errors are:

(1) accidentally putting a number as a credit when it was a debit (or vise versa)
(2) transferring only part of a journal entry (i.e. just the debit or just the credit)
(3) using the wrong amount when transferring the entry into the T-accounts.
(4) Incorrectly calculating the ending balance in a T-account.

Luckily, a tool has been developed that can help you find some of these common errors—a trial balance. A trial balance is an internal document which lists all of the account names in one column and their ending balances in the appropriate debit or credit column. After you add up all the debit amounts and get a total, then add up all of the credit amounts and get a total – the two totals should be the same (i.e. they should balance.) We're just 'trying' it out to be sure everything balances, so it is called a 'trial balance.'

But wait, this section is labeled the *unadjusted* trial balance…what gives? In order to accurately report revenues and expenses on the income statement, certain 'adjustments' need to be made to some of the accounts. Without these adjustments the income statement may not provide a reliable, all-inclusive calculation of a company's net income. Just to ensure that you are kept riveted, we will not discuss adjustments any further until Chapter 4 so, stay tuned!

If the total debits and total credits are not the same when you prepare your trial balance, subtract one total from the other total and see what the difference is between the two totals. If the difference is:

- The same amount as one of your T-account balances, you probably forgot to put that total on your trial balance.
- Double the amount of a specific transaction, you may have summarized a debit as a credit or a credit as a debit in one of the affected T-accounts.
- Evenly divisible by 9, you probably reversed the order of two digits in a number (ie. 54 vs.45), or left a zero off of the end of a number (60 vs. 600). This type of error is called a transposition error.
- Evenly divisible by 3, you may have hit the key above or below the one you intended to hit (like 4 instead of 7) with your numeric keypad.
- Double the amount of a specific account balance, you probably put a debit balance amount into the credit column or put a credit balance amount into the debit column.

One final comment before we complete this topic, even if total debits = total credits and everything balances, it doesn't necessarily mean you haven't made mistakes. You may have debited Equipment for 300…but, you *should* have debited Supplies. This error will *not* cause your trial balance to be out of balance, but an error has been made.

Review of Revenues and Expenses
You've now had the opportunity to see a variety of transactions involving operating activities (and there's a bunch of 'em!) This is a great place to do a quick summary of all the information we've covered about revenues, expenses,

and journal entries. The exhibits presented in your text are duplicated here. Don't gloss over them! These accrual-basis revenue and expense transactions must be understood thoroughly. Take the time to study and learn the information contained in the tables presented in each of the following sections.

Revenues are recorded when a business completes its promise to provide goods or services to its customers. Since this may not occur when cash is received by the business, three separate cases were examined: (1) when cash is received at the *same* time as the promised acts are performed (middle panel), (2) when cash is received *before* the promised acts are performed (left panel), and (3) when cash is received *after* the promised acts are performed. See if you can match the panels with the landscaping examples provided earlier in this chapter.

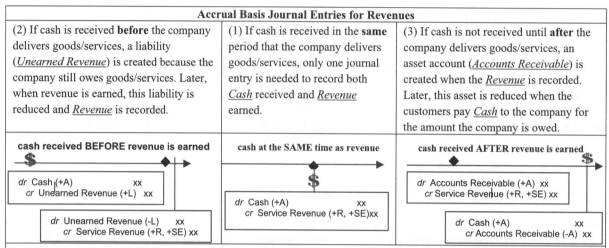

Accrual Basis Journal Entries for Revenues

(2) If cash is received **before** the company delivers goods/services, a liability (*Unearned Revenue*) is created because the company still owes goods/services. Later, when revenue is earned, this liability is reduced and *Revenue* is recorded.

(1) If cash is received in the **same** period that the company delivers goods/services, only one journal entry is needed to record both *Cash* received and *Revenue* earned.

(3) If cash is not received until **after** the company delivers goods/services, an asset account (*Accounts Receivable*) is created when the *Revenue* is recorded. Later, this asset is reduced when the customers pay *Cash* to the company for the amount the company is owed.

Explanation: In the three different situations above, the diamond (♦) indicates the point in time at which the company performs the promised act of delivering to the customer goods/services. The dollar sign ($) indicates the point in time at which the company receives cash from the customer for the promised act.

Accrual-basis accounting requires that expenses be recorded when they are incurred, not necessarily when the cash is paid. Recall that expenses are incurred when the items acquired do not have a future economic benefit to the company or when assets already owned by the company are used up. Like revenues, the timing of the payment for the item and the time when the expense is incurred create three possibilities: (1) when cash is paid at the *same* time the expense is incurred (middle panel), (2) when cash is paid *before* the expense is incurred (left panel), and (3) when cash is paid *after* the expense is incurred. See if you can match the panels with the insurance and supplies examples provided earlier in this chapter.

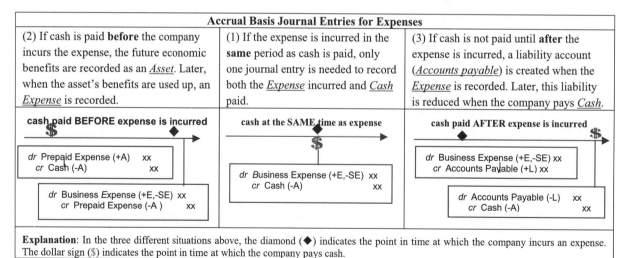

Accrual Basis Journal Entries for Expenses

(2) If cash is paid **before** the company incurs the expense, the future economic benefits are recorded as an *Asset*. Later, when the asset's benefits are used up, an *Expense* is recorded.

(1) If the expense is incurred in the **same** period as cash is paid, only one journal entry is needed to record both the *Expense* incurred and *Cash* paid.

(3) If cash is not paid until **after** the expense is incurred, a liability account (*Accounts payable*) is created when the *Expense* is recorded. Later, this liability is reduced when the company pays *Cash*.

Explanation: In the three different situations above, the diamond (♦) indicates the point in time at which the company incurs an expense. The dollar sign ($) indicates the point in time at which the company pays cash.

EVALUATE THE RESULTS

Learning Objective 5
Describe the limitations of
the income statement.

Income Statement Limitations
Though the income statement is a good indicator of a company's operating performance, there are some misconceptions about the income statement. One common misconception is that net income equals the amount of cash generated by a business. This is not the case. Secondly, the income statement does not indicate an increase or decrease in the *value* of a business. Finally, the measurement income *is not* simply a matter of counting. While each of these three things may impact the income statement, *none* of them is accurate in defining what an income statement provides to users of financial statements.

REVIEW THE CHAPTER

Chapter Summary
LO1. Describe common operating transactions and select appropriate income statement account titles.
- ❖ The *income statement* reports net income, which is calculated by combining:
  - o **Revenues**–amounts charged to customers for sales of goods or services provided
  - o **Expenses**–costs of business activities undertaken to earn revenues
- ❖ See Exhibit 3.1 in your text for basic income statement format and Exhibit ksjdfksdlkdncreases in assets or settlements of liabilities from peripheral activities

LO2. Explain and apply the revenue and matching principles.
- ❖ The two key concepts underlying accrual basis accounting and the income statement are
  - o **Revenue principle** – recognize revenues when they are earned
  - o **Matching principle** – recognize expenses when are incurred in generating revenue

LO3. Analyze, record, and summarize the effects of operating transactions, using the accounting equation, journal entries, and T-accounts.

- ❖ The expanded transaction analysis model includes revenues and expenses as subcategories of retained earnings

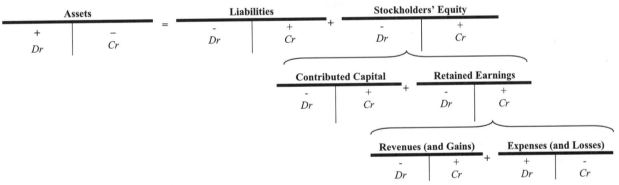

- ❖ In journal entry format,
  - o Revenue increases are recorded with credits
  - o Expense increases are recorded with debits

LO4. Prepare an Unadjusted Trial Balance.
- ❖ The unadjusted trial balance is a list of
  - o All accounts and their unadjusted balances
  - o It is used to check on the equality of recorded debits and credits

LO5. Describe limitations of the income statement.
- ❖ Does not indicate whether the company is bringing in more cash than it is spending.
- ❖ Does not directly measure the change in value of a company during the period.
- ❖ Estimation plays a key role when measuring income.

READ AND RECALL QUESTIONS

After you read each section of the chapter, answer the related Read and Recall Questions below.

> ## LEARNING OBJECTIVE
> *After studying the section of the chapter, you should be able to:*
> 1. Describe common operating transactions and select appropriate income statement account titles

Operating Transactions and Income Statement Accounts
What do **revenues** represent to a business? What do **expenses** represent to a business?

Which is the most important thing to remember about revenues, (1)when the money is received or (2) when customers receive the good or were provided the services?

What needs to happen before an expense can be reported on the income statement?

How is net income calculated? Give at least one other name that Net Income.

Explain the Time Period Assumption. Why is it important?

Cash Basis Accounting
Why isn't cash-basis accounting a good measure of financial performance?

Accrual Basis Accounting
Which basis of accounting is required by Generally Accepted Accounting Principles? Why?

What is the *rule of accrual*?

> ## LEARNING OBJECTIVE
> *After studying the section of the chapter, you should be able to:*
> 2. Explain and apply the revenue and matching principles

Revenue Principle – Revenue Recognition
When are revenues recognized in accrual-basis accounting? What is the key factor in determining when to report revenues?

List the three different points when cash can be received in relation to when the company has performed what it promised.

What causes the creation of an Unearned Revenue account? What type of account is it? What does the amount in this account represent? Are revenues reported at the time the money is received? Why or why not? When is this account reduced?

What causes the creation of an Accounts Receivable account? What type of account is it? What does the amount in this account represent? Are revenues reported at the time the account receivable is created? Why? When is this account reduced?

The Matching Principle – Expense Recognition
According to the matching principle, when are expenses recorded? Why is this important in calculating net income?

List the three different points when cash can be paid in relation to when the related expenses are incurred to generate revenue.

When cash is paid before the cost is incurred to generate revenue, what kind of account is created? Why is it recorded as an asset?

Give an example of a cost that is immediately recorded as an expense.

LEARNING OBJECTIVE
After studying the section of the chapter, you should be able to:
3. Analyze, record, and summarize the effects of operating transactions, using the accounting equation, journal entries, and T-accounts.

The Expanded Accounting Equation
Stockholders equity represents the stockholders' investment in the company which comes from what two sources?

Complete the following: Revenues and expenses are subcategories within the _____ account.

Why are Revenues and Expenses initially accumulated in separate accounts?

For each set of bolded items in parenthesis below, circle the correct answer.
Revenues are recorded on the **(left, right)** side of the T-account which is the **(debit, credit)** side. Expenses are recorded on the **(left, right)** side of the T-account which is the **(debit, credit)** side.

Complete the expanded transaction analysis model by inserting (1) a "+" or "-" sign and (2) a "dr" or "cr" into each side of each of the t-accounts shown below. (NOTE: the Assets have been done for you.)

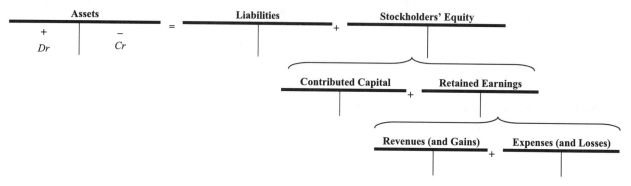

Transaction Analysis, Recording, and Summarizing
In the Unearned Revenue account, what does the word *unearned* mean?

Complete the following statements:
The right to collect money is an asset called _____.

When costs are incurred before they are paid, a liability is created called _____.

Calculating Account Balances
Describe how the ending balance in an account is determined.

Calculate the ending balance of the following accounts using this method.

Prepaid Insurance		
Beg. Bal. 4,500		
5,000	3,000	
End. Bal. ?		

Unearned Revenues		
	Beg. Bal.	6,700
7,200		4.300
	End. Bal.	?

(prepaid insurance:
$4,500 + $5,000 – $3,000 = $6,500;
unearned revenues:
$6,700 + $4,300 – $7,200 = $3,800)

Study Guide, Chapter 3

┌───┐
│ **LEARNING OBJECTIVE**   │
│ *After studying the section of the chapter, you should be able to:*   │
│ 4. Prepare an unadjusted trial balance   │
└───┘

Unadjusted Trial Balance

Name the three typical mistakes described in the text that might be discovered by preparing an unadjusted trial balance?

If you have an error in the unadjusted trial balance and the difference between total debits and total credits is evenly divisible by 9, what type of mistake have you probably made? What is this type of error called?

If the unadjusted trial balance balances, no errors have been made in the recording process. Is this is a true statement? Why or why not?

Review of Revenues and Expenses

Complete the following statements about revenues, under the accrual-basis of accounting:

(1) Cash can be received *before* the promised acts are performed which creates a(n) _____ account called

_____.

(2) Cash can be received at the *same time* the promised acts are performed which creates the same results as the _____ basis of accounting.

(3) Cash can be received *after* the promised acts are performed which creates a(n) _____ account called

_____.

Match the following journal entries (a, b, and c) to it correct description in the previous section (1, 2, or 3)

_____ (a) *dr* Cash   xxx
         cr Service Revenue   xxx

_____ (b) *dr* Accounts Receivable   xxx
         cr Service Revenue   xxx

_____ (c) *dr* Cash   xxx
         cr Unearned Revenues   xxx

Complete the following statements about expenses, under the accrual-basis of accounting:

(1) Cash can be paid *before* the company incurs an expense which creates a(n) _____ account called

_____.

(2) Cash can be paid at the *same time* the company incurs an expense which creates the same results as the _____ basis of accounting.

(3) Cash can be paid *after* the company incurs an expense which creates a(n) _____ account called

_____.

Match the following journal entries (a, b, and c) to its correct description in the previous section (1, 2, or 3)

_____ (a) *dr* Business Expense   xxx
           cr Accounts Payable   xxx

_____ (b) *dr* Business Expense   xxx
           cr Cash   xxx

_____ (c) *dr* Prepaid Expense   xxx
           cr Cash   xxx

LEARNING OBJECTIVE

After studying the section of the chapter, you should be able to:
5. Describe limitations of the income statement

Income Statement Limitations

Complete the following statement: One common misconception about the income statement is that some people think net income equal the amount of _____ generated by the business during the period.

Net income measures the change in the value of a company during a period. Do you agree with this statement? Why or why not?

Accounting involves some counting and precision, estimation also plays a key role when measuring income. Do you agree with this statement? Why or why not?

SUPPLEMENT – ACCOUNT NAMES

The following is a more complete list of revenues and expenses.

Account # and **Name**	**Description**
Revenues	
Sales Revenues	sales of products in the ordinary course of business
Service Revenues	sales of services in the ordinary course of business
Rental Revenues	amounts earned by renting out company property
Interest Revenues	amounts earned on savings accounts and certificates of deposit
Dividend Revenues	dividends earned from investing in other companies
Expenses	
Cost of Goods Sold	cost of products sold in the ordinary course of business
Repairs & Maintenance	cost of routine maintenance and upkeep of building/equipment
Advertising Expense	cost of advertising services obtained during the period
Depreciation Expense	cost of plant and equipment used-up during the period
Insurance Expense	cost of insurance coverage for the current period
Salaries & Wages Expense	cost of employees' salaries and wages for the period
Rent Expense	cost of rent for the period
Supplies Expense	cost of supplies used-up during the period
Transportation Expense	cost of freight to transport goods out to customers
Utilities Expense	cost of power, light, heat, internet, and telephone for the period
Amortization Expense	cost of intangible assets use-up or expired during the period
Interest Expense	interest charged on outstanding debts owed
Income Tax Expense	taxes charged on reported earnings

FINANCIAL ANALYSIS TOOLS

1. Unadjusted Trial Balance: Here is a quick and dirty snapshot of an unadjusted trial balance.

<table>
<tr><td colspan="3" align="center">Company Name
Trial Balance
Date</td></tr>
<tr><td></td><td>Debits</td><td>Credits</td></tr>
<tr><td>Cash</td><td>$ xxx</td><td></td></tr>
<tr><td>Notes Receivable</td><td>xxx</td><td></td></tr>
<tr><td>Accounts Receivable</td><td>xxx</td><td></td></tr>
<tr><td>Prepaid Insurance</td><td>xxx</td><td></td></tr>
<tr><td>Equipment</td><td>xxx</td><td></td></tr>
<tr><td>Land</td><td>xxx</td><td></td></tr>
<tr><td>Accounts Payable</td><td></td><td>xxx</td></tr>
<tr><td>Unearned Revenues</td><td></td><td>xxx</td></tr>
<tr><td>Notes Payable</td><td></td><td>xxx</td></tr>
<tr><td>Contributed Capital</td><td></td><td>xxx</td></tr>
<tr><td>Retained Earnings</td><td></td><td>xxx</td></tr>
<tr><td>Dividends</td><td>xxx</td><td></td></tr>
<tr><td>Service Revenue</td><td></td><td>xxx</td></tr>
<tr><td>Wages Expense</td><td>xxx</td><td></td></tr>
<tr><td>Insurance Expense</td><td>xxx</td><td></td></tr>
<tr><td>General and Administrative Expense</td><td>xxx</td><td></td></tr>
<tr><td>Interest Expense</td><td>xxx</td><td></td></tr>
<tr><td>Income Tax Expense</td><td>xxx</td><td></td></tr>
<tr><td align="center">Totals</td><td>$ xxx</td><td>$ xxx</td></tr>
</table>

HELPFUL STUDY TIP

1. Distinguishing Revenues from Assets, and Expenses from Liabilities. In this chapter you learned that it's easy to figure out what items go on the income statement because it only contains two items: Revenues and Expenses. However, sometimes it can be a bit tricky figuring out which accounts are revenues and which accounts are expenses. So, here's a run down of: the most commonly confused accounts, why people confuse them, and how to figure out what type of account they *really* are.

Account Name	Why Confusing?	How to figure it out	What they really are and where they belong
Accounts Receivable	Because they are part of the entry to record revenues earned *on account,* they are often confused with revenues. *They are not revenues. They do not belong on the income statement.*	Anytime you see the word *Account* in an account name, the account belongs somewhere on the *Balance Sheet.* The word Receivable means we will *receive* money, which is a good thing (assets are good things)	Accounts Receivable are *Assets* and will always be found on the *Balance Sheet.*
Accounts Payable	Like the previous example, since this is part of the entry to record expenses *on account* they are often confused with expenses. *They are not expenses. They do not belong on the income statement.*	Again, anytime you see the word *Account* in an account name, the account belongs somewhere on the *Balance Sheet.* The word Payable means we will *pay* money, which is a bad thing (liabilities are bad things)	Accounts Payable are *Liabilities* and will always be found on the *Balance Sheet.*

Account Name	Why Confusing?	How to figure it out	What they really are and where they belong
Unearned Revenues	When the word *Revenues* is part of the account name, it seems like a no-brainer, it must be a revenue! Unfortunately, in this particular situation, you would be wrong. *These are not revenues. They do not belong on the income statement.*	Focus instead on the *first* word, **Unearned.** Anytime you see the word **Unearned** in an account name, you still *owe the customer* something. Notice that 'un' means opposite or didn't. So *unearned* means 'didn't earn'. If you 'didn't earn' Revenues, that's a bad thing because you must still *earn them!* (liabilities are bad things)	Unearned Revenues are **Liabilities** and will always be found on the **Balance Sheet.**
Prepaid Expenses	Like the previous example, When the word *Expenses* is part of the account name, it seems like a no-brainer, it must be an expense! Unfortunately (again), in this situation, you would be wrong. *These are not expenses. They do not belong on the income statement.*	Again, focus on the *first* word, **Prepaid.** Anytime you see the word **Prepaid** in an account name, it means you paid for something *already* (before you used it up!) Anything that is already paid for is a good thing! (assets are good things)	Prepaid Expenses are **Assets** and will always be found on the **Balance Sheet.**

SELF-TEST QUESTIONS AND EXERCISES
MATCHING
1. *Match each of the key terms listed below with the appropriate textbook definition below.*

_____ Accrual Basis Accounting   _____ Revenue Principle

_____ Cash Basis Accounting   _____ Revenues

_____ Expense   _____ Time period assumption

_____ Matching Principle   _____ Trial Balance

_____ Net Income   _____ Unearned Revenue

A. Excess of revenues over expenses
B. A list of accounts and their balances used to check the quality of recorded debits and credits
C. A liability representing a company's obligation to provide goods or services to customers in the future
D. Cost of business necessary to earn revenues
E. Requires that expenses be recorded in the same period as the revenues they generate, not necessarily in the period when cash is paid for them
F. Assumes the life of a business can be divided into shorter time periods
G. Sales of goods or services to customers
H. Reports revenues when they are earned and expenses when they are incurred
I. Requires that revenues be recorded when they are earned, not necessarily when the cash is received for them
J. Reports revenues when cash is received and expenses when cash is paid

TRUE-FALSE QUESTIONS
For each of the following, enter a T or F in the blank to indicate whether the statement is true or false.

_____1. (LO1) Revenues represent the costs incurred in providing customers with goods or services.

_____2. (LO1) Net income is calculated as Expenses – Revenues.

_____3. (LO1) The time period assumption assumes that the long life of a company can be divided into shorter periods of time.

_____4. (LO1) The cash basis of accounting measures performance very well when transactions are conducted using credit rather than cash.

_____5. (LO2) The only method allowed for external reporting purposes according to generally accepted accounting principles (GAAP) is the accrual-basis of accounting.

_____6. (LO2) Accrual basis accounting records revenues when the company has time to record them and expenses when the company has the cash to pay for them.

_____7. (LO2) The revenue principle requires that revenues be recorded when they are earned, not necessarily when cash is received for them.

_____8. (LO2) When cash is received before the promised acts are performed, revenues for accrual accounting and cash basis accounting are the same.

_____9. (LO2) The matching principle requires that expenses be recorded in the period in which they are incurred to generate revenues, rather than the period in which the cash is paid for them.

_____10. (LO2) When cash for an insurance policy is paid before the policy is used, an asset account is created called Prepaid Insurance.

_____11. (LO3) Stockholders' Equity has two subaccounts called contributed capital and unearned revenues.

_____12. (LO3) Contributed capital is generated by the company itself through profitable operations.

_____13. (LO3) Each type of revenue and expense is accumulated in retained earnings to make it easier to determine the retained earnings balance.

_____14. (LO3) Revenues are recorded as credits and Expenses are recorded as debits.

_____15. (LO3) When cash is received before the company performs the promised acts, an asset account (Accounts Receivable) is created when the Revenue is recorded.

_____16. (LO3) When cash is not paid until after the expense is incurred, a liability account (Accounts Payable) is created when the Expense is recorded.

_____17. (LO3) The ending balance in a T-account is determined by adding the amounts on the "+" side and subtracting the amounts on the "–".

_____18. (LO4) One of the most common types of recording errors is incorrectly calculating the ending balance in a T-account.

_____19. (LO4) There are times when an error has occurred, but it will not cause your trial balance to be out of balance.

_____20. (LO5) The measurement of income is simply a matter of counting.

MULTIPLE CHOICE QUESTIONS
Choose the best answer or response by placing the identifying letter in the space provided.

_____1. (LO1) Net Income is calculated as
  a. unearned revenue – expenses
  b. revenues – expenses
  c. expenses – revenues
  d. assets – liabilities

_____2. (LO1) Which of the following is *not* a true statement regarding the income statement?
   a. revenues are recorded based on the matching principle
   b. it reports the financial effects of business activities that occurred during just the current period
   c. if expenses are greater than revenues the company has a net loss (rather than net income)
   d. all of these are true statements regarding the income statement

_____3. (LO2) The accrual basis of accounting records revenues when _____ and expenses when _____
   a. cash is received; cash is paid
   b. earned, incurred
   c. cashed is received, incurred
   d. earned, cash is paid

_____4. (LO2) Which of the following are allowed for external reporting under GAAP?
   a. cash-basis accounting
   b. accrual-basis accounting
   c. both a. and b.
   d. none of the above

_____5. (LO2) The _____ defines when a company reports its revenues from providing goods or services to customers
   a. matching principle
   b. time period assumption
   c. revenue principle
   d. president

_____6. (LO2) Assuming Claremont Corporation had the following transactions in August, what is the amount of revenue Claremont Corporation must report on its income statement for August?
   ➢ Provided services of $1,000 to Monal Izza, Inc. Claremont will bill Monal Izza in September.
   ➢ Cash of $600 was received for services rendered in August.
   ➢ Received $200 from the sale of gift certificates.
   a. $ 600
   b. $1,000
   c. $1,600
   d. $1,800

_____7. (LO2) Assuming Claremont Corporation had the following transactions in November, what is the amount of expenses that Claremont must report on its income statement for November?
   ➢ Paid $1,200 for an insurance policy that covers November and December
   ➢ Received a bill for $500 for radio advertisements that ran during October
   ➢ Paid November, December, and January rent in advance at a total cost of $4,500
   a. $1,700
   b. $2,100
   c. $2,600
   d. $6,200

_____8. (LO3) Which of the following is *not* a category or subcategory of Stockholders' Equity?
   a. contributed capital
   b. unearned revenues
   c. expenses or losses
   d. retained earnings

_____ 9. (LO3) Which of the following is a true statement about revenue and expense accounts?
   a. revenue and expense accounts are not affected in the same way as all stockholders' equity accounts
   b. increases in revenue are recorded on the left and increases in expenses are recorded on the right
   c. revenue accounts are affected any time cash is received
   d. none of the above are true statements regarding revenue and expense accounts

_____ 10. (LO3) Which of the following describes the debit and credit accounts affected when a company sells $500 of gift certificates?
   a. debit Cash $500; credit Revenues $500
   b. debit Revenues $500; credit Cash $500
   c. debit Unearned Revenues $500; credit Cash $500
   d. debit Cash $500; credit Unearned Revenues $500

_____ 11. (LO3) Which of the following describes the debit and credit accounts affected when a company provides $1,200 of Services to customers in June that will be billed to the customer in July?
   a. debit Revenues $1,200; credit Unearned Revenues $1,200
   b. debit Accounts Payable $1,200; credit Revenues $1,200
   c. debit Accounts Receivable; credit Revenues $1,200
   d. debit Revenues $1,200; credit Accounts Receivable $1,200

_____ 12. (LO3) What are the debit and credit accounts affected when the customer in the previous questions pays the entire bill in July?
   a. debit Cash $1,200; credit Accounts Receivable $1,200
   b. debit Cash $1,200; credit Revenues $1,200
   c. debit Accounts Receivable $1,200; credit Cash $1,200
   d. debit Cash $1,200; credit Unearned Revenues $1,200

_____ 13. (LO3) When a company debits Prepaid Rent for $6,000 and credits Cash for $6,000 which of the following best describes the transaction that was made?
   a. the company paid $6,000 rent in advance of using it
   b. the company incurred and paid $6,000 rent for the current period
   c. the company received $6,000 rent from a customer for the current period
   d. the company received $6,000 rent from a customer in advance of the customer using it

_____ 14. (LO3) Which of the following situations would require a debit to Cash and a credit to Unearned Revenue?
   a. cash is received after the company delivers goods/services
   b. cash is received before the company delivers goods/services
   c. cash is received in the same period that the company delivers goods/service
   d. the company has earned revenue that was previously unearned

_____ 15. (LO3) Which of the following describes the debit and credit accounts affected in April when a company runs an ad in the local newspaper for $200 in April, the bill will be paid in May?
   a. debit Accounts Receivable $200; credit Revenues $200
   b. debit Prepaid Advertising $200; credit Accounts Payable $200
   c. debit Accounts Payable $200; credit Advertising Expense $200
   d. debit Advertising Expense $200; credit accounts Payable $200

_____ 16. (LO3) What are the debit and credit accounts affected when the entire bill in the previous question is paid in May?
   a. debit Accounts Receivable $200; credit Cash $200
   b. debit Accounts Payable $200; credit Cash $200
   c. debit Accounts Payable $200; credit Advertising Expense $200
   d. debit Advertising Expense $200; credit Cash $200

_____17. (LO4) When recording transactions by hand, mistakes can be made. Which of the following errors is *not* a common mistake made when recording transactions?
    a. summarizing a debit in the credit column (or vice versa)
    b. recording the wrong amount
    c. forgetting to summarize both sides of a journal entry
    d. all of these are common mistakes made when recording transactions.

_____18. (LO4) If your trial balance doesn't balance and the difference between the debits and credits is twice the amount of an account balance, which of the following errors did you most likely make?
    a. You may have included an account balance in the wrong column of the trial balance
    b. You may have reversed the order of two digits in a number or left a zero off of the end of a number
    c. You may have hit the key above or below the one you intended to hit
    d. You probably forgot to include the account balance in your trial balance.

_____19. (LO4) Which of the following is *not* true regarding the trial balance?
    a. Amounts reported on the trial balance are obtained from the ledger (T-accounts)
    b. the accounts still have to be adjusted before we can prepare financial statements that follow generally accepted accounting principles
    c. if total debits equal total credits no errors were made in recording transactions
    d. all of these are true regarding the trial balance

_____20. (LO5) Which of the following is a misconception about the income statement?
    a. net income does not equal cash generated by the company during the period
    b. net income measures the change in the value of a company
    c. measuring income involves more than just counting
    d. all of these are misconceptions about accounting.

EXERCISES

Record your answer to each exercise in the space provided. Show your work.

Exercise 3-1. Identifying and Recording Revenues (LO2)

Note: Exercises 3-1, 3-2, 3-3, and 3-4 are sequential problems and should be done in order.

The following transactions are October 2008 revenue-related activities for **Mannie's Miniature Golf, Inc.**, which operates several miniature golf courses. If revenue is to be recognized in October, indicate the amount. If revenue is not to be recognized in October, explain why.

	Activity	Amount or Explanation
a.	Mannie's collected $3,700 from customers for Miniature Golf Games played in October.	
b.	Mannie's sold Dollie's Day Care $1,500 worth of gift certificates that they will use during the remainder of the year.	
c.	Mannie's sent a bill for $425 to a customer for a birthday party held at the course on October 31. The bill will be paid in November.	
d.	Mannie's collected $800 from customers for credit sales made in September.	
e.	Mannie's sold Dollie's Day Care another $400 of gift certificates to be used during the remainder of the year.	

Exercise 3-2. Identifying Expenses (LO2)

The following transactions are October 2009 expense-related activities for Mannie's Miniature Golf, Inc., which operates several miniature golf courses. If an expense is to be recognized in October, indicate the amount. If an expense is not to be recognized in October, explain why.

	Activity	Amount or Explanation
f.	Paid for an insurance policy covering October, November, and December for $1,500.	
g.	Paid employees $900 in wages for work they provided in October.	
h.	Received a bill for $350 for ads in the local newspapers that ran in October. Mannie's will pay this bill in November.	
i.	Paid the October, November, and December rent in advance for a total of $4,500.	
j.	Paid the utility bill of $600 for services received and billed in October.	

Exercise 3-3. Using the Transaction Analysis Approach with Revenues and Expenses (LO2)

1. Using the Transactions Analysis approach illustrated in the text, (1) analyze the following transactions of **Mannie's Miniature Golf, Inc.** for October of 2009, (2) record the corresponding journal entry, and (3) summarize the results in the T-accounts: Step 3 for transactions (a) – (j) should be recorded in the ledger (T-accounts) provided immediately following transaction (j).

(a) Mannie's collected $3,700 from customers for Miniature Golf Games played in October.

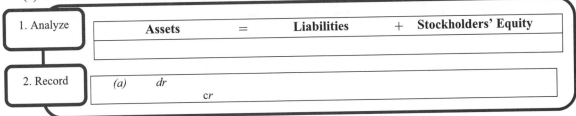

3. Summarize the transactions effects in T-accounts. (See T-accounts after transaction (j.))

(b) Sold Dollie's Day Care $1,500 worth of gift certificates that they will use during the remainder of the year.

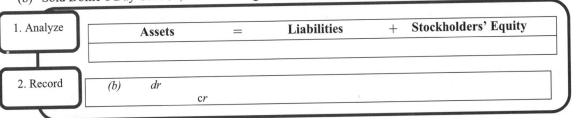

3. Summarize the transactions effects in T-accounts. (See T-accounts after transaction (j.))

(c) Mannie's sent a bill for $425 to a customer for a birthday party held at the course on October 31. The bill will be paid in November.

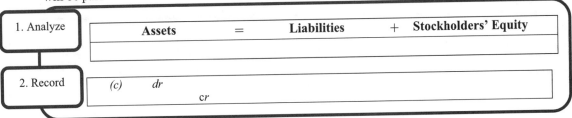

3. Summarize the transactions effects in T-accounts. (See T-accounts after transaction (j.))

(d) Mannie's collected $800 from customers for credit sales made in September.

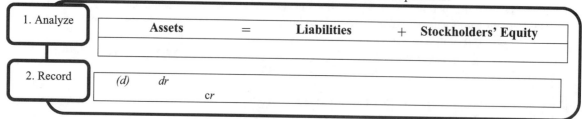

3. Summarize the transactions effects in T-accounts. (See T-accounts after transaction (j.))

(e) Sold Dollie's Day Care another $400 of the gift certificates that they will use the remainder of the year.

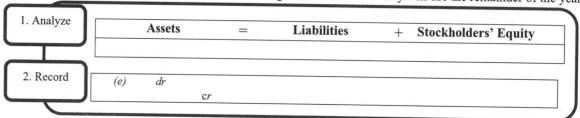

3. Summarize the transactions effects in T-accounts. (See T-accounts after transaction (j.))

(f) Paid for an insurance policy covering October, November, and December for $3,000.

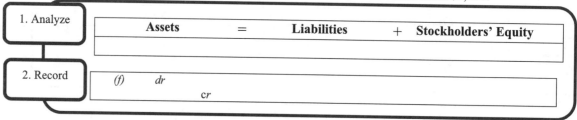

3. Summarize the transactions effects in T-accounts. (See T-accounts after transaction (j.))

(g) Paid employees $2,000 in wages for work they provided in October.

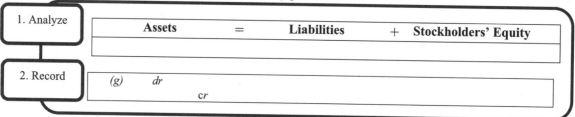

3. Summarize the transactions effects in T-accounts. (See T-accounts after transaction (j.))

(h) Received a bill for $350 for ads in the local newspapers that ran in October. Mannie's will pay this bill in November.

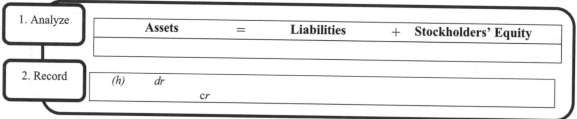

3. Summarize the transactions effects in T-accounts. (See T-accounts after transaction (j.))

(i) Paid the October, November, and December rent in advance for a total of $6,000.

<table>
<tr><td>1. Analyze</td><td>**Assets**</td><td>**=**</td><td>**Liabilities**</td><td>**+**</td><td>**Stockholders' Equity**</td></tr>
<tr><td></td><td colspan="5"></td></tr>
<tr><td>2. Record</td><td colspan="5">(i)   dr
          cr</td></tr>
</table>

    3. Summarize the transactions effects in T-accounts. (See T-accounts after transaction (j.))

(j) Paid the utility bills of $600 for services received and billed in October.

<table>
<tr><td>1. Analyze</td><td>**Assets**</td><td>**=**</td><td>**Liabilities**</td><td>**+**</td><td>**Stockholders' Equity**</td></tr>
<tr><td></td><td colspan="5"></td></tr>
<tr><td>2. Record</td><td colspan="5">(j)   dr
          cr</td></tr>
</table>

    3. Summarize the transactions effects in T-accounts.

Cash (A)		Accounts Payable (L)		Golf Revenue (R)	
+	-	-	+	-	+
beg bal 13,000			beg bal 7,400		beg bal 0

Accounts Receivable (A)		Unearned Revenues (L)		Wages Expense (E)	
+	-	-	+	+	-
beg bal 16,100			beg bal 0	beg bal 0	

Prepaid Insurance (A)		Common Stock (SE)		Advertising Expense (E)	
+	-	-	+	+	-
beg bal 0			beg bal 15,000	beg bal 0	

(continued)

Prepaid Rent (A)		Retained Earnings (SE)		Utilities Expense (L)	
+	-	-	+	+	-
beg bal 0			beg bal 6,700	beg bal 0	

Exercise 3-4. Preparing an Unadjusted Trial Balance, Income Statement and Balance Sheet from T-Accounts. (LO2, LO3, LO4)

Part A.

Using the October 31, 2009 balances of the T-accounts prepared in the previous exercise, prepare an unadjusted Trial Balance for **Mannie's Miniature Golf, Inc.** (HINT: Use only the ending account balances)

Mannie's Miniature Golf, Inc.		
Unadjusted Trial Balance		
As of October 31, 2009		
Account Name	**Debits**	**Credits**
Cash	$	$
Accounts Receivable		
Prepaid Insurance		
Prepaid Rent		
Accounts Payable		
Unearned Revenues		
Common Stock		
Retained Earnings		
Golf Revenues		
Wages Expense		
Advertising Expense		
Utilities Expense		
Totals	$	$

Part B. Prepare an Income Statement.

Using the Unadjusted Trial Balance created in Part A., prepare an Income Statement for the month of October for Mannie's Miniature Golf, Inc.

Mannie's Miniature Golf, Inc.		
Income Statement		
For the Month Ended October 31, 2009		
Revenues:		
Golf Revenue		$
Expenses:		
Wages Expense	$	
Advertising Expense		
Utilities Expense		
Total Expenses		
Net Income		$

Part C. Prepare a Balance Sheet.

Using the unadjusted trial balance and Income Statement from Part A., prepare a Classified Balance Sheet (on following page) for **Mannie's Miniature Golf, Inc.** as of October 31, 2009. (HINT: Calculate Ending Retained Earnings first using the following: Beginning Retained Earnings + Net Income)

Mannie's Miniature Golf, Inc.		
Balance Sheet		
October 31, 2009		
Assets		
Current assets:		
Cash	$	
Accounts Receivable		
Prepaid Insurance		
Prepaid Rent		
Total Assets	$	
Liabilities and Stockholders' Equity		
Current liabilities:		
Accounts Payable	$	
Unearned Revenues		
Total liabilities		
Stockholders' equity:		
Contributed Capital	$	
Retained Earnings		
Total stockholders' equity		
Total liabilities and stockholders' equity	$	

Exercise 3-5. Determining Financial Statement Effects of Operating Activities Involving Revenues and Expenses (LO2)

The following transactions are August 2008 activities of Alvin's Alleys, which operates several bowling alleys. For each of the following transactions, complete the spreadsheet, indicating the amount of the effect (+ for increase and − for decrease) of each transaction. Write NE if there is no effect. The first transaction has been done for you. (HINT: Remember that revenues and expenses affect the balance sheet because they are subcategories of retained earnings.)

Transaction	Balance Sheet			Income Statement		
	Asset	Liability	Stockholders' Equity	Revenues	Expenses	Net Income
a) Alvin's paid $600 for the August utilities.	-600	NE	-600	NE	+600	-600
b) Alvin's had $2,100 of credit sales made to customers in August.						
c) Alvin's paid $3,000 to employees for work in August.						
d) Purchased anti-fungal spray for golf shoe rentals for $400 on account.						
e) Alvin's collected $9,500 from customers for games played in August.						
f) Bob's purchased $1,800 in insurance for coverage from August 1 through November 1.						
g) Alvin's borrowed $30,000 from a bank, signing a short-term note.						
h) The Fowler's Bowling League purchased gift certificates of $2,500 as prizes for the league tournament.						
i) Purchased bowling equipment of $20,000 with cash.						
j) Alvin's paid $900 for repairing the bowling pin re-set machine for lane 7.						

| | Balance Sheet | | | Income Statement | | | *(continued)* |
Transaction	Asset	Liability	Stockholders' Equity	Revenues	Expenses	Net Income
k) Alvin's received $500 from customers in transaction (b).						
l) Paid $100 on accounts payable.						
m) Incurred and paid interest expense on account $120						

Exercise 3-6. Recording Journal Entries and Posting to T-Accounts (LO2, LO3, LO5)

For each transaction (a) – (n) in **Exercise 3-5**, record the journal entry.

Date	Transaction	Debit	Credit
(a)			
(b)			
(c)			
(d)			
(e)			
(f)			
(g)			
(h)			
(i)			
(j)			
(k)			
(l)			
(m)			

Cash (A)		Accounts Payable (L)		Bowling Revenue (R)	
+	-	-	+	-	+
beg bal 13,000			beg bal 0		beg bal 0

Accounts Receivable (A)		Unearned Revenues (L)		Wages Expense (E)	
+	-	-	+	+	-
beg bal 0			beg bal 0	beg bal 0	

Bowling Supplies (A)		Notes Payable (L)		Repairs Expense (E)	
+	-	-	+	+	-
beg bal 0			beg bal 0	beg bal 0	

Prepaid Insurance (A)		Common Stock (SE)		Utilities Expense (E)	
+	-	-	+	+	-
beg bal 0			beg bal 13,000	beg bal 0	

Bowling Equipment (A)		Retained Earnings (SE)		Interest Expense (E)	
+	-	-	+	+	-
beg bal 0			beg bal 0	beg bal 0	

Exercise 3-7. Inferring Transactions and Preparing an Unadjusted Trial Balance (LO2, LO3, LO4)

TurboTurf, Inc. operates a full-service, professional lawn-maintenance business. It performs general lawn-care maintenance year-round. It is based in a rental space in a local strip mall. During its first month of business ending March 31, 2008, TurboTurf, Inc. completed eight transactions with dollar effects indicated in the following schedule (NOTE: Each *column* contains one transaction one transaction, not the row):

Dollar Effect of Each of the Eight Transactions

Accounts	(a)	(b)	(c)	(d)	(e)	(f)	(g)	(h)	Ending Balance
Cash	$40,000	$(1,000)	$(20,000)	$(1,500)	$9,800		$ 800	$ (2,500)	$
Accounts Receivable					3,800				
Supplies		3,200							
Prepaid Expenses				1,500					
Equipment			20,000						
Accounts Payable		2,200				910			
Unearned Revenue							800		
Contributed Capital	40,000								
Lawn Revenue					13,600				
Wages Expense								2,500	
Utilities Expense						910			

Part A.

Write a brief explanation of Transactions (a) – (h). Include any assumptions that you made.

(a)

(b)

(c)

(continued)

(d)

(e)

(f)

(g)

(h)

Part B.
Compute the ending balance in each account, in the space provided on the table, and prepare an unadjusted trial balance for TurboTurf, Inc. on March 31, 2008.

Account Name	Debits	Credits
TurboTurf, Inc.		
Unadjusted Trial Balance		
As of March 31, 2008		
Cash		
Accounts Receivable		
Supplies		
Prepaid Insurance		
Equipment		
Accounts Payable		
Unearned Revenues		
Contributed Capital		
Lawn Revenues		
Wages Expense		
Utilities Expense		
Totals	$	$

SOLUTIONS TO SELF-TEST QUESTIONS AND EXERCISES

MATCHING
1.

H	Accrual Basis Accounting	I	Revenue Principle
J	Cash Basis Accounting	G	Revenues
D	Expense	F	Time period assumption
E	Matching Principle	B	Trial Balance
A	Net Income	C	Unearned Revenue

TRUE-FALSE QUESTIONS
1. F – Revenues represent the sales of goods or services to customers.
2. F – Net income is calculated as Revenues – Expenses.
3. T
4. F – Generally speaking, cash basis accounting doesn't measure financial performance very well when transactions are conducted using credit rather than cash because there can be a significant delay between the time an activity occurs and the time it impacts the bank account balance.
5. T
6. F – Accrual basis accounting reports revenues when they are earned and expenses when they are incurred.
7. T

8. F – When cash is received before the company performs the promised act, a liability account is created until the promised act is performed by the company.
9. T
10. T
11. F – Stockholders' equity subaccounts are contributed capital and retained earnings
12. F – Retained earnings is generated by the company itself through profitable operations.
13. F – Each type of revenue and expense is accumulated in a separate account, making it easier to identify the amount to report for each of these line items on the income statement.
14. T
15. F – When cash is received before the company performs the promised acts, a liability account is created called Unearned Revenues.
16. T
17. T
18. T
19. T
20. F – While accounting does involve some counting and precision, estimation also plays a key role when measuring income.

MULTIPLE CHOICE QUESTIONS

1. B	6. C	11. C	16. B
2. A	7. B	12. A	17. D
3. B	8. B	13. A	18. A
4. B	9. D	14. B	19. C
5. C	10. D	15. D	20. B

EXERCISES

Exercise 3-1. Identifying and Recording Revenues (LO2)

	Activity	Amount or Explanation
a.	Mannie's collected $3,700 from customers for Miniature Golf Games played in October.	$3,700
b.	Sold Dollie's Day Care $1,500 worth of gift certificates that they will use during the remainder of the year.	Revenue is recognized when the promised act is performed, that will occur when the gift certificates are redeemed.
c.	Mannie's sent a bill for $425 to a customer for a birthday party held at the course on October 31. The bill will be paid in November.	$425
d.	Mannie's collected $800 from customers for credit sales made in September.	The sale was recorded in September, this is simply collecting the money the customer promised to pay at that time.
e.	Sold Dollie's Day Care an additional $400 of gift certificates that they will use the remainder of the year.	Revenue is recognized when the promised act is performed, that will occur when the gift certificates are redeemed.

Exercise 3-2. Identifying Expenses (LO2)

	Activity	Amount or Explanation
f.	Paid for an insurance policy covering October, November, and December for $1,500.	$500
g.	Paid employees $900 in wages for work they provided in October.	$900
h.	Received a bill for $350 for ads in the local newspapers that ran in October. Mannie's will pay this bill in November.	$350
i.	Paid the October, November, and December rent in advance for a total of $4,500.	$1,500
j.	Paid the utility bills of $600 for services received and billed in October.	$600

Exercise 3-3. Using Transaction Analysis. (LO2)

(a) Mannie's collected $3,700 from customers for Miniature Golf Games played in October.

1. Analyze

Assets	=	Liabilities	+	Stockholders' Equity
Cash + 3,700				Golf Revenue + 3,700

2. Record

(a)	dr Cash...(+A)..	3,700	
	cr Golf Revenue...(+R, +SE).............		3,700

3. Summarize the transactions effects in T-accounts. (See T-accounts after transaction (j.))

(b) Sold Dollie's Day Care $1,500 worth of gift certificates that they will use during the remainder of the year.

1. Analyze

Assets	=	Liabilities	+	Stockholders' Equity
Cash + 1,500		Unearned Revenue +1,500		

2. Record

(b)	dr Cash (+A)...	1,500	
	cr Unearned Revenue (+L)...............		1,500

3. Summarize the transactions effects in T-accounts. (See T-accounts after transaction (j.))

(c) Mannie's sent a bill for $425 to a customer for a birthday party held at the course on October 31. The bill will be paid in November.

1. Analyze

Assets	=	Liabilities	+	Stockholders' Equity
Accounts Receivable +425				Golf Revenue + 425

2. Record

(c)	dr Accounts Receivable...(+A)......................	425	
	cr Golf Revenue (+R, +SE)...............		425

3. Summarize the transactions effects in T-accounts. (See T-accounts after transaction (j.))

(d) Mannie's collected $800 from customers for credit sales made in September.

1. Analyze

Assets	=	Liabilities	+	Stockholders' Equity
Cash + 800				
Accounts Receivable −800				

2. Record

(d)	dr Cash...(+A)	800	
	cr cr Accounts Receivable...(-A).........		800

3. Summarize the transactions effects in T-accounts. (See T-accounts after transaction (j.))

(e) Sold Dollie's Day Care an additional $400 of the gift certificates that will be used later in the year.

1. Analyze

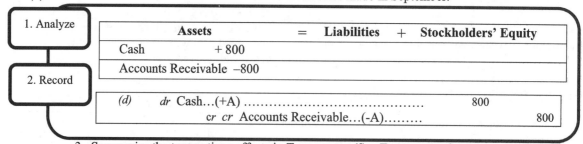

Assets	=	Liabilities	+	Stockholders' Equity
Cash + 400		Unearned Revenue +400		

2. Record

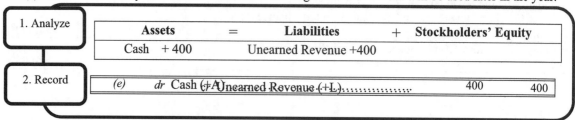

(e)	dr Cash (+A) cr Unearned Revenue (+L).................	400	400

(f) Paid for an insurance policy covering October, November, and December for $3,000.

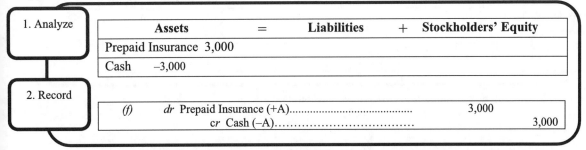

1. Analyze	Assets	=	Liabilities	+	Stockholders' Equity
	Prepaid Insurance 3,000				
	Cash –3,000				

2. Record			
	(f) *dr* Prepaid Insurance (+A)...	3,000	
	cr Cash (–A)………………………………		3,000

   3. Summarize the transactions effects in T-accounts. (See T-accounts after transaction (j.))

(g) Paid employees $2,000 in wages for work they provided in October.

1. Analyze	Assets	=	Liabilities	+	Stockholders' Equity
	Cash –2,000				Wages Expense (+E) – 2,000

2. Record			
	(g) *dr* Wages Expense (+E, –SE)...	2,000	
	cr Cash (–A)………………………………..		2,000

   3. Summarize the transactions effects in T-accounts. (See T-accounts after transaction (j.))

(h) Received a bill for $350 for ads in the local newspapers that ran in October. Mannie's will pay this bill in November.

1. Analyze	Assets	=	Liabilities	+	Stockholders' Equity
			Accounts Payable +350		Advertising Expense (+E), (–SE) – 350

2. Record			
	(h) *dr* Advertising Expense(+E, –SE)...................................	350	
	cr Accounts Payable (+L)……………………		350

   3. Summarize the transactions effects in T-accounts. (See T-accounts after transaction (j.))

(i) Paid the October, November, and December rent in advance for a total of $6,000.

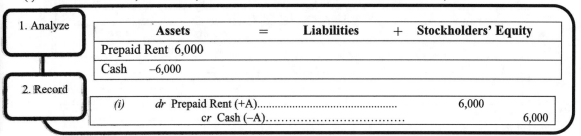

1. Analyze	Assets	=	Liabilities	+	Stockholders' Equity
	Prepaid Rent 6,000				
	Cash –6,000				

2. Record			
	(i) *dr* Prepaid Rent (+A)..	6,000	
	cr Cash (–A)………………………………		6,000

   3. Summarize the transactions effects in T-accounts. (See T-accounts after transaction (j.))

(j) Paid the utility bills of $600 for services received and billed in October.

1. Analyze

Assets	=	**Liabilities**	+	**Stockholders' Equity**
Cash –600				Utilities Expense (+E) – 600

2. Record

(a)   *dr* Utilities Expense (+E, –SE)..   600
         cr Cash (–A)…………………..   600

3. Summarize the transactions effects in T-accounts.

+ Cash (A) -				Accounts Payable (L)				Golf Revenue (R)	
beg bal 13,000				-	+			-	+
(a) 3,700	(f) 3,000				beg bal 7,400				beg bal 0
(b) 1,500	(g) 2,000				(h) 350				(a) 3,700
(d) 800	(i) 6,000								(c) 425
(e) 400	(j) 600			end bal 7,750					
end bal 7,800									end bal 4,125

Accounts Receivable (A)			- Unearned Revenues (L) +			Wages Expense (E)	
+	-			beg bal 0		+	-
beg bal 16,100	(d) 800			(b) 1,500		beg bal 0	
(c) 425				(e) 400		(g) 2,000	
end bal 15,725				end bal 1,900		end bal 2,000	

Prepaid Insurance (A)			Common Stock (SE)			Advertising Expense (E)	
+	-		-	+		+	-
beg bal 0				beg bal 15,000		beg bal 0	
(f) 3,000				end bal 15,000		(h) 350	
end bal 3,000						end bal 350	

Prepaid Rent (A)			Retained Earnings (SE)			Utilities Expense (L)	
+	-		-	+		+	-
beg bal 0				beg bal 6,700		beg bal 0	
(i) 6,000				end bal 6,700		(j) 600	
end bal 6,000						end bal 600	

Exercise 3-4. Preparing an Unadjusted Trial Balance, Income Statement and Balance Sheet from T-Accounts. (LO2, LO3, LO4)
Part A.

Mannie's Miniature Golf, Inc.		
Unadjusted Trial Balance		
As of October 31, 2009		
Account Name	**Debits**	**Credits**
Cash	$ 7,800	
Accounts Receivable	15,725	
Prepaid Insurance	3,000	
Prepaid Rent	6,000	
Accounts Payable		$ 7,750
Unearned Revenues		1,900
Common Stock		15,000
Retained Earnings		6,700
Golf Revenues		4,125
Wages Expense	2,000	
Advertising Expense	350	
Utilities Expense	600	
Totals	$ 35,475	$ 35,475

Part B. Prepare an Income Statement.

<table>
<tr><td colspan="3" align="center">Mannie's Miniature Golf, Inc.
Income Statement
For the Month Ended October 31, 2009</td></tr>
<tr><td>Revenues:</td><td></td><td></td></tr>
<tr><td>Golf Revenue</td><td></td><td>$ 4,125</td></tr>
<tr><td>Expenses:</td><td></td><td></td></tr>
<tr><td>Wages Expense</td><td>$ 2,000</td><td></td></tr>
<tr><td>Utilities Expense</td><td>600</td><td></td></tr>
<tr><td>Advertising Expense</td><td>350</td><td></td></tr>
<tr><td>Total Expenses</td><td></td><td>2,950</td></tr>
<tr><td>Net Income</td><td></td><td>$ 1,175</td></tr>
</table>

Part C. Prepare a Balance Sheet.

<table>
<tr><td colspan="3" align="center">Mannie's Miniature Golf, Inc.
Balance Sheet
October 31, 2009</td></tr>
<tr><td colspan="3" align="center">Assets</td></tr>
<tr><td>Current assets:</td><td></td><td></td></tr>
<tr><td>Cash</td><td></td><td>$ 7,800</td></tr>
<tr><td>Accounts Receivable</td><td></td><td>15,725</td></tr>
<tr><td>Prepaid Insurance</td><td></td><td>3,000</td></tr>
<tr><td>Prepaid Rent</td><td></td><td>6,000</td></tr>
<tr><td>Total Assets</td><td></td><td>$ 32,525</td></tr>
<tr><td colspan="3">Liabilities and Stockholders' Equity</td></tr>
<tr><td>Current liabilities:</td><td></td><td></td></tr>
<tr><td>Accounts Payable</td><td></td><td>$ 7,750</td></tr>
<tr><td>Unearned Revenues</td><td></td><td>1,900</td></tr>
<tr><td>Total liabilities</td><td></td><td>9,650</td></tr>
<tr><td>Stockholders' equity:</td><td></td><td></td></tr>
<tr><td>Contributed Capital</td><td>$ 15,000</td><td></td></tr>
<tr><td>Retained Earnings (6,700 + 1,175)</td><td>7,875</td><td></td></tr>
<tr><td>Total stockholders' equity</td><td></td><td>22,875</td></tr>
<tr><td>Total liabilities and stockholders' equity</td><td></td><td>$ 32,525</td></tr>
</table>

Exercise 3-5. Determining Financial Statement Effects of Operating Activities Involving Revenues and Expenses (LO2)

Transaction	Balance Sheet			Income Statement		
	Asset	Liability	Stockholders' Equity	Revenues	Expenses	Net Income
a) Alvin's paid $600 for the August utilities.	-600	NE	-600	NE	+600	-600
b) Alvin's had $2,100 of credit sales made to customers in August.	+2,100	NE	+2,100	+2,100	NE	+2,100
c) Alvin's paid $3,000 to employees for work in August.	-3,000	NE	-3,000	NE	+3,000	-3,000
d) Purchased anti-fungal spray for golf shoe rentals for $400 on account.	+400	+400	NE	NE	NE	NE
e) Alvin's collected $9,500 from customers for games played in August.	+9,500	NE	+9,500	+9,500	NE	+9,500
f) Bob's purchased $1,800 in insurance for coverage from August 1 through November 1.	+1,800 -1,800	NE	NE	NE	NE	NE

(continued)

		Balance Sheet			Income Statement		
Transaction	Asset	Liability	Stockholders' Equity	Revenues	Expenses	Net Income
g) Alvin's borrowed $30,000 from a bank, signing a short-term note payable.	+30,000	+30,000	NE	NE	NE	NE
h) The Fowler's Bowling League purchased gift certificates of $2,500 as prizes for the league tournament.	+2,500	+2,500	NE	NE	NE	NE
i) Purchased bowling equipment of $20,000.	+20,000 -20,000	NE	NE	NE	NE	NE
j) Alvin's paid $900 for repairing the bowling pin re-set machine for lane 7.	-900	NE	-900	NE	+900	-900
k) Alvin's received $500 from customers in transaction (b)	+500 -500	NE	NE	NE	NE	NE
l) Paid $100 on accounts payable.	-100	-100	NE	NE	NE	NE
m) Incurred and paid $120 Interest expense	-120	NE	-120	NE	+120	-120

Exercise 3-6. Recording Journal Entries and Posting to T-Accounts (LO2, LO3, LO5)

Date	Transaction	Debit	Credit
(a)	Utilities Expense	600	
	Cash		600
(b)	Accounts Receivable	2,100	
	Bowling Revenue		2,100
(c)	Wages Expense	3,000	
	Cash		3,000
(d)	Bowling Supplies	400	
	Accounts Payable		400
(e)	Cash	9,500	
	Bowling Revenue		9,500
(f)	Prepaid Insurance	1,800	
	Cash		1,800
(g)	Cash	30,000	
	Notes Payable		30,000
(h)	Cash	2,500	
	Unearned Revenues		2,500
(i)	Bowling Equipment	20,000	
	Cash		20,000
(j)	Repairs Expense	900	
	Cash		900
(k)	Cash	500	
	Accounts Receivable		500
			(continued)

Date	Transaction	Debit	Credit
(l)	Accounts Payable	100	
	Cash		100
(m)	Interest Expense	120	
	Cash		120

Cash (A)

+		-	
beg bal	13,000	(a)	600
(e)	9,500	(c)	3,000
(g)	30,000	(f)	1,800
(h)	2,500	(i)	20,000
(k)	500	(j)	900
		(l)	100
		(m)	120
28,980			

Accounts Payable (L)

-		+	
(l)	100	beg bal	0
		(d)	400
			300

Bowling Revenue (R)

-		+	
		beg bal	0
		(b)	2,100
		(e)	9,500
			11,600

Accounts Receivable (A)

+		-	
beg bal	0	(k)	500
(b)	2,100		
1,600			

Unearned Revenues (L)

-		+	
		beg bal	0
		(h)	2,500
			2,500

Wages Expense (E)

+		-	
beg bal	0		
(c)	3,000		
3,000			

Bowling Supplies (A)

+		-	
beg bal	0		
(d)	400		
400			

Notes Payable (L)

-		+	
		beg bal	0
		(g)	30,000
			30,000

Repairs Expense (E)

+		-	
beg bal	0		
(j)	900		
900			

Prepaid Insurance (A)

+		-	
beg bal	0		
(f)	1,800		
1,800			

Common Stock (SE)

-		+	
		beg bal	13,000
		end bal	13,000

Utilities Expense (E)

+		-	
beg bal	0		
(a)	600		
600			

Bowling Equipment (A)

+		-	
beg bal	0		
(i)	20,000		
20,000			

Retained Earnings (SE)

-		+	
		beg bal	0

Interest Expense (E)

+		-	
beg bal	0		
(m)	120		
120			

Exercise 3-7. Inferring Operating Transactions and Preparing an Unadjusted Trial Balance (LO2, LO3, LO4)

Part A.

(a) The owners of the business invested $40,000 in exchange for common stock in the business.

(b) The business purchased $3,200 of Supplies and paid $1,000 Cash for part of the cost, putting the remaining $2,200 balance on an Account Payable

(c) The business purchased $20,000 of equipment, paying all of it in Cash.

(d) The business paid $1,500 Cash for some kind of prepaid expense. You might assume they paid Rent in advance or perhaps Insurance in advance of its being used by the business.

(e) The company performed lawn maintenance services of $13,600. They received $9,800 in Cash and the remaining $3,800 are Accounts Receivable which the business will receive in cash at a later date.

(f) The business incurred $910 of Utilities and will pay them later.

(g) The business received cash of $800 from customers for services that will be performed some time in the future. No services have yet been performed.

(h) The business paid employees Cash for services rendered, $800.

Part B.

Accounts	(a)	(b)	(c)	(d)	(e)	(f)	(g)	(h)	Ending Balance
Cash	$ 40,000	$ (1,000)	$ (20,000)	$ (1,500)	$ 9,800		$ 800	$ (2,500)	$ 25,600
Accounts Receivable					3,800				3,800
Supplies		3,200							3,200
Prepaid Expenses				1,500					1,500
Equipment			20,000						20,000
Accounts Payable		2,200				$ 910			3,110
Unearned Revenue							800		800
Contributed Capital	40,000								40,000
Lawn Revenue					13,600				13,600
Wages Expense								2,500	2,500
Utilities Expense						910			910

TurboTurf, Inc.		
Unadjusted Trial Balance		
As of March 31, 2008		
Account Name	**Debits**	**Credits**
Cash	$ 25,600	
Accounts Receivable	3,800	
Supplies	3,200	
Prepaid Insurance	1,500	
Prepaid Rent	20,000	
Accounts Payable		$ 3,110
Unearned Revenues		800
Contributed Capital		40,000
Lawn Revenues		13,600
Wages Expense	2,500	
Utilities Expense	910	
Totals	$ 57,510	$ 57,510

Any time your balance sheet does not balance don't panic! Failing to balance means you've made an error somewhere. Compare the Total Assets Amount to the Liabilities + Stockholders Equity amount and subtract! The difference between the two amounts should be compared to the following list of common accounting errors:

1. If the difference is the *same as* one of your account balances, you probably forgot to include the account on the balance sheet.
2. If the difference is *twice* the amount of *an account balance*, you may have reported the account in the wrong category of A, L, or SE.
3. If the difference is *two times* the amount of *a particular transaction,* you may have posted a debit as a credit or a credit as a debit in your T-accounts.
4. If the difference can be *evenly divided by 9,* you may be reversed the order of two digits in a number (i.e. 54 instead of 45), or left a zero off of the end of a number (93 instead of 930).

CHAPTER 4
ADJUSTMENTS, FINANCIAL STATEMENTS,
AND THE QUALITY OF FINANCIAL REPORTING

ORGANIZATION OF THE CHAPTER

Understand the business	**Study the accounting methods**	**Evaluate the results**	**Review the chapter**
- Why adjustments are needed	- Making required adjustments - Preparing an adjusted trial balance and financial statements - Closing temporary accounts	- The quality of adjusted financial statements	- Demonstration case - Chapter summary - Key terms - Practice material

CHAPTER FOCUS SUGGESTIONS

Review

Chapters 2 and 3 emphasized two important financial statements and the types of activities that are presented on each. The day-to-day results of operations in a business are revealed in the income statement, while critical investment and financing information are shown on the balance sheet. With this information under our belts, we're ready to delve a little deeper into important *additions* to these financial statements that make them even *more* useful to external users.

Introduction

The need to have up-to-date and complete information in an accounting system is critical. Without it, decision-making may be poor—at best, and devastating—at worst. Therefore, at the end of every accounting period adjustments are made to the financial statements to ensure that they contain *all* of the information needed for sound decision making. In addition, these adjustments are required by Generally Accepted Accounting Principles to help ensure that financial statements include the financial results of *all* the company's activities for the period.

This chapter explains why adjustments are necessary in accrual-basis accounting, shows you how to determine what adjustments are needed, and provides the journal entries to accomplish this. Then, you'll see how these adjustments impact external users and we'll wrap it up with an overview of the entire chapter.

UNDERSTAND THE BUSINESS
Why Adjustments Are Needed

> **Learning Objective 1**
> Explain why adjustments are needed.

Every day we use cash. So, as individuals we tend to focus on money for every-day transactions. But, in a business, cash is not always received at the same time that revenues are earned and cash is not always paid at the time expenses are incurred. Because of this difference in the timing of cash receipts and revenues earned, as well as the timing of cash paid and expenses incurred, *adjusting journal entries* are made.

These adjusting journal entries serve to *update* the revenues and expenses already recorded to include any that haven't been recorded yet due to timing differences. Without the inclusion of these revenues, net income would be less than it should be. Similarly, without the inclusion of these expenses, net income would be more than it should be. So, making these adjustments helps to make certain that the information presented on the income statement and the balance sheet is accurate. Adjustments are needed to ensure:

- Revenues are recorded when earned (the revenue principle)
- Expense are recorded in the same period as the revenues to which they relate (the matching principle)
- Assets are reported at amounts representing the economic benefits that remain at the end of the current period, and
- Liabilities are reported at amounts owed at the end of the current period that will require a future sacrifice of resources

Generally, adjustments are grouped into two categories: (1) deferral adjustments and (2) accrual adjustments.

1. Deferral Adjustments.

To *defer* something means to postpone it, or put it off until later. For accounting purposes, it means to put off reporting the item on the income statement until later, either an expense or a revenue. Deferrals occur when money has changed hands, but the revenue hasn't been earned yet and/or the expense hasn't been incurred yet.

We've already dealt with deferral situations in Chapter 3! When the business paid for a full year's insurance policy, we did not record this as Insurance Expense, it was put into a Prepaid Insurance account. The insurance can only be expensed when each month that the policy covers has passed. A portion of this 'prepaid' amount can be expensed once each month of coverage has passed. This is an example of an expense that is deferred.

The same type of thing occurs with revenues. When customers purchase gift certificates, for example, they've paid for goods or services in advance. The amount received cannot be reported as revenue until we have performed the promised act. This amount is placed, instead, into an Unearned Revenue account. When the customers use the gift certificates, then it can be reported as income. The earnings are deferred until the gift certificate is used.

At some point journal entries will need to be made to show that: some of the prepaid insurance has been used up (because the months of coverage have passed), and (2) some of the gift certificates have been redeemed by customers. Deferral adjustments are the journal entries we make to record these types of events. Two things to remember about deferral adjustments are:

a) *Deferral adjustments are used to reduce amounts previously deferred on the balance sheet and to increase corresponding accounts on the income statement.* These adjustments will update the T-accounts for the types of situations just described. The portion of Unearned Revenues (gift certificates) that are now earned (redeemed) will be recorded and the amount of prepaid insurance that has been used up (because a portion of the coverage period has elapsed) will also be recorded.

b) *Each deferral adjustment involves either a pair of asset and expense accounts, or a pair of liability and revenue accounts*

   ❖ **Asset and Expense accounts** – These adjustments update amounts that were originally recorded on the balance sheet as Prepaid Expenses but, have now been incurred (according to the Matching Principle.) The required entry will transfer amounts from prepaid accounts (assets) to expense accounts (expenses) as shown in the following illustration:

	Balance Sheet	Income Statement	
	(FROM: these Prepaid accounts)	(TO: these Expense accounts)	
Assets	Supplies ⟶	Supplies Expense	**Expenses**
	Prepaid Rent ⟶	Rent Expense	
	Prepaid Insurance ⟶	Insurance Expense	

   ❖ **Revenue and Liability Accounts** – These adjustments update amounts that were originally recorded on the balance sheet as Unearned Revenue, that have now been earned (according to the Revenue Principle.) The required entry will transfer amounts from unearned revenue accounts (liabilities) to revenue accounts (income) as shown in the following illustration:

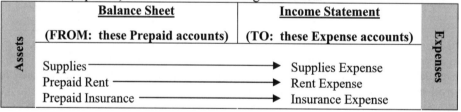

	Balance Sheet	Income Statement	
	(FROM: these Unearned accounts)	(TO: these Revenue accounts)	
Liabilities	Unearned Ticket Revenue ⟶	Ticket Sales Revenue	**Revenues**
	Unearned Subscriptions Revenue ⟶	Subscriptions Revenue	

2. Accrual Adjustments:

a) *Accrual adjustments are used to recognize revenue or expenses when they occur, prior to receipt or payment of cash and to adjust corresponding balance sheet accounts.* Accrual adjustments are needed when a transaction has occurred, but has not yet been recorded. This usually occurs when the service or act has been performed by the business (revenue earned), but the cash has not yet been received, or when an expense has been incurred, but the cash has not yet been paid.

b) *Each accrual adjustment involves a pair of asset and revenue accounts, or a pair of liability and expense accounts.*

   ❖ **Asset and Revenue accounts** – These adjustments record amounts earned (according to the Revenue Principle) that have not yet been received in cash creating a Receivable (asset) on the balance sheet. The entry required will create a Receivable (asset) and report Revenue (income) earned.

	Balance Sheet	**Income Statement**	
Assets	Interest Receivable ⟶	Interest Revenue	**Revenues**
	Rent Receivable ⟶	Rent Revenue	

   ❖ **Liability and Expense accounts** – These adjustments record amounts incurred (according to the Matching Principle) that have not yet been paid in cash, creating a Payable (liability) on the balance sheet. The entry required will create a Payable (liability) and report Expenses (incurred).

	Balance Sheet	**Income Statement**	
Liabilities	Income tax payable ⟶	Income Tax Expense	**Expenses**
	Wages Payable ⟶	Wages Expense	
	Interest Payable ⟶	Interest Expense	

The previous four tables show the nuts-and-bolts of deferral adjustments and accrual adjustments. Notice that *without exception, every* adjustment involves both an income statement account and a balance sheet account. This is true regarding every adjusting entry.

STUDY THE ACCOUNTING METHODS

> **Learning Objective 2**
> Prepare adjustments needed at the end of the period.

Making Required Adjustments

The adjustments just described are made at the end of an accounting period just before financial statements are prepared. There are three steps in the process: (1) Analyze accounts to determine the necessary adjustments; (2) Record adjustments as **adjusting journal entries**; and (3) Summarize the adjustments in the T-accounts. At this point another trial balance, called the **adjusted trial balance** will be prepared. As the name indicates, it is prepared after all adjusting entries have been recorded and posted. The adjusted trial balance helps to locate any errors that may have been made journalizing and posting the adjusting entries.

Adjustment Analysis, Recording, and Summarizing

Identifying the accounts that need adjusting can be a little tough. The starting point is the unadjusted trial balance. Since it contains a listing of *all* accounts, it will be easier to identify those that require adjusting because we can see every account. Use the information in the **Helpful Hints** as a guide in determining the accounts to be adjusted. Then apply the following steps to determine the amount of the adjustment and the journal entry necessary to complete it.

We'll begin by analyzing the accounts on the trial balance to determine the necessary adjustments. The Unadjusted Trial Balance for LandShapes Unlimited on the following page is for the month of October. Lots of transactions have occurred throughout the month and they are reflected in the 'new' balances of the accounts. Each account that requires adjustment on the unadjusted trial balance is noted by the explanation of the required adjustment.

Account Name	Debits	Credits	Explanation of Adjustments Needed
	LandShapes Unlimited		
	Unadjusted Trial Balance		
	As of October 31, 2009		
Cash	$18,000		
Landscaping supplies	1,200		Reduce for supplies used up during October
Accounts receivable	5,800		Increase for Landscaping provided but not yet collected
Interest receivable	0		Increase for October interest due us on note receivable
Prepaid rent	3,000		Reduce for prepaid October rent benefits used up
Notes receivable	6,000		
Truck	20,000		
Accumulated depreciation		$ 0	Adjust for equipment benefits used up in October
Accounts payable		3,800	
Unearned revenues		600	Reduce for gift certificates redeemed in October
Wages payable		0	Increase for October wages not yet paid
Income tax payable		0	Increase for taxes owed on October income generated
Interest payable		0	Increase for interest owed on unpaid note in October
Notes payable		25,000	
Contributed capital		20,000	
Retained earnings		0	
Dividends declared	0		Increase for dividends declared in October
Landscape revenue		15,400	Increase for Landscaping services provided
Interest Revenue		0	Increase for interest earned on uncollected note
Wages expense	7,200		Increase for employee work provided for October
Rent expense	0		Increase for expense incurred for October rent
Depreciation expense	0		Increase for expense of using equipment in October
Utilities expense	1,600		
Advertising expense	2,000		
Landscaping supplies expense	0		Increase for supplies used up in October
Interest expense	0		
Income tax expense	0		Increase for taxes on income generated in October
Totals	$64,800	$64,800	

Deferral Adjustments
Remember, the purpose of deferral adjustments is to update amounts that have been previously deferred on the balance sheet.

a) **_Supplies Used During the Period_**

Supplies were initially recorded as an asset, but you determine that, of the $1,200 of supplies purchased during October, only $300 of supplies still remain on your supply shelf (on-hand) at the end of October. Since you have been given the amount left on the shelf, the rest of the supplies must have been *used up* and the matching principle requires that we expense the amount 'used', so we will need to expense $900 ($1,200 - $300).

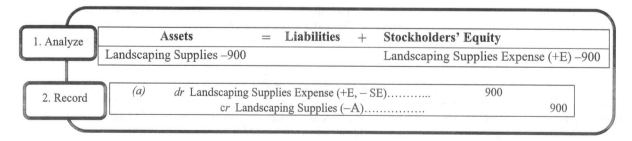

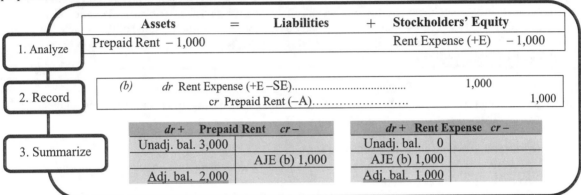

	3. Summarize	*dr* + Landscaping supplies *cr* –		*dr* + Landscaping Supplies Expense *cr* –	
		Unadj. bal. 1,200		Unadj. bal. 0	
			AJE (a) 900	AJE (a) 900	
		Adj. bal. 300		Adj. bal. 900	

b) *Rent Benefits Expire During the Period*

Your monthly rent is $1,000. You paid the amount shown in the prepaid rent account on October 1 ($3,000). It is now October 31. You need to determine the amount of prepaid rent that has been used up. Since it was paid on October 1, it must cover all of October's rent, $1,000 ($1,000 * 1 month.) This will leave two month's rent in the prepaid rent account that has not yet been used.

1. Analyze

Assets	=	Liabilities	+	Stockholders' Equity
Prepaid Rent – 1,000				Rent Expense (+E) – 1,000

2. Record

(b)	*dr* Rent Expense (+E –SE).................................	1,000	
	cr Prepaid Rent (–A)………………….		1,000

3. Summarize

dr + Prepaid Rent *cr* –		*dr* + Rent Expense *cr* –	
Unadj. bal. 3,000		Unadj. bal. 0	
	AJE (b) 1,000	AJE (b) 1,000	
Adj. bal. 2,000		Adj. bal. 1,000	

c) *Depreciation is Recorded for Use of Equipment*

When you look back at adjusting journal entry *(a)*, notice that when supplies are used by a business, those supplies are actually gone from existence. They are no longer on the shelf. So, when the entry is made to show the usage of supplies, the asset account (supplies) is reduced, showing this literal removal of items on the shelf.

However, when we use our furniture, vehicles, buildings, etc., we don't actually 'remove' portions of it from existence. The whole truck is still there, all of the furniture is still there, etc., they are simply a little older and perhaps a bit more tattered. Therefore, when we expense these items, a new expense is created – Depreciation Expense.

Depreciation is the process of allocating the cost of long-lived assets to the accounting periods in which they are used. In an effort to make this distinction *on paper* (i.e. in the T-accounts), we've got to be a little bit creative. We keep the *entire* purchase price in the T-account of the asset being used (i.e. Furniture, Equipment, etc.) as a reminder that the whole item still exists. But, we still have to show that there's *less* of the item left to use.

Therefore, a new account is created as an offset to the asset account. This account will keep a running total of the amount of the asset's cost that has been used up so far. This new account is called Accumulated Depreciation. You can think of this account as a 'holding-tank' that holds all of the depreciation taken on the truck since it was purchased. An account like this that holds amounts separately (rather than taking amounts directly out of the Truck account) is called a **contra-account**.

The amount in the contra-account is then subtracted from the amount in the related asset account to show how much of the asset's original cost 'remains' to be used up. In our example, it is estimated that the depreciation on the truck for the current month is $500. Note here that the small x is used to denote a posting to a contra account.

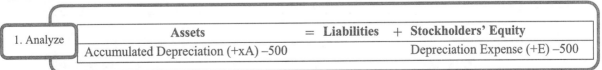

	1. Analyze	Assets	= Liabilities	+ Stockholders' Equity
		Accumulated Depreciation (+xA) –500		Depreciation Expense (+E) –500

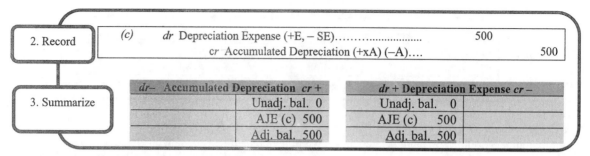

| 2. Record | (c) | dr Depreciation Expense (+E, – SE)……….................. | 500 | |
| | | cr Accumulated Depreciation (+xA) (–A)…. | | 500 |

3. Summarize	dr– **Accumulated Depreciation** cr +		dr + **Depreciation Expense** cr –	
		Unadj. bal. 0	Unadj. bal. 0	
		AJE (c) 500	AJE (c) 500	
		Adj. bal. 500	Adj. bal. 500	

Notice that the adjusting entry did not directly impact the Truck account; that account still has a balance of $20,000 (the original price of the truck). But, the accumulated depreciation account has *more* in it…it has accumulated and includes the depreciation taken this month. The truck's *carrying value* is reduced because the accumulated depreciation is subtracted from the Truck account when it is presented (or carried) on the balance sheet. This difference of $19,500 ($20,000 – $500) is also called **book value**. It shows that some of the vehicle has been used up, and the difference is how much of the truck's cost remains to be used-up in future years. On the balance sheet, it will look like this:

Truck	$20,000	Original cost of the truck
Accumulated Depreciation	(500)	Running total of all recorded depreciation on the truck
Truck, net of accumulated depreciation	$19,500	

There are four things to note about this adjusting entry:
- Accumulated depreciation is a balance sheet account and Depreciation Expense is an income statement account.
- By recording depreciation in accumulated depreciation separate from the equipment account, you can report both the original cost of the truck and a running total of the amount of the truck that has been depreciated (in this example, $500 of the truck's usefulness has been used up.)
- A contra-account is always recorded in a way that opposes the account it offsets. This means that if the normal account (truck) has a debit balance the contra-account (accumulated depreciation) will have a credit (or offsetting) balance to the truck.
- The amount of depreciation depends on the method used for calculated it (see Chapter 9)

d) *Gift Certificates Redeemed for Service*
This is the only deferral adjustment that involves revenues. The best example of this type of adjustment is the purchase of gift certificates by customers. In this situation, we have received money that we haven't done a blasted thing to earn yet! This means that we owe (liability) the customer something--sales, a game of pool, landscape maintenance, whatever the gift certificate was good for. Until it is provided to the customer we *owe* them. We may not owe them actual *money,* but we owe them the sale or the game of pool. Either way, *we owe them* something. That's why it is a liability.

At the end of the accounting period, we determine how many of the gift certificates have been redeemed and that determines how much of the revenue is actually earned and how much remains to be provided to customers at a later date. So, assume LandShapes Unlimited provides gift certificates for landscaping and they've sold $600 of gift certificates this month. By the end of the month, $550 of the certificates were redeemed.

1. Analyze	**Assets**	**=**	**Liabilities**	**+**	**Stockholders' Equity**
			Unearned Revenues – 550		Landscape Revenue (+R) +550

| 2. Record | (d) | dr Unearned Revenues (–L)…………………………… | 550 | |
| | | cr Landscape Revenue (+R, +SE)……. | | 550 |

3. Summarize	dr– **Unearned Revenues** cr +		dr – **Landscape Revenue** cr +	
		Unadj. bal. 600		Unadj. bal. 15,400
	AJE (d) 550			AJE (d) 550
		Adj. bal. 50		Adj. bal. 15,950

In this situation, you were given the amount of the adjustment. That isn't always the case, sometimes you will have to calculate the amount. As a result of the entry, Unearned Revenue has been reduced by the amount that is now earned, and Landscape Revenue has been increased by the same amount.

Accrual Adjustments
These adjustments include transactions that have occurred, but have not yet been recorded.

e) *Revenues Earned But Not Yet Recorded*
Oftentimes, companies that provide services on credit, have performed the services but have not yet recorded them in the accounting system. This entry ensures that this type of transaction is recorded when the promised act has occurred (per the revenue principle.) Assume LandShapes Unlimited provided landscaping services to a long-time customer for $1,500 and told the customer that in lieu of cash now, they would send them a bill for the services. Since the services were performed in October, the revenue must be reported in October, no matter when the customer pays.

	Assets	= Liabilities	+ Stockholders' Equity
1. Analyze	Accounts Receivable + 1,500		Landscape Revenue (+SE, +R) +1,500

2. Record

(e)	dr Accounts Receivable (+A).......................................	1,500	
	cr Landscape Revenue (+R, +SE).............		1,500

3. Summarize

dr + Accounts Receivable cr –		dr – Landscape Revenue cr +	
Unadj. bal. 5,800			Unadj. bal. 15,400
AJE (e) 1,500			AJE (d) 550
Adj. bal. 7,300			AJE (e) 1,500
			Adj. bal. 17,450

f) *Wages Expense Incurred But Not Yet Recorded*
Assume employees earn $400 per day and are paid on Fridays. If October 31 falls on a Tuesday, that means $800 of expense was incurred in October, and won't be paid to employees (thus not recorded) until Friday. The matching principle requires that the two days of wages that occurred in October....must be recorded in October, no matter when the employees are actually paid. Look at the following illustration to better visualize this situation:

	Monday 10/30	Tuesday 10/31	Wednesday 11/1	Thursday 11/2	Friday 11/3
Employee earnings	$400	$400	$400	$400	$400
Employee paid					$2,000

$800
These two days wages belong in October.

$1,200
These three days wages belong in November.

The following entry records the two days wages from October into Wages Expense for the month of October.

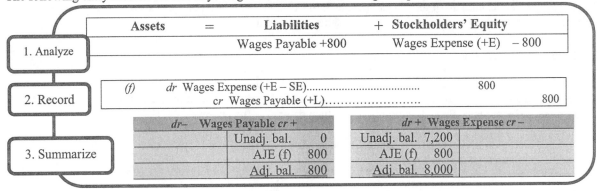

	Assets	=	Liabilities	+ Stockholders' Equity
1. Analyze			Wages Payable +800	Wages Expense (+E) – 800

2. Record

(f)	dr Wages Expense (+E – SE).......................................	800	
	cr Wages Payable (+L)........................		800

3. Summarize

dr– Wages Payable cr +		dr + Wages Expense cr –	
	Unadj. bal. 0	Unadj. bal. 7,200	
	AJE (f) 800	AJE (f) 800	
	Adj. bal. 800	Adj. bal. 8,000	

The unadjusted balance in the Wages expense account represents all of the wages that have been *paid* to employees during the month of October. The accrual adjustment records the final two days worth of wages for October that have not yet been recorded because they won't be paid until November 3 (Friday).

g) *Interest Earned But Not Yet Recorded*

Assume Landshapes Unlimited has a customer that signed a $6,000 note receivable. The customer currently owes $50 in interest on the note to LandShapes Unlimited for the month of October.

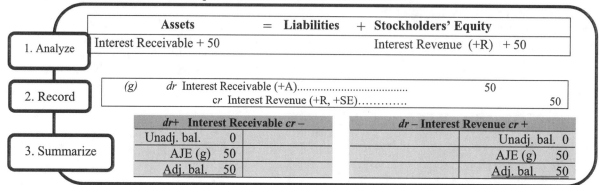

Notice that the amount of the Notes Receivable didn't change. This is an entry to accrue the *interest* on the note only. The balance of the note can only change when a customer collection is made. But, LandShapes Unlimited earns interest on the note every month…whether the customer has paid it or not.

h) *Interest Incurred But Not Yet Recorded*

LandShapes Unlimited owes the bank $25,000 on a note payable. LandShapes currently owes the bank $150 interest on the note. Do not confuse this situation with the adjustment made in *(g)*. While both situations result in accruals of interest, in that case, the interest was *earned* by LandShapes since a customer owed *them* the money on the note, causing the recording of a receivable and revenues. In this case, the interest charges were *incurred* by LandShapes because they owe *the bank* the money on the note, causing the recording of expenses and a payable.

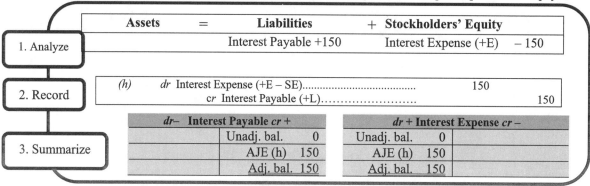

Notice that the amount of the Notes Payable didn't change. This is an entry to accrue the *interest* on the note only. The balance of the note can only change when a payment is made.

i) *Income Taxes Incurred But Not Yet Recorded*

LandShapes Unlimited is required to pay taxes on its income at a rate of 30%. The amount of taxes owed for October must be accrued and recorded in October in accordance with the matching principle. In order to determine the amount of taxes owed, LandShapes Unlimited needs to calculate its income (after all adjusting journal entries have been made) before tax. Using this figure, it will then determine the tax owed.

Let's start with the revenue and expense amounts from the unadjusted trial balance and adjust these totals for the adjusting journal entries we've made:

	Revenues	Expenses	
Unadjusted Totals	$ 15,400	$ 10,800	($7,200 + $1,600 + $2,000)
Adjustments: (a)		+900	
(b)		+1,000	
(c)		+500	
(d)	+550		
(e)	1,500		
(f)		800	
(g)	50		
(h)		150	
Adjusted Totals	$ 17,500	– $ 14,150	= $3,350 Adjusted income before tax

The adjusted income before tax is the figure used to calculate the taxes owed. Since the tax rate for LandShapes Unlimited is 30%, total taxes due are $1,005 ($3,350 * 30%.)

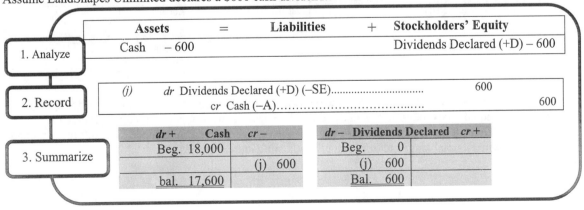

Additional Comments

Two points need to be made now: (1) Adjusting journal entries **never affect the cash account.** (2) Dividends are *not* an expense of the company (that is why this entry is not shown until *after* the calculation of income tax expense. Dividends are distributions of profits that corporations give out to their owners (shareholders.) The board of directors determines whether or not dividends will be given to shareholders by officially declaring them. If the board declares dividends, the corporation pays the shareholders those dividends.

Since dividends are distributions of earnings, they are taken out of the retained earnings account. They represent the amount of earnings that are *not* retained in the business. Instead, they are pulled out of the corporation and given to the owners so that owners can share in the success of the company!

j)   *Dividends Declared and Paid*
Assume LandShapes Unlimited declares a $600 cash dividend.

Preparing the Adjusted Trial Balance

The adjusted trial balance, like the unadjusted trial balance in Chapter 3, is prepared to check that the accounts are still in balance after journalizing and posting entries. The only difference is that these are adjusting journal entries so, we prepare an adjusted trial balance (meaning after adjusting entries). Preparing it involves nothing more than copying the ending balances in the T-accounts and adding them up. If the trial balance balances, you are ready to prepare the financial statements.

Learning Objective 3
Prepare an adjusted trial balance

After journalizing and posting the adjusting journal entries in this chapter, the T-accounts have the following balances. Note that all balances from the unadjusted trial balance are labeled **Unadj. Bal.** Adjusting journal entries are labeled **ADJ** followed by the specific letter of the entry in parenthesis. Finally, the adjusted balance is labeled as **Adj. bal.** If no changes occurred in the balance as a result of adjusting entries, the unadjusted and adjusted balances are the same and will be used to prepare the adjusted trial balance.

dr + Cash (A) cr –		
Unadj. Bal. 18,000	ADJ (j)	600
Adj. bal. 17,400		

dr + Landscaping Supplies (A) cr –		
Unadj. Bal. 1,200	ADJ (a)	900
Adj. bal. 300		

dr + Accounts Receivable (A) cr –		
Unadj. Bal. 5,800		
ADJ (e) 1,500		
Adj. bal. 7,300		

dr + Interest Receivable (A) cr –		
Unadj. Bal. 0		
ADJ (g) 50		
Adj. bal. 50		

dr + Prepaid Rent (A) cr –		
. Bal. 3,000	ADJ (b)	1,000
Adj. bal. 2,000		

dr + Notes Receivable (A) cr –		
Unadj. Bal. 6,000		

dr + Truck (A) cr –		
Unadj. Bal. 20,000		

dr – Accumulated Depreciation (xA) cr +		
	Unadj. Bal.	0
	ADJ (c)	500
	Adj. bal.	500

dr – Accounts Payable (L) cr +		
	Unadj. Bal.	3,800

dr – Unearned Revenue (L) cr +		
ADJ (d) 550	Unadj. Bal.	600
	Adj. bal.	50

dr – Wages Payable (L) cr +		
	Unadj. Bal.	0
	ADJ (f)	800
	Adj. bal.	800

dr – Income Taxes Payable (L) cr +		
	Unadj. Bal.	0
	ADJ (i)	1,005
	Adj. bal.	1,005

dr – Interest Payable (L) cr +		
	Unadj. Bal.	0
	ADJ (h)	150
	Adj. bal.	150

dr – Notes Payable (L) cr +		
	Unadj. Bal.	25,000

dr – Contributed Capital (SE) cr +		
	Unadj. Bal.	20,000

dr – Retained Earnings (SE) cr +		
	Unadj. Bal.	0

dr + Dividends Declared(D) cr –		
Unadj. Bal. 0		
ADJ (j) 600		
Adj. bal. 600		

dr – Landscape Revenue (R) cr +		
	Unadj. Bal.	15,400
	ADJ (d)	550
	ADJ (e)	1,500
	Adj. bal.	17,450

dr – Interest Revenue (R) cr +		
	Unadj. Bal.	0
	ADJ (g)	50
	Adj. bal.	50

dr + Wages Expense (E) cr –		
Unadj. Bal. 7,200		
ADJ (f) 800		
Adj. bal. 8,000		

dr+ Rent Expense (E) cr–		
Unadj. Bal. 0		
ADJ (b) 1,000		
Adj. bal 1,000		

dr + Depreciation Expense (E) cr –		
Unadj. Bal. 0		
ADJ (c) 500		
Adj. bal 500		

dr+ Utilities Expense (E) cr–		
Unadj. Bal. 1,600		

dr+ Advertising Expense (E) cr–		
Unadj. Bal. 2,000		

dr+ Landscaping Supplies Expense (E) cr–		
Unadj. Bal. 0		
ADJ (a) 900		
Adj. bal. 900		

dr + Interest Expense (E) cr –		
Unadj. Bal. 0		
ADJ (h) 150		
Adj. bal. 150		

dr+ Income Tax Expense (E) cr–		
Unadj. Bal. 0		
ADJ (i) 1,005		
Adj. bai. 1,005		

From these balances the adjusted trial balance (shown on the following page) is prepared. Once again, verify that total debits equal total credits on the adjusted trial balance. If they do, you're ready to prepare the financial statements. Don't forget that just because you balance on an adjusted trial balance...doesn't mean that no mistakes were made when journalizing, and/or posting the adjusting journal entries.

Now, we're ready to prepare the financial statements. The adjusted trial balance is used for this purpose. The best part is that each number on the adjusted trial balance will only be used **once.** So, once a number has been used, it can be 'marked off' and not used again. When statements are prepared, we prepare them in a specific order: (1) the income statement, (2) the statement of retained earnings, and (3) the balance sheet.

The income statement is easy to prepare. Simply copy the income statement account balances (revenues and expenses) from the adjusted trial balance using the format presented in Chapter 2, and you're done! Notice that expenses are listed in order from the largest dollar amount to the smallest dollar amount (except taxes, which are always shown last because they are calculated last.)

Next, we'll prepare the statement of retained earnings. Notice that the amount of retained earnings on the adjusted trial balance is the *beginning retained earnings*. The *ending* balance must be calculated (on the statement of retained earnings) so that this ending balance may be used on the balance sheet. The income statement gives us the figure that will be added to the beginning retained earnings amount, and we finish it up by subtracting out the dividends declared. The Income Statement and Retained Earnings Statement for LandShapes, Unlimited, are shown below.

LandShapes Unlimited Adjusted Trial Balance October 31, 2009		
	Debits	**Credits**
Cash	$17,400	
Landscaping Supplies	300	
Accounts Receivable	7,300	
Interest Receivable	50	
Prepaid Rent	2,000	
Notes Receivable	6,000	
Truck	20,000	
Accumulated Deprecation		500
Accounts Payable		3,800
Unearned Revenues		50
Wages Payable		800
Income taxes Payable		1,005
Interest Payable		150
Notes Payable		25,000
Contributed Capital		20,000
Retained Earnings		0
Dividends Declared	600	
Landscape Revenue		17,450
Interest Revenue		50
Wages Expense	8,000	
Rent Expense	1,000	
Depreciation Expense	500	
Utilities Expense	1,600	
Advertising Expense	2,000	
Landscaping Supplies Expense	900	
Interest Expense	150	
Income Tax Expense	1,005	
Totals	$ 68,805	$ 68,805

LandShapes, Unlimited Income Statement For the Month Ended October 31, 2009		
Revenues:		
Landscape Revenue	$17,450	
Interest Revenue	50	
		17,500
Expenses:		
Wages Expense	$8,000	
Advertising Expense	2,000	
Utilities Expense	1,600	
Rent Expense	1,000	
Landscaping Supplies Expense	900	
Depreciation Expense	500	
Interest Expense	150	
Income Tax Expense	1,005	
Total Expenses		15,155
Net Income		$2,345

LandShapes, Unlimited Statement of Retained Earnings For the Month Ended October 31, 2009	
Retained Earnings, October 1, 2009	$0
Add: Net Income	2,345
	2,345
Less: Dividends Declared	(600)
Retained Earnings, October 31, 2009	$1,745

Note that the Net Income figure is used when In preparing the statement of retained earnings This is why the income statement is prepared First...the net income figure is needed to Prepare the next statement. You will shortly see that the ending retained earnings figure Will be needed in preparing the final statement

Preparing the Balance Sheet

Like the income statement, the balance sheet is prepared by simply copying the adjusted trial balance figures (except retained earnings) and, using the statement format presented in Chapter 3. At this point, the only accounts on the unadjusted trial balance that have not been used yet are all be Balance Sheet accounts. Be careful about these three things:

(1) Be sure you classify assets and liabilities as current if they will be used up, turned into cash, or fulfilled within 12 months,

(2) Accumulated Depreciation is *subtracted* from the Truck account in the asset section, and

(3) Use the retained earnings figure just calculated on the statement of retained earnings for the retained earnings figure on the balance sheet. ***Do not use the retained earnings figure from the adjusted trial balance.*** Besides, we already used this number and it is no longer available (remember each number is used only once).

The balance sheet for LandShapes, Unlimited follows:

LandShapes Unlimited Balance Sheet October 31, 2009		
Assets		
Current assets:		
Cash	$17,400	
Notes Receivable	300	
Accounts Receivable	7,300	
Interest Receivable	50	
Prepaid Insurance	2,000	
Total Current Assets		$27,050
Investments:		
Notes Receivable		6,000
Property, Plant, and Equipment:		
Truck	$20,000	
Accumulated Depreciation	(500)	
Total Property, Plant, and Equipment		19,500
Total Assets		$52,550
Liabilities and Stockholders' Equity		
Current liabilities:		
Accounts Payable	$3,800	
Unearned Revenues	50	
Wages Payable	800	
Interest Payable	150	
Income Taxes Payable	1,005	
Total Current Liabilities		5,805
Long-Term Liabilities:		
Notes Payable		25,000
Total liabilities		30,805
Stockholders' equity:		
Contributed Capital	$20,000	
Retained Earnings	1,745	
Total stockholders' equity		21,745
Total Liabilities and Stockholders' Equity		$52,550

> This number comes from the Retained Earnings statement

Preparing the Statement of Cash Flows and Notes to the Financial Statements

Your head is probably swimming right now with all of the information contained in this Chapter, so I'm sure you won't mind if we postpone coverage of these topics to later chapters.

Closing the Income Statement and Dividend Accounts

Remember way back in Chapter 3 (ah, those were the good old days) when you learned that revenues and expenses, were all subcategories in Retained Earnings? Well, it's baaaaacccckkk! These accounts, along with dividends declared, are referred to as *temporary* accounts. That is, they contain dollar amounts *temporarily* and then those amounts are deleted, zapped, zeroed–out, or removed so that the business can start the new year out fresh with nothing in these accounts.

You've actually experienced something like this yourself! When you receive your paycheck it probably contains a column called Year-to-Date Earnings. This contains all of your cumulative earnings, etc. for the entire year. However, on December 31, your employer wipes out all that information so that you can start all over again in the following year, with zero dollar amounts in every category. This allows you to keep track of your income on an annual basis.

A business has to do the exact same thing with its earnings. After financial statements are prepared, the company can start with a clean slate (zero balances) in these accounts for next year. This is accomplished with closing entries. The only purpose of closing entries is to zero out the temporary accounts (revenues, expenses, and dividends) and to transfer these amounts into retained earnings. The retained earnings account and all of the balance sheet accounts are *permanent* accounts. They are not zeroed-out at the end of the accounting period. Rather, the amounts in these accounts, at the end of the accounting period, become the beginning balances of those accounts in the following year. So, these *permanent* accounts and their balances continue to exist even after the temporary accounts are closed. So, to summarize, closing entries serve two purposes:

1. *To transfer net income (or loss) and dividends to Retained Earnings.* Once the closing entries are prepared and posted, the balance in the Retained Earnings account will agree with the amount calculated on the Statement of Retained Earnings, and the amount on the Balance Sheet. All of these now contain the *ending balance.*

2. *To establish zero balances in all income statement and dividend accounts.* Once the closing entries are prepared and posted, the balances in all of the temporary accounts will be reset to zero so that they are ready to start accumulating next year's information. Closing entries follow the same debit/credit format used for the transaction journal entries presented in Chapters 2 and 3, as well as the adjusting entries presented earlier in this chapter. Two closing entries are required:

a. Debit each revenue account for the amount of its credit balance and credit each expense account for the amount of its debit balance. The difference will be put into the Retained Earnings account. This difference should be the amount reported as Net Income (or Net loss) on the current income statement. If a credit is needed to make debits = credits, Net Income was reported on the income statement. If a debit is needed to make debits = credits, a Net Loss was reported on the income statement.

CJE 1. Close revenue and expense accounts:

dr Landscape Revenue (-R) 17,450	
dr Interest Revenue (-R). 50	
cr Wages Expense (-E)	8,000
cr Advertisng Expense (-E)	2,000
cr Utilities Expense (-E)	1,600
cr Rent Expense (-E)	1,000
cr Landscaping Supplies Expense (-E)	900
cr Depreciation Expense (-E)	500
cr Interest Expense (-E)	150
cr Income Tax Expense (-E)	1,005
cr Retained Earnings (+SE)	2,345

b. Credit the dividends declared account for the amount of its debit balance and debit Retained Earnings for the same amount.

CJE 2. Close dividends declared account:

> dr Retained Earnings (-SE)   600
>   cr Dividends Declared (-D)   600

After posting the closing entries, the T-accounts will have the following balances:

dr + Cash (A) cr –			
Unadj. Bal.	18,000	ADJ (j)	600
Adj. bal.	17,400		

dr + Landscaping Supplies (A) cr –			
Unadj. Bal.	1,200	ADJ (a)	900
Adj. bal.	300		

dr + Accounts Receivable (A) cr –			
Unadj. Bal.	5,800		
ADJ (e)	1,500		
Adj. bal.	7,300		

dr + Interest Receivable (A) cr –			
Unadj. Bal.	0		
ADJ (g)	50		
Adj. bal.	50		

dr + Prepaid Rent (A) cr –			
Unadj. Bal.	3,000	ADJ (b)	1,000
Adj. bal.	2,000		

dr + Notes Receivable (A) cr –			
Unadj. Bal.	6,000		

dr + Truck (A) cr –			
Unadj. Bal.	20,000		

dr – Accumulated Depreciation (xA) cr+			
		Unadj. Bal.	0
		ADJ (c)	500
		Adj. bal.	500

dr – Accounts Payable (L) cr +			
		Unadj. Bal.	3,800

dr – Unearned Revenue (L) cr +			
ADJ (d) 550		Unadj. Bal.	600
		Adj. bal.	50

dr – Wages Payable (L) cr +			
		Unadj. Bal.	0
		ADJ (f)	800
		Adj. bal.	800

dr – Income Taxes Payable (L) cr +			
		Unadj. Bal.	0
		ADJ (i)	1,005
		Adj. bal.	1,005

dr – Interest Payable (L) cr +			
		Unadj. Bal.	0
		ADJ (h)	150
		Adj. bal.	150

dr – Notes Payable (L) cr +			
		Unadj. Bal.	25,000

dr – Contributed Capital (SE) cr +			
		Unadj. Bal.	20,000

dr – Retained Earnings (SE) cr +			
CJE (2)	600	Unadj. Bal.	0
		CJE (1)	2,345
		Closed bal.	1,745

dr + Dividends Declared(D) cr –			
Unadj. Bal.	0	CJE (2)	600
ADJ (j)	600		
Closed bal.	0		

dr – Landscape Revenue (R) cr +			
CJE (1) 17,450		Unadj. Bal.	15,400
		ADJ (d)	550
		ADJ (e)	1,500
		Closed bal.	0

dr – Interest Revenue (R) cr +			
CJE (1)	50	Unadj. Bal.	0
		ADJ (g)	50
		Closed bal.	0

dr + Wages Expense (E) cr –			
Unadj. Bal.	7,200	CJE (1)	8,000
ADJ (f) 800			
Closed bal.	0		

dr + Rent Expense (E) cr –			
Unadj. Bal.	0	CJE (1)	1,000
ADJ (b)	1,000		
Closed bal.	0		

dr + Depreciation Expense (E) cr –			
Unadj. Bal.	0	CJE (1)	500
ADJ (c)	500		
Closed bal.	0		

dr + Utilities Expense (E) cr –			
Unadj. Bal. 1,600		CJE (1)	1,600
Closed bal.	0		

dr + Advertising Expense (E) cr –			
Unadj. Bal.	2,000	CJE (1)	2,000
Closed bal.	0		

dr + Landscaping Supplies Expense (E)cr –			
Unadj. Bal.	0	CJE (1)	900
ADJ (a)	900		
Closed bal .	0		

dr + Interest Expense (E) cr –			
Unadj. Bal.	0	CJE (1)	150
ADJ (h)	150		
Closed bal.	0		

dr + Income Tax Expense (E) cr –			
Unadj. Bal.	0	CJE (1) 1,005
ADJ (i)	1,005		
Closed bal.	0		

Post-Closing Trial Balance

As with every other 'trial balance' the purpose of the post-closing trial balance is to ensure that all of the accounts remain in balance after recording and posting the closing entries. The post-closing trial balance should list only balance-sheet (permanent) accounts because all of the income statement accounts and the dividends declared account have been zeroed out. In addition, the Retained Earnings account balance should now reflect the ending balance calculated on the Statement of Retained Earnings.

The post-closing trial balance is prepared using the closed balances in the T-accounts. The post-closing trial balance, for LandShapes Unlimited after closing journal entries have been made and posted, is on the following page:

EVALUATE THE RESULTS
The Quality of Adjusted Financial Statements

While you probably hear lots of hoopla about
fraud and mismanagement of funds by managers
and accountants, it has been found that overall,
adjustments significantly improve the quality of
financial statements. This helps financial
statement users make better use of past
information and predicting future results.

REVIEW THE CHAPTER

CHAPTER SUMMARY
LO1. Explain why adjustments are needed.
- ❖ Adjustments are needed to ensure:
  - o Revenues are recorded when earned (the revenue principle)
  - o Expenses are recorded when incurred to generate revenues (the matching principle)
  - o Assets are reported at amounts representing the economic benefits that remain at the end of the current period, and
  - o Liabilities are reported at amounts owed at the end of the current period that will require a future sacrifice of resources.

	LandShapes Unlimited Post-Closing Trial Balance October 31, 2009		
		Debits	**Credits**
Cash		$17,400	
Landscaping Supplies		300	
Accounts Receivable		7,300	
Interest Receivable		50	
Prepaid Rent		2,000	
Notes Receivable		6,000	
Truck		20,000	
Accumulated Deprecation			500
Accounts Payable			3,800
Unearned Revenues			50
Wages Payable			800
Income taxes Payable			1,005
Interest Payable			150
Notes Payable			25,000
Contributed Capital			20,000
Retained Earnings			1,745
Totals		$ 53,050	$ 53,050

LO2. Prepare adjustments needed at the end of the period
- ❖ The process for preparing adjustments includes:
  1) Analyzing the unadjusted balances in the pair of balance sheet and income statement accounts to be adjusted, and calculating the amount of the adjustment needed, using a timeline where appropriate
  2) Prepare an adjusting journal entry to make the adjustment
  3) Summarizing the adjusting journal entry in the applicable ledger (T-accounts)
- ❖ Adjusting entries never affect the Cash account.

LO3. Prepare an adjusted trial balance
- ❖ An adjusted trial balance is a list of all accounts showing their
  - o 'adjusted' debit or credit balances in the appropriate column
  - o Providing a check on the equality of the total debits and total credits

LO4. Prepare financial statements
- ❖ Adjusted account balances are used in preparing the following financial statements (in this order):
  - o Income Statement: Revenues – Expenses = Net Income
  - o Statement of Retained Earnings: Beginning Retained Earnings + Net Income – Dividends Declared = Ending Retained Earnings
  - o Balance Sheet: Assets = Liabilities + Stockholders' Equity
- ❖ The Statement of Cash Flows and Notes to the Financial Statements are important components of adjusted financial statements, but they will be studied in later chapters.

LO5. Explain the closing process
- ❖ Closing journal entries are required to:
  - o Transfer net income (or loss) and dividends declared into retained earnings, and
  - o Prepare all temporary accounts for the following year by establishing zero balances in these accounts.

- Temporary accounts include: revenues, expenses, and dividends
  ❖ Two closing journal entries are necessary:
    o Zero out the Income Statement accounts. This entry requires the following steps:
      ▪ Debit each revenue account
      ▪ Credit each expense account
      ▪ Record the difference (equal to net income) in retained earnings
    o Zero out the Dividends declared account. This entry requires the following steps:
      ▪ Credit the dividends declared account for the amount of its balance and,
      ▪ Debit retained earnings for the same amount

LO6. Explain how adjustments affect information quality.
  ❖ Research shows that overall, adjustments
    o Significantly improve the quality of financial statements
    o By allowing financial statement users to better:
      ▪ Evaluate past decisions and
      ▪ Predict future financial results

READ AND RECALL QUESTIONS
After you read each section of the chapter, answer the related Read and Recall Questions below.

LEARNING OBJECTIVE
After studying the section of the chapter, you should be able to:
1. Explain why adjustments are needed

Adjusting journal entries are needed to ensure what four things?

1. Deferral Adjustments
Briefly explain the purpose of deferral adjustments.

Describe the two specific situations requiring deferral adjustments. Why are these adjustments required?

Complete the following statement:
Each deferral adjustment involves either a pair of _____ and _____ accounts, or _____ and _____ accounts.

2. Accrual Adjustments
Briefly explain the purpose of accrual adjustments.

Describe the two specific situations that require accrual adjustments. Why are these adjustments required?

Complete the following statement:

Each accrual adjustment involves either a pair of _____ and _____ accounts, or _____ and _____ accounts.

Deferral and/or accrual adjustments *always* include accounts from which two financial statements?

LEARNING OBJECTIVE
After studying the section of the chapter, you should be able to:
2. Prepare adjustments needed at the end of the period

Briefly describe the three steps necessary in preparing adjusting journal entries.

Briefly explain why each of the following accounts on an unadjusted trial balance would need to adjusted at the end of an accounting period : (1) Supplies, (2) Prepaid Rent, (3) Truck, and (4) Unearned Revenues

Examples of Deferral Adjustments

> **HINT: All of the adjustments in this section can be solved exactly like the examples presented in the text. If you have difficulty solving them, refer to the deferral examples presented in the text. The adjusted balances for each account are shown in italics immediately following the example.**

(a) *Supplies Used During the Period*
The unadjusted trial balance at March 31 shows the following account balances:

Supplies	$1,500
Supplies Expense	0

Upon counting the supplies on hand at the end of March, you have determined that $1,000 remain on the shelves. Use the three step process shown in the chapter to complete the following by filling in the missing information:

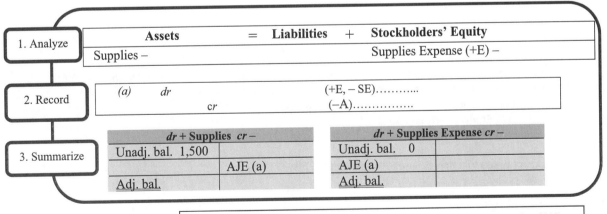

> *Adjusted balances: Supplies $1,000 ($1,500 - $500; Supplies Expense $500 ($0 +$500)*

(b) Rent Benefits Expire During the Period

The unadjusted trial balance at March 31 shows the following account balances:

Prepaid Rent: $8,100 (representing rent for March, April, and May)

Rent Expense   0

As of March 31, one month of rent had expired.

Use the three step process shown in the chapter to complete the following by filling in the missing information:

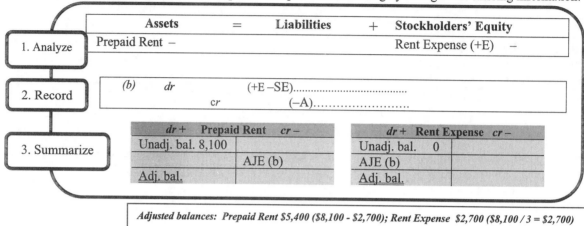

Adjusted balances: Prepaid Rent $5,400 ($8,100 - $2,700); Rent Expense $2,700 ($8,100 / 3 = $2,700)

(c) Property and Equipment (Accumulated Depreciation) – Depreciation Expense

Before reviewing this deferral adjustment, answer the following questions:

What is carrying value? Is carrying value of equipment increased or decreased by the adjusting journal entry?

Briefly describe depreciation.

What type of an account is *accumulated depreciation*?

Now, we're ready for the practice adjustment. Assume that the business purchased equipment in March for $30,000.

The unadjusted trial balance at March 31 shows the following account balances:

Equipment: $30,000 (purchased on March 1)

Accumulated Depreciation: 0

Depreciation Expense   0

The manager determined that depreciation for March is $250.

Page 116

Study Guide, Chapter 4

Use the three step process shown in the chapter to complete the following by filling in the missing information.

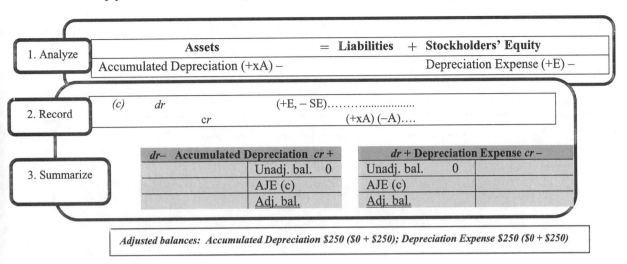

1. Analyze	**Assets**	=	**Liabilities**	+	**Stockholders' Equity**
	Accumulated Depreciation (+xA) –				Depreciation Expense (+E) –

2. Record	(c)	dr	(+E, – SE)………….................
		cr	(+xA) (–A)….

3. Summarize		

dr– Accumulated Depreciation cr +		dr + Depreciation Expense cr –	
	Unadj. bal. 0		Unadj. bal. 0
	AJE (c)		AJE (c)
	Adj. bal.		Adj. bal.

Adjusted balances: Accumulated Depreciation $250 ($0 + $250); Depreciation Expense $250 ($0 + $250)

(d) Gift Certificates Redeemed for Service
The unadjusted trial balance at March 31 shows the following account balances:

Unearned Revenues:	$600
Service Revenue:	$12,300

On the last day of March, it was determined that $450 of gift certificates had been redeemed, but not yet recorded by the business.
Use the three step process shown in the chapter to complete the following by filling in the missing information.

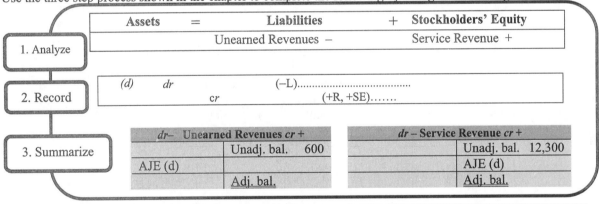

1. Analyze	**Assets**	=	**Liabilities**	+	**Stockholders' Equity**
			Unearned Revenues –		Service Revenue +

2. Record	(d)	dr	(–L)………………………………….
		cr	(+R, +SE)…….

3. Summarize		

dr– Unearned Revenues cr +		dr – Service Revenue cr +	
	Unadj. bal. 600		Unadj. bal. 12,300
AJE (d)			AJE (d)
	Adj. bal.		Adj. bal.

Adjusted balances: Unearned Revenues $150 ($600 - $450); Service Revenue $12,750 ($12,300 + $450)

Examples of Accrual Adjustments

HINT: All of the adjustments in this section can be solved exactly like the examples presented in the text. If you have difficulty solving them, refer to the deferral examples presented in the text. The adjusted balances for each account are shown in italics immediately following the example.

e) Revenues Earned But Not Yet Recorded
The unadjusted trial balance at March 31 shows the following account balances:

Accounts Receivable:	$1,100
Service Revenue:	$12,750 (after recording the previous transaction)

On the last day of March, it was determined that $300 of revenue had been earned but not yet recorded by the business.

Use the three step process shown in the chapter to complete the following by filling in the missing information.

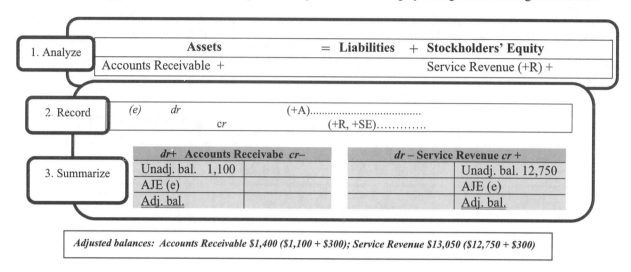

1. Analyze	**Assets**	=	**Liabilities**	+	**Stockholders' Equity**
	Accounts Receivable +				Service Revenue (+R) +

2. Record

(e)   dr   (+A).....................................
              cr   (+R, +SE)............

3. Summarize

dr+ **Accounts Receivabe** *cr–*	
Unadj. bal. 1,100	
AJE (e)	
Adj. bal.	

dr – **Service Revenue** *cr +*	
	Unadj. bal. 12,750
	AJE (e)
	Adj. bal.

Adjusted balances: Accounts Receivable $1,400 ($1,100 + $300); Service Revenue $13,050 ($12,750 + $300)

f) *Wages Expense Incurred But Not Yet Recorded*

The unadjusted trial balance at March 31 shows the following account balances:

Wages Payable:	$0
Wages Expense:	$7,000

On the last day of March, it was determined that employee wages incurred in March had not yet been recorded by the business.

Assume employees earn $300 per day and are paid on Fridays and that March 31 falls on a Tuesday.
Fill in the missing amounts on the following table:

	Monday 3/30	Tuesday 3/31	Wednesday 4/1	Thursday 4/2	Friday 4/3
Employee earnings	$300	$300	$300	$300	$300
Employee paid					$1,500

$_____
These two days wages belong in March. $_____
These three days wages belong in April.

Use the three step process shown in the chapter to complete the following by filling in the missing information.

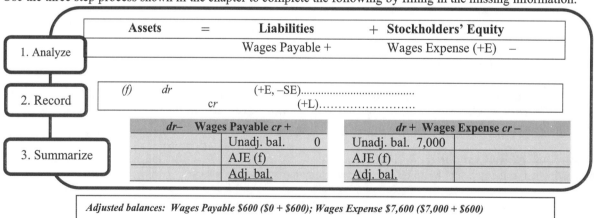

	Assets	=	**Liabilities**	+	**Stockholders' Equity**
1. Analyze			Wages Payable +		Wages Expense (+E) –

2. Record

(f)   dr   (+E, –SE)...................................
              cr   (+L)........................

3. Summarize

dr– **Wages Payable** *cr +*	
	Unadj. bal. 0
	AJE (f)
	Adj. bal.

dr + **Wages Expense** *cr –*	
Unadj. bal. 7,000	
AJE (f)	
Adj. bal.	

Adjusted balances: Wages Payable $600 ($0 + $600); Wages Expense $7,600 ($7,000 + $600)

(g) Interest Earned But Not Yet Recorded
The unadjusted trial balance at March 31 shows the following account balances:

Interest Receivable:	$0
Interest Revenue:	$0

The business has a Note Receivable of $30,000. At the end of March it was determined that interest of $150 had been earned on the note but not recorded.

Use the three step process shown in the chapter to complete the following by filling in the missing information.

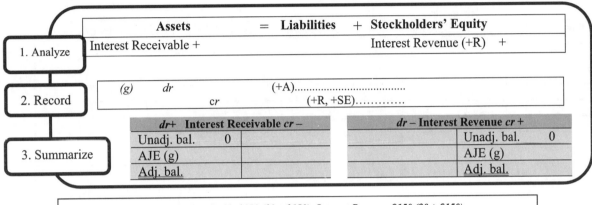

Adjusted balances: Interest Receivable $150 ($0 + $150); Interest Revenue $150 ($0 + $150)

(h) Interest Incurred But Not Yet Recorded
The unadjusted trial balance at March 31 shows the following account balances:

Interest Payable:	$0
Interest Expense:	$0

The business has a Note Payable of $15,000. At the end of March it was determined that interest of $100 had been incurred on the note but not recorded.

Use the three step process shown in the chapter to complete the following by filling in the missing information.

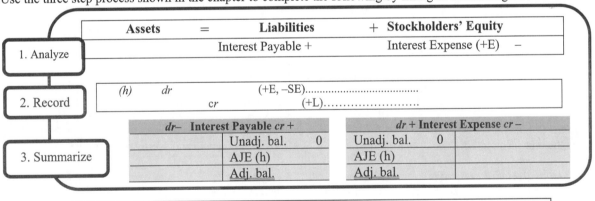

Adjusted balances: Interest Payable $100 ($0 + $100); Interest Revenue $100 ($0 + $100)

(i) Income Taxes Incurred But Not Yet Recorded
Before reviewing this accrual adjustment, answer the following question:
How is income tax expense calculated?

Assume the transactions above are the only transactions for this business. Therefore, the revenues and expenses BEFORE the above accrual and deferral adjustments are the unadjusted balances and are provided on the table shown on the following page. The business pays income tax at an average rate equal to 40% of its income before taxes. No income tax has been recorded for March. Complete the table and determine the Adjusted Income Before Tax (HINT: Adjusted totals should be: Revenues $13,200 and Expenses $11,150)

	Revenues	Expenses	
Unadjusted totals:	$12,300	$7,000	Balances provided from adustments (d) and (f)
Adjustments:			
(a)			
(b)			
(c)			
(d)			
(e)			
(f)			
(g)			
(h)			
Adjusted totals:			= $ Adjusted Income before Tax

Use the three step process shown in the chapter to complete the following by filling in the missing information.

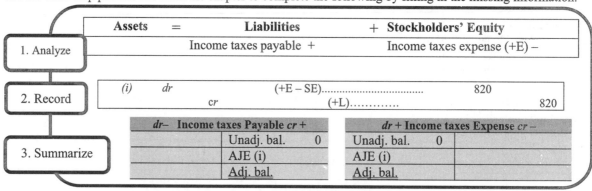

Adjusted balances: Income Taxes Payable $820 ($0 + $820); Income Tax Expense $0 ($0 + $820)
Tax calculation: ($13,200 – $11,150 = $2,050 * 40% = $820)

Additional Comments
What is the one account that *none* of these adjusting entries affected? Is this normal? Why or why not?

(j) Dividends Declared and Paid
The unadjusted trial balance at March 31 shows the following account balances:

        Cash: $6,400
        Dividends Declared: $0

The business declared and paid a $200 dividend on March 31.

Use the three step process shown in the chapter to complete the following by filling in the missing information.

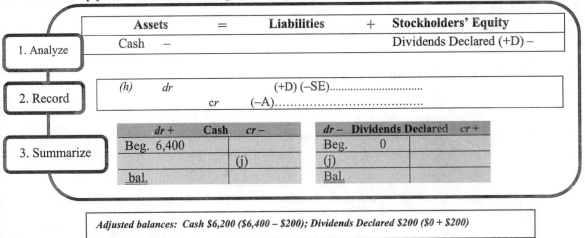

Adjusted balances: Cash $6,200 ($6,400 – $200); Dividends Declared $200 ($0 + $200)

LEARNING OBJECTIVE
After studying the section of the chapter, you should be able to:
3. Prepare an adjusted trial balance

Preparing the Adjusted Trial Balance
What distinguishes a trial balance from an adjusted trial balance? How is it prepared?

When financial statements are prepared using the adjusted trial balance, each account on the adjusted trial balance is used how many times on either the income statement, the statement of retained earnings, or the balance sheet?

LEARNING OBJECTIVE
After studying the section of the chapter, you should be able to:
4. Prepare adjusted financial statements

Income Statement and Statement of Retained Earnings
Which statement is usually prepared first? Why?

Does the Retained Earnings figure taken from the Adjusted Trial Balance represent the 'beginning-of-year' balance or the 'end-of-year' balance? Explain.

Preparing a Balance Sheet
How is the account Accumulated Depreciation treated on the Balance Sheet? Why?

Is the Retained Earnings figure used for the Balance Sheet taken from the adjusted trial balance? Why or why not?

Closing Income Statement and Dividend Accounts
Name the two subcategories of Retained Earnings.

What are temporary accounts? Name three temporary accounts.

What are permanent accounts? Name three permanent accounts.

What type of journal entries are used to zero out temporary accounts at the end of accounting year? What two purposes do they serve?

How many journal entries are needed to zero-out the temporary accounts?

Post-Closing Trial Balance
After the closing entries are posted what will be the balance in all of the temporary accounts? Once the closing process is complete, which T-account finally has the balance indicated on the Balance Sheet? Why?

What is a post-closing trial balance?

The Quality of Adjusted Financial Statements
Comment on the following statement: Managers and accountants frequently report assets and revenues that don't exist or they fail to report liabilities and expenses that do exists.

FINANCIAL ANALYSIS TOOLS

1. Impact of Adjusting Journal Entries on Balance Sheet and Income Statement—A summary

<table>
<tr><td colspan="2" align="center">Impact of Adjusting Journal Entries on the Balance Sheet</td></tr>
<tr>
<td>

Current Assets:
(Accruals of Revenues create or increase the following accounts):
    Accounts Receivable
    Interest Receivable
(Deferral adjustments of expenses eliminate or reduce the following accounts):
    Inventories
    Prepaid Expenses

      Total current assets
Non-Current Assets:
(Deferral adjustments of expenses eliminate or reduce the following accounts):

    Property and Equipment
    Intangible assets

</td>
<td>

Current Liabilities:
(Accruals of expenses create or increase the following accounts):
    Accounts Payable
    Interest payable
    Wages Payable
    Utilities Payable
    Income Taxes Payable
(Deferral adjustments of expenses eliminate or reduce the following accounts):
    Unearned Revenue
      Total current liabilities
Non-Current Liabilities:
(Accrual and deferral adjustments usually do not impact these accounts)
Stockholders' Equity
(Accrual and Deferral adjustments usually do not impact these accounts)

</td>
</tr>
</table>

<table>
<tr><td colspan="1" align="center">Impact of Adjusting Journal Entries on the Income Statement</td></tr>
<tr><td>**Revenues:**</td></tr>
<tr><td>*(Accrual and Deferral adjustments to revenue increase revenues)*</td></tr>
<tr><td>**Expenses:**</td></tr>
<tr><td>*(Accrual and Deferral adjustments to expenses increase expenses)*</td></tr>
<tr><td>**Income before Income Taxes:**</td></tr>
<tr><td>*(Accruals to income tax expense create or increase the following account):*
    Income Tax Expense</td></tr>
<tr><td>**Net Income**</td></tr>
<tr><td>*(The net effect of accrual and deferral adjustments can increase or decrease net income)*</td></tr>
</table>

HELPFUL STUDY TIPS

1. The most difficult task in adjusting the accounts is figuring out *which* accounts need adjusting in the first place! In an effort to help you make this determination, this section provides you with a simple way to identify some typical accounts that usually need to be adjusted at the end of an accounting period.

   Let's begin with *deferral adjustments*. Here's an example. Let's say you went to the grocery store and bought a 64 ounce bottle of ketchup. You are having hamburgers for dinner this evening. You squirt out some of the ketchup and stop dead in your tracks. Why? Because you need to dash into the kitchen and update your shopping list on the refrigerator door. You mark out the 64 ounces and change it to 63 ounces. You do this each time someone in your family uses the ketchup bottle. Right? WRONG! If you do this, you probably need serious psychological counseling. NO ONE is this meticulous about keeping things up-to-date. More likely what happens is that the next time you go grocery shopping, you check your bottle of ketchup in the refrigerator and notice that it only has a couple of squirts left.

   The thing is, you haven't been keeping track of its *usage* during the month (you've been putting it off (*deferring* it), so you only know some of it has been used up when you check for it periodically. This is *exactly* how most adjustments work. People can't be bothered to keep everything up-to-date by the minute. It takes too much time and, quite frankly, it isn't worth all the effort to be that precise. Instead, businesses will occasionally (at the end of an accounting period), scan their accounts and determine which accounts are 'ketchup-like' accounts. Is there stuff in this account that needs to be brought up-to-date since it was purchased or paid for? That's what we're going to do now!

Since *every* adjustment affects both an income statement account and a balance sheet account, this seems like a logical place to begin our search. Let's start with the balance sheet. Look at the following list of common balance sheet accounts and see if you can visualize which accounts may have been 'used-up' or 'expired' (because we deferred showing the usage or earnings) since the original entry was made. Remember we're only looking for *deferral* adjustments for now. So, look for things that were paid for already, but some of it may have been used, expired, or earned since the payment was recorded.

Asset	"ketchup-analysis"
Cash	Cash is never adjusted, so we can skip this asset.
Notes Receivable	This has not expired or been used up since we got it.
Accounts Receivable	This has not expired or been used up since we got it.
Supplies	This is a prime candidate for a deferral adjustment. Supplies are purchased (like ketchup) and probably used all period long without the Supplies account ever being updated to match the actual amount of supplies on the shelf.
Prepaid Insurance	This is another candidate for a deferral adjustment. Insurance is purchased 'in-bulk'. Usually the policy covers many months or years. The policy is purchased, recorded as an asset, and probably never thought about again, even as these months of insurance are used-up.
Equipment	This is also a candidate for a deferral adjustment. It may not seem obvious at first…but, you pay for the car (even if it is with a bank loan) before you use it. Again, you probably don't even consider that every time you drive it (use it) some portion of that usage should be reported as an expense. But, most businesses wait until the end of the accounting period to show this usage.
Accounts Payable	This has not expired or been used up since we got it.
Unearned Revenues	This is the most common type of liability deferral adjustment. Some customers pay a business for services they do not intend to use until some future date. This is like the gift certificates described earlier. It could not be considered revenue when the money was received because the business has done nothing to *earn* that money yet. Until it performs the service or fulfills the sale it *owes* (liability) the customer, it cannot report earnings. Many businesses will wait until the end of the period to report the revenues that resulted from customers 'cashing in' their gift certificates.
Notes Payable	This has not expired or been used up since we got it.
Stockholder Equity Accounts	These have not expired or been used up since we got them.

2. Now, that you know how to identify accounts that might be affected by deferral adjustments, let's turn our attention to those that will be impacted by accrual adjustments. These are actually much more difficult to identify. Deferral adjustments are easy because you are trying to reduce (adjust) the balance of accounts that *already exist!* So, it's a simple matter of identifying the accounts (already existing on a trial balance) that need to be updated.

Accrual adjustments, on the other hand, often create balance sheet accounts that *had no balance in them prior to the adjustment.* They are transactions that are totally *missing* from the books altogether. You have to be a bit of a detective to figure these out. But, it can be done, and *all remaining accounts are suspects!* So, let's revisit the list from the deferral discussion, but we're only going to worry about the accounts that we decided were *not* potential deferral adjustment accounts. (The others will not be shown again, in an effort to save space.) Here's a hint! ***All accrual adjustments either create some type of a receivable (asset) or they create some type of a payable (liability). ALWAYS!***

Asset	"ketchup-analysis"
Cash	Cash is rarely ever adjusted, so we can skip this asset.
Notes Receivable	This is a prime candidate for an accrual adjustment and it will be a *receivable* that is created. But, what the company has earned but probably not yet recorded is the *interest earned* on the note. This account may generate an *Interest Receivable* account.
Accounts Receivable	This is another candidate for an accrual adjustment. If there are any sales or services that we've provided this period and simply haven't recorded yet. Another *account receivable* may be added to any already existing.
Accounts Payable	This has potential in that there may be purchases or expenses we've incurred this period and simply haven't recorded yet. Another *account payable* may be added to any already existing.
Notes Payable	This has potential for an accrual adjustment because we probably owe interest on this note but haven't recorded it yet. This *interest expense* we've incurred will create an *interest payable* on the balance sheet.
Stockholder Equity Accounts	This is the one that many students forget to accrue. If we declare dividends to our stockholders', it may not have been recorded yet. We still must pay them, so it will create a *payable* on the balance sheet.

Hopefully, these hints have helped to identify the accounts that need to be adjusted a bit more easily. With this information, you can now use the steps from the text to determine the amount of the adjustment and journal entries necessary.

SELF-TEST QUESTIONS AND EXERCISES

MATCHING

1. *Match each of the key terms listed below with the appropriate textbook definition.*

_____ Accrual Adjustments   _____ Deferral Adjustments

_____ Adjusted Trial Balance   _____ Depreciation

_____ Adjustments   _____ Permanent Accounts

_____ Carrying Value   _____ Posting

_____ Closing Journal Entries (CJEs) _____ Post-Closing Trial Balance

_____ Contra-Account   _____ Temporary Accounts

A. An account that is an offset to, or a reduction of, another account.
B. To move balances from the temporary accounts to where they belong, in retained earnings.
C. Used to track financial results for a limited period of time by having their balances zeroed-out at the end of each accounting year.
D. Used to recognize revenues or expenses when they occur, prior to receipt or payment of cash and to adjust corresponding balance sheet accounts.
E. Prepared as the last step in the accounting cycle to check that debits equal credits and all temporary accounts have been closed.
F. An amount that an asset or liability is reported at in the financial statements; also called book value.
G. Used to reduce amounts previously deferred on the balance sheet and to increase corresponding accounts on the income statement.
H. A list of all accounts and their adjusted balances used to check on the equality of recorded debits and credits.
I. Made at the end of every accounting period to report revenues and expenses in the proper period and assets and liabilities at appropriate amounts.
J. Used to track financial results from year to year by carrying their ending balances into the next year.
K. The process of entering the effects of a journal entry into the accounts affected by it.

L. The process of allocating the cost of buildings, vehicles, and equipment to the accounting periods in which they are used.

TRUE-FALSE QUESTIONS
For each of the following, enter a T or F in the blank to indicate whether the statement is true or false.

_____1.   (LO1) Adjustments involve only income statement accounts.

_____2.   (LO1) Adjustments help ensure, among other things, that revenues are recorded when earned (Revenue Principle).

_____3.   (LO1) Deferral adjustments include transactions that were not previously recorded and accrual adjustments update accounts for transactions previously recorded.

_____4.   (LO1) Each deferral adjustment involves a pair of asset and expense accounts, or liability and revenue accounts.

_____5.   (LO1) Each accrual adjustment involves a pair of asset and revenue accounts or liability and expense accounts.

_____6.   (LO2) There is a two-step procedure used for determining and recording adjustments: 1) Determine the necessary adjustments, and 2) summarize their affects in the accounts.

_____7.   (LO2) Prepaid expense adjustments are accrual adjustments.

_____8.   (LO2) Carrying value is the amount an asset or liability is reported at in the financial statements.

_____9.   (LO2) Depreciation results because of the cost principle, which states that when equipment is used to generate revenue in the current period, part of its cost should be transferred to an expense account in that period.

_____10. (LO2) A contra-account is an offset to, or a reduction of, another account.

_____11. (LO2) Depreciation Expense is a running total of the amount that has been depreciated.

_____12. (LO2) The word 'unearned' in the Unearned Revenue account means that the company has no obligation to provide anything in the future.

_____13. (LO2) Adjusting journal entries never involve cash.

_____14. (LO2) Dividends are used by a corporation to distribute profits to stockholders as a return on their investment in the corporation.

_____15. (LO3) An adjusted trial balance is prepared before adjusting journal entries have been posted.

_____16. (LO3) The balance for each account in the adjusted trial balance will be reported only once on either the income statement, statement of retained earnings, or balance sheet.

_____17. (LO3) An adjusted trial balance helps verify that the total debits equal the total credits after adjustments are made.

_____18. (LO4) The amount of Retained Earnings on the adjusted trial balance is ending Retained Earnings and will be shown on the balance sheet as well.

_____19. (LO5) Closing entries are used to transfer net income (or loss) and dividends to Retained Earnings, and to establish a zero balance in all income statement and dividends accounts.

_____20. (LO6) Most managers use adjustments to mislead financial statement users, or are fraudulent adjustments. That's why nearly all accountants and managers are in jail.

MULTIPLE CHOICE QUESTIONS
Choose the best answer or response by placing the identifying letter in the space provided.

_____1. (LO1) Which of the following is *not* a reason for recording adjustments?
- a. to ensure that expenses are recorded in the same period as the revenues to which they relate (the matching principle)
- b. assets are reported at amounts representing the economic benefits that remain at the end of the current period
- c. revenues are recorded in the same period as the cash is received (the revenue principle)
- d. all of these are reasons for recording adjustments

_____2. (LO1) Which of the following correctly describes deferral adjustments?
- a. it involves a pair of asset and liability accounts, or revenue and expense accounts
- b. they are used to reduce amounts previously deferred on the balance sheet and to increase corresponding accounts on the income statement
- c. they are needed if assets and revenues are generated in the current period but haven't been recorded yet.
- d. none of these correctly describes deferral adjustments

_____3. (LO1) All of the following are possible deferral adjustment accounts except:
- a. unearned revenue
- b. supplies expense
- c. accounts payable
- d. transport truck

_____4. (LO1) Which of the following is *not* a possible accrual adjustment account?
- a. interest receivable
- b. wages payable
- c. income tax expense
- d. prepaid rent

_____5. (LO2) Assume Jenson Co. paid rent of $75,000 on October 1 for the following five months. It is now December 31, what amount should Jenson Co. use for its adjusting journal entry?
- a. $30,000
- b. $45,000
- c. $60,000
- d. $75,000

_____6. (LO2) Greene Enterprises owns $600,000 of Property and Equipment as of June 1. At that time they also had $133,000 of Accumulated Depreciation. It is estimated that the depreciation for June is $12,500. What will the balance in the Accumulated Depreciation account be after the adjustment is made for June?
- a. $120,500
- b. $145,500
- c. $587,500
- d. $612,500

_____7. (LO2) Customers had paid $6,000 to Inamorata Inc. in May for work to be completed at a later date. By August, it is determined that $3,500 of the work had still not been completed. Assuming all prepayments are initially recorded in Unearned Revenues, the amount of Revenue to be recorded from this adjustment is:
   a. $9,500
   b. $6,000
   c. $3,500
   d. $2,500

_____8. (LO2) Jolly Grime & Co. began the year with $950 of supplies. By the end of the year, they had $150 on-hand. The adjustment to record this entry includes:
   a. a debit to Supplies of $150
   b. a credit to Supplies of $150
   c. a debit to Supplies Expense of $800
   d. a credit to Supplies Expense of $800

_____9. (LO2) On February 1, Gergle Inc. took out a loan for $10,000 that was due in one year. At the end of March it was determined that Gergle had incurred $150 of interest on this loan. The adjustment to record the interest includes:
   a. a debit to Interest Expense for $150
   b. a debit to Interest Expense for $10,000
   c. a credit to Interest Expense for $150
   d. a credit to Interest Expense for $10,000

_____10. (LO2) Traynor Limited invested in a CD at the bank on October 1. The CD will pay $100 interest on December 31. The entry to record the interest includes:
   a. a debit to Interest Expense for $100
   b. a debit to Interest Payable for $100
   c. a credit to Interest Receivable for $100
   d. a credit to Interest Revenue for $100

_____11. (LO2) Assume Gargoyle Inc. had Revenues before adjustments of $32,000 and Expenses before adjustments of $26,000. After adjustments were made, Revenues were $36,500 and Expenses were $29,800. If Gargoyle has an average tax rate of 40%, what how much should be accrued for income tax expense?
   a. $2,400
   b. $2,680
   c. $880
   d. $0 because there was a net loss

_____12. (LO2) Which of the following statements is *not* true regarding adjusting entries?
   a. adjusting entries nearly always involve Cash
   b. deferral adjustments are made to reduce amounts previously deferred on the balance sheet and to increase corresponding accounts on the income statement
   c. accrual adjustments are made to recognize revenue or expenses when they occur prior to the receipt or payment of cash to adjust corresponding balance sheet accounts
   d. accrual adjustments cannot be made for salaries, utilities, or property taxes

_____13. (LO3) The calculation of book value of equipment is:
   a. Cost + Accumulated Depreciation
   b. Cost + Depreciation Expense
   c. Cost – Deprecation Expense
   d. Cost – Accumulated depreciation

_____14. (LO3) Which of the following is *not* true regarding the adjusting journal entry for equipment?
   a. The amount of depreciation depends on the method used for calculating it
   b. Accumulated depreciation is an income statement account and depreciation expense is a balance sheet account
   c. By recording depreciation in Accumulated depreciation separate from the Equipment account, you can report both the original cost of equipment and a running total of the amount that has been depreciated
   d. A contra-account is always recorded in a way that opposes the account it offsets

_____15. (LO3) Which of the following is *not* a true statement regarding dividends?
   a. dividends are an expense of the business
   b. dividends are a return to stockholders for having invested in the business
   c. the decision to pay a dividend is made, on behalf of the stockholders, by the board of directors
   d. all of the above are true statements regarding dividends

_____16. (LO3) The adjusted trial balance is:
   a. prepared only at the end of each accounting year to move temporary account balances into retained earnings
   b. prepared after temporary accounts have a zeroed balance and as a final check that all debits equal credits after this accounting cycle is complete
   c. the process of entering the effects of a journal entry into the accounts affected by it
   d. a list of all accounts and their adjusted balances to check on the equality of recorded debits and credits

_____17. (LO4) One account does *not* contain the ending balance in its account until *all* closing entries have been completed. Which Financial Statement contains the account described?
   a. income statement
   b. statement of retained earnings
   c. statement of cash flows
   d. none of the above contain the account described

_____18. (LO6) Which of the following are true statements about the closing journal entries?
   a. they transfer net income (or loss) to Retained Earnings
   b. they transfer dividends to Retained Earnings
   c. they establish zero balances in all income statement and the dividends declared accounts
   d. all of the above are true statements about closing journal entries

_____19. (LO6) Two closing entries are needed at the end of the accounting period; which of the following is *not* a part of the closing entries?
   a. debiting each revenue for the amount of its balance
   b. crediting each expense for the amount of its balance
   c. debiting dividends declared for the amount of its balance
   d. all of the above are part of closing entries

_____20. (LO6) Which of the following are true statements regarding the effect of adjustments on information quality?
   a. most managers and accountants report assets and revenues that don't exist, or fail to report liabilities and expenses that do exist
   b. it is rare that adjustments have helped financial-statement users better judge how well a company is performing
   c. company financial statements are influenced by management's frequent, fraudulent manipulation of numbers
   d. none of the above are true statements regarding the effect of adjustments on information quality

EXERCISES
Record your answer to each exercise in the space provided. Show your work.

Exercise 4-1. Matching Transactions with Type of Adjustment (LO1)
Match each transaction with the type of adjustment that will be required, by entering the appropriate letter in the space provided. *Note: Exercises 4-1, and 4-2 are sequential problems and should be done in order.*

Transaction

_____ 1. At year-end Wages expense of $600 has been incurred, but not yet paid or recorded.

_____ 2. $800 of Revenue that was collected in advance earlier this year has now been earned.

_____ 3. At year-end $100 interest has been earned on a note receivable. It will be collected next year.

_____ 4. Store supplies were purchased throughout the year for $400, and $50 of the Store supplies remained on hand (unused) at year-end

_____ 5. A twelve-month insurance policy on the building was paid for $1,200 on October 1. At year end, some of the policy had expired.

Type of Adjustment
A. Accrual Adjustment
B. Deferral Adjustment

Exercise 4-2. Determining Financial Statement Effects and Recording Adjusting Journal Entries (LO2)

Part A. For each of the transactions in **Exercise 4-1**, indicate the accounting equation effect as illustrated in the chapter, and the adjusting journal entry required at year-end. Use the following format, indicating + for increases, – for decreases. For transactions affecting Stockholders' Equity, indicate the effect total stockholders' equity as well as the effect on the specific subaccount.

Transaction 1:

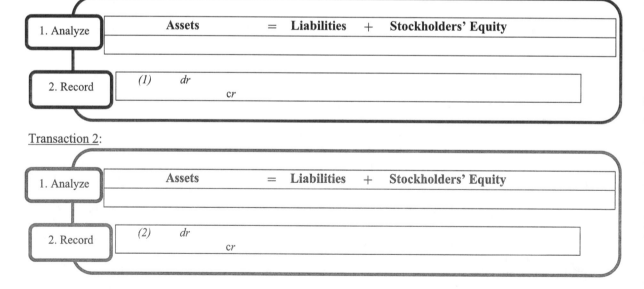

Transaction 2:

Transaction 3:

1. Analyze	Assets	=	Liabilities	+	Stockholders' Equity

2. Record	(3) dr
	cr

Transaction 4:

1. Analyze	Assets	=	Liabilities	+	Stockholders' Equity

2. Record	(4) dr
	cr

Transaction 5:

1. Analyze	Assets	=	Liabilities	+	Stockholders' Equity

2. Record	(5) dr
	cr

Exercise 4-3. Prepare Adjusting Journal Entries. (LO2)

Prepare adjusting entries, dated December 31, 2009, for each of the following transactions. Assume that you are adjusting the related accounts as of the end of the year and that no adjustments have been made.

(a) The Company had $3,500 of office supplies on hand January 1, 2009, purchased $5,400 of office supplies during 2009, and had $950 of office supplies on hand December 31, 2009.

dr _____   _____

    cr _____   _____

(b) Employees work five days per week and are paid $45,000 every other Friday. The year ends on December 31, 2009. Employees worked eight days in December. They will be paid on January 2, 2010.

dr _____   _____

    cr _____   _____

(c) The company rents out a portion of its office space to a small business owner. The rental agreement requires an advance payment of $12,000 for six months' rent. The advanced payment received from the small business owner was recorded as unearned revenue when it was received on August 1, 2009.

dr _____   _____

    cr _____   _____

(d) The accounting department sends out bills to customers every Friday and records the revenue earned at that time. The last bills were sent Friday, December 26, 2009. Services performed on December 29, 30 and 31, amounted to $18,500. This amount has not yet been recorded.

dr _____ _____
  cr _____ _____

(e) On November 1, 2009, a three-year insurance premium of $18,720 was paid for coverage beginning on that date. The payment was recorded in the prepaid insurance account.

dr _____ _____
  cr _____ _____

(f) On September 1, the company purchased equipment for $51,000. Estimated *annual* depreciation is $10,200 has not yet been recorded.

dr _____ _____
  cr _____ _____

Exercise 4-4. Prepare an Adjusted Trial Balance. (LO4)

Note: Exercises 4-4, and 4-5 are sequential problems and should be done in order.
LaLuz Company has the following adjusted accounts and balances at year-end (July 31, 2008.)

Accounts Payable	325	Depreciation Expense	200	Prepaid Expenses	70
Accounts Receivable	250	Income Taxes Expense	205	Rent Expense	500
Accrued Liabilities	100	Income Taxes Payable	50	Retained Earnings	1,140
Accumulated Depreciation	230	Interest Expense	60	Salaries Expense	420
Buildings and Equipment	1,625	Interest Revenue	40	Sales Revenue	3,710
Cash	180	Inventories	590	Unearned Revenue	170
Contributed Capital	475	Land	2,390		
Cost of Goods Sold	1,450	Long-term debt	1,700		

Prepare an adjusted trial balance for LaLuz Company as of July 31, 2008. (HINT: Accounts should be listed in appropriate order.)

LaLuz Company Adjusted Trial Balance July 31, 2008	Debits	Credits
	$	

Totals		$	$

Exercise 4-5. Prepare Closing Entries. (LO6)

Using the Adjusted Trial Balance prepared in Exercise 4-4, prepare the closing entry for LaLuz Company for the year ending July 31, 2008.

1. *dr* _____
    dr _____
       cr _____
       cr _____
       cr _____
       cr _____
       cr _____
       cr _____
       cr _____

Why is there only *one* closing entry for LaLuz instead of two?

Exercise 4-6. Recording Adjusting Journal Entries and Preparing an Adjusted Trial Balance (LO2, LO4)
Note: Exercises 4-6, 4-7, and 4-8 are sequential problems and should be done in order.

Kerns Company prepared the following unadjusted trial balance at the end of its second year of operations ending December 31, 2009.

Kerns Corporation Trial Balance December 31, 2009		
	Debits	**Credits**
Cash	$ 34,000	
Notes Receivable	5,000	
Accounts Receivable	19,500	
Interest Receivable		
Prepaid Insurance	12,000	
Equipment	72,000	
Accumulated Deprecation		13,200
Land	200,000	
Accounts Payable		32,000
Unearned Revenues		18,300
Interest Payable		
Income Taxes Payable		
Dividends Payable		
Notes Payable		60,000

Contributed Capital		120,000
Retained Earnings		34,700
Dividends Declared		
Service Revenue		86,800
Interest Revenue		
Wages Expense	19,500	
Utilities Expense	3,000	
Insurance Expense		
Depreciation Expense		
Interest Expense		
Income Tax Expense		
Totals	$ 365,000	$ 365,000

Other data not yet recorded at December 31, 2009.

a. Interest earned on note receivable $150
b. Insurance expired during 2009, $11,500
c. Depreciation expense for 2009, $14,400
d. Unearned Revenues earned in 2009, $15,000
e. Interest incurred on the note payable in 2009, $4,800
f. Income Taxes for 2009, $18,525
g. Dividends Declared in 2009, $10,500

Part A. Prepare the adjusting journal entries (*a*) through (g) for 2009.

(a) *dr* _____ _____
    cr _____ _____

(b) *dr* _____ _____
    cr _____ _____

(c) *dr* _____ _____
    cr _____ _____

(d) *dr* _____ _____
    cr _____ _____

(e) *dr* _____ _____
    cr _____ _____

(f) *dr* _____ _____
    cr _____ _____

(g) *dr* _____ _____
    cr _____ _____

Part B. Using the following unadjusted T-accounts, determine the adjusted balances in each account and prepare an adjusted trial balance as of December 31, 2009.

dr + Cash (A) cr –	dr– Notes Payable (L) cr +	dr – Service Revenue (R) +cr
Unadj. bal 34,000	Unadj. bal 60,000	Unadj. bal 86,800

dr + Notes Receivble (A) cr –	dr– Accounts Payable (L) cr +	dr – Interest Revenue (R) +cr
Unadj. bal 5,000	Unadj. bal 32,000	Unadj. bal 0

dr + Accounts Receivable (A) cr –	dr– Unearned Revenues (L) cr +	dr + Wages Expense (E) cr –
Unadj. bal 19,500	Unadj. bal 18,300	Unadj. bal 19,500

dr + Interest Receivable (A) cr –	dr– Interest Payable (L) cr +	dr + Utilities Expense (E) cr –
Unadj. bal 0	Unadj. bal 0	Unadj. bal 3,000

dr + Prepaid Insurance (A) cr –	dr– Income Taxes Payable (L) cr +	dr + Insurance Expense (E) cr –
Unadj. bal 12,000	Unadj. bal 0	Unadj. bal 0

dr + Land (A) cr –	dr– Dividends Payable (L) cr +	dr + Depreciation Expense (E) cr –
Unadj. bal 200,000	Unadj. bal 0	Unadj. bal 0
		Unadj. bal 34,000

dr + Equipment (A) cr –	dr– Contributed Capital (SE) cr +	dr + Interest Expense (E) cr –
Unadj. bal 72,000	Unadj. bal 120,000	Unadj. bal 0

dr–Accumulated Depreciation cr +	dr– Retained Earnings (SE) cr +	dr + Income Tax Expense (E) cr –
Unadj. bal 13,200	Unadj. bal 34,700	Unadj. bal 0

dr+ Dividends Declared (SE) cr –
Unadj. bal 0

Part C. Prepare an Adjusted Trial Balance (LO4)

Using the T-accounts from Part B, prepare an adjusted trial balance as of December 31, 2009 for Kerns Company using the form on the following page.

(HINT: The totals for the adjusted trial balance should be $413,375)

<table>
<tr><td colspan="3">Kerns Corporation
Adjusted Trial Balance
December 31, 2009</td></tr>
<tr><td></td><td>Debits</td><td>Credits</td></tr>
<tr><td>Cash</td><td></td><td></td></tr>
<tr><td>Notes Receivable</td><td></td><td></td></tr>
<tr><td>Accounts Receivable</td><td></td><td></td></tr>
<tr><td>Interest Receivable</td><td></td><td></td></tr>
<tr><td>Prepaid Insurance</td><td></td><td></td></tr>
<tr><td>Equipment</td><td></td><td></td></tr>
</table>

Accumulated Deprecation		
Land		
Notes Payable		
Accounts Payable		
Unearned Revenues		
Interest Payable		
Income Taxes Payable		
Dividends Payable		
Contributed Capital		
Retained Earnings		
Dividends Declared		
Service Revenue		
Interest Revenue		
Wages Expense		
Utilities Expense		
Insurance Expense		
Depreciation Expense		
Interest Expense		
Income Tax Expense		
Totals		

Exercise 4-7. Reporting an Income Statement, Statement of Retained Earnings, and Balance Sheet (LO5)
Refer to **Exercise 4-6**.

Part A. Using the adjusted trial balance in Exercise 4-6, prepare an Income Statement for Kerns Company for 2009. (Use the Income Statement form on the following page)

Part B. Using the adjusted trial balance in Exercise 4-6, prepare a Statement of Retained Earnings for Kerns Company for 2009. (Use the Statement of Retained Earnings form on the following page.)

Part C. Using the adjusted trial balance in Exercise 4-6, prepare a Balance Sheet (on the following page) for Kerns Company as of December 31, 2009. (NOTE: Assume all Notes Receivable and Payable are short-term)

HINT: Total Assets should be $303,550

Part A.

Kerns Corporation
Income Statement
For the Year Ended December 31, 2009

Revenues:		
Service Revenue		$
Interest Revenue		
Total Revenues		
Expenses:		
Wages Expense	$	
Depreciation Expense		
Insurance Expense		
Utilities Expense		
Interest Expense		
Total Expenses		

Income before Income Taxes	
Income Taxes Expense	
Net Income	$

Part B.

	Kerns Corporation Statement of Retained Earnings For the Year Ended December 31, 2009
Retained Earnings, January 1, 2009	$
Add: Net Income	
Subtotal	
Less: Dividends Declared	
Retained Earnings, December 31, 2009	$

Part C.

Kerns Corporation
Balance Sheet
December 31, 2009

Assets

Current assets:

Cash		$
Notes Receivable		
Accounts Receivable		
Interest Receivable		
Prepaid Insurance		
Total Current Assets		$

Property, Plant, and Equipment:

Land		$
Equipment	$	
Accumulated Depreciation		
Total Property, Plant, and Equipment		
Total Assets		$

(continued)

Liabilities and Stockholders' Equity

Current liabilities:

Accounts Payable	$
Unearned Revenues	
Interest Payable	
Income Taxes Payable	
Dividends Payable	
Notes Payable	
Total liabilities	$

Stockholders' equity:

Contributed Capital	$
Retained Earnings	
Total stockholders' equity	
Total Liabilities and Stockholders' Equity	$

Exercise 4-8. Recording Closing Entries (LO6)
Refer to Exercise 4-6.

Part A.
Using the adjusted trial balance prepared in Exercise 4-6, prepare the closing journal entries for 2009.
1. Close revenue and expense accounts:

dr _____
dr _____
       cr _____
       cr _____
       cr _____
       cr _____
       cr _____
       cr _____
       cr _____

2. Close the dividends declared account:

dr _____
       cr _____

Part B.
Refer back to Exercise 4-5. Why did you prepare *one* closing entry on that exercise and *two* for this exercise?

SOLUTIONS TO SELF-TEST QUESTIONS AND EXERCISES
MATCHING
1.

D	Accrual Adjustments		G	Deferral Adjustments
H	Adjusted Trial Balance		L	Depreciation
I	Adjustments		J	Permanent Accounts
F	Carrying Value		K	Posting
B	Closing Journal Entries		E	Post-Closing Trial Balance
A	Contra-Account		C	Temporary Accounts

TRUE-FALSE QUESTIONS
1. F – Adjustments involve both income statement and balance sheet accounts.
2. T
3. F – Deferral adjustments update accounts for transactions previously recorded and accrual adjustments include transactions that were not previously recorded.
4. T
5. T
6. F – There is a 3-step process for adjustments: 1) Determine the necessary adjustment, 2) record the required adjusting journal entries, and 3) Summarize the results in the accounts.
7. F – Prepaid adjustments are deferral adjustments
8. T
9. F – This statement describes the Matching Principle, not the Cost Principle.
10. T
11. F – This statement describes Accumulated Depreciation.
12. F – It means that the company has an obligation to provide something in the future.
13. T
14. T
15. F – An adjusted trial balance is prepared after adjusting journal entries have been posted.
16. T

17. T
18. F – The amount of Retained Earnings on the adjusted trial balance is beginning retained earnings. The amount calculated on the statement of retained earnings is used on the balance sheet.
19. T
20. F – While some managers may have used adjustments to mislead, overall, adjustments significantly improve the quality of financial statements.

MULTIPLE CHOICE QUESTIONS

1. C	6. B	11. B	16. D
2. B	7. D	12. A	17. B
3. C	8. C	13. D	18. D
4. D	9. A	14. B	19. C
5. B	10. D	15. A	20. D

EXERCISES

Exercise 4-1. Matching Transactions with Type of Adjustment (LO1)

_____A_____ 1. At year-end Wages expense of $600 has been incurred, but not yet paid or recorded.

_____B_____ 2. $800 of Revenue that was collected in advance earlier this year, has now been earned.

_____A_____ 3. At year-end $100 interest has been earned on a note receivable. It will be collected next year.

_____B_____ 4. Store supplies were purchased throughout the year for $400, and $50 of the Store supplies remained on hand (unused) at year-end

_____B_____ 5. A twelve-month insurance policy on the building was paid for $12,000 in October. At year end, some of the policy had expired.

Exercise 4-2. Determining Financial Statement Effects and Recording Adjusting Journal Entries (LO2)
Transaction 1:

1. Analyze	Assets	=	Liabilities	+	Stockholders' Equity
			Wages Payable +600		Wages Expense (+E) − 600

2. Record	(1)	dr Wages Expense (+E – SE)..	600	
		cr Wages Payable (+L).........................		600

Transaction 2:

1. Analyze	Assets	=	Liabilities	+	Stockholders' Equity
			Unearned Revenues −800		Service Revenue (+R) +800

2. Record	(2)	dr Unearned Revenues (–L)..	800	
		cr Landscape Revenue (+R, +SE).......		800

Transaction 3:

1. Analyze	Assets	=	Liabilities	+	Stockholders' Equity
	Interest Receivable + 100				Interest Revenue (+R) + 100

2. Record	(3)	dr Interest Receivable (+A)..	100	
		cr Interest Revenue (+R, +SE)............		100

Transaction 4:

1. Analyze	Assets	=	Liabilities	+	Stockholders' Equity
	Store Supplies –350				Store Supplies Expense (+E) –350

2. Record	(4)	dr Store Supplies Expense (+E, – SE)………..	350	
		cr Store Supplies (–A)…………….		350

Transaction 5:

1. Analyze	Assets	=	Liabilities	+	Stockholders' Equity
	Prepaid Insurance – 300				Insurance Expense (+E) – 300

2. Record	(5)	dr Insurance Expense (+E –SE)………………………………	300	
		cr Prepaid Insurance (–A)…………………..		300

Exercise 4-3. Prepare Adjusting Journal Entries. (LO 3)

a.
dr	Office Supplies Expense	7,950	
cr	Office Supplies		7,950
	($3,500 + $5,400 – $950)		

b.
dr	Wages Expense	36,000	
cr	Wages Payable		36,000
	($45,000/10 days = $4,500 per day);		
	($4,500 * 8 days)		

c.
dr	Unearned Revenue	10,000	
cr	Rent Revenue		10,000
	($12,000/6 = $2,000 per month);		
	($2,000 * 5 months)		

d.
dr	Accounts Receivable	18,500	
cr	Service Revenue		18,500

e.
dr	Insurance Expense	1,040	
cr	Prepaid Insurance		1,040
	($18,720/3 = $6,240 per year);		
	($6,240/12 = $520 per month);		
	($520 * 2 months)		

f.
dr	Depreciation Expense	3,400	
cr	Accumulated Depreciation		3,400
	($10,200/12 = $850 per month);		
	($850 * 4 months)		

Exercise 4-4. Prepare an Adjusted Trial Balance. (LO4)

LaLuz Company Adjusted Trial Balance July 31, 2008	Debits	Credits
Cash	$ 180	
Accounts Receivable	250	
Inventories	590	
Prepaid Expenses	70	
Buildings and Equipment	1,625	
Accumulated Deprecation		230
Land	2,390	
Accounts Payable		325
Unearned Revenue		170
Accrued Liabilities		100
Income Taxes Payable		50
Long-term debt		1,700
Contributed Capital		475
Retained Earnings		1,140
Sales Revenue		3,710
Interest Revenue		40
Cost of Goods Sold	1,450	
Salaries Expense	420	
Rent Expense	500	
Depreciation Expense	200	
Interest Expense	60	
Income Tax Expense	205	
Totals	$ 7,940	$ 7,940

Exercise 4-5. Prepare Closing Entries. (LO6)

1.	dr	Sales Revenue	3,710	
	dr	Interest Revenue	40	
	cr	Cost of goods sold		1,450
	cr	Salaries Expense		420
	cr	Rent Expense		500
	cr	Depreciation Expense		200
	cr	Interest Expense		60
	cr	Income Tax Expense		205
	cr	Retained Earnings		915

There is only one closing entry because LaLuz did not declare any dividends for this year.

Exercise 4-6. Recording Adjusting Journal Entries and Preparing an Adjusted Trial Balance (LO2, LO4)
Part A.

(a)	dr	Interest Receivable........................	150	
	cr	Interest Revenue...............		150
(b)	dr	Insurance Expense.......................	11,500	
	cr	Prepaid Insurance..............		11,500
(c)	dr	Depreciation Expense..................	14,400	
	cr	Accumulated Depreciation...		14,400
(d)	dr	Unearned Revenues......................	15,000	
	cr	Service Revenue............		15,000

(e)	*dr*	Interest Expense.........................	4,800
	cr	Interest Payable................	4,800
(f)	*dr*	Income Taxes Expense..................	18,525
	cr	Income Taxes Payable.......	18,525
(g)	*dr*	Dividends Declared.....................	10,500
	cr	Dividends Payable............	10,500

Part B.

dr + **Cash (A)** *cr −*	
Unadj. bal 34,000	
Adj. Bal. 34,000	

dr− **Notes Payable (L)** *cr +*	
	Unadj. bal 60,000
	Adj. Bal. 60,000

dr − **Service Revenue (R)** *+cr*	
	Unadj. bal 86,800
	ADJ (d) 15,000
	Adj. Bal.101,8 00

dr + **Notes Receivble (A)** *cr −*	
Unadj. bal 5,000	
Adj. Bal. 5,000	

dr− **Accounts Payable (L)** *cr +*	
	Unadj. bal 32,000
	Adj. Bal. 32,000

dr − **Interest Revenue (R)** *+cr*	
	Unadj. bal 0
	ADJ (a) 150
	Adj. Bal. 150

dr + **Accounts Receivable (A)** *cr −*	
Unadj. bal 19,500	
	ADJ (d) 15,000
Adj. Bal. 19,500	

dr− **Unearned Revenues (L)** *cr +*	
	Unadj. bal 18,300
	Adj. Bal. 3,300

dr + **Wages Expense (E)** *cr −*	
Unadj. bal 19,500	
Adj. Bal. 19,500	

dr + **Interest Receivable (A)** *cr −*	
Unadj. bal 0	
ADJ (a) 150	
Adj. Bal. 150	

dr− **Interest Payable (L)** *cr +*	
	Unadj. bal 0
	ADJ (e) 4,800
	Adj. Bal. 4,800

dr + **Utilities Expense (E)** *cr −*	
Unadj. bal 3,000	
Adj. Bal. 3,000	

dr + **Prepaid Insurance (A)** *cr −*	
Unadj. bal 12,000	
	ADJ (b) 11,500
Adj. Bal. 500	

dr− **Income Taxes Payable (L)** *cr +*	
	Unadj. bal 0
	ADJ (f) 18,525
	Adj. Bal. 18,525

dr + **Insurance Expense (E)** *cr −*	
Unadj. bal 0	
ADJ (b) 11,500	
Adj. Bal. 11,500	

(continued)

dr + **Land (A)** *cr −*	
Unadj. bal 200,000	
Adj. Bal. 200,000	

dr− **Dividends Payable (L)** *cr +*	
	Unadj. bal 0
	ADJ (g) 10,500
	Adj. Bal. 10,500

dr + **Depreciation Expense (E)** *cr −*	
Unadj. bal 0	
ADJ (c) 14,400	
Adj. bal 14,400	

dr + **Equipment (A)** *cr −*	
Unadj. bal 72,000	
Adj. Bal. 72,000	

dr− **Contributed Capital (SE)** *cr +*	
	Unadj. bal 120,000
	Adj. Bal. 120,000

dr + **Interest Expense (E)** *cr −*	
Unadj. bal 0	
ADJ (e) 4,800	
Adj. Bal. 4,800	

*dr−***Accumulated Depreciation** *cr +*	
	Unadj. bal 13,200
	ADJ (c) 14,400
	Adj. Bal. 27,600

dr− **Retained Earnings (SE)** *cr +*	
	Unadj. bal 34,700
	Adj. Bal. 34,700

dr + **Income Tax Expense (E)** *cr −*	
Unadj. bal 0	
ADJ (f) 18,525	
Adj. Bal. 18,525	

dr+ **Dividends Declared (SE)** *cr −*	
Unadj. bal 0	
ADJ (g) 10,500	
Adj. Bal. 10,500	

Part C.

Kerns Corporation Adjusted Trial Balance December 31, 2009	Debits	Credits
Cash	$ 34,000	
Notes Receivable	5,000	
Accounts Receivable	19,500	
Interest Receivable	150	
Prepaid Insurance	500	
Land	200,000	
Equipment	72,000	
Accumulated Deprecation		27,600
Notes Payable		60,000
Accounts Payable		32,000
Unearned Revenues		3,300
Interest Payable		4,800
Income Taxes Payable		18,525
Dividends Payable		10,500
Contributed Capital		120,000
Retained Earnings		34,700
Dividends Declared	10,500	
Service Revenue		101,800
Interest Revenue		150
Wages Expense	19,500	
Utilities Expense	3,000	
Insurance Expense	11,500	
Depreciation Expense	14,400	
Interest Expense	4,800	
Income Tax Expense	18,525	
Totals	$ 413,375	$ 413,375

Exercise 4-7. Reporting an Income Statement, Statement of Retained Earnings, and Balance Sheet (LO5)
Part A.

Kerns Corporation
Income Statement
For the Year Ended December 31, 2009

Revenues:		
Service Revenue		$ 101,800
Interest Revenue		150
Total Revenues		101,950
Expenses:		
Wages Expense	$ 19,500	
Depreciation Expense	14,400	
Insurance Expense	11,500	
Utilities Expense	3,000	
Interest Expense	4,800	
Total Expenses		53,200
Income before Income Taxes		48,750
Income Taxes Expense		18,525
Net Income		$ 30,225

Part B.

Kerns Corporation
Statement of Retained Earnings
For the Year Ended December 31, 2009

Retained Earnings, January 1, 2007	$ 34,700
Add: Net Income	30,225
Subtotal	64,925
Less: Dividends Declared	10,500
Retained Earnings, December 31, 2007	$ 54,425

Part C.

Kerns Corporation
Balance Sheet
December 31, 2009

Assets

Current assets:			
Cash		$ 34,000	
Notes Receivable		5,000	
Accounts Receivable		19,500	
Interest Receivable		150	
Prepaid Insurance		500	
Total Current Assets			$ 59,150
Property, Plant, and Equipment:			
Land		$200,000	
Equipment	$72,000		
Accumulated Depreciation	(27,600)	44,400	
Total Property, Plant, and Equipment			244,400
Total Assets			$303,550

(continued)

Liabilities and Stockholders' Equity

Current liabilities:		
Accounts Payable	$32,000	
Unearned Revenues	3,300	
Interest Payable	4,800	
Income Taxes Payable	18,525	
Dividends Payable	10,500	
Notes Payable	60,000	
Total liabilities		$129,125
Stockholders' equity:		
Contributed Capital	$120,000	
Retained Earnings	54,425	
Total stockholders' equity		174,425
Total Liabilities and Stockholders' Equity		$303,550

Exercise 4-8. Recording Closing Entries (LO6)
Part A.
1. Close revenue and expense accounts

dr		Service Revenue (-R)...................	101,800	
dr		Interest Revenue (-R)...................	150	
	cr	Utilities Expense (-E).........		19,500
	cr	Utilities Expense (-E).........		3,000
	cr	Insurance Expense (-E).......		11,500
	cr	Depreciation Expense (-E)...		14,400
	cr	Interest Expense (-E).........		4,800
	cr	Income Tax Expense (-E)....		18,525
	cr	Retained Earnings (+SE)....		30,225

2. close the dividends declared account

dr		Retained Earnings (-SE)................	10,500	
	cr	Dividends Declared (-D)......		10,500

Part B.
When closing entries are made, it is only necessary to close temporary accounts that currently *have a balance.*
There was no balance in the dividends declared account so it didn't need to be zeroed-out. In short, Kerns
Corporation declared dividends in 2009 while LaLuz declared no dividends.

ORGANIZATION OF THE CHAPTER

Understand the business	**Study the accounting methods**	**Evaluate the results**	**Review the chapter**
- The needs of financial statement users - The financial reporting environment	- Financial statement formatting - Independent external audit - Releasing financial information	- Comparison to common benchmarks -Financial statement ratio analyses	- Demonstration case - Chapter summary - Key terms - Practice material

CHAPTER FOCUS SUGGESTIONS

Review

Now that you've got solid knowledge of the basic financial statements, we can go a bit deeper into 'what they mean' to the user. Aside from the numbers themselves, what can we learn from these statements about the business we are interested in? How can we manipulate, rearrange, and analyze the numbers on the statements to provide a little deeper insight into what makes the company tick? How can we compare the results of this company to another company when one is a multi-million dollar Fortune 500 company and the other is an up-and-coming babe in the woods? Well, welcome to the exciting world of Chapter 5! It's time to roll up your sleeves and get ready to dig in!!

Introduction

This chapter centers on the analyses performed by financial statement users in obtaining information about a business from its financial statements. It's not enough to simply review a company's performance in a previous year. Analysis requires a certain amount of 'digging' to compile data from a variety of sources and reduce it to understandable and useful information for financial decision-making. This chapter will introduce you to the analytical tools and information resources available to financial statement users in making investment decisions. You'll also see how some managers might be tempted to misreport financial results, and what how the enactment of new legislation helps to prevent it from occurring.

UNDERSTAND THE BUSINESS

The Needs of Financial Statement Users
There are four primary groups of people who use financial statements for decision-making. While each group uses the information for different purposes, the need for analytical tools is common to all of them.

> **Learning Objective 1**
> Explain the needs of financial statement users.

Managers
Management relies on accounting information to help the business run smoothly. Marketing, investment, employment, and sales decisions depend heavily on the accounting information received by management *and* how this information is interpreted. When used in this manner, accounting information fulfills a *management* function.

Directors
Directors is a short title used to describe the Board of Directors in a corporation. Elected by the stockholders, these individuals are essentially a 'watch-dog' group. They ensure that the decisions made by management are in the best interests of the stockholders. When used to watch over the management in a business, accounting information fulfills a *governance* function.

Creditors
Since creditors essentially allow a business the opportunity to pay for goods and services *after* they've been purchased or used. Creditors must be able to determine the likelihood of receiving the *payment* for those goods and services. A company's financial statements need to reassure creditors that the company will be able to repay them.

Occasionally, banks will put certain restrictions on the business as an additional bit of 'insurance'. The bank might require that a business maintain a minimum cash balance at all times. These types of requirements are referred to as **loan covenants**. When used to administer contracts, accounting information fulfills a *contracting* function.

Investors

Investors (and their advisors) are interested in the financial strength of a company and, consequently, a company's value. The ability use financial statements to predict a company's financial performance in the future is critical. For this reason, investors are interested in information that will help them evaluate the current financial strength of the business, and its potential for growth. This information helps investors to place some kind of value on the business. When accounting information is used to measure stock prices, it fulfills a *valuation* role.

Here is a summary of how financial information is used and the different functions it performs:

Users	Uses
Managers	Management (Run the business)
Directors	Governance (Oversee the business)
Creditors	Contracting (Administer business contracts)
Investors	Valuation (Value the business)

The Financial Reporting Environment

Recent high-profile cases involving fraud and mismanagement by high-level managers have fueled the drive for changes in the financial reporting environment. In this section, we look more closely at what caused these scandals and the response to them by accounting regulators.

<table>
<tr><td>Learning Objective 2
Describe the environment for financial reporting, including the Sarbanes-Oxley Act of 2002.</td></tr>
</table>

Accounting Fraud

Three things are required in order for fraud to occur: (1) An incentive for someone to commit the fraud, (2) An opportunity for someone to commit the fraud, and (3) The person committing the fraud has to have a character such that they will rationalize and conceal the fraud. Fraud investigators refer to these as the *fraud triangle*.

1. ***Incentive to Commit Fraud*** –
   The incentives for managers to commit fraud can be divided into two categories: (a) Creating Business Opportunities, and (b) Satisfying personal greed.

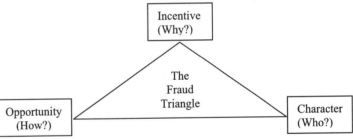

   a. ***Creating Business Opportunities:*** There is tremendous pressure for managers to produce favorable financial results in order to:
      - ➤ **Satisfy Loan Covenants:** Complying with loan covenants is critical for management.. Failure of a company to meet specific financial targets, as specified in the loan covenants, could cause the lender to impose the following penalties:
        - o Higher interest rates charged to company
        - o Immediate repayment of the entire loan
        - o Extra collateral required to secure the loan
      - ➤ **Increase Equity Financing:** The successful operations of the company lead to higher stock prices, thus managers may feel the need to exaggerate the company's financial performance.
      - ➤ **Attract Business Partners:** In order to establish and/or maintain relationships with suppliers, or other business partners, the company must be strong, stable, and self-sufficient. The company may intentionally misrepresent a company's financial stability to ensure continued relationships with these business partners.

b. *Satisfying Personal Greed:* Financial incentives to successful managers can be extremely rewarding. Management performance can be rewarded in three ways:

   > **Enhance Job Security:** To keep their high-salary, prestigious positions, managers must show superior financial performance and management abilities. Financial operating results of a company are a leading indicator of management performance.

   > **Increase Personal Wealth:** One perk of management is that they are often rewarded with stock in the company. The more the value of the stock increases, the more wealth the manager acquires.

   > **Obtain a Bigger Paycheck:** The 'year-end' bonus, which is often directly linked to financial performance of the company, can substantially increase the earnings of management. The more profitable the company, the higher the bonus.

2. **Opportunity to Commit Fraud** – If there are weaknesses available when analyzing, recording, and summarizing financial information, the opportunities to 'get around' the system and commit fraud are greatly increased. Reducing the likelihood that someone can 'get around' the system's intended purpose is dependent on the system's *internal controls*. Nothing can completely eliminate fraud, but following the policies and procedures of a company's internal controls can greatly increase the system's effectiveness at preventing and detecting fraud. Internal controls are covered in Chapter 6.

3. **Character to Rationalize and Conceal Fraud** – Most people operate their lives with a sense of fairness, honesty, and concern for others. But, people that commit fraud have developed a sense of personal entitlement that outweighs their sense of what is 'right'. Some are thought to be egotistical, have the ability to lie easily, and/or get associates and co-workers to look the other way when a fraud has been committed.

The Sarbanes-Oxley Act of 2002

In response to the many financial frauds and scandals that occurred during the 1990s and 2000s, Congress passed the **Sarbanes-Oxley (SOX) Act of 2002**. The collapse of *Enron,* and the problems with *WorldCom* (now *Verizon*), shook many people's confidence in the financial markets. SOX is an attempt to improve the financial reporting environment and restore investor confidence in the U.S markets. Every company whose stocks are traded on a U.S. stock exchange is required to comply with SOX. Major provisions of SOX include:

1. **Counteract Incentives for Committing Fraud:** The penalties for willful misrepresentation of a company's financial results is much higher, and includes:
   a. Fines up to $5 million
   b. Jail sentences up to 20 years, with the ability of the judge to require consecutive jail terms for each violation.

2. **Reduce Opportunities for Fraud:** The portion of SOX having the most profound, wide-reaching impact on business owners, managers, and accountants, is the requirement that businesses must have improved internal controls over financial reporting. SOX intends to achieve this in three ways:
   a. Managers must review how well their company's internal controls worked during the year and issue a report that indicates whether the controls over financial reporting operated effectively.
   b. The company's board of directors is required to establish an audit committee made up of independent directors to oversee financial matters of the company. This includes the hiring of the external auditors who determine whether or not a company's financial were prepared according to GAAP.
   c. In addition to determining whether the company is in compliance with GAAP, external auditors are now required to test the effectiveness of the company's internal controls and issue a report that indicates whether they agree with the conclusions of the internal control report issued by management.

3. **Encourage Good Character in Employees:** While this goal is, admittedly, a difficult one to achieve, SOX attempts to make it easier for honest employees to disclose the deeds of dishonest employees without fear of reprisals. It does so by:
   a. Requiring companies are required to adopt a code of ethics for their senior financial officers.

b. Requiring audit committees to create tip lines that the company's employees can use to secretly communicate concerns about questionable accounting or auditing practices done by others.

c. Affording legal protection to these *whistle-blowers* so they aren't retaliated against by those perpetrating the fraud.

STUDY THE ACCOUNTING METHODS

In this section, we introduce three aspects of the accounting process that improve the quality of financial statements and make them more informative for users are. They are: (1) enhance the format of financial statements, (2) obtain an independent external audit, and (3) release additional financial information.

> **Learning Objective 3**
> Prepare a comparative balance sheet, multi-step income statement, and statement of stockholders' equity.

Financial Statement Formatting

The statements shown in previous chapters are somewhat simplified compared to those that are actually published in the business world. In this section, we enhance the financial statements by providing users with more complete information.

Comparative Financial Statements: **Comparative financial statements** make is easy for user to compare account balances from one period to the next. These are financial statements (income statement, balance sheet, etc.) that contain two or more columns of numbers, with each column representing the financial results for different time periods.

1. *Multistep Income Statements:* Previous chapters used a format for presenting the income statement that used a single grouping of revenues and a single grouping of expenses. This type of format is called a **single-step income statement.** A more comprehensive income statement format is called the **multi-step income statement.** Both formats derive the same figure for Net Income. However, the multi-step income statement provides more detailed information for the user. The LandShapes, Unlimited Income Statement from Chapter 4 is presented again, this time using a multi-step format. Note the following new subtotals:

LandShapes, Unlimited Income Statement For the Month Ended October 31, 2009		
Landscape Revenue		$17,450
Expenses:		
Wages Expense	$8,000	
Advertising Expense	2,000	
Utilities Expense	1,600	
Rent Expense	1,000	
Landscaping Supplies Expense	900	
Depreciation Expense	500	
Total Operating Expenses		14,000)
Income from Operations		3,450
Interest Income	50	
Interest Expense	(150)	(100)
Income before Income Tax Expense		3,350
Income Tax Expense		(1,005)
Net Income		$2,345

- **Income from Operations** – Investors and creditors are most interested in a company's ability to sustain itself with its core business activities. This subtotal includes the results of the core activities of the business. Peripheral activities (like interest revenue and interest expense are presented separately from the core operations of the business since they aren't critical to the success (or failure) of the business.

- **Income before Income Tax Expense** – The next new subtotal shows the company's profits before taxes are deducted. This is a valuable subtotal because the average tax rates of one company can vary substantially from the rates of its competitors. Following this subtotal is Net Income. Note that this amount is the same regardless of the format used – multi-step or single-step.

2. *Statement of Stockholders' Equity:* In previous chapters, a statement of retained earnings was prepared to show that retained earnings is increased by net income and reduced by dividends and/or net loss. However, there is another component to stockholders' equity – Contributed Capital. A Statement of Stockholders' Equity shows comprehensive changes to stockholders' equity including changes in Retained Earnings and changes in Contributed Capital as well. After incorporating all changes, the ending figures for Retained Earnings and Contributed Capital will be identical to the figures presented on the balance sheet.

Independent External Audit

Basically, the auditor's job is to see that everyone follows the rules. Publicly traded companies are required, by the SEC, to have their internal controls and financial statements audited by external auditors. These audits are performed by CPAs (Certified Public Accountants) who are independent of the company, hired by the company's audit committee, and required to provide their opinion as to whether or not they believe that the company's financial statements were prepared according to GAAP, in all material respects.

Learning Objective 4
Describe other significant aspects of the financial reporting process, including external audits and the distribution of financial information

Since it would be impossible (and cost a fortune) to have auditors verify every single transaction in the company, auditors are never 100% certain that GAAP has been followed. So, auditors design their audits to detect **material** misstatements and omissions on the financial statements. This allows them to provide an opinion, with reasonable assurance, regarding whether the financial statements are fairly reported. At the completion of the audit, a report is issued by the auditors indicating the results. A 'passing grade' is called an **unqualified audit opinion.** If the statements do not follow GAAP or if auditors were unable to perform the necessary tests to determine whether or not GAAP was followed, the report will contain a **qualified audit opinion.**

Releasing Financial Information

Preliminary Releases

About three to five weeks after the end of an accounting period, most public companies announce quarterly and annual earnings by sending news agencies a press release. It includes key figures, management's discussion of the results, and attachments with a condensed income statement and balance sheet. This information is fairly reliable because it isn't released until the information it contains has been verified by management and/or the auditors. After issuing press releases, many companies broadcast an internet conference call that allows analysts to probe senior management with questions about the press release.

Financial Statement Release

Several weeks following a press release, the company will issue a formal quarterly or annual report. An **annual report** has two sections. The first section contains photos, commentaries, and an overall glowing picture of the company. The second part of the report contains the financial section—the 'meat' of the report. The following table shows the most common information contained in an annual report:

Name of Financial Section	Information Presented
1. Summarized financial data	• key figures covering a period of 5 or 10 years.
2. Management's discussion and analysis (MD&A)	• an honest and detailed analysis of the company's financial condition and operating results, a must-read for any serious financial statement user.
3. Management's report on internal control	• statements that describe management's responsibility for reporting adequate internal control over financial reporting and that report on the effectiveness of these controls during the year.
4. Auditor's report	• the auditor's conclusion about whether GAAP was followed (and, for public companies, whether the internal controls were effective.)
5. Comparative financial statements	• a multi-year presentation of the four basic financial statements.
6. Financial statement notes	• further information about the financial statements; crucial to understanding the financial statement data.
7. Recent stock price data	• brief summary of highs and lows during the year.
8. Unaudited quarterly data	• condensed summary of each quarter's results.
9. Directors and officers	• a list of who's overseeing and running the company.

A Quarterly Report is a much more condensed, less-glossy, and unaudited version of the annual report. It contains a short letter to stockholders, followed by condensed versions of: the income statement, balance sheet, and statement of cash flows for the quarter. The statement of retained earnings is often omitted. Though not as informative as an annual report, it provides *timely* information because it is prepared every three months.

1. **_Securities and Exchange Commission (SEC) Filings_** – To ensure sufficient, relevant information is available to investors, the SEC requires public companies to electronically file certain reports. Some of these reports contain more information than what is required in the company's quarterly or annual reports. These reports (usually referred to by numbers) are:

a. **Form 10K** – an annual report that includes 30 significant business risks that the company faces and outlines the business strategies for addressing those risks.

b. **Form 10Q** – quarterly reports

c. **Form 8K** – a current events report including significant business events that occur between financial statement dates, such as the acquisition of another company, a change in year-end, or a change in auditor.

These reports are available to the public as soon as the SEC receives them from EDGAR (Electronic Data Gathering and Retrieval Service), usually several weeks before the annual reports are issued.

2. _**Investor Information Websites**_ – There are literally thousands of investor information websites on the internet. Some sections of the sites provide very useful financial ratios, etc. A few great sites for evaluating and predicting a company's performance are:

- Press Release conference call archives: **biz.yahoo.com/cc**
- SEC Filings: Click on "Search for Company Filings" at www.sec.gov
- EDGAR: **edgarscan.pwcglobal.com**

While there are many more sites where financial information about a company can be found, a word of caution is in order. As with any information obtained from the internet, it is difficult to determine which sites contain good information and which don't. Oftentimes, unaudited data are used on these sites and/or the formulas used for ratio calculations are not provided. So, the information may not be reliable. Luckily, you can calculate many of these ratios yourself using the tools provided in the next section.

EVALUATE THE RESULTS

> **Learning Objective 5**
> Compare the results to common benchmarks.

Comparison to Common Benchmarks

In order to adequately evaluate information on financial statements, you should be able to compare it to something else. Points of comparison like this are known as 'benchmarks.' Some common benchmarks are:

1. _**Prior Periods**_ – When you compare a company's current period results with its own results for a previous period, you can more easily gauge its performance over time. For instance, you can compare net income this year against net income amounts from previous years. This comparison of the same company over a series of prior time periods is called **time-series analysis**.

2. _**Competitors**_ – To get a better perspective of how a company is doing within its industry, most analysts compare a company to its competitors within a particular industry. When a comparison is made across companies that compete in the same section of an industry, it is called **cross-sectional analysis.**

Financial Statement Ratio Analysis

> **Learning Objective 6**
> Calculate and interpret the debt-to-assets, asset turnover, and net profit margin ratios.

**The goal of ratio analysis is to get to the heart of how well each company performed given the resources it had available.**

1. _**A Basic Business Model:**_ The success (or failure) of running a business can be broken down into four elements:

   a. Obtain financing from lenders and investors, which is used to invest in assets.

   b. Invest in assets, which are used to generate revenues.

   c. Generate revenues, which lead to producing net income.

   d. Produce net income, which is needed to comfort lenders, satisfy investors, and provide resources for future expansion.

From this description a business model can be developed that provides a framework for understanding the ratios that are introduced next. Ratios provide measures of key business results, often examining relationships between one element of the business and the next. Think of ratios as ways to measure key relationships within a business.

The basic business model looks like this:

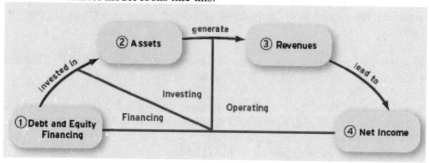

2. **_Financial Statement Ratios:_** Refer to the basic business model for these three links: (1) debt and equity financing is invested in assets, (2) assets are used to generate revenues, and (3) revenues lead to net income. These links are the basis for the three following financial ratios.

    a. **_Debt-to-Assets Ratio:_** This ratio compares total liabilities to total assets. It is usually calculated to three decimal places, and can be expressed as a percentage by multiplying the result by 100. It indicates the proportion of total assets that are financed by debt. This is important because debt must be repaid whether a company is doing well financially or not. The higher this ratio, the riskier the financing strategy of the company. Worst case scenario if a company is unable to repay its debt is bankruptcy.

    b. **_Asset Turnover Ratio:_** This ratio compares total revenue to average total assets. It is usually calculated to two decimal places and is not expressed as a percentage. It indicates the revenue per dollar invested in the assets of the business. The higher the ratio, the more efficient the business is at utilizing assets. A lower ratio indicates a business with idle assets that generate no income for the business.

    c. **_Net Profit Margin Ratio:_** This ratio measures the amount of net income (profit) generated from each dollar of revenue. It is usually calculated to three decimal places and can be expressed as a percentage by multiply the result by 100. It is an important ratio because it is an indicator of how well the company has controlled costs.

(The formulas for each of these ratios, explanation of ratios as percentages, comparisons, and why we average items, are covered in the **Helpful Hints** later in the chapter.)

There are many other financial statement ratios that evaluate other things, such as:
- o Profitability Ratios – measures the ability of a company to generate income in the current period.
- o Solvency Ratios – measures the company's ability to use current assets to pay its liabilities
- o Liquidity Ratios – measures the ability of the company to repay lenders when debt matures

    A few new ratios will be introduced in upcoming chapters, when the information presented is more closely related to each.

REVIEW THE CHAPTER

Chapter Summary
LO1. Explain the needs of financial statement users.
   ❖ The four main financial statement users are:
- o Managers, who use accounting information to run the business.
- o Directors, who use accounting information to oversee the business.
- o Creditors, who use accounting information to administer business contracts.

o   Investors, who use accounting information to value the business.

LO2. Describe the environment for financial reporting, including the Sarbanes-Oxley Act of 2002.
- ❖ For someone to commit fraud, three things must exists:
  - o   The incentive.
  - o   The opportunity.
  - o   The character to rationalize and conceal.
- ❖ Incentives that motivate managers to misreport financial results include:
  - o   Creating business opportunities by:
    - ▪ Satisfying loan covenants
    - ▪ Increasing equity financing, and
    - ▪ Attracting business partners.
  - o   Satisfying personal greed by
    - ▪ Enhancing job security
    - ▪ Increasing personal wealth
    - ▪ Obtaining a bigger paycheck
- ❖ The Sarbanes-Oxley (SOX) Act of 2002 introduced new requirements to:
  - o   Reduce the incentive to commit fraud by
    - ▪ Introducing stiffer penalties
  - o   Limit opportunities to commit fraud by
    - ▪ Improving internal controls through
      - • Management reporting
      - • Audit committee functions
      - • External audit reporting
  - o   Attempted to support employees of good character by
    - ▪ Confronting those of poor character

LO3. Prepare a comparative balance sheet, multistep income statement, and statement of stockholders' equity.
- ❖ Comparative financial statements include separate columns for each period's results.
- ❖ A multistep income statement includes subtotals to
  - o   Separate core and peripheral results
  - o   Highlight the effect of income taxes
- ❖ The statement of stockholders' equity
  - o   Which replaces the statement of retained earnings
  - o   Has columns for each stockholders' equity account
    - ❖ Show the factors that increased and decreased these account balances during the period

LO4. Describe other significant aspects of the financial reporting process, including external audits and the distribution of financial information.
- ❖ Financial information can be distributed through:
  - o   Press releases
  - o   SEC filings
  - o   Investor information web sites
  - o   Quarterly and annual reports
- ❖ Press releases typically include:
  - o   Key figures
    - ❖ Sales revenues
    - ❖ Net income
  - o   Management's discussion of the results
  - o   Attachments containing a condensed income statement and balance shet
- ❖ SEC Forms:
  - o   Form 10-K is:
    - ❖ the SEC's version of the annual report
    - ❖ Which includes:

- Annual financial statements
- Auditor's report
- Management's discussion and analysis
- Stock price data
- Other financial schedules

o Form 10-Q is:
  ❖ The SEC's version of the quarterly report
  ❖ Which includes:
    - Quarterly financial statements
    - Management's discussion and analysis
o Form 8-K is:
  ❖ The SEC's form that companies use to:
    - Report significant current events, such as
      o Changes in auditors
      o Press releases issued
      o Acquisitions of other companies

LO5. Compare results to common benchmarks.
  ❖ Common benchmarks include:
    o Prior periods (used in time-series analysis)
    o Competitors (used in cross-sectional analysis)

LO6. Calculate and interpret the debt-to-assets, asset turnover, and net profit margin ratios.
  ❖ Debt-to-Total Assets ratio:
    o Calculated by dividing total liabilities by total assets.
    o It indicates the percentage of assets financed by debt.
    o As an indicator of risk, the higher the ratio, the riskier the financing strategy.
  ❖ Asset Turnover Ratio:
    o Calculated by dividing sales revenue for the period by average total assets held during the period.
      ▪ Average Total Assets is usually calculated by adding the beginning and ending total assets together and dividing by 2.
    o It indicates how well assets are used by the company to generate sales
    o The higher the ratio, the greater the efficiency.
  ❖ Net Profit Margin ratio:
    o Calculated by dividing net income by sales revenue
    o It indicates a company's ability to control expenses.
    o The higher the ratio, the better the company's performance.

READ AND RECALL QUESTIONS
After you read each section of the chapter, answer the related Read and Recall Questions below.

LEARNING OBJECTIVE
After studying the section of the chapter, you should be able to:
1. Explain the needs of financial statement users.

The Needs of Financial Statement Users
List the four main groups of people who use financial statements for decision-making.

Complete the following statement: Managers at all levels within a company use accounting information to
_____. What is the function of accounting information in this situation?

What is the term 'directors' short for? What is the function of accounting information when it is used by directors?

What is one type of decision that creditors make using financial information? Define a *loan covenant*. What is the function of accounting information when it is used by creditors to administer contracts?

Why do investors use accounting information? What is the function of accounting information in this situation?

LEARNING OBJECTIVE
After studying the section of the chapter, you should be able to:
2. Describe the environment for financial reporting, including the Sarbanes-Oxley Act of 2002.

The Financial Reporting Environment
Name the three things required in order for fraud to occur. What are these three things referred to by fraud investigators?

What are the two incentive categories that drive some managers to misreport financial information?

What are the three *creating business opportunities* incentives discussed that may compel management to misrepresent financial information? Briefly describe each.

What are the three *satisfying personal greed* incentives discussed that may compel management to misrepresent financial information? Briefly describe each.

What are *internal controls*? How can they reduce the opportunities to commit fraud?

Describe what is meant by a 'character to rationalize and conceal fraud'.

Briefly describe SOX. What is SOX an abbreviation of?

What are the two penalties enacted by SOX intended to counteract incentives for committing fraud?

List three ways SOX requires managers to reduce opportunities for fraud.

How does SOX make it easier for honest employees to disclose the deeds of dishonest employees?

LEARNING OBJECTIVE
After studying the section of the chapter, you should be able to:
3. Prepare Comparative Balance Sheets, a Multi-step Income Statement, and a Statement of Stockholders' Equity.

Financial Statement Formatting
What are comparative financial statements? What are they used for?

What is a single-step income statement? What is a multi-step income statement? Which figure is the same on both?

Are peripheral activities listed before or after 'income from continuing operations'? Why?

Why is 'income before income tax expense' an important subtotal?

How does a Statement of Stockholders' Equity differ from a Statement of Retained Earnings?

After studying the section of the chapter, you should be able to:
4. Describe other significant aspects of the financial reporting process, including the external audits and the distribution of financial information.

Independent External Audit
Who performs audits? Why?

What does it mean to receive an *unqualified* audit report? Why is this important? What does it mean when a company receives a *qualified* report?

Releasing Financial Information
Describe the information provided in a Press Release. When is it issued? Is this information reliable? Why or why not?

Is an internet conference call useful for decision makers? Why or why not?

What is contained in each of the two sections of an annual report?

How does a Quarterly Report differ from an Annual Report? Which statement is often omitted from Quarterly Report? What is the primary benefit derived from quarterly reports?

Name three items contained in the financial section of an annual report and briefly describe each.

What are the three reports that public companies must file with the SEC? Briefly describe each.

Where are these reports available to the public? When are they made available?

What is one problem faced by investors when using Information Websites? Why is this important?

LEARNING OBJECTIVE
After studying the section of the chapter, you should be able to:
5. Compare the results to common benchmarks.

Comparison to Common Benchmarks
What are benchmarks? Why are they helpful in analyzing financial information?

What are two commonly used benchmarks? Give a brief definition of each.

What is the difference between a *time-series analysis* and a *cross-sectional analysis*?

LEARNING OBJECTIVE
After studying the section of the chapter, you should be able to:
6. Calculate and interpret the debt-to-assets, asset turnover, and net profit margin ratios.

Financial Statement Ratio Analysis
What are the four elements of the basic business model?

What do ratios provide?

Which ratio isn't shown as a percentage? Which ratio uses averages?

What does the *Debt-to-Assets Ratio* determine? Calculate the Debt-to-assets ratio for a company with Total Assets of $200,000 and Total Liabilities of $120,000.

Page 158

Study Guide, Chapter 5

What does the *Asset Turnover Ratio* measure? Calculate the Asset Turnover ratio for a company with Sales Revenue of $600,000; last years' Total Assets of $100,000 and this years' Total Assets of $200,000.

What does the *Net Profit Margin Ratio* measure? Calculate the Net Profit Margin for a company with Sales Revenue of $600,000 and Net Income of $51,000.

Assuming all the ratios you just calculated are for the same company, give a brief analysis of the company based on your calculations. What could you compare this information with that would allow you to make a more accurate analysis?

FINANCIAL ANALYSIS TOOLS
(NOTE: The icons in the last column are explained in the **Helpful Hints** section of this chapter.)

1. **Debt-to-Assets Ratio:**
   - ➤ This ratio is used to determine the percentage of assets financed by debt.
   - ➤ It is an indicator of the company's financing risk.
   - ➤ It is usually calculated to three decimal places
   - ➤ This ratio can be expressed as a percentage by multiplying the result by 100.
   - ➤ The higher the ratio, the more the financing risk.
   - ➤ For example, a ratio of 30% is much less risky than a ratio of 70%

Debt-to-Assets Ratio $= \dfrac{\text{Total Liabilities}}{\text{Total Assets}}$	

2. **Asset Turnover Ratio:**
   - ➤ This ratio is used to determine how well assets are used to generate sales.
   - ➤ The higher the ratio, the better the efficiency.
   - ➤ Since this is a 'turnover' ratio, it is expressed as the *number of times* average total assets were *turned over* during the period.
   - ➤ This ratio is not expressed as a percentage.
   - ➤ The higher the ratio, the better the efficiency.
   - ➤ For example, a ratio of .98 times is not as efficient as a ratio of 2.87 times.

Asset Turnover Ratio $= \dfrac{\text{Sales Revenue}}{\text{Average Total Assets}}$	

3. **Net Profit Margin Ratio:**
   - ➤ This ratio is used to determine a company's ability to generate sales while controlling expenses.
   - ➤ It is usually calculated to three decimal places
   - ➤ This ratio is can be expressed as a percentage by multiplying the result by 100.
   - ➤ The higher the ratio, the better the performance.

➢ For example, a ratio of 3.74% is not as good as a ratio of 6.45%

| Net Profit Margin Ratio | = | Net Income / Sales Revenue | |

HELPFUL STUDY TIP

This discussion explains the icons shown in the **Finding Financial Information** section immediately preceding.

With ratio analysis, you are always dividing one number by another number. Sometimes, you just take the numbers provided and divide. Other times, you have to 'average' some numbers on the bottom *before* you figure out the ratio. By far, the most common question from students trying to master ratio analysis is, "How do I know when to use an amount given on the bottom, and when I have to use an average?" This is an excellent question and now you'll learn an easy way to make this determination.

First, bear with me while I tell my little story here. Its purpose will make sense in a minute. At this point, I like to bring up the movie Titanic. Everyone remembers this movie. This movie is a whole, exciting, 3-hour long event, right? That's because: It's a movie (remember that)! Now, recall the scene where Rose is on the bow of the ship standing with her arms outspread. This is usually the scene they use for all of the movie posters. But, it's really just a tiny *part* of the movie (one frame of thousands), right? That's because: It's a photograph (remember that, too!)

If you try to compare the *movie* to a dinky little *photo,* it's nearly impossible! You can compare a movie to another movie, or a photo to another photo…but, it is pretty doggone hard to get a real sense of a movie with a photo. This brings us to the accounting connection.

The Income Statement (and all of the items on it) includes the revenues and expenses for the *entire period!* So, it's like a *movie* event lasting an entire, exciting month, quarter, or year. Whereas, the Balance Sheet (and all of the items on it), includes the assets, liabilities, and stockholders' equity balances for a *specific instant in time.* So, it's like *one photograph* or *one snapshot* taken from the entire movie. The point is – you can compare movie items (income statement) to other movie items, no problem. You can also compare snapshot items (balance sheet) to other snapshot items, no problem. The problem occurs when you try to compare (in a ratio calculation) a movie item to a snapshot item.

In order to *compare* them with any kind of accuracy, we try to convert the snapshots into a movie! Have you ever seen those little books with tons of drawings in them? If you flip the pages quickly, it looks like a man running across the pages? Well, that's just a bunch of snapshots all put together to create a rough kind of movie. We try to accomplish this 'making a movie' out of lots of snapshots in accounting by *averaging* the balance sheet items (snapshots). Unfortunately, we usually only have *two* snapshots…which is a pretty crummy movie. But, two snapshots is a better movie than one snapshot!!

The table below shows you how to we'll use this information and some icons to help with ratio analysis:

Ratio	Accounts used	Statement	Icon	Result	Percent?
Net Profit Margin	Net Income / Sales Revenue	Income Statement / Income Statement		No problem. Both are 'movie' items. Just divide. You're comparing an Income Statement account to an Income Statement account. It's all good!	When the icons are the same, the ratio is expressed as a %
Debt-to-Assets	Total Debt / Total Assets	Balance Sheet / Balance Sheet		No problem. Both are 'snapshot' items. Just divide. You're comparing a Balance Sheet account to a Balance Sheet account. It's all good!	When the icons are the same, the ratio is expressed as a %

| Asset Turnover | Sales Revenue / Average Total Assets | Income Statement / Balance Sheet | | Houston, we have a problem! You're comparing an Income Statement account (movie item) to a Balance Sheet account (snapshot item). This requires that you *average* the snapshots to 'convert' them into movies. | When the icons are *not* the same, the ratio is expressed as a decimal |

SELF-TEST QUESTIONS AND EXERCISES

MATCHING

1. *Match each of the key terms listed below with the appropriate textbook definition.*

_____ Asset Turnover Ratio

_____ Comparability

_____ Comparative financial statements

_____ Consistency

_____ Cross-Sectional Analysis

_____ Debt-to-Assets Ratio

_____ Loan Covenants

_____ Material Misstatements

_____ Multi-step income statement

_____ Net Profit Margin Ratio

_____ Qualified Audit Opinion

_____ Sarbanes-Oxley (SOX) Act

_____ Single-step income statement

_____ Time-Series Analysis

_____ Unqualified Audit Opinion

A. Large enough to influence the decisions of financial statement users.
B. Indicates how well assets are being used to generate revenues by dividing total assets into total revenue.
C. Compares the results of one company with those of others in the same section of the industry.
D. Reports alternative measure of income by calculating subtotals for core and peripheral business activities.
E. The qualitative characteristic of accounting information that makes cross sectional analysis appropriate.
F. Indicates that either the financial statements do not follow GAAP or the auditors were not able to complete the tests needed to determine whether the financial statements followed GAAP.
G. Indicates that the financial statements are presented in accordance with GAAP.
H. A set of regulations passed by Congress in 2002 in an attempt to improve financial reporting and restore investor confidence.
I. Compares a company's results for one period to its own results over a series of time periods.
J. Terms of a loan agreement which, if broken, entitle the lender to renegotiate loan terms.
K. Indicates how well expenses are controlled by dividing net income by revenue.
L. Report numbers for two or more time periods to make it easy for user to compare account balances from one period to the next.
M. Indicates financing risk by computing the proportion of total assets financed by debt.
N. Reports net income by subtracting a single group of expenses from a single group of revenues.
O. The qualitative characteristic of accounting information that makes time-series analysis appropriate.

TRUE-FALSE QUESTIONS

For each of the following, enter a T or F in the blank to indicate whether the statement is true or false.

_____1. (LO1) Managers use accounting information to help evaluate the financial strength of a business and estimate its value.

_____2. (LO1) Stockholders elect directors as a watch-dog group.

_____3. (LO1) When accounting information is used to measure stock prices, it is being used in a contracting role.

_____4. (LO2) The four things required in order for fraud to occur are collectively referred to as the fraud rectangle.

_____5. (LO2) Managers may misrepresent financial results to *create business opportunities* such as increasing equity financing, attracting business partners, and increasing personal wealth.

_____6. (LO2) Cash bonuses are an example of managers *satisfying personal greed* by increasing personal wealth.

_____7. (LO2) Nothing can completely eliminate fraud, but following the policies and procedures of a company's internal controls can greatly increase the system's effectiveness at prevents and detecting fraud.

_____8. (LO2) Persons who perform fraudulent acts have difficulty lying or getting associates and co-workers to look the other way when a fraud has been committed.

_____9. (LO2) SOX was enacted in an attempt to improve the financial reporting environment and restore investor confidence in the US.

_____10. (LO2) SOX greatly increased the penalties for willful misrepresentation of a company's financial results include : fines up to $5 million, jail sentences up to 20 years and the ability of the judge to require consecutive jail terms for each offense.

_____11. (LO2) SOX requires external auditors to test the effectiveness of the company's internal controls and issue a report that indicates whether they agree with the conclusions of the internal report issued by management.

_____12. (LO3) The three aspects of the accounting process that improve the quality of financial statements and make them more informative for users are: enhance the format of financial statements, obtain a biased external audit, and release additional financial information.

_____13. (LO3) Comparative financial statements contain two or more columns of numbers, with each column representing the financial results for different time periods.

_____14. (LO3) New subtotals found on a multiple-step income statement are: *income from operations* and *income before income tax expense*.

_____15. (LO4) Getting a qualified audit report is a good thing because a qualified report means that the company meets the qualifications required for GAAP.

_____16. (LO4) A press release usually includes key figures, management's discussion of the results, and attachments with a condensed income statement and balance sheet.

_____17. (LO4) There is very little difference between annual and quarterly reports.

_____18. (LO4) Forms 10K, 10-Q, and 8-K are reports included as part of the company's press release to news agencies.

_____19. (LO5) Common points of comparison (benchmarks) for a business are prior periods and competitors.

_____20.   (LO6) An business that is efficient at utilizing its assets to generate revenues is indicated by a low asset turnover ratio.

MULTIPLE CHOICE QUESTIONS

Choose the best answer or response by placing the identifying letter in the space provided.

_____1. (LO1) All of the following are groups of primary users of financial statements *except:*
   a. board of directors
   b. auditors
   c. managers
   d. creditors

_____2. (LO1) Which of the following is *not* a business function that is fulfilled by accounting information?
   a. contracting
   b. reliance
   c. valuation
   d. governance

_____3. (LO1) Which of the following are true statements?
   a. directors are stockholders' representatives
   b. creditors use accounting information, among other things, to administer business contracts
   c. investors ultimately, are interested in valuing the business
   d. all of the above are true statements

_____4. (LO1) Accounting information used to meet the requirements of loan covenants fulfills which function?
   a. management
   b. governance
   c. contracting
   d. valuation

_____5. (LO2) Which of the following is *not* part of the fraud triangle?
   a. Opportunity to commit fraud
   b. Good internal controls
   c. Incentive to commit fraud
   d. Character to rationalize and conceal fraud

_____6. (LO2) Which of the following is an example of the *satisfying personal greed* incentive for committing fraud?
   a. Satisfy loan covenants
   b. Attract business partners
   c. enhance job security
   d. all of the above are examples of satisfying personal greed

_____7. (LO2) Which of the following is *not* a goal of SOX?
   a. Reduce opportunities for fraud
   b. Encourage good character in employees
   c. counteract incentives for committing fraud
   d. creating business opportunities

_____8. (LO3) A subtotal that can be found on a multi-step income statement that was not included on the single-step income statement is:
   a. Net income
   b. income from operations
   c. revenues
   d. retained earnings

_____9.   (LO4) Which of the following is a true statement regarding an unqualified opinion?
a.   auditors were unable to complete tests needed to determine if the statements follow GAAP
b.   the financial statements appear to have been prepared using GAAP
c.   accuracy is ensured because every transaction is checked
d.   it is a failing grade

_____10.   (LO4) Which of the following is a true statement regarding preliminary releases?
a.   It is also known as a press release
b.   The information is fairly reliable because it isn't released until the information it contains has been verified by management and/or the auditors
c.   it is issued about three to five weeks after the end of an accounting period
d.   all of the above are true statements regarding preliminary releases

_____11.   (LO4) Which of the following will *not* be found in the financial section of a company's annual report?
a.   management's discussion and analysis
b.   financial statement notes
c.   recent stock price data
d.   audited quarterly data

_____12.   (LO4) Which of these is *not* an SEC filing discussed in the chapter for public companies?
a.   form 8-Q
b.   form 8-K
c.   form 10-Q
d.   form 10-K

_____13.   Which of the following are useful web sites for finding information about a company?
a.   Edgarscan.pwcglobal.com
b.   TheStreet.com
c.   Iknoweverything.com
d.   Fool.com

_____14.   (LO5) Which of the following is a true statement regarding comparison to common benchmarks?
a.   comparing the same company over a series of prior time periods is referred to as time-series analysis
b.   in order to adequately evaluate information on financial statements, it is useful to have benchmarks
c.   comparing the results of one company with the results of competitors within a particular industry is referred to as cross-sectional analysis
d.   all of the above are true statements regarding comparison to common benchmarks

_____15.   (LO6) Which of the following is *not* a part of the business model?
a.   obtain financing
b.   invest in assets
c.   generate expenses
d.   produce net income

_____16.   (LO6) Which of the following statements are true regarding ratio analysis?
a.   Other useful ratios assess a company's profitability, solvency, and liquidity
b.   Ratios often examine relationships between one element of the business and the next
c.   Think of ratios as ways to measure key relationships within a business
d.   All of these are true statements regarding ratio analysis

Use the following information in answering questions 11, 12, 13, and 14. Selected information for Aik Company is shown below:			
Net Sales	$100,000	Net Income	$24,000
Average Total Assets	$180,000	Total Debt	$75,000
Total Assets (current)	$150,000		

_____17. (LO7) Using the information presented for Aik Company, what is the Asset Turnover Ratio?
   a. .24
   b. .56
   c. .13
   d. .67

_____18. (LO6) Using the information presented for Aik Company, what is the Net Profit Margin Ratio?
   a. 41.67%
   b. 13.33%
   c. 18.00%
   d. 24.00%

_____19. (LO6) Using the information presented for Aik Company, what is the Debt-to-Assets Ratio?
   a. 41.67%
   b. 20.00%
   c. 50.00%
   d. 24.00%

_____20. (LO6) Using the information presented for Aik Company, and the ratios calculated, which of the following best describes Aik's financial situation?
   a. Aik is an incredibly strong company financially, is well-managed and should continue on as it has been. Nothing needs to change.
   b. Aik is an incredibly weak company financially, is horribly-managed and will certainly have to declare bankruptcy if current trends continue.
   c. Aik has some strong points and some areas that could be improved; income, assets and debt should be carefully monitored and adjusted as needed
   d. none of the are true statements

EXERCISES
Record your answer to each exercise in the space provided. Show your work.

Exercise 5-1. Matching Sarbanes-Oxley (SOX) Requirements with the Fraud Triangle (LO2)
Following are significant changes introduced by the Sarbanes-Oxley (SOX) Act of 2002. Match each SOX change to the corresponding component of The Fraud Triangle each is aimed at preventing. (Note: There may be more than one answer for each blank, *but* each letter is only used once.

_____ 1. Incentives for Committing Fraud (Why?)

_____ 2. Opportunities for Committing Fraud (How?)

_____ 3. Personal Characteristics that allow fraud to be concealed (Who?)

A. Code of ethics.
B. Internal control audit by external auditors.
C. Whistle-blower protection. Stronger oversight by directors.
D. Internal control report from management.
E. Anonymous tip lines.
F. Stiffer fines and prison terms.
G. Stronger oversight by directors.

Exercise 5-2. Preparing and Interpreting Financial Statements (LO3, 6)

The following are account balances taken from the records of Calamazoo Enterprises for 2008 and 2009. From this information, prepare comparative multi-step income statements for Calamazoo on December 31, 2009. (Hint: It is customary to show the most current year's information first.)

	2008	2009
Cost of Sales	595	685
General & Administrative Expenses	52	83
Income Tax Expense	16	20
Interest Expense	8	25
Sales Revenues	827	1,013
Sales and Marketing Expenses	100	125
Total Assets	500	562
Total Liabilities	151	400

Required:

1. Prepare comparative multi-step income statements for Calamazoo for December 31, 2008 and 2009. (HINT: It is customary in accounting to show the most current year's information first)

	Year Ended December 31	
	2009	2008
Sales Revenues		
Expenses:		
Cost of Sales		
Sales and Marketing Expenses		
General & Administrative Expenses		
Total Operating Expenses		
Income from Operations		
Interest Revenue		
Income before Income Tax Expense		
Income Tax Expense		
Net Income		

2. Calculate the Asset Turnover Ratios, Debt-to-Assets Ratios, and Net Profit Margin Ratios for 2009 and 2008.
   a. Asset Turnover: (assume total assets of $450 for 2007.)
   2009:

   2008:

   b. Debt-to-Assets Ratios:
   2009:

   2008:

   c. Net Profit Margin Ratios:
   2009:

   2008:

3. Comment on the performance of Calamazoo's performance.

Exercise 5-3. Matching Events With Concepts (LO3)

Following are accounting concepts covered in Chapters 2 through 5. Match each event (on the following page) with the concept that is being violated by entering the appropriate letter in the space provided. Use one letter for each blank.

_____ Comparability	_____ Relevance
_____ Conservatism	_____ Reliability
_____ Consistency	_____ Revenue Principle
_____ Cost Principle	_____ Separate Entity
_____ Full Disclosure Principle	_____ Unit of Measure
_____ Matching Principle	

A. Purchased Land for $100,000. A current appraisal by a respected appraiser places the value of the Land at $175,000. The amount in the account was increased to reflect the new value.

B. A specific method of accounting for inventory is *used industry-wide*. The company elected to use a different method for inventory valuation purposes, but has not disclosed this information.

C. Because the office equipment and the owner's home are insured through the same agent, both are paid from the company account and charged to insurance expense.

D. Due to a series of significant errors by the previous accountant and the lack of time to find them, the errors were charged to Miscellaneous Expenses since it was the most descriptive account for these errors.

E. Pet Rocks purchased for $25,000 can be replaced for $5,000. No adjustment is made to show this loss in value.

F. A new treasurer was recently hired because the previous treasurer (employed 3 years) was recently indicted on federal charges for embezzlement. *Since the charge was not related to this company*, the information was not deemed to be important to investors.

G. All money collected from customers is reported as earnings, including gift certificates.

H. A major lawsuit of $2,500,000 is pending and it is likely we will have to pay at least some portion of this award. We haven't included it in the annual report because it hasn't been settled yet.

I. Equipment purchased from a Canadian supplier was paid in Canadian currency and recorded in that currency.

J. Computer equipment was classified as Equipment last year and classified as a Current Asset this year since it is only going to last another year.

K. Employee salaries earned during the last week of December will not be recorded until January because that's when the pay period ends.

Exercise 5-4. Matching Information Items and Definitions with Information Releases Made by Public Companies (LO4)

Following are various financial reports issued by public companies. Match each report with its related definition and the information items that would most likely be found on each by entering the appropriate letter(s) in the space provided. (Note: There may be more than one answer for each report, *but* each letter is only used once.)

_____ 1. Annual Report	_____ 4. Form 10-Q
_____ 2. Form 8-K	_____ 5. Quarterly Report
_____ 3. Press Release	_____ 6. Form 10-K

A. Annual report filed by public companies with the SEC that contains detailed financial information.
B. Recent stock price data.
C. Detailed discussion of the company's business risks and strategies.
D. Brief, report to the stockholders, normally containing condensed income statement, balance sheet, and statement of cash flows (unaudited).
E. Summarized financial data for 5- or 10-year period.
F. Initial announcement of change in auditors.
G. Detailed notes to financial statements.
H. A company-prepared news announcement that is normally distributed to major news agencies.
I. Contains glossy pictures and glowing commentaries about the company's success.
J. Report of special events (e.g. auditor changes, mergers and acquisitions) filed by public companies with the SEC.
K. These often omit the statement of retained earnings and notes to the financial statements.
L. Comprehensive report containing the four basic financial statements, statements by management and auditors, and other descriptions of the company's activities.
M. Additional management discussion and required schedules not found elsewhere.
N. Initial announcement of quarterly earnings.
O. Quarterly report filed by public companies with the SEC that contains unaudited financial information.

Exercise 5-5. Determining the Effects of Transactions on the Accounting Equation. (LO6)
Note: Exercises 5-5, and 5-6 are sequential problems and should be done in sequence.

Littlestow Company is a manufacturer of children's beds (race cars, etc.). Listed here are selected aggregate transactions from the first quarter of a recent year. Complete the following table, indicating the sign (+ for increase, - for decrease, and NE for no effect) and amount of the effect of each transaction. Provide an account name for any revenue or expense transactions included in stockholders' equity. Consider each item independently. The first one has been done for you.

(a) Issued $40,000 of stock for cash.
(b) Recorded Services provided on account for $5,000.
(c) Purchased $60,000 equipment on a note payable.

Transaction	Assets	Liabilities	Stockholders' Equity
Initial Balance	100,000	50,000	50,000
(a)	+40,000	NE	+40,000
Balance	140,000	50,000	90,000
(b)			
Balance			
(c)			
Balance			

Exercise 5-6. Determining the Effects of Transactions on Debt-to-Assets, Asset Turnover, and Net Profit Margin Ratios. (LO6)

Part A. Using the transactions (a) – (c) in **Exercise 5-5**, re-calculate the Debt-to-Assets, Asset Turnover, and Net Profit Margin Ratios after each transaction. Consider each item independently. The initial balances have been calculated for you. (Note: when calculating average total assets for the asset turnover, use $75,000 for beginning assets for all calculations. A column for calculating average total assets has been provided to assist you. The actual ratio should be placed in the table for **Part B.**)

HINT: Use the "Balance" rows from Exercise 5-5 to perform all calculations. For example, when calculating the ratios for *(a)*, use the Balance row immediately below transaction *(a)*.

Calculations:

	Debt-to-Assets	Average Total Assets	Asset Turnover	Net Profit Margin
Init.	$\dfrac{50,000}{100,000}$	$\dfrac{75,000 + 100,000}{2}$	$\dfrac{280,000}{87,500}$	$\dfrac{70,000}{280,000}$
(a)				
(b)				
(c)				

Part B. Use the ratios calculated in Part A to complete the following table. Each ratio calculated in Part A should be written in the appropriate 'New' Ratio Column for that transaction. Compare the 'new' ratio to the one from the previous transaction. Indicate whether the effect of the transaction on the ratio was an increase, a decrease, or there was no effect on the ratio. (use + for increase, - for decrease, NE for no effect.) (NOTE: All ratios should be rounded to two decimal points.)

Transaction	Debt-to-Assets (+, –, NE, CD)	New Debt-to-Assets Ratio	Asset Turnover (+, –, NE, CD)	New Asset Turnover Ratio	Net Profit Margin (+ –, NE, CD)	New Profit Margin Ratio
Initial Ratios	NE	50.00%	NE	3.20	NE	25.00%
(a)						
(b)						
(c)						

Part C.
1. Transactions (a), (b), and (c) caused the asset turnover ratio to decrease, why was the decrease larger for transactions (a) and (c) than transaction (b)?

2. Transaction (a) caused the Debt-to-Assets ratio to decrease substantially. Why?

Exercise 5-7. Analyzing and Interpreting Asset Turnover and Net Profit Margin. (LO6)
Cridium Corporation has many stores throughout the U.S. Presented here are select amounts from Cridium's income statement and balance sheet.

	2009	2008	2007
Net Sales	$11,687	$11,098	$10,741
Net Income	315	304	289
Total Assets	7,321	5,004	2,753
Total Liabilities	4,253	2,114	1,258

Required:
1. Compute the asset turnover and net profit margin ratios for 2009 and 2008.

	2009	2008
Asset Turnover		
Net Profit Margin		

2. Would investment analysts be more likely to increase or decrease their estimates of stock value on the basis of these changes? Explain what the changes in these two ratios mean.

3. Compute the debt-to-assets ratio for 2009 and 2008.

	2009	2008
Debt-to-Assets		

4. Would credit analysts be more likely to increase or decrease their estimates of Cridium's ability to repay lenders on the basis of this change? Explain by interpreting what the change in this ratio means.

SOLUTIONS TO SELF-TEST QUESTIONS AND EXERCISES

MATCHING
1.

B	Asset Turnover Ratio	D	Multi-step income statement
E	Comparability	K	Net Profit Margin Ratio
L	Comparative financial statements	F	Qualified Audit Opinion
O	Consistency	H	Sarbanes-Oxley (SOX) Act
C	Cross-Sectional Analysis	N	Single-step income statement
M	Debt-to-Assets Ratio	I	Time-Series Analysis
J	Loan Covenants	G	Unqualified Audit Opinion
A	Material Misstatements		

TRUE-FALSE QUESTIONS
1. F – Managers use accounting information to run the business.
2. T
3. F – When accounting information is used in this way, it is a valuation role.
4. F – the three things required in order for fraud to occur are referred to as the fraud triangle.
5. F – the creation of business opportunities are: satisfy loan covenants, increase equity financing, and attract business partners
6. F – this is an example of managers satisfying personal greed by obtaining a bigger paycheck.

7. T
8. F – persons who perform fraudulent acts do not have difficulty doing these things.
9. T
10. T
11. T
12. F – the aspects are: enhance the format of financial statements, obtain an independent external audit, and release additional financial information.
13. T
14. T
15. F – An unqualified report is good. A qualified report means that the company's financial statements don't follow GAAP or that tests needed to make that determination couldn't be performed.
16. T
17. F – Quarterly reports are often unaudited, highly condense, and often omit the statement of retained earnings.
18. F – these are reports required SEC filing for public companies, not press release information.
19. T
20. F – efficiency in this area is denoted by a high asset turnover ratio

MULTIPLE CHOICE QUESTIONS

1. B	6. C	11. D	16. D
2. B	7. D	12. A	17. B
3. D	8. B	13. C	18. D
4. C	9. B	14. D	19. C
5. B	10. D	15. C	20. C

EXERCISES

Exercise 5-1. Matching Sarbanes-Oxley (SOX) Requirements with the Fraud Triangle (LO2)

F	1. Incentives for Committing Fraud (Why?)
B, D, G	2. Opportunities for Committing Fraud (How?)
A, C, E	3. Personal Characteristics that allow fraud to be concealed (Who?)

Exercise 5-2. Preparing and interpreting financial statements (LO3, LO6)

1. Prepare comparative multi-step income statements for Calamazoo for December 31, 2008 and 2009.

Calamazoo Enterprises Income Statement		
	Year Ended December 31,	
	2009	**2008**
Sales Revenues	$ 1,013	$ 827
Expenses:		
Cost of Sales	685	595
Sales and Marketing Expenses	125	100
General & Administrative Expenses	83	52
Total Operating Expenses	893	747
Income from Operations	120	80
Interest Expense	25	8
Income before Income Tax Expense	95	72
Income Tax Expense	20	16
Net Income	$ 75	$ 56

2. a. Asset Turnover:
    2009: $1,013 / (500 + 562)/2 = 1.91 times
    2008: $827 / (450 + 500) / 2 = 1.74 times

b. Debt-to-Assets Ratios:
2009: 400 / 562 * 100 = 71.2%
2008: 151 / 500 * 100 = 30.2%

c. Net Profit Margin Ratios:
2009: 75 / 1,013 * 100 = 7.40%
2008: 56 / 827 * 100 = 6.77%

3. Comment on the performance of Calamazoo's performance.
The Asset turnover has increased from 1.74 to 1.91 times, indicating a greater efficiency in using assets to generate sales. However, the debt-to-assets ratio has increased substantially from 30.2% to 71.2%, indicating a huge portion of assets are now being financed by debt. This could be a very disturbing trending since the net profit margin ratio, while it is higher, is not even one percentage point higher. The large amount of interest charges also reduced income taxes, but is this enough of a reduction to justify the debt? This leads one to question whether the incurrence of such a large amount of debt was worth the 0.63% increase in the net profit margin ratio. Since interest expense charges more than tripled, from 8 to 25, you have to wonder if Calamazoo can sustain this level of profitability for long.

Exercise 5-3. Matching Events With Concepts (LO3)

B	Comparability		F	Relevance
E	Conservatism		D	Reliability
J	Consistency		G	Revenue Principle
A	Cost Principle		C	Separate Entity
H	Full Disclosure Principle		I	Unit of Measure
K	Matching Principle			

Exercise 5-4. Matching Information Items and Definitions with Information Releases Made by Public Companies (LO4)

B, E, G, I, L	1. Annual Report		O	4. Form 10-Q
C, F, J	2. Form 8-K		D, K	5. Quarterly Report
H, N	3. Press Release		A, M	6. Form 10-K

Exercise 5-5. Determining the Effects of Transactions on the Balance Sheet and Income Statement. (LO6)

Transaction	Assets	Liabilities	Stockholders' Equity
Initial Amounts	100,000	50,000	50,000
(a)	+40,000	NE	+40,000
Balance	140,000	50,000	90,000
(b)	+5,000	NE	+5,000
Balance	145,000	50,000	95,000
(c)	+60,000	+60,000	NE
Balance	205,000	110,000	95,000

Exercise 5-6. Determining the Effects of Transactions on Debt-to-Assets, Asset Turnover, and Net profit Margin Ratios. (LO6)

Part A. *Calculations:*

	Debt-to-Assets	Average Total Assets	Asset Turnover	Net Profit Margin
Init.	$\dfrac{50{,}000}{100{,}000}$	$\dfrac{75{,}000 + 100{,}000}{2}$	$\dfrac{280{,}000}{87{,}500}$	$\dfrac{70{,}000}{280{,}000}$
(a)	$\dfrac{50{,}000}{140{,}000}$	$\dfrac{75{,}000 + 140{,}000}{2}$	$\dfrac{280{,}000}{107{,}500}$	$\dfrac{70{,}000}{280{,}000}$
(b)	$\dfrac{50{,}000}{145{,}000}$	$\dfrac{75{,}000 + 145{,}000}{2}$	$\dfrac{285{,}000}{110{,}000}$	$\dfrac{75{,}000}{285{,}000}$
(c)	$\dfrac{110{,}000}{205{,}000}$	$\dfrac{75{,}000 + 205{,}000}{2}$	$\dfrac{285{,}000}{140{,}000}$	$\dfrac{75{,}000}{285{,}000}$

Part B.

Transaction	Debt-to-Assets (+, –, NE, CD)	New Debt-to-Assets Ratio	Asset Turnover (+, –, NE, CD)	New Asset Turnover Ratio	Net Profit Margin (+ –, NE, CD)	New Profit Margin Ratio
Initial Ratios	NE	50.00%	NE	3.20	NE	25.00%
(a)	–	35.71%	–	2.60	NE	25.00%
(b)	–	34.48%	–	2.59	+	26.32%
(c)	+	53.66%	–	2.04	NE	26.32%

Part C.

1. Transactions (a), (b), and (c) caused the asset turnover ratio to decrease, why was the decrease larger for transactions (a) and (c) than transaction (b)?

This takes a bit of analysis. The asset turnover ratio combines information from the balance sheet and income statement, so transactions (or lack of) from BOTH statements will affect this ratio. Transactions (a) and (c) both increased assets. This would cause the Average Total Assets to increase. However, there was no corresponding increase in Net Income because of these two transactions. Remember that this turnover measures a company's efficiency in *using its assets to generate income*. If the company gets more assets, but those assets do not generate any additional income, that is an inefficient use of assets and the ratio will go down...A LOT. However, transaction (b) generated both new assets *and* more revenues. So, while the ratio may have decreased, it was only a very slight decrease because the new assets were, in fact, used to generate more income, indicating a more efficient use of the assets.

2. Transaction (a) caused the Debt-to-Assets ratio to decrease substantially. Why?
The Debt-to-Assets ratio measures the percentage of assets that are financed with debt. Transaction (a) increased assets, but did so without incurring debt. Instead it received the cash by selling stock. When a huge amount of assets are financed through stockholders rather than debt, the debt ratio goes down in a big way.

Exercise 5-7. Analyzing and Interpreting Asset Turnover and Net Profit Margin. (LO1, LO2)
1. Compute the asset turnover and net profit margin ratios for 2009 and 2008.

	2009	2008
Asset Turnover	11,687 / [(7,321 + 5,004)/2]= 11,687 / 6,162.50 = 1.90 times	11,098 / [(5,004 + 2,753)/2] = 11,098 / 3,878.50 = 2.86 times
Net Profit Margin	315 / 11,687 = 2.70%	304 / 11,098 = 2.74%

2. Would investment analysts be more likely to increase or decrease their estimates of stock value on the basis of these changes? Explain what the changes in these two ratios mean.
Investment analysts would likely decrease their estimates of stock value based on these changes. The Asset Turnover Ratio measures how efficiently the business uses its assets to generate revenues. The higher this ratio, the better a company is using its assets. Since the asset turnover ratio for Cridium decreased substantially, it indicates that the company has lots of assets that are idle or not being used properly in generating income. The profit margin ratio measures the percentage of revenues that remain in the business after covering all of its expenses for the period. The higher this percentage the better the company is at controlling its costs. This ratio also decreased from

2008 to 2009, indicating that the company is not generating enough sales and/or not adequately controlling costs. The decline in the asset turnover ratio coupled with the decline in the profit margin ratio would cause many business analysts to decrease their estimates of Cridium's stock value.

3. Compute the debt-to-assets ratio for 2009 and 2008.

	2009	2008
Debt-to-Assets	4,253 / 7,321 = 58.09%	2,114 / 5,004 = 42.25%

4. Would credit analysts be more likely to increase or decrease their estimates of Cridium's ability to repay lenders on the basis of this change? Explain by interpreting what the change in this ratio means.

Credit analysts would likely decrease their estimates of Cridium's ability to repay lenders on the basis of this change. The debt-to-assets ratio measures the percentage of total assets that are financed with debt. The higher this percentage, the more likely the business will not be able to pay off its debt. Anytime this ratio is higher than 50%, there is a very large amount of debt and the risk is greater that the company will be unable to make its payments in a timely manner. Since the ratio increase over 37.49%, [(58.09 – 42.25) / 42.25) creditors should be concerned about Cridium's ability to pay off the debt…especially considering the bad news generated from the other two ratios.

Copyright © 2008 The McGraw-Hill Companies, Inc.

Page 174   Study Guide, Chapter 5

CHAPTER 6

INTERNAL CONTROL AND FINANCIAL REPORTING
FOR CASH AND MERCHANDISING OPERATIONS

ORGANIZATION OF THE CHAPTER

Understand the business - Operating Cycles - Internal control	Study the accounting methods - Controlling and reporting cash - Controlling and reporting inventory purchases and sales transactions	Evaluate the results - Gross profit analysis	Review the chapter - Demonstration case - Chapter summary - Key terms - Practice material

CHAPTER FOCUS SUGGESTIONS

Review

Now that you've dealt with the accounting cycle and the financial statements generated from it, we're ready to get into some specific concerns about accounting operations. I'll bet you know people who can't seem to figure out what they've done with their money. They seem to have no control over their spending, lending, or bank accounts. They're probably always behind on their bills or often borrowing money in an effort to keep up. These same people are probably constantly running to the store for items they ran out of during the month. They need to learn how to control their money and other assets. One purpose of this chapter is to provide you with tools that help gain control over assets like cash and inventory.

Introduction

Like the people described above, businesses also need tools to control assets, but on a much larger scale. A business needs to have enough cash available to pay debts as they come due, without missing out on investment opportunities if additional funds become available. Inventories must be sufficient to meet the expectations of customers without having so many available that they become spoiled, stale, damaged, obsolete, or stolen. Most companies have some way of tracking the sale and purchase of inventories so that these pitfalls can be avoided. In addition to inventory issues, cash has its own special problems. It is the asset most susceptible to theft or loss because it can be: (1) easily carried and (2) used for any purpose, which make it especially attractive to thieves.

In addition to the controls used to protect assets like cash and inventory, this chapter also describes a merchandiser's operations and financial statements, and what makes it different from other types of businesses.

UNDERSTAND THE BUSINESS

Learning Objective 1
Distinguish service, merchandising, and manufacturing operations.

Service, Merchandising, and Manufacturing Operating Activities
Based on what they sell to generate revenues, there are three different types of businesses *(1) service companies, (2) merchandising companies,* and *(3) manufacturing companies.*

A service company sells services rather than physical goods (e.g. attorneys, doctors, landscapers, etc.) A merchandising company sells goods that have been obtained from a supplier and a manufacturing company sells goods that it has made itself.

Each of these company types has its own operating cycle. An operating cycle is a series of activities that a company undertakes to generate sales and, ultimately, cash. The operating cycle of a service company is the easiest. As illustrated on the right, it uses cash to provide services that are sold to customers and then it collects the cash from the customers.

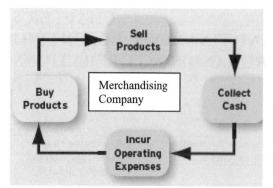

The operating cycle of a merchandiser is slightly more complex, as illustrated on the left. It uses cash to buy inventory, sells the inventory to customers and collects the cash from those customers.

The operating cycle of a manufacturing company is nearly identical to that of a merchandiser except that rather than purchasing the inventories that are ready to sell to its customers, the manufacturer purchase raw materials that it uses to make the products that it sells to customers. A manufacturing company's operating cycle is illustrated below.

All of these companies need to have control over their operations if they want to be successful. In order to achieve this, companies have a variety of procedures and policies in place called *internal controls*.

Internal Controls

> **Learning Objective 2**
> Explain common principles of internal control.

Recall from Chapter 5 that public companies are now required, by the Sarbanes-Oxley (SOX) Act of 2002 to have independent auditors assess the effectiveness of their internal controls. Effective internal controls play an essential role in creating an ethical business environment and ultimately in improving financial performance. Though there are twenty control principles for senior managers, we focus on five of the basic principles that you are most likely to come across in business.

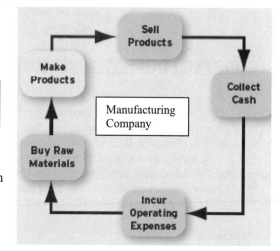

Principles of Internal Control
Since the number of specific controls that a business can put into place to accomplish its goals is nearly endless, we will focus on five internal controls related to merchandising operations. They are:

1. *Establish Responsibility* – Assign each task to only one employee because it allows you to determine who caused any errors or thefts that may occur.

2. *Segregate Duties* – This involves assigning responsibilities so that one employee can't make a mistake or commit a dishonest act without someone else discovering it. It is most effective when responsibilities for related activities are assigned to two or more people, and when the responsibilities for record-keeping are assigned to people who do not also handle the assets that they are accounting for. To do this, management should:
    a. Never give one individual responsibility for all of the following tasks related to any given transaction:
        *   Initiating
        *   Approving, and
        *   Recording
    b. Separate the responsibilities of:
        *   Physically handling assets, and
        *   Recording transactions related to that asset

3. *Restrict Access* – Access to items that can be stolen, etc. should be restricted and only provided on an as-needed basis. Some examples include:
    a. Valuable assets should be physically locked up.
    b. Other assets and/or important information should be secured electronically
    c. Access should be provided on an as-needed basis (if it is not needed to fulfill an assigned responsibility, access should not be allowed)

4. ***Document Procedures*** – Without documents, a company wouldn't know what transactions have already been or still need to be entered into its accounting system. Most companies assign a sequential number to each document and then verify at the end of every accounting period that each document number corresponds to one, and only one, entry in the accounting system.

5. ***Independently Verify*** – various independent verifications include:
   a. Hire an internal auditor to check that the work done by others within the company is appropriate and supported by documentation.
   b. Part of a person's job can be to verify information (e.g. verify a customer's driver's license number.)
   c. Compare the company's information to information kept by an independent third party. An example of this would be a *bank reconciliation*.

Limitations of Internal Control
Internal controls cannot detect and prevent all instances errors or fraud. People can make mistakes, work with other people (collude) to get around the controls in place, or disarm (override) controls.

STUDY THE ACCOUNTING METHODS

<table>
<tr><td>**Learning Objective 3**
Perform the key control of reconciling cash to bank statements.</td></tr>
</table>

Controlling and Reporting Cash
Cash controls are important since cash is the asset most likely to be stolen. To help protect cash, all businesses should: (1) keep a limited amount of cash on hand, (2) prevent unauthorized writing of checks from the bank account, and (3) prepare a *bank reconciliation* regularly to account for differences between the balance on the bank statement and the balance in the checkbook. This method of double-checking the accuracy of checkbook records is usually prepared monthly by most businesses.

Need for Reconciliation
The balance in the checkbook and the balance on the bank statement can differ for two primary reasons: (1) there are some items that you have recorded in the check register that the bank didn't know about when the bank statement was prepared, or (2) the bank has recorded some items that you didn't know about until you received the bank statement. Common examples of these differences are listed in the following table:

Bank may not know about	You may not know about
1. Errors made by the bank	3. Interest the bank has put into your account
2. Time Lags:	4. Electronic Funds Transfers (EFT)
a. Deposits that you made recently.	5. Service charges taken out of your account.
b. Checks that you wrote recently.	6. Customer checks you deposited that bounced
	7. Errors made by you

1. ***Bank errors.*** Banks do make mistakes. If you find a bank error, contact the bank and have them correct it. But, you don't have to change your bank records.

2. ***Time Lags.*** These occur very frequently. Neither of the following situations requires you to adjust your bank records.
   a. **Deposits in Transit:** If you deposit $50 in the bank today and your bank statement comes in the mail tomorrow, the deposit you just made will not be listed. But, you know you made the deposit. There is a time lag between the time you made the deposit and the time the bank records it. These are called deposits in transit.
   b. **Outstanding Checks:** The same type of thing occurs with checks. If you write a check today for $100, it will not be listed on the bank statement that comes in the mail tomorrow. But, again, you know you wrote this check. These are called outstanding checks.

3. ***Interest Deposited.*** Most people don't know how much interest has been earned on a bank account until the bank statement arrives indicating the amount of the interest. When you know how much the interest is, it can be added to your checkbook balance.

4. **_Electronic Funds Transfer (EFT)._** With the explosion of internet banking, there has been a big increase in direct deposits and automatic bill payments. Often, the exact dollar amount of the transaction will not be known until the bank statement arrives. At that time, your check register will need to be updated.

5. **_Service Charges._** These charges are usually taken directly out of your checking account and you don't know the exact amount of the charges until you get the bank statement. The checkbook will need to be updated for these charges.

6. **_Bounced Checks._** When you make a deposit, the bank usually immediately increases your account for the amount of the deposit. Sometimes there are checks in the deposit that the bank is unable to collect because the check writer does not have enough money in the account to cover the check. These are called NSF (not sufficient funds) checks. When the bank discovers that there is not enough money in the writer's account to pay for the check, the bank removes the amount of the check from your checking account. The checkbook will need to be updated for these bounced checks.

7. **_Checkbook Errors._** These are errors made in the checkbook or items that mistakenly haven't been recorded yet (usually ATM transactions). The checkbook will need to be updated for these errors and/or omissions.

The Bank Statement
Refer to the textbook for an example of a bank statement.

Bank Reconciliation
Usually the ending cash balance shown on the bank statement will not agree with the ending cash balance shown in your Cash account (checkbook). The true balance in the account is usually *neither* the amount on the bank statement nor the amount in the checkbook since *both* amounts are unaware of one or more transactions of the other. In order to determine the true balance in the account, these two differing amounts must be reconciled. This reconciled amount is the figure that will be shown as Cash on the balance sheet (you always wondered where that number came from, didn't you?) Here are the steps in preparing a Bank Reconciliation.

1. **_Identify the deposits in transit._** These are the deposits that have been made, but have not yet cleared the bank. Therefore, the bank is unaware of them and, once identified, these items are
- **Added to the <u>Bank Statement</u> balance** because the bank will eventually add them to your account

2. **_Identify the outstanding checks._** These are checks that have been written on the account, but have not yet cleared the bank. Therefore, the bank is unaware of them and, once identified, these items are
- **Subtracted from the <u>Bank Statement</u> balance** because the bank will eventually subtract them from your account.

3. **_Record Other Transactions on the bank statement._**
   a. **Interest Received.** This is on the bank statement and the checkbook is not aware of it yet. So, this item must be
- **Added to the <u>Checkbook</u> balance.**

   b. **Electronic funds transfers (EFTs).** These are on the bank statement and the checkbook is not aware of them yet. So, depending on whether the transfer was a deposit or a withdrawal, these items must be:
- **Added to the <u>Checkbook</u> balance** if it was an EFT DEPOSIT.
- **Subtracted from the <u>checkbook</u> balance** if it was an EFT WITHDRAWAL

   c. **NSF checks.** These are deposits of a customer's recorded earlier. The bank is now informing us that the customer did not have enough cash in their account to cover this check. So, the bank subtracted it out of your cash account. The checkbook is unaware of it until now, and this item must be

- **Subtracted from the <u>Checkbook</u> balance**

  d. **Service Charges**. The amount charged by the bank for service charges is not known until the bank statement is received, then this item must be
  - **Subtracted from the <u>Checkbook</u> balance.**

4. *Determine the impact of book errors (if any)*. After performing all of the steps, you may discover errors made in the checkbook. If so, determine the amount of the error and whether it must be
   - **Added to the <u>Checkbook</u> balance** (if it is an error that increases your checking account)
   - **Subtracted from the <u>Checkbook</u> balance** (if it is an error that decreases your checking account)

It is important to note that only Steps 3 and 4 affect *the checkbook*. This is significant because only items that affect the checkbook require journal entries on the company's books to update the account. Once the up-to-date cash balance is determined, there are journal entries that must be prepared in order to bring the Company's *Cash* (checkbook) balance to the reconciled *Cash* amount.

The items on the Bank Statement side of the reconciliation *do not need to be recorded* since the bank records its own transactions. Once the checkbook entries are recorded, the *Cash* account in the checkbook should contain the reconciled amount.

Reporting Cash and Cash Equivalents:
For financial reporting, Cash includes:
- Cash deposited with banks (including checks, money orders, or bank drafts)
- Cash on hand (also called petty cash)
- Cash Equivalents – Short-term, highly liquid investments *purchased* within three months of maturity.
  - Because they are readily convertible into known amounts of cash, and
  - So near to maturity that there is little risk their value will change

Controlling and Reporting Inventory Transactions

<table>
<tr><td>

Merchandisers have the bulk of their money invested in inventory and they spend a great deal of time and money tracking it. The following table shows the three roles accounting plays in the inventory management process:
</td><td>

Learning Objective 4
Explain the use of a perpetual inventory system as a control.
</td></tr>
</table>

Accounting for Inventory MUST PROVIDE management with:
1. Up-to-date information on the cost and quantity of inventory so managers can make informed decisions.

2. Accurate information for preparing financial statements
    -Inventory is reported as an asset on the balance sheet until it is sold
    -When inventory is sold it is removed from the balance sheet and reported on the income statement as
    Cost of Goods Sold (an expense)

3. Information that controls inventory and helps protect it from theft.

Businesses use one of two types of inventory accounting systems: *perpetual* or *periodic*.

Perpetual Inventory System
The grocery store you shop at probably uses a perpetual inventory system. This type of system updates the number of units and cost of each unit every time inventories are purchased, sold, or returned. The scanner that rings up your purchases serves two purposes:

1. It calculates and records the Sales Revenue for each product you bought, and
2. It removes from the grocery store's inventory records both
   - The product you bought and
   - Its cost to the grocery store.

This constant, continual, or *perpetual* updating of the records for every transaction keeps the *Inventory* and *Cost of Goods Sold* accounts current at all times. A physical count should be done periodically in order to discover shrinkage (see discussion under *Inventory Control*)

Periodic Inventory System

This system is more like the one *you* probably use at home for keeping track of your groceries. You can't be bothered with the tremendous detail of keeping track of every grocery item you buy, use, and return. So, instead you probably only update everything occasionally or *periodically*, usually at the *end of an accounting period*.

This method doesn't keep detailed records of inventories sold or still on-hand, so it is **necessary** to physically *count* everything remaining on the shelves at the end of the accounting period. The value of the items you counted that still remain on the shelves is considered the ending *Inventory* for that period. It is assumed everything else that was purchased must have been sold (Cost of Goods Sold).

Inventory Control

The following are benefits derived from using a perpetual inventory system:

- Good documentation of inventory transactions in a perpetual inventory system allows businesses to keep just the right quantity of products on the shelves for the right amount of time.
- It also allows a business to estimate how much inventory might be missing due to shrinkage (another name for inventory lost as a result of theft, fraud, and errors).

The following model can be used to estimate the amount of shrinkage in a company using a perpetual inventory system:

1. Determine units that are on–hand at the beginning of the period.
2. Monitor every piece of inventory entering and exiting your stock during the period.
   a. Add Purchases.
   b. Subtract goods Sold
3. Count the inventory to determine what is actually there (this step should be performed at least once per year to ensure accounting records are accurate and shrinkage is detected)

There are three possible outcomes from this process:

Inventory Records *exactly match* physical count	No errors, losses, theft, or shrinkage of any kind occurred
Inventory Records are *more than* physical count	The system thinks there should be *more inventory* on-hand than the physical count has shown. The difference in the two amounts indicates errors, losses, theft, or shrinkage has occurred
Inventory Records are *less than* physical count	There is likely an error somewhere, it is unusual for a business to have *more* inventory on-hand than its records indicate it should

This type of monitoring cannot be done in a periodic inventory system because up-to-date records are not maintained. The only means of determining an ending inventory count......is to count inventory! It assumes all other items were sold. So, if anything is missing, you will never know...missing items will be considered sold! This inability to track inventories is a huge disadvantage to using a periodic inventory system.

At one time, the cost of setting up and maintaining a perpetual inventory system was prohibitive, except for the most successful of businesses. But, now the technology available is very inexpensive and a business will likely have difficulty surviving in today's world unless perpetual inventory records are maintained.

Because of the prevalence of perpetual inventory systems in business, the perpetual inventory system is covered in-depth. The periodic system is included in this chapter as a supplement. Your instructor will determine whether or not you will be covering the periodic system in your class.

Inventory Purchase and Sales Transactions

Learning Objective 5
Analyze purchase and sales transactions under a perpetual inventory system.

Purchases

In a perpetual system, all inventory purchases are recorded directly into the *Inventory* account. Most companies purchase inventory on account, so if we assume a company purchased $10,700 of Inventory on credit, the journal entry and corresponding effects on the accounting equation are:

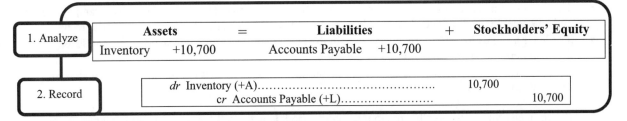

	Assets	=	Liabilities	+	Stockholders' Equity
1. Analyze	Inventory +10,700		Accounts Payable +10,700		

2. Record

dr Inventory (+A)...	10,700	
cr Accounts Payable (+L).......................		10,700

Transportation Cost

Did you ever purchase anything on the Internet? Of course! Who hasn't? What was the one additional cost you knew would be part of every purchase? Yup! Shipping and Handling! Businesses have to pay it too! The inventory you purchase would not be on your shelves unless you were able to get them into your business. This cost is considered part of the cost of the inventory purchased. Costs that are necessary to get the inventory into 'salable condition' are charged to the inventory account. Assuming the shipping cost (often called Freight-In) for the previous transaction is $300 and is paid in cash, it is recorded like this:

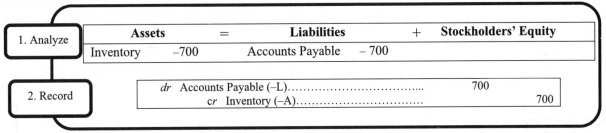

	Assets	=	Liabilities	+	Stockholders' Equity
1. Analyze	Inventory +300				
	Cash −300				

2. Record

dr Inventory (+A)..	300	
cr Cash (−A)...		300

Purchase Returns and Allowances

Sometimes inventory items arrive damaged, the wrong color, or for some other reason are returned to the vendor or a reduction in price is requested (called an 'allowance'.) In our example, if $700 of the inventory purchased was returned because it was damaged, these *purchase returns and allowances* will reduce inventory, and therefore, will be recorded like this:

	Assets	=	Liabilities	+	Stockholders' Equity
1. Analyze	Inventory −700		Accounts Payable − 700		

2. Record

dr Accounts Payable (−L).................................	700	
cr Inventory (−A)................................		700

Purchase Discounts

Since inventory is often purchased on account, payment is usually made some time after the purchase. Vendors often give discounts on the purchase price of the inventory to those who pay off their accounts early. The company provides *terms* that indicate how much of a discount will be given (in percentage terms) assuming the balance is paid within a specified number of days after the purchase. Given the following terms:

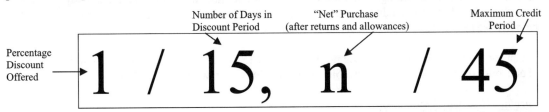

These terms are read as 'one-fifteen, net forty-five', and each element of these terms has a significant meaning:

- The first number is the percentage of the discount offered on the purchase price of the inventory (i.e. 1%)

- The second number represents the number of days from the invoice date that the purchaser can pay the bill and still receive the discount. This is called the 'Number of days in the discount period.' (i.e. 15 days)
- The letter *n* stands for *net*. This means that, in the event that payment is *not* made within the 15 day discount period, the full (net) amount of the invoice is due
- The last number indicates the number of days from the invoice date that the full payment is due even if the discount is not taken (i.e. 45 days)

If a company fails to pay by the maximum credit period date, the seller can: (1) charge interest on the invoice, (2) deny any further credit to the purchaser, and/or (3) collections efforts can be pursued.
A purchase discount is accounted for in two steps:

1) The purchase is recorded at its full cost (as if no discount is taken) because when the company buys the goods, they don't know if they will be taking advantage of the discount or not.

2) When payment is made, two possibilities exist, either payment is made:
   a) **Within the discount period**-in this case, inventory is reduced by the amount of the purchase discount. This may seem illogical but remember that the inventory account was debited for the full purchase price. If that recorded price wasn't the price actually paid, the amount currently recorded for inventory is incorrect. The purchase price recorded for *Inventory* on the books is too high and must be reduced by the amount of the discount so that the inventory reflects the true price paid.

   b) **After the discount period**-no adjustment is made since the original purchase was recorded at full cost and full cost was actually paid! Everything is correct just as it was initially recorded.

Assume the purchase recorded earlier had terms of 1/15, n/45 and is now being paid. Don't forget that $700 of the original $10,700 purchase was returned. So, the company only owes $10,000 at the time payment is made. If the original purchase was made on April 1, the time line (to the right) illustrates the situation.

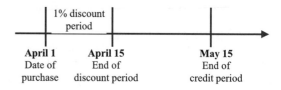

Assuming payment is made within the discount period, on or before April 15. The following entry would be recorded.

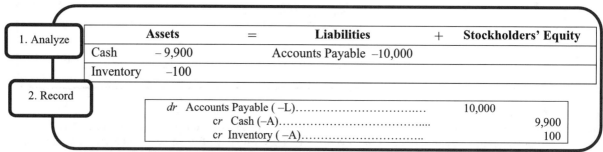

Note that the discount ($10,000 * 1%) is credited to inventory. The full amount of the invoice ($10,000) is removed from accounts payable (even though you didn't have to pay that much), and the amount actually paid for the items is credited to cash. The $100 credit to inventory removes the discount amount from the amount originally recorded for the purchase ($10,000). This is correct since you only paid $9,900...not $10,000 for the goods.

If payment for the inventory was not made until *after* April 15, the full $10,000 would have to be paid for the purchase. Then, both the debit to accounts payable and the credit to cash would be $10,000.

Summary of Purchase-Related Transactions
You've been presented with an example of each of the purchase-related transactions. The affect on the inventory account of each transaction is summarized in the following T-account.

Study Guide, Chapter 6

dr +	Inventory (A)			-- cr
	Bal. Fwd.	+ 0		
	Purchases	+10,700	−700	**Purchase Returns and Allowances**
	Transportation	+ 1,000	−100	**Purchase Discounts**
Cost of Goods Available for Sale		=10,900		

Sales

A sale is considered complete when the *ownership* of the goods has been transferred to the customer. The exact moment when the ownership transfer occurs can vary considerably. So, most businesses use a sales agreement to determine the transfer of ownership. Most use one of the following points in time:

   a) **FOB Shipping Point** – when the goods leave the *shipping* department (i.e. the premises) of the seller
   b) **FOB Destination** – when the goods reach their *destination* at the customer's premises

This text assumes that all sales are FOB Shipping Point (when the goods leave the shipping department of the seller).

In either situation, when a sale occurs, *two* entries are required in a perpetual inventory system:
   (1) Record an increase in *Sales Revenue* and a corresponding increase in either *Cash* (for a cash sale) or *Accounts Receivable* (for a sale on account), and

   (2) Record a reduction in the store's *Inventory* account and a corresponding increase in *Cost of Goods Sold*.

For example, assume your store sells $2,100 of goods on account. These items cost your store $1,260. At the time of the sale, the following entries would be made:

1. Analyze	**Assets**	**= Liabilities +**	**Stockholders' Equity**
	Accounts Receivable +2,100		Sales Revenue (+R, +SE) +2,100
	Inventory −1,260		Cost of Goods Sold (+E, –SE) –1,260

2. Record	
dr Accounts Receivable (+A).............................	2,100
cr Sales Revenue (+R, +SE).....................	2,100
dr Cost of Goods Sold (+E, –SE)..........................	1,260
cr Inventory (–A).......................................	1,260

The first entry records the amount you will collect from the customer for the goods you sold to them and the second entry records the fact that the cost of this inventory has been removed from the shelves and expensed (though Cost of Goods Sold doesn't have the word *expense* in its name, it is the largest expense a merchandising company has.)

The difference between the sales price of the inventory sold and the price paid by the seller for the inventory $840 ($2,100 – $1,260) is called **gross profit**. Though this figure isn't actually recorded in the entry, its effect has been recorded simply by recording Sales Revenue (a credit of $2,100) and Cost of Goods Sold (a debit of $1,260).

Sales Returns and Allowances

If the customer in the previous example bought unacceptable goods and wants to return them to your store, you would take the item back (for a full refund) or the customer can choose to keep the goods if you give them a partial refund for their troubles. These are referred to as *Sales Returns and Allowances*. If the items are returned, we sort of have to 'undo' a portion of the entries that were made at the time of the sale.

So, assuming the customer returns $100 worth of items sold and these items cost you $60, it is basically just a 'reversal' of the previous set of entries…with one small exception. When something is returned to a store, the original sales receipt cannot be 're-recorded' or deleted…instead, a 'new' receipt is created with the 'return' recorded on it. This serves to offset the original sale that was recorded earlier. Since the actual sale cannot be 'un-sold', we create an *offsetting* account to hold the return…called Sales Returns and Allowances, and the following is recorded:

1. Analyze	Assets	=	Liabilities	+	Stockholders' Equity
	Accounts Receivable –100				Sales Ret. & Allow (+xR, –SE) –100
	Inventory + 60				Cost of Goods Sold (–E, +SE) + 60

2. Record

dr Sales Returns and Allowances (+xR, –SE)………….. 100
    cr Accounts Receivable (–A)………………   100

dr Inventory (+A)…………………………………….. 60
    cr Cost of Goods Sold (–E, +SE)……………..   60

    Notice that this entry serves two purposes: (1) it decreases the amount of money the customer owes you as well as reducing your sales (after all, if a customer returns something, it wasn't actually a sale), and (2) it puts the item back into your inventory and removes the item's 'cost' from the expenses.

Sales Discounts

As a business, you want your customers to pay you as quickly as possible, so you can use the cash for more inventory, to pay wages, etc. When you sell customers goods on account, you may offer them a discount on the original invoice price if you receive the money promptly. These are called *sales discounts*. They are calculated in much the same way as the purchase discounts described earlier. Note, however, that there is no effect on the *Inventory*. When you collect money from a customer for an amount billed, the customer only sends you the money, not the stuff they bought, too! There are two parts to completing this entry:

1) The sale is originally recorded at its full price because when the company sells the goods, they don't know if a customer will take advantage of the discount or not.

2) When payment is made two possibilities exist, either you collect the money from the customer:
   a) **Within the discount period** – in this case, the full amount of the receivable is removed (remember that the customer's sale was recorded at the FULL amount) from the accounts receivable account. The cash the customer pays is less than the amount showing in the receivable. The difference between the two figures is the amount of the discount.
   b) **After the discount period** – No adjustment is made since the original sale was recorded at full amount and the full amount was actually received by the customer! Everything is correct just as it was initially recorded.

    Assume the previous sale for $2,000 ($2,100 original sales price – $100 sales return) on account was recorded on June 5, with terms of 2/10, n/30. You collect $1,960 from the customer on June 15 (the last day of the discount period qualifies for the full discount.) On the date of the collection, the following entry would be made:

1. Analyze	Assets	=	Liabilities	+	Stockholders' Equity
	Cash +1,960				Sales Discounts (+xR, –SE) –40
	Account Receivable –2,000				

2. Record

dr Cash (+A)…($2,000 - $40)…………………….... 1,960
dr Sale Discounts (+xR, –SE)…($2,000 * 2%)…. 40
    cr Accounts Receivable (–A)…………..   2,000

    If the money is not collected from the customer by the last day of the discount period, they will have to send you the full amount of the invoice owed ($2,000). One final thing should be mentioned about sales discounts.

These are not the same type of discounts you and I receive when a department store has a 'sale'. Sales discounts (as described here) are rarely given to individuals like you and I, they are primarily offered to businesses. In our example, this type of discount is given specifically for *early collection of a receivable, not because of a sale.*

Summary of Sales-Related Transactions

Let's revisit the income statement now, and see how all of the information we've covered thus far affects it. The Sales Discounts and Sales Returns & Allowances accounts are *contra-revenue* accounts. So, on the income statement they are offsets to revenues. The difference between the Sales Revenues and these contra-revenues is the net sales or the actual dollar amount you expect to collect from customers. It is calculated like this:

Sales Revenue		$ 2,100
Less: Sales Returns and Allowances	$ 100	
Sales Discounts	40	(140)
Net Sales		$ 1,960

As a business, however, you don't want to give away the farm! Businesses are very careful to guard this information and don't normally release it to anyone outside of the company. If competitors had this information, they could use it to better compete against your business. Instead, the income statement will often simply begin with the Net Sales figure, as shown here:

<table>
<tr><td>

Learning Objective 6
Analyze a merchandiser's multi-step income statement.

</td><td colspan="3">

Company A
Income Statement
For the Month Ended June 30, 2009

</td></tr>
</table>

EVALUATE THE RESULTS

Gross Profit Analysis

Bottom-line? Businesses have to sell stuff for more money than they paid to buy it. After covering the cost of the stuff they sell, any remaining amount covers their operating costs first and, then profits (hopefully). In order to easily identify how much of the sales dollars cover each of these major chunks (cost of goods sold, other expenses, and profit), most businesses present the income statement in a multi-step format.

Net Sales		$1,960
Cost of Goods Sold		1,200
Gross Profit		760
Expenses:		
Selling Expenses	xx	
General and Administrative Expenses	xx	
Operating Income		xx
Interest Income and Other Revenues	xx	
Interest Expenses and other Expenses	xx	
Income Tax Expense		xx
Net Income		$xxx

Look at the income statement provided in the previous section, notice how Cost of Goods Sold is shown separately from the other expenses. The amount remaining from sales after covering cost of goods sold is also shown. It is called Gross Profit (also called Gross Margin or just Margin.) Basically, it represents the amount left after covering the cost of the stuff that was sold. This amount is all that remains to cover operating costs and (hopefully) a profit. When the expenses of running the business are deducted from this amount, the remaining amount is called *operating income.* This is the income earned from operating the business and before covering the income taxes on those earnings.

Gross Profit Percentage

It can be very difficult to compare one business to another or do any other kind of analysis when you only use the dollar amounts on financial statements. For example, let's compare the following companies:

	Company A	Company B
Net Sales	$ 40,000	$ 100,000
Cost of Goods Sold	30,000	90,000
Gross Profit	10,000	10,000

Both companies have gross profit of $10,000, but they are vastly different from one another. The key is: how much gross profit is generated from each dollar of sales? To determine this, we perform the following calculation:

	Gross Profit			(Net Sales – Cost of Goods Sold)		
Gross Profit Percentage =	Net Sales	*	100	or	Net Sales	*	100

The **gross profit percentage** measures how much above cost a company sells its products. It is used to:
  (1) Analyze changes in the company's operations over time,
  (2) Compare one company to another, and
  (3) Determine whether a company is earning enough on each sale to cover its operating expenses.

A higher percentage indicates a company that has more resources available to cover operating expenses, and, therefore, more available to earn a profit. After calculating this ratio for the two companies in our example, all other things being equal, it appears as if Company A is in a much better position.

	Company A	Company B
Gross Profit Percentage	(10,000 / 40,000) * 100 = 25%	(10,000 / 100,000) * 100 = 10%
Analysis	This company has about 25¢ of every sales dollar remaining to contribute towards operating costs and company profits	This company has about 10¢ of every sales dollar remaining to contribute towards operating costs and company profits

Now 25¢ might not sound like a lot to you, but remember this is 25¢ for every *dollar* in sales! I'd much rather have a quarter leftover from every buck of sales I earn, than a dime, wouldn't you?

Comparing Operating Results Across Companies and Industries
The gross profit percentages will vary widely among differing industries. For instance, fine jewelers have very high gross margins simply because they have fewer sales and must cover all of their costs based on a small number of sales. Whereas, discount chains like Wal-Mart can operate (and be highly profitable) on a much smaller gross margin because they have such an enormous volume of sales.

Companies operating within the same industry have varying percentages in gross profit rates as well. All of those marketing classes you have to take are very relevant here. A business trying to find a small niche in the industry can be very profitable, but must charge higher prices in order to meet the specific needs of their customers. Health-conscious people will shop in a 'specialty' food store like *Wild Oats* or *Whole* Foods. But they pay a premium for the privilege.

SUPPLEMENT A – PERIODIC INVENTORY SYSTEMS
While a perpetual inventory system tracks Cost of Goods Sold and Inventory every time a sale is made, a periodic system assumes *everything* that isn't on your shelves at the end of the accounting period (or returned) *must* have been sold! Consequently, a periodic inventory system only updates the inventory at the *end of the accounting period*. Determining the amount of inventory sold, under a periodic inventory system, is a four-step process:

1. **Determine beginning inventory**—To get this amount, simply use the inventory figure from *last year's* balance sheet.

2. **Track this period's purchases**—This step is actually referring to 'Net Purchases'. That is, all *Purchases* reduced by *Purchase Returns and Allowances* and *Purchase Discounts*.

3. **Determine the Cost of ending inventory**—This is accomplished by taking a physical count of the units of inventory on the shelves at the end of the accounting period. This count is then multiplied by the cost of each unit of inventory to determine the cost of the ending inventory.

4. **Calculate the cost of goods sold**—Notice that this is essentially a 'catch-all' account under the periodic inventory system. Any inventory items that *weren't* considered in one the three previous steps are *assumed* to have been sold! As you can see, this is a *huge* and *completely erroneous* assumption. It is the same as saying that all the groceries you bought this year were eaten! But, we all know that some of it was spoiled, lost, destroyed, stolen, or taken by to school by your child who is determined to feed every child in their school.

This is why the periodic system is quickly being replaced by the perpetual system. It is nearly impossible to track theft, loss, spoilage, etc. because these items are all lumped into Cost of Goods Sold by the erroneous assumption that everything you bought is either *still there on the shelves* or *was sold.* In other words, it assumes there is *never any theft, loss, or spoilage!!*

The previous four steps can be summarized using the following Cost of Goods Sold calculation:

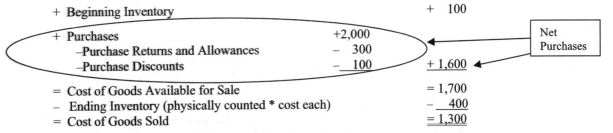

+ Beginning Inventory		+ 100	
+ Purchases	+2,000		Net Purchases
–Purchase Returns and Allowances	– 300		
–Purchase Discounts	– 100	+ 1,600	
= Cost of Goods Available for Sale		= 1,700	
– Ending Inventory (physically counted * cost each)		– 400	
= Cost of Goods Sold		= 1,300	

Comparison of the Accounting Process Used in Periodic and Perpetual Systems

The entries for both systems are compared and summarized in the following table using these transactions:

Jan. 1	Beginning inventory: 800 units, at unit cost of $50.
April 14	Purchased: 1,100 additional units on account, at unit cost of $50.
Nov. 30	Sold: 1,300 units on account, at unit sales price of $83.
Dec. 31	Counted: 560 units, at unit cost of $50.

Periodic Records	Perpetual Records
A. Record purchases.	**A. Record purchases.**
April 14, 2009:	April 14, 2009:
dr Purchases (+A) (1,100 units at $50) 55,000	*dr* Inventory (+A) (1,100 units at $50) 55,000
cr Accounts payable (+L). 55,000	*cr* Accounts payable (+L) 55,000
B. Record sales (but not cost of goods sold).	**B. Record sales and cost of goods sold.**
November 30, 2009:	November 30, 2009:
dr Accounts receivable (+A) 107,900	*dr* Accounts receivable (+A) 107,900
cr Sales revenue (+R, +SE) (1,300 units at $83)... 107,900	*cr* Sales revenue (+R, +SE) (1,300 at $83)... 107,900
	dr Cost of goods sold (+E, –SE) 65,000
No cost of goods sold entry	*cr* Inventory (–A) (1,300 units at $50). . . 65,000
C. Record end-of-period adjustments.	**C. Record end-of-period adjustments.**
At end of period, compute cost of goods sold using the four-step process and adjust the inventory accounts.	At the end of the accounting period, the balance in the Cost of Goods Sold account is reported on the income statement. It is not necessary to compute cost of goods sold because the Cost of Goods Sold account is up-to-date. Also, the Inventory account shows the ending inventory amount reported on the balance sheet. A physical inventory count is still necessary to assess the accuracy of the perpetual records and identify theft and other forms of shrinkage. Any shrinkage would be recorded by reducing the Inventory account and increasing an expense account (such as Inventory Shrinkage or Cost of Goods Sold). This illustration assumes shrinkage is detected amounting to $2,000.
1. Beginning inventory (last period's ending) $40,000	
2. Add net purchases 55,000	
Cost of goods available for sale $95,000	
3. Deduct ending inventory	
(physical count—560 units at $50) 28,000	
4. Cost of goods sold $67,000	
December 31, 2009:	
Transfer beginning inventory and net purchases to cost of goods sold: (act *as if* all goods were sold)	No entry
dr Cost of goods sold (+E, –SE) 95,000	
cr Inventory (–A) (beginning) 40,000	
cr Purchases (–A) 55,000	
Adjust the cost of goods sold by subtracting the amount of ending inventory still on hand: (recognize that not all goods were sold)	
dr Inventory (+A) (ending) 28,000	
cr Cost of goods sold (–E, +SE) 28,000	*(continued)*

Assets		=	Liabilities		+	Stockholder Equity		Assets		=	Liabilities		+		Stockholder Equity
Purchases	+55,000		Accts Pay	+55,000				Inventory	+55,000	=	Accts. Pay	+55,000			107,900
Acct. Rec	+107,900					Reven.	+107,900	Acct. Rec	+107,900					Reven	+107,900
Inventory	-40,000					COGS	-95,000	Inventory	-65,000					COGS	-65,000
Purchases	-55,000						+42,900								
Inventory	+28,000						+30,000								
Total	+95,900			+55,000			+42,900		+97,900			+55,000			+42,900

REVIEW THE CHAPTER

Chapter Summary

LO1. Distinguish service, merchandising, and manufacturing operations.
- ❖ Service Companies
  - o Sell services rather than physical goods, therefore,
  - o Their income statements shows costs of *services* rather than cost of *goods sold*
- ❖ Merchandise companies sell goods that have been obtained from a supplier
  - o Retail merchandise companies sell directly to consumers
  - o Wholesale merchandise companies sell to retail merchandise companies
- ❖ Manufacturing companies sell goods that they have made themselves

LO2. Explain common principles of internal control
- ❖ The concept of internal controls is broad.
- ❖ Most employees working within a company will encounter five basic principles:
  - o Establish responsibility for each task
  - o Segregate duties so that
    - ▪ One employee cannot perform *all* of the following for a single transaction:
      - • Initiate
      - • Record
      - • Approve
      - • Handle
  - o Restrict access to those employees who have been assigned responsibility
  - o Document procedures performed
  - o Independently verify work done by others inside and outside the business

LO3. Perform the key control of reconciling cash to bank statements
- ❖ The bank reconciliation requires determining two categories of items:
  - o Those that have been recorded in the company's books, but not in the bank's statement of account
  - o Those that have been reported in the bank's statement of account, but not in the company's books.
    - ▪ This category of items provides the data needed to adjust the Cash records to the balance reported on the balance sheet

LO4. Explain the use of a perpetual inventory system as a control.
- ❖ Perpetual inventory systems protect against undetected theft because
  - o They provide an up-to-date record of inventory that should be on hand at any given time
    - ▪ This inventory record can be compared to a count of the physical quantity that is actually on hand
- ❖ Perpetual inventory systems serve to promote efficient and effective operations because
  - o They are updated every time inventory is
    - ▪ Purchased
    - ▪ Sold
    - ▪ Returned

LO5. Analyze purchase and sales transactions under a perpetual inventory system.
- ❖ In a perpetual inventory system, the *Inventory* account
  - o Is increased every time inventory is purchased
  - o Should include any costs needed to get the inventory into a condition and location ready for sale

- For example, Transportation-In
- ❖ In a perpetual inventory system, the purchaser's *Inventory* account is
  - o Decreased whenever the purchaser returns goods to the supplier
  - o Decreased whenever the purchases purchaser is given a discount for prompt payment
- ❖ In a perpetual inventory system, the seller's *Inventory* account is
  - o Decreased every time inventory is sold
  - o The decrease in inventory is accompanied by an increase in an expense account for the cost of goods sold.
- ❖ In a perpetual inventory system, two entries are made every time inventory is sold
  - o One entry records the sale
    - And corresponding debit to cash or accounts receivable
  - o The other entry records the cost of the goods sold
    - And corresponding credit to inventory
- ❖ Net sales are reduced by recording the following contra-revenues:
  - o *Sales Discounts*
  - o *Sales Returns and Allowances*

LO6. Analyze a merchandiser's multi-step income statement.
- ❖ One of the key items in a merchandiser's multi-step income statement is Gross Profit which is:
  - o A subtotal calculated as
    - Net Sales – Cost of Goods Sold
  - o The Gross Profit Percentage:
    - Is calculated as:
      - Gross Profit / Net Sales * 100
    - It measures the amount of gross profit that is included in each dollar of sales

READ AND RECALL QUESTIONS
After you read each section of the chapter, answer the related Read and Recall Questions below.

Introduction
What can happen to a business' inventories that remain on the shelves for too long? Why is Cash the asset most susceptible to theft or loss?

LEARNING OBJECTIVE
After studying the section of the chapter, you should be able to:
1. Distinguish service, merchandising, and manufacturing operations.

Service, Merchandising, and Manufacturing Operating Activities
Define a service company, a merchandising company, and a manufacturing company.

Briefly describe the operating cycle of each type of company.

What is meant by the term *internal controls*?

Internal Controls

What is the essential role of a company's system of internal control?

What are the five basic principles of internal control you are most likely to come across in business?

What is *segregation of duties*? How should management ensure that duties have been segregated?

How should access be restricted for items that can be stolen, etc.?

Define what is meant by document procedures.

What is independent verification? Give two examples of this.

What are the limitations of internal control? How can they be circumvented?

┌───┐
│ **LEARNING OBJECTIVE**   │
│ *After studying the section of the chapter, you should be able to:*   │
│ 3. Perform the key control of reconciling cash to bank statements   │
└───┘

Controlling and Reporting Cash

What three controls should be followed when dealing with cash?

What causes a checkbook balance to differ from a bank statement?

How can these differences be accounted for? Why is this procedure a necessary internal control for cash?

What is a *time lag* event? Give two examples of a time lag event. Who is usually unaware of these events, the bank or the company? Will the company have to adjust its cash records for these items? Why or why not?

Give five examples of events that the company may not be aware of. Will the company need to adjust its cash records for these items? Why or why not?

What is an NSF check? How is it handled on a bank reconciliation?

Which amount is the true balance in the cash account: The checkbook balance or the bank statement? Why?

What are the first two steps in preparing a bank reconciliation? Are these items placed on the Bank Statement side or the Company's Books side of the bank reconciliation? Why?

What types of transactions are included in step three of the bank reconciliation? Are these items placed on the Bank Statement side or the Company's Books side of the bank reconciliation? Why?

How are errors dealt with on a bank reconciliation? Are they placed on the Bank Statement side or the Company's Books side of the bank reconciliation? Why?

Are items on the Bank Statement side of the reconciliation recorded on the books? Why or why not?

What types of items are included in "Cash"? Define a Cash Equivalent.

LEARNING OBJECTIVE
After studying the section of the chapter, you should be able to:
4. Explain the use of a perpetual inventory system as a control

Controlling and Reporting Inventory Transactions
What are the three roles played by the accounting system in the inventory management process?

How often are inventory items updated in a perpetual inventory system? What purpose do bar code readers serve in the check-out line of a business? Which accounts will always contain updated balances in a perpetual inventory system?

How is ending inventory determined in a periodic inventory system?

For inventory control purposes, which method provides the most benefits? What are they?

How did a perpetual inventory system allow Wal-Mart to achieve phenomenal productivity gains?

What is *shrinkage*?

What are the three steps used to determine an estimate of shrinkage? Which two figures are compared in making this determination?

LEARNING OBJECTIVE
After studying the section of the chapter, you should be able to:
5. Analyze purchase and sales transactions under a perpetual inventory system

Inventory Purchase and Sales Transactions
In what account are all purchases recorded in a perpetual inventory system? What accounts are normally debited and credited for an inventory purchase?

Why are transportation charges considered an inventory cost? What is another name for transportation charges? What accounts are normally debited and credited for transportation charges on inventory?

What is a *purchase return*? What is a *purchase allowance*? What accounts are debited and credited for purchase returns and allowances?

Why are *purchase discounts* given? Define each element in the following terms: 3/15, n/30 Assuming a company had an original purchase price of $12,000 for inventory and paid within the discount period, how much would the company pay on that date? What would the journal entry be at that time?

Complete the following T-account using the correct terminology

	+	Inventory (A)	--	
Bal. Fwd.	1,000			
_____	15,500	500	_____	
_____	600	450		
_____	16,150	_____		

What do most sales agreements list as the two possible points in times that a transfer of ownership has occurred? Which one is used throughout this text?

How many entries are made at the time of sale in a perpetual inventory system? What accounts are debited and credited for a sale on account?

What is gross profit? How is it calculated?

What are Sales Returns and Allowances? How many journal entries are needed to record a Sales Return? Why?

Compare a Sales Return to a Purchase Return. How do they differ? How are they alike? What is a *contra-revenue*? Give an example of a contra-revenue.

What accounts are debited and credited for a Sales Return?

What is offered to a customer to encourage prompt payment on an account receivable? What are the two parts involved? What accounts are debited and credited in this situation?

What are the two possibilities when a payment is made by a customer? What is the difference in each?

Complete the following partial income statement (assuming the seller provides this information on the income statement) using the correct terminology.

Revenues:		
Sales Revenue		$ 9,000
Less: _____	$ 250	
_____	100	350
_____		$ 8,650

How can monitoring sales returns and allowances help a business control costs? Why do sellers often omit this information from the income statement?

LEARNING OBJECTIVE
After studying the section of the chapter, you should be able to:
6. Analyze a merchandiser's multi-step income statement

Gross Profit Analysis
What is the purpose of showing Gross Profit on an income statement?

Why is the *multi-step* income statement format informative to users? What subtotals might you see on a multi-step income statement?

Gross Profit Percentage
What is the gross profit percentage? How is it calculated? What three things does this ratio measure? All else being equal, a *lower* ratio indicates what?

SUPPLEMENT A – PERIODIC INVENTORY SYSTEMS

Periodic Inventory Systems
What is the four-step process for determining the amount of inventory sold in a periodic inventory system?

What is Net Purchases? How is it calculated?

Why is the periodic inventory method a poor system for tracking theft, loss, or spoilage of inventory?

What is the calculation that summarizes the four-step process for determining the amount of inventory sold in a periodic system?

FINANCIAL ANALYSIS TOOLS

1. Net Sales and Gross Profit – Now that we've added so many new things to the income statement, here it is with all the bells and whistles. Pay special attention to the bolded areas, which were introduced in this chapter.

Whoever Company		
Income Statement		
For the Year Ended December 31, 2009		
Revenues:		
Sales Revenue		**$ 36,000**
Less: Sales Returns and Allowances	**$ 500**	
Sales Discounts	**120**	**(620)**
Net Sales		**$ 35,380**
Cost of Goods Sold		**(16,800)**
Gross Profit		**18,580**
Expenses:		
Selling Expenses	4,970	
General and Administrative Expenses	3,420	(8,390)
Operating Income		10,190
Interest Income and Other Revenues	116	
Interest Expenses and other Expenses	(441)	(325)
Income before Income Tax Expense		9,865
Income Tax Expense		(2,400)
Net Income		$7,465

2. Gross Profit Percentage- To determine the amount of gross profit included in every dollar of sales, calculate the gross profit margin percentage:

$$\text{Gross Profit Percentage} = \frac{\text{Gross Profit}}{\text{Net Sales}} * 100 = \frac{(\text{Net Sales} - \text{Cost of Goods Sold})}{\text{Net Sales}} * 100$$

HELPFUL STUDY TIP

1. **Bank Reconciliations**-Many students have difficulty with the bank reconciliation. The reconciliation itself isn't too horrifying, but trying to figure out *which* items need to be journalized and which don't can be frustrating. In your accounting class, you have probably already discovered the value of having 'check figures' for exercises and problems. These 'check figures' are an indicator to you about whether your homework is correct or incorrect. Without this helpful information, you wouldn't have a clue if your assignments were correct or not.

   Well, think of the Bank Statement side of the bank reconciliation as your 'check figure' for the Company's Books side of the Bank Reconciliation. In fact, one of the reasons the Bank Statement side is prepared first is because there are usually fewer differences (and fewer errors made by the bank) than there are differences or errors made by the business. Just think of how many times *you* have made an addition or subtraction error in your checkbook!

   So, the bank statement side is a good 'check figure' to shoot for when determining the Company's cash figure on the books. Since the Bank Statement side is nothing more than a check figure, it makes sense that the items affecting this side *should not be recorded in the company's books.* Armed with this information, it is clear that the only items that should be recorded on the books are those items on the *Company's books* side of the bank reconciliation.

   Furthermore, we all remember the hint from Chapter 2, Deposits=Debits and Checks=Credits, right? This little tidbit of information will help you when journalizing bank reconciliation entries as well! If the item on the Company's Books side of the reconciliation is something that is added (the equivalent of a deposit), it will be debited to the Cash account. If the item is something that is subtracted (the equivalent of a check) on the reconciliation, it will be credited to the Cash account. For example, if there is interest of $64 earned on the bank account, it will be an addition to the Company's Books side of the reconciliation (the equivalent of a deposit=debit). So, the corresponding entry will be:

dr Cash (+A)	64	
cr Interest Revenue (+R, +SE)		64

   Similarly, if there is a $30 bank service fee, it will be a subtraction from the Company's Books side of the reconciliation (the equivalent of a check=credit). So, the corresponding entry will be:

dr Other Expenses (+E, -SE)	30	
cr Cash (-A)		30

   The only thing you have to do, is figure out what the offsetting debit/credit will be for each entry (i.e. Interest Revenue, Other Expenses)

SELF-TEST QUESTIONS AND EXERCISES

MATCHING
1. *Match each of the key terms listed below with the appropriate textbook definition.*

_____ Bank Reconciliation	_____ Periodic Inventory System
_____ Cash	_____ Perpetual Inventory System
_____ Cash Equivalent	_____ Purchase Discounts
_____ Gross Profit	_____ Purchase Returns and Allowances
_____ Gross Profit Percentage	_____ Sales Discounts
_____ Internal Controls	_____ Sales Returns and Allowances
_____ Manufacturing Company	_____ Segregation of Duties
_____ Merchandising Company	_____ Service Company
_____ NSF Check	_____ Time Lags

A. An internal report prepared to verify the accuracy of both the bank statement and the cash accounts of a business or individual.
B. An internal control that involves separating employees' duties so that the work of one person can be used to check the work of another person.
C. A reduction in cost of purchases associated with unsatisfactory goods.
D. Short-term, highly liquid investments purchased within three months of maturity.
E. Sells services rather than physical goods.
F. A ratio indicating the percentage of profit earned on each dollar of sales, after considering the cost of the products sold.
G. Arise when the check writer (your customer) does not have enough funds to cover the amount of the check also, another name for a bounced check.
H. Sells goods that have been obtained from a supplier.
I. A cash discount received in exchange for the prompt payment of a purchase on account.
J. Examples of these include Deposits in Transit and Outstanding Checks.
K. Net sales minus cost of goods sold. It is a subtotal, not an account.
L. Includes money or any instrument that banks will accept for deposit and immediate credit to a company's account, including currency, checks, money orders, or bank drafts.
M. A cash discount given to customers for the prompt payment of an account receivable.
N. Inventory records are updated at the end of the accounting period. To determine how much merchandise has been sold a physical count at the end of the period is required.
O. A reduction given to customers after goods have been sold that and found unsatisfactory.
P. Sells goods that it has made itself.
Q. Methods that a company uses to protect against theft of assets, to enhance the reliability of accounting information, to promote efficient and effective operations, and to ensure compliance with applicable laws and regulations.
R. The inventory records are updated every time inventory is bought, sold, or returned; they are often combined with bar codes and optical scanners.

TRUE-FALSE QUESTIONS
For each of the following, enter a T or F in the blank to indicate whether the statement is true or false.

_____ 1. (LO1) Cash and some inventory items are attractive to thieves because they're easy to carry and easy to hide.

_____ 2. (LO1) Merchandising companies sell products they've produced themselves from raw materials.

_____ 3. (LO2) SOX rules have led companies to strengthen their internal controls and better inform financial statement users about how effective their accounting systems are in producing accurate financial statements.

_____ 4. (LO2) Assigning responsibilities so that one employee can't make a mistake or commit a dishonest act without someone else discovering it, is referred to as segregation of duties.

_____ 5. (LO3) As an enhancement of document procedures, most companies assign a sequential number to each document and then check at the end of every accounting period that each document number corresponds to one, and only one, entry in the accounting system.

_____ 6. (LO3) The process of identifying the differences between cash records and the bank's records is called a bank statement.

_____ 7. (LO3) Common reasons for differences on the bank side of the reconciliation are time lags.

_____ 8. (LO3) You will only need to adjust your cash records for items identified as those 'your bank may not know about.'

_____ 9. (LO3) To the bank, your account is a liability that decreases when you take money out (debit the liability) and it increases when you deposit money (credit the liability).

_____ 10. (LO3) Cash refers to currency and checks but does not include money orders or bank drafts.

_____ 11. (LO4) The two types of inventory accounting systems are: periodic and perpetual.

_____ 12. (LO4) A major benefit of the periodic inventory system is the ability for a business to estimate shrinkage.

_____ 13. (LO5) A purchaser should include in its Inventory account any costs needed to get its inventory into a condition and location ready for sale.

_____ 14. (LO5) Inventory transportation cost is also referred to as Freight-out.

_____ 15. (LO5) For the terms, 1/15, n/45 the 15 refers to the percentage discount available if items are paid for within the discount period.

_____ 16. (LO5) In a perpetual inventory system all purchases, purchase discounts, purchase returns and allowances, and transportation charges related to inventory are included in the inventory account.

_____ 17. (LO5) A contra-revenue account reduces the total in a revenue account.

_____ 18. (LO5) In a perpetual inventory system two journal entries are required to record a sale on account, but not for a cash sale.

_____ 19. (LO5) Sales discounts, as discussed in this chapter, refer to the discount a consumer gets when buying clearance items at a reduced selling price.

_____ 20. (LO6) The Gross Profit Percentage is calculated as: (Gross Profit/Net Sales) * 100.

_____ 21. (Sup) In a periodic inventory system it is not necessary to compute Cost of Goods Sold because this account is already up-to-date.

MULTIPLE CHOICE QUESTIONS

Choose the best answer or response by placing the identifying letter in the space provided.

_____1.   (LO1) Which of the following is *not* one of the three types of business based on its operating activities?
   a.   Manufacturer
   b.   Merchandiser
   c.   Service
   d.   Corporation

_____2.   (LO2) From the perspective of the CFO, the broad concept of internal controls does *not* include which of the following?
   a.   Hiring good employees
   b.   Instilling ethical principles
   c.   Setting strategic objectives for the company
   d.   All of the above are examples of internal control

_____3.   (LO2) Which of the following is *not* a common principle of internal control?
   a.   Combine duties
   b.   Ensure transactions are authorized and properly recorded
   c.   Establish responsibility
   d.   All of these are common principles of internal control

_____4.   (LO3) Which of the following are differences that the bank doesn't know about?
   a.   Outstanding check
   b.   Interest deposited
   c.   NSF checks
   d.   None of the above are differences the bank doesn't know about

_____5.   (LO3) What is the proper order of the steps in preparing a bank statement?
   1.   Determine the impact of book errors
   2.   Identify the outstanding checks
   3.   Record other transactions on the bank statement
   4.   Identify the deposits in transit
   a.   1, 2, 3, 4
   b.   2, 1, 4, 3
   c.   4, 3, 2, 1
   d.   4, 2, 3, 1

_____7.   (LO3) Which of the following items is *not* a difference that is journalized to bring Cash up-to-date?
   a.   Service charges
   b.   Deposits in transit
   c.   Company error
   d.   NSF check

_____8.   (LO3) Which of the following is considered a cash equivalent?
   a.   Check
   b.   Short-term highly liquid investments purchased within three months of maturity
   c.   Money order
   d.   All of these are examples of cash equivalents

_____9.   (LO4) Which of the following is *not* a true statement regarding inventory systems?
   a.   Periodic systems require that inventory be physically counted at the end of the period
   b.   Bar codes and optical scanners are used extensively in a periodic inventory system
   c.   Perpetual systems update accounting records every time an item is bought, sold, or returned.
   d.   Perpetual inventory systems allow managers to estimate shrinkage

_____10. (LO4) Which of the following are *not* examples of shrinkage?
  a. Fraud
  b. Theft
  c. Errors
  d. All of these are examples of shrinkage

_____11. (LO5) Based on the following information, estimate the amount of inventory that is missing for Jones
     Co. Purchases are $10,000; Ending inventory (physically counted) is $2,000; Goods Sold are $9,000
     and Beginning Inventory (physically counted) is $4,000
  a. $1,000
  b. $2,000
  c. $3,000
  d. $5,000

_____12. (LO5) Which of the following accurately describes how purchase-related transactions affect Inventory?
  a. Purchases + transportation in + purchase returns and allowances + purchase discounts
  b. Purchases – transportation in – purchase returns and allowances – purchase discounts
  c. Purchases – transportation in + purchase returns and allowances + purchase discounts
  d. Purchases + transportation in – purchase returns and allowances – purchase discounts

_____13. (LO5) Determine the cost of Goods Available for Sale for Sloan Company, assuming the following:
  - Purchases $50,000
  - Purchase Discounts $1,000
  - Transportation $3,500
  - Purchase Returns and Allowances $4,000
  - Beginning Inventory $6,000
  a. $35,500
  b. $47,500
  c. $57,500
  d. $54,500

_____14. (LO5) Which of the following does *not* describe purchase transactions under a perpetual inventory
     system?
  a. Costs incurred after the inventory is ready for sale are included in the inventory account
  b. Purchases of equipment for internal use are not recorded in the inventory account
  c. Since discounts actually reduce the purchaser's inventory cost, it is recorded as a reduction in
     inventory
  d. Most purchases are charged to Accounts Payable because purchases are usually charged

_____15. (LO5) Which of the following is *not* considered a transfer of ownership for purposes of recording a sale?
  a. When the goods leave the shipping department at the seller's premises
  b. When a customer takes the goods to the checkout and agrees to pay for them using cash or credit
  c. When an order is placed by the customer
  d. When the goods reach their destination at the customer's premises

_____16. (LO5) In recording a Sale under a perpetual inventory system, which of the following accounts is *not*
     affected?
  a. Sales Returns and Allowances
  b. Cost of Goods Sold
  c. Inventory
  d. Sales Revenue

_____17. (LO5) Which of the following are *not* considered contra-accounts?
  a. Sales returns and allowances
  b. Accumulated depreciation
  c. Cost of goods sold
  d. Sales discounts

_____18. (LO5) Klem Corp. makes a $1,000 sale to a customer with terms of 2/15, n/45. $200 of the merchandise is later returned by the customer. Assuming payment is made within the discount period, what is the total amount the customer will remit to Klem Corp. in payment of its account?
   a. $800
   b. $784
   c. $980
   d. $1,000

_____19. (LO5) What is the calculation for Net Sales?
   a. Sales + sales returns and allowances + sales discounts
   b. Sales + sales returns and allowances – sales discounts
   c. Sales – sales returns and allowances + sales discounts
   d. Sales – sales returns and allowances – sales discounts

_____20. (LO6) Given the following information, determine the gross profit percentage for Zane Industries, Inc.

Net Sales	$100,000
Operating Expenses	$20,000
Income Tax Expense	$4,500
Cost of Goods Sold	$65,000

   a. 80%
   b. 65%
   c. 35%
   d. 15%

EXERCISES
Record your answer to each exercise in the space provided. Show your work.

Exercise 6-1. Identifying Service, Merchandising, and Manufacturing Operations (LO1)
Match each of the operating cycle descriptions to the type of business it describes.

Operating Cycle Descriptions	Type of Business
_____ 1. Use cash to buy raw materials to make inventory, sell the inventory to customers and collect cash from those customers.	A. Service Company.
_____ 2. Use cash to provide services that are sold to customers and then collect cash from those customers.	B. Merchandising Company.
_____ 3. Use cash to buy inventory, sell the inventory to customers and collect cash from those customers.	C. Manufacturing Company.

Exercise 6-2. Identifying Internal Controls Principles (LO2)
Match each of the following explanations of internal control principles to the internal control principle it describes.

Explanation	Internal Control Principles
_____ 1. Prepare documents to show activities that have occurred.	A. Establish Responsibility.
_____ 2. Assign each task to only one employee.	B. Segregate Duties.
_____ 3. Check the work of others.	C. Restrict Access.
_____ 4. Do not provide access to assets or information unless it is needed to fulfill assigned responsibilities.	D. Document Procedures.
_____ 5. Do not make one employee responsible for all parts of a transaction.	E. Independently Verify.

Exercise 6-3. Organizing Items on the Bank Reconciliation and Journal Entries (LO2)

Part A.

Indicate whether the following amounts are added (+) or subtracted (–) from the company's books or the bank statement side of a bank reconciliation.

	Reconciling Item	Company's Books	Bank Statement
a.	Bank service charge of $25		
b.	Bounced check from a customer for $600		
c.	Deposits in transit of $1,200		
d.	Interest earned of $32		
e.	Outstanding checks of $845		

Part B. For each of the reconciling items a – e in **Part A,** record the journal entry required. If a journal entry is not required, write No Entry Required and explain why no entry is required for the reconciling item.

a. *dr* _____   _____

   cr _____   _____

b. *dr* _____   _____

   cr _____   _____

c. *dr* _____   _____

   cr _____   _____

d. *dr* _____   _____

   cr _____   _____

e. *dr* _____   _____

   cr _____   _____

Exercise 6-4. Identifying Outstanding Checks and Deposits in Transit, Preparing a Bank Reconciliation, and Journal Entries. (LO2)

The March 2009 Bank Statement for Stewart Company and the cash T-account for March 2009 follows:

Bank Statement

Date	Checks	Deposits	Other	Balance
Mar. 1				$42,630
2	$500			42,130
3		$9,000		51,130
4	630			50,500
5	820			49,680
9	950			48,730
10	2,370			46,360
15		12,000		58,360
21	4,330			54,030
24	36,000			18,030
25	400			17,630
30		4,000		21,630
30			Interest earned 54	21,684
31			Service charge 25	21,659

+	Cash (A)	-
Mar. 1 Balance 40,680		Checks written
Deposits		Mar. 5 950
Mar. 2 9,000		7 2,370
1 3 12,000		1 5 4,330
2 8 4,000		1 7 36,000
3 1 18,000		2 0 400
		2 7 6,580
		2 9 7,734
		3 0 5,520

Outstanding checks at the end of **February** were for $630, $500, and $820. No deposits were in transit at the end of February.

Part A: Identify and list the deposits in transit and the outstanding checks at the end of March.

Deposits in Transit	Outstanding Checks
Total Deposits in Transit	Total Outstanding Checks

Part B. Prepare a bank reconciliation for March.

STEWART COMPANY
Bank Reconciliation
For the Month Ending March 31, 2009

Bank Statement		Company's Books	
Ending cash balance per bank statement	$	Ending cash balance per books	$
Additions:		Additions:	
Deductions:		Deductions:	
Up-to-date ending cash balance	$	Up-to-date ending cash balance	$

Part C. Give any journal entries that the company should make as a result of the bank reconciliation.

1. *dr* _____   _____
    cr _____   _____

2. *dr* _____   _____
    cr _____   _____

Part D.
1. Why are the journal entries in Part C necessary?

2. After the reconciliation journal entries are posted, what balance will be reflected in the cash account of the company?

3. If the company also has $500 on hand, which is recorded in a different account called "Cash on Hand," what total amount of cash should be reported on the March 31, 2009 balance sheet?

Exercise 6-5. Inferring Shrinkage Using a Perpetual Inventory System. (LO3)

Calculate the amount of shrinkage for each of the following independent cases:

Cases	Beginning Inventory	Purchases	Cost of Goods Sold	Ending Inventory (As counted)	Shrinkage
A	600	1,700	1,500	300	
B	300	1,300	400	880	
C	200	1,800	600	540	
D	520	2,200	1,700	390	

Exercise 6-6. Recording Purchases, Purchase Discounts, and Purchase Returns Using a Perpetual Inventory System (LO4)

During the months of June and July, Noquest Eons Corporation purchased goods from two suppliers. The sequence of events was as follows:

June	8	Purchased goods for $6,800 from Lube Inc. with terms 1/15, n/45
	10	Returned goods costing $800 to Lube Inc. for full credit.
	13	Purchased goods from Maas Corp. for $12,000 with terms of 2/10, n/30
	22	Paid the balance owed to Lube Inc.
July	12	Paid Maas in full.

Part A.
Assuming that Noquest Eons uses a perpetual inventory system, prepare journal entries to record the transactions.

Jun 8   *dr* _____   _____
         cr _____   _____

Jun 10   *dr* _____   _____
         cr _____   _____

Jun 13   *dr* _____   _____
         cr _____   _____

Jun 22   *dr* _____   _____
         cr _____   _____
         cr _____   _____

Jul 12   *dr* _____   _____
         cr _____   _____

Part B.
Calculate the cost of inventory as of July 31 Noquest Eons assuming there was no beginning inventory. (HINT: Use a T-account.)

Inventory	

Exercise 6-7. Recording Net Sales with Credit Sales, Sales Returns, and Sales Discounts (LO5)

The following transactions were selected from among those completed by Peglet's Retail Store in 2009.

27   Sold 10 items of merchandise to Balboa Bodyworks at a total selling price of $9,000; terms 3/10, n/30. The goods cost Peglet's $6,000
28   Sold 20 items of merchandise to Craig's Supply Shop at a total selling price of $15,000; terms 3/10, n/30. The goods cost Peglet's $9,500

Oct   2   Balboa Bodyworks returned one of the items purchased on the 27th. The item was defective, and credit was given to the customer.
5   Balboa Bodyworks paid the account balance in full.
30   Craig's Supply Shop paid in full for the invoice of September 28, 2009.

Part A.
Prepare journal entries to record the transactions, assuming Peglet's Retail Store uses a perpetual inventory system.

Sept 27   dr   _____   _____
          cr   _____   _____

          dr   _____   _____
          cr   _____   _____

Sept 28   dr   _____   _____
          cr   _____   _____

          dr   _____   _____
          cr   _____   _____

Oct 2   dr   _____   _____
          cr   _____   _____

          dr   _____   _____
          cr   _____   _____

Oct 5   dr   _____   _____
          dr   _____   _____
          cr   _____   _____

Oct 30   dr   _____   _____
          cr   _____   _____

Part B.
Assuming that sales returns, sales discounts, and credit card discounts are reported as contra-revenues, compute net sales, Cost of Goods Sold, and Gross Profit for the two months ended October 31, 2009.

Sales			$ _____
Less: Sales Returns And Allowances	$ _____		
Sales Discounts	_____		_____
Net Sales			_____
Cost of Goods Sold			_____
Gross Profit			_____

Exercise 6-8. Determining the Effects of Sales, Sales Discounts, and Sales Returns and Allowances on Income Statement Categories (LO5)

Roscoe Coat Company records sales returns and allowances, sales discounts, and credit card discounts as contra-revenues. Complete the following table, indicating the amount and direction of effect (+ for increase, - for decrease, and NE for no effect) of each transaction on Roscoe.

April   8   Roscoe sold merchandise to Coat Corral at a selling price of $6,500, with terms 1/15, 1/45
       21   Collected cash due from Coat Corral
       23   Sold merchandise to Outer Warehouse, Inc. at a selling price of $8,000 with terms 3/10, n/30
       25   Outer Warehouse, Inc. returned $600 of merchandise.
May   3   Outer Warehouse, Inc. paid the amount due.

Transaction	Sales Revenues	Sales Returns and Allowances	Sales Discounts	Net Sales
April 8				
April 21				
April 23				
April 25				
May 3				

Exercise 6-9. Recording Sales and Purchase Transactions with Discounts and Returns. (LO4, 5)

a.	Sold merchandise for cash (cost of merchandise $40,000)	$ 67,000
b.	Received merchandise returned by customers as unsatisfactory, for cash refund (original cost of merchandise $1,800)	$3,000
c.	Purchased merchandise from Giant Grocers Company with terms 2/10, n/30	12,000
d.	Purchased merchandise from Other Suppliers with terms 3/10, n/30	25,000
e.	Purchased office supplies for future use in the store; paid cash	4,000
f.	Purchased office equipment for use in store; paid cash	42,000
g.	Returned defective goods to Other Suppliers.	2,000
h.	Freight on merchandise purchased; paid cash	800
i.	Paid Giant Grocers Company after the discount period	12,000
j.	Paid Other Suppliers within the 3% discount period	22,310

a.   dr   _____   _____

      cr   _____   _____

      dr   _____   _____

      cr   _____   _____

b.   dr   _____   _____

      cr   _____   _____

      dr   _____   _____

      cr   _____   _____

c.   dr   _____   _____

      cr   _____   _____

d. dr _____   _____

    cr _____   _____

e. dr _____   _____

    cr _____   _____

f. dr _____   _____

    cr _____   _____

g. dr _____   _____

    cr _____   _____

h. dr _____   _____

    cr _____   _____

i. dr _____   _____

    cr _____   _____

j. dr _____   _____

    cr _____   _____

    cr _____   _____

Exercise 6-10. Inferring Missing Amounts Based on Income Statement Relationships. (LO6)

Supply the missing dollar amounts for the 2008 Income Statement of Stevenson Company for each of the following independent cases.

Cases	Sales Revenue	Sales Ret. & Allow.	Net Sales	Cost of Goods Sold	Gross Profit	Operating Expenses	Net Income
A	$120,000	?	$115,000	$85,000	$30,000	?	$8,000
B	?	1,000	102,000	?	43,000	30,000	13,000
C	305,000	5,000	?	200,000	?	30,000	70,000
D	42,000	600	41,400	?	18,400	14,900	?
E	135,000	17,000	118,000	88,000	?	?	(10,000)

Calculations:

Exercise 6-11. Adjusting Gross Profit Percentage on the Basis of a Multi-Step Income Statement. (LO6)

The following summarized data were provided by the records of Dynasty Incorporated for the year ended December 31, 2009:

Sales of merchandise for cash	$697,000
Sales of merchandise on credit	45,000
Cost of goods sold	409,000
Selling expense	182,000
Administrative expense	65,000
Sales returns and allowances	15,000
Income tax expense	20,000

Required:

1. Based on these data, prepare a multi-step income statement (showing both gross profit and operating income.)

2. What is the amount of gross profit? What was the gross profit percentage? Explain what these two amounts mean.

Exercise 6-12. Journalizing Sales and Purchase Transactions Using a Periodic Inventory System (Supplement)

Kringle Incorporated, is a junk food cooperative. Kringle uses a periodic inventory system. .Beginning inventory consisted of 500 units each costing $20. The following transactions (summarized) have been selected from 2007

a.	Purchased 1,700 units of merchandise, on account, at a unit cost of $20
b.	Sold 1,600 units on account, at unit sales price of $53
c.	Counted: 600 units at unit cost of $20

Required:

1. Journalize the entries to record (a) the purchase, (b) the sale, (c) the end-of-period adjustment to transfer beginning inventory and net purchases to cost of goods sold, and (d) the end-of-period adjustment to adjust the cost of goods sold by subtracting the amount of ending inventory still on hand.

a. *dr* _____ _____

    cr _____ _____

b. *dr* _____ _____

    cr _____ _____

No Cost of Goods Sold Entry

c. *dr* _____ _____

    cr _____ _____

    cr _____ _____

d. *dr* _____ _____

    cr _____ _____

2. Calculate Cost of Goods sold.

SOLUTIONS TO SELF-TEST QUESTIONS AND EXERCISES

MATCHING

1.

A	Bank Reconciliation		N	Periodic Inventory System
L	Cash		R	Perpetual Inventory System
D	Cash Equivalent		I	Purchase Discounts
K	Gross Profit		C	Purchase Returns and Allowances
F	Gross Profit Percentage		M	Sales Discounts
Q	Internal Controls		O	Sales Returns and Allowances
P	Manufacturing Company		B	Segregation of Duties
H	Merchandising Company		E	Service Company
G	NSF Check		J	Time Lags

TRUE-FALSE QUESTIONS

1. F – They are easy to carry and ready-to-use.
2. F – Merchandising companies sell products they've purchased ready-to-sell from suppliers.
3. T
4. T
5. T
6. F – It is referred to as a bank reconciliation.
7. T
8. F – Adjustments requiring you to adjust your cash records are items 'you may not know about'.
9. T
10. F – Cash includes any instrument that banks will accept for deposit and immediate credit to a company's account, including money orders or bank drafts.
11. T
12. F – This is a benefit of the perpetual inventory system.
13. T
14. F – Transportation costs are also called Freight-in. Freight-out to deliver goods to customers is a selling expense.
15. F – The 15 in this set of terms refers to as the number of days in the discount period.
16. T
17. T
18. F – All sales in a perpetual inventory system require two journal entries whether they are cash or credit sales.
19. F – Sales discounts in this chapter are reductions in price given in business to business transactions for prompt payment.
20. T
21. F – A Cost of Goods Sold account doesn't *exist* in a periodic inventory system. It must be computed using a four-step process.

MULTIPLE CHOICE QUESTIONS

1. D	6. D	11. C	16. A
2. D	7. B	12. D	17. C
3. A	8. B	13. D	18. B
4. A	9. B	14. A	19. D
5. D	10. D	15. C	20. C

EXERCISES

Exercise 6-1. Identifying Service, Merchandising, and Manufacturing Operations (LO1)

	Operating Cycle Descriptions	Type of Business
C	1. Use cash to buy raw materials to make inventory, sell the inventory customers and collect cash from those customers.	A. Service Company.
A	2. Use cash to provide services that are sold to customers and then collect cash from those customers.	B. Merchandising Company.
B	3. Use cash to buy inventory, sell the inventory to customers and collect cash from those customers.	C. Manufacturing Company.

Exercise 6-2. Identifying Internal Controls Principles (LO2)

	Explanation	Internal Control Principles
D	1. Prepare documents to show activities that have occurred.	A. Establish Responsibility.
A	2. Assign each task to only one employee.	B. Segregate Duties.
E	3. Check the work of others.	C. Restrict Access.
C	4. Do not provide access to assets or information unless it is needed to fulfill assigned responsibilities.	D. Document Procedures.
B	5. Do not make one employee responsible for all parts of a transaction.	E. Independently Verify.

Exercise 6-3. Organizing Items on the Bank Reconciliation and Journal Entries (LO2)

Part A.

	Reconciling Item	Company's Books	Bank Statement
a.	Bank service charge of $25	−25	
b.	Bounced check from a customer for $600	−600	
c.	Deposits in transit of $1,200		+1,200
d.	Interest earned of $32	+32	
e.	Outstanding checks of $845		−845

Part B.

a.	dr	Other Expenses (+E, - SE)	25	
	cr	Cash (-A)		25
		To record service charge deducted by bank		

b.	dr	Accounts Receivable (+A)	600	
	cr	Cash (-A)		600
		To record check refused by bank; customer still owes		

c.   *This is on the bank side of the reconciliation and so it is not recorded on the company's books.*

d.	dr	Cash (+A)	32	
	cr	Interest Revenue (+R, +SE)		32
		To record interest received from the bank.		

e.   *This is on the bank side of the reconciliation and so it is not recorded on the company's books.*

Exercise 6-4. Identifying Outstanding Checks and Deposits in Transit, Preparing a Bank Reconciliation, and Journal Entries. (LO2)

Part A: Identify and list the deposits in transit and the outstanding checks at the end of March.

Deposits in Transit		Outstanding Checks	
Mar. 31	$18,000	Mar. 27	$ 6,580
		Mar. 29	$ 7,734
		Mar. 30	$ 5,520
Total Deposits in Transit	$18,000	Total Outstanding Checks	19,825

Part B. Prepare a bank reconciliation for March.

STEWART COMPANY
Bank Reconciliation
For the Month Ending March 31, 2009

Bank Statement		Company's Books	
Ending cash balance per bank statement	$21,659	Ending cash balance per books	$19,796 *
Additions		Additions	
(1) Deposits in Transit	18,000	(1) Interest Earned	54
	39,659		19,850
Deductions		Deductions	
(1) Outstanding checks	19,834	(1) Service charge	25
Up-to-date ending cash balance	$19,825	Up-to-date ending cash balance	$19,825

* $40,680 + 9,000 + 12,000 + 4,000 + 18,000 - 950 - 2,370 - 4,330 - 36,000 - 400 - 6,580 - 7,734 - 5,520$

Part C. Give any journal entries that the company should make as a result of the bank reconciliation.

1. dr   Cash (+A)   54
        cr   Interest Revenue (+R, +SE)   54
                To record interest received from bank

2. dr   Other expenses (+E, -SE)   25
        cr   Cash (-A)   25
                To record service charge from bank

Part D.
1.   These entries bring the current cash balance on the Company's books to the up-to-date balance shown on the bank reconciliation. This amount is reported in the balance sheet.

2.   The balance in the cash account will be $19,825 (the reconciled balance from the bank reconciliation) after posting the reconciliation journal entries.

3.   The cash reported on the balance sheet would be $20,325 including the cash on hand.

Exercise 6-5. Inferring Shrinkage Using a Perpetual Inventory System. (LO3)

Cases	Beginning Inventory	Purchases	Cost of Goods Sold	Ending Inventory (As counted)	Shrinkage
A	600	1,700	1,500	300	500
B	300	1,300	400	880	320
C	200	1,800	600	540	860
D	520	2,200	1,700	390	630

A: $600 + 1,700 - 1,500 - 300 = 500$; B: $300 + 1,300 - 400 - 880 = 320$; C: $200 + 1,800 - 600 - 540 = 860$;
C: $200 + 1,800 - 600 - 540 = 860$; D: $520 + 2,200 - 1,700 - 390 = 630$

Exercise 6-6. Recording Purchases, Purchase Discounts, and Purchase Returns Using a Perpetual Inventory System. (LO4)

Part A.

Jun 8	dr	Inventory (+A)	6,800	
	cr	Accounts Payable-Lube Inc. (+L)		6,800
		To record purchase on account		

Jun 10	dr	Accounts Payable-Lube Inc. (-L)	800	
	cr	Inventory (-A)		800
		To record purchase return		

Jun 13	dr	Inventory (+A)	12,000	
	cr	Accounts Payable-Maas Corp (+L)		12,000
		To record purchase on account		

Jun 22	dr	Accounts Payable-Lube Inc. (-L) ($6,800 - $800)	6,000	
	cr	Inventory (-A) ($6,000 * 1%)		60
	cr	Cash (-A) ($6,000 – 60)		5,940
		To record payment within the discount period		

Jul 12	dr	Accounts Payable-Maas Corp. (-L)	12,000	
	cr	Cash (-A)		12,000
		To record payment after the discount period		

Part B.

Inventory	
6,800	800
12,000	60
17,940	

Exercise 6-7. Recording Net Sales with Credit Sales, Sales Returns, and Sales Discounts (LO5)

Part A.

Sept 27	dr	Accounts Receivable-Balboa Bodyworks (+A)	9,000	
	cr	Sales Revenues (+R, +SE)		9,000

	dr	Cost of Goods Sold (+E, -SE)	6,000	
	cr	Inventory (-A)		6,000
		To record sale on account-Balboa Bodyworks		

Sept 28	dr	Accounts Receivable-Craig's Supply Shop (+A)	15,000	
	cr	Sales Revenue (+R, +SE)		15,000

	dr	Cost of Goods Sold (+E, -SE)	9,500	
	cr	Inventory (-A)		9,500
		To record sale on account-Craig's Supply Shop		

Oct 2	dr	Sales Returns and Allowances ($9,000/10) (+xR, -SE)	900	
	cr	Accounts Receivable-Balboa Bodyworks (-A)		900

	dr	Inventory ($6,000/10) (+A)	600	
	cr	Cost of Goods Sold (+E, -SE)		600
		To record customer return of defective merchandise		

Oct 5	dr	Cash (+A) ($8,100 – 243)	7,857	
	dr	Sales Discounts (+xR, -SE) ($8,100 * 3%)	243	
	cr	Accounts Receivable-Balboa Bodyworks (-A)		8,100
		Paid balance on account less return and discount		

| Oct 30 | dr | Accounts Payable-Craig's Supply Shop (-L) | 15,000 | |
| | cr | Cash (-A) | | 15,000 |

Part B.

Sales	(9,000 + 15,000)		$ 24,000
Less:	Sales Returns And Allowances	$ 900	
	Sales Discounts	243	1,143
Net Sales			22,857
Cost of Goods Sold (6,000 + 9,500 – 600)			14,900
Gross Profit			$ 7,957

Exercise 6-8. Determining the Effects of Sales, Sales Discounts, Credit Card Sales, and Sales Returns and Allowances on Income Statement Categories (LO5)

Transaction	Sales Revenues	Sales Returns and Allowances	Sales Discounts	Net Sales
April 8	+ 6,500	NE	NE	+6,500
April 21	NE	NE	+65	-65
April 23	+8,000	NE	NE	+8,000
April 25	NE	+600	NE	-600
May 3	NE	NE	+222	-222

Exercise 6-9. Recording Sales and Purchase Transactions with Discounts and Returns. (LO4, 5)

| a. | dr | Cash (+A) | 67,000 | |
| | cr | Sales Revenue (+R, +SE) | | 67,000 |

	dr	Cost of Goods Sold (+E, -SE)	40,000	
	cr	Inventory (-A)		40,000
		To record cash sales		

| b. | dr | Sales Returns and Allowances (+xR, -SE) | 3,000 | |
| | cr | Cash (-A) | | 3,000 |

	dr	Inventory (+A)	1,800	
	cr	Cost of Goods Sold (-E, +SE)		1,800
		To record customer return of defective goods		

c.	dr	Inventory (+A)	12,000	
	cr	Accounts Payable-Giant Grocers Company (+L)		12,000
		To record inventory purchases on account		

d.	dr	Inventory (+A)	25,000	
	cr	Accounts Payable-Other Suppliers (+L)		25,000
		To record inventory purchases on account		

e.	*dr*	Office Supplies (+A)		4,000	
	cr	Cash (-A)			4,000
		To record purchase of office supplies for cash			
f.	*dr*	Office Equipment (+A)		42,000	
	cr	Cash (-A)			42,000
		To record purchase of office equipment for cash			
g.	*dr*	Accounts Payable-Other Suppliers (-L)		2,000	
	cr	Inventory (+A)			2,000
		To record return of defective goods to suppliers			
h.	*dr*	Inventory (+A)		800	
	cr	Cash (-A)			800
		To record payment for freight on inventory purchases			
i.	*dr*	Accounts Payable-Giant Grocers Company (-L)		12,000	
	cr	Cash (-A)			12,000
		To record payment for inventory after discount period			
j.	*dr*	Accounts Payable-Other Suppliers (25,000-2,000) (-L)		23,000	
	cr	Inventory (-A) ($23,000 * 3%)			690
	cr	Cash (-A)			22,310
		To record payment within the discount period			

Exercise 6-10. Inferring Missing Amounts Based on Income Statement Relationships. (LO6)

Cases	Sales Revenue	Sales Ret. & Allow.	Net Sales	Cost of Goods Sold	Gross Profit	Operating Expenses	Net Income
A	$120,000	*5,000*	$115,000	$85,000	$30,000	*22,000*	$8,000
B	*103,000*	1,000	102,000	*59,000*	43,000	30,000	13,000
C	305,000	5,000	*300,000*	200,000	*100,000*	30,000	70,000
D	42,000	600	41,400	*23,000*	18,400	14,900	*3,500*
E	135,000	17,000	118,000	88,000	*30,000*	*40,000*	(10,000)

Calculations:
A: 120,000-115,000=5,000   30,000-8,000=22,000
B: 1,000+102,000=103,000   102,000-43,000=59,000
C: 305,000-5,000=300,000   300,000-200,000=100,000 or 30,000+70,000=100,000
D: 41,400-18,400=23,000   18,400-14,900=3,500
E: 118,000-88,000=30,000   30,000-30,000=0 Net Income.

To make income negative by 10,000 expenses had to be 10,000 *more* than gross profit or 30,000+ 10,000=40,000

Exercise 6-11. Adjusting Gross Profit Percentage on the Basis of a Multi-Step Income Statement. (LO6)

1.

Dynasty Incorporated		
Income Statement		
For the Year Ended December 31, 2009		
Revenues:		
Sales Revenue		$ 742,000
Sales Returns and Allowances		15,000
Net Sales		727,000
Cost of Goods Sold		409,000
Gross Profit		318,000
Expenses:		
Selling Expense	$ 182,000	
Administrative Expense	65,000	
Total Operating Expenses		247,000
Operating Income		71,000
Income Tax Expense		20,000
Net Income		$ 51,000

2. Gross profit is $318,000
    Gross profit percentage is (318,000/727,000) * 100 = 43.74%

Gross profit represents the amount the company earned from selling goods *after* covering the cost of the goods that were sold. Basically, it is the amount remaining from sales to cover costs of operations and (hopefully) a profit. The gross profit percentage indicates how much above cost a company sells its products. A higher gross profit percentage means that, all else being equal, a company will have more resources to cover operating expense, leading to a greater net income.

Exercise 6-12. Journalizing Sales and Purchases Transactions Using Periodic Inventory System (Suppl)

a.	dr	Purchases (1,700 X $20) (+A)	34,000	
	cr	Accounts Payable (+L)		34,000
		To record purchases on account		
b.	dr	Accounts Receivable (1,600 X $53) (+A)	84,800	
	cr	Sales Revenue (+R, +SE)		84,800
		To record sales on account		
		No Cost of Goods Sold Entry		
c.	dr	Cost of Goods Sold (10,000 + 34,000) (+E, -SE)	44,000	
	cr	Inventory (500 X $20) (-A)		10,000
	cr	Purchases (1,700 X $20) (-A)		34,000
		Transfer beg. inv. and net purch. to cost of goods sold		
d.	dr	Inventory (600 X $20) (-A)	12,000	
	cr	Cost of Goods Sold		12,000
		Remove ending inventory from cost of goods sold		

2. Calculate Cost of Goods sold.

Beginning Inventory (500 X $20)	10,000
Add: Purchases (1,700 X $20)	34,000
Cost of Goods Available for Sale	44,000
Deduct: Ending Inventory (600 X $20)	12,000
Cost of Goods Sold	32,000

CHAPTER 7
REPORTING AND INTERPRETING
INVENTORIES AND COST OF GOODS SOLD

ORGANIZATION OF THE CHAPTER

Understand the business	**Study the accounting methods**	**Evaluate the results**	**Review the chapter**
- Inventory management decisions - Types of inventory	- Balance sheet and income statement reporting - Inventory costing methods - Lower of cost or market	- Inventory turnover analysis - Impact of costing methods	- Demonstration case - Chapter summary - Key terms - Practice material

CHAPTER FOCUS SUGGESTIONS

Review
Now that we've looked at the perpetual and periodic inventory systems, we're going to continue our journey into the exciting world of inventory. We will see that there is more than one way to account for inventory costs. So, without any further ado, heeeere's Inventory!

Introduction
Suppose you're having a barbeque tonight and you've got some ribs in the freezer. They cost $2.00 a pound on sale. You bought some more this week in anticipation of the event, but those cost $2.75 a pound. How do you know which ribs are being served to your guests, are they eating the $2.00 a pound ribs or the $2.75 a pound ribs? You probably didn't bother to identify which were which when you cooked 'em. Well, businesses have a similar problem when they sell goods to customers. Since every purchase of inventory is likely to be at a different unit price, how does a business know how much to charge to cost of goods sold when the sale is recorded and how much to assume is unsold and still on their shelves as ending inventory? It seems unlikely that accounting rules would allow a business to pick and choose which costs go where.

Well, believe it or not, they kind of do! Generally accepted accounting principles allow businesses to choose from several different methods when determining Cost of Goods Sold and Ending Inventory. This allows businesses some freedom in selecting an option that best fits their business environment. However, because of these multiple options, it is important that you understand all four methods and how they work.

UNDERSTAND THE BUSINESS

> **Learning Objective 1**
> Describe inventory management goals.

Inventory Management Decisions
Inventory managers want to (1) maintain a sufficient quantity of inventory to meet customer needs, (2) ensure inventory quality meets the customers' expectations and the company's standards, and (3) minimize the costs of acquiring and carrying inventory (including costs related to purchasing, production, storage, spoilage, theft, obsolescence, and financing.) Another important factor for many businesses is: innovation. Running out of popular items can create stock-outs, lost sales, and customer dissatisfaction. On the other hand, having too many slow-moving inventory items increases storage costs, interest costs (on short-term borrowings), and may lead to losses if inventories become outdated and the business is unable to sell them.

> **Learning Objective 2**
> Describe the different types of inventory.

Types of Inventory
Inventory includes goods that are (1) held for sale in the normal course of business, or (2) used to produce goods for sale. Inventory for manufacturers is different than inventories for merchandisers. Merchandisers typically *purchase* their inventories so they usually only have *one type* of inventory: Merchandise Inventory. Manufacturers *produce* their inventories from scratch so they usually have *three types* of inventory and each one represents a different stage in the manufacturing process:

(1) Raw Material Inventory: This consists of items that are *entered* into production and used to produce the finished product. For example, if you make clothing, your raw materials would be fabric, buttons, zippers, thread, etc.

(2) Work in Process Inventory: This consists of the raw materials that have been *started* into production and are in the process of being manufactured. Continuing the previous example, the business has taken all the raw materials necessary to create a bathrobe, and has begun assembling the bathrobe. It is a 'bathrobe' in process.

(3) Finished Goods inventory: When the work in process inventory is complete, it becomes Finished Goods inventory. These are goods that have been completed and are ready for sale. It would consist of all of the bathrobes that are finished and ready to sell to customers.

Before we dig into the specifics of inventory valuation, there are a couple of other inventory definitions that need to be introduced: consignment goods and goods in transit.

- **Consignment Goods**. These are goods that a company is holding and selling for the owner of the goods. Usually, the owner doesn't want to sell the goods himself, so he has someone else sell the good for him – for a fee. The business holding the goods *does not own* these goods. They remain the property of owner.

- **Goods in Transit**. These are goods that are being transported. They are not owned by the company transporting them. They belong to the company that owns them and is having them transported. Ownership of these items is determined by the sales agreement (see Chapter 6). The sales agreement is either:
    o *FOB Shipping Point:* The FOB point is the point at which ownership transfers to the buyer. So, in this case, ownership of the **inventory has passed to the buyer the moment it leaves the seller's premises.** So, while the goods are in transit, they belong to the **buyer.**
    o *FOB Destination:* In this case, the ownership of the inventory **passes to the buyer when the buyer receives it.** So, while the goods are transit, they belong to the *seller.*

STUDY THE ACCOUNTING METHODS

Balance Sheet and Income Statement Reporting
Here are some characteristics of inventory:
(1) When listing these inventories on the balance sheet, they are *all considered current assets.* They are considered current because it is expected that they will be used up or sold and converted into cash within one year.
(2) Inventories are recorded at cost, which includes:
- Purchase price.
- Additional costs to prepare the goods for sale.
    o Freight-in (increase to inventory cost).
    o Purchase discounts (reduction of inventory cost)
    o Purchase returns and allowances (reduction of inventory cost).

When these goods are sold, their cost is removed from the corresponding inventory account and reported on the income statement as a brand new, huge expense—Cost of Goods Sold. When a company sells inventories, the single largest expense they have to cover from the sale is: *the cost of the thing they just sold!* Businesses don't get this stuff for free, it costs them something. This cost (and how much of the revenue is left once its cost has been covered) is a *very* important item on the income statement. In fact, the income statement likes to summarize these specific elements in the following manner:

Sales	(number of units sold * sales price per unit)
– Cost of Goods Sold (CGS)	(number of units sold * cost per unit)
= Gross Profit.	

Gross profit represents how much profit was made on the item after covering the item's cost, but before covering any other operating expenses. The following shows the relationship between cost of goods sold on the income statement and inventory on the balance sheet:

Beginning inventory (BI)	$40,000
+ Purchases of merchandise during the year (P)	+ 55,000
= Goods available for sale (GAFS)	= 95,000
– Ending inventory (EI)	- 35,000
= Cost of goods sold (CGS)	= $60,000

Notice that the two numbers above the circle (Beginning Inventory and Purchases) equal the circled amount and the two numbers below the circle (Ending Inventory and Cost of Goods Sold) also equal the circled amount. This will always be true. This relationship can also be represented in the inventory T-account like this:

+ **Merchandise Inventory (A)** -			
Beginning inventory	$40,000		
Purchases of inventory	55,000	Cost of goods sold	60,000
Ending inventory	$35,000		

Inventory Costing Methods

Learning Objective 3
Compute costs using four inventory costing methods.

When inventory costs change over time, it isn't obvious what costs should be used to determine the cost of goods sold and which should be used to determine the cost of the ending inventory. So, generally accepted accounting principles provide four methods of accounting for inventory costs:

- Specific Identification
- First-In, First-Out (FIFO)
- Last-In, First-Out (LIFO)
- Weighted Average

These methods give four alternatives for splitting the total dollar amounts of **Goods Available for Sale** between the Ending Inventory and the Cost of Goods Sold.

1.   Specific Identification Method

This method is most often used with inventories of high dollar value and low volume of sales, like Diamond Solitaire Engagement Rings. It requires keeping track of the purchase cost of each individual item. This is relatively easy to do with diamond solitaire engagement rings since they are unique and expensive. It would not make sense to do this with ¾" wood nails because they all look identical (no matter when they were purchased) and the cost of each individual nail is very small.

The Specific Identification method is the only method that is based on the actual flow of goods from the shelves to the customers. The remaining three methods are not based on the *actual flow of goods*. Instead they are based on an *assumed flow of goods from the shelves to the customers* – thus the term *cost flow assumptions*. It should be noted that generally accepted accounting principles **do not require that a company use a cost flow assumption that mirrors its actual physical flow.**

2.   First-In, First-Out (FIFO) Method

This method assumes that the cost of the oldest goods (the first ones in), are the first costs used to calculate cost of goods sold (the first ones out). This leaves the newer costs remaining on your shelves in the ending inventory. Determining Cost of Goods Sold and Ending Inventory under this method is a two-step process:

Step 1:   Every time inventory is purchased, it is placed on the shelf so that the oldest purchase is on the bottom of the shelf (usually beginning inventory) and the newest purchases are placed on the top shelf. In total, these costs are the total Goods available for Sale. The total cost of all the shelves together equal the **Goods Available for Sale.**

Let's assume the following:

	Units	Cost per Unit	Total Cost
December 10 purchase	1,500	$21	$31,500
September 8 purchase	300	20	6,000
July 16 purchase	1,200	18	21,600
April 5 purchase	800	14	11,200
Beginning Inventory	200	12	2,400
Total Goods Available for Sale	4,000		$72,700
Sales (in units)	3,500		

Step 2: As inventories are sold, they are removed, first, from the *bottom* shelf (assume the shaded area of the preceding table are the shelves) so that the first inventory items placed on the shelves (beginning inventory – the first items in) are the first inventory items sold off the shelves (first items out or sold off the shelves). Once all sales are accounted for (3,000 units in our example), the only items remaining on the shevles are the latest purchases (those on the top shelves.) FIFO allocates the *oldest* (first-in) unit costs to *cost of goods sold* and the *newest* (most recent purchase) unit costs to *ending inventory*.

Cost of Goods Sold (first-in are first out)	Units	Cost per Unit	Total Cost
December 10 purchase 1,000 sold (1,500 – 500)	1,000	$21	$21,000
September 8 purchase (all sold)	300	20	6,000
July 16 purchase (all sold)	1,200	18	21,600
April 5 purchase (all sold)	800	14	11,200
Beginning Inventory (all sold)	200	12	2,400
Total Cost of Goods Sold (FIFO)	3,500		$62,200

Ending Inventory (most recent purchase)	Units	Cost per Unit	Total Cost
What's left on the shelf are from the most recent purchase			
December 10	500	$21	$10,500

3.   Last-In, First-Out (LIFO) Method
This method assumes that the cost of the newest goods (the last ones in) are the first costs used to calculate cost of goods sold (first ones out), and that the oldest costs are the ones remaining in the ending inventory. Determining Cost of Goods Sold and Ending Inventory under this method is a two-step process:

Step 1. Every time inventory is purchased it is placed onto the shelves exactly as they were under the FIFO method. The oldest purchase is on the bottom shelve (usually beginning inventory) and the newest purchases are on the top shelves. In total, once again, these costs are the Goods Available for Sale. Since this amount is the same we will use the original inventory shelves from the FIFO example. The only difference is the way we empty them!

Step 2. Here's where we see the difference between the methods. Under the LIFO inventory method, each item sold is treated as if its cost were removed in sequence from the *top shelf* (the most recent purchases) and work our way down. Once all sales are accounted for, the only items remaining on the shelves are the oldest inventory items (those on the bottom shelves.) LIFO allocates the *newest* unit costs to *cost of goods sold* and the *oldest* unit costs to *ending inventory*. The cost flows for LIFO are exactly the opposite of the cost flows for FIFO. Assume the same 3,500 units are sold, but now we'll use LIFO to determine their cost.

Cost of Goods Sold (Last-in)	Units	Cost per Unit	Total Cost
December 10 purchase (all sold)	1,500	$21	31,500
September 8 purchase (all sold)	300	20	6,000
July 16 purchase (all sold)	1,200	18	21,600
April 5 purchase 1,000 sold (800 – 300)	500	14	7,000
Total Cost of Goods Sold	3,500		$66,100

Ending Inventory	Units	Cost per Unit	Total Cost
What's left on the shelf are from the oldest purchases			
Beginning Inventory	200	$12	$ 2,400
April 5	300	14	4,200
Total Ending Inventory	500		$6,600

The following table compares the results of the two methods when prices are increasing and decreasing. Notice that even though they're called *inventory* costing methods, the name of the costing method *describes the unit costs used to calculate Cost of Goods Sold.* The name doesn't mention the unit costs remaining in Ending Inventory *at all*!

	FIFO	LIFO
Inventory (Balance Sheet)	Newest	Oldest
Cost of Goods Sold (Income statement)	Oldest (first-in)	Newest (last –in)

4. Weighted Average Cost Method

This method is, essentially, the polar opposite of Specific Identification. Weighted Average Costing is used for high volume, low cost items like nails, toothpaste, etc.—items that are all pretty much identical to one another. For this type of item, there's no need to identify specific purchase costs with each item sold. We simply mix them all in a big bin and sell them! Doesn't matter if some nails sold are from the first, second, tenth, or one thousandth purchase, we want to treat them all the same. The steps are kind of weird for this one:

Step 1a. Determine the number of units and cost of goods available for sale in the same manner as the other two methods. In this case, take special note of the *total number of inventory units* placed onto the shelves and the *total calculated cost of inventory* (goods available for sale) placed onto the shelves.

Step 2a. Calculate the weighted average cost per unit as:

$$\text{Weighted Average Cost per Unit} = \frac{\$\$\$\$}{\#\,\text{Units}} = \frac{\text{Total cost of Goods Available for Sale}}{\text{Total Number of Units Available for Sale}} = \frac{\$72,700}{4,000} = \$18.175$$

Again, there is no difference in the total goods available for sale or the total number of units available for sale. The inventory available to sell...is the inventory available to sell. The only difference (for *any* of these methods) is how we assume item costs are *removed from* the shelves when we sell them.)

Step 2b. Assign the same weighted average unit cost to cost of goods sold and ending inventory (all are given exactly the same cost each.)

Cost of Goods Sold (Average Cost)	Units	Cost per Unit	Total Cost
Total Cost of Goods Sold	3,500	$18.175	$63,612.50

Ending Inventory	Units	Cost per Unit	Total Cost
Total Ending Inventory	500	$18.175	$9,087.50

Financial Statement Effects of Inventory Costing Methods

So, what was the point of all these calculation options? Well, they are what determine the dollar amount of the journal entry we record when goods are sold. For example, assume that the 3,500 units sold in the previous examples were sold for $30 each. Recall that two entries are required to record a sale when you are using a perpetual inventory system. The first entry records the sale, like this:

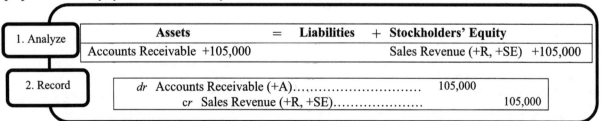

1. Analyze	Assets	=	Liabilities	+	Stockholders' Equity
	Accounts Receivable +105,000				Sales Revenue (+R, +SE) +105,000

2. Record

```
dr  Accounts Receivable (+A)............................    105,000
        cr  Sales Revenue (+R, +SE)......................               105,000
```

Study Guide, Chapter 7

The sales portion of the entry is the same regardless of the inventory costing method used. However, the *second entry* is the one that is affected by the inventory costing method used by the business. Had the company used the FIFO inventory costing method (refer back to where we performed the FIFO calculations), the second entry would be:

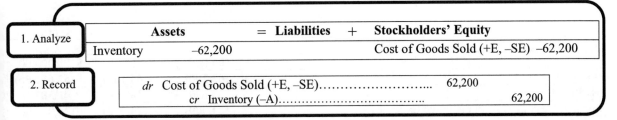

1. Analyze	Assets	= Liabilities	+	Stockholders' Equity
	Inventory −62,200			Cost of Goods Sold (+E, −SE) −62,200

2. Record	dr Cost of Goods Sold (+E, −SE)........................ 62,200
	cr Inventory (−A)..................................... 62,200

If the business had used the LIFO costing method, the journal entry would be identical *except* for the dollar amount used for the entry. Under LIFO (again, referring back to where the LIFO calculations were performed), the following entry would be made to record the Cost of Goods Sold and corresponding reduction of inventory:

1. Analyze	Assets	= Liabilities	+	Stockholders' Equity
	Inventory −66,100			Cost of Goods Sold (+E, −SE) −66,100

2. Record	dr Cost of Goods Sold (+E, −SE)........................ 66,100
	cr Inventory (−A)..................................... 66,100

Finally, assuming the business used the Weighted Average costing method, the journal entry would be the same as the previous two, *except* for the dollar amount used for the entry. Under Weighted Average (again, referring back to where the Weighted Average calculations were performed), the following entry would be made to record the Cost of Goods Sold and corresponding reduction of inventory:

1. Analyze	Assets	= Liabilities	+	Stockholders' Equity
	Inventory −63,612.50			Cost of Goods Sold (+E, −SE) −63,612.50

2. Record	dr Cost of Goods Sold (+E, −SE)........................ 63,612.50
	cr Inventory (−A)..................................... 63,612.50

It is important to note that the journal entry itself, *never changes* —only the dollar *amount used* to *make* the journal entry changes, depending on the cost flow assumption used for calculating inventory.

FIFO, LIFO, and Weighted Average Costing methods differ only in how they allocate the Goods Available for Sale between Cost of Goods Sold and Ending Inventory. If the lowest dollar costs are allocated to Ending Inventory, it means the higher dollar costs are allocated to Cost of Goods Sold. This means a *higher dollar amount* is subtracted from net sales resulting in a lower *Gross Profit*. This occurs only because of the *inventory method* used by the business. The table below summarizes the effect of using each of the three inventory methods and its effect on the Income Statement and Balance Sheet.

Highest Dollar Amount of...	When Costs are Increasing	When Costs are Decreasing
Inventory	FIFO	LIFO
Cost of Goods Sold	LIFO	FIFO
Gross Profit	FIFO	LIFO
Net Income	FIFO	LIFO

To better illustrate these effects, a comparison of the Income Statement for each of these cost flow assumptions follows. Take a few minutes to compare the effects noted on the previous table, to the information presented here. Since this example assumes an inflationary period, the results on the statements will be the same as the table column labeled "When Costs are Increasing."

	FIFO	LIFO	Weighted Average
Income Statement (I/S) Effects			
Sales	$105,000	$105,000	$105,000.00
Cost of Goods Sold	**(62,200)**	**(66,100)**	**(63,612.50)**
Gross Profit	**42,800**	**38,900**	**41,387.50**
Selling and General & Administrative Expenses	(24,000)	(24,000)	(24,000.00)
Income from Operations	18,800	14,900	17,387.50
Other Revenue (Expenses)	1,200	1,200	1,200.00
Income before Income Taxes	20,000	16,100	18,587.50
Income Tax Expense (30%)	(6,000)	(4,830)	(5,576.25)
Net Income	$ 14,000	$ 11,270	$ 13,011.25
Balance Sheet (B/S) Effects			
Inventory	**$10,500**	**$6,600**	**$9,087.50**
Beginning Inventory	$ 2,400	$ 2,400	$ 2,400.00
Plus: Purchases	70,300	70,300	70,300.00
Goods Available for Sale	72,700	72,700	72,700.00
Minus: Ending Inventory (on the balance sheet)	**(10,500)**	**(6,600)**	**(9,087.50)**
Cost of Goods Sold (on the income statement)	**62,200**	**66,100**	**63,612.50**

We know that (1) this is a period of rising prices because beginning inventory only cost $12 each and the prices of each subsequent purchase steadily increased. Per the table, when prices are increasing, LIFO will give the highest cost of goods sold – $66,100. Because this amount is *subtracted* from sales in determining gross profit (and net income), this will also result in the lowest amount of gross profit ($38,900) and the highest net income ($11,270) of the three methods. It also results in the lowest Ending Inventory of the three methods – $6,600.

Notice that the effect on Net Income is the same as the effect on Gross Profit for each scenario. In other words, if gross profit is higher, then net income is also higher. If gross profit is lower, then net income is also lower. This is because Net Income is calculated directly from gross profit (simply subtract the expenses, and other income/expense items.) So, both subtotals are derived from the same initial amount: gross profit.

Remember, that the *only difference* between these three income statements is the inventory cost flow assumption being used. Since the Weighted Average method tends to smooth out any fluctuations in price and 'average' them, it will never result in the highest or lowest cost of the items.

Recall that managers are allowed to select any of the four methods for inventory costing purposes. Because the choice made can have a significant impact on income and assets, managers don't make this decision lightly. For example, the situation created by the LIFO inventory costing method during periods of rising costs, results in the lowest net income. Why would a manager want to *decrease* net income? Isn't that how managers are evaluated...by having a *profitable* business?

Well, the answer is: higher income leads to higher *income tax expense*! This cost is a *real, physical, out of pocket cost that must be absorbed by the company.* Whereas, the impact of an inventory costing method is a cost that can only be seen *on paper.*

So, if a manager is evaluated on the basis of *keeping costs down,* LIFO (during a period of rising prices), effectively saves the company money in the form of lower income taxes. Lower taxes mean more cash in the till to use for other purposes and this makes the manager look good. If, however, a manager is evaluated *solely* on the basis of making a profit...the bigger the better, FIFO would be the better choice because it generates the highest profit (during periods of rising prices), resulting in large bonuses, raises, etc. for the manager.

Because of the ability to manipulate income by switching back and forth (as needed) between methods, both GAAP and the tax laws prevent a manager from playing musical chairs with inventory methods. A business may only change its inventory costing method if it will improve the *accuracy* of financial statements.

Additional Inventory Cost Flow Computations

While you now understand the flow of costs using each of the three methods, and that the terms FIFO and LIFO refer to the costs that are allocated to *Cost of Goods Sold,* not ending inventory, its time to inform you of the bad news. Seldom is it the *Cost of Goods Sold* that is calculated first. Usually, it is the *ending inventory!* Why? Because businesses count inventory at the end of the year and it is easier to calculate the costs allocated to these items than it is to determine the cost of goods sold. So, oftentimes, a business will determine the costs in ending inventory *first,* then subtract that from the goods available for sale and 'force out' the cost of goods sold figure.

Lower of Cost or Market

> **Learning Objective 4**
> Explain why inventory is reported at the lower of cost or market.

Normally, assets are reported at their original cost. But, sometimes inventory values can fall *below original cost.* This decrease in value occurs because (1) it is easily replaced by identical goods at a lower cost, or (2) it has become outdated or damaged. In either case, when the inventory values fall below cost, the inventories are 'marked down' to this lower market value. This is known as the *lower of cost or market (LCM) rule.* Its purpose is to prevent a business from showing assets at *more than they are worth.*

For example, assume a company has 1,000 units of inventory on-hand that originally cost $20 each. However, the replacement cost of the inventory has fallen to $17 per item. The original cost ($20) is compared to the 'new' replacement cost ($17) and the *lower* of the two amounts is used to value the inventory. In our example, since the replacement cost is lower and the original cost is the amount currently shown in the inventory account, the following journal entry is required to reduce the amount in the inventory account.

1. Analyze	**Assets**	**= Liabilities**	**+**	**Stockholders' Equity**
	Inventory −3,000			Inventory Write-down (+E, −SE) −3,000

2. Record		
	dr Inventory Write-down (+E, −SE)...................	3,000	
	cr Inventory (−A)..		3,000

The write down is calculated as the difference between the original cost and the replacement cost times the number of items in inventory [($20 − $17) * 1,000]. Most companies will report this write-down amount as a normal operating expense, because inventory price fluctuations are a normal part of doing business.

If the replacement cost of the inventory had been *higher* than cost (i.e. $22), no entry would be made because the amount in the inventory account *is* already the lower of the two figures. GAAP does not allow companies to *increase* costs to the decrease costs to market value, thus the name – *lower* of cost or market value.

Sometimes, errors are made in estimating the correct market value of inventory. Errors like this are common and have an impact on the financial statements. The impact of these kinds of errors is discussed in Supplement B of this chapter.

EVALUATE THE RESULTS

> **Learning Objective 5**
> Compute and interpret the inventory turnover ratio.

Inventory Turnover Analysis

When inventory account balances change from one period to the next, it is easy to figure out what caused the increase or decrease...if you work there, just ask around! But, financial statement users don't have this luxury, they have to use analytical methods to determine the reasons for increases or decreases in inventory levels. One tool used for this purpose is Inventory Turnover Analysis.

Here's the basic idea of inventory turnover analysis: when a company buys goods, inventories go up, and when it sells goods, inventories go down. This buying and selling process is repeated over and over many times during an accounting period. The inventory turnover essentially calculates the *number of times this process occurs* during a period. It is calculated as follows:

$$\text{Inventory Turnover Ratio} = \frac{\text{Cost of Goods Sold}}{\text{Average Inventory}} = \left[\frac{\text{Cost of Goods Sold}}{\text{Beginning Inventory} + \text{Ending Inventory}}\right] / 2$$

A higher ratio indicates that inventory moves more quickly from when it is purchased to its ultimate sale to a customer. This reduces storage and obsolescence costs. So, increases in the ratio indicate:
- efficient purchase or production techniques
- high product demand

Whereas, sudden declines in this ratio may indicate:
- that inventory management is getting shoddy
- there's been an unexpected drop in demand for a product.

The overall impact of a high inventory turnover ratio includes:
- Reduced costs for inventory:
    - Storage – since the inventory isn't in the business for long, costs for storing it are low
    - Obsolescence – since the inventory is sold quickly, the likelihood of it becoming outdated, stale, etc. are very low
- Since there is less of the company's money tied up in inventory, there are additional funds available to the company for:
    - Investing – thus earning interest income or some other type of return on the funds
    - Reducing Borrowings – using the excess funds to pay off debt that the company has, thus reducing interest expense charges.
    - There is extra cash available to the company

Some people have difficulty evaluating the 'number of times' inventory is purchased and sold, so this ratio can be converted to the average number of Days to Sell. This is calculated as:

$$\text{Days to Sell} = \frac{365}{\text{Inventory Turnover Ratio}}$$

This basically tells you, on average, how many *days* it takes for this buying/selling process to take place.

Comparison to Benchmarks
These ratios should not be evaluated *solely* on the information presented earlier. You need to consider the type of business you are dealing with as well. For example, if you calculate an inventory turnover of 14.6 times (Days to sell of 25 days) for a business. That looks like a pretty good ratio. But, what if I tell you that this is the turnover for a company that is a Fresh Flower Shop? Well, not so good....we got lots of dead flowers. So, consider other things besides the 'rules of thumb' when evaluating inventory turnover.

The Impact of Inventory Costing Methods

> **Learning Objective 6**
> Explain how accounting methods affect evaluations of inventory management.

Since inventory and cost of goods sold are the primary components of the inventory turnover ratio and the days to sell, the method used for inventory costing affects the results of both calculations. This can cause problems if you are trying to evaluate the financial statements of different businesses. In an effort to prevent confusion, GAAP requires that businesses using the LIFO inventory costing method must also report their results of operations using FIFO in the notes to the financial statements. This is a relatively easy conversion for accountants and the result will be something called a LIFO Reserve. For this reason, many companies prefer to compare the ratio results only to its own results in previous periods, or with a company that uses the same inventory costing method.

SUPPLEMENT A – APPLYING FIFO AND LIFO IN A PERPETUAL INVENTORY SYSTEM

Throughout this chapter, the inventory costing methods presented were calculated under the *periodic* inventory system though most systems today incorporate a *perpetual* inventory system. Then, why is the emphasis on the periodic system? There are some good reasons for this:

1. The FIFO and Specific Identification methods provide the same results regardless of whether they are calculated using a perpetual system or a periodic system. Differences only arise when using:
   a. LIFO
   b. Weighted Average
2. Most businesses keep their books on a FIFO basis throughout the year and, if they use LIFO for reporting purposes, will simply prepare an end-of-period adjusting entry to report inventory on a LIFO basis. In doing this, inventory purchases are recorded throughout the accounting period, but Cost of Goods Sold is not determined until the *end* of the accounting period (via the adjusting entry) thus *behaving* like a periodic system.
3. Companies typically adjust their records at year-end to match a physical count of the inventory on-hand. So, in effect, they are using a periodic system anyway.
4. The periodic system is easier to demonstrate and understand so it is usually the preferred method for illustration purposes.

Even so, it is good to know how to calculate inventories using a perpetual inventory system. The biggest difference is that, when a sale is made, only the inventory actually on the shelves as of the date of the sale can be used to calculate the Cost of Goods Sold and Inventory amounts.

Assume the following transactions occurred in a business that uses the LIFO method:

Jan 1	Beginning Inventory 100 units costing $60 each
April 12	Purchased 200 units at $63 each
June 20	Sold 120 units
Aug 5	Purchased 300 units at $65 each
Nov 16	Sold 250 units

Date	Event	# of Units	Unit Cost	Units after Event		Unit Costs after Event	Inventory Cost after Event
On April 12, the company had the following inventory after the purchase				Beg.	200	$63	12,600
					100	60	6,000
		Total					18,600
On June 20, the company had the following inventory after the sale (120 @ $63)					80	63	5,040
					100	60	6,000
		Total					11,040
On August 5, the company had the following inventory after the purchase					300	65	19,500
					80	63	5,040
					100	60	6,000
		Total					30,540
On November 16, the company had the following inventory after the sale (250 @ $65)					50	65	3,250
					80	63	5,040
					100	60	6,000
		Total					14,290

The calculation is exactly the same as shown in the chapter (everything is sold off of the top shelf), *except* that items are removed from the shelves on the actual *date of sale*. In the body of the chapter, all calculations were made at the *end* of the accounting period as if all *sales were made on the last day of the year*, and as if all inventories were available at that time. Now, you can see that when a sale is made under the perpetual inventory system, the unit costs can only be taken from the *items actually on the shelves at the time the sale occurred*. This meticulous record-keeping is perfect for the computer, but was quite tedious to do by hand.

Also, when costs are rising, the perpetual LIFO Cost of goods sold will be *lower* than the periodic LIFO cost of goods sold (like we calculated in the chapter.) Since perpetual LIFO cost of goods sold is lower, income will be higher. Thus, income taxes will be higher also. If income taxes will be lower simply by using a periodic LIFO inventory rather than a perpetual LIFO why *wouldn't* companies prefer to keep the records in the manner described in the chapter here. That is, wait until the end of the accounting period and adjust cost of goods sold and ending inventory then, *as if they were using a periodic system.*

SUPPLEMENT B – THE EFFECTS OF ERRORS IN ENDING INVENTORY

As mentioned in the chapter, errors in inventory can occur when the LCM rule is not applied properly to ending inventory. But, errors can occur for a variety of other reasons as well:

1. Failure to apply the LCM rule is considered an error (as already mentioned)
2. Incorrect quantities or unit costs were used in calculations,
3. A variety of other reasons.

In any event, inventory errors can have a significant impact on the balance sheet and the income statement. Ending inventory is on the balance sheet and cost of goods sold is on the income statement. If items are sold, they can't be in ending inventory and if items are in ending inventory, they haven't been sold. Therefore, an error made in ending inventory affects both the balance sheet and the income statement. Since ending inventory in the current year is also the beginning inventory in the following year, an error in ending inventory also affects the calculation of cost of goods sold in the following year (and thus net income) as well.

To show how inventory errors affect net income, we will assume that a company has identical income and inventory amounts for two years in a row. Ending inventory *if no errors are made* should always be $10,000. In the following situation, assume that ending inventory was understated by $4,000 in the current year.

Two-Year Income Effects of Inventory Error

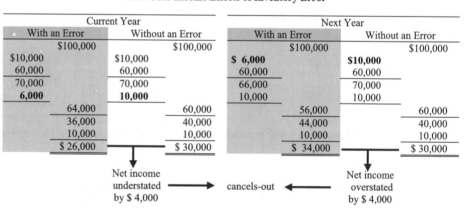

An understatement of ending inventory by $4,000 in the current year, results in a understatement of Net Income of $4,000 ($26,000 vs. $30,000) in the current year. If the error is not detected and corrected, it will become the beginning inventory in the next year, causing an offsetting *overstatement* of net income in the next year ($34,000 vs. $30,000). By the end of the second year, assuming no other errors are made in ending inventory, the combined result of the errors will have offset each other. Therefore, inventory errors are ultimately self-correcting, assuming no additional errors are made in calculating subsequent ending inventory amounts.

REVIEW THE CHAPTER

Chapter Summary
LO1. Describe inventory management goals.
❖   Make or buy:
   o   A sufficient *quantity*
   o   Of *quality* and *innovative* products
   o   At the lowest possible *cost*
   o   So they can be sold to earn the desire amount of gross profit

LO2. Describe the different types of inventory.
❖   Merchandise inventory is
   o   Bought by merchandisers in a ready to sell format
❖   Merchandisers have
   o   *Raw Materials Inventory* – that enter a manufacturer's production process where they become
   o   *Work in Process Inventory* – as the raw materials start to become processed
   o   *Finished Goods Inventory* – production that has been further transformed and will ultimately sold to customers

LO3. Compute costs using four inventory costing methods.
❖   Any of four generally accepted methods can be used to allocate the Cost of Goods Available for Sale between:
   o   Cost of Goods Sold (Goods that are sold), and
   o   Ending Inventory (goods that remain on hand at the end of the accounting period)
❖   *Specific Identification* assigns costs to Ending Inventory and Cost of Goods Sold
   o   By tracking and identifying each specific item of inventory
❖   *FIFO* assigns costs such that:
   o   Cost of Goods Sold is assigned the first costs into the business (oldest)
   o   Ending Inventory is assigned the last costs into the business (most recent)
❖   *LIFO* assigns costs such that:
   o   Cost of Goods Sold is assigned the last costs into the business (most recent)
   o   Ending Inventory is assigned the first costs into the business (oldest)
❖   *Weighted Average Cost* assigns costs such that:
   o   The weighted average cost per unit of inventory is assigned equally to Cost of Goods Sold and Ending Inventory

LO4. Explain why inventory is reported at the lower of cost or market (LCM).
❖   The LCM rule ensures that inventory assets are not reported at more than they are worth.

LO5. Compute and interpret the inventory turnover ratio.
❖   The inventory turnover ratio measures the efficiency of inventory management.
❖   It reflects how many times (on average) inventory was acquired and sold during the period.
❖   Inventory Turnover Ratio is calculated as:
   o   Cost of Goods Sold / Average Inventory

LO6. Explain how accounting methods affect evaluations of inventory management.
❖   To help financial statement users compare the inventory levels and ratios of companies that use different inventory cost flow assumptions:
   o   LIFO companies also report FIFO numbers in their financial statement notes
      ▪   Most companies use a LIFO reserve to show how FIFO numbers are converted into LIFO numbers.

READ AND RECALL QUESTIONS

After you read each section of the chapter, answer the related Read and Recall Questions below.

> **LEARNING OBJECTIVE**
> *After studying the section of the chapter, you should be able to:*
> 1. Describe inventory management goals

Inventory Management Decisions

List the three goals of inventory managers. What types of problems could occur when these goals aren't being met? What was the fourth factor that Oakley's Managers listed as the final factor that drives their inventory decisions?

> **LEARNING OBJECTIVE**
> *After studying the section of the chapter, you should be able to:*
> 2. Describe the different types of inventory

Types of Inventory

What two general types of goods are included in inventory?

List the type(s) of inventories held by *merchandisers*. How is each acquired?

List the type(s) of inventories held by *manufacturers*. How is each acquired?

What are consignment goods? Who owns these goods?

How is the ownership of goods in transit determined?

Briefly define (1) FOB shipping point and (2) FOB destination.

What are the two primary characteristics of inventory?

Name four items that would be included in the cost of inventories.

Balance Sheet and Income Statement Reporting
What is gross profit? How is Gross profit calculated?

Define *goods available for sale.* Goods available for sale are ultimately allocated between what two items?

On what financial statement can each be found?

What is the formula for calculating *Cost of Goods Sold?* How many components are needed for the calculation?

LEARNING OBJECTIVE
After studying the section of the chapter, you should be able to:
3. Compute costs using four inventory costing methods

Inventory Costing Methods
List the four inventory costing methods. What is the purpose of an inventory costing method?

Why is the specific identification method impractical for costing toilet paper?

Complete the following statement: The _____ method is the only method that is based on the _____ flow of goods.

Complete the following statement: _____ do not require that a company use a _____ flow that mirrors its _____ flow.

Define FIFO. What is FIFO an abbreviation for? Under this method, which costs are allocated to Cost of Goods Sold? Which are allocated to Ending Inventory?

Define LIFO. What is LIFO an abbreviation for? Under this method, which costs are allocated to Cost of Goods Sold? Which are allocated to Ending Inventory?

When referring to "First-In, First Out" and "Last-In, First Out", the name describes how the unit the costs are allocated to which of the following: (circle one)

Cost of Goods Sold   **Ending Inventory**

What is unique about how items are valued using the Weighted Average Cost method?

Complete the following statement: The _____ itself, *never changes* – only the _____ *used* to *make* the_____ changes, depending on the _____ assumption for calculating inventory.

When costs are rising, which method provides a higher cost of goods sold amount? Higher ending inventory amount? Higher net income?

Why might a company want to use a method that produces the lowest Net Income?

Additional Inventory Cost Flow Computations
What is meant by 'forcing out' the cost of goods sold?

LEARNING OBJECTIVE
After studying the section of the chapter, you should be able to:
4. Explain why inventory is reported at the lower of cost or market

---

Lower of Cost or Market
Why might inventory values fall below its original cost? When this occurs what valuation rule is used?

What is the purpose of this rule? If replacement cost is higher than the original cost, will the inventory be restated to the higher amount? Why or why not?

LEARNING OBJECTIVE
After studying the section of the chapter, you should be able to:
5. Compute and interpret the inventory turnover ratio

Inventory Turnover Analysis
Define inventory turnover. What is an inventory turnover ratio and how is it calculated?

Would a business normally prefer a high inventory turnover ratio or a low inventory turnover ratio? Explain.

What two results might does an increase in the inventory turnover ratio indicate?

What is *Days to Sell*? Why might it be calculated?

Why should you be careful when evaluating all inventory turnover ratios using the same criteria and rules of thumb for all companies?

LEARNING OBJECTIVE
After studying the section of the chapter, you should be able to:
6. Explain how accounting methods affect evaluations of inventory management

---

The Impact of Inventory Costing Methods
Why would the inventory costing method used by a company alter the outcome of the inventory turnover ratio and the days to sell?

How does GAAP enhance comparability due to the differences in inventory costing methods? Explain.

FINANCIAL ANALYSIS TOOLS
1. To determine how frequently inventory turns over during the period, calculate the inventory turnover ratio:

$$\text{Inventory Turnover Ratio} = \frac{\text{Cost of Goods Sold}}{\text{Average Inventory}}$$

Calculate the following to express the inventory turnover ratio in terms of number of days to sell:

$$\text{Days to Sell} = \frac{365}{\text{Inventory Turnover Ratio}}$$

HELPFUL STUDY TIP

1. **Inventory Costing Methods: FIFO.** Many students confuse FIFO and LIFO. You may be able to do the calculations perfectly, but do them backwards! Here's an easy way to visualize the two methods so that they make more sense intuitively. FIFO is the most frequently used method of inventory costing—and with good reason! This is the natural flow of items in a business. Ever buy milk? When you go to the store to buy milk you might notice the guys in the back putting out the new milk. Have you ever noticed how they do that? They push the *old milk* to the front of the shelf. The old milk is the *first milk they brought into the store.* The milk guys also want it to be the *first milk SOLD from the store!* Otherwise, they'll get stuck with a bunch of spoiled milk. This is the perfect example of FIFO costing. SO, when you work your problems on FIFO, simply imagine selling milk at the grocery store! It will work every time! (I know, I know, you cheat and dig way back on the shelf to make sure you get the freshest milk, but pretend that you sent your 12 year-old to buy it.)

2. **Inventory Costing Methods: LIFO.** The actual flow of most businesses is FIFO, but believe it or not, some companies actual flow is LIFO! Can't think of one? Well, it's STEEL. Ever seen steel produced? It is actually created in gigantic flat slabs weighing many, many tons. When one slab is finished, it is placed on top of the previous one like this:

Last slab put on pile ⟶ _____ ⟵ First slab sold from the pile

                        _____

First slab put on pile ⟶ _____ ⟵ Last slab sold from the pile

Because the slabs are so heavy, it would be ludicrous to force them to sell the *first slab put on the pile.* That would entail lifting all of the other 40 tons of slabs off of the one on the bottom of the stack. Then pulling out the one at the bottom and selling it! So, as you can readily see, it actually makes sense for companies selling steel slabs to sell them such that the *last slab put on the pile, is the first slab sold from the pile* (LIFO.) Now, when you calculate using the LIFO costing method, you can simply picture the steel slabs!

SELF-TEST QUESTIONS AND EXERCISES

MATCHING

1. *Match each of the key terms listed below with the appropriate textbook definition.*

_____ Cost of Goods Sold Equation		_____ Inventory
_____ Days to Sell		_____ Inventory Turnover
_____ First-in, First-out (FIFO)		_____ Last-in, First out (LIFO)
_____ FOB Destination		_____ Lower of Cost or Market (LCM)
_____ FOB Shipping Point		_____ Specific Identification
_____ Goods Available for Sale		_____ Weighted Average Cost

A. A term of sale indicating that goods are owned by the customer the moment they leave the seller's premises.
B. The process of buying and selling inventory.
C. Assumes that the costs of the first goods purchased, are the costs of the first goods sold.
D. Goods that are held for sale in the normal course of business or are used to produce other goods for sale.
E. BI + P – EI.
F. A valuation rule that requires the inventory account to be reduced when the value of the inventory falls to an amount less than its cost.
G. The inventory costing method that identifies the cost of the specific item that was sold.
H. Assumes that the cost of the last goods purchased are the costs of the first goods sold.
I. A measure of the average number of days from the time inventory is bought to the time it is sold.
J. The sum of beginning inventory and purchases for the period.
K. A term of sale indicating that goods are owned by the seller until they are delivered to the customer.
L. Uses a weighted average unit cost of the goods available for sale for both cost of goods sold and ending inventory.

TRUE-FALSE QUESTIONS

For each of the following, enter a T or F in the blank to indicate whether the statement is true or false.

_____1.   (LO1) One of the primary goals of managers who make inventory decisions is to ensure inventory quality meets customers' expectations and company standards.

_____2.   (LO2) Raw Materials inventory includes manufactured goods that are complete and ready for sale.

_____3.   (LO2) Consignment inventory refers to goods a company is holding on behalf of the goods' owner.

_____4.   (LO2) If a sale is made FOB shipping point, inventory belongs to the customer at the moment it leaves the seller's premises.

_____5.   (LO2) Inventory is reported on the income statement as Cost of Goods Sold.

_____6.   (LO3) The four inventory costing methods are alternative ways to split the total dollar amount of goods available for sale between ending inventory and purchases.

_____7.   (LO3) The specific identification method is the best method to use when a company sells large quantities of similar items.

_____8.   (LO3) Most inventory cost flow assumptions are not based on the actual physical flow of the goods on and off the shelves, but on the assumed flow of costs from the balance sheet to the income statement.

_____9.   (LO3) The actual physical flow of goods cannot differ from the cost flow assumption used.

_____10. (LO3) LIFO assumes that the costs for the oldest goods are used first to calculate cost of goods sold and the newer costs are left to calculate ending inventory.

_____11. (LO3) In LIFO each item sold is treated as if its cost were removed in sequence from the top of a stack beginning with the most recent purchases.

_____12. (LO3) The name of the costing method describes how to calculate the costs that remain in ending inventory.

_____13. (LO3) The specific identification method uses the same unit cost to assign dollar amounts to cost of goods sold and ending inventory.

_____14. (LO3) The LIFO, FIFO, and Weighted Average methods differ only in how they allocate the cost of goods available for sale to cost of goods sold and ending inventory.

_____15. (LO3) Generally accepted accounting principles allow managers to choose LIFO one period, FIFO the next, and then back to LIFO, depending on whether unit costs are rising or declining during the period.

_____16. (LO4) When the value of inventory increases to an amount higher than its cost, the LCM rule is followed and the inventory is reported at the replacement cost.

_____17. (LO4) The failure to estimate the market value of inventory appropriately is one of the most common types of financial statement errors.

_____18. (LO5) A higher inventory turnover ratio indicates that inventory moves more quickly from purchase (or production) to the ultimate customer, increasing storage and obsolescence costs.

_____19. (LO5) With inventory turnover rates varying between industries and companies, it's most useful to compare a company's turnover with its own results from prior periods.

_____20. (LO6) GAAP requires that companies using LIFO must report what their inventory balance would have been had they used FIFO, in the notes to the financial statements.

MULTIPLE CHOICE QUESTIONS
Choose the best answer or response by placing the identifying letter in the space provided.

_____1.   (LO1) Which of the following is *not* a primary goal of inventory managers?
     a.   minimize costs of acquiring and carrying inventory
     b.   ensure inventory quality meets customers' expectations and company standards
     c.   maintain a sufficient quantity of inventory to meet customer needs
     d.   all of these are goals of inventory managers

_____2.   (LO1) Which of the following is *not* a cost of acquiring and carrying inventory?
     a.   storage
     b.   gross profit
     c.   obsolescence
     d.   theft

_____3.   (LO2) Which of the following is *not* a type of inventory?
     a.   Finished goods
     b.   FOB destination
     c.   work in process
     d.   all of the above describe inventory

_____4.   (LO2) Inventory costs include all of the following, *except*:
     a.   Purchase price of the goods
     b.   Cost of transporting inventory to the seller's premises
     c.   Cost of transporting inventory to the buyer's premises
     d.   All of the above are inventory costs

_____5.   (LO2) Which of the following correctly depicts the Cost of Goods Sold Equation?
     a. $BI + P - EI = CGS$
     b. $BI - P + EI = CGS$
     c. $EI + P - BI = CGS$
     d. $EI - P + BI = CGS$

Use the following information to answer questions 6, 7, 8, 9, and 10.

Jan 1	Beginning Inventory has	7 units @ $20 each
Apr 13	Purchased	8 units @ $22 each
Aug 31	Purchased	25 units @ $25 each
Dec 28	Sold	30 units

_____6.   (LO3) What is the Cost of Goods Available for Sale?
     a. $250
     b. $691
     c. $735
     d. $941

_____7.   (LO3) What is Cost of Goods Sold using the FIFO costing method?
     a. $250
     b. $691
     c. $735
     d. $941

_____8. (LO3) What is Cost of Goods Sold using the LIFO costing method?
   a. $250
   b. $691
   c. $735
   d. $941

_____9. (LO3) What is Cost of Goods Sold using the Weighted Average costing method? (Round the unit cost to three decimal places)
   a. $669.99
   b. $705.75
   c. $735.00
   d. cannot be determined from the information given

_____10. (LO3) Using the cost of goods sold equation, and assuming the ending inventory is determined to be $240.00, what is the Cost of Goods Sold?
   a. $421
   b. $701
   c. $901
   d. Cannot be determined without more information

_____11. (LO3) Which of the following is *not* a true statement regarding inventory costing methods?
   a. when unit costs are rising, FIFO provides the highest cost of goods sold
   b. when unit costs are rising, FIFO provides the highest net income
   c. when unit costs are falling, LIFO provides the highest ending inventory
   d. when unit costs are rising FIFO provides the highest gross profit

_____12. (LO3) Which of the following is *not* true regarding the inventory costing methods?
   a. Managers are not free to choose LIFO one period, FIFO the next, and then back to LIFO
   b. Companies can use different inventory methods for different product lines of inventory as long as the methods are used consistently over time
   c. the LIFO conformity rule allows you to use different costing methods for financial statement reporting and for income tax reporting
   d. all of the above are true statements regarding inventory costing methods

_____13. (LO4) Why might inventory prices fall below its recorded cost?
   a. the inventory can be easily replaced by identical goods at a lower cost
   b. innovations in technology have made the inventory item less expensive to produce
   c. the inventory has become damaged
   d. all of the above represent reasons why inventory might fall below its recorded cost

_____14. (LO4) Klink Company has 2,000 units of Charm-Glo on hand at the end of the accounting period. The Charm-Glo cost Klink $85 each. Due to obsolescence, the replacement price of Charm-Glo has fallen to $75 each. What amount will be used in the entry to write-down the inventory?
   a. $20,000
   b. $150,000
   c. $170,000
   d. GAAP does not allow inventory write-downs because it violates the cost principle

_____15. Which of the following are true statements regarding LCM?
   a. one of the most common types of financial statement errors is to estimate the market value of inventories incorrectly
   b. it ensures that inventories are always reported at what they are worth
   c. replacement cost must be used when inventories fall below or rise above original cost
   d. market value can fall below cost when an item can be easily replaced by identical goods at a higher cost

_____16. (LO5) Which of the following are *not* true statements regarding inventory turnover?
  a. the Days to Sell provides the same information as the inventory turnover, but in an easier to understand format
  b. a higher ratio could lead to investment income because funds will be freed up for other purposes
  c. a sudden decline indicates that sales have improved and the product line is being properly marketed
  d. more efficient purchasing and production will cause this ratio to be higher

Use the following information to answer questions 17, and 18.	
Jan 1 Inventory	$62,000
Dec 31 Inventory	$73,000
Cost of Goods Sold	$330,000
Net Sales	$700,000

_____17. (LO5) What is the inventory turnover for this company?
  a. 4.89 times
  b. 7.05 times
  c. 8.31 times
  d. none of the above is the correct inventory turnover amount

_____18. (LO5) What is the average Days to Sell?
  a. 43.92 days
  b. 51.77 days
  c. 74.64 days
  d. none of the above is the correct days to sell amount

_____19. (LO6) Which of the following is *not* a true statement regarding inventory costing methods?
  a. FIFO will give the same results under a periodic or perpetual inventory system
  b. the inventory turnover ratio and the days to sell are affected by the cost flow assumption used
  c. companies that choose to use the FIFO costing method must report what their inventory balance would have been using LIFO
  d. all of the above are true statements

_____20. (LO6) Which of the following is *not* true regarding the impact of inventory costing methods?
  a. for an older established business using LIFO, the cost of ending inventory reported on the balance sheet can be much higher when valued under FIFO
  b. it is best to compare a company only to its own results from prior periods or to another company that uses the same cost flow assumption
  c. the inventory costing method used has no impact on the inventory turnover or days to sell calculations
  d. all of the above are true statements

EXERCISES
Record your answer to each exercise in the space provided. Show your work.

Exercise 7-1. Solving for Unknown Values Using the Cost of Goods Sold Equation (LO2)
Complete the following table by using the Cost of Goods Sold equation to solve for the missing value in each case.

	Case 1	Case 2	Case 3	Case 4
Beginning Inventory	$48,000	?	45,000	10,000
Purchases	152,000	801,000	216,000	?
Ending Inventory	39,000	23,000	?	8,000
Cost of Goods Sold	?	900,000	210,000	74,100

Exercise 7-2. Matching Financial Statement Effects to Inventory Costing Methods (LO3)
Complete the following table by indicating whether the FIFO or LIFO inventory costing method would lead to the effects noted in the rows, for each of the circumstances described in the columns.

	1. Rising Costs	2. Declining Costs
a. Highest Ending Inventory		
b. Highest Cost of Goods Sold		
c. Highest Net Income		
d. Lowest Ending Inventory		
e. Lowest Cost of Goods Sold		
f. Lowest Gross Profit		

Exercise 7-3. Inferring Missing Amounts Based on Income Statement Relationships. (LO3)
Supply the missing dollar amounts for the 2008 income statement of Clark Retailers for each of the following independent cases: (HINT: Use the Cost of Goods Sold Equation; and the Income Statement format when appropriate.

Case	Sales Revenue	Begin. Invent.	Purchases	Total Available	Cost of Ending Inventory	Cost of Goods Sold	Gross Profit	Oper. Expen.	Oper. Income (or Loss)
A	900	?	700	850	?	?	300	?	(100)
B	840	50	500	?	125	?	?	140	?
C	675	210	480	?	?	?	?	110	75
D	1,490	?	620	?	340	?	?	300	473
E	?	300	?	?	250	750	450	350	?

Exercise 7-4. Analyzing and Interpreting the Financial Statement Effects of FIFO, LIFO, and Weighted Average. (LO3)
Solar Company uses a periodic inventory system. At the end of the annual accounting period, December 31, 2009, the accounting records provided the following information:

Transactions	Units	Unit Cost
Inventory, December 31, 2008	10,800	$20
For the Year 2009:		
Purchase, March 15	18,000	$24
Purchase, September 20	34,200	$26
Sale, June 10 (sold for $52 per unit)	22,000	
Sale, October 2, (sold for $56 per unit)	33,000	
Operating Expenses (excluding income tax expense), $1,500,000		

Required:
1. Compute the cost of goods sold under (a) FIFO; (b) LIFO, and (c) Weighted Average

FIFO	LIFO	Weighted Average

2. Prepare an income statement that shows 2009 amounts for the FIFO method in one column, the LIFO method in another column, and the weighted average method in a final column. Include the following line-items in the income statement: sales, cost of goods sold, gross profit, operating expenses, and operating income.

Solar Company Income Statement For the Year Ended December 31, 2009	FIFO	LIFO	Weighted Average
Sales			
Cost of Goods Sold			
Gross Profit			
Operating Expenses			
Operating Income			

3. Compare the operating income and the ending inventory amounts that would be reported under the three methods. Explain the similarities and differences.

	FIFO	LIFO	Weighted Average
Ending Inventory			
Operating Income			

Calculations:

Exercise 7-5. Choosing LIFO vs. FIFO When Costs are Rising and Falling. (LO3)
Complete the following table using the information that follows the table.

	Costs Rising				Costs Falling			
	Situation A FIFO		Situation B LIFO		Situation C FIFO		Situation D LIFO	
Sales Revenue		$15,000		$15,000		$15,000		$15,000
Beginning Inventory	$2,000		$		$		$	
Purchases	8,400							
Goods available for sale	10,400							
Ending inventory	2,400							
Cost of goods sold		8,000						
Gross profit		7,000						
Operating expenses		4,000		4,000		4,000		4,000
Operating income		3,000						
Income tax expense (25%)		750						
Net income		$ 2,250		$		$		$

Required:
1. Complete the previous table for situations A – D using the following assumptions, Situation A has been completed for you as an example:

	Situation A and Situation B	Situation C and Situation D
Beginning Inventory	500 units @ $4.00 = $2,000	500 units @$6.00 = $3,000
Purchases	1,400 units @ $6.00 = $8,400	1,400 units @ $4.00 = $5,600
Total	10,400	8,600

Calculations:

Study Guide, Chapter 7

2. Describe the relative effects on operating income as demonstrated by requirement 1 when costs are rising and when costs are falling.

3. Describe the relative effects on income taxes for each situation

4. Would you recommend FIFO or LIFO? Explain.

Exercise 7-6. Reporting Inventory at the Lower of Cost or Market (LO4)
Rabbitson Appliances is preparing the annual financial statements dated December 31, 2008. Ending inventory information about the five major items stocked for regular sale follows:

Item	Ending Inventory, 2008		
	Quantity On hand	Unit Cost When Acquired (FIFO)	Replacement Cost (Market) at Year-End
Daring Dishwashers	225	$100	$110
Fabulous Freezers	320	$75	$80
Raring Refrigerators	40	$300	$285
Stupendous Stoves	65	$150	$145
Wonderful Washers	500	$275	$250

Required:
Part A.
Using the following table, compute the amount that should be reported for the 2008 ending inventory using the LCM rule applied to each item.

Item	Quantity	Cost per Item	Market per Item	LCM per item	Total LCM
Daring Dishwashers					
Fabulous Freezers					
Raring Refrigerators					
Stupendous Stoves					
Wonderful Washers					
Total					

Part B.
What is the journal entry to write-down the inventory?

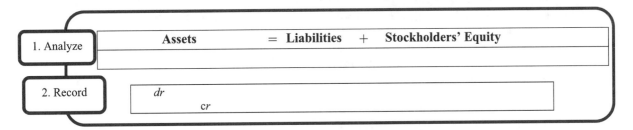

Exercise 7-7. Analyzing and Interpreting the Inventory Turnover Ratio and Days to Sell (LO5)
Sirius Industries, Inc. produces recliners. It reported the following amounts in its financial statements.

	2009	2008	2007
Net Sales Revenue	$26,000,000	$18,000,000	$12,000,000
Cost of Goods Sold	18,500,000	12,000,000	6,700,000
Average Inventory	1,900,000	1,500,000	1,200,000

Required:
1. Determine the inventory turnover ratio and average days to sell inventory for 2009, 2008, and 2007.

2. Comment on any trends, and compare the effectiveness of inventory managers at Sirius to inventory managers at its main competitor, Xenon, where inventory turns over 6.21 times per year (58.78 days to sell). Both companies use the FIFO inventory costing method.

SOLUTIONS TO SELF-TEST QUESTIONS AND EXERCISES

MATCHING
1.

E	Cost of Goods Sold Equation	D	Inventory
I	Days to Sell	B	Inventory Turnover
C	First-in, First-out (FIFO)	H	Last-in, First out (LIFO)
K	FOB Destination	F	Lower of Cost or Market (LCM)
A	FOB Shipping Point	G	Specific Identification
J	Goods Available for Sale	L	Weighted Average Cost

TRUE-FALSE QUESTIONS
1. T
2. F – Raw materials inventory includes materials that eventually are processed further to produce finished goods.
3. T
4. T
5. F – Inventory is reported on the balance sheet as a current asset.
6. F – They split goods available for sale between ending inventory and cost of goods sold.
7. F – The specific identification method is not realistic when large quantities of similar items are sold.
8. T
9. F – The actual physical flow of goods can differ from the cost flow assumption.
10. F – This is a description of FIFO.
11. T
12. F – The name of the costing method describes the cost of the units that were sold.
13. F – This is a description of the weighted average cost method.
14. T
15. F – The constant switching would make it difficult to compare financial results across periods, so GAAP does not allow this.

16. F – Increases in inventory value are not recorded in the inventory account, LCM only records decreases.
17. T
18. F – This indicates a decrease in storage and obsolescence costs.
19. T
20. T

MULTIPLE CHOICE QUESTIONS

1. D	6. D	11. A	16. C
2. B	7. B	12. C	17. A
3. B	8. C	13. D	18. C
4. C	9. B	14. A	19. C
5. A	10. B	15. A	20. C

EXERCISES

Exercise 7-1. Solving for Unknown Values Using the Cost of Goods Sold Equation (LO2)

	Case 1	Case 2	Case 3	Case 4
Beginning Inventory	$48,000	*122,000*	45,000	10,000
Purchases	152,000	801,000	216,000	*72,100*
Ending Inventory	39,000	23,000	*51,000*	8,000
Cost of Goods Sold	*161,000*	900,000	210,000	74,100

Case 1: 48,000 + 152,000 – 39,000 = 161,000   Case 2: 23,000 + 900,000 – 801,000 = 122,000
Case 3: 45,000 + 216,000 – 210,000 = 51,000   Case 4: 8,000 + 74,100 – 10,000 = 72,100

Exercise 7-2. Matching Financial Statement Effects to Inventory Costing Methods (LO3)

	1. Rising Costs	2. Declining Costs
a. Highest Ending Inventory	FIFO	LIFO
b. Highest Cost of Goods Sold	LIFO	FIFO
c. Highest Net Income	FIFO	LIFO
d. Lowest Ending Inventory	LIFO	FIFO
e. Lowest Cost of Goods Sold	FIFO	LIFO
f. Lowest Gross Profit	LIFO	FIFO

Exercise 7-3. Inferring Missing Amounts Based on Income Statement Relationships. (LO3)

Case	Sales Revenue	Begin. Invent.	Purchases	Total Available	Cost of Ending Inventory	Cost of Goods Sold	Gross Profit	Oper. Expen.	Oper. Income (or Loss)
A	900	*150*	700	850	*250*	*600*	300	*400*	(100)
B	840	50	500	*550*	125	*425*	*415*	140	*275*
C	675	210	480	*690*	*200*	490	*185*	110	75
D	1,490	*437*	620	*1,057*	340	*717*	*773*	300	473
E	*1,200*	300	*700*	*1,000*	250	750	450	350	*100*

Case A: (2) 900 – 300 = 600 COS; 300 – (-100) or 300 + 100 = 400 Oper Exp; (1) 850 – 700 = 150 BI;
850 – 600 = 250 EI
Case B: (1) 50 + 500 = 550 (GAFS); 550 – 125 = 425 COS; (2) 840 – 425 = 415 GP; 415 – 140 = 275 Oper. Inc
Case C: (2) 75 + 110 = 185 GP; 675 – 185 = 490 COS; (1) 480 + 210 = 690 GAFS; 690 – 490 = 200 EI
Case D: (2) 473 + 300 = 773 GP; 1,490 – 773 = 717 COS (1) 717 + 340 = 1,057 GAFS; 1,057 – 620 = 437 BI
Case E: (2) 450 – 350 = 100 Oper Inc; 450 + 750 = 1,200 Rev (1) 750 + 250 = 1,000 GAFS; 1,000 – 300 = 700 P

Copyright © 2008, The McGraw-Hill Companies, Inc.
Study Guide, Chapter 7   Page 241

Exercise 7-4. Analyzing and Interpreting the Financial Statement Effects of FIFO, LIFO, and Weighted Average. (LO3)

1. Compute the cost of goods sold under (a) FIFO; (b) LIFO, and (c) Weighted Average

FIFO	LIFO	Weighted Average
(10,800) ($20) = $216,000	(34,200) ($26) = $889,200	(10,800) ($20) = $216,000
(18,000) ($24) = $432,000	(18,000) ($24) = $432,000	(18,000) ($24) = $432,000
(26,200) ($26) = $681,200	(2,800) ($20) = $56,000	(34,200) ($26) = $889,200
Total $1,329,200	Total $1,377,200	63,000 $1,537,200
		$1,537,200/63,000 = $24.40
		(55,000) ($24.40) = $1,342,000

2.

Solar Company Income Statement For the Year Ended December 31, 2009			
	FIFO	**LIFO**	**Weighted Average**
Sales (22,000) ($52) + (33,000) ($56)	$ 2,992,000	$ 2,992,000	$ 2,992,000
Cost of Goods Sold	1,329,200	1,377,200	1,342,000
Gross Profit	1,662,800	1,614,800	1,650,000
Operating Expenses	1,500,000	1,500,000	1,500,000
Operating Income	162,800	114,800	150,000

3.

	FIFO	**LIFO**	**Weighted Average**
Ending Inventory	$208,000	$160,000	$195,200
Operating Income	$ 162,800	$ 114,800	$ 150,000

Calculations: FIFO 1,537,200 – 1,329,200; LIFO 1,537,200 – 1,377,200;
Weighted Average 1,537,200 – 1,342,000

Inventory amounts are higher using FIFO (making the balance sheet *appear* stronger) and a higher operating income (making the company *look* more profitable.) Whereas, the LIFO costing method provides a lower operating income and will, therefore, have a lower income tax expense than the other methods.

All three methods are similar in that ending inventory can be calculated by subtracting the cost of goods sold from goods available for sale. All have the same Sales and Operating Expenses regardless of the inventory method used. All ending inventory figures can be verified by 'proving' the ending inventory using the appropriate costing method.

The methods differ because they assume different flows of costs in determining cost of goods sold. They also differ in that each will provide different cost of goods sold and operating income amounts even though the same inventory items were sold in all three scenarios.

4. Which inventory costing method may be preferred by Solar Company for income tax purposes? Explain.
For tax purposes, Solar Company would be most concerned about lowering their income tax bill, so they would prefer to use the LIFO inventory cost method for tax purposes. This method provides Solar with the lowest operating income of the three methods, and therefore, will have the lowest income tax expense.

Exercise 7-5. Choosing LIFO vs. FIFO When Costs are Rising and Falling. (LO3)

| | Costs Rising | | Costs Falling | |
	Situation A FIFO	Situation B LIFO	Situation C FIFO	Situation D LIFO
Sales Revenue	$15,000	$15,000	$15,000	$15,000
Beginning Inventory	$2,000	$2,000	$3,000	$3,000
Purchases	8,400	8,400	5,600	5,600
Goods available for sale	10,400	10,400	8,600	8,600
Ending inventory	2,400	1,600	1,600	2,400
Cost of goods sold	8,000	8,800	7,000	6,200
Gross profit	7,000	6 200	8,000	8,800
Operating expenses	4,000	4,000	4,000	4,000
Operating income	3,000	2,200	4,000	4,800
Income tax expense (25%)	750	550	1,000	1,200
Net income	$ 2,250	$ 1,650	$ 3,000	$ 3,600

Required:
1. Calculations:

Situation A: FIFO: COS: 500 @ $4 and 1,000 @ $6 = $8,000; EI: $10,400 – $8,000 = $2,400

Situation B: LIFO: COS: 1,400 @ $6 and 100 @ $4 = $8,800; EI: $10,400 – $8,800 = $1,600

Situation C: FIFO: COS: 500 @ $6 and 1,000 @ $4= $7,000; EI: $ 8,600 – $7,000 = $1,600

Situation D: LIFO: COS: 1,400 @ $4 and 100 @ $6 = $6,200; EI: $8,600 – $6,200 = $2,400

2. Describe the relative effects on operating income as demonstrated by requirement 1 when costs are rising and when costs are falling.
When prices are rising FIFO provides a higher profit for the business than LIFO making the company look more profitable. When prices are falling, LIFO provides a higher profit for the business than FIFO. In fact, FIFO looks positively ghastly! It provides the lowest ending inventory and the lowest net income, making both the income statement and the balance appear worse than they are in reality.

3. Describe the relative effects on income taxes for each situation
When prices are rising, LIFO provides the lowest income tax expense, which will please the company. When prices are falling FIFO provides the highest profit with a higher income tax expense as well, which will make the company unhappy.

4. Would you recommend FIFO or LIFO? Explain.
An inventory pricing method should not be chosen on the bases of maximizing profits or minimizing income tax expense. It should be selected because it is the method that most clearly reflects the results of operations and improves the accuracy of financial results.

Exercise 7-6. Reporting Inventory at Lower of Cost of Market (LO4)

Part A.

Item	Quantity	Cost per Item	Market per Item	LCM per item	Total LCM
Daring Dishwashers	225	$100	$110	$100	$22,500
Fabulous Freezers	320	$75	$80	$75	$24,000
Raring Refrigerators	40	$300	$285	$285	$11,400
Stupendous Stoves	65	$150	$145	$145	$9,425
Wonderful Washers	500	$275	$250	$250	$125,000
Total					$192,325

Part B.
The total inventory cost is:
(225) ($100) + (320) ($75) + (40) ($300) + (65) ($150) + (500) ($275) = $205,750
Amount of write-down is: 205,750 – 192,325 = $13,425

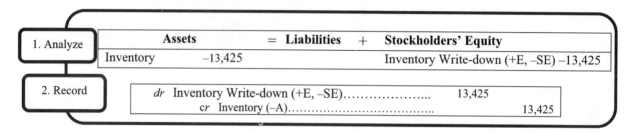

Exercise 7-7. Analyzing and Interpreting the Inventory Turnover Ratio and Days to Sell (LO5)
1. Determine the inventory turnover ratio and average days to sell inventory for 2009, 2008, and 2007.

2004: Turnover: 18,500,000/1,900,000 = 9.74 times   Days to sell: 365/9.74 = 37.5 days
2003: Turnover: 12,000,000/1,500,000 = 8.00 times   Days to sell: 365/8 = 45.63 days
2002: Turnover: 6,700,000/1,200,000=5.58 times   Days to sell: 365/5.58 = 65.41 days

2. Comment on any trends, and compare the effectiveness of inventory managers at Sirius to inventory managers at its main competitor, Xenon, where inventory turns over 6.21 times per year (58.78 days to sell). Both companies use the FIFO inventory costing method.

Compared to its competitor, Sirius seems to be increasing its efficiency and effectiveness of operations for inventory. It may have found a technological advancement that decreases its production time, or has increased its product demand. This means it has also reduced it storage and obsolescence costs in the past three years. They're doing great!

CHAPTER 8
REPORTING AND INTERPRETING RECEIVABLES,
BAD DEBT EXPENSE, AND INTEREST REVENUE

ORGANIZATION OF THE CHAPTER

Understand the business	Study the accounting methods	Evaluate the results	Review the chapter
- Pros and cons of Extending credit	- Accounts receivable and bad debts - Notes receivable and interest revenue	- Receivable turnover analysis	- Demonstration case - Chapter summary - Key terms - Practice material

CHAPTER FOCUS SUGGESTIONS

Review
In Chapter 7 you learned about the different inventory cost flow assumptions, the balance sheet presentation of inventory assuming a lower of cost or market approach (LCM), and an analysis of the speed with which inventories are sold from a company's shelves with the inventory turnover ratio. Now, we turn our attention to another balance sheet item: Accounts Receivable.

Introduction
When a company sells a product to a customer and allows the customer to pay for the product at a later date, the company cannot be certain that they will, in fact, ever collect the amount owed by the customer for these goods. It is a virtual certainty that some customers will not pay. Unfortunately, it is not possible for *any* business to identify who these *bad* customers will be. Accounting recognizes this uncertainty and provides a way to *estimate* the dollar amount of receivables that will not be collected by a business. This way management can report, in a timely manner, estimates of how much money will be collected on customer accounts providing financial statements users a realistic basis for making decisions.

This chapter focuses on what managers must consider when evaluating extending credit to customers, how this decision can affect a company's accounting methods, and the tools users can have to evaluate accounts receivable management practices.

> **Learning Objective 1**
> Describe the trade-offs of extending credit.

UNDERSTAND THE BUSINESS

Pros and Cons of Extending Credit
Many businesses don't sell to consumers; instead they sell to retail businesses. When a business is dealing with another business, it must determine whether or not to extend credit (sell goods to the retailer on account) or not. If credit is not provided to retailers, it is likely that the company will lose business since its competitors are likely extending credit to its business customers. A business has to determine whether the advantage gained from extending the credit is greater than the following disadvantages of extending credit to its customers:

1. *Increased Wage costs.* Since no one will extend credit blindly, a business incurs costs because it will need additional employees to:
   a. Determine whether each customer is creditworthy
   b. Track how much each customer owes, and
   c. Follow-up with each customer to collect the receivable.

2. *Bad debt costs.* No matter how careful a business is in extending credit to customers, eventually some customers will end up only paying a portion of their bill (due to disputes, etc.) or in the worst case, a business will not collect *any* of the amount due from an individual customer. These *Bad Debts* can be a substantial additional cost of extending credit.

3. **Delayed receipt of cash.** A frequently overlooked cost of extending credit is that, even if the full amounts are collected from customers, there is a 30-60 day delay between the time the sale is made and the time the customer actually sends payment. If this delay forces the business to take on a short-term loan collected, there will be interest charges associated with the loan that could have been avoided had the money been available at the time of sale.

Even given all of these risks, most businesses find that the hefty boost in revenues from extending credit outweighs all of these risks. Similar advantages and disadvantages arise when a business is deciding whether to provide customers with notes receivable. A *note receivable* is created when a formal written contract is established outlining the terms by which a company will receive amounts it is owed.

The biggest differences between accounts receivable and notes receivable are that notes receivable:
- Usually charge interest on the outstanding balance of the note.
- Usually have a higher legal status than an account receivable
- However, a new note must be created for every transaction, so they are not used frequently.

Notes tend to be used only when the business takes on a great deal of risk, like:
- Large dollar-value items (like cars) are sold
- Sales are made to customers that have no established credit history or a poor credit history

STUDY THE ACCOUNTING METHODS

> **Learning Objective 2**
> Estimate and report the effects of uncollectible accounts.

Accounts Receivable and Bad Debts
The sad truth about accounts receivable (amounts owed to a business by its customers) is that some of them will never be collected by the company. These unpaid receivables are called Bad Debts. There are two accounting principles that are relevant to this discussion of accounts receivable and Bad Debts.

1. **The Conservatism Principle** – The idea behind this principle is that you should not make your financial statements look 'better' than they really are. So, accounts receivable need to be shown on the balance sheet at the amount that the company actually expects to collect from customers. This amount is called the *net realizable value* of the accounts receivable.
2. **The Matching Principle** – This principle requires that all expenses incurred (including bad debts) in generating the current year's....must be recorded in the same year as the related income it helped generate.

In order to adhere to both of these requirements, we reduce both accounts receivable and net income by the amount of credit sales that are included in receivable and net income this period, but which the company believes it will never collect in cash. In other words, assume that you have credit sales of $200,000 all of which have not yet been collected and are, therefore, also reported as accounts receivable. If you think that you will only collect $196,000 of those receivables, it would be inappropriate to report the entire $200,000 as accounts receivable. Furthermore, one of the costs incurred (expense) in generating that $200,000 of receivables is that *some of them will go bad and not be collected...ever!* So, the related expense must also be reported.

Unfortunately, you don't know *who* will default or *how much* the amount of the default will be. You will certainly find out who will not pay, but it will probably occur in a later accounting period...after you've exhausted all efforts to collect it. However, the matching principle will not allow you to wait until a later period to record the costs of the bad debts on the current period's income statement because that pesky matching principle requires you to record the expense of the bad debts in the *same period as the related sale occurred.*

Huh? You say. How can we reduce receivables and record bad debts for amounts... if we don't even *know* who the bad guys are yet or how much money we will be unable to collect from them? It's like a bad western! Well, accounting has found a way to accomplish all of that too! Generally accepted accounting principles require that you estimate the amount of the bad debts in the period when the sale is recorded. Later, when you know the bad guys and the amounts with certainty, your records can be adjusted. This approach requiring an estimation of bad debts is called the **allowance method.** It is a two-step process, and here's how it works:

1) Record an estimated bad debt expense in the period in which the sale takes place by making an adjusting journal entry at the end of that accounting period.

2) Remove ("write off") specific customer balances in the period they are determined to be uncollectible.

1. Record Estimated Bad Debt Expense

Bad Debt Expense is an estimate of the credit sales made this period that won't ever be collected from customers. The first step in accounting for bad debts is to record this estimate in the accounting system. When credit sales are made, both accounts receivable and Sales Revenue are increased. So, it makes sense to offset both of these accounts when some of the credit sales are deemed to be uncollectible. Therefore, both the income statement and the balance sheet will be affected by an entry to record an estimate of bad debts.

At the end of each accounting period, an adjustment is made to reduce accounts receivable (using a contra-asset account called Allowance for doubtful accounts) and reduce net income (using an expense account called Bad Debt Expense.) At the end of 2008, the journal entry to record this estimate is:

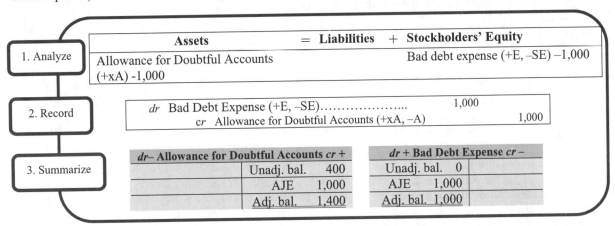

Recall that we can't credit Accounts Receivable because *we don't know who is going to default yet!* So, we credit a *contra-asset* account instead called **Allowance for Doubtful Accounts** (also referred to as Allowance for Bad Debts or Allowance for Uncollectible Accounts.) This account works much like the Accumulated Depreciation account discussed in Chapter 4. In that case, Accumulated Depreciation was subtracted from (netted against) the related asset account (Equipment, Building, etc.) It is also a permanent account, so the adjusted balance in the allowance for doubtful accounts will carry forward from one accounting period to the next. On the other hand, bad debt expense is a temporary account, and its balance will be zeroed out at the end of the accounting period. Therefore, as illustrated in the previous T-accounts, the allowance account and bad debt expense will rarely have the same account balance.

The Allowance for Doubtful Accounts is also subtracted from its related asset account: Accounts Receivable. The result of this subtraction is called **Net Accounts Receivable** and it represents the amount of the receivables the company actually expects to collect (net realizable value). Because of this 'new' terminology, you may have difficulty figuring out whether *Accounts Receivable* is referring to the amount *before* the subtraction or the amount *after* the subtraction. Therefore, we will refer to the amount *before* the subtraction as **Gross Accounts Receivable** and the amount *after* the subtraction as **Net Accounts Receivable,** like this:

Balance Sheet Presentation	2008	Explanation
Gross accounts receivable	$ 28,000	Total amount owed to the company
Less: Allowance for doubtful accounts	(1,400)	Amount unlikely to be collected
Net accounts receivable	26,600	Amount likely to be collected (net realizable value)

2. Remove ("Write-off") Specific Customer Balances

A company will work diligently to collect amounts owed to them. But, ultimately someone will fail to pay. When it has been determined that a customer will simply never pay, the customer's account receivable must be removed from the company's books. Since at least *one* of the 'bad' customers has been identified, they can also be removed from the allowance account as well. (Remember that the allowance account was used because, at the time the Bad Debts Expense entry was made the company *didn't know who* would default.) Now, the company *knows* at least one of the customers who has defaulted. The removal of this customer from the accounts receivable of the business is referred to as a **Write-off.** It should be noted that the following entry is the *worst way to remove a receivable from the books.* When a company makes this entry, it can ruin someone's credit because this type of information is typically sent to credit reporting agencies.

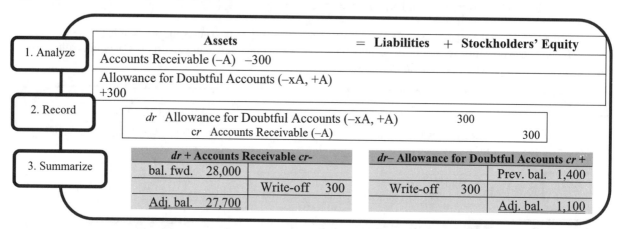

Note a couple of things here: (1) this entry does not affect the income statement at all. The estimated bad debts were recorded in the period that the corresponding sale was made. (2) the entry merely transferred the bad debt from one balance sheet account to another. Notice the following 'before' the write-off and 'after' the write-off presentations on the following balance sheet. The individual components of Net Accounts Receivable have been reduced by the $300. However, the Net Accounts Receivable was $26,600 before the write-off and it is *still* $26,600 after the write-off. Why? Because the Allowance for doubtful accounts was our 'estimate' of the total dollars we expected to go bad and, at the time of the entry, we *didn't know who those customers would be.*

Balance Sheet Presentation-Before	2008	Balance Sheet Presentation-After	2008
Gross accounts receivable	$28,000	Gross accounts receivable	$ 27,700
Less: Allowance for doubtful accounts	(1,400)	Less: Allowance for doubtful accounts	(1,100)
Net accounts receivable	26,600	Net accounts receivable	26,600

Once an individual bad debt is identified, the actual gross accounts receivable can be reduced, and this individual is no longer part of the 'allowance' account because the Allowance for doubtful accounts represents the *unidentified* amounts the company expects it will not collect. Since this individual and the amount owed have been identified, we can remove them from the Allowance for Doubtful Accounts balance, and remove the specific Account Receivable from the books. Note how the Net Accounts Receivable is reported both *before* the write-off and *after* the write-off. This is similar to transferring $300 from checking to savings. It doesn't change the *value* of your assets, only where you've placed them.

Summary of the Allowance Method

The following table summarizes the steps required when using the Allowance Method of accounting for bad debts, the entries needed for each step, when the entries are made, and the effect of the entries on the financial statements.

Step:	Timing:	Journal Entry:	Financial Statement Effects:	

			Balance Sheet	Income Statement
. Record adjustment for estimated bad debts	End of the period in which sales are made	*dr* Bad Debt Expense (+E,-SE) *cr* Allowance for Doubtful Accounts (+xA, -A)	Gross accounts receivable — *no effect* Less: Allowance — increase Net accounts receivable — decrease	Revenues — *no effect* Expenses 　Bad Debt Expense — increase Net Income — decrease
. Identify and write off actual bad debts	As accounts are determined uncollectible	*dr* Allowance for Doubtful Accounts (-xA, +A) *cr* Accounts Receivable (-A)	Gross accounts receivable — decrease Less: Allowance — decrease Net accounts receivable — *no effect*	Revenues — *no effect* Expenses 　Bad Debt Expense — *no effect* Net Income — *no effect*

Estimating Bad Debts

As indicated earlier, at the end of an accounting period an adjusting journal entry is made to record an estimate of bad debts for the current period. There are two methods businesses use to determine the *dollar amount* of the estimate for this entry: (1) Aging of accounts receivable method, or (2) Percentage of credit sales method. Both are acceptable for GAAP, but the aging of accounts receivable method is the most common. The aging method is presented here and the percentage method will is included as Chapter Supplement A.

Aging of Accounts Receivable Method. This approach, often referred to as the Balance Sheet approach (because the estimate is based on a balance sheet account – Accounts Receivable) is the most commonly used approach in business. It basically assumes that the longer an uncollected accounts receivable has been on the books, the more likely it will never be collected. Therefore, the 'older' the account balance, the more likely the company will never collect the balance owed by the customer. So, this method is based on the *age* of the receivables. A receivable that is 60 days overdue has a better chance of being collected than a receivable that is 120 days overdue. Let's continue with our ongoing example and assume that it is now December 31, 2009 (for simplicity, we will assume that none of the account balances have changed since the write-off entry presented earlier.) There are three steps for estimating bad debts using this method:

1) Prepare an aged listing of accounts receivable, with totals for each aging category, like this:

Customer	Total	Number of Days Unpaid			
		0-30	30-60	60-90	Over 90
Abernathy, Inc	$ 456	$ 210	$ 141	$ 63	$ 42
....	....	....	....	....	....
Zengla Corporation	1,200	752	448		
Total Receivables	$ 27,700	$ 16,376	$ 6,270	$ 3,238	$ 1,816
x Estimated bad debt rates		1%	5%	25%	50%
= **Estimated uncollectible**	$ 2,196	$ 164	$ 314	$ 810	$ 908

2) Estimate bad debts loss percentages for each category. Usually, percentages are higher as the age of each category increases.

3) Compute the total estimate by:
   - Multiplying the totals in step 1 by the percentages in step 2, (i.e. $16,376 * 1%; $6,270 * 5%; etc.) and
   - Then summing across all aging categories. The total across all aging categories represents the balance that the Allowance for Doubtful Accounts will need to be adjusted to at the end of the period (i.e. $2,196 = $164 + $314 + $810 + $908)

It is important to point out that the amount just calculated ($2,196) is *not the amount of the adjustment*. Rather, this figure represents the balance that should be in the allowance for doubtful accounts *after the adjustment is made*. Since the allowance for doubtful accounts is a permanent account, it usually has an existing balance that must be considered when determining the amount of the adjustment.

Based on our aging it has been determined that the balance in the account should be $2,196. Since there is already a balance of $1,100 in the account (see T-account balances after the write-off previously) we only need to add an additional $1,096 ($2,196 – $1,100) to bring the account to the calculated amount. Therefore, the adjusting journal entry is:

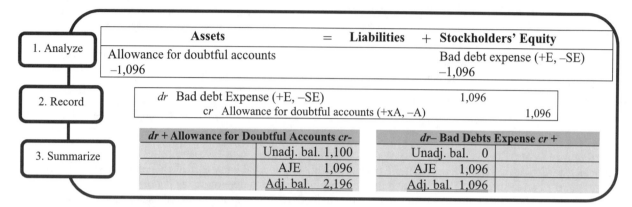

Notice that after this entry is posted, the Bad Debts Expense of $1,096 will be reported on the income statement and the Allowance for Doubtful Accounts will have a balance of $2,196 as calculated earlier – *not the amount of the adjusting journal entry*. The amount recorded as Bad Debt Expense will be whatever amount is required to make the allowance account have the calculated balance of $2,196.

Though the allowance for doubtful accounts normally has a credit balance, at times, it may have a debit balance just prior to recording the adjusting journal entry. This can occur when the company had a larger amount of write-offs during the period, than were estimated in the allowance for doubtful accounts. In other words, our estimate was too small to accommodate all of the bad debts written off…resulting in a debit balance in the allowance for doubtful accounts. To determine the dollar amount of the adjustment in this situation, calculate the amount needed in the allowance account (just as before). But, instead of subtracting this from the balance in the allowance account, you will need to add it.

For example, assume the adjusted balance in the allowance for doubtful accounts had been a debit balance of $200 (instead of the credit balance of $1,100 in the previous example). The amount required in the allowance for doubtful accounts has not changed ($2,196). However, in order to have this amount in the allowance account after the adjustment has been made, the adjustment must be $2,396 ($2,196 + $200), as the following example shows:

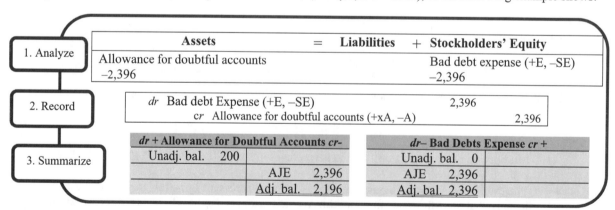

Other Issues

Revising Estimates
As illustrated in the previous situation, sometimes an estimate for bad debts is not the same as the amount of bad debts actually written off in a period. In practice, we do not attempt to revise the original estimate that was made.

Instead, we simply play 'catch-up' at the end of the current accounting period. This is illustrated by the last example. The estimate for 2008 was too low, causing a debit balance in the allowance for doubtful accounts at the end of 2008. But, no changes were made to the 2008 estimate. Instead, when the 2009 adjustment is made, it is for a larger amount to accommodate the additional write-offs that weren't originally estimated for 2008.

Account Recoveries

Sometimes, after you've written off a bad debt as uncollectible, the unimaginable happens. The customer pays the amount they owe you – let's assume it is $100! When a customer pays you an amount that was previously written off as a bad debt, it is called a *recovery*. To record this event, there are two journal entries required. First, since the customer was written off in a manner that adversely affected their credit, this 'bad way' of removing the accounts receivable from the books must be reversed. The effect of this is to reinstate the receivable on your books, so that the account receivable can be removed the 'nice' way – with a debit to Cash. These two entries are shown in the following illustration.

dr Accounts Receivable (+A) 100	
cr Allowance for doubtful accounts (+xA, –A)	100
dr Cash (+A) 100	
cr Accounts Receivable (–A)	100

Alternative Methods

Some small businesses use a method called the Direct Write-off Method. This method is *not allowed* under GAAP because it violates both the matching and conservatism principles. However, it *is* acceptable for tax purposes according to the Internal Revenue Service (IRS.) Because of its potential use, this method is discussed in Supplement B of this Chapter.

> **Learning Objective 3**
> Compute and report interest on notes receivable.

Notes Receivable and Interest Revenue

Accounting for notes receivable and accounts receivable are similar except that notes receivable charge interest from the day they are created, whereas interest on accounts receivable is usually only charged when the account is overdue.

Calculating Interest

To calculate interest on a note, you need to know three things: (1) the principal of the note which is simply the amount of the note, (2) the interest rate charged on the note, and (3) the time period covered in the interest calculation. It is calculated as:

$$\text{Interest} = \text{Principal} * \text{Rate} * \text{Time}$$

The interest rate is always specified in annual terms (i.e. 10% annually) even when the note is less than one year in length. So, when the time period being calculated is less than one year, the Time portion of the calculation must be adjusted. For example, if the interest is calculated for 2 months, the 'time' would be calculated as 2/12 (2 months out of 12 months). This ensures that the interest calculated only covers two months out of the entire year that the rate is based on. Assume a business has a note receivable for $20,000 with an interest rate of 8% annually, and the note is due in 9 months. The note is dated October 1, 2009.

To calculate the total interest on this note (through June of 2010) we multiply all three figures together: $20,000 * 8% * 9/12 = $1,200. However, the interest on a note is usually only paid once or twice per year. That means that as the month's go by, interest on the note needs to be accrued in accordance with the revenue recognition principle. The accrual is usually done on the last day of the accounting period. This situation is depicted in the following time line:

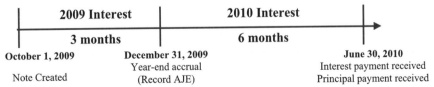

2009 Interest	2010 Interest
3 months	6 months
October 1, 2009	**June 30, 2010**
Note Created	Interest payment received Principal payment received

(December 31, 2009 — Year-end accrual (Record AJE))

Sometimes it can be difficult to understand the difference between the time period included in the accrual of interest and the time period covered by the payment of interest. So, let's look carefully at that time line. On December 31, 2009, adjusting entries are made to record items that have occurred, but haven't been recorded yet. On that Date, three months of interest have accrued on the note (October, November, and December). Though the interest won't be collected until June 30, 2010, the revenue principle requires that we recognize this income in the period in which it was earned (2009.) Therefore, three months of interest are earned in 2009 must be recorded as income in 2009.

This example illustrates the four key events that occur with any note: (1) establishing the note; (2) accruing interest earned but not received; (3) recording interest payments received; and (4) recording principal payments received. These will be individually covered next….stay tuned!

1. Establishing a Note Receivable

Using the example just illustrated, let's prepare the entry to record the note (assuming it was created in exchange for cash), the following entry would be made.

1. Analyze	Assets	= Liabilities	+	Stockholders' Equity
	Cash −20,000			
	Notes Receivable +20,000			

2. Record		
	dr Notes Receivable (+A)………………..	20,000	
	cr Cash (−A)…………………………...		20,000

2. Accruing Interest Earned

Revenue must be recorded when it is earned, not when the money is received. This requires a business to report the interest earned on notes receivable as the months go by, *even though no cash has been received.* This will be done as an adjusting entry on December 31, 2009. Even though this is a 9-month note, don't be fooled into calculating the interest for nine months. By December 31, the company hasn't *earned* the entire 9 months—only October, November, and December! So, it has only earned interest for 3 months!

A common mistake made when calculating interest accrued is using the fraction 3/9, (since only 3 of the 9 months have been earned). But, remember the interest rate is an *annual* rate. So, the time element of the interest calculation needs to ensure that only three months interest out of the year is charged on the note. So, to ensure that the time element portion of the calculation covers only three months out of the year, the time portion of the calculation is shown like this: 3/12. The formula would be:

Interest	=	Principal	*	Rate	*	Time
$400	=	$20,000	*	8%	*	3/12

Note that the remaining six months of interest on the note will be reported in 2010, so we don't need to worry about that interest until next year, when the note is collected. Therefore, the adjusting journal entry to record interest earned is:

1. Analyze	Assets	= Liabilities	+	Stockholders' Equity
	Interest Receivable +400			Interest Revenue (+R, +SE) +400

2. Record		
	dr Interest Receivable (+A………………….	400	
	cr Interest Revenue (+R, +SE)…………….		400

3. Recording Interest Received

On June 30, 2010, two things happen:

(1) Interest for the *entire 9 months* is received and
(2) Principle of the note is also received.

This means two separate entries need to be made in order to record both of these events. Here's the first entry:

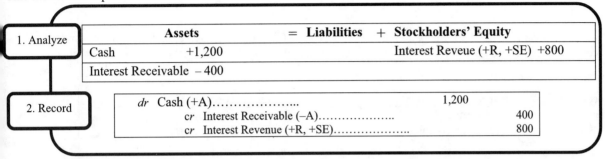

1. Analyze	Assets		= Liabilities	+ Stockholders' Equity
	Cash	+1,200		Interest Reveue (+R, +SE) +800
	Interest Receivable	– 400		

2. Record

```
dr  Cash (+A)......................              1,200
        cr  Interest Receivable (–A)...................          400
        cr  Interest Revenue (+R, +SE)...................         800
```

This entry requires a bit of explanation. The entry made on December 31, 2009 did not include the *receipt of any cash* for the interest accrued at that time! It only recorded how much interest had actually been *earned* in 2009 for October, November, and December. Since this was a 9-month note and 3-months of it had already been *earned and recorded* as of December 31, the remaining 6-months (January, February, March, April, May, and June) of the 9-month note need to be recorded as Revenue in 2010. Furthermore, *none* of the money for the entire 9-month period has been received by the company yet. So, to calculate the amount of Cash the company is actually going to receive in interest on June 30, the following interest calculation is made:

Interest	=	Principal	*	Rate	*	Time
$1,200	=	$20,000	*	8%	*	9/12

However, 3 months of the interest has already been accrued in Interest Receivable. Since the company is now receiving it, we can eliminate the accrued amount in the account ($400). The remaining 6 months of interest must be reported as interest revenue for the current year in the amount of $800 as follows:

Interest	=	Principal	*	Rate	*	Time
$800	=	$20,000	*	8%	*	6/12

4. Recording Principal Received

All of your efforts in the previous entry probably made you forget that *two entries need to be made at the time the note matures.* Relax! The second entry is much easier. It simply records the receipt of the principal and elimination of the Notes Receivable on the books.

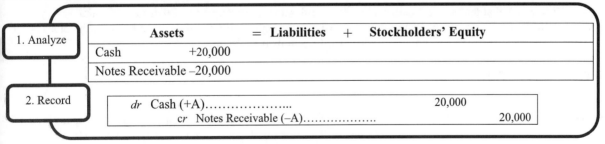

1. Analyze	Assets		= Liabilities	+	Stockholders' Equity
	Cash	+20,000			
	Notes Receivable	–20,000			

2. Record

```
dr  Cash (+A)......................              20,000
        cr  Notes Receivable (–A)...................          20,000
```

Accounting for Uncollectible Notes

Sometimes, customers fail to pay the Notes Receivable (and interest) to the business. When the collection of a note receivable and its corresponding interest is in doubt, an allowance account should be established for the notes receivable.

EVALUATE THE RESULTS

Learning Objective 4
Compute and interpret the
receivables turnover ratio.

Receivables Turnover Analysis

Financial statement users need to know how well a business is managing its credit-granting and collection activities. One tool used to evaluate these activities is called a ***Receivables Turnover Ratio***. Accounts Receivable increases when a business sells goods on account and decreases as collections are made on those accounts. The number of times this process of selling and collecting occurs during a period (on average) is measured by the receivables turnover.

To illustrate, assume a company has net sales of $100,000. January 1 Receivables are $5,000 and December 31 receivables are $6,000. The ratio would be calculated as follows:

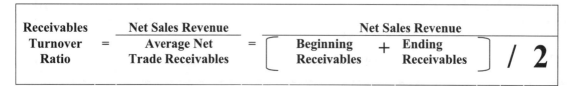

Average Receivables are: $5,500 = (5,000 + 6,000) / 2
Therefore, the receivables turnover is: 18.18 = $100,000 / 5,500

The higher this ratio, the more quickly the company collects its receivables and the more cash it has available for other things. If this ratio is low, it may mean that collections are sluggish or that the company is too liberal in granting credit to customers. You should also keep in mind topics covered previously in the chapter, bad debts. Analysts watch the accounts receivable turnover closely because a sudden decrease in the ratio may indicate that:

- A company is recording sales that they expect will likely be returned later by the customer
- The company is lengthening credit period to entice customers to buy as much as possible (a practice known as *channel stuffing*)

The accounts receivable turnover ratio calculated earlier is 18.18. Is this good? Well, most people can't tell if a receivables turnover ratio of 18.18 is good or not in terms of the appropriate management of receivables. A more logical evaluation can be made based on *how many days, on average, did it take for the business to collect from its customers.* This is exactly what is measured by the ***Days to Collect.*** This is calculated as follows:

$$\text{Days to Collect} = \frac{365}{\text{Receivables Turnover Ratio}}$$

In our example, the days to collect would be: 20.08 = 365 / 18.18

This means that the business collected its receivables approximately every 20 days. This is more understandable to most people than 18.18 times per year. Knowing the number of days, on average, that it takes for a business to collect receivables is more useful to management than 18.18 times.

Comparison to Benchmarks

Credit Terms

One reason that the Days to Collect is such a useful measurement is that you can compare it to the company's stated collections policy. For instance, if the credit terms for the company illustrated in this analysis were 2/10, n/30, this would be a great turnover. The Days to Collect was approximately every 20 days. Based on the credit terms, customers have the full 30 days to pay, but the 20 days to collect indicates that some of its customers are paying *sooner than* every 30 days. This indicates that some customers are taking advantage of the discount. This is good!!! On the other hand, if the company's credit terms are n/10, this is horrible, customers aren't paying on time!

Other Companies

Because there is such a big range in ratios between industries, it is difficult to compare the results of your company to that of other companies. Therefore, you should compare a company's Accounts Receivable Turnover Ratio and Days to Collect with other companies in the same industry or with that company's results from previous periods.

Speeding Up Collections

Factoring Receivables

Collection of receivable is critical for generating the cash needed to pay for a company's business activities. When collecting from customers becomes difficult, the company's collections department starts calling customers incessantly for payment. Unfortunately, this method of speeding up collections has some drawbacks: (1) it is expensive and time-consuming for the business, and (2) it can irritate customers to the point that they will take their business elsewhere.

A more attractive alternative is for the company to *sell* the receivables to another business (called a factor.) The specifics of this *factoring* arrangement are:
- You sell your outstanding receivables to the factor (for a fee)
- The factor takes over all of the collections efforts on the receivables sold
- The factor gives you the use of your money now (less their fee)
- Your employees are free to perform other duties.

The following disadvantages may result from factoring arrangements:
- Factoring may send a negative message because it is often seen as a last resort for collecting accounts.
- The factoring fee can be very high – as much as 3% of the receivables sold.

Reporting the factoring fee depends on the frequency with which a company factors its receivables. If a company factors its receivables frequently, the fee is reported on the income statement as a selling expense. If the company factors its receivable infrequently, the fee is reported as part of the company's non-operating section of the income statement as Other Expense.

Credit Card Sales

Another method of speeding up the collection of cash from sales is to accept national credit cards (Visa, MasterCard, American Express, and Discover) as a method for customers to pay for goods. The greatest advantage of accepting credit cards as payment for sales is that credit card receipts can be deposited directly into a company's bank account – just like cash! The acceptance of credit cards also reduces the amount of bad debts suffered by a company because these sales are considered cash in the bank.

However, there are some costs associated with the acceptance of credit cards: (1) Credit card companies charge a fee to each business that accepts the card from customers as payment for goods and services. The fee is about 3% of the total sales price. For some companies, 3% may be a small price to pay for the advantages received in return; for others, the disadvantages may exceed the benefits derived from the arrangement. Each company must make this decision based on its own situation.

SUPPLEMENT A – PERCENTAGE OF CREDIT SALES METHOD

The percentage of credit sales method is another method used for estimating bad debts. It determines the dollar amount of the entry based by multiplying the current year's credit sales times the historical percentage of the company's bad debt losses. Since the adjustment is based on Sales, and Sales are reported on the income statement, this method is often referred to as the *Income Statement Approach*.

Assuming that the company has $100,000 of net credit sales and an historical Bad Debt Rate of 1%, the amount of the adjusting journal entry to record the estimate of bad debts would be determined as follows:

Dollar amount of Bad Debt Expense this Year	=	Credit Sales this Year	*	Historical Bad Debt Rate
$1,000	=	$100,000	*	1%

The accounts debited and credited in this entry are identical to those debited and credited when the aging of accounts receivable method is used. The only things that differ between the two are:

1. The method used to calculate the dollar amount of the adjusting journal entry.
2. The amount used to record the adjusting journal entry
3. The existing balance in the Allowance for Doubtful Accounts is completed ignored for this method.

Based on this, the entry to record the estimate of bad debts would be:

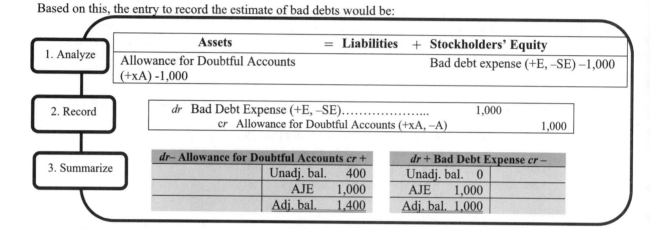

| | 1. Analyze | **Assets** | **= Liabilities** | **+ Stockholders' Equity** |

Assets: Allowance for Doubtful Accounts (+xA) -1,000

Stockholders' Equity: Bad debt expense (+E, –SE) –1,000

2. Record

| *dr* Bad Debt Expense (+E, –SE)……………….. | 1,000 | |
| *cr* Allowance for Doubtful Accounts (+xA, –A) | | 1,000 |

3. Summarize

dr– Allowance for Doubtful Accounts *cr* +			*dr* + Bad Debt Expense *cr* –	
	Unadj. bal.	400	Unadj. bal. 0	
	AJE	1,000	AJE 1,000	
	Adj. bal.	1,400	Adj. bal. 1,000	

SUPPLEMENT B – DIRECT WRITE-OFF METHOD

There is an alternative to account for bad debts called the Direct Write-off method. This method is allowed for tax purposes but not for financial reporting purposes because it doesn't follow GAAP. The reason the direct write-off is not considered GAAP is because it disregards both the conservatism and matching principles.

It fails to follow the conservatism principle because no estimates of bad debts are made, *all* receivables are reported as being collectible at the end of the accounting period (no Allowance for Doubtful Accounts). Assuming that all customers will pay the balances due to the business is an unrealistic and overly optimistic stance.

Regarding its failure to adhere to the matching principle, the Direct Write-off method records Bad Debt Expense when the receivable is deemed to be uncollectible rather than in the period the corresponding sale was actually made. So, the matching principle is violated. Assuming that all efforts to collect a $600 accounts receivable have been exhausted, the company decides to write-off the receivable. Under the direct write-off method, the following entry would be made in the period that the receivable is deemed to be uncollectible:

| *dr* Bad Debts Expense (+E, -SE)……………. …………… 600 | |
| *cr* Accounts Receivable (- A)……….…………… …………… | 600 |

REVIEW THE CHAPTER

Chapter Summary
LO1. Describe the trade-offs of extending credit
- ❖ By extending credit to customers, a company is likely to attract a greater number of customers willing to buy from it.
- ❖ The additional costs of extending credit include:
  - o Increased wage costs
  - o Bad debt costs
  - o Delayed receipt of cash

LO2. Estimate and report the effects of uncollectible accounts

- ❖ Under generally accepted accounting principles, companies must use the allowance method to account for uncollectibles. This method involves the following steps:
    1. Estimate and record uncollectibles with an end-of-period adjusting journal entry that
        - Increases Bad debts expense (with a debit)
        - Increases the Allowance for doubtful accounts (with a credit)
    2. Identify and write-off specific customer balances in the period they are determined to be uncollectible.
- ❖ The Adjusting Journal Entry in Step 1
    - o Reduces net income
    - o Reduces net accounts receivable.
- ❖ The Write-off in Step 2
    - o Has offsetting effects on
        - Accounts receivable and
        - Allowance for doubtful accounts
    - o Ultimately resulting in no net effect on
        - Accounts Receivable, net or
        - Net Income

LO3. Compute and report interest on notes receivable

- ❖ Interest is calculated by :
    - o Principle * interest rate * time period
        - ❖ Where time period is the number of months out of 12
- ❖ As time passes and interest is earned on the note, accountants must record an adjusting journal entry that accrues the interest revenue that is receivable on the note.

LO4. Compute and interpret the receivables turnover ratio

- ❖ The receivables turnover ratio measures the effectiveness of credit-granting and collection activities.
    - o It reflects how many times Average Trade Receivables were *recorded* and *collected* during the period.
- ❖ Analysts and creditors watch this ratio because a sudden decline in it may mean that
    - o A company is extending payment deadlines in an attempt to prop up lagging sales, or
    - o Is recording sales that later will be returned by customers.

READ AND RECALL QUESTIONS

After you read each section of the chapter, answer the related Read and Recall Questions below.

LEARNING OBJECTIVE

After studying the section of the chapter, you should be able to:

1. Describe the trade-offs of extending credit to customers

Pros and Cons of Extending Credit

What benefits do managers achieve in granting credit to customers?

What additional costs will a business incur by extending credit to its customers? Briefly describe each. Is this trade-off worthwhile? Why or why not?

What is a note receivable? How is it distinguished from an account receivable?

Accounts Receivable and Bad Debts
What is the conservatism principle? How does it apply to accounting for accounts receivable?

How are Net Accounts Receivable calculated? What does this subtotal represent?

How does the matching principle affect the accounting for accounts receivable?

Explain the Allowance Method.   What is the two-step process it follows?

What is Bad Debt Expense? What account is credited when recording Bad Debt Expense? Why? When is this entry made on the company's books?

What type of account is the Allowance for Doubtful Accounts? Will the balance in the Allowance for Doubtful Accounts be the same as the balance in the Bad Debt Expense account? Why or why not?

What is meant by the term *write-off*? Why is this entry made? When is it made? What statement(s) are affected by this entry?

What are the two main steps of the allowance method? Describe the timing of each. List the financial statement effects of each.

Estimating Bad Debts
What are the two methods used to estimate bad debt expense? Briefly describe each.

What is another name for the aging of accounts receivable method? Why is this name used?

How is Bad Debt Expense determined using the **Aging of Accounts Receivable** method? What financial statement accounts does this method focus on?

Is the beginning balance of the Allowance for Doubtful Accounts taken into consideration when determining the amount of Bad Debt Expense under the aging of accounts receivable method? Why or why not?

Describe the three step process for estimating Bad Debt Expense using the aging method.

Other Issues
When estimates of bad debts from a previous period were not correct, how is it handled? Why?

When a bad debt is recovered, how many entries are needed to record the collection? Why?

What method is allowed by the Internal Revenue Service (IRS) for tax purposes in accounting for bad debts? Is this method acceptable for GAAP? Why or why not?

LEARNING OBJECTIVE
After studying the section of the chapter, you should be able to:
3. Compute and report interest on notes receivable

Notes Receivable and Interest Revenue
Define a note receivable.

What is the interest formula?

Why is an adjusting journal entry needed to record interest earned on a note receivable?

What are the four steps required to account for notes receivable?

Ignoring dollar amounts, what account is debited and what account is credited when *establishing a Note Receivable*?

Ignoring dollar amounts, what account is debited and what account is credited when *accruing interest earned* on a Note Receivable?

Ignoring dollar amounts, what account is debited and what accounts are credited when *recording interest received* on a Note Receivable?

Ignoring dollar amounts, what account is debited and what account is credited when *recording principal received* on a Note Receivable?

How are uncollectible notes treated?

LEARNING OBJECTIVE
After studying the section of the chapter, you should be able to:
4. Compute and interpret the receivables turnover ratio

Receivables Turnover Analysis
What is a *receivables turnover*? How is it calculated? Which is better, a high turnover ratio or a low turnover ratio? Explain.

What is *days to collect*? How is it calculated?

Why are credit terms important in analyzing the Accounts Receivable Turnover Ratio and Days to Collect?

Describe what a *factoring* arrangement is. Why would a business consider factoring its accounts receivable?

What are the potential drawbacks of entering into a factoring agreement?

Why might a company choose to accept national credit cards as a means of payment from customers?

FINANCIAL ANALYSIS TOOLS

1. **Receivables Turnover Ratio.** This ratio is used to determine the average number of times that accounts receivable are recorded and collected during the period. The accounts receivable turnover tells you two things:
   - The number of times receivables turn over during the period
   - A higher ratio means a faster turnover.

$$\text{Receivables Turnover Ratio} = \frac{\text{Net Sales Revenue}}{\text{Average Net Trade Receivables}} = \frac{\text{Net Sales Revenue}}{\left[\text{Beginning Receivables} + \text{Ending Receivables}\right] / 2}$$

2. **Days to Collect.** This ratio is used to express the receivables turnover ratio in terms of the number of days needed, on average, to collect receivables. The days to collect tells you two things:
   - Average number of days from a sale on account to its collection
   - A higher number means a longer time to collect.

$$\text{Days to Collect} = \frac{365}{\text{Receivables Turnover Ratio}}$$

HELPFUL STUDY TIP (Skip this tip if your instructor does not cover the percentage of sale method covered in the Chapter Supplement.)

1. Many students have difficulty distinguishing between the Percent of Sales approach and the Aging of Accounts Receivable approach of Estimating Bad Debts using the allowance method. Specifically, it is difficult to determine when you're supposed to consider the current balance in the Allowance for doubtful accounts and when you aren't. So, let's tackle this problem! First, let's take a look at the entry that is made at the end of the year as an adjusting entry for bad debts. It is:

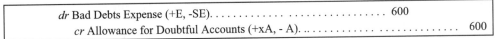

   dr Bad Debts Expense (+E, -SE)............................ 600
        cr Allowance for Doubtful Accounts (+xA, - A)............................ 600

   Notice that the entry affects both Expenses (an *income* statement) accounts and, ultimately, *net* accounts receivable (a *balance sheet*) account. When it comes to making this entry, you have two different accountants trying to prove their way is best. There are the *Income Statement* accountants who believe that the only thing that matters in this life is: The Bottom Line... Net Income...The Matching Principle. As far as they are concerned nothing on the balance sheet matters (Accounts Receivable? Who cares? Allowance for Doubtful Accounts? Not a concern!)

   What *the income statement* folks believe is that the only important numbers in the world are *Revenues, Expenses, and Net Income*. So, in terms of the adjusting entry, they only care about the Bad Debt *Expense* portion of the entry and (more importantly) *don't care* about the effect the entry might have on *the balance sheet accounts—like* the Allowance for Doubtful Accounts. Therefore, this method *completely and totally ignores any balance currently in the Allowance for Doubtful Accounts because it's on the balance sheet.* All that matters is that the Bad Debt Expense is correctly matched against current year Sales (which conveniently is *exactly* what the Percent of Sales approach is based on!!!

   Then we've got the other side of the fence, the *Balance Sheet* accountants believe that the only thing that matters in this life is: Net Accounts Receivables – the actual amount of receivables assumed to be collectible.

Who cares about Revenue and Expense for the *whole reporting period?* The real issue is simply this: The Balance Sheet accountants don't care how many sales occurred, or the percentage of those sales that may go bad because the fact is: All of these sales have been collected already *except* the amounts currently in Accounts Receivable!!! If there are $300,000 in Accounts Receivable at the end of the year, the most a company can possibly *fail to collect is $300,000!!* Why mess with a percentage of credit sales when most of those sales have already been collected?

Instead, let's focus on the ones that *haven't been collected!* These *uncollected* receivables are the only amounts that can possibly go bad. Determine the amount of *current* receivables that are probably not going to be collected and simply subtract that from the total Accounts Receivables on the books, and you're done! You've determined the amount of receivables that probably won't be collected and have subtracted it from the total receivables leaving *only the receivables you expect to collect,* Net Accounts Receivables.

To ensure that the amount calculated based on an aging of accounts receivable is the *final ending amount in the Allowance for doubtful accounts,* we must take into consideration any amount that is *already in the allowance account* before *the adjusting entry is made.*

It is important to note that *neither a debit balance nor a credit balance remaining in the Allowance account at the end of accounting period is an error!* It simply means that the estimate that was a bit off. Not a mistake, just an estimate slightly off the mark. Think of your budget for groceries. Perhaps you budget $400 per month in groceries (an estimate.) Did you mess up your estimate if one month you spent $415.32 and another month you spent $391.07? Of course not! The $400 was just an estimate and your actual figures are close enough! That's why no one is overly concerned if the Allowance account has a small debit balance or a small credit balance before the adjusting entry is made. Under this method, it is 'adjusted' to the new estimate of losses.

SELF-TEST QUESTIONS AND EXERCISES

MATCHING
1. *Match each of the key terms listed below with the appropriate textbook definition.*

_____	Accounts Receivable	_____	Factoring
_____	Aging of Accounts Receivable Method	_____	Interest Formula
_____	Allowance for Doubtful Accounts	_____	Percentage of Credit Sales Method
_____	Allowance Method	_____	Receivables Turnover Ratio
_____	Bad Debt Expense	_____	Notes Receivable
_____	Days to Collect	_____	Write-off
_____	Direct write-off		

A. A method of accounting that reduces accounts receivable (as well as net income) for an estimate of uncollectible accounts (bad debts).
B. Estimates bad debts based on the historical percentage of sales that lead to bad debt losses (also called the income statement approach.)
C. A non-GAAP alternative to the allowance method of accounting for uncollectible accounts.
D. The act of removing an uncollectible account and its corresponding allowance from the accounting records.
E. A measure of the average number of days from the time a sale is made on account to the time it is collected.
F. Amounts owed to a business by its customers.
G. Principal times the annual interest rate times the time period covered in the interest calculation equal interest calculated.
H. Estimates uncollectible accounts based on the age of each account receivable (also called the balance sheet approach)
I. A promise that requires another party to pay the business according to a written agreement.
J. An arrangement where receivables are sold to another company for immediate cash, net of a fee.

K. A contra-asset that is subtracted from Accounts Receivable on the balance sheet in determining Net Accounts Receivable.
L. The estimated amount of this period's credit sales that customers will fail to pay.
M. It determines the number of times the process of selling and collecting on account occurs during the period.

TRUE-FALSE QUESTIONS

For each of the following, enter a T or F in the blank to indicate whether the statement is true or false.

_____1. (LO1) Businesses who fail to extend credit to customers risk losing sales to their competitors.

_____2. (LO1) Most businesses believe that the costs outweigh the benefits of extending credit to customers.

_____3. (LO1) A Note Receivable is created when a formal written contract is established outlining the terms by which a company will receive amounts it is owed and interest is generally charged on any outstanding balances.

_____4. (LO2) The term "trade" describes receivables that arise when goods or services are sold on credit.

_____5. (LO2) Conservatism requires that a business report Accounts Receivable at the total it would collect if everyone paid rather than the amount it actually expects to collect.

_____6. (LO2) The matching principle requires that the cost of bad debts be recorded in the period that a receivable is determined to be uncollectible.

_____7. (LO2) The Allowance for Doubtful Accounts contains the estimated dollar value of the accounts receivable that will not be collected.

_____8. (LO2) Write-offs do not affect income statement accounts.

_____9. (LO2) There are two methods allowed by GAAP for estimating bad debts: the Direct Write-off method and the Aging of Accounts Receivable method.

_____10. (LO2) The aging of accounts receivable method gets its name from the fact that this method has been used to estimate bad debts for ages and ages.

_____11. (LO2) The allowance for doubtful accounts normally has a credit balance, so if you have a situation where there is a debit balance in this account, you have made an error that must be corrected.

_____12. (LO2) There are two entries required to record the recovery of a bad debt that has been written off.

_____13. (LO2) The direct write-off method is a widely-used GAAP method for recording bad debts.

_____14. (LO3) The formula to calculate interest is Interest = Principal Owed x Interest Rate x Time

_____15. (LO3) When recording interest received, credits may be made to the following accounts: Interest Receivable and Interest Revenue.

_____16. (LO4) The Receivables Turnover Ratio calculates how many times, on average, the process of selling and collecting is repeated over and over during the period.

_____17. (LO4) A high accounts receivable turnover ratio is an indicator that sales are being recorded, that are likely to be returned later.

_____18. (LO4) The Days to Collect measures something completely different than the receivables turnover, therefore both must be calculated for every company.

_____19. (LO4) Credit terms are insignificant and largely ignored when calculating the Days to Collect.

_____20. (LO4) Factoring is a mathematical and efficient tool for accurately determining the dollar amount of bad debts for an accounting period.

MULTIPLE CHOICE QUESTIONS
Choose the best answer or response by placing the identifying letter in the space provided.

_____1.   (LO1) Which of the following is an advantage of extending credit to customers?
   a.   it allows businesses to remain competitive
   b.   delayed receipt of cash
   c.   increased employee costs
   d.   bad debt costs

_____2.   (LO2) The allowance method is justified by the
   a.   revenue principle and matching principle
   b.   revenue principle and cost principle
   c.   matching principle and cost principle
   d.   matching principle and conservatism principle

_____3.   (LO2) Which of the following does *not* describe the allowance method?
   a.   it reduces accounts receivable
   b.   it records an estimate of bad debt expense at the end of the accounting period
   c.   it removes specific customer balances as an adjusting journal entry
   d.   it reduces Net Income

_____4.   (LO2) Accounts receivable are normally reported on the Balance Sheet as
   a.   gross receivables + bad debt expense
   b.   gross receivables – bad debt expense
   c.   gross receivables + allowance for doubtful accounts
   d.   gross receivables – allowance for doubtful accounts

_____5.   (LO2) The entry to write-off actual bad debts has the following effect on the financial statements:
   a.   decrease net accounts receivable and decrease net income
   b.   no effect on net accounts receivable and no effect on net income
   c.   decrease net accounts receivable and no effect on net income
   d.   no effect on net accounts receivable and decrease net income

_____6.   (LO2) Which of the following is a true statement regarding account recoveries after an account receivable has been written off as a bad debt?
   a.   An entry must be made to reverse the write-off
   b.   The recovery does not affect Net Income
   c.   An entry must be made to record the collection
   d.   All of these are true statements regarding account recoveries

_____7.   (LO2) Gage company uses the aging of accounts receivable method for estimating bad debts. Based on the aging, it was determined that estimated bad debts amounted to $1,500. The allowance for doubtful accounts had a $400 debit balance prior to recording the adjusting journal entry. The amount of the adjusting journal entry for Gage Company is:
   a. $400
   b. $1,100
   c. $1,500
   d. $1,900

_____8. (LO2) Which of the following is true regarding the Aging of Accounts Receivable method?
   a. the older an account receivable, the less likely it will be collected
   b. it is not allowed under GAAP for estimating bad debt expense
   c. this method is also known as the income statement approach
   d. it focuses on computing the dollar amount of bad debts expense

_____9. (LO2) Which of the following is *not* a method of estimating bad debts that is allowed by generally accepted accounting principles?
   a. Aging of accounts receivable
   b. Direct write-off method
   c. Percentage of credit sales method
   d. All of these are allowed by GAAP

_____10. (LO2) All of the following are true statements regarding accounts receivable and bad debts, *except*
   a. *Accounts receivable, net* on the balance sheet, is computed by subtracting bad debt expense from accounts receivable.
   b. Write-offs do not affect income statement accounts.
   c. Most managers find that the gross profit to be gained from selling on account to business customers is greater than the additional costs incurred to do so.
   d. All of the above are true statements regarding accounts receivable and bad debts.

_____11. (LO3) Which of the following does *not* describe a note receivable?
   a. each typically outlines the terms by which a company will receive amounts it is owed
   b. it is viewed as providing a stronger legal claim than accounts receivable
   c. the interest rate is always stated in monthly terms
   d. interest accruals are usually required at the end of each accounting period on a note receivable.

_____12. (LO3) A note receivable is received on August 1 that is due in 8 months. When calculating the interest accrual on December 31 for this note, the fraction that should be used for the *time* portion of the calculation is:
   a. 4/8 (or 1/2)
   b. 5/8
   c. 5/12
   d. 8/12

_____13. (LO3) On September 1, 2008, a business received a $25,000 note. The agreement indicated that 10% interest would be paid on the note and the note matured on September 1, 2009. What is the amount of interest that must be reported as earnings on December 31, 2008?
   a. $ 0.00
   b. $ 625.00
   c. $ 833.33
   d. $ 2,500.00

_____14. (LO4) Which of the following *does not* describe the receivables turnover?
   a. when a company sells goods or services on credit, its receivables balance goes up
   b. as it collects from its customers, its receivables balance goes down
   c. a sudden decline may indicate that the company is stuffing the channel
   d. it is also known as Average Days' Sales Uncollected

_____15. (LO4) A business has Net Sales Revenue of $250,000; beginning receivables of $5,000 and ending receivables of $75,000. What is the receivables turnover ratio?
   a. 3.13 times
   b. 3.33 times
   c. 6.25 times
   d. 16.00 times

_____16. (LO4) Refer to question 12. What is the Days to Collect for the company in question 12?
   a. 36.00 days
   b. 43.82 days
   c. 58.40 days
   d. 110.00 days

_____17. (LO4) Refer to questions 12 and 13. Assuming the last three years Days to Collect were 34.2 days, 33.9 days, and 36.0 days, what do the current year figures suggest?
   a. the company has tightened its credit policies
   b. the company may be stuffing the channel
   c. the company has factored receivables
   d. all of the above

_____18. (LO4) All of the following are options when receivables collections are slow *except:*
   a. hound customers for payments
   b. sell the receivables
   c. don't allow the customer on the business premises until payment is received
   d. all of the above are options when receivables collections are slow

_____19. (LO4) Which of the following is *not* true regarding Factoring?
   a. cash is received less a factor fee
   b. the factor has the right to collect the outstanding amounts owed by your customers
   c. the factoring fee must be reported on the income statement as a selling expense
   d. all of the above are true statements regarding factoring

_____20. (Sup) Which of the following does *not* describe the Percentage of Credit Sales method of estimating bad debts?
   a. a historical percentage is multiplied by the balance in the accounts receivable account
   b. it focuses on the income statement accounts
   c. the calculated amount is used for the adjusting journal entry without considering beginning balances in any accounts
   d. all of the above are true statements regarding the percentage of credit sales method

EXERCISES
Record your answer to each exercise in the space provided. Show your work.

Exercise 8-1. Recording Accounts Receivable Transactions using the Allowance Method for Bad Debts; Effects on the Financial Statements (LO2)

Indulged Doggies is an elite dog-sitting service with operations throughout the southwest. The 'customers' under its care are provided walks, meals, companionship, games, and plenty of hugs. All services provided are billed to customers. Indulged Doggies uses the Allowance method to account for bad debts.

Part A. Prepare journal entries for each of the following transactions at Indulged Doggies:

a. On May 1, a customer balance for $2,000 from a prior year was considered uncollectible and was written off.
b. On August 12, a customer paid $700 on a balance that had been written off last year.
c. On December 31, a summary entry to record revenue for the year was made for $224,000.
d. On December 31, a summary entry to record customer collections for the year was made for $160,000.
e. On December 31, Bad debt Expense is estimated to be $3,500 (assume no balance in the allowance account).

a. dr _____ _____

    cr _____   _____

b. dr _____ _____

    cr _____   _____

    dr _____ _____

    cr _____   _____

c. dr _____ _____

    cr _____   _____

d. dr _____ _____

    cr _____   _____

e. dr _____ _____

    cr _____   _____

Part B. Complete the following table, indicating the amount and effect (+ for increase, - for decrease, and NE for no effect) transactions a. – e.

Transaction	Net Receivables	Net Sales	Income from Operations
a.			
b.			
c.			
d.			
e.			

Exercise 8-2. Recording and Reporting Allowance for Doubtful Accounts Using Aging of Accounts Receivable Method (LO2)

Berebos Company uses the aging approach to estimate bad debt expense. The balance of each account receivable is aged on the basis of four time periods, and the average loss rate for each time period are shown in the following table:

	Time Period	Receivables Amount	Uncollectible Percentage
a.	1 – 30 days old	$ 142,000	½ %
b.	31 – 90 days old	68,000	20 %
c.	91 – 120 days old	39,000	50%
d.	Over 120 days old	25,000	70%
	Total	$ 274,000	

At December 31, 2008 (end of the current year), the Allowance for Doubtful Account has a $540 credit balance before the end-of-period adjusting entry is made.

Required:
1. Prepare the appropriate bad debt expense adjusting entry for the year 2008.
   Calculations:

   dr _____   _____

   cr _____   _____

2. Assume the unadjusted balance in the Allowance for Doubtful Accounts had a $850 debit balance, what would be the amount bad debt expense adjusting entry for the year 2008?

Exercise 8-3. Recording Accounts Receivable Transactions Using the Allowance Method (LO2)

Kolio Inc. is a large drug manufacturing facility. Assume the company recently reported the following amounts in its unadjusted trial balance as of December 31, 2009.

	Debits	**Credits**
Accounts Receivable	$65,000	
Allowance for Doubtful Accounts		$ 655
Sales		$ 875,000

Required (each of the following are independent assumptions):
1. Assume Kolio uses the aging of accounts receivable method and estimates that $6,841 of Accounts Receivable will be uncollectible. Prepare the adjusting journal entry required at December 31, 2009 for recording bad debt expense.

   dr _____   _____

   cr _____   _____

2. Repeat requirement 1, except this time assume the unadjusted balance in Kolio's allowance for doubtful accounts at December 31, 2009 was a debit balance of $230.

   dr _____   _____

   cr _____   _____

Exercise 8-4. Using the Interest Formula to Compute Interest (LO3)

Complete the following table by computing the missing amounts (?) for the following independent cases.

Principal Amount on Note Receivable	Annual Interest Rate	Time Period	Interest Earned
a. $ 29,000	12%	9 months	?
b. ?	10%	3 months	1,825
c. $200,000	8%	?	16,000
d. $ 81,000	?	8 months	5,940

Exercise 8-5. Recording Notes Receivable Transactions, Including Accrual Adjustment for Interest (LO3)

Dive-In Incorporated rents low-end offices to businesses with credit difficulties. Dive-In recently received a $12,000, 5 month, 14% note to settle an unpaid balance owed by one of its customers. Prepare journal entries to record the following transactions for Dive-In Incorporated:

Year	Date	Event
2008	October 1	The note is accepted by Dive-In Incorporated causing the company to replace the account receivable with a note receivable.
	December 31	Dive-In adjusted its books for interest earned through December 31, 2008.
2009	February 28	Dive-In receives the principal and interest of the note on its maturity date.

Oct 1 dr _____ _____

           cr _____   _____

Dec 31 dr _____ _____

           cr _____   _____

Feb 28 dr _____ _____

           cr _____   _____

           cr _____   _____

           cr _____   _____

Exercise 8-6. Analyzing and Interpreting Receivables Turnover Ratio and Days to Collect (LO4)

A recent Annual report for Move-It-Or-Lose-It, an express delivery service, contained the following data:

		Current Year	Previous Year
Accounts Receivable		$ 275,000	$ 201,000
Less: Allowance for Doubtful Accounts		9,000	10,000
Net accounts Receivable		266,000	191,000
Net Sales (assume all on credit)		1,750,000	1,600,000

Required:

1. Determine the Receivables Turnover ratio and Days to Collect for the current year.

Receivables Turnover

Days to Collect

2. Assuming the Receivables Turnover was 8.31 in the previous year and 9.47 the year before that, explain the current trend. Does it look as if receivables management in Move-It-Or-Lose-It is moving (forward) or losing (ground)? Explain.

Exercise 8-7. Recording and Reporting Accounts Receivable and Notes Receivable Transactions (LO2, 3)

Hey-Balers 'R' Us is a supplier of farm balers. Most of its sales are made on account, but some particularly large orders are sold in exchange for notes receivable. Hey-Balers 'R' Us reported the following balances in its December 31, 2009 unadjusted trial balance:

Account	Debit	Credit
Accounts Receivable	$4,550,000	
Allowance for doubtful accounts		$ 9,000
Bad debt expense	0	
Interest receivable	0	
Interest revenue		0
Notes receivable	210,000	
Sales on account		18,500,000
Sales in exchange for notes		210,000

Notes receivable consist of principal amounts owed by a customer on a 3-year, 6% note accepted on July 1, 2009. The note requires the customer to make annual interest payments on June 30, 2010, 2011, and 2012. Hey-Balers 'R' Us has no concerns about the collectibility of this note. Hey-Bales 'R' Us does estimate, however, that 4% of its gross accounts receivable will be uncollectible.

Required:

1. Prepare the December 31, 2009 adjusting journal entries related to accounts receivable and notes receivable.

Dec 31   *dr*   _____   _____
          cr   _____   _____

Dec 31   *dr*   _____   _____
          cr   _____   _____

2. Show how the adjusted balances for the balance sheet accounts will be reported on Hey-Balers 'R' Us' classified balance as of December 31, 2009.

Hey-Balers 'R' Us		
Balance Sheet		
December 31, 2009		
Assets		
Current assets:		
Cash	$	xx
Accounts Receivable		
Less: Allowance for Doubtful Accounts		
Interest Receivable		
Total Current Assets	$ xxxxx	$ xxxxx

SOLUTIONS TO SELF-TEST QUESTIONS AND EXERCISES

MATCHING

1.

F	Accounts Receivable		J	Factoring
H	Aging of Accounts Receivable Method		G	Interest Formula
K	Allowance for Doubtful Accounts		B	Percentage of Credit Sales Method
A	Allowance Method		M	Receivables Turnover Ratio

L	Bad Debt Expense		I	Notes Receivable
E	Days to Collect		D	Write-off
C	Direct write-off			

TRUE-FALSE QUESTIONS

1. T
2. F – Most businesses believe the benefits outweigh the costs of extending credit to customers.
3. T
4. T
5. F – Conservatism requires that a business report receivables at the amount that is actually expected to be collected.
6. F – It requires that the cost of bad debts be recorded in the period that the related credit sale was made.
7. T
8. T
9. F – They are the Percentage of Credit Sales method and the Aging of Accounts Receivable method.
10. F – The aging of accounts receivable method gets its name from the fact that it bases the estimate of bad debts on the 'age' of each amount in accounts receivable.
11. F – A debit can occur in the allowance account when a company has recorded write-offs that exceed its previous estimates. No error corrections are necessary.
12. T
13. F – the direct write-off method is allowed for income tax reporting, but it is not GAAP
14. T
15. T
16. T
17. F – This is the description for a low accounts receivable turnover ratio.
18. F – The days to collect presents the same information as the receivables turnover, it is simply easier to interpret.
19. F – credit terms allow you to compare the day to collect with the length of the credit period to gain a sense of whether customers are complying with the stated policy.
20. F – Factoring is an arrangement where receivables are sold to another company for cash less a factoring fee.

MULTIPLE CHOICE QUESTIONS

1.	A	6.	D	11. C		16. C	
2.	D	7.	D	12. C		17. B	
3.	C	8.	A	13. C		18. C	
4.	D	9.	B	14. D		19. C	
5.	B	10.	A	15. C		20. A	

EXERCISES

Exercise 8-1. Recording Accounts Receivable Transactions using the Allowance Method for Bad Debts; Effects on the Financial Statements (LO2)

Part A. Prepare journal entries for each of the following transactions at Indulged Doggies:

a.	dr	Allowance for Doubtful Accounts	2,000	
	cr	Accounts Receivable		2,000
b.	dr	Accounts Receivable	700	
	cr	Allowance for Doubtful Accounts		700
	dr	Cash	700	
	cr	Accounts Receivable		700
c.	dr	Accounts Receivable	224,000	

cr		Dog-sitting Revenue		224,000

d.   *dr*   Cash   160,000
        cr   Accounts Receivable   160,000

e.   *dr*   Bad Debt Expense   3,500
        cr   Allowance for Doubtful Accounts   3,500

Part B. Complete the following table, indicating the amount and effect (+ for increase, - for decrease, and NE for no effect) transactions a. – e.

Transaction	Net Receivables	Net Sales	Income from Operations
a.	NE	NE	NE
b.	NE	NE	NE
	−700	NE	NE
c.	+224,000	+224,000	+224,000
d.	−160,000	NE	NE
e.	−3,500	NE	−3,500

Exercise 8-2. Recording and Reporting Allowance for Doubtful Accounts Using Aging of Accounts Receivable Method (LO2)

1.   Prepare the appropriate bad debt expense adjusting entry for the year 2008.

(142,000)	(.005)	=	710
(68,000)	(.20)	=	13,600
(39,000)	(.50)	=	19,500
(25,000)	(.70)	=	17,500
			51,310

Since there is currently a $540 credit balance in the Allowance for Doubtful Accounts, and we've just determined that the amount should be $51,310 *after* the adjusting entry is made, the adjusting entry must be made for $50,770 ($51,310 – $540)

dr   Bad Debts Expense   50,770
    cr   Allowance for Doubtful Accounts   50,770

2.   If the unadjusted balance in the Allowance for Doubtful Accounts had a $850 debit balance, what would be the amount bad debt expense in 2008?

If there is currently a debit balance in the Allowance for Doubtful Accounts, there *still* must be a balance of $51,310 *after* the adjustment is made. Since there is a debit balance, the entry must be large enough to eliminate the current debit of $850 *and* the $51,310 that should be the ending balance in the account after the entry is made. So, the entry has to credit the account for the sum of *both these amounts combined* ($850 + $51,310) or $52,160. The $850 will zero out the current debit balance of $850 and then we still need to have the $51,310 balance in the account, so *both* amounts need to be credited to the allowance for doubtful accounts.

Exercise 8-3. Recording Accounts Receivable Transactions Using the Allowance Method (LO2)

1.   This method is concerned with the balance sheet, so the *dollar amount* of bad debt expense is irrelevant. The real concern is: The allowance account *must have a balance of $6,841* after this entry is made. End of story.

dr   Bad Debt Expense ($6,841 – $655)   6,186
    cr   Allowance for Doubtful Accounts   6,186

2. The point is: worry about what is currently in the allowance account *only if you are doing the aging of accounts receivable method.* Otherwise, the amount in the account is irrelevant.

dr	Bad Debt Expense ($6,841 + $230)	7,071
cr	Allowance for Doubtful Accounts	7,071

Exercise 8-4. Using the Interest Formula to Compute Interest (LO3)

Principal Amount on Note Receivable	Annual Interest Rate	Time Period	Interest Earned
a. $ 29,000	12%	9 months	**2,610**
b. **$ 73,000**	10%	3 months	1,825
c. $200,000	8%	**12 months or 1 year**	16,000
d. $ 81,000	**11%**	8 months	5,940

Calculations:

a. $29,000 x 12% x 9/12 = $2,610

b. 3/12 x 10% x Principal = $1,825
.025 x Principal = $1,825
Principal = $1,825 / .025
Principal = $73,000

c. $200,000 x 8% x Time = $16,000
$16,000 x Time = $16,000
Time = $16,000 / $16, 000
Time = 1 (year) or 12 months.

d. $81,000 x 8/12 x Rate = $5,940
$54,000 x Rate = $5,940
Rate = $5,940 / $54,000
Rate = .11 or 11%

Exercise 8-5. Recording Notes Receivable Transactions, Including Accrual Adjustment for Interest (LO3)

Oct 1	dr	Notes Receivable	12,000	
	cr	Accounts Receivable		12,000
Dec 31	dr	Interest Receivable ($12,000) (14%) (3/12)	420	
	cr	Interest Revenue		420
Feb 28	dr	Cash	12,700	
	cr	Notes Receivable		12,000
	cr	Interest Receivable		420
	cr	Interest Revenue ($12,000) (14%) (2/12)		280

Exercise 8-6. Analyzing and Interpreting Receivables Turnover Ratio and Days to Collect (LO4)

1.
Accounts Receivable Turnover = Net Sales/Average Accounts Receivable. First, we'll calculate the bottom figure, average accounts receivable. This is really based on average NET Accounts Receivable (Gross Accounts Receivable – Allowance for Doubtful Accounts).

($266,000 + $191,000) / 2 = $228,500 Average Net Accounts Receivable

Next, we put the result into the original formula:
$1,750,000 / $228,500 = 7.66 times

Days to Collect = 365 / Accounts Receivable Turnover.
365 / 7.66 = 47.65 days

2. Because the Days to collect is easier to interpret than the Accounts Receivable Turnover, we first convert prior years' turnovers into Days to Collect.

	Accounts Receivable Turnover	Days to Collect
Current Year	7.66	47.65 days
Prior Year	8.31	43.92 days
Year before that	9.47	38.54 days

It looks like the average number of days to collect has steadily increased in the past three years by nearly 10 days (from 38.54 days to 47.65 days). This might be explained a number of ways: (1) They have changed their credit policies and extended the length of time for customers to pay in an effort to attract more business from competitors; (2) They may be 'stuffing the channel' and allowing customers a longer-than-normal period of time to pay their accounts in order to lure them from competitors or prevent them from leaving to competitors; (3) They have poor collections policies and need to tighten their policies and procedures and be more aggressive in collections efforts. They may wish to considering a factoring relationship if necessary.

Exercise 8-7. Recording and Reporting Accounts Receivable and Notes Receivable Transactions (LO2, 3)
1.

Dec 31	dr	Bad Debts Expense ($4,550,000) (4%) – $9,000	173,000	
	cr	Allowance for Doubtful Accounts		173,000

Dec 31	dr	Interest Receivable ($210,000) (6%) (6/12)	6,300	
	cr	Interest Revenue		6,300

2. Show how the adjusted balances for the above balance sheet accounts will be reported on Hey-Balers 'R' Us' classified balance as of December 31, 2009.

Hey-Balers 'R' Us		
Balance Sheet		
December 31, 2009		
Assets		
Current assets:		
Cash		$ xx
Accounts Receivable	4,550,000	
Less: Allowance for Doubtful Accounts	182,000	4,368,000
Interest Receivable		6,300
Total Current Assets	$ XXXXX	$ XXXXX

CHAPTER 9
REPORTING AND INTERPRETING LONG-LIVED TANGIBLE AND INTANGIBLE ASSETS

ORGANIZATION OF THE CHAPTER

Understand the business - Definition and classification of long-lived assets	**Study the accounting methods** - Tangible assets - Intangible assets	**Evaluate the results** - Management decisions - Turnover analysis - Impact of depreciation differences	**Review the chapter** - Demonstration case -Chapter summary - Key terms - Practice material

CHAPTER FOCUS SUGGESTIONS

Review
The primary focus of Chapters 7 and 8 were the current assets on the balance sheet. You learned about perpetual inventory systems and the journal entries required to record the purchase and sale of items for a merchandising business. Then you turned your attention to accounts and notes receivable. You worked with the allowance method estimate bad debt expense, learned to write off bad debts, and dealt with various transactions involving notes receivable. Finally, each chapter introduced useful tools for evaluating a business. These ratios are invaluable to users, both internal and external, for decision-making.

Introduction
Now we're ready to turn the spotlight on long-lived tangible and intangible assets. You'll need to understand what long-lived assets are and why they're important for decision-making. Then we'll cover the accounting methods and procedures used to track these assets. Finally, you'll learn the tools used to help determine how well the company is using these assets.

UNDERSTAND THE BUSINESS

Learning Objective 1 Define, classify, and explain the nature of long-lived assets.

Definition and Classification of Long-Lived Assets
Long-lived assets are business assets acquired for use over one or more years. They are not purchased for resale rather, they are 'productive' assets that enable the business to produce the goods or services that are sold to customers. Notice that when you buy these items, you intend to keep them *longer than one year*. There are two major classes of long-lived assets, they are:

Tangible assets
Tangible means 'touchable'. Tangible assets are those assets that you can physically touch, they have substance. Examples of tangible assets include: land, buildings, vehicles, machinery, office equipment, furniture and fixtures, etc. These are collectively referred to as Property, Plant, and Equipment on the balance sheet. These assets are also called fixed assets.

Intangible assets
These assets are hard to pin down because they have no physical substance, but they have special rights. We *force physical substance on them* by putting them *on paper—legal documents* which spell out these legal rights. Intangible assets include: copyrights, trademarks, patents, brand names, licensing rights, etc. These intangible assets only have physical substance because we put them on a piece of paper.

Natural Resources
In addition to the major classes of long-lived assets, natural resources include assets such as oil wells, timber, and precious mineral/gem mines. Natural resources are depleted over time. The accounting for natural resources is covered in Chapter Supplement A.

Learning Objective 2
Apply the cost principle to the
acquisition of long-lived assets.

Tangible Assets

We'll begin our discussion with the (1) acquisition, (2) use, and (3) disposal of tangible long-lived assets. Before jumping too deeply into this topic, a few new terms need to be introduced:

- Land Improvements – these are improvements made to land that deteriorate over time. Land is assumed to last forever. Land improvements include things like:
  - o Sidewalks
  - o Pavement
  - o Landscaping
- Construction in Progress – this is an account that contains the costs of building or constructing new buildings and equipment. When the construction is completed, the costs are removed from this account and put into the corresponding Buildings or Equipment account.

1. Acquisition of Tangible Assets

The cost principle states that all reasonable and necessary costs of acquiring and preparing an asset for use should be recorded as the cost of the asset. When costs are recorded as assets (rather than expenses) it is called **capitalizing** the costs.

Deciding whether costs should be expensed or capitalized is a matter of judgment. Remember that we subtract expenses from revenues to determine net income. If a manager is evaluated on the basis of profits generated, there is a huge incentive for the manager to record costs as assets (capitalize them) rather than record them as expenses. This section of the chapter, therefore, focuses on identifying which costs should be capitalized and which should be expensed.

In order to capitalize (record as an asset) *initial* costs at the point of acquisition *the cost must be considered necessary for acquiring and preparing the asset for its intended use.* The following table lists the types of costs that are capitalized when purchasing Land, Buildings, and Equipment.

Acquisition Costs that are Capitalized		
Land	**Buildings**	**Equipment**
Purchase price	Purchase/Construction Cost	Purchase/Construction cost
Legal Fees	Legal Fees	Sales Taxes
Survey Fees	Appraisal Fees	Transportation Costs
Broker's Commissions	Architect Fees	Installation Costs

If a company buys land, buildings, or equipment and incurs demolition, renovation, or repair costs before it can be used, these additional costs would be capitalized as a cost of the corresponding item. They are capitalized because they are incurred to get the asset ready for its intended purpose.

When assets are purchased in a lump sum, called a Basket Purchase, the lump sum purchase price is allocated to each asset on the basis of its market value. The purchase price must be split out like this because each asset purchased is used-up over different lengths of time, which is important for depreciation purposes (covered later in the chapter). For example, assume you purchased land, buildings, and equipment as a basket purchase for $500,000. It is determined that the land makes up 45% of the value of the assets; the buildings are 35%; and the equipment is 20%. Therefore, the $500,000 would be allocated as follows:

Land	Buildings	Equipment	Total
($500,000) (45%) = $225,000	($500,000) (35%) = $175,000	($500,000) (20%) = $100,000	$500,000

Now, let's concentrate on the Land, assume that in addition to the allocated price above, the following costs were incurred. Razed (demolished) an old shed on the land (in anticipation of putting a new building on it); incurred surveying fees of $1,000, legal fees of $4,000, and broker's commissions of $10,000. The journal entry to record the purchase of the land depends on how payment is made for these costs (including the buildings and equipment).

These costs are added to the basket cost of the land to determine the amount recorded:

Allocated price	$225,000
Surveying fees	1,000
Legal fees	4,000
Broker's Commissions	10,000
Total purchase price of land	$240,000

a. Cash Purchase

If cash was paid for the entire transaction, the following entry would be made for the land (the entry for the Buildings and Equipment would be similar):

	Assets		= Liabilities	+ Stockholders' Equity
1. Analyze				
	Cash	−515,000		
	Land	+240,000		
2. Record	Building	+175,000		
	Equipment	+100,000		

dr Land (+A)..	240,000	
dr Building (+A)..	175,000	
dr Equipment (+A)......................................	100,000	
cr Cash (−A)..		515,000

b. Credit Purchase

Assuming these assets were purchased by paying cash for the surveying fees, legal fees, and broker's commission and signing a note payable for everything else, the entry would be:

	Assets		=	Liabilities	+ Stockholders' Equity
1. Analyze					
	Cash	−15,000		Notes Payable +500,000	
	Land	+240,000			
2. Record	Building	+175,000			
	Equipment	+100,000			

dr Land (+A)..	240,000	
dr Building (+A)..	175,000	
dr Equipment (+A)......................................	100,000	
cr Cash (−A)..		15,000
cr Notes Payable (+L)...............................		500,000

Finally, not all acquisitions of fixed assets are capitalized. Oftentimes, the cost of items purchased is such a small dollar amount, that it isn't worth the trouble of recording them as fixed assets. This is perfectly acceptable because immaterial (relatively small dollar) amounts will not affect users' analysis of and decisions made regarding the financial statements. Other costs that are routinely expensed are: insurance, interest on loans to purchase fixed assets, and ordinary repairs and maintenance of fixed assets.

2. Use of Tangible Assets
a. Maintenance Costs Incurred during Time of Use

Just like you have to do regular maintenance on your automobile, home, etc. to keep it running in tip-top condition, a business incurs regular maintenance costs to keep its long-lived assets running smoothly. There are two categories of maintenance performed on long-lived assets:

i. *Ordinary repairs and maintenance* – these types of repairs are intended to maintain the productive capacity of the asset for a short period of time so they are recorded as expenses in the current period. Characteristics of ordinary repairs and maintenance are that they:
- Are routine maintenance and upkeep
- Tend to be recurring
- Have relatively small costs per occurrence
- Examples are: changing spark plugs on a vehicle, or oiling the mechanism of motorized equipment.

ii. *Extraordinary repairs, replacements, and additions* – These types of repairs bring the asset to a *better* condition and higher usefulness than it was before so their costs are added to the corresponding asset account. Characteristics include are that they:
- Occur infrequently
- Involve large dollar amounts
- Increase an asset's economic usefulness in the future through
  o Increased efficiency
  o Increased capacity
  o Longer life
- Examples are: Additions, major overhauls, complete reconditioning, and major replacements and improvements.

b. *Depreciation Expense*

> **Learning Objective 3**
> Apply various depreciation methods as future economic benefits are used up over time.

There is another expense of tangible assets that needs to be reported – **Depreciation.** Recall that expenses are not recorded until the item has been 'used'. Furthermore, since long-lived assets are recorded as assets rather than expenses, *nothing* is reported as expense when the asset is acquired. But, you *know* these assets have been used throughout the period. Depreciation expense is how we *allocate the cost of an asset over the periods it is actually used.*

This process is required in order to be in accordance with the *matching principle* which requires that we *match* expenses to the period that the corresponding revenue was earned. We do this by moving a portion of the asset's cost from the balance sheet to the income statement as an expense in the period the asset is used to generate revenue.

The Depreciation Expense is reported on the income statement in the current period, usually as a selling or general and administrative expense. The amount of deprecation that has accumulated since the asset's acquisition is reported on the balance sheet as a contra-asset account called Accumulated Depreciation. The original cost of the asset less the accumulated depreciation taken on the asset is the asset's **book (or carrying) value.** Book value is not an indicator of the asset's value, it simply shows how much of an asset's cost has not yet been expensed or recovered. In order to determine how much depreciation to record, you need three items:

1. *Asset Cost.* This includes all capitalized costs for the asset being depreciated.

2. *Residual Value.* This is an estimated amount that the company expects to receive when it ultimately disposes of the asset. This can be compared to the amount you might expect to receive when you 'trade-in' a vehicle. (Residual value is known by many similar names, such as: trade-in value, scrap value, salvage value, disposal value, etc.)

3. *Useful Life.* This is an estimate of the asset's useful economic life *to the company.* It can be expressed in terms of years or productive capacity. (i.e. a car may have a useful life of 3 *years* or 100,000 *miles*) Land is the only tangible asset that is assumed to have a unlimited useful life, and is therefore, *not depreciated.*

Essentially, with depreciation, we are trying to allocate the amount of an asset's cost that is *used-up* every period (utilized by a business) to generate revenues. We subtract any residual value from the asset's cost in calculating depreciation, because we expect to recover (or get back) that portion of its cost when we dispose of it. So, the only portion of an asset's cost that can be depreciated is: Cost – Residual Value, known as Depreciable Cost.

The adjusting journal entry to record depreciation is:

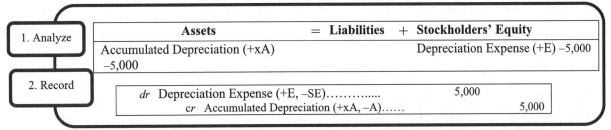

	Assets	= Liabilities	+ Stockholders' Equity
1. Analyze	Accumulated Depreciation (+xA) −5,000		Depreciation Expense (+E) −5,000

2. Record	*dr* Depreciation Expense (+E, −SE)............	5,000
	cr Accumulated Depreciation (+xA, −A)......	5,000

You probably have a general idea of what depreciation is now, but here's the kicker—companies are allowed to use one of several different methods for calculating depreciation (for external financial reporting purposes). Each method will produce a different amount of depreciation, so it is important to understand how each method works and how to accurately analyze the differences.

c. Alternative Depreciation Methods
This text covers the three most common depreciation methods:

- Straight-line
- Units-of-Production (also referred to as Units-of-Activity)
- Declining-Balance

i. **Straight-line Method.** This method allocates the same amount of depreciation to each accounting period over its estimated useful life. Let's assume that a company purchased Equipment for $23,000 on January 1, 2009; its residual value is estimated to be $3,000; and it has an estimated useful life of 4 years. Depreciation is calculated as follows:

$$(\text{Cost} - \text{Residual Value}) \quad \times \quad \frac{1}{\text{Useful Life}} \quad = \quad \text{Depreciation Expense}$$

$$(\$23,000 - \$3,000) \quad \times \quad \frac{1}{4} \quad = \quad \$5,000$$

The depreciable cost of the equipment ($23,000 - $3,000) is multiplied by the straight-line rate (1/4) to calculate the annual depreciation ($5,000.) Accountants use a *depreciation schedule* to show the depreciation, accumulated depreciation, and book value for the entire useful life of an asset like this:

Year (A)	Computation (B)	INCOME STATEMENT Depreciation Expense (C)	BALANCE SHEET Cost (D)	BALANCE SHEET Accum. Deprec. (E) [Prior yr (E) + (C)]	BALANCE SHEET Book Value (F) [(D) − (E)]
At acquisition			$23,000	-	$23,000
2009	($23,000-$3,000) x ¼	$5,000	23,000	$5,000	18,000
2010	($23,000-$3,000) x ¼	5,000	23,000	10,000	13,000
2011	($23,000-$3,000) x ¼	5,000	23,000	15,000	8,000
2012	($23,000-$3,000) x ¼	5,000	23,000	20,000	3,000

Column (C) is the amount of the adjusting journal entry to record depreciation expense for the corresponding year. Columns (D, E, and F) are reported on the balance sheet (book value) at the end of the accounting period.

Note that *straight-line* depreciation suggests:
- Depreciation expense is a *constant* (i.e. $5,000) amount each year.
- Accumulated depreciation increases by an equal amount each year ($5,000).
- Book value decreases by an equal amount ($5,000) each year.

At the end of the asset's life, accumulated depreciation ($20,000) equals the asset's depreciable cost ($23,000 – $3,000), and book value ($3,000) equals the asset's residual value.

NOTE: Accountants rely primarily on judgment to determine the amounts used for useful life and residual value (for all depreciation methods). Because these amounts are difficult to estimate, depreciation calculations should be updated regularly.

ii. ***Units-of-Production Method.*** This method also allocates the asset's depreciable cost over its useful life. BUT, useful life is based on the estimated total production from the equipment. Assume that the equipment is a trench-digger and it is estimated that the equipment will be used to dig an estimated 50,000 hours over its useful life. During 2009, the equipment was used for 10,000 hours; 13,000 in 2010; 12,000 in 2011; and 15,000 in 2012. The formula is now calculated as:

$$\frac{(\text{Cost} - \text{Residual Value})}{\text{Estimated Total Production}} \quad \text{X} \quad \text{Actual Production} \quad = \quad \text{Depreciation Expense}$$

$$\frac{(\$23,000 - \$3,000)}{50,000 \text{ hours}} \quad \text{X} \quad 10,000 \quad = \quad \$4,000 \text{ in } 2009$$

Year (A)	Computation (B)	INCOME STATEMENT Depreciation Expense (C)	Cost (D)	BALANCE SHEET Accum. Deprec. (E) [Prior yr (E) + (C)]	Book Value (F) [(D) – (E)]
At acquisition			$23,000	-	$23,000
2009	[($23,000 -3,000)/50,000]x10,000	$4,000	23,000	$4,000	19,000
2010	[($23,000 -3,000)/50,000]x13,000	5,200	23,000	9,200	13,800
2011	[($23,000 -3,000)/50,000]x12,000	4,800	23,000	14,000	9,000
2012	[($23,000 -3,000)/50,000]x15,000	6,000	23,000	20,000	3,000

Dividing book value by the estimated total production (hours) results in an estimated depreciation expense of $0.40 *per hour of usage* [($23,000 - $3,000) / 50,000] for the equipment. Forty cents of depreciation will be taken every hour the equipment is used. Notice that in order to use this method, the company must also provide the actual production achieved every accounting period since the rate is based on production rather than years. The amounts for depreciation expense, accumulated depreciation, and book value will vary from period to period with this method.

iii. ***Declining-balance Method.*** This method expenses higher depreciation amounts in the early years of an asset's life and lower amounts in the later years. Because of this speeding-up (acceleration) of expense in the early years, it is often referred to as an *accelerated depreciation* method. A depreciation rate is applied to the asset's *book value* at the beginning of the period to determine the depreciation expense.

Notice that this method *does not* use depreciable cost to calculate depreciation expense, it uses *book value*. The declining-balance rate is based on the straight-line rate. The straight-line rate is usually doubled. This *doubling* of the straight-line rate led to this method being referred to as the *double-declining-balance* method. Using the same piece of equipment as the last two examples, had the Double-Declining-Balance method been applied, the depreciation for 2009 would be:

$$(\text{Cost} - \text{Accumulated Depreciation}) \quad \text{X} \quad \frac{2}{\text{Useful Life}} \quad = \quad \text{Depreciation Expense}$$

$$(\$23,000 - \$0) \quad \text{X} \quad \frac{2}{4} \quad = \quad \$11,500$$

Year (A)	Computation (B)	INCOME STATEMENT Depreciation Expense (C)	BALANCE SHEET		
			Cost (D)	Accum. Deprec. (E) Prior yr (E) + (C)	Book Value (F) (D) – (E)
At acquisition			$23,000	-	$23,000
2009	$23,000 * 2/4	$11,500	23,000	$11,500	11,500
2010	$11,500 * 2/4	5,750	23,000	17,250	5,750
2011	$5,750 * 2/4	2,750 ~~2,875~~	23,000	20,000 ~~20,125~~	3,000 ~~2,875~~
2012		~~0~~	23,000	20,000	3,000
	$20,000 – $17,250 = $2,750				

Notice the following regarding the declining-balance method:

- This method is calculated using *beginning book value* not *depreciable cost* as with the previous methods.
- This method *completely ignores residual value* in its calculation.
   o However, the rule still applies that the book value *must equal residual value* after all depreciation has been taken on the asset. This requires diligence on the part of the accountant. The accumulated depreciation must be carefully monitored to ensure that book value does not go below salvage value, even if it means *altering the calculated depreciation in the final year of the asset's useful life.*

Notice in 2011, had the calculated amount of depreciation expense been taken ($2,875), the book value of the asset would be *below residual value!* The residual value is $3,000 and book value would have been $2,875 Therefore, a smaller amount of depreciation must be taken in 2011, than was calculated using double-declining balance. The amount is determined by taking the depreciable cost of the asset ($20,000), and subtracting the accumulated depreciation taken *as of the previous year* ($17,250.) This provides the exact dollar amount that can be depreciated in the final year without taking book value below the residual value.

4. ***Summary.*** The amount of depreciation expense taken in each year of an asset's life depends on the method used. Since depreciation expense can vary, net income will also vary based on the depreciation method used. After the asset has been fully depreciated at the end of its life, regardless of the method used, the total amount of depreciation will equal the asset's depreciable cost.

Managers are allowed to choose any *rational and systematic* depreciation method they wish as long as the method(s) used is (are) described in the notes to the financial statements (as required by the full-disclosure principle.) Furthermore, different methods may be used for different assets, as long as the method used for each group is *used consistently over time* allowing users to compare across time periods with ease. In general,

- Straight-line is preferred because it is the easiest to use and understand, and it also matches depreciation to revenues evenly throughout an asset's life
- Units-of-production is best when asset use fluctuates significantly from period to period.
- Declining-balance works best with assets that are the most productive when they are new and quickly use up their usefulness as they get older.

d. Tax Depreciation.

The methods described in this chapter, thus far, are depreciation methods allowed for *external financial reporting purposes.* However, tax laws require that another method be used to determine depreciation expense of tangible assets for *income tax reporting purposes.* Because of this, companies usually keep two separate sets of books, one for financial reporting purposes and the other for tax purposes. It is *both legal and ethical to maintain separate records for tax and financial reporting purposes.* This is true because the objectives of GAAP and the Internal Revenue Code (IRC) are different. The IRS allows companies to deduct larger amounts of tax depreciation in the early years of an asset's life in order to encourage economic renewal and growth.

Since amounts of depreciation will differ for tax and financial reporting purposes, income will differ for tax purposes and financial reporting purposes as well. Tax savings will result in the early years of an asset's life and decrease in the later years. This 'putting off' or delaying tax liability is called deferred taxes. The deferral is temporary, since ultimately, the same amount of depreciation is taken at the end of the asset's useful life.

Essentially, this delaying of taxes illustrates *the least and the latest rule*. This means that taxpayers want to pay the *least* amount of tax that is legally permissible, and at the *latest* possible date. A business is no different, if the business can defer (put off) paying taxes legally, IT WILL! Many corporate income tax deferrals are the direct result of differences in depreciation methods used for tax versus financial reporting purposes.

3. Asset Impairment Losses

Depreciation is not intended to report assets at their current values, it is merely supposed to report how much of an asset's cost has been 'used'

> **Learning Objective 4**
> Explain the effect of asset impairment on the financial statements.

over time in generating revenues. So, when events or changed circumstances cause the estimated future cash flow of the asset to fall below its book value, it results in an asset *impairment*.

If this happens, the asset's book value should be *written-down* to what the asset is now worth (fair value) and the amount of the write-down should be reported as an impairment loss. This loss is reported in the "Other Expenses and Losses" section of the income statement rather than as a part of operating income. (If the loss is substantial, a note to the financial statements should be included.) Assume an asset's book value is $30,000 and its estimated future cash flows are $20,000, an impairment loss of $10,000 ($20,000 - $30,000) is incurred. The journal entry would be:

1. Analyze	**Assets**	**=**	**Liabilities**	**+**	**Stockholders' Equity**
	Equipment (–A) –10,000				Loss Due to Impairment of Assets (+E) –10,000

2. Record	
dr Loss Due to Impairment of Assets (+E, –SE).........	10,000
cr Equipment (–A).....................................	10,000

4. Disposal of Tangible Assets

When a business decides it no longer needs a long-lived asset, it may *voluntarily* dispose of it. The business may trade it in, sell it, or trash it. In other cases a business may *involuntarily* dispose of an asset due to damage, fires, accidents, etc. The disposal of an asset usually requires two journal entries in order to:

> **Learning Objective 5**
> Analyze the disposal of long-lived tangible assets.

a. *Update the depreciation expense and accumulated depreciation accounts* through the date of disposal.
b. *Record the disposal.* The asset's cost and accumulated depreciation must be removed from the books (since this is typically only done once per year, as an adjusting entry)

   i.   Remove the asset's cost and accumulated depreciation (through the date of disposal) from the accounts
   ii. The amount received from the disposal (if any) minus the asset's book value determines the "Gain" or "Loss" on disposal.
   iii. The Gain or Loss is reported on the income statement under
      1. Other Revenues and Gains – if a gain results
      2. Other Expenses and Losses – if a loss results

Assume a business owns a piece of machinery that cost $120,000. It has been depreciated using the straight-line method assuming a 10-year useful life with no residual value. The machinery was sold for $40,000 cash. The accumulated depreciation through the date of sale was $75,000. The entry to record the gain or loss on disposal is:

1. Analyze	**Assets**		**=**	**Liabilities**	**+**	**Stockholders' Equity**
	Cash	+40,000				Loss on Sale (+E) –5,000
	Accumulated Depreciation	–75,000				
	Equipment	–120,000				

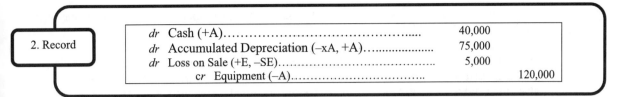

2. Record	dr Cash (+A)...	40,000	
	dr Accumulated Depreciation (–xA, +A).....................	75,000	
	dr Loss on Sale (+E, –SE).....................................	5,000	
	cr Equipment (–A)......................................		120,000

A common mistake is to remove only the net book value (NBV) of $45,000 ($120,000 - $75,000) from the Equipment account. It is important that you reduce both the Equipment account (for the full cost of the asset disposed of) and the accumulated depreciation account (for the full amount of accumulated depreciation on the asset through the date of disposal).

Intangible Assets

Intangible assets are long-lived assets that have no physical substance. They are given substance through legal documentation. Types of intangible assets include:

- *Trademarks.* A special name, image, or slogan identified with a product or company. Those registered with the US Patent and Trademark Office use the symbol ®, while those unregistered use the symbol ™

- *Copyrights.* Gives the owner the exclusive right to publish, use, and sell a literary, musical, artistic, or dramatic work for a period not exceeding 70 years after the author's death.

- *Patents.* An exclusive right granted by the federal government, providing the owner exclusive rights to use, manufacture, or sell the patented item for 20 years. The intent is to encourage inventors by preventing others from copying their ideas.

- *Licensing Rights.* These are limited permissions to use something according to specific terms and conditions.

- *Franchises.* This is a contractual right to sell certain products or services, use certain trademarks, or perform activities in a geographical region. It normally involves an up-front fee and an on-going percentage of profits.

- *Goodwill.* This is the most frequently reported intangible asset. It represents all of the 'intangible' things that help make a business profitable. It includes things like favorable location, established customer base, great reputation, and a top-notch staff. GAAP requires that this intangible be purchased in order to be recorded on the books.

1. Acquisition, Use, and Disposal of Intangible Assets

a. *Acquisition.* Intangibles are only recorded as assets if they have been *purchased*. If the intangible is internally developed or constructed by the business, the costs must be reported as *research and development* expenses. The reason why intangibles must be purchased in order to be reported is because the 'inventor' typically thinks the 'invention' is worth more than anyone else thinks its worth. The only way to *prove* what the invention is *really* worth is to see what *someone else is willing to pay for it.* So, if no one will buy it, it ain't worth squat.

The value of purchased Goodwill is sort of determined on a fall-out basis. In other words, assume you're willing to pay $1,000,000 for a business, and it has been determined that the **net assets** (total assets – total liabilities) of the business are only worth $850,000. There must be some *unidentifiable, intangible* reason why you are willing to pay $150,000 *more* than this business is supposedly worth. The answer is Goodwill (also called the *cost in excess of net assets acquired*) and it is calculated as: Purchase Price – Fair Market value of Identifiable assets and liabilities.

2. Use. So, how are intangible assets accounted for *after* the purchase? Everything depends on its whether they are deemed to have a limited or unlimited life.

- **Limited life** – In this case, the cost is allocated on a straight-line basis over its useful life. This is called **amortization.** Typically, there is no residual value for an intangible asset because it has no value at the end of its life. Amortization Expense is reported on the income statement and deducted directly from the intangibles account on the balance sheet. For example, assume a Patent is purchased for $25,000. Amortization Expense would be $1,250 per year ($25,000 / 20) and recorded like this:

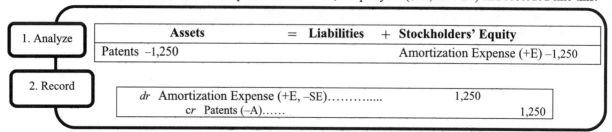

1. Analyze	Assets	= Liabilities	+ Stockholders' Equity
	Patents –1,250		Amortization Expense (+E) –1,250

2. Record

dr Amortization Expense (+E, –SE)............ 1,250
    cr Patents (–A)...... 1,250

- **Unlimited life** – these intangibles are not amortized. However, they are periodically checked for possible impairment. If an intangible asset is impaired, its book value is written down to its fair value.

3. Disposal. The rules regarding impairment and disposal for tangible assets also apply for intangible assets. Gains and losses will be determined on the basis of the cash (if any) received minus the book value of the asset on the date of disposal.

EVALUATE THE RESULTS

> **Learning Objective 7**
> Interpret the fixed asset turnover ratio.

Management Decisions
Businesses have the dubious task of accurately forecasting the right amount to invest in long-lived assets. An estimate that is too low indicates missed opportunities to earn revenues while an estimate that is too high indicates the company will have excessive costs that reduce profits.

Turnover Analysis
As a means to evaluate how management uses its assets to produce revenues, a *fixed asset turnover ratio* can be calculated:

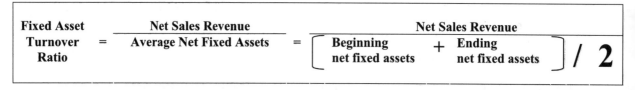

$$\text{Fixed Asset Turnover Ratio} = \frac{\text{Net Sales Revenue}}{\text{Average Net Fixed Assets}} = \frac{\text{Net Sales Revenue}}{\left[\begin{array}{c}\text{Beginning net fixed assets} + \text{Ending net fixed assets}\end{array}\right] / 2}$$

This ratio measures the sales dollars generated from each dollar invested in fixed assets. In general, a high or increasing ratio, relative to the industry's average or the company's prior periods, suggests a more effective use of fixed assets.

You can't *always* evaluate based strictly upon the turnover results alone. A declining ratio may be the result of a company acquiring additional assets in anticipation of higher future sales, which is a strong indicator. Similarly, an increasing ratio may be the result of renting assets rather than buying them. This ratio varies widely by industry because capital intensity (the need for tangible assets) varies widely.

> **Learning Objective 8**
> Describe the factors to consider when comparing across companies.

The Impact of Depreciation Differences
As you know, different methods of calculating depreciation result in vastly different amounts of depreciation expense reported in any one year. Using the equipment example used in this chapter, the following table summarizes the Depreciation Expense, Accumulated Depreciation, and Book Value, using each of the three depreciation methods we've covered.

Yr.	Straight-Line			Units-of-Activity			Declining Balance		
	Deprec. Expense	Accum. Deprec.	Book Value	Deprec. Expense	Accum. Deprec.	Book Value	Deprec. Expense	Accum. Deprec.	Book Value
2009	5,000	5,000	18,000	4,000	4,000	19,000	11,500	11,500	11,500
2010	5,000	10,000	13,000	5,200	9,200	13,800	5,750	17,250	5,750
2011	5,000	15,000	**8,000**	4,800	14,000	9,000	2,750	20,000	**3,000**
2012	5,000	20,000	3,000	6,000	20,000	3,000	0	20,000	3,000

All three methods result in accumulated depreciation of $20,000 at the end of 2012. However, Depreciation Expense for 2009 under the declining balance method is *more than twice* the amount calculated under the straight-line method. The impact on Net income of using the declining balance method will be to substantially reduce income in the early years, and increase income in the later years, for no other reason than because of *the depreciation method used.*

The method used will also affect the gain or loss reported when the asset it sold. Assume this asset is sold on the last day of 2011 for $7,000. Under the straight-line method, the book value on that date is $8,000. The company would *receive* $7,000 and *give up* an asset with a book value of $8,000. This will result in a Loss of $1,000 ($7,000 – $8,000.) Had the exact same sale occurred under the declining-balance method, a $4,000 gain ($7,000 – $3,000) would have resulted. Under this method, the asset is fully depreciated! This illustrates why financial statement users must have a basic understanding of depreciation methods and the impact that they have on net income (as well as net assets.)

Our example focused on the company using different depreciation methods but the *useful life and residual value* were the same. If either of these two components were changed, the computations would result in differing amounts of depreciation expense, accumulated depreciation, and book value. Differences in useful lives occur because of: (1) the type of equipment used by each company, (2) the frequency of repairs and maintenance, (3) the frequency and duration of use, and (4) the degree of conservatism in management's estimates.

Because of all the differences that occur from the use of different depreciation methods, some companies have resorted to evaluating businesses *without including* these figures. One popular way this is accomplished is with a subtotal called **EBITDA,** which stands for 'Earnings Before Interest, Taxes, Depreciation, and Amortization.' This lets analysts evaluate the business without worrying about variations in income caused by differing depreciation methods.

SUPPLEMENT A – NATURAL RESOURCES

Natural resources include oil wells, mineral deposits, timber tracts, etc.. They provide the raw materials for products sold by company like *Exxon Mobil* and *International Paper.* A natural resource, when first acquired, is recorded based on the cost principle. The allocation of the cost over the periods the natural resource is used by the company is based on the matching principle. The allocation of a natural resource over the period of its extraction or harvesting is called **depletion.** The units-of-production method is frequently used to compute depletion.

While depletion is similar to depreciation and amortization, it differs in one important way: When a natural resource is depleted (i.e. an oil well), the company obtains additional inventory (oil). Since this process is required in order to get the inventory, depletion costs are added to the cost of the inventory, rather than expensed during the period.

For example, assume a timber tract costing $400,000 is depleted over its estimated cutting period based on a 'cutting' rate of approximately 25% per year, it would be depleted by $100,000 ($400,000 * 25%) per year. The entry to record the depletion would be:

1. Analyze	Assets	=	Liabilities	+ Stockholders' Equity
	Timber Inventory +100,000			
	Timber Tract −100,000			

2. Record	
	dr Timber Inventory (+A).............................. 100,000
	cr Timber Tract (−A)................................ 100,000

SUPPLEMENT B – CHANGES IN DEPRECIATION

Changes In Estimate

Depreciation expense calculations are based on two estimates: *useful life* and *residual value*. The estimates of these amounts are made at the time the asset is acquired. At some point during the life of the asset, one or both of these estimates may need revision. When it is determined that one or both of these estimates should be revised, or if the asset's cost has changed (due to extraordinary repairs or additions), the *current undepreciated balance* (book value) less any updated residual value, should be allocated over the *remaining estimated life* beginning in the year the estimates were revised. This is called a **prospective change in estimate.**

To illustrate, assume a machine originally cost $110,000 has a salvage value of $10,000 and is being depreciated over 10 years using straight-line. At the beginning of the 4th year, it was determined that the estimated life should have been 15 years and the residual value should be $11,000. To calculate the *new* annual *straight-line* depreciation, the original formula is altered slightly:

$$(\textbf{Book Value} - \textit{New Residual Value}) \quad X \quad \frac{1}{\textit{Remaining Life}} \quad = \quad \text{Depreciation Expense}$$

$$(\$80{,}000 * - \$11{,}000) \quad X \quad \frac{1}{12 **} \quad = \quad \$5{,}750 ***$$

---

*The book value is calculated in the normal way for the first three years:

($110,000 - $10,000) / 10 = $10,000 per year.
Since it was owned for 3 full years before the estimates were revised, a total of $30,000 ($10,000 x 3) has been depreciated by the *beginning* of the 4th year. So, the book value at the beginning of year 4 is:

	Cost	$110,000
−	Accumulated Depreciation	30,000
=	Book Value	80,000

** The *remaining life* at the beginning of the 4th year is the *new* useful life estimate *less* the number of years the machine has been depreciated *so far!* (15 − 3 = 12)

*** This is the amount of depreciation that will be expensed for years 4 – 15 based on the changes in estimate.

A company may also change depreciation methods, though such a change requires significant disclosures. This topic is covered in Intermediate Accounting texts. GAAP states that changes in accounting estimates and depreciation methods should only be made when a new estimate or accounting method 'better measures' the periodic income of the business.

Partial Year Calculations

It is extremely rare for a company to dispose of a long-lived asset on the first or last day of an accounting period. So, we frequently need to calculate depreciation for time periods shorter than one year. For straight-line and declining-balance, you simply take the annual depreciation expense and multiply it by the fraction of the year that you are calculating depreciation for. For example, if you have annual depreciation charges calculated as $5,000, but you only need to calculate depreciation for 9 months. You would calculate the depreciation like this:

$$\$5,000 * 9/12 = \$3,750$$

The units-of-production method does not require any modification in the calculation for partial years because it is based on actual production for the period. If the period of time covered by the depreciation is less than one year, then the actual production will simply be less than a year's normal production.

REVIEW THE CHAPTER

Chapter Summary
LO1. Define, classify, and explain the nature of long-lived assets
- ❖ Long-lived assets are those that a business retains for long periods of time for use in the course of normal operations rather than for sale. They may be divided into:
  - o Tangible Assets including: Land, buildings, and equipment; OR
  - o Intangible Assets including: Goodwill, patents, and franchises

LO2. Apply the cost principle to the acquisition of long-lived assets
- ❖ Acquisition cost of property, plant, and equipment is:
  - o The cash-equivalent purchase price, plus
  - o All reasonable and necessary expenditures made to acquire and prepare the asset for its intended use.
- ❖ Expenditures made *after* the asset is in use are:
  - o Expensed (and considered ordinary repairs and maintenance expense) if:
    - ▪ they recur frequently
    - ▪ involve relatively small amounts, and
    - ▪ do not directly lengthen the asset's useful life.
  - o Capitalized as a cost of the asset if:
    - ▪ They provide benefits for one or more accounting periods beyond the current period
    - ▪ Included in this category are:
      - • Extraordinary repairs
      - • Replacements
      - • Additions

LO3. Apply various depreciation methods as future economic benefits are used-up over time
- ❖ In conformity with the matching principle,
  - o The cost of long-lived tangible assets (less any estimated residual value) is allocated to depreciation expense over each period benefited by the assets
- ❖ Because of depreciation
  - o The book value of an asset declines over time, and
  - o Net income is reduced by the amount of the expense
- ❖ Common depreciation methods include:
  - o Straight-line (a constant amount over time)
  - o Unit-of-production (a variable amount over time)
  - o Double-declining balance (a decreasing amount over time)

LO4. Explain the effect of asset impairment on the financial statements
❖ When events or changes in circumstances reduce the estimated future cash flows of a long-lived asset below its book value, the
  o Book value of the asset should be written down, and
  o Amount of the write-down should be reported as an impairment loss

LO5. Analyze the disposal of long-lived tangible assets.
❖ When assets are disposed of through sale or abandonment
  o Record additional depreciation arising since the last adjustment was made
  o Remove the cost of the old asset and its related accumulated depreciation
  o Recognize the cash proceeds (if any)
  o Recognize any gains or losses when the asset's book value is not equal to the cash received

LO6. Analyze the acquisition, use, and disposal of long-lived intangible assets
❖ Intangible assets are recorded at cost, but only when *purchased*
  o The costs of most *internally developed* intangible assets are expensed as research and development when incurred
❖ Intangibles are reported at book value on the balance sheet
❖ Amortization is calculated for intangibles with limited useful lives using the straight-line method
❖ Intangibles with unlimited useful lives, including goodwill, are not amortized, but are reviewed for impairment

LO7. Interpret the fixed asset turnover ratio.
❖ The fixed asset turnover ratio measures the company's efficiency at using its investment in property, plant, and equipment to generate sales
  o Higher turnover ratios imply greater efficiency

LO8. Describe factors to consider when comparing across companies
❖ Companies in different industries require different levels of investments in long-lived assets. Beyond that, you should consider:
  o Whether there are differences in
    ▪ depreciation methods,
    ▪ estimated useful lives, and
    ▪ estimated residual values can affect
  o Because differences in any of these can affect
    ▪ the book value of long-lived assets
    ▪ the ratios calculated using these book values
    ▪ any gains or losses reported at the time of asset disposal

READ AND RECALL QUESTIONS
After you read each section of the chapter, answer the related Read and Recall Questions below.

LEARNING OBJECTIVE
After studying the section of the chapter, you should be able to:
1. Define, classify, and explain the nature of long-lived assets

---

Definition and Classification of Long-Lived Assets
What is a long-lived asset? Name and define the two broad types of long-lived assets?

LEARNING OBJECTIVE
After studying the section of the chapter, you should be able to:
2. Apply the cost principle to measure the acquisition of long-lived assets

Tangible Assets
Briefly describe the following: (1) Land Improvements; (2) Construction in Progress

What costs are considered part of the cost of a tangible asset? What is meant by the term *capitalizing* costs?

How is the determination made about whether to expense or capitalize a cost?

List three or four costs (besides Land) that are capitalized in the Land account.

What is a *basket purchase*? How are the costs of a basket purchase allocated to the individual assets?

Assuming a company purchased a Building for $1,000,000, what account(s) would be debited and what account(s) would be credited for the transaction?

How would the previous entry differ if $200,000 of the purchase price was paid in cash and the balance owed was put on a note?

Use of Tangible Assets
Explain the types of expenditures that are considered *ordinary repairs and maintenance*. How often are these types of expenditures made?

Explain the types of expenditures that are considered *extraordinary repairs, replacements, and/or additions*. How often are these types of expenditures made? What specifically differentiates these expenditures from ordinary repairs and maintenance?

Define *depreciation*. What principle or assumption requires that depreciation expense be recorded? What account is debited when recording depreciation and what account is credited?

What type of account is *accumulated depreciation?* What does the balance in the account represent? Define *book value*. How is it calculated?

What three amounts are necessary to calculate depreciation?

Define *residual value* and *useful life*. What is *depreciable cost?* How is it determined?

LEARNING OBJECTIVE
After studying the section of the chapter, you should be able to:
3. Apply various depreciation methods as the future economic benefits are used-up over time

---

Depreciation Methods
How is *straight-line* depreciation calculated? What does (1 / Useful Life) represent? Explain what a *depreciation schedule* is.

Complete the following for the straight-line method: (1) Depreciation Expense is a _____ amount each year. (2) Accumulated depreciation _____ by an equal amount each year; and (3) Book value _____ by the same equal amount each year.

What two elements are estimated in calculating straight-line depreciation? Why should these estimates be updated regularly?

What are the two steps performed when calculating Units-of-Production depreciation? How is useful life defined under this method? What *additional* information must be provided in order to calculate depreciation at the end of the accounting period under this method? Why?

Complete the following: Under the declining-balance method, depreciation expense is _____ in the early years of an asset's life and _____ in the later years. This is why it is sometimes called a(n) _____ depreciation method.

What is the declining-balance rate based on?   What is the declining-balance rate used in the text?   Which amount is *not* included in the formula for computing depreciation expense under this method, though it is for the other methods?

Complete the following: Managers are allowed to choose any _____ and _____ depreciation methods, provided that they describe them in their financial statement _____.

Complete the following: _____ typically is used when asset use fluctuates significantly from period to period. _____ methods apply best to assets that are most productive when they are new and quickly lose their usefulness as they get older.

Why do differing depreciation methods for book and tax purposes cause deferred income taxes? What is the least and latest rule?

LEARNING OBJECTIVE
After studying the section of the chapter, you should be able to:
4. Explain the effect of asset impairment on the financial statements

Asset Impairment Losses
Define an asset impairment. What is the proper accounting treatment for an impairment?

How are the income statement and balance sheet affected by the recording of an asset impairment?

LEARNING OBJECTIVE
After studying the section of the chapter, you should be able to:
5. Analyze the disposal of long-lived tangible assets

Disposal of Tangible Assets
Explain the difference between a *voluntary* disposal vs. an *involuntary* disposal. Why are two journal entries necessary to record the disposal of an asset?

How is the gain or loss on disposal calculated? Where is the gain or loss reported in the income statement? Why?

Intangible Assets
List four types of intangible assets.

What is the most frequently reported intangible assets?

Acquisition, Use, and Disposal
What is required in order for an intangible cost to be recorded as an asset? If a cost cannot be recorded as an intangible asset, how is it reported? What amount is used to record an intangible asset?

Define *net assets*. Why is this concept important in calculating goodwill?

What is *amortization*? When can intangible assets be amortized? When would an intangible asset *not* be eligible for amortization?

Management Decisions
What might occur if a business underestimates the amount to invest in long-lived assets? If it overestimates?

What does the Fixed Asset Turnover measure? How is it calculated?

The Impact of Depreciation Differences
Which elements of the depreciation calculation are estimates that can vary the results of the depreciation expense calculation? Why is an understanding of the different depreciation methods important for financial statement users?

How does the depreciation method used affect the gain or loss on disposal of an asset? Why?

What effect do estimates of *useful life* and *residual value* have on the income statement? What measure is popular in analyzing financial statements without having to evaluate the impact of differences in depreciation and amortization methods?

Supplement A – Natural Resources
What is a natural resource?

Define depletion.

What is the primary difference between how depletion is recorded versus how depreciation and amortization are recorded? Why?

Supplement B – Changes in Depreciation
When the useful life and/or residual value of an asset changes, how is it accomplished?

Why is partial years' depreciation necessary? Which method never has to worry about partial years' depreciation? Why?

FINANCIAL ANALYSIS TOOLS

1. The following table summarizes the calculation for each of the three depreciation methods:

Method	Computation
Straight-line	(Cost – Residual Value) x 1 /Useful Life
Units-of-production	[(Cost – Residual Value) / Estimated Total Production] x Actual Production
Double-declining-balance	(Cost – Accumulated Depreciation) x 2 /Useful Life

2. The Fixed Asset Turnover Ratio is calculated as:

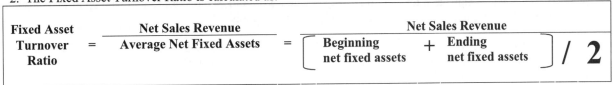

HELPFUL STUDY TIP

1. **Calculating the Gain or Loss on Disposal of an Asset:** Your head is probably swimming right now with all of the information covered in this chapter. You may be wondering, "How am I possibly going to remember all of this?" Well, I can help you out with one area, anyway: calculating the gain or loss on an asset upon its disposal. Trying to remember all of the calculations involved can be overwhelming. So, here is a sure-fire, quick, and easy way to calculate the gain or loss on sale of an asset. The key is letting the *journal entry* do all the work. There are four steps in this process and all four involve the journal entry. Just follow these steps, and it will work EVERY TIME.

   Let's go through an example. Assume that the journal entry to update depreciation through the date of disposal has already been made so all of the accounts are up-to-date. A company sold a machine for $16,000. The machine cost $33,000 and has accumulated depreciation of $20,000 through the date of disposal. Follow these steps to make the journal entry:

   Step 1. *Credit the asset account for the machine's original cost.* This step removes the asset from the books. An asset has a normal debit balance. So, if you want to remove it from the books you have to credit it. (NOTE: Leave some space above this entry because you're going to have some debits pretty soon!)

   > cr Machinery (-A) 33,000

   Step 2. *Debit the asset's Accumulated Depreciation account for the full amount in the Accumulated Depreciation account for this asset.* When you get rid of an asset, you have to get rid of *everything* associated with the asset, including the entire amount of its Accumulated Depreciation. This step removes the accumulated depreciation of the asset from the books. (NOTE: when you do this step leave a blank line between the entry from step 1 and this entry as shown.) This is why you left some space above the first entry.

   > dr Accumulated Depreciation (+xA, -A)   20,000
   >
   > cr Machinery (-A) 33,000

   Step 3. *Debit Cash for the amount receive from the disposal (if any).* This step simply records the amount received on the sale. If no cash was received, you simply *skip this step and go straight to step 4!!*

   > dr Cash (+A)   16,000
   > dr Accumulated Depreciation . . (+xA, -A)   20,000
   >
   > cr Machinery (-A) 33,000

   Step 4. *Fill in the Blank!* This is the best part and why you left the blank space in step 2. If you look back at the 'incomplete' entry in step 3, you will see that the total debits ($16,000 + $20,000 = $36,000) *do not* equal total credits ($33,000.) This is where the 'fill in the blank comes in. To make this entry balance you need a $3,000 credit. (NOTE: always 'fill in' an amount on the side (debit or credit) with the smallest total—$33,000 in our example, that will make it total up to the bigger side—$36,000). To make $33,000 'add up to' $36,000 an additional $3,000 is needed on the credit side of the entry, like this:

   > dr Cash (+A)   16,000
   > dr Accumulated Depreciation   20,000
   >   cr Gain on Sale of Machinery 3,000
   >   cr Machinery (-A) 33,000

   Now, all you need is an account name! Gains and losses act like Revenues and Expenses. That is, Revenues are Credits and Gains are also credits! Expenses are Debits and Losses are also Debits! Since you needed a CREDIT to make this entry balance, it must be a GAIN on sale of Machinery! Had it been a Loss, in step 4 you would have needed a debit to balance. If there *is no gain or loss,* the entry will balance after step 3!

SELF-TEST QUESTIONS AND EXERCISES

MATCHING
1. *Match each of the key terms listed on the following page with the appropriate textbook definition.*

_____	Amortization	_____	Impairment
_____	Book values	_____	Licensing Right
_____	Capitalize	_____	Long-lived assets
_____	Copyright	_____	Net assets
_____	Declining-balance method	_____	Ordinary Repairs and Maintenance
_____	Depletion	_____	Patent
_____	Depreciable Cost	_____	Research and development
_____	Depreciation	_____	Residual value
_____	EBITDA	_____	Straight-line method
_____	Extraordinary Repairs	_____	Trademark
_____	Franchise	_____	Units-of-production method
_____	Goodwill	_____	Useful life

A. A special name, image, or slogan identified with a product or company.
B. A measure of operating performance that some managers and analysts use in place of net income.
C. The limited permission to use property according to specific terms and conditions set out in a contract.
D. A depreciation method that allocates the cost of an asset over its useful life based on the relationship of its periodic output to its total estimated output.
E. A right to exclude others from making, using, selling, or importing an invention.
F. The estimated amount to be recovered at the end of the company's estimated useful life of an asset.
G. A depreciation method that assigns more depreciation to the early years of an asset's life and less depreciation to the later years.
H. To record a cost as an asset, rather than an expense.
I. The portion of an asset's cost that will be used in generating revenue.
J. Expenditures for routine operating upkeep of long-lived assets and are recorded as expenses.
K. The process of allocating a natural resource's cost over the period of its extraction or harvesting.
L. A contractual right to sell certain products or services, use certain trademarks, or perform activities in a certain geographical region.
M. The allocation of the cost of long-lived tangible assets over their productive lives using a systematic and rational method.
N. A depreciation method that allocates the cost of an asset in equal periodic amounts over its useful life.
O. The shorthand term used to refer to assets minus liabilities.
P. The expected service life of an asset to the present owner.
Q. The acquisition cost of an asset less accumulated depreciation.
R. The name given to allocating the cost of intangible assets over their limited useful lives.
S. A form of protection provided to the original authors of literary, musical, artistic, dramatic, and other works of authorship.
T. Expenditures that may someday lead to patents, copyrights, or other intangible assets, but the uncertainty about their future benefits requires that they be expensed.
U. Resources owned by a business that will enable it to produce the goods and services that are sold to customers
V. Expenditures that increase a tangible asset's economic usefulness in the future and are recorded as increases in asset accounts, not as expenses
W. The premium a company pays to obtain the favorable reputation associated with another company.
X. Occurs when the cash to be generated by an asset is estimated to be less than the carrying value of that asset.

TRUE-FALSE QUESTIONS

For each of the following, enter a T or F in the blank to indicate whether the statement is true or false.

_____1.   (LO1) Long-lived assets are any assets that will be used up within the next year.

_____2.   (LO1) Intangible assets are assets you can see and touch such as land and buildings.

_____3.   (LO2) Capitalized costs include all reasonable and necessary costs of acquiring and preparing an asset for use, in accordance with the cost principle.

_____4.   (LO2) A 'basket purchase' splits the cost between each asset in proportion to the tax benefits provided to the company. Those assets providing a higher tax benefit are allocated more cost.

_____5.   (LO2) Replacements and additions are capitalized in the appropriate asset account because they increase the usefulness of the asset beyond its original condition.

_____6.   (LO2) Long-lived tangible assets are essentially prepaid costs, depreciation is the method used for allocating that cost to the future periods benefited in accordance with the matching principle.

_____7.   (LO2) To calculate depreciation expense, three elements are needed: Book value, Residual Value, and Useful Life.

_____8.   (LO3) Units-of-production is an accelerated depreciation method.

_____9.   (LO3) Book value of an asset cannot be lower than residual value under any of the depreciation methods, even when the asset is fully depreciated.

_____10. (LO3) It is both illegal and unethical for a business to maintain separate records for tax and financial reporting purposes.

_____11. (LO4) Asset impairment losses are considered expenses since the asset was used for normal operations.

_____12. (LO5) Two entries must be made for an asset disposal: one updates the depreciation expense and accumulated depreciation accounts, while the other records the actual disposal of the asset.

_____13. (LO5) Gain or loss on asset disposal is determined by taking the resources received from the disposal and subtracting the depreciable cost of the asset.

_____14. (LO6) The most frequently reported intangible assets are trademarks since virtually every product can be readily identified by them.

_____15. (LO6) Goodwill results when the purchase price of a business is greater than the value of its net assets.

_____16. (LO6) Intangible assets with an unlimited or indefinite life are amortized over a maximum of forty years.

_____17. (LO7) When the proper investment in long-lived assets is underestimated, excessive costs are incurred that will reduce profitability.

_____18. (LO7) A high or increasing fixed asset turnover ratio, generally speaking, indicates a more effective use of fixed assets whereas a low or declining ratio usually means the opposite.

_____19. (LO8) It is possible for a company to report a loss on sale using one depreciation method, but a gain on sale using another depreciation method even if the same amount is received for the sale.

_____20. (Supp) Depletion is the process of allocating an intangible asset's cost over the period of its extraction or harvesting.

MULTIPLE CHOICE QUESTIONS

Choose the best answer or response by placing the identifying letter in the space provided.

_____1. (LO1) Long-lived assets are classified as:
   a.   amortizable and non-amortizable
   b.   ordinary and extraordinary
   c.   tangible and intangible
   d.   research and development

_____2. (LO2) Capitalizing costs that are a lot like rent
   a.   is an example of land improvements
   b.   is an example of construction in progress
   c.   is standard practice in accounting
   d.   was a recent example of accounting fraud committed at WorldCom

_____3. (LO2) How much of the following costs relative to a building purchase should be capitalized?
   ➢ Closing agreement price for the building; $1,200,000
   ➢ Survey Fees; $12,000
   ➢ Architect Fees; $25,000
   ➢ Legal Fees; $31,000
   ➢ Repair of parking lot lights; $5,000
   a. $ 1,256,000
   b. $ 1,261,000
   c. $ 1,268,000
   d. $ 1,273,000

_____4. (LO2) Which of the following is *not* a characteristic of extraordinary repairs, replacements, and additions?
   a.   they occur frequently
   b.   they are capitalized in the appropriate asset account
   c.   they increase the efficiency, capacity or extend the useful life of the asset
   d.   they involve large amounts of resources

_____5. (LO2) The acquisition cost of an asset less accumulated depreciation describes:
   a.   depreciable cost
   b.   gain or loss on sale of an asset
   c.   net assets
   d.   book value

> **The following information will be used in answering questions 6 – 9.**
> Conejo Company purchased a piece of equipment for $50,000 on January 3 of year 1. It estimates the equipment will have an estimated useful life of 8 years (or 200,000 hours) and a $4,000 residual value.

_____6. (LO3) Using the straight-line method, what is the book value at the end of year 3?
   a. $ 17,250
   b. $ 18,750
   c. $ 28,750
   d. $ 32,750

_____7. (LO3) Using the Units-of-Production method, calculate the accumulated depreciation at the end of year 4 assuming actual production is:

➤ Year 1   20,000   ➤ Year 3   18,000
➤ Year 2   33,000   ➤ Year 4   28,000

a. $ 22,770
b. $ 22,230
c. $ 24,750
d. $ 25,250

_____8. (LO3) Using the Double Declining Balance Method, what is depreciation expense for year 2?
a. $ 9,375
b. $ 9,625
c. $ 11,500
d. $ 12,500

_____9. (Supplement) Assuming the straight line method is being used, the company revises the estimates for residual value and useful life of the asset at the beginning of year 4. The new residual value is $5,000 and the new useful life from the date of purchase is 13 years. The new annual depreciation expense is: (HINT: use your answers from question 7)
a. $ 2,775.00
b. $ 3,083.33
c. $ 3,275.00
d. $ 3,638.89

_____10. (LO3) Which of the following is *not* a characteristic of the declining-balance method?
a. it is an accelerated depreciation method
b. it is based on a multiple of the straight-line rate
c. residual value is not included in the formula for computing depreciation expense
d. the rate is applied to the asset's depreciable cost in determining depreciation expense for the period

_____11. (LO3) Which of the following is a true statement regarding tax depreciation?
a. managers are not willing to pay the extra cost of maintaining two sets of books: one for tax purposes and one for financial reporting purposes
b. the internal revenue code is designed to discourage certain behaviors that are thought to benefit society
c. the least and latest rule is an unethical, illegal scheme designed to make money
d. none of these are true statements regarding tax depreciation

_____12. (LO4) Which of the following is *not* a true statement regarding impairment losses?
a. an impairment loss occurs when estimated future cash flows of an asset fall below their book value
b. impairment losses are extremely rare because they violate the conservatism principle
c. book value should be written down and the amount of the write-down reported as an impairment loss
d. impairment losses are reported below operating income in the bottom part of the income statement

_____13. (LO5) Which of following is *not* a true statement regarding the disposal of tangible assets?
a. a disposal requires a journal entry to remove the asset from the accounts
b. gain or loss on disposal is calculated as the difference between the resources received from the disposal and the accumulated depreciation of the disposed asset
c. disposals may be voluntary or involuntary
d. a disposal requires a journal entry to update the depreciation expense and accumulated depreciation accounts

_____14. (LO2) Which of the following describes the treatment of costs of an intangible asset that is being self-constructed or internally developed?
   a.   licensing right
   b.   goodwill
   c.   patent
   d.   research and development

_____15. (LO6) Which of the following is *not* considered a type of intangible asset?
   a.   licensing rights
   b.   copyright
   c.   mineral deposits
   d.   all of these are considered intangible assets

_____16. (LO6) Which of the following is *not* considered a true statement regarding intangible assets?
   a.   nearly all intangible assets must be purchased in order to be recorded as an asset on the balance sheet
   b.   the excess of the purchase price of a business over the value of its net assets is referred to as a Gain on Purchase of a business
   c.   amortization is similar to depreciation except that amortization is applied to intangible assets and depreciation is applied to tangible assets
   d.   intangibles have no value at the end of their useful lives

_____17. (LO7) Assuming a business has Net Sales Revenue of $800,0000; beginning net fixed assets of $200,000; ending net fixed assets of $250,000; and Net Income of $120,000, what is the fixed asset turnover ratio?
   a.   0.28 times
   b.   0.53 times
   c.   3.56 times
   d.   4.00 times

_____18. (LO7) Which of the following statements about the fixed asset turnover ratio is *not* true?
   a.   Renting assets has the effect of increasing the fixed asset turnover ratio because a company can generate revenues using fixed assets that are not reported on the balance sheet
   b.   the fixed asset turnover ratio measures the sales dollars generated by each dollar invested in fixed assets
   c.   a high or increasing turnover ratio suggests a more effective use of fixed assets
   d.   a low or declining ratio always means a company is inefficient in using its fixed assets

_____19. (LO8) Which of the following is *not* a true statement regarding depreciation differences?
   a.   the gain or loss on the sale of two *identical, fully depreciated*, pieces of equipment will not differ if the company uses straight-line depreciation for one and units of production for the other
   b.   even if two companies have the same number of customers and the same total revenues, the net income will differ if the companies use two different GAAP depreciation methods
   c.   changes in estimates of residual value have no impact on any prior years' depreciation calculations
   d.   all of the above are true statements regarding depreciation differences

_____20. (Supplement) Which of the following is *not* a reason useful lives may vary?
   a.   significant changes in technology that make the asset obsolete more quickly
   b.   the frequency of repairs and maintenance
   c.   the degree of conservatism in management's estimates
   d.   all of the above are reasons that useful lives may vary

EXERCISES
Record your answer to each exercise in the space provided. Show your work.

Exercise 9-1. Identifying and Classifying Capital and Revenue Expenditures (LO1, 2, 6)
For each of the following expenditures, indicate the treatment of the expenditure and its related nature. Use the abbreviations shown on the right. The first one has been done for you as an example.

Transaction	Treatment	Nature
(1) Complete reconditioning of machine	C	M
(2) Power and natural gas used by machine		
(3) Appraisal fee on Building		
(4) Amounts paid to develop a faster machine		
(5) Amount paid for the purchase of a patent		
(6) Closing Costs on purchase of land		
(7) Sales tax on machine		
(8) Annual property taxes on Land		
(9) Transportation charges on new machinery		

Treatment	
C	Capitalize
E	Expense

Nature	
L	Land
B	Building
M	Machinery
I	Intangible
N	Not Capitalized

Exercise 9-2. Computing Depreciation under Alternative Methods. (LO3)
Storm Corporation purchased a machine at the beginning of the year at a cost of $75,000. The estimated useful life is 5 years, and the residual value is $6,600. Assume that the estimated productive life the machine is 120,000 units. Annual production was: Year 1–16,000; Year 2–28,000; Year 3–30,000; Year 4–20,000; Year 5–26,000

Required:
Complete a depreciation schedule for each of the following depreciation methods.

a. Straight-Line

Year (A)	Computation (B)	Depreciation Expense (C)	Accum. Deprec. (D) Prior yr (D) + (C)	Book Value (E) Cost – (D)
At acquisition				
1				
2				
3				
4				
5				

b. Units-of-Production

Year (A)	Computation (B)	Depreciation Expense (C)	Accum. Deprec. (D) Prior yr (D) + (C)	Book Value (E) Cost – (D)
At acquisition				
1				
2				
3				
4				
5				

c. Double-Declining Balance

Year (A)	Computation (B)	Depreciation Expense (C)	Accum. Deprec. (D) Prior yr (D) + (C)	Book Value (E) Cost − (D)
At acquisition				
1				
2				
3				
4				
5				

Exercise 9-3. Identifying Asset Impairment. (LO4)

For each of the following scenarios, indicate whether the asset has been impaired (Y for yes and N for no) and, if so, how much loss should be recorded?

Asset	Book Value	Estimated Future Cash Flows	Is Asset Impaired?	If yes, amount of loss?
a. Equipment	$ 112,000	$ 80,000		$
b. Machine	43,000	39,000		
c. Trademark	300,000	340,000		
d. Store House	19,000	7,000		

Calculations:

Exercise 9-4. The Effect of Book Value on an Asset Disposal. (LO5)

Part A.

Park and Shop operates at the local Mall. Drivers shuttle customers from their parking spot to the mall entrance. When customers are done shopping, drivers return the customers to their parked vehicle. Park and Shop recently sold a shuttle van for $12,000. The original price of the van was $43,000 and depreciation had been recorded on the van for 3 years. Give the journal entry for the disposal of the van, assuming that:

a. The accumulated depreciation was $35,000

b. The accumulated depreciation was $31,000

c. The accumulated depreciation was $29,000

Part B.

Based on the preceding situations explain how the amount of depreciation recorded affects the amount of the gain or loss on disposal.

Exercise 9-5. Computing and Reporting the Acquisition and Amortization of Intangible Assets (LO6)
Part A.
Rolle Company purchased a patent for $65,000 on January 1, 2009. It is expected to have a useful life of 20 years. Compute the amortization of the patent for the year ended December 31, 2009

Part B.
Bonnie Doodles™ has been in business for 20 years and has developed a number of loyal customers for its home-baked dog snacks. Poorina Dog Chews offered to purchase Bonnie Doodles™ for $4,300,000. The market value of Bonnie Doodles™ assets and liabilities is $3,500,000 when the offer is made. The internally developed Trade Name of Bonnie Doodles™ is valued at $500,000.

(1) How much has Poorina Dog Chews included for intangibles in its offer of $4,300,000? List the name and amount of each intangible.

(2) Assuming Bonnie Doodles™ accepts this offer, which company will report goodwill on its balance sheet?

Exercise 9-6. Computing and Evaluating the Fixed Asset Turnover Ratio (LO7)
The following information was reported by Beg Lad Two Inc. (BLT) for 2006:

Net fixed assets (beginning of year)	$ 980,000
Net fixed assets (end of year)	1,350,000
Net sales for the year	636,000
Net income for the year	75,000

(1) Compute the company's fixed asset turnover ratio for the year.

(2) What can you say about BLT's fixed asset turnover when compared to its competitor's ratio of .75?

SOLUTIONS TO SELF-TEST QUESTIONS AND EXERCISES

MATCHING

R	Amortization		X	Impairment
Q	Book value		C	Licensing Right
H	Capitalize		U	Long-lived assets
S	Copyright		O	Net assets
G	Declining-balance method		J	Ordinary Repairs and Maintenance
K	Depletion		E	Patent
I	Depreciable Cost		T	Research and development
M	Depreciation		F	Residual value
B	EBITDA		N	Straight-line method
V	Extraordinary Repairs		A	Trademark
L	Franchise		D	Units-of-production method
W	Goodwill		P	Useful life

TRUE-FALSE QUESTIONS

1. F – Long-lived assets will *not* be used up within the next year.
2. F – Intangible assets have special rights, but no physical substance.
3. T
4. F – Basket purchases are split between each asset in proportion to the market value of the assets as a whole.
5. T
6. T
7. F – The three elements needed are Asset Cost, Residual Value, and Useful Life.
8. F – Declining-balance is an accelerated depreciation method.
9. T
10. F – It is both legal and ethical for a business to maintain separate records for tax and financial reporting purposes.
11. F – Asset impairments work *like* expenses but are not technically considered expenses because they arise from peripheral or incidental activities rather than normal operations.
12. T
13. F – Gain or loss on asset disposal is determined by taking the resources received from the disposal and subtracting the book value of the asset.
14. F – The most frequently reported intangible asset is Goodwill.
15. T
16. F – Intangible assets with an unlimited or indefinite life are not amortized.
17. F – This describes the result if proper investment in long-lived assets is overestimated.
18. T
19. T
20. F – Depletion is the process of allocating a natural resource's cost over the period of its extraction or harvesting.

MULTIPLE CHOICE QUESTIONS

1. C	6. D	11. D	16. B
2. D	7. A	12. B	17. C
3. A	8. A	13. B	18. D
4. A	9. A	14. D	19. D
5. D	10. D	15. C	20. D

EXERCISES

Exercise 9-1. Identifying and Classifying Capital and Revenue Expenditures   (LO1, 2, 6)

Transaction	Treatment	Nature
(1) Complete reconditioning of machine	C	M
(2) Power and natural gas used by machine	E	N
(3) Appraisal fee on Building	C	B
(4) Amounts paid to develop a faster machine	E	N
(5) Amount paid for the purchase of a patent	C	I
(6) Closing Costs on purchase of land	C	L
(7) Sales tax on machine	C	M
(8) Annual property taxes on Land	E	N
(9) Transportation charges on new machinery	C	M

Exercise 9-2. Computing Depreciation under Alternative Methods. (LO3)

a. Straight-Line

Year (A)	Computation (B)	Depreciation Expense (C)	Accum. Deprec. (D) Prior yr (D) + (C)	Book Value (E) Cost – (D)
At acquisition			-	$75,000
1	($75,000-$6,600) x 1/5	$13,680	$13,680	61,320
2	($75,000-$6,600) x 1/5	13,680	27,360	47,640
3	($75,000-$6,600) x 1/5	13,680	41,040	33,960
4	($75,000-$6,600) x 1/5	13,680	54,720	20,280
5	($75,000-$6,600) x 1/5	13,680	68,400	6,600

b. Units-of-Production

Year (A)	Computation (B)	Depreciation Expense (C)	Accum. Deprec. (D) Prior yr (D) + (C)	Book Value (E) Cost – (D)
At acquisition			-	$75,000
1	[($75,000-$6,600) / 120,000] x 16,000	$9,120	$9,120	65,880
2	[($75,000-$6,600) / 120,000] x 28,000	15,960	25,080	49,920
3	[($75,000-$6,600) / 120,000] x 30,000	17,100	42,180	32,820
4	[($75,000-$6,600) / 120,000] x 20,000	11,400	53,580	21,420
5	[($75,000-$6,600) / 120,000] x 26,000	14,820	68,400	6,600

c. Double-Declining Balance

Year (A)	Computation (B)	Depreciation Expense (C)	Accum. Deprec. (D) Prior yr (D) + (C)	Book Value (E) Cost – (D)
At acquisition			-	$75,000
1	($75,000-$0) x 2/5	$30,000	$30,000	45,000
2	($75,000-$30,000) x 2/5	18,000	48,000	27,000
3	($75,000-$48,000) x 2/5	10,800	58,800	16,200
4	($75,000-$58,800) x 2/5	6,480	65,280	9,720
5	($75,000-$65,280) x 2/5	~~3,888~~	~~69,168~~	~~5,832~~
	$68,400-65,280 = 3,120	3,120	68,400	6,600

Exercise 9-3. Identifying Asset Impairment. (LO4)

Asset	Book Value	Estimated Future Cash Flows	Is Asset Impaired?	If yes, amount of loss?
a. Equipment	$ 112,000	$ 80,000	Y	$32,000
b. Machine	43,000	39,000	Y	4,000
c. Trademark	300,000	340,000	N	N/A
d. Store House	19,000	7,000	Y	12,000

Exercise 9-4. The Effect of Book Value on an Asset Disposal. (LO5)
Part A.
a. The accumulated depreciation was $35,000

    dr Cash (+A). 12,000
    dr Accumulated Depreciation .(+xA, -A) 35,000
        cr Gain on Sale of Machinery (+R, +SE) 4,000
        cr Machinery (-A) 43,000

b. The accumulated depreciation was $31,000

    dr Cash (+A). 12,000
    dr Accumulated Depreciation . .(+xA, -A) 31,000
        cr Machinery (-A) 43,000

c. The accumulated depreciation was $29,000

    dr Cash (+A). 12,000
    dr Accumulated Depreciation . (+xA, -A). 29,000
    dr Loss on Sale of Machinery (+E, -SE) 2,000
        cr Machinery (-A) 43,000

Part B.
When the depreciation recorded is high (perhaps an accelerated depreciation method), more depreciation is taken resulting in a lower book value. Since the book value is lower than the other situations, the $12,000 received from the sale resulted in a gain. When the depreciation recorded is low (perhaps units-of-production), less depreciation is taken resulting in a higher book value. Since the book value is higher than the cash received, a loss results from the sale. When the depreciation recorded causes the book value of the asset to be exactly the same amount as the money received from the sale, there is no gain or loss.

Exercise 9-5. Computing and Reporting the Acquisition and Amortization of Intangible Assets (LO6)
Part A.
Rolle Company purchased a patent for $65,000 on January 1, 2007. It is expected to have a useful life of 20 years. Compute the amortization of the patent for the year ended December 31, 2007
$65,000 / 20 = 3,250

Part B.
Bonnie Doodles™ has been in business for 20 years and has developed a number of loyal customers for its home-baked dog snacks. Poorina Dog Chews offered to purchased Bonnie Doodles™ for $4,300,000. The market value of Bonnie Doodles™ assets and liabilities is $3,500,000 when the offer is made. The internally developed Trade Name of Bonnie Doodles™ is valued at $500,000.

(1) How much has Poorina Dog Chews included for intangibles in its offer of $4,300,000? List the name and amount of each.

Trade Name:	$500,000
Goodwill: (4,300,000 – 3,500,000 -500,000)	$300,000
Total	$800,000

(2) Assuming Bonnie Doodles™ accepts this offer, which company will report goodwill on its balance sheet?
Poorina Dog Chews

Exercise 9-6. Computing and Evaluating the Fixed Asset Turnover Ratio. (LO7)
Compute the company's fixed asset turnover ratio for the year.
$636,000 / [(980,000 + 1,350,000) / 2] = .55

What can you say about BLT's fixed asset turnover when compared to its competitor's ratio of .75?
It appears as if BLT is not using its fixed assets efficiently as compared to its competitor. However, it may be that BLT purchased a number of fixed assets in anticipation of increased sales in the following year. A thorough analysis of the financials is recommended.

CHAPTER 10
REPORTING AND INTERPRETING
LIABILITIES

ORGANIZATION OF THE CHAPTER

Understand the business	**Study the accounting methods**	**Evaluate the results**	**Review the chapter**
- Decisions related to Liabilities	- Measurement of liabilities	- Current ratio analysis	- Demonstration case
- Reporting liabilities	- Current liabilities	- Times interest earned ratio	-Chapter summary
	- Long-term liabilities	- Common features of debt	- Key terms
		- Unrecorded liabilities	- Practice material

CHAPTER FOCUS SUGGESTIONS

Review

In Chapters 8 and 9, you learned everything you ever wanted to know about accounts receivable and long-lived assets, and then some! Much to your dismay, you discovered that following GAAP doesn't necessarily mean there's only *one* right way to do things. There may be three (straight-line, units-of-production, or declining-balance) You also discovered new tools for evaluating businesses (a couple of turnovers and ratios.) Well, we certainly don't want to disappoint you now! Like a good soap opera, the saga continues in Chapter 10. So, grab a bowl of cereal and settle in for a while. This chapter is a bit long!

Introduction

In this chapter we cover the accounting procedures and financial ratios used to report and interpret liabilities, and how they affect credit ratings. If a business is unable to pay its bills when they come due it may be headed to bankruptcy court sometime in the future. You certainly don't want to be holding their stock or their note payable should that scenario play out. So, evaluating whether a company is able to meet its debt obligations is of the utmost concern to both investors and creditors.

UNDERSTAND THE BUSINESS

> **Learning Objective 1**
> Explain how the reporting of liabilities assists decision makers.

Decisions Related to Liabilities

Anyone who loans money to others (even if it's just $10 to your brother) wants to know if the money will be repaid. One way to determine this is to see how much this individual owes *everyone else*. Logically, we all know that if someone owes a lot of money to other people, it wouldn't be a wise decision to lend them more!

Reporting Liabilities

However, if one individual owes $100,000 on a building mortgage and another individual owes $100,000 on a five-month note payable, there's a huge difference! Though both owe the same amount, the first person has a number of years to repay the debt, whereas the second person only has five months to pay off the same amount! For this reason, we classify liabilities as **current liabilities** (amounts due within one year or one operating cycle which ever is longer) or long-term liabilities. We'll deal with the long-term debt later in the chapter. For now, let's focus on current liabilities.

STUDY THE ACCOUNTING METHODS

> **Learning Objective 2**
> Explain how to account for common types of current liabilities.

Measurement of Liabilities

A company must record a liability when a transaction or event obligates the company to give up assets or services in the future. The amounts reported on the balance sheet as liabilities result from any or all of the following events:

1) ***The initial amount of the liability.*** This is the amount that a creditor would accept to settle the liability immediately after the transaction or event occurred. This is often called its *cash-equivalent.*

2) **Additional amounts owed to the creditor.** Debt will increase when additional obligations arise. Some additional charges arise simply because of the passage of time! We know this all too well as *Interest.*

3) **Payments or services provided to the creditor.** Debt is lowered when payments are made or services are provided to the creditor.

Current Liabilities

1. Accounts Payable

Purchasing goods and services on credit from other companies involves three stages: (1) order the goods/services; (2) receive the goods/services; and (3) pay for the goods/services. Liabilities are recorded when the company is 'obligated to give up assets or services.' The liability that is created at the point of obligation is Accounts Payable. A major benefit of purchasing on account is that suppliers don't charge interest on unpaid balances unless they are overdue.

2. Accrued Liabilities

When a business incurs an expense in one accounting period and makes payment in a subsequent accounting period, an adjusting entry is required at the time the expense is incurred. These types of adjustments create **accrued liabilities.** The following accrued liabilities are discussed in this section: (1) Accrued Salaries, (2) Accrued Payroll Taxes, and (3) Accrued Income taxes.

    a.   Accrued Salaries Most workers receive their paychecks sometime *after* rendering the services to the company. So, at the end of the accounting period, there are wages that have been *earned* by the employees but have not yet been *paid.* These unpaid salaries are recorded as a liability called *salaries payable.* Assuming salaries owed at the end of the period – 12/31/08 are $6,000, the entry to record them would be:

1. Analyze	Assets	=	Liabilities	+	Stockholders' Equity
			Salaries Payable +6,000		Salaries Expense (+E) –6,000

2. Record			
	dr Salaries and Wages Expense (+E, –SE)...............	6,000	
	cr Salaries Payable (+L)......		6,000

    Most companies also include the cost of employment benefits earned by employees but not yet paid. These benefits include: retirement programs, vacation time, and health insurance.

    b.   Accrued Payroll Taxes In addition to accrued salaries, the company is required to withhold amounts from employees for federal, state, and local income taxes, as well as Social Security, and Medicare taxes. The company is responsible for additional payroll taxes over and above the amounts withheld from employees, including federal unemployment taxes and state unemployment taxes.

        a.   Employee Income Taxes All businesses are required to withhold income taxes from every employee's pay. Businesses collect the money and submit it to the appropriate governmental agencies throughout the year. This amount withheld is recorded as a liability of the company because the company owes this money to the governmental agencies on behalf of the employees.

        b.   FICA Taxes FICA is short for the Federal Insurance Contributions Act and consists of employee and employer contributions for Medicare and Social Security. In 2007, companies were required to withhold 1.45% of each employee's gross wages for Medicare and 6.2% of employees gross wages (up to $97,500) for Social Security.

        Many businesses combine the Medicare and Social Security into one percentage 7.65% (1.45% Medicare + 6.2% Social Security.) This 7.65% represents the *employee's* contribution. The *employer* is required to ante up the exact same amount into the kitty. Thus, the company actually *owes* a total of 2.9% (1.45% employees + 1.45% company) for Medicare and 12.4% (6.2% employees + 6.2% company) for Social Security.

In reality, recording payroll isn't as simple as the previous entry because all of the withheld items must be recorded and deducted from the employee's pay. The journal entry that is made every time payroll is earned by employees to record the amounts to be paid to employees (after withholding the items discussed previously) must be made. *Plus* another entry is made to record the payroll taxes owed by the company itself! These two entries are:

1. Analyze	Assets	=	Liabilities	+ Stockholders' Equity
	Cash –4,941		Withheld Income Taxes Payable +600	Salaries and Wages Expense (+E) –6,000
			FICA Taxes Payable +459	

2. Record

dr Salaries and Wages Expense (+E, –SE)……….	6,000	
cr Withheld Income Taxes Payable (+L)…		600
cr FICA Taxes Payable (+L)……………		459
cr Cash (–A)……………………………		4,941

The amount actually paid to employees is $4,941. The withheld amounts ($600, $459) are liabilities that will be paid to the government on the employee's behalf. The gross wages ($6,000) are an expense to the company.

Employers are also required to pay payroll taxes. The FICA taxes withheld from the employees must be matched by the company. So, an additional entry is required to record the employer's responsibility.

1. Analyze	Assets	=	Liabilities	+ Stockholders' Equity
			FICA Taxes Payable +459	Payroll Tax Expense (+E) –459

2. Record

dr Payroll Tax Expense (+E, –SE)……….......	459	
cr FICA Taxes Payable (+L)……		459

c.   ***Accrued Income Taxes***   Just like you and me, a business must pay income taxes on its taxable earnings. Corporate income taxes are reported annually on a Form 1120. Taxable income is multiplied by a tax rate, which for most large corporations is about 35%. Corporate income taxes are due two and a half months after year-end, although most corporations are required to make estimated tax payments during the year.

3. Notes Payable
Assume a company borrows $30,000 from a local bank on October 1, 2008. It is a 10-month note, charging 8% interest annually. Interest payments are due March 1, 2009 and August 1, 2009. The principal is to be repaid at maturity, August 1, 2009. The following time line illustrates the transactions on the note.

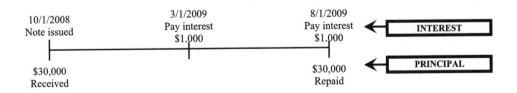

Study Guide, Chapter 10

Page 309

Three journal entries are required to account for this note:

a. **_The Note is Issued and the Cash is Received._** On the date the note is received, the following entry must be made:

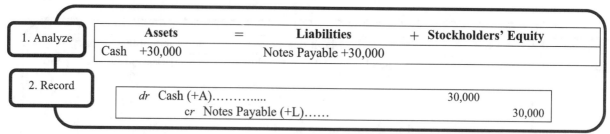

b. **_Interest is owed at the end of the accounting period_.** Nobody lends money for free. There is a 'fee' for the time that money is lent. This is called *Interest*. Interest represents the amount charged for the use of money. Every lender charges a different amount for the use of the money. This is referred to as an *interest rate*. To determine the amount of interest charged on a note we use the following formula:

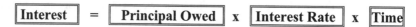

While principal and interest are pretty straight-forward, the *time* component is the tricky one. This is computed based on the length of time you are calculating the interest. When the note's length is stated in

- *months* (as is the case for our example), time is expressed in months. So, if you calculate interest for the *entire term of this loan,* the time would be expressed as 10/12. This means you wish to calculate interest on 10 months out of 12 months (1 year.) The bottom number of the time fraction will *always be 12 if the maturity of the note is expressed in months!* **_ALWAYS_** (the number on the bottom -12- only changes if the length of the loan is expressed in something other than months, such as days.)
- if we wish to calculate the amount of interest that is owed on the note *as of* December 31, 2008 (end of the accounting period), the time element is expressed as 3/12. We use this amount because we are only calculating interest for the length of time we've had the note as of December 31. We've had it for all of October, November, and December—3 months out of the whole year—12. (NOTE: the length of the note (10 months) is totally irrelevant for this calculation. We are only interested in calculating interest on how many months *this year* we owe interest on). Therefore, the amount of interest accrued is $600 ($30,000 x 8% x 3/12.) This calculates interest for the period of October through December of 2008.

Notice that a payable is recorded because we *owe* this interest to the company. The first interest payment isn't due until March 1, but the matching principle requires that we report this interest expense in the period it was incurred.

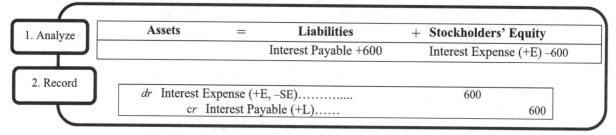

c. **_Record Payments made to the Lender_.** Now, it is time for the first interest payment, March 1, 2009. Pay close attention here because its kind of tricky. On this date, the company will pay for *five full months of interest.* However, *three of those months have already been recorded and a liability accrued.* So, a portion of the payment will pay off the $600 recorded in December and a portion of the payment will be for interest incurred in January and February of 2009. The entry made for the first interest payment is:

1. Analyze	Assets	=	Liabilities	+	Stockholders' Equity
	Cash −1,000		Interest Payable −600		Interest Expense (+E) +400

2. Record		
dr Interest Expense (+E, −SE).............	400	
dr Interest Payable (−L)......	600	
cr Cash (−A)......		1,000

The interest expense of $400 ($30,000 * 8% * 2/12) represents the amount of interest incurred for January and February of 2009. The cash payment of $1,000 ($30,000 * 8% * 5/12) represent the five months of interest that have been incurred since the loan was taken out on October 1, 2008.

Since no end of period accrual will be made again before the note matures, the full interest amount due on August 1 (maturity date) can *all be expensed when payment is made* (remember this is a 10-month note and five months of interest have already been reported, so only five months remain unpaid when the note matures on August 1) as follows:

1. Analyze	Assets	=	Liabilities	+	Stockholders' Equity
	Cash −1,000				Interest Expense (+E) −1,000

2. Record		
dr Interest Expense (+E, −SE).............	1,000	
cr Cash (−A)......		1,000

Finally, at maturity, the original amount borrowed (principal) must also be repaid:

1. Analyze	Assets	=	Liabilities	+	Stockholders' Equity
	Cash −30,000		Notes Payable −1,000		

2. Record		
dr Notes Payable (−L).............	30,000	
cr Cash (+L)......		30,000

4. *Current Portion of Long-term Debt*
When anyone has a debt that extends beyond one-year in length, (think of your car loan or mortgage), it is a long-term debt. However, you intend to pay off some of that debt *within the current year*. So, the chunk of principal that we expect to pay off within the *current year* must be reported as a *current liability*. We sort of chop up the total amount due into two separate chunks: (1) the amount to be paid off within the current year (current portion of long-term debt), and (2) the amount to be paid off after the current year (long-term debt). Assuming you have a long-term debt of $200,000 and you expect to pay $50,000 of it within the current year, it would be presented on the balance sheet as follows:

Current Liabilities:
Current portion of long-term debt	$50,000
Long-term debt	150,000
Total Liabilities	$ 200,000

We don't actually create a separate account for this current portion, nor is an entry made. It is just split on the balance sheet. The reclassification of long-term debt into current liabilities is necessary so that the balance sheet accurately reports the dollar amount of existing liabilities that will be paid in the upcoming year (current liabilities.)

5. Additional Current Liabilities

a. Sales Tax Payable Most states require retail companies to charge sales tax. Retailers collect sales tax from customers at the time of sale and remit payment to the state. Until payment is made to the state, the sales tax collected by the retailer is reported as a current liability. It is *not an expense* of the company. Assuming an individual purchases a refrigerator for $800 and the sales tax is 6%, the entry made by the retailer would be:

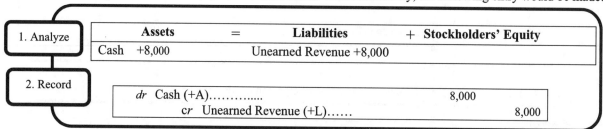

The sales tax payable of $48 ($800 * 6%) will be paid to the state and/or local governments that assess it.

b. Unearned Revenue When companies receive money for goods or services *before* the goods or services are provided, there are two journal entries required to account for these unearned revenues:

    i.   **Receive Cash and Create a Liability.** Assume the State Symphony Organization, sells season tickets to its performances. If $8,000 of season tickets were sold in July, the following entry would be made:

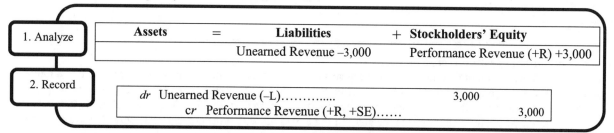

    ii.   **Fulfill Part of the Liability and Earn Revenue.** The Symphony doesn't earn the money until its has performed each concert. Assuming that on December 31, $3,000 of the performances had been earned, the following entry would be made:

1. Analyze	Assets	=	Liabilities	+ Stockholders' Equity
			Unearned Revenue –3,000	Performance Revenue (+R) +3,000

2. Record			
	dr Unearned Revenue (–L)...............		3,000	
	cr Performance Revenue (+R, +SE)......			3,000

At that time, the symphony still owes its patrons $5,000 of performances. Every time another performance is made, the Symphony earns a portion of the $5,000 remaining and no longer *owes* that performance to the patrons.

Long-term Liabilities

Borrowing funds can be done through a private loan agreement or by publicly issued debt certificates. In a private placement, the company finds a lender and negotiates terms for a loan. These types of borrowings are treated exactly like the notes payable discussed earlier except that the maturity of the note extends beyond one year.

> **Learning Objective 3**
> Analyze and record bond liability transactions.

However, when a company needs a very large sum of money, a single lender can not finance the entire amount, so the company sets up publicly issued debt certificates, which is accomplished in three phases: (1) standard terms are set that apply to *every lender,* then (2) the company finds interested lenders, and (3) the money is

                                                        Study Guide, Chapter 10

borrowed from these lenders. These types of loan arrangements are referred to as *bonds*. The terms, interest rate, and date of repayment (maturity date) are detailed in the *bond certificate*. When a company 'sells' these certificates, it actually creates a loan called Bonds Payable. The company receives the cash in exchange for its promise to repay the lenders according to the terms stated on the bond certificates.

Bonds Payable

Bond certificates state the interest payments, a maturity date, and the amount to be paid at maturity (call face value) and are usually $1,000 per bond. Assume $200,000 of bonds are issued (sold) to lenders on January 1, 2009. The bonds will pay $200,000 at maturity (January 1, 2013) and have an interest rate of 8% which is paid annually on January 1.

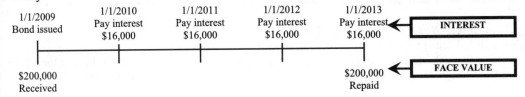

A. **_Accounting for Bonds Issued at Face Value_**

There are four types of entries required when accounting for bonds: (1) the initial bond issuance; (2) interest amounts owed to the lender; (3) interest payments made to the lender; (4) removal of the bond liability when it is paid at maturity (item 2 and much of item 3 are detailed in the supplements to this chapter, item 4 is covered later in this chapter.)

1. **_Issue the Bonds and Receive Cash_.** The journal entry made by the borrower on January 1, 2009 is:

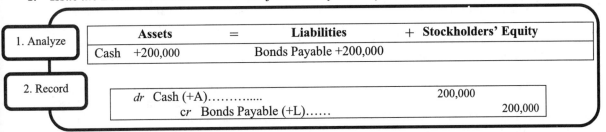

2. **_Owe Interest at the End of the Accounting Period_.** We calculate interest on a bond just as we do for interest on a note. Interest of $16,000 ($200,000 x 8% x 12/12) is recorded on December 31, 2009 as follows:

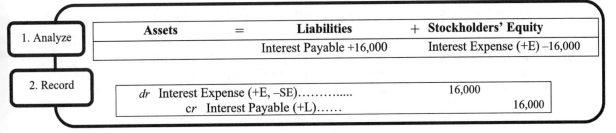

3. **_Pay the Lenders._** On January 1, 2009 the preceding liability is paid as shown:

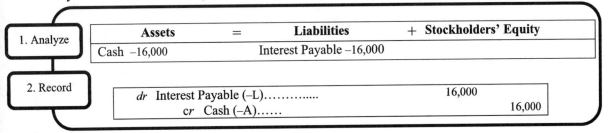

The accrual of interest expense (Step 2) and the interest payments (Step 3) will continue every year until the maturity date of the bonds. At maturity, the bonds will be fully repaid and the following entry will be made:

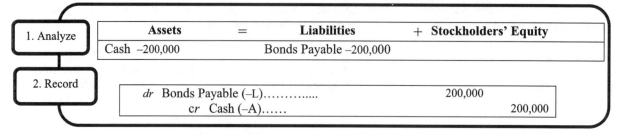

1. Analyze	Assets	=	Liabilities	+	Stockholders' Equity
	Cash −200,000		Bonds Payable −200,000		

2. Record	
dr Bonds Payable (−L)..............	200,000
cr Cash (−A)......	200,000

B. Accounting for Bonds Issued Below or Above Face Value

Before we tackle this topic, a little explanation is in order. In order to issue bonds, a company has to go through many regulatory hurdles, approvals, and have them printed up on fancy paper with a seal and everything. One of the things a company must do, long before the bonds are actually printed up, is select the interest rate that will be paid on the bonds.

Once selected, the rate is printed on the fancy bond along with other important information. When the time comes to actually sell the bonds to lenders, the interest rate may not be what the lenders expect from this company given the economic conditions in the market. In this case, two possibilities can occur.

- Bonds Sold at a Discount – The interest rate printed (stated) on the bonds is 8%, but bondholders expect to earn 10%. It would be extremely difficult to change the rate of interest we've specified on the bond. So, we do the only thing we can do – have a 'sale' on bonds! That is, we reduce (or discount) the selling price to make them more attractive to lenders.

- Bonds Sold at a Premium – If we assume the stated rate on the bonds is still 8%, but this time lenders only expect to earn 6% on our bonds, the opposite situation occurs. We still can't change our interest rate, but we aren't going to give away the extra 2% we're paying on the bonds for free, so….we ask our lenders to pay a little bit extra (a premium) for the bonds.

The point is, that bonds will sell at different amounts (other than face) if the stated interest rate printed on the bond differs from the rated desired by lenders. Before we go any further, in order to thoroughly understand the complexities of bonds, you need to be familiar with the terminology associated with them. So, let's take a couple of minutes to cover this new terminology:

1. *Face value.* The value printed on the 'face' of the bond certificate. It is also called other names such as Par Value and Stated Value.

2. *Stated Interest Rate.* The interest rate printed on the 'face' of the bond. This is also called other names such as Coupon Rate and Contract Rate.

3. *Issue Price (proceeds).* Regardless of what is actually printed on the bond certificate, the issue price is the amount actually *received* by the company when it sells the bond. Lenders calculate what the bond is *really worth* using something called a *present value* calculation (covered in Appendix C.) In this chapter, we will assume this calculation has already been made and the results have been presented. Bond dealers and news reports typically quote the bond issue price as a percentage of the face value of the bond, but they omit the percentage (%) symbol.
   For instance, if the calculation determined that the bond should be sold for less than the face amount, say 85% of $1,000 (the rate is always based on the price of *one* bond), the bond is said to be selling at 85 (the percent sign is not mentioned, but everyone knows that 85 means 85%). So, in this case each bond would sell for $850 ($1,000 x 85%.)

4. **Market Interest Rate** The interest rate the lenders in the bond market demand from a bond (and use in their present value calculations to determine the bond issue price). This rate also known by other names, such as: yield, discount rate, and effective-interest rate.

You probably have a headache from trying to force all this junk into your head. Well, go take an aspirin and when you get back, we'll continue. Ok? Ready? Some common questions that come up right about now are: (1) why would lenders pay a premium, and (2) why would issuers sell for less than the face – a discount? Well, the important thing to remember here is that no one is really getting more or less than the current market situation requires. The point isn't to try to get more or less for something....the purpose is to equalize everything, so that you wouldn't care one iota if you received 10% on someone else's bonds or received 8% on this company's bonds...but, paid less for the bond because of it. You should be indifferent to either one....they are the same.

C. Accounting for Bonds Issued at a Discount

Of course none of this makes any sense until you see it in action. A bond issued at a discount (less than the face of the bond) means that the lender receives *everything printed on the bond certificate*, because that's what he's buying! That is, the lender *will* receive the face value of the bond (at maturity) and *will* receive the interest rate stated on the bond certificate every year. However, the lender receives all of this by paying *less than $200,000* for it! There's a "Sale" on bonds at the mall! Why? Assume lenders expect to earn 10% on the bonds (recall that these bonds only pay 8%.) There's not a soul in the world that will pay $200,000 for these bonds because the stated rate (8%) is too low. However, the lender will pay $ 187,318 (quoted as 93.659—the selling price of these bonds is calculated in the Supplement of this chapter.) The borrower's entry on January 1, 2009 is:

	Assets	=	Liabilities	+ Stockholders' Equity
1. Analyze	Cash +187,318		Bonds Payable +200,000	
			Discount on Bonds Payable (+xL) −12,682	

2. Record	dr Cash (+A)..............	187,318	
	dr Discount on Bonds Payable (+xL, −L)......	12,682	
	cr Bonds Payable (+L)......		200,000

Notice that the bonds are recorded at face value ($200,000) which is the amount the borrower must repay at maturity. Since only $187,318 was received, that is the amount that must be shown on the balance sheet for this bond, so the discount ($12,682) will be subtracted from the face value on the balance sheet. The *discount on bonds payable* account is a *contra-liability* account. It offsets the liability—bonds payable. The net amount presented on the balance sheet $187,318 ($200,000 – $12,682) is called the *carrying value* of the bond.

The fact that the borrower must repay more than they received when the bond was issued is the adjustment for difference in interest rates. So, in effect, the $12,682 represents additional interest that the issuer is paying to lenders for the bond. **The discount gave the borrower less money than they will have to repay at maturity. This increases the total cost of borrowing (because of the extra 2% that the lenders have demanded.)**

The matching principle requires that we match the interest charges on this bond with the period that it benefits. This is accomplished by allocating a portion of the Discount on Bonds Payable to each accounting period (called *amortizing* the discount) until the bond matures in four years. There are two methods used to accomplish this allocation: (1) the straight-line method (covered in Supplement A), and (2) the effective-interest method (covered in Supplement B, Supplement C will combine the best of both methods.) GAAP requires that the effective-interest method be used unless the straight-line method does not materially differ from the effective-interest method. This might be a good spot to take a break before moving on.

D. Accounting for Bonds Issued at a Premium

Whew! OK. Now we discuss bonds issued at a premium. A bond issued at a premium (more than the face of the bond) means that the lenders receive *everything printed on the bond certificate.* So once again, the lender *will* receive the face value of the bond (at maturity) and *will* receive the interest rate stated on the bond certificate.

However, this time, the interest rate stated on the bond certificate is *higher* than lenders expect, so they are willing to pay *more than $200,000 for these bonds!* This kind of situation can be compared with the following: Assume there's a blizzard outside and there's only *one* heater left in the city. *Everyone wants it and they'll pay* *more for it.* Assume lenders expect to earn 6% on bonds (recall that these bonds pay 8%.) All the lenders in the city will clamor for these bonds because the rate paid on them is higher than they expect. So, the lender is willing to pay $ 213,862 (quoted as 106.931—the selling price of these bonds is calculated in the Supplement of the chapter). The entry on January 1, 2009 is:

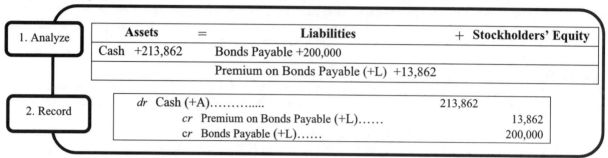

The bonds, once again, are recorded at face value ($200,000) which is the amount the borrower must repay at maturity. However, this time $213,862 was received, and this amount must be shown on the balance sheet for this bond, so the premium ($13,862) will be added to the face value on the balance sheet. The *premium on bonds payable* account is an *adjunct* account, meaning that it is added to the balance of an account. It is added to the liability—bonds payable. The combined amount presented on the balance sheet $213,862 ($200,000 + 13,862) is also called the *carrying value* of the bond.

The fact that the borrower repays less than they received when the bond was issued is the adjustment for difference in interest rates. So, in effect, the $13,862 represents a reduction in the interest that the issuer is paying to lenders for the bond. **The premium gave the borrower more money than they will have to repay at maturity. This reduces the total cost of borrowing (the extra 2% the bond is paying over and above what at the lenders have demanded.)**

The matching concept requires that we match the interest charges on this bond with the periods that it benefits (called *amortizing* the premium). This is accomplished by allocating a portion of the Premium on Bonds Payable to each accounting period until the bond matures in four years. Again, the mechanics of this are covered in Supplements A, B, and C. You're through the worst of it now. Hang in there we're almost done with Bonds!

E. Early Retirement of Debt
Usually a bond (debt) is paid-off (retired) at maturity. But, sometimes the borrower wants to pay it off early. The borrower may have additional cash lying around with nothing better to do, so why not pay off the bonds! This is especially important because this also removes any interest expense associated with the bonds.

With no bond interest expense charges on the income statement, net income looks much better because the business earns a higher profit. If interest rates have fallen since the last bond issuance, the company may have a new bond issuance. They can use the proceeds from the new issuance to pay off the amounts still owed on the old issuance, and do it at a lower *stated* interest rate in the future.

Three financial effects result from the retirement of bonds before their maturity: (1) cash is paid by the borrower; (2) the borrower's bond liability is eliminated; and (3) either a gain arises or a loss is incurred, depending on what the bonds are worth in the marketplace at the time of the retirement.

- A gain results if the cash paid to retire the bonds is less than the carrying value of the bonds.
- A loss results if the cash paid to retire the bonds is more than the carrying value of the bonds.

Let's assume that a company has $500,000 face value bonds that were issued at face value. Seven years later the company decides to retire them at 110 ($500,000 * 110%). The journal entry to record the retirement is:

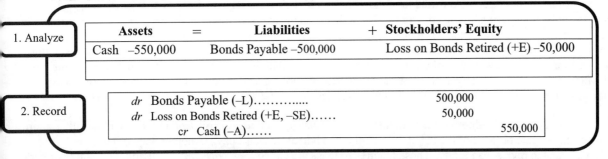

1. Analyze	Assets	=	Liabilities	+ Stockholders' Equity
	Cash –550,000		Bonds Payable –500,000	Loss on Bonds Retired (+E) –50,000

2. Record		
dr Bonds Payable (–L).............	500,000	
dr Loss on Bonds Retired (+E, –SE)......	50,000	
cr Cash (–A)......		550,000

Because the company had to pay more than to retire the bonds ($550,000) than the carrying value ($500,000), a loss was incurred. The loss on bond retirement would be reported on the income statement with Other Expenses and Losses between 'operating income' and 'income before income taxes'. There is no premium or discount on the bonds because they were issued at face. Retirement of bonds involving a premium or discount will be covered in intermediate accounting.

EVALUATE THE RESULTS

> **Learning Objective 4**
> Interpret the current ratio and the times interest earned ratio.

In order to determine the ability of another person or company to pay you what it owes, you must determine whether the company has enough assets available, and whether the company has the ability to generate additional resources in the future to pay off the debt. If it appears that the company may not be able to pay you, what are your options?

Current Ratio
The ability of a company to pay amounts it currently owes is called *liquidity*. A common ratio used to evaluate liquidity is the *current ratio:*

$$\text{Current Ratio} = \frac{\text{Current Assets}}{\text{Current Liabilities}}$$

This ratio measures whether the company has enough current assets to pay off its current liabilities. Generally, a higher ratio suggests a company with better liquidity. An old 'rule of thumb' was that this ratio should be between 1.00 and 2.00, but many companies today can successfully keep this ratio under 1.00 through sound management techniques. But for others a ratio below 1.0 can still be a cause for concern. Many banks offer businesses a *line of credit* which provides cash to the business as needed (up to a specified limit.) This allows a company to borrow on an as-needed basis saving them a great deal in interest charges.

Times Interest Earned Ratio
Because current liabilities only include the *unpaid* interest payments as of the balance sheet date (omitting any *future* interest charges), the current ratio is woefully lax in evaluating the company's ability to pay *future* interest charges. One way to analyze its ability to pay future interest charges is to evaluate the company's ability to cover interest charges with its net income in the *past.* The measure used most often for this evaluation is called the *times interest earned ratio.*

$$\text{Times Interest Earned Ratio} = \frac{\text{Net Income + Interest Expense + Income Tax Expense}}{\text{Interest Expense}}$$

This ratio adds Interest Expense and Income Tax Expense *back to net income.* This is done because the ratio evaluates how many *times* interest was covered *before financing and taxes.* This ratio measures the amount of resources generated for each dollar of interest expense. Generally, a high ratio is better than a low ratio, indicating a net income 'cushion' in the event profitability declines in the future. **A ratio less than one indicates that the company *does not* generate enough income to cover its interest expense.** This can be a serious hurdle to overcome because most companies can only survive a couple of years like this before declaring bankruptcy.

Common Features of Debt

Learning Objective 5
Describe the additional liabilities information reported in the notes to the financial statements.

Lenders and borrowers often use terminology that is unique to debt-financed transactions. Without a solid knowledge of these terms and their meanings, you could well be floundering in a sea of words. So, in this section we cover some of the most common terms used when dealing with debt. To reduce the risk of a loan, some lenders require borrowers to offer specific assets as security to creditors. This means that if the borrower does not pay its liability, the creditor may take ownership of the assets used as security. Another name for security is collateral. This type of situation occurs when you buy a car. The car is security on the loan and if you fail to pay, they can repossess the car. A loan associated with this type of situation is called *secured debt*.

Sometimes a creditor will lend money without security, call *unsecured debt*, but they will usually require a higher interest rate because of the increased risk that the borrower won't pay. Another way to reduce risk is to allow lenders to revise loan terms. These features in loans are called *loan covenants*. The following table provides a quick and dirty summary of these (and other) terms.

Loan Terms	What They Mean	Effects
Security	Security guarantees that the borrower's assets will be given to the creditor if the borrower doesn't pay.	Reduces risk to creditors, making them willing to accept a lower interest rate.
Loan Covenants	Allows the creditor to force immediate repayment of the loan if the borrower violates these terms.	Reduces risk to creditors, making them willing to accept a lower interest rate.
Seniority	Debt designated as "senior" is paid first in the event of bankruptcy, followed by "subordinated" debt.	Reduces risk to senior creditors, making them willing to accept a lower interest rate.
Convertibility	Gives the creditor an option to accept the borrower's stock as payment for the outstanding loan.	Gives greater control to creditors, reducing their risk and making them willing to accept a lower interest rate.
Callability	Gives the borrower control over the decision to fully repay the lender before the loan's maturity date.	Gives greater control to borrowers, increasing creditors' risk and causing them to demand a higher interest rate.

Unrecorded Liabilities

Believe it or not, some accounting rules *require* that certain liabilities *not* be reported on the balance sheet. One situation like involves contingent liabilities.

A *contingent liability* is a *potential* liability that arises out of past transactions or events. The company cannot determine whether it will owe anything or for what amount, until a future event occurs or fails to occur. Perhaps the most common contingent liabilities in a business are lawsuits. There may be a lawsuit pending against a company, but unless and until a determination has been made on the lawsuit, the company has no idea if it will owe anything or how much it would be required to pay if it is determined that a liability exits.

Failure to record the liability just discussed is *not* unethical or illegal. Debt should not be recorded unless it is probable that the debt will be owed. Many companies notify financial statement users of these unrecorded liabilities in the notes to the financial statements.

SUPPLEMENT A – STRAIGHT-LINE AMORTIZATION OF BOND DISCOUNT AND PREMIUM

Straight-Line Amortization of Bond Discount

Earlier in this chapter, a bond was issued for $187,318 resulting in a discount of $12,682 ($200,000 - $187,318.) It was noted that in order to be in compliance with the matching principle, a portion of the discount had to be allocated to each of the four years in the life of the bond.

The straight-line method is one way to accomplish this. Essentially, the straight-line method allocates an equal portion of the discount to each of the four years: $12,682 / 4 = $3,171. Since the Discount on bonds Payable is a debit balance account, when interest is accrued, this account must be credited, until it is all used-up (at maturity.) Therefore, the entry on December 31, 2009 for this bond would be:

1. Analyze	Assets	=	Liabilities	+ Stockholders' Equity
			Interest Payable +16,000	Interest Expense (+E) –19,171
			Discount on Bonds Payable (–xL) +3,171	

2. Record			
	dr Interest Expense (+E –SE).............	19,171	
	cr Discount on Bonds Payable (–xL, +L)......		3,171
	cr Interest Payable (+L)......		16,000

Interest payable is calculated based upon the amount that must be paid according to the face of the bond (the bond certificate), $16,000 ($200,000 * 8% * 12/12). Interest expense is this amount plus the amortized portion of additional cost of the bond incurred because we had to sell it for less than its face value $19,171 ($16,000 + 3,171.)

Upon payment of the interest on January 1, 2010, the *interest payable* is debited and *cash* is credited for $16,000. These entries are made every year until the discount is fully amortized to zero. Notice that a discount causes *interest expense* to be higher than the actual interest payment. This is what was meant in chapter when it mentioned that a discount, effectively, creates a higher cost of borrowing.

Straight-Line Amortization of Bond Premium

Just like the discount, a premium ($13,860 in our chapter example) must also be spread over the life of the bond. Using the straight-line method, the amortization of premium each year is: $13,862 / 4 = $3,466. This amount is *subtracted* from interest expense as shown in this annual journal entry:

1. Analyze	Assets	=	Liabilities	+ Stockholders' Equity
			Interest Payable +16,000	Interest Expense (+E) –12,534
			Premium on Bonds Payable –3,466	

2. Record		
	dr Interest Expense (+E –SE).............	12,534
	dr Premium on Bonds Payable (–L)......	3,466
	cr Interest Payable (+L)......	16,000

In this situation, the interest payable is the same (remember you are required to pay what is shown on the face of the bonds, regardless of what you sold them for. Interest expense is this amount less the 'extra' amortized portion we received when we sold the bonds for more than face value $12,534 ($16,000 – $3,466.)

Upon payment of the interest on January 1, 2010, the *interest payable* is debited and *cash* is credited for $16,000. These entries are made every year until the premium is fully amortized to zero. Notice that a premium causes *interest expense* to be lower than the actual interest payment. This is what was meant in chapter when it mentioned that a premium, effectively, creates a lower cost of borrowing.

SUPPLEMENT B – EFFECTIVE-INTEREST AMORTIZATION OF BOND DISCOUNT AND PREMIUM

The *effective-interest method* is a superior method of accounting for bonds since it accurately *calculates* interest expense every period by multiplying the true cost of borrowing (Market Rate of Interest) by the amount of money actually owed to lenders (Issue Price.) The amount owed to lenders is the carrying value of the bond.

       The effective-interest method is based on the concept of present value. In a nutshell, present value says that the sooner the money is received, the more valuable it is. For example, if I offer you $10,000 and you have a choice of receiving the money today or one year from now....which would you choose? Today! Of course! The reason is that the money received today could be invested at the going interest rate (say 10%) and one year from now you would have *more* than $10,000. Had you chosen the other scenario, you would only have $10,000 a year from now.

       In order to calculate the present value of something, you need the following information: (1) the amount(s) to be received in the future, (2) the length of time between now and then; and (3) the interest rate you expect to earn on the money during that time. Some of this information is available on the face of the bond. There are actually two separate cash flows that a lender will receive from the borrower: (1) the face amount of the bond--$200,000 in our scenario, and (2) the annual interest payments on the $200,000 at 8% interest.

       The present values (current worth) of these future cash flows are calculated using the present value techniques illustrated in Appendix C, based on the *market rate of interest that the lender expects to earn on the bonds*. The results of these present value calculations, using three different market rates of interest, are shown in the following table:

	|--------Market Interest Rates--------|	
	6%	8%	10%
Present value of $200,000 (face value)			
paid four years from now	$158,420	$147,006	$136,600
Present value of $16,000 (interest)			
paid once a year for four years	55,442	52,994	50,718
Amount to sell the bonds for	**$ 213,862**	**$ 200,000**	**$ 187,318**

       Notice that if the stated rate on the bond certificate (8%) is the same as what the lender wants to earn in the market (middle column), the bond *sells for its face amount!* When the amount lenders want to earn in the market is *less* (6% column) than what the stated rate on the bond certificate (8%), the lender is willing to pay more for the bond than its face value ($213,862—a premium.) Whereas, if the rate the lender wants to get in the market is *more* (10% column) than the stated rate, the lender pays less than the face value of the bond ($187,318—a discount.)

Effective-Interest Amortization of Bond Discount
When a bond sells for less than its face, the true cost of borrowing is greater than the interest rate stated on the face of the bond. So, the interest expense is calculated on the actual funds received using the true market rate of interest when the funds were received. This interest charge of $18,732 ($187,318 x 10% x 12/12) is actually greater than the 8% paid to the lender, $16,000.

       Under the effective interest method, the true cost of the interest is calculated and charged to interest expense and the stated rate is paid to the lender. The difference between the two amounts is removed (amortized) from the discount on bonds payable account. Discount on bonds payable is a debit balance account, when interest is accrued, this account must be credited, until it is all used-up (at maturity.) Therefore, the entry on December 31, 2009 for this bond would be:

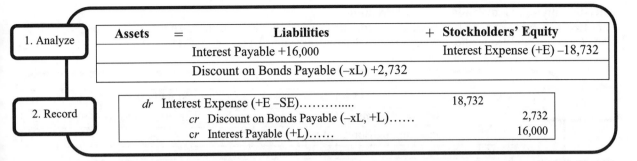

1. Analyze	Assets	=	Liabilities	+ Stockholders' Equity
			Interest Payable +16,000	Interest Expense (+E) –18,732
			Discount on Bonds Payable (–xL) +2,732	

2. Record	dr Interest Expense (+E –SE)…………...	18,732	
	cr Discount on Bonds Payable (–xL, +L)……		2,732
	cr Interest Payable (+L)……		16,000

As shown earlier, the interest expense is calculated based on the amount of funds received ($187,318) using the rate that lenders expect to receive (10%). The amount of the discount on bonds payable that is amortized of $2,732 is simply the difference between the amount of interest calculated on the funds you received for the bonds and the amount of interest you are required to pay ($18,732 – $16,000).

Upon payment of the interest on January 1, 2010, the *interest payable* is debited and *cash* is credited for $16,000. It is important to note that under both the straight-line method and the effective interest method, the amount of the payment is the same ($16,000). The only differences between the two methods are:

(1) the amount of the discount that is amortized each period,
(2) how it is calculated, and
(3) the corresponding interest expense recorded each year.

Under both methods, the interest expense is higher than the actual amount paid to show the higher cost of borrowing.

Now, let's show the journal entry for the accrual a year later on December 31, 2010. Interest expense is always calculated on the carrying value of the bonds. In the previous year, the carrying value was $187,318 (Face value – Discount on bonds payable: $200,000 – 12,682.) This year the interest is also calculated on the carrying value of the bonds. But it has changed! Since $2,732 of the discount was charged to expense in the previous entry, there is only $9,950 in the discount on bonds payable now ($12,682– 2,732). So, the carrying value of the bond is now $190,050 ($200,000 – $9,950). Interest expense will now be $19,005 ($190,050 x 10% x 12/12). So, the entry is:

1. Analyze	Assets	=	Liabilities	+ Stockholders' Equity
			Interest Payable +16,000	Interest Expense (+E) –19,005
			Discount on Bonds Payable (–xL) +3,005	

2. Record	dr Interest Expense (+E –SE)…………...	19,005	
	cr Discount on Bonds Payable (–xL, +L)……		3,005
	cr Interest Payable (+L)……		16,000

Notice a couple of things:
(1) the carrying value is higher than it was last year. This is because some of the discount on bonds payable was removed last year ($2,732) so there is a smaller amount of discount that is *subtracted from the face value in determining carrying value;*
(2) the interest expense is higher than it was last year. This is because the carrying value has *increased.* The carrying value is slowly making its way *up to the face value of the bonds.* Since interest is calculated on carrying value, a higher carrying value results in higher interest charges. When the carrying value is $200,000 ($200,000 – 0 discount), the bond will have matured and can be paid off at face value.

Effective-Interest Amortization of Bond Premium

The effective interest method is applied to a premium in exactly the same manner as it is with a discount. The true market rate is multiplied by the carrying value to determine the interest expense: ($213,862 x 6% x 12/12= 12,832), only this time, a debit is needed to balance the entry:

1. Analyze	Assets	=	Liabilities	+ Stockholders' Equity
			Interest Payable +16,000	Interest Expense (+E) –12,832
			Premium on Bonds Payable –3,168	

2. Record		
dr Interest Expense (+E –SE)…………...	12,832	
dr Premium on Bonds Payable (–L)……	3,168	
cr Interest Payable (+L)……		16,000

Upon payment of the interest on January 1, 2010, the *interest payable* is debited and *cash* is credited for $16,000. Again, the amount of the payment ($16,000) is the same under both the straight-line method and the effective interest method. The only differences between the two methods are *(1) the amount of the premium that is amortized each period, (2) how it is calculated, and (3) the corresponding interest expense recorded each year.* Under both methods, the interest expense is lower than the actual amount paid to show the lower cost of borrowing. This makes sense because the bond pays 8%, but we effectively only have to pay 6%, a lower rate.

Now, let's show the same journal entry for the accrual a year later on December 31, 2010. Interest expense is always calculated on the carrying value of the bonds. In the previous year, the carrying value was $213,862 (Face value + Premium on bonds payable: $200,000 + 13,862.) This year the interest is also calculated on the carrying value of the bonds. But it has changed again! Since $3,168 of the premium reduced the expense in the previous entry, there is only $10,694 in the premium on bonds payable now ($13,862 – 3,168). So, the carrying value is now $210,694 ($200,000 + $10,694). Interest expense will now be $12,642 ($210,694 x 6% x 12/12). So, the entry is:

1. Analyze	Assets	=	Liabilities	+ Stockholders' Equity
			Interest Payable +16,000	Interest Expense (+E) –12,642
			Premium on Bonds Payable –3,358	

2. Record		
dr Interest Expense (+E –SE)…………...	12,642	
dr Premium on Bonds Payable (–L)……	3,358	
cr Interest Payable (+L)……		16,000

Again, notice a couple of things:
(1) the carrying value is lower than it was last year. This is because some of the premium on bonds payable was amortized last year ($3,168) so there is a smaller amount of premium that is *added to the face value in determining carrying value;*
(2) the interest expense is lower than it was last year. This is because the carrying value has *decreased.* The carrying value is slowly making its way *down to the face value of the bonds.* Since interest is calculated on carrying value, a lower carrying value results in lower interest charges. When the carrying value is $200,000 ($200,000 + 0 premium), the bond will have matured and can be paid off at face value.

SUPPLEMENT C – SIMPLIFIED APPROACH TO BOND ACCOUNTING USING EFFECTIVE-INTEREST AMORTIZATION

NOTE: Check with your instructor (or course outline) to see whether you are expected to read this supplement.

This approach is a short cut method for accounting for bond transactions. It involves removing some of the accounts from the analysis presented in Supplements A and B. Many students have difficulty visualizing how a *reduction* in a contra-liability account can *increase* the carrying value of the bond. This method is meant to show you this in a simple, clear-cut manner.

Essentially, we will eliminate the Discount or Premium on Bonds payable accounts, and instead use *one* account to represent the carrying value of the bonds—Bonds Payable, net. Now, all entries that impact the carrying value of the bond, will be debited and/or credited to the Bonds Payable, net account. This removes the added complexity of a Discount or Premium account when journalizing transactions to account for (1) the initial bond issuance, (2) additional amounts owed to lenders for interest, (3) payments to the lenders, and (4) removal of the bond liability when it is retired.

Accounting for Bonds Issued Below Face Value

1. Initial Bond Issuance. So, let's re-work the discount presented earlier in this chapter, using the simplified approach. The bonds were issued on January 1, 2009, at $187,318 (a market rate of 10%). The face amount of the bond is $200,000 and the stated rate is 8%. So the journal entry to record this is:

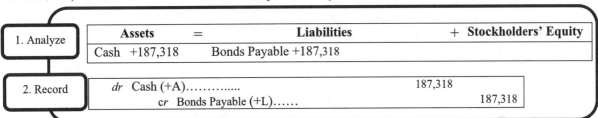

1. Analyze	Assets	=	Liabilities	+ Stockholders' Equity
	Cash +187,318		Bonds Payable +187,318	

2. Record	*dr* Cash (+A)...............	187,318	
	cr Bonds Payable (+L)......		187,318

Notice that no discount on bonds payable is recorded and the Bonds payable is not recorded at face value ($200,000). This is because the *net amount* of the value less the discount on bonds payable is recorded in *one account,* Bonds Payable, net. In this manner, the Bonds Payable, net account *always show the true liability of the bonds.*

2. Interest owed and Paid.

Interest Owed. Another benefit of this approach is that you don't have to select a method of amortizing (straight-line vs. effective-interest) because there is *no discount or premium to amortize!* Furthermore, we can now calculate the true amount of interest expense on the bond using a slight variation of the formula shown earlier in this chapter. We will use:

$$\text{INTEREST} = \text{AMOUNT OWED} \times \text{MARKET INTEREST RATE} \times \text{TIME}$$

Assume that the amount owed is equal to the carrying value of the bond at the beginning of the period (i.e. the amount in the Bonds Payable, net account.) So, the interest accrual at December 31, 2009 would be $18,732 recorded as follows:

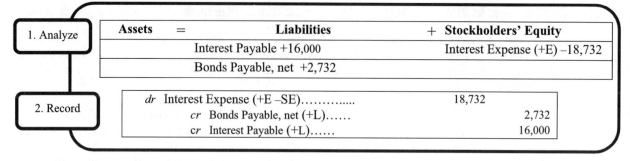

Interest Paid. When payment is made, the journal entry to record it is:

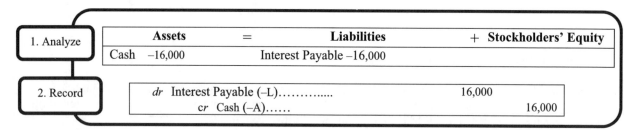

Interest Owed. The entire process must be done again in the next accounting period. On December 31, 2008, interest is calculated on the Bonds Payable, net *at the beginning of the accounting period* $190,050 (187,318 + 2,732). The interest expense is $19,005 (190,050 x 10%) and the entry is:

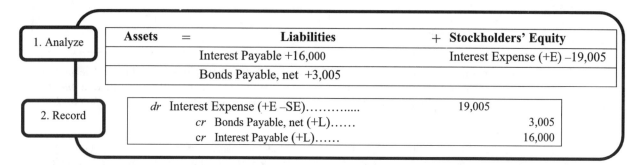

The payment of the interest on January 1, would be:

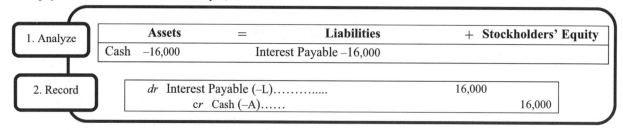

These journal entries to accrue interest and pay interest will continue until the bonds mature or are retired. However, the carrying value (Bonds Payable, net) will change every time, so the interest expense amount will differ for each entry.

Accounting for Bonds Issued Above Face Value

Accounting for a premium follows exactly the same procedures as for a discount. The only difference is that the premium decreases interest expense, and therefore, a debit will be made to the Bonds Payable, net for the initial issuance. Again, using the example in this chapter, assume the bonds were issued at $213,860 (a market rate of 6%). The entry to record the issuance would be:

1. Analyze	Assets	=	Liabilities	+ Stockholders' Equity
	Cash +213,862		Bonds Payable, net +213,862	

2. Record	dr Cash (+A).............	213,862
	cr Bonds Payable, net (+L)......	213,862

The interest is calculated on the carrying value at the beginning of the period (Bonds Payable, net) and is $12,832.

1. Analyze	Assets	=	Liabilities	+ Stockholders' Equity
			Interest Payable +16,000	Interest Expense (+E) –12,832
			Bonds Payable, net –3,168	

2. Record	dr Interest Expense (+E –SE).............	12,832	
	dr Bonds Payable, net (–L)......	3,168	
	cr Interest Payable (+L)......		16,000

Notice that the interest expense is lower than the interest to be paid, showing the true cost of the loan. Since the going rate is 6% and this bond pays 8%, the 'true' interest is lower than the 8% stated rate on these bonds. The entries to accrue and pay interest continue until the bond matures or is retired.

The payment of the interest on January 1, would be:

1. Analyze	Assets	=	Liabilities	+ Stockholders' Equity
	Cash –16,000		Interest Payable –16,000	

2. Record	dr Interest Payable (–L).............	16,000	
	cr Cash (–A)......		16,000

REVIEW THE CHAPTER

Chapter Summary

LO1. Explain how the reporting of liabilities assists decision makers.
- ❖ Liabilities are any probable future sacrifices of economic benefits that arise from past transactions
  - o Examples include accounts payable, accrued liabilities, notes payable, and bonds payable
- ❖ Liabilities are classified as current if due to be paid with current assets within the current operating cycle of the business or within one year of the balance sheet date (whichever is longer).
  - o All other liabilities are considered long-term.

LO2. Explain how to account for common types of current liabilities.
- ❖ Liabilities are initially reported at their cash equivalent value, which is
  - o The amount of cash that a creditor would accept to settle the liability immediately after the transaction or event occurred

- ❖ Liabilities are
  - ○ increased whenever additional obligations arise (including interest), and
  - ○ reduced whenever the company makes payments or provides services to the creditor.

LO3. Analyze and record bond liability transactions.
- ❖ For most public issuances of debt (bonds), the amount borrowed by the company does not equal the amount repaid at maturity.
  - ○ The effect of a bond discount is to provide the borrower with less money than the value stated on the face of the bond
    - ▪ This increases the cost of borrowing at an interest rate above the interest rate stated on the bond.
  - ○ The effect of a bond premium is to provide the borrower more money than the face value of the bond
    - ▪ This decreases the cost of borrowing at an interest rate below the interest rate stated on the bond.
- ❖ Interest expense reports the cost of borrowing, which equals:
  - ○ The periodic interest payments plus the amount of the bond discount, amortized in that interest period, or
  - ○ The periodic interest payments minus the amount of the bond premium amortized in that interest period.

LO4. Interpret the current ratio and times interest earned ratio.
- ❖ The current ratio measures liquidity, which is:
  - ○ The company's ability to pay its current liabilities using its current assets.
- ❖ The times interest earned ratio measures a company's ability to meets its interest obligations with resources generated from its profit-making activities.

LO5. Describe the additional liabilities information reported in the notes to the financial statements.
- ❖ The notes to the financial statements describe:
  - ○ Specific features of debt
    - ▪ Significant financial commitments (such as contingent liabilities)
- ❖ A contingent liability is:
  - ○ A potential liability that has arise as a result of a past transaction or event.
  - ○ Its ultimate outcome will not be known until a future event occurs or fails to occur.

READ AND RECALL QUESTIONS
After you read each section of the chapter, answer the related Read and Recall Questions below.

INTRODUCTION
When a credit rating agency gives a company a grade of AAA, what does it mean? What if the grade is D?

LEARNING OBJECTIVE
After studying the section of the chapter, you should be able to:
1. Explain how the reporting of liabilities assists decision makers

---

Decisions Related to Liabilities
What two questions should be asked before extending credit to another company? Why are they important?

Define *current liabilities.*   What is a classified Balance Sheet? List three types of current liabilities presented in this chapter and give a brief explanation of each.

LEARNING OBJECTIVE
After studying the section of the chapter, you should be able to:
2. Explain how to account for common types of current liabilities

Measurement of Liabilities
What three things determine the dollar amount reported for liabilities on the balance sheet? Define a *cash-equivalent* amount.

Current Liabilities
List the three stages involved in the purchase of goods and services on credit.

Define *accrued liabilities.* Give three examples. How are they presented on the balance sheet?

List the payroll taxes that are withheld from employee's salaries when paying employees? Which payroll taxes are paid by *both the employer and the employee?* How are payroll tax liabilities presented on the balance sheet?

Define *accrued income taxes.* How do they differ from accrued *payroll* taxes? What is a Form 1120?

What are the two components of a *note payable?* Why are three journal entries required for a note payable?

What is the calculation for computing interest expense? Explain the how the *time* element of this calculation is determined.

What account(s) is (are) debited and credited to record the issuance of the note and receipt of cash?

What account(s) is (are) debited and credited to record any interest owed by the end of the accounting period on a note payable?

What account(s) is (are) debited and credited to record payments made to the lender on a note payable?

Explain what is meant by the *current portion of long-term debt.* How is it presented on the balance sheet?

Are Sales Taxes expensed by a company? Why or why not? What account(s) is (are) debited and credited when recording Sales that include Sales Taxes?

How many entries are required to record *unearned revenues?* What are the journal entries?

LEARNING OBJECTIVE
After studying the section of the chapter, you should be able to:
3. Analyze and record bond liability transactions

Long-term Liabilities
What are the two ways to obtain corporate financing? List the three steps required for each.

List the four events that must be recorded when accounting for bonds.

Use the information in this table to answer all of the following bond questions.

Face Value of the Bond	$100,000
Issue Date	September 1, 2008
Maturity Date	September 1, 2009
Stated Rate	7%

Assume the bond is issued at face value. What is the journal entry to record the issuance?

What is the entry to record interest owed on December 31, 2008?

When bonds are sold at less than face value, what is it called? Why might this occur?

Define the following terms: (a) Face Value; (b) Stated Interest Rate; (c) Issue Price; (d) Present Value; (d) Market Interest Rate.

Complete the following statements:

a. When a bond has a Stated Interest Rate of 7% , and lenders expect a 9% Market Interest Rate, the bond will sell for _____.

b. When a bond has a Stated Interest Rate of 7% , and lenders expect a 5% Market Interest Rate, the bond will sell for _____.

c. When a bond has a Stated Interest Rate of 7% , and lenders expect a 6% Market Interest Rate, the bond will sell for _____.

Complete the following statements:
a. The amounts listed on the bond certificate (face value and stated interest rate) are used only to determine

_____.

b. The Issue Price and Market Interest Rate are used to determine _____ and _____.
Assume the bond (presented previously) was issued at 95. What is the journal entry to record the issuance?

What type of account is *Discount on Bonds Payable?* How will bonds that were issued at a discount be reported on the balance sheet? Why?

Complete the following: The effect of the discount is to provide the borrower _____ money than what is repaid at maturity, which _____ the cost of borrowing.

Explain how this effect is achieved.

Assume the bond (presented previously) was issued at 103. What is the journal entry to record the issuance?

How will bonds be that were issued at a premium be reported on the balance sheet? Why?

Complete the following: The effect of the premium is to provide the borrower _____ money than what is repaid at maturity, which _____ the cost of borrowing.

Explain how this effect is achieved.

Assume the $100,000 bond was issued at face and retired 5 years later at 101. What is the journal entry to record the early retirement of the bond?

Where would the gain or loss on retirement of bonds be shown in the income statement?

LEARNING OBJECTIVE
After studying the section of the chapter, you should be able to:
4. Interpret the current ratio and times interest earned ratio

Current Ratio

The ability to pay liabilities as they come due in the short-run is called _____. A common way to evaluate this is to calculate the _____.

How is the Current Ratio calculated? Evaluate the following statement: When the current ratio is less than one, the company is in trouble.

Times Interest Earned Ratio

To evaluate a company's ability to cover its interest expense in the future, most analysts calculate a _____.

How is the Times Interest Earned Ratio calculated? Why are Interest Expense and Income Tax Expense added back to net income in calculating this ratio? What does this ratio measure?

Comment on the following statement: A negative Times Interest Earned Ratio basically says that the company does *not* generate enough income to cover its interest expense.

Common Features of Debt
Define the following terms: (a) Security; (b) Loan Covenants; (c) Seniority; (d) Convertibility; (e) Callability

LEARNING OBJECTIVE
After studying the section of the chapter, you should be able to:
5. Describe the additional liabilities information reported in the notes to the financial statements

Unrecorded Liabilities
List a situation in which properly following accounting rules can lead to unrecorded liabilities?

What is a *contingent liability?* Give an example of a contingent liability. Is it unethical or illegal to have unrecorded liabilities? Explain.

FINANCIAL ANALYSIS TOOLS

1. **Current Ratio.** To determine how well a company is able to use its current assets to pay its current liabilities:

$$\text{Current Ratio} = \frac{\text{Current Assets}}{\text{Current Liabilities}}$$

2. **Times Interest Earned Ratio.** To determine the amount of income generated by the company (before interest and taxes) for each dollar of interest expense.

$$\frac{\text{Times Interest}}{\text{Earned Ratio}} = \frac{\text{Net Income} + \text{Interest Expense} + \text{Income Tax Expense}}{\text{Interest Expense}}$$

HELPFUL STUDY TIP

1. "Bonds are a bunch of &%$^#@!!!" This is the type of comment heard frequently from introductory accounting students. So, let's try to make them a little bit easier to swallow. The entries for recording bond issuance, interest payments, and pay-out at maturity aren't too bad *if bonds are issued at face value.* Unfortunately, how many times do you think that happens? Like never, dude! So, first we'll learn some hints on how to properly identify bonds sold at a premium and bonds sold at a discount. Then, we'll go over some tricks to help you make the journal entries for these pesky little bonds.

   First of all, forget all the rules, entries, etc. about bonds. In fact, let's talk about heaters. You know those little space heaters you can get at the local discount store for about $50? Assume that it's August, 100 degrees outside, and humidity is 95%. How many heaters do you think are being sold? How about zero, zip, not a single one! The only hope the store has of selling these babies is to slash the price dramatically and hope that someone out there in the city is looking ahead to the bitterly cold winters you always have. This 'discounting' (while an admittedly unusual example) is basically what occurs when bonds are issued at a discount. Demand for the product just ain't out there! You need to entice buyers a bit, and you do this by slashing the price or discounting it.

   Alternatively (and this really happened where I live one year), assume it's bitterly cold out, the coldest day anyone can remember on record. Snow has downed power lines all over the city so, even if you have a home heated with natural gas, the pilot lights have electric ignitions. Power has been out across the city for two days, and newscasters anticipate it will be about four more days before the power is fully restored. Let me tell you, people were in the stores ripping each other to shreds for one of those little oil-based space heaters. Businesses were charging up to $300 each...and getting it! This is an example of something in such high demand people are willing to pay more than the marked price for it, or a premium.

So, when you do the journal entry to record the sale or issuance of a bond (with either a premium or a discount), it can be confusing trying to figure out which amount is debited to cash and which amount is credited to bonds payable. It's all the same stinking bond, right? To help you with this dilemma, we need to bring back some examples from this chapter. See if you can figure out which case deals with a discount and which case deals with a premium.

Case A: In one situation, assume lenders expect to earn 6% on bonds (these are $200,000 and they pay 8%.) So, the lender is willing to pay $ 213,862 (quoted as 106.931).
Case B: In the other situation, assume lenders expect to earn 10% on bonds (these are $200,000 bonds and they pay 8%.) However, the lender will pay $ 187,318 (quoted as 93.659).

Nearly everyone see immediately that Case A represents a bond issued at a premium and Case B a bond issued at a discount. But, that doesn't help with the journal entry. Let's start with Case A. There are two dollar amounts here for the bond ($200,000 and $213,862.) I refer to one of these as an 'ugly' number and the other as a 'pretty' number.

The pretty number (in any bond problem) usually has a whole bunch of zeros in it. The ugly number is usually just a bunch of ugly numbers. So, can you figure out the ugly one and the pretty one for Case A? Good! Now, here's the rule: ***upon issuance, the ugly number is always debited to cash and the pretty number is always credited to bonds payable.*** So, let's do that! Just skip a line between the debit and the credit entries (because of the premium/discount) and you have:

dr Cash (+A) …………………………… 213,862		⇐ Ugly number debited
cr Bonds payable (+L) …………………	200,000	⇐ Pretty number credited

But, we still need to make the entry balance. So, we simply 'fill in the blank'. We need a credit of $13,860 to make this balance. We know this is a premium because the company got more (Cash) than it expected (Bonds Payable) for the bond. Therefore, the credit must be to Premium on Bonds Payable!!

dr Cash (+A) …………………………… 213,862		
cr Premium on Bonds Payable…………	13,862	⇐ fill in the blank (amt. to balance)
cr Bonds payable (+L) …………………	200,000	

See! Easy! Now, look at Case B and follow the same rules: Debit the ugly number to cash and credit the pretty number to bonds payable, leaving a blank line in between them.

dr Cash (+A) …………………………… 187,318		⇐ Ugly number debited
cr Bonds payable (+L) …………………	200,000	⇐ Pretty number credited

Now, fill in the blank. This time, we need a debit of 12,680 to make the entry balance. We know this is a discount because the company got less (Cash) than it expected (Bonds Payable) for the bond. Therefore, the debit must be to Discount on Bonds payable (another hint: Discount=Debit!)

dr Cash (+A) …………………………… 187,318		
dr Discount on bonds payable (+xL, -L) …… 12,682		⇐ Fill in the blank (amt. to balance)
cr Bonds payable (+L) …………………	200,000	

SELF-TEST QUESTIONS AND EXERCISES

MATCHING
1. *Match each of the key terms listed below with the appropriate textbook definition.*

_____ Accrued Liabilities	_____ Line of Credit
_____ Contingent Liability	_____ Liquidity
_____ Current Liabilities	_____ Market Interest Rate
_____ Current Ratio	_____ Premium
_____ Discount	_____ Present Value
_____ Effective-Interest Method (Supplement B)	_____ Stated Interest Rate
_____ Face Value	_____ Straight-Line Method (Supplement A)
_____ Issue Price	_____ Times Interest Earned Ratio

A. Bonds are issued at this when the issue price is greater than the face value.
B. A prearranged agreement that allows a company to borrow any amount of money at any time, up to a prearranged limit.
C. Report the liability for expenses that have been incurred but not paid at the end of the accounting period.
D. Based on a mathematical calculation that determines the amount that one or more payments made in the future are worth today. .
E. Measures the extent to which earnings before taxes and financing costs are sufficient to cover interest incurred on debt.
F. The ability to pay current obligations.
G. Allocates the amount of bond discount (or premium) evenly over each period of the bond's life to adjust interest expense for differences between its stated interest rate and market interest rate.
H. The amount of money that a lender pays (and the company receives) when a bond is issued (sold).
I. The rate stated on the face of the bond, which is used to compute interest payments.
J. The rate of interest that lenders demand from a bond.

(continued)

K. Short-term obligations that will be paid with current assets within the current operating cycle or one year, whichever is longer.
L. A potential liability that has arisen as a result of a past transaction or event whose outcome will not be known until a future event occurs or fails to occur.
M. Bonds are issued at this when the issue price is less than the face value.
N. Used to evaluate liquidity, which is the ability to pay current obligations.
O. The payment made when the bond matures.
P. Allocates the amount of bond discount (or premium) using the market interest rate resulting in an expense equal to the true cost of borrowing.

TRUE-FALSE QUESTIONS
For each of the following, enter a T or F in the blank to indicate whether the statement is true or false.

_____1. (LO1) Liabilities are debts or probable obligations that result from past transactions and will be paid with assets or services.

_____2. (LO2) A Cash equivalent is the amount of cash that a creditor would accept to settle the liability one year after the transaction or event has occurred.

_____3. (LO2) Accrued liabilities are usually reported with an adjusting entry at the end of an accounting period.

_____4. (LO2) Companies are essentially collection agencies for the government when income taxes are withheld from employees pay.

_____5. (LO2) FICA is short for Financial Insurance Contributions Act.

_____6. (LO2) Assuming no interest has been accrued, the payment for interest on a note payable includes a debit to Interest Expense and a credit to Cash.

_____7. (LO2) Sales tax collected from customers is recorded as an expense to the business and charged to account called Sales Tax Expense.

_____8. (LO2) A company can obtain long-term financing through a private placement, or publicly issued debt certificates.

_____9. (LO3) When the market rate of a bond is 11% and the stated rate is 9% the bonds will sell at a premium.

_____10. (LO3) The issue price of a bond is the value printed on the bond certificate.

_____11. (LO3) The issue price and the market interest rate are used only to determine cash payments on a bond.

_____12. (LO3) When bonds are issued at a discount, an account called Discount on Bonds Payable is debited for the difference between the issue price of the bonds and the face value of the bonds.

_____13. (LO3) The effect of a premium is to provide the borrower less money than is repaid at maturity, which increases the total cost of borrowing.

_____14. (LO3) When bonds are retired before maturity, a gain is reported if the cash paid to retire the bonds is less than the carrying value of the bonds.

_____15. (LO4) The current ratio measures the current line of credit offered to a business by a financial institution.

_____16. (LO4) The times interest earned ratio is calculated by dividing Net Income + Interest Expense + Income Tax Expense by Interest Expense.

_____17. (LO4) Callability gives the borrower control over the decision to fully repay the lender before the loan's maturity date.

_____18. (LO4) Loan covenants reduce risk to borrowers, making them willing to accept a lower interest rate.

_____19. (LO5) A contingent liability is an actual liability whose amount is not yet known and the company must wait for a future event to occur or fail to occur to determine the amount of the liability.

_____20. (Supplements A and B) The Effective-interest method of amortizing bonds is considered conceptually superior because it correctly calculates interest expense by multiplying the true cost of borrowing times the amount of money actually owed to lenders.

MULTIPLE CHOICE QUESTIONS

Choose the best answer or response by placing the identifying letter in the space provided.

_____1. (LO1) Current liabilities are defined as:
  a. short-term obligations that will be paid with current liabilities within the current operating cycle or one year, whichever is longer
  b. short term obligations that will be paid with current liabilities within the current operating cycle or one year, whichever is shorter
  c. short-term obligations that will be paid with current assets within the current operating cycle or one year, whichever is longer
  d. short-term obligations that will be paid with current assets within the current operating cycle or one year, whichever is shorter

_____2. (LO2) The dollar amount reported for liabilities is the result of all of the following, *except*:
  a. the initial amount of the liability
  b. amounts contingent upon a future event
  c. payments or services provided to the creditor
  d. additional amounts owed to the creditor

_____3. (LO2) Which of the following is *not* an example of an accrued liability?
  a. FICA payable
  b. notes payable
  c. liability for income taxes payable
  d. interest payable

_____4. (LO2) Interest expense on a Note Payable is calculated as:
  a. payment amount * interest rate * time
  b. principal owed * interest rate * time
  c. present value * interest rate * time
  d. none of the above is the calculation for interest expense

_____5. (LO2) Which of the following is a true statement regarding unearned revenues?
  a. unearned revenues represent revenues that have been earned before the money is received
  b. the entry to record the cash receipt includes a debit to Unearned Revenues and a credit to Cash
  c. the entry to record the portion of the unearned revenues that were earned includes a debit to Service Revenue and a credit to Unearned Revenues
  d. none of the above is a true statement regarding unearned revenues

_____6. (LO3) Which of the following is *not* a true statement about ways to obtaining corporate financing?
  a. a private placement is just like notes payable except that it extends more than one year
  b. to obtain corporate financing using publicly issued debt certificates, the company first finds a lender, then sets the loan terms, and finally borrows the money
  c. standard terms are set, with publicly issued debt, that will apply to each potential lender
  d. interested lenders 'buy' bonds by providing money to the company in exchange for the company's promise to repay the lender according to the terms stated on the bond certificate

_____7. (LO3) When accounting for bonds, accountants are *not* concerned with:
  a. removal of the interest when the liability is paid off
  b. payments to the lender
  c. the initial bond issuance
  d. additional amounts owed to the lender for interest

_____8. (LO3) Which of the following is *not* used to determine cash payments on a bond?
   a. face value
   b. market interest rate
   c. stated interest rate
   d. all of the above are used to determine cash payments on a bond

_____9. (LO3) Which of the following are terms associated with the selling price of a bond?
   a. issue price
   b. present value
   c. market interest rate
   d. all of the above are terms associated with the selling price of a bond

_____10. (LO3) Which of the following is a true statement regarding bonds issuances?
   a. when the stated rate is less than the market interest rate, the bond will sell at a discount
   b. when the stated rate is equal to the market interest rate, the bond will sell at a premium
   c. when the stated rate is greater than the market interest rate, the bond will sell at face value
   d. when the stated rate is greater than the discount rate, the bond will sell at a discount

_____11. (LO3) Which of the following indicates bonds selling at a premium?
   a. bonds sell at 98.20
   b. bonds sell at 100.00
   c. bonds sell at 103.25
   d. none of the above indicates bonds selling at a premium

_____12. (LO3) The journal entry to record the issuance of bonds selling at a discount includes a debit to cash, a credit to bonds payable and:
   a. a credit to Discount on Bonds Payable
   b. a debit to Discount on Bonds Payable
   c. a debit to Interest Expense
   d. a credit to Interest Expense

_____13. (LO3) All of the following are true regarding bond issuances *except:*
   a. The effect of a discount is to increase the total cost of borrowing
   b. The effect of a premium is to decrease the total cost of borrowing
   c. A premium provides the borrower more money than what is repaid at maturity
   d. All of the above are true statements regarding bond issuances

_____14. (LO3) The journal entry to record an early retirement of debt, resulting in a Loss, includes:
   a. a debit to Bonds Payable, and a debit to Loss on Bonds Retired
   b. a debit to Bonds Payable, and a credit to Loss on Bonds Retired
   c. a credit to Bonds Payable, and a debit to Loss on Bonds Retired
   d. a credit to Bonds Payable, and a credit to Loss on Bonds Retired

_____15. (LO4) Which of the following is a true statement regarding the current ratio and the times interest earned ratio?
   a. the ability to earn amounts due in the future is called liquidity
   b. a line of credit is a prearranged agreement that allows a company to borrow any amount of money at any time, up to a prearranged limit
   c. a low current ratio is a good indicator because it means the company has a low amount of debt to pay
   d. a high interest earned ratio indicates that a business is highly unlikely to cover its interest payments in the future

_____16. (LO4) Assuming the following for a company, calculate the times interest earned ratio.
  ➤ Net Income $20,500
  ➤ Interest Payable   2,000
  ➤ Interest Expense   6,200
  ➤ Current Liabilities   24,000
  ➤ Income Tax Expense   9,500
  a.   16 times
  b.   15.16 times
  c.   9.71 times
  d.   5.84 times

_____17. (LO4) Assuming the following information, calculate the current ratio:
  ➤ Current Assets $200,000
  ➤ Net Income   25,000
  ➤ Interest Payable   1,000
  ➤ Current Liabilities   150,000
  a.   0.125 to 1
  b.   0.750 to 1
  c.   1.333 to 1
  d.   1.500 to 1

_____18. (LO4) Which of the following loan features increases the risk to the creditors?
  a.   callability
  b.   seniority
  c.   security
  d.   loan covenants

_____19. (LO4) Which of the following loan features gives greater control to creditors?
  a.   convertibility
  b.   callability
  c.   subordination
  d.   all of the above give greater control to creditors

_____20. (LO5) When could a contingent liability be recorded as a liability?
  a.   When the amount is possible and the amount can be estimated
  b.   When the amount is possible and the amount can be estimated
  c.   when the liability is likely, and the amount can be estimated
  d.   none of the above are situations in which a contingent liability should be recorded as a liability

EXERCISES
Record your answer to each exercise in the space provided. Show your work.

Exercise 10-1. Reporting Payroll Costs with Discussion (LO2)
Colombo Company completed the salary and wage payroll for June 2009. The payroll provided the following details:

Salaries and wages earned	$345,000
Employee income taxes withheld	69,000
Union dues withheld	4,500
Insurance premiums withheld	2,600
FICA taxes withheld	24,668

Required:

1. Prepare the journal entry to record the payroll for June, including employee deductions (but excluding employer FICA taxes.)

> dr   _____
>   cr   _____
>   cr   _____
>   cr   _____
>   cr   _____
>   cr   _____

2. Prepare the journal entry to record the employer's FICA taxes.

> dr   _____
>   cr   _____

3. Assume the amounts owed to governmental agencies and other organizations are paid on July 8, 2009. Prepare the journal entry to record the payment.

> dr   _____
> dr   _____
> dr   _____
> dr   _____
>   cr   _____

4. What was the total labor cost for the company? Explain.

Exercise 10-2. Reporting Interest and Long-term Debt (including Current Portion) (LO2)
Cladbery Chocolatiers used a promissory note to borrow $800,000 on October 1, 2008, at an annual interest rate of 8%. The note is to be repaid in annual installments of $160,000, plus accrued interest, on every September 30, until the note is paid in full (on September 30, 2013).

Required:

1. Prepare the journal entry to be recorded on October 1, 2008

> dr   _____
>   cr   _____

2. Prepare the journal entry to be recorded on December 31, 2008

> dr   _____
>   cr   _____

3. Prepare the journal entry to be made on September 30, 2009 to (a) record the payment of interest, and (b) to record the first principle payment.

a.
> dr   _____
> dr   _____
>   cr   _____

b.

```
dr
        cr                                              _____

                                                                _____
```

4. Show how the note would be reported (and any other liabilities resulting from the note) on the Balance Sheet on December 31, 2009.

Exercise 10-3. Recording and Reporting Current Liabilities. (LO2)
During 2009, ChinaWorks Inc. completed the following transactions. The accounting period ends December 31.

a. Collected rent revenue on October 31, 2009 of $15,000 for office space that ChinaWorks rented to another business. The rent collected was for 3 months from November 1, 2009 through January 31, 2010 and was credited in full to Unearned Rent Revenue.

b. ChinaWorks, Inc. sells china cabinets. For December, sales totaled $11,600, plus a 5% sales tax.

Required:
1. Give (a) the journal entry for the collection of rent on October 31, 2009, and (b) the adjusting journal entry on December 31, 2009.
a.

```
dr
        cr                                              _____

                                                                _____
```

b.

```
dr
        cr                                              _____

                                                                _____
```

2. Give the journal entry to record the sales of china cabinets in December.

```
dr
        cr                                              _____
        cr                                              _____

                                                                _____
```

Exercise 10-4. Preparing Journal Entries to Record Issuance of a Bond, Accrual of Interest, and Payments of Interest, and Early Retirement. (LO3)
On January 1, 2009, Unified Triacting Corporation (UTC) issued $700,000 bonds that mature in 8 years. The bond has a stated interest rate of 7%. The bond was issued at face value and pays interest annually on January 1.

Required:
1. Prepare the journal entry to record the bond issuance.

```
dr
        cr                                              _____

                                                                _____
```

2. Prepare the journal entry to accrue interest on December 31, 2009.

dr

    cr   _____

                             _____

3. Prepare the journal entry to record the interest payment on January 1, 2010.

dr

    cr   _____

                             _____

4. Assume the bond was retired immediately after the first interest payment on January 1, 2010, at a quoted price of 101 ½ . Prepare the journal entry to record the early retirement of the bond.

dr

dr

    cr

Exercise 10-5. Comparing Bonds Issued at Par, Discount, and Premium. (LO3)

Alive! Inc., whose annual accounting period ends on December 31, issued the following bonds:

    Date of bonds: January 1, 2008

    Maturity amount and date: $500,000 due in 10 years (December 31, 2017)

    Interest: 12% per year payable each December 31

    Date sold: January 1, 2008

Required:

1. Provide the following amounts to be reported on January 1, 2008 financial statements immediately after the bonds are issued.

		Case A Issued at 100	Case B Issued at 97	Case C Issued at 104
a.	Bonds Payable			
b.	Unamortized discount or premium			
c.	Bonds payable, net			

Computations:

2. Record the journal entry for the issuance of bonds for each Case:

Case A:
    dr

        cr

Case B:
    dr

    dr

        cr

Case C:
    dr

        cr

        cr

Exercise 10-6. Calculating the Current Ratio and Times Interest Earned Ratio (LO4)

At a recent year-end, a company reported the following amounts in its financial statements:

	Current Year	Prior Year
Total Current assets	$48,744	$41,325
Total Current liabilities	42,874	28,193
Interest and other debt expense	6,022	765
Income tax expense	4,615	8,850
Net income	8,174	10,965

Required:

1. Compute the current ratio and times interest earned ratio for the current year and the prior year.

2. Did the company appear to have increased or decreased its ability to pay current liabilities and future interest obligations as they become due? Why?

Exercise 10-7. Recording Bond Issuance and Interest Payment (Straight-line Amortization) (Supplement A)

Part A.

Denko Company issued $600,000, 10-year, bonds on January 1, 2009. The stated interest rate was 9%. Interest is payable annually on January 1.

The bonds were issued for $732,479. Using straight-line amortization, prepare journal entries to record:

(a) the bond issuance on January 1, 2009

> dr _____
>   cr _____
>   cr _____

(b) the accrual of interest on December 31, 2009

> dr _____
> dr _____
>   cr _____

Part B.

Assume, instead that the bonds were issued at $529,326. Using straight-line amortization, prepare journal entries to record:

(a) the bond issuance on January 1, 2009

> dr _____
> dr _____
>   cr _____

(b) the accrual of interest on December 31, 2009

```
dr
    cr                                          _____
    cr                                                      _____
                                                            _____
```

Exercise 10-8. Recording Bond Issuance and Interest Payment (Effective-Interest Amortization) (Supplement B)

Plenko Company issued $1,200,000, 10-year bonds on January 1, 2009. The stated interest rate is 6%. Interest is payable annually on January 1.

Part A.

The bonds were issued for $1,038,954 at a market rate of interest of 8%. Interest is payable annually on January 1. Using effective-interest amortization, prepare journal entries to record:

(a) the bond issuance on January 1, 2009,

```
dr
dr                                              _____
    cr                                          _____
                                                            _____
```

(b) the accrual of interest on December 31, 2009 (the market rate is 8%)

```
dr
    cr                                          _____
    cr                                                      _____
                                                            _____
```

Part B

Assume, instead that the bonds were issued at $1,292,657 at a market rate of interest of 5%. Using effective-interest amortization, prepare journal entries to record:

(a) the bond issuance on January 1, 2009,

```
dr
    cr                                          _____
    cr                                                      _____
                                                            _____
```

(b) the accrual of interest on December 31, 2009 (the market rate is 5%)

```
dr
dr                                              _____
    cr                                          
                                                            _____
```

Exercise 10-9. Recording Bond Issuance and Interest Payment (Simplified Approach to Effective-Interest Amortization) (Supplement C)

Refer to Exercise 10-8. Rework Parts A and B using the Simplified Approach to Effective-Interest Amortization.
Part A.
The bonds were issued for $1,038,954. Interest is payable annually on January 1. Using effective-interest amortization, prepare journal entries to record:

(a) the bond issuance on January 1, 2009

> dr
>
>   cr   _____

(b) the accrual of interest on December 31, 2009 (the market rate is 8%)

> dr   _____
>
>   cr
>
>   cr   _____

Part B

Assume, instead that the bonds were issued at $1,292,657. Using effective-interest amortization, prepare journal entries to record:

(a) the bond issuance on January 1, 2009

> dr   _____
>
>   cr   _____

(b) the accrual of interest on December 31, 2009 (the market rate is 5%)

> dr   _____
>
> dr   _____
>
>   cr   _____

SOLUTIONS TO SELF-TEST QUESTIONS AND EXERCISES

MATCHING
1.

C	Accrued Liabilities	B	Line of Credit
L	Contingent Liability	F	Liquidity
K	Current Liabilities	J	Market Interest Rate
N	Current Ratio	A	Premium
M	Discount	D	Present Value
P	Effective-Interest Method (Supplement B)	I	Stated Interest Rate
O	Face Value	G	Straight-Line Method (Supplement A)
H	Issue Price	E	Times Interest Earned Ratio

TRUE-FALSE QUESTIONS
1. T
2. F – A cash equivalent is the amount of cash that a creditor would accept to settle the liability immediately after the transaction or event occurred.
3. T
4. T
5. F – FICA is short for Federal Insurance Contributions Act.
6. T
7. F – Retailers collect sales tax from consumers and forwards it to the state government. It is not an expense because the company simply collects and passes on the sales tax.
8. T

9. F – When the market rate is higher than the stated rate, the bonds sell at a discount because the bonds pay less than the market and, therefore, aren't worth as much.
10. F – The issue price is the amount of money that a lender pays (and the company receives) when a bond is issued.
11. F – The face value and the stated interest rate are used only to determine cash payments.
12. T
13. F – This describes the effect of a discount, not a premium.
14. T
15. F – The current ratio measures the liquidity of a company.
16. T
17. T
18. F – Loan covenants reduce risk to creditors, making them willing to accept a lower interest rate.
19. F – It is a potential liability arising as a result of past transactions or events, but the company is unable to determine whether it actually will liable until a future event occurs or fails to occur.
20. T

MULTIPLE CHOICE QUESTIONS

1. C	6. B	11. C	16. D
2. B	7. A	12. B	17. C
3. B	8. B	13. D	18. A
4. B	9. D	14. A	19. A
5. D	10. A	15. B	20. C

EXERCISES

Exercise 10-1. Reporting Payroll Costs with Discussion (LO2)

1. Prepare the journal entry to record the payroll for June, including employee deductions (but excluding employer FICA taxes.)

dr Compensation expense (+E, -SE)	345,000	
cr Liability for employee income taxes withheld (+L)		69,000
cr Union Dues Payable. .(+L).		4,500
cr Employee insurance premiums payable. (+L)		2,600
cr FICA payable (+L)		24,668
cr Cash (-A)		244,232

2. Prepare the journal entry to record the employer's FICA taxes.

dr Compensation expense (+E, -SE)	24,668	
cr FICA payable (+L)		24,668

3. Assume the amounts owed to governmental agencies and other organizations are paid on July 8, 2009. Prepare the journal entry to record the payment.

dr Liability for employee income taxes withheld (-L).	69,000	
dr Union Dues Payable (-L)	4,500	
dr Employee Insurance Premiums payable (-L).	2,600	
dr FICA Payable (-L)	49,336	
cr Cash (-A)		125,436

4. What was the total labor cost for the company? Explain.

Paying for labor involves more than simply paying salaries. There are additional payroll costs paid by an employer as well. It must match the FICA withheld from employees and pay state and federal unemployment taxes. Also, while not shown in this example, there are the additional costs borne by the employer for vacations, health insurance (if covered by employer), sick days earned by the employee, and any matching costs to retirement funds (if paid by employer). It can be very expensive to pay for labor. In our example, the cost is: $369,668 ($345,000 + $24,668)

Exercise 10-2. Reporting Interest and Long-term Debt (including Current Portion) (LO2)

1. Prepare the journal entry to be recorded on October 1, 2008

dr Cash (+A) 800,000
    cr Notes payable (+L)   800,000

2. Prepare the journal entry to be recorded on December 31, 2008

dr Interest Expense (+E, -SE). 16,000
    cr Interest Payable (+L). ($800,000x 8% x 3/12) 16,000

3. Prepare the journal entry to be made on September 30, 2009 to (a) record the payment of interest, and (b) to record the first principle payment.

dr Interest payable (-L) 16,000
dr Interest Expense (+E, -SE). ($800,000 x 8% x 9/1 . .48,000
    cr Cash (-A). .. ($800,000 x 8% x 12/12) .... .64,000

dr Notes Payable (-L) 160,000
    cr Cash   160,000

4. Show how the note would be reported (and any other liabilities resulting from the note) on the Balance Sheet on December 31, 2009.

NOTE: Interest is calculated based on the unpaid balance of the note ($800,000 – $160,000) x 8% x 3/12 = $12,800

Current Liabilities:

Current portion of long-term debt	$ 160,000
Interest Payable	12,800
Total Current Liabilities	$ 172,800
Long-term debt	480,000
Total Liabilities	$ 652,800

Exercise 10-3. Recording and Reporting Current Liabilities. (LO2)

1. Give (a) the journal entry for the collection of rent on October 31, 2009, and (b) the adjusting journal entry on December 31, 2009.

a.   *dr* Cash (+A)   15,000
        cr Unearned revenue (+L)   15,000

b.   *dr* Unearned revenue (-L) ($15,000/3) x 2.........   10,000
        cr Rent revenue (+R, +SE)   10,000

2. Give the journal entry to record the sales of china cabinets in December.
        dr Cash (+A)   12,180
        cr Sales tax payable (+L) ($11,600 x 5%) ...   580
        cr Sales revenue (+R, +SE)   11,600

Exercise 10-4. Preparing Journal Entries to Record Issuance of a Bond, Accrual of Interest, and Payments of Interest, and Early Retirement. (LO3)

1. Prepare the journal entry to record the bond issuance.
dr Cash (+A)   700,000
    cr Bonds payable (+L)   700,000

2. Prepare the journal entry to accrue interest on December 31, 2009.
dr Interest expense (+E,-SE) 49,000
    cr Interest payable (+L) 49,000
        ($700,000 x 7%x 12/12)

3. Prepare the journal entry to record the interest payment on January 1, 2010.
dr Interest payable (-L) 49,000
    cr Cash (-A) 49,000

4. Assume the bond was retired immediately after the first interest payment on Janaury 1, 2010, at a quoted price of 101 ½ . Prepare the journal entry to record the early retirement of the bond.
dr Bonds payable (-L) 700,000
dr Loss on bonds retired (+E, -SE) 10,500
    cr Cash (-A) ...($700,000 x 101 ½ %)....................... 710,500

Exercise 10-5. Comparing Bonds Issued at Par, Discount, and Premium. (LO3)

		Case A Issued at 100	Case B Issued at 97	Case C Issued at 104
a.	Bonds Payable	500,000	500,000	500,000
b.	Unamortized discount or premium	-	15,000	20,000
c.	Bonds payable, net	500,000	485,000	520,000

Computations:
Case B: c. ($500,000 x 97% = $485,000); b. $500,000 – $485,000 = $15,000 discount
Case C: c. ($500,000 x 104% = $520,000); b. $520,000 – $500,000 = $20,000 premium

2. Record the journal entry for the issuance of bonds for each Case:
Case A:
dr Cash (+A) 500,000
    cr Bonds payable (+L) 500,000

Case B:
dr Cash (+A) 485,000
dr Discount on bonds payable (+xL, -L) 15,000
    cr Bonds payable (+L) 500,000

Case C:
dr Cash (+A) 520,000
    cr Premium on bonds payable (+L) 20,000
    cr Bonds payable (+L) 500,000

Exercise 10-6. Calculating the Current Ratio and Times Interest Earned Ratio (LO4)
1. Compute the current ratio and times interest earned ratio for the current and prior years.

Current year: Current Ratio: $48,744 / $42874= 1.14 to 1
                Times Interest Earned Ratio: ($8,174 + $6,022 + $4,615) / $6,022 = 3.12 times

Prior year: Current Ratio: $41,325 / $28,193 = 1.47 to 1
                Times Interest Earned Ratio: ($10,965 + $765 + $8,850) / $765 = 26.9 times

2. OUCH! This company is hurting and could be in serious trouble. While the current ratio still appears to be relatively strong, it has decreased quite a bit from last year. The times interest earned ratio really took a dive! Last year interest was earned nearly 27 times. But this year it nose-dived to a mere 3 times. This appears to be bad news for this company....UNLESS it used a large number of its current resources for a planned expansion and investment in long-lived assets, which it financed through a large bond issuance. This would explain the loss of current assets and the huge increase in interest charges. You can only be certain if you work there, or have been following the company closely for a while.

Exercise 10-7. Recording Bond Issuance and Interest Payment (Straight-line Amortization) (Supplement A)
Part A.
(a) The bond issuance on January 1, 2009
dr Cash (+A) 732,479
      cr Premium on bonds payable (+L) ($732,479 – $600,000)   132,479
      cr Bonds payable (+L)   600,000

(b) The accrual of interest on December 31, 2009
dr Interest expense (+E, -SE) ($54,000 – $13,248)................. 40,752
dr Premium on bonds payable (–L) ($132,479/10). 13,248
      cr Interest payable (+L) . .($600,000 x 9% x 12/12).   54,000

Part B.
(a) the bond issuance on January 1, 2009
dr Cash (+A) 529,326
dr Discount on bonds payable (+xL, -L) ($600,000 – $529,326).... 70,674
      cr Bonds payable (+L)   600,000

(b) the accrual of interest on December 31, 2009
dr Interest expense (+E, -SE) ($54,000 + $7,067)... 61,067
      cr Interest payable (+L) ($600,000 x 9% x 12/12)..........   54,000
      cr Discount on bonds payable (-xL, +L) ($70,674 / 10)...   7,067

Exercise 10-8. Recording Bond Issuance and Interest Payment (Effective-Interest Amortization) (Supplement B)

Part A.
The bonds were issued for $1,038,954. Interest is payable annually on January 1. Using effective-interest amortization, prepare journal entries to record:
(a) The bond issuance on January 1, 2009
dr Cash (+A) 1,038,954
dr Discount on bonds payable (+xL, -L) ($1,200,000 – $1,038,954) 161,046
      cr Bonds payable (+L)   1,200,000

(b) The accrual of interest on December 31, 2009
dr Interest expense (+E, -SE) ($1,038,954 x 8% x 12/12)............ 83,116
      cr Interest payable (+L) ($1,200,000 x 6% x 12/12)........   72,000
      cr Discount on bonds payable (-xL, +L) ($83,116 – $72,000)   11,116

Part B
Assume, instead that the bonds were issued at $1,292,657. Using effective-interest amortization, prepare journal entries to record:
(a) The bond issuance on January 1, 2009
dr Cash (+A) 1,292,657
      cr Premium on bonds payable (+L) ($1,292,657–$1,200,000)   92,657
      cr Bonds payable (+L) 1,200,000

(b) The accrual of interest on December 31, 2009
dr Interest expense (+E, -SE) ($1,292,657 x 5% x12/12)..... 64,633
dr Premium on bonds payable (–L) ($72,000 – $64,633) 7,367
      cr Interest payable (+L) . .($1,200,000 x 6% x 12/12).   72,000

Exercise 10-9. Recording Bond Issuance and Interest Payment (Simplified Approach to Effective-Interest Amortization) (Supplement C)

Refer to Exercise 10-8. Rework Parts A and B using the Simplified Approach to Effective-Interest Amortization.

Part A.

The bonds were issued for $1,038,954. Interest is payable annually on January 1. Using effective-interest amortization, prepare journal entries to record:

(a) The bond issuance on January 1, 2009

dr Cash (+A) 1,038,954

       cr Bonds payable, net (+L)   1,038,954

(b) The accrual of interest on December 31, 2009

dr Interest expense (+E, -SE) ($1,038,954 x 8%)..................... 83,116

       cr Interest payable (+L) ($1,200,000 x 6% x12/12)..........   72,000

       cr Bonds Payable, net (-xL, +L) ($83,116 – $72,000)......   11,116

Part B

Assume, instead that the bonds were issued at $1,292,657. Using effective-interest amortization, prepare journal entries to record:

(a) The bond issuance on January 1, 2009

dr Cash (+A) 1,292,657

       cr Bonds payable, net (+L)   1,292,657

(b) The accrual of interest on December 31, 2009

dr Interest expense (+E, -SE) ($1,292,657 x 5% x 12/12)......... 64,633

dr Bonds Payable, net (–L) ($72,000 – $64,633) 7,367

       cr Interest payable (+L) . .($600,000 x 9% x 12/12).   72,000

CHAPTER 11
REPORTING AND INTERPRETING
STOCKHOLDERS' EQUITY

ORGANIZATION OF THE CHAPTER

Understand the business	Study the accounting methods	Evaluate the results	Review the chapter
- Corporate ownership - Equity versus debt financing	- Common stock transactions - Stock dividends and stock splits - Preferred stock - Retained earnings	- Earnings per share (EPS) - Return on Equity (ROE) - Price Earnings (P/E) ratio	- Demonstration case -Chapter summary - Key terms - Practice material

CHAPTER FOCUS SUGGESTIONS

Review

Chapter 10 discussed both short-term and long-term liabilities. A number of expenses are accrued at the end of an accounting period including payroll, payroll taxes, and income taxes. Unearned revenues were also covered. But, long-term financing via a public offering was the crux of the chapter. Bonds are a major source of external financing when large amounts of capital are needed for expansion and growth. However, not all major financing is accomplished from external sources. A primary consideration for capital financing is through current and potential stockholders.

UNDERSTAND THE BUSINESS

Corporate Ownership

Corporations have the ability to raise large amounts of money because investors can easily participate in a corporation's ownership. Corporations are able to do this because:

> **Learning Objective 1**
> Explain the role of stock in financing a corporation.

- ■ **Shares of stock can be purchased in small amounts**. There are some corporations that allow an investor to purchase only one share of stock.
- ■ **Ownership interests are transferable**. Shares of public companies are regularly bought and sold on established markets.
- ■ **Stockholders are not liable for the corporation's debt**. Creditors have no legal claim to the personal assets of stockholders like they do on personal assets belonging to owners of sole proprietorships and partnerships.

A corporation exists separate and apart from its owners, or in legalese, a corporation is a *separate legal entity*. It is allowed to own assets, incur debt, sue others, be sued, and enter into contracts independent of its stockholders. Since the owners are typically not on the premises of the business their rights are heavily regulated. Application to the state is required for new corporations and, upon approval, the state issues a charter or *articles of incorporation*. Each state has its own laws regarding corporate organization. Since Delaware has the most favorable rules, many of the largest corporations are incorporated there.

In its most basic form, a corporation must have one type of stock, appropriately called **common stock.** The benefits received by the owners of common stock include:

- ■ *Voting Rights.* For each share of stock owned, you are entitled to one vote on important issues.
- ■ *Dividends.* Stockholders receive a share in the corporation's profits when distributed as dividends.
- ■ *Residual Claim.* If the company declares bankruptcy, stockholders' get a share in remaining assets after creditors have been paid.
- ■ *Preemptive Rights.* Existing stockholders may be given the first chance to buy newly issued stock before it is offered to others.

Equity Versus Debt Financing

When a company needs large amounts of long-term financing, the board of directors will have to decide whether to obtain it by issuing new stock to investors (called *equity financing*) or borrowing the money from lenders (called *debt financing*). Each has its own advantages and disadvantages, as shown in the following list:

Advantages of Equity Financing:
- **Equity does not have to be repaid.** Debt must be repaid or refinanced.
- **Dividends are Optional.** Interest must be paid on debt.

Advantages of Debt Financing:
- **Interest on debt is tax deductible.** Dividends on stock are not tax deductible.
- **Debt does not change stockholder control.** In contrast, a stock issue gives new stockholders the right to vote and share in the earnings, diluting existing stockholders' control.

STUDY THE ACCOUNTING METHODS

Learning Objective 2
Explain and analyze common stock transactions.

Common Stock Transactions

Stockholders' Equity in a corporation consists of the following accounts:
1. **Contributed Capital.** This is the amount of capital the company received from investors' contributions, in exchange for the company's stock.
2. **Retained Earnings.** This represents the cumulative amount of net income earned by the company less the cumulative amount of dividends declared since the corporation was first organized. It is sometimes referred to as Earned Capital.
3. **Treasury Stock.** These are shares that were previously owned by stockholders but have been bought back and are now held by the corporation.

Authorization, Issuance and Repurchase

When the state grants a charter to a corporation, it indicates the maximum number of shares that the corporation can sell, called the **authorized** shares. Of course, the company doesn't max out this limit on the first day! Only some of these authorized shares will actually be sold. Shares that have actually been sold to investors are called **issued** shares. Shares that have been issued and not bought back by the corporation are called **outstanding** shares. Sometimes, a company may purchase its own stock that was previously sold to someone else. When a company buys some of its own previously issued shares, it is called **treasury stock.** While treasury stock is held by the corporation, the shares are not entitled to voting rights, dividends, or any of the other stockholder rights listed earlier in the chapter.

1. **Stock Authorization.** The specific rights and characteristics of stock are authorized and defined in the corporate charter before stock can be issued. One characteristic determined by the corporate charter is the stock's **par value.** This is a token amount and in no way relates to the actual *market value* of the stock. It is the minimum amount that stock can be issued for *legally*. Some states no longer require that a par value be specified on stock issuances and allow corporations to issue **no-par value stock.** No-par stock is just like par value stock, except that it does not have a specified *legal* value per share.

2. **Stock Issuance.** The sale of stock by the corporation to an investor is called a *stock issuance*. When a corporation issues stock for the very first time it is called an IPO (initial public offering) or 'going public.' Once a company's stock has been traded on the market, any additional issuances are referred to as *seasoned new issues*. Regardless of the type of issuance, they are accounted for the same way. Assume Jones, Inc. issued 50,000 of its $2.00 par common stock for $25 per share. Jones, Inc. would record the following entry:

1. Analyze	Assets	=	Liabilities	+	Stockholders' Equity	
	Cash +1,250,000				Common Stock (+SE)	+100,000
					Additional paid-in capital (+SE)	+1,150,000

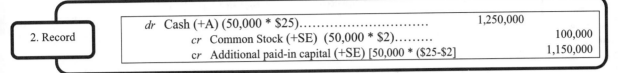

2. Record	dr Cash (+A) (50,000 * $25)................................	1,250,000	
	cr Common Stock (+SE) (50,000 * $2)..........		100,000
	cr Additional paid-in capital (+SE) [50,000 * ($25-$2]		1,150,000

Look at the dollar amount that is credited to the common stock account. It is the *par value* of each share sold. Only the par value of the stock issued can be put into the Common Stock account regardless of the issue price of the stock. The only exception to this is if the company is issuing *no par stock*, then the entire amount of the cash received is credited to the Common Stock account.

Stock Sold between Investors. The examples shown thus far illustrate transactions between the issuing corporation and the buyer of the stock. After this initial sale of stock to the investor, the investor is free to sell these shares to other investors. This is a personal sale between the individuals involved and is not a recordable event for the corporation. The entries discussed in this chapter only apply to *initial* sales of stock (initial public offerings or seasoned new issues) by the corporation.

Stock Used to Compensate Employees. To encourage employees to work hard for a corporation, they are often offered stock options. Stock options allow employees to buy the company's stock at a predetermined price during a specified period of time. The assumption is that if employees are also owners of the business, the success of the business will be important to them. If the stock prices rise, the employees can exercise the stock options and buy the stock at the predetermined price – usually a bargain price. If the stock prices fall, the employees will not exercise the option, and will have lost nothing.

3. ***Repurchase of Stock***
Sometimes a corporation purchases its own stock from existing shareholders for the following reasons:

   a. To distribute excess cash to stockholders.
   b. To send a signal to investors that the company itself believes its own stock is worth purchasing.
   c. To obtain shares that can be reissued as payment for purchases of other companies
   d. To obtain shares to reissue to employees as part of employee stock ownership plans

Usually, when a company repurchases its own stock, the stock is accounted for based on the cost of the shares to the company. This is called the *cost method*. Assume Jones, Inc. purchased 5,000 of its own shares at $22 per share. The entry is:

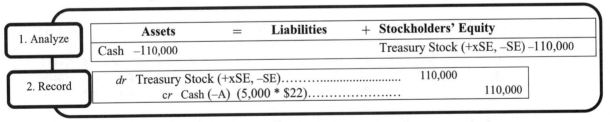

| 1. Analyze | **Assets** | **=** | **Liabilities** | **+ Stockholders' Equity** |
| | Cash –110,000 | | | Treasury Stock (+xSE, –SE) –110,000 |

| 2. Record | dr Treasury Stock (+xSE, –SE)........................... 110,000 | |
| | cr Cash (–A) (5,000 * $22)..................... 110,000 | |

The entire cost of the treasury stock $110,000 is debited to the treasury stock account. The account *Treasury Stock is not an asset!!!* Instead, it is a contra-equity account and is subtracted from total stockholders' equity on the balance sheet. It may seem odd, but it does make sense. These shares are owned by the company, and since a company can't own itself, the cost of the shares it owns must be subtracted from the amount owned by the 'real' owners—stockholders' equity.

4. ***Reissuance of Treasury Stock***
Upon selling treasury stock, GAAP does not allow a corporation to report a gain or loss on the sale of *its own stock* because owner transactions are not considered *profit-making activities*. Assume that Jones, Inc. reissued 1,000 of the treasury shares for $24 per share. The entry to record the reissuance is:

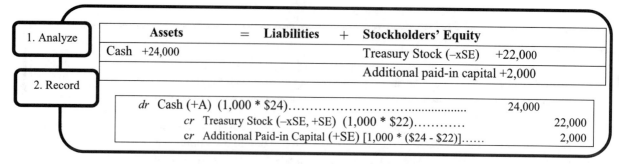

1. Analyze	Assets	= Liabilities	+	Stockholders' Equity	
	Cash +24,000			Treasury Stock (–xSE) +22,000	
2. Record				Additional paid-in capital +2,000	

dr Cash (+A) (1,000 * $24)... 24,000
 cr Treasury Stock (–xSE, +SE) (1,000 * $22)............ 22,000
 cr Additional Paid-in Capital (+SE) [1,000 * ($24 - $22)]...... 2,000

The Treasury stock is removed from the account at the same price it was purchased for $22,000. The additional $2.00 per share received by the corporation from the reissuance, $2,000 is 'extra' capital. So, it is appropriately placed into the Additional Paid-In Capital account

If treasury stock is reissued at a price *below* the amount paid for the treasury stock, the difference is a reduction in *Additional Paid-in Capital.* Let's assume that Jones, Inc. reissued another 500 shares at $21 per share, the entry is:

1. Analyze	Assets	= Liabilities	+	Stockholders' Equity	
	Cash +10,500			Treasury Stock (–xSE) +11,000	
2. Record				Additional paid-in capital (–SE) –500	

dr Cash (+A) (500 * $21)... 10,500
dr Additional Paid-in Capital (–SE) [500 * ($22 - $21)]............ 500
 cr Treasury Stock (–xSE, +SE) (500 * $22) 11,000

In this case, the corporation paid more for the treasury stock than the received when it was reissued. The Additional paid-in capital account absorbs the difference of $500.

5. **Dividends on Common Stock**

> **Learning Objective 3**
> Explain and analyze cash dividends, stock dividends, and stock split transactions.

There are really *two* different expectations of investors when they purchase stock. They expect to be paid a portion of the profits (dividends) and they expect the value of their investment to go up (stock value.) Investors preferring that little or no dividends be paid out on their stock are primarily interested in the value of the stock increasing. They purchased the stock as a 'growth' investment.

Other investors would rather receive some of the profits right now. They are more interested in the dividends paid by the corporation and purchased the stock as an 'income' investment. Typically these are people, such as retirees, seeking a steady cash flow from their investment. No corporation is legally obligated to pay dividends. It is a decision made by the board of directors. Unless the board declares a dividend, none are paid to stockholders. There are three important dates related to dividends:

a. ***Declaration Date.*** The **declaration date** is the date on which the board officially approves (declares) a dividend. Once declared, the dividend is a legal liability of the company. Both Dividends Declared and Dividends Payable are increased by a declaration. The dividends declared account is a temporary account that will be closed to Retained earnings at the end of the accounting period. Remember that dividends are distributions of the corporation's accumulated prior earnings. Dividend payments represent the portion of accumulated prior earnings that the business *does not retain.*

Assume Jones, Inc. declares .07 cents per share dividends to its 46,500 shares outstanding (50,000 – 5,000 + 1,000 + 500). Notice that dividends are not given to the treasury shares still held by the corporation. Only those that have been reissued receive dividends. The following journal entry is made:

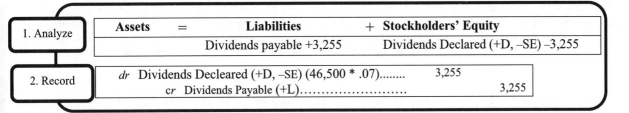

1. Analyze	Assets	=	Liabilities	+	Stockholders' Equity
			Dividends payable +3,255		Dividends Declared (+D, –SE) –3,255

2. Record	*dr* Dividends Decleared (+D, –SE) (46,500 * .07)........ 3,255
	cr Dividends Payable (+L)........................ 3,255

b. ***Date of Record.*** *Date of Record.* The **record date** always follows the declaration date. It is the date that the list of current stockholders is made by the corporation. The individuals on this list are the only ones who will receive the dividend declared earlier. The corporation needs some time to identify who will actually receive the dividends that were declared. There is no journal entry on this date.

c. ***Date of Payment.*** The **payment date** is the date on which the dividend is paid to the individuals on the list prepared on the date of record. The entry made on this date is:

1. Analyze	Assets	=	Liabilities	+	Stockholders' Equity
	Cash –3,255		Dividends payable –3,255		

2. Record	*dr* Dividends payable (–L)............................... 3,255
	cr Cash (–A)....................................... 3,255

On the date of payment *Cash* is paid to shareholders for the dividend. This is pointed out so that you will notice that two things are necessary in order for a company to declare cash dividends:

- *Sufficient Retained Earnings.* There must be enough profits in the business to cover the amount of dividends declared. If there are no profits (even if the company has tons of cash), there is nothing to 'share' with stockholders. State law often limits cash dividends to the amount of Retained Earnings. A company's payment of cash dividends may be further restricted if it has existing loan covenants with a bank that requires a minimum amount of cash be available at all times, in accordance with the loan agreement. Because of the severe limitations these types of covenants can have on a corporation, GAAP requires that companies disclose this information in the notes to the financial statements.
- *Sufficient cash.* If there is no cash (even if there are tons of profits), there's no money to give to stockholders so the company can't really 'share' the profits with owners. Remember ***Retained Earnings is NOT Cash!***

Stock Dividends and Stock Splits

Stock Dividends
Some dividends involve the stockholder receiving additional shares of *stock* rather than *cash.* These are called **stock dividends.** They involve a distribution of stock to stockholders on a pro rata basis at no cost to the stockholder. The phrase *pro rata* means that each stockholder receives additional shares equal to the percentage of shares held. So, if a stockholder owns 15% of the stock, they would receive 15% of any additional shares issued from the stock dividend.

Stock dividends are a subject of much debate. They do not really increase the wealth of stockholders like a cash dividend. If you own 10% of the company's stock before the stock dividend, you still own 10% of the stock *after* the stock dividend. It's just that 10% represents a few more shares than it did before.

So, why would a company issue stock dividends if they have no value? Well, the primary reason is: ***It reduces the market price per share of the stock.*** When stock prices are so high that new investors won't buy them, there is a need to reduce the price. If you check your local newspaper for stock prices, you will see that most shares are selling for less than $200 per share. When more stock is issued, the price of the stock declines. This is because the more people there are sharing ownership, the *less each individual share is worth*. To accomplish this price reduction, many companies will declare one huge stock dividend (100% stock dividends are common.) This has the effect of *doubling* the number of shares out there. With twice as many shares issued, the value of each is cut in half.

When a stock dividend occurs, the company is essentially buying the stock for the stockholders. Though the shareholder isn't required to pay for the shares, the shares must be 'paid for' because they haven't been issued yet (this isn't treasury stock). The only way to accomplish this is to use some of the company's Retained Earnings (or Additional Paid-in Capital). Overall, there is no effect on the corporation of this 'transfer'. It is similar to a situation where you would transfer $1,000 from Savings to Checking. Your overall wealth hasn't changed a bit...you've simply redistributed it.

Large stock dividends (more than 20% - 25% of outstanding shares) have a significant effect on stock price. Therefore, they aren't 'sold' at the current market price. Instead they are 'sold' at par value...the minimum price that a share can be sold for by law. Assume Jones, Inc. declared a 100% stock dividend when the stock was selling for $35 per share. After the dividend, there will be 93,000 shares outstanding (46,500 already issued + 46,500 * 100% stock dividend.) In other words, the company will issue *another* 46,500 shares for a total of 93,000 shares *after the* dividend. The entry would be:

	Assets	=	Liabilities	+	Stockholders' Equity
1. Analyze					Retained Earnings +93,000
					Common Stock +93,000

2. Record
dr Retained Earnings (–SE) (46,500 * 100% * $2)....... 93,000
cr Common Stock (+SE)......................... 93,000

Notice that, even though the stock currently sells for $35 per share, the large stock dividend is recorded at the minimum legal amount of $2.00 per share. The following table shows the corporation's stockholders' equity account balances before and after the 100% stock dividend.

Stockholders' Equity	Before a 100% Stock Dividend	After 100% Stock Dividend
Number of shares outstanding	46,500	93,000
Par value per share	$2.00	186,000
Total par value outstanding	$93,000	$186,000
Retained Earnings	400,000	307,000
Total Stockholders' Equity	$493,000	$493,000

A small stock dividend is a distribution of less than 20 – 25% of the outstanding stock. The accounting treatment for a small stock dividend is to require a transfer equal to the current price of the stock; whereas, with a large stock dividend the amount of the transfer is the minimum required by law – par value.

Notice that *total stockholders' equity* increased by $93,000 (46,500 shares * $2 par) and it also decreased by $93,000. Many companies call a 100% stock dividend a 'stock split effected as a stock dividend.' This is not true. A stock split is *completely different* and the two should never be confused. A stock dividend *can never be a stock split!* Why? Read on!

Stock Splits
The biggest difference between a stock dividend and a stock split is that a stock split has no effect *on **any** account in stockholders' equity*. In fact, it doesn't even require a journal entry. So, it costs the shareholders *nothing, zip, zero*. This is vastly different from the $93,000 of retained earnings that was used in the last example. The problem is that a stock dividend requires the use of *retained earnings*. It uses those hard earned profits to *buy more stock*. Most stockholders would rather that retained earnings be available later for some *cash dividends!* But, no! It's gone!

On the other hand, stock splits are like taking what you've got, giving it back, and getting at least twice as much in return! Splits are described as 2 for 1, 3 for 1, 4 for 1, etc. A 4 for 1 stock split gives the owner *four* shares in exchange for each *one* they currently own. So, if you own 100 shares and a 4 for 1 split is declared, you now have 400 shares (100 * 4). Neither cash nor retained earnings are affected by a stock split.

Instead, the par value is simply reduced. If par value was $2.00, a 4 for 1 would reduce the par to 50 cents ($2.00 / 4). So, you quadruple the number of shares and reduce the par to ¼. Essentially, the dollar amount of the stock on the books has not changed at all! Assume Jones, Inc. effects a 4 for 1 stock split on its outstanding 93,000 shares. There will now be 372,000 shares and the par value of each will now be 50 cents ($2.00/4). These two changes offset one another exactly, so no journal entry is needed as shown below.)

Stockholders' Equity	Before a 4 for 1 Stock Split	After a 4 for 1 Stock Split
Number of shares outstanding	93,000	372,000
Par value per share	$2.00	0.50
Total par value outstanding	$186,000	$186,000
Retained Earnings	307,000	307,000
Total Stockholders' Equity	$493,000	$493,000

Stock splits tend to be used when the financial situation looks a bit rocky. This is because no retained earnings are used to issue the extra shares of stock. You may need that retained earnings to declare cash dividends in the future. So, if you expect financial struggles in the future, you don't want to use up precious resources that you may need later.

Stock dividends tend to be used when companies anticipate a rosy financial picture. You don't care if Retained Earnings is reduced because you anticipate that future earnings will bring the retained earnings right back up! In fact, it can show a bit of confidence. Finally, this almost creates a third reason: *companies declare stock dividends as a signal to financial statement users that the company expects strong financial performance in the near future.*

Preferred Stock
Preferred stock differs from common stock, primarily, on the number of rights granted to each.

- *Preferred stock generally is not granted voting rights.* Those who want some control over the operations of the company will not be attracted to preferred stock since voting rights are generally not given to preferred stockholders. Common shareholders like preferred stock because it enables the company to raise funds without reducing the control of the common stockholders,
- *Preferred stock is less risky.* The word 'preferred' basically means they get everything before the common shareholders do (they are 'preferred'.) They receive dividends first, and any assets remaining after paying creditors if the company folds.
- *Preferred stock typically has a fixed dividend rate.* Preferred stock is usually defined as a percent. 6% preferred; 5% preferred, etc. This 'percentage' refers to the amount of the dividend that will be paid annually to the preferred shareholders, if declared. The percentage refers to a percentage of par value. So, $50 par, 6% preferred means that a $3.00 dividend ($50 * 6%) will be paid to preferred shareholders annually, if declared.

Assume Jones, Inc. issues 5,000 shares of $100 par value 7% preferred stock for $175. The following entry is made:

1. Analyze	Assets	=	Liabilities	+ Stockholders' Equity	
	Cash +875,000			Preferred Stock (+SE)	+500,000
				Additional paid-in capital (+SE)	+375,000

2. Record		
dr Cash (+A) (5,000 * $175).............................	875,000	
cr Preferred Stock (+SE) (5,000 * $100).........		500,000
cr Additional paid-in capital (+SE) [5,000 * ($175-$100]		375,000

Dividends on Preferred Stock

Two customary dividend preferences are granted to preferred shareholders because they forego so many rights given to the common shareholders. The two most common dividend preference are called current and cumulative.

1. *Current Dividend Preference*

This preference requires that the current year's preferred dividends be paid to the preferred shareholders before the common receive dividends. If no other preferences exist, the common shareholders may receive their dividends. This preference is always a feature of preferred dividends.

Assume Jones, Inc. declares a $30,000 dividend in the current year. The preferred shareholders receive their preference first $35,000 (5,000 x 7% x $100). If there weren't enough dividends declared (as in this case) to cover the current year preference, the preferred receive the entire declaration ($30,000) and forfeit the remaining amount of $5,000 for this period. If $50,000 in dividends is declared in the following year, the preferred will received their entire $35,000 *current* preference and the remainder will be distributed to the common shareholders $15,000 ($50,000 - $35,000).

2. *Cumulative Dividend Preference*

This preference says that if all or part of the preferred stock's current dividend is not paid in full, the *cumulative unpaid amount,* known as **dividends in arrears,** must be paid before any future common dividends can be paid.

Using the previous example, assume that the preferred stock is *cumulative preferred.* In the first year, when $30,000 was declared, the preferred shareholders still receive just the $30,000. But, now the $5,000 unpaid amount is in arrears the following year. So, when the $50,000 is declared in the following year, the $5,000 arrearage must be paid first, leaving $45,000.

At this point, the preferred are all caught up for last year and we can start distributing the current year's preference. Don't forget that the preferred shareholders also get their current year dividend of $35,000 first, leaving $10,000 ($50,000 – $5,000 arrearage, – $35,000 current) for the common shareholders. Dividends in arrears are not actually *declared* so they are not a legal liability. Remember that only $30,000 was actually declared in the first year, so the $5,000 cannot be shown as a liability on the books in that year. But, the full disclosure principle requires that the arrearage be shown in the notes to the financial statements. Boy, those notes are becoming more and more important aren't they?

Retained Earnings

Retained Earnings represents the company's total earnings that have been retained in the business and, therefore, not distributed to stockholders (as dividends). This account balance increases each year the company reports net income and decrease each year that the company reports a net loss, or declares cash or stock dividends to the stockholders. In the event that a company accumulates more net losses than it does net income over the year, retained earnings will have a negative or debit balance. In that case, the amount would be (1) shown in parenthesis on the balance sheet, (2) deducted when computing total stockholders' equity, and (3) typically called an accumulated deficit rather than retained earnings.

EVALUATE THE RESULTS

> **Learning Objective 5**
> Analyze the earnings per share (EPS), return on equity (ROE), and price/earnings (P/E) ratios.

Earnings Per Share (EPS)

The granddaddy of all ratios is (drum roll please) Earnings Per Share (EPS.) This ratio reports how much profit (net income) is earned by each share of common stock outstanding (treasury stock doesn't get any). While this calculation can get pretty hairy, in its most basic form, it is calculated as:

$$\text{Earnings per Share} = \frac{\text{Net Income}}{\text{Average Number of Common Shares Outstanding}}$$

This ratio is usually reported on the income statement directly below net income or in the notes to the financial statements. It is typically calculated at the end of every quarter, and end of each year. Earnings per Share is important because it is what most investors use for predicting future stock prices and future dividends. Good earnings this year mean good dividends next year.

EPS also allows you to easily compare a company over time. Since it is a *per share* amount, it is adjusted for any additional shares issued, etc. thus providing a clearer picture of how the any increases (or decreases) will affect each individual investor.

Word to the wise, EPS is not the best measure for comparing one company with another company. There are too many reporting differences that can exist between two companies: depreciation methods, inventory methods, bad debt estimation methods, treasury stock methods, etc. You also need to consider the cost of each share of stock. Two companies may have identical EPS, but if one costs only $50 per share and the other costs $200, they can't be compared to one another. So, while it is an effective and widely used measure for comparing a company with itself or time, it is not appropriate for comparing across companies.

Return on Equity (ROE)

Like EPS, the **Return on Equity** reports a company's return to investors. However, rather than relate net income to the average *number* of shares outstanding, the ROE ratio relates net income to the average *dollars* of stockholder investment and earnings reinvested. Since this ratio compares dollars to dollars, it can be appropriately compared across companies. A higher ratio indicates that stockholders are likely to enjoy greater returns. It is calculated as follows:

$$\text{Return on Equity} = \frac{\textbf{Net Income}}{\textbf{Average Stockholders' Equity}}$$

This percentage is calculated from the company's point of view. It does not necessarily reflect what each individual investor pays to acquire the company's stock nor does it represent the current value of all outstanding stock. The accounts are not updated for changes in market value. They still reflect the dollar amount paid for the *initial issuance* of the stock. It is likely worth much more than that. So, every individual stockholder actually earns a different return than that calculated by the ROE.

Price/Earnings (P/E) Ratio

The **Price/Earnings Ratio** is a basic way to determine the value investors place on a company's common stock. It measures how many times more than current year's earnings investors are willing to pay for a company's stock. Generally, a relatively high P/E ratio means that investors expect the company to improve in the future and increase its profits, so they have factored the future earnings into the current stock price. A relatively low P/E ratio usually means that strong future performance isn't expected. Since these ratios vary widely across industries, they are most meaningful when comparing a company over time with itself or with competitors in the same industry.

$$\text{Price/Earnings (P/E)} = \frac{\textbf{Current stock price (per share)}}{\textbf{Earnings Per share (annual)}}$$

SUPPLEMENT A – ACCOUNTING FOR EQUITY IN SOLE PROPRIETORSHIPS, PARTNERSHIPS, AND OTHER BUSINESS FORMS

Owner's Equity for a Sole Proprietorship

A sole proprietorship is an unincorporated business owned by one person. There are only two owners' equity accounts: (1) a capital account for the proprietor (B. Cordova, Capital) and (2) a drawing (or withdrawal) account for the proprietor (B. Cordova, Drawings.)

The capital account contains investments by the owner and any cumulative income or loss. The drawing account records the owner's withdrawals of cash or other assets from the business. This account will be closed at the end of the accounting period (much like dividends for a corporation.) After closing entries have been prepared and posted, the capital account contains all cumulative investments and withdrawals by the owner, and all cumulative earnings of the business.

Bud Cordova started a retail store by investing $100,000 of personal savings in January 2009. The journal entry follows:

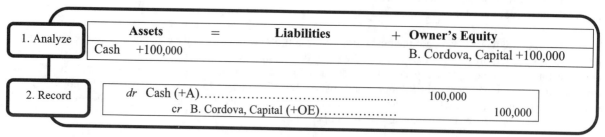

	1. Analyze		Assets	=	Liabilities	+	Owner's Equity	
			Cash +100,000				B. Cordova, Capital +100,000	

2. Record	dr Cash (+A)... 100,000
	cr B. Cordova, Capital (+OE)................. 100,000

Each month during the year, Bud withdrew $700 cash from the business for personal living costs. Accordingly, each month the following journal entry was made:

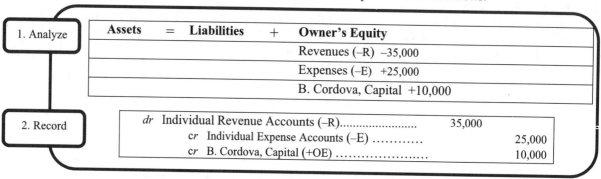

1. Analyze		Assets	=	Liabilities	+	Owner's Equity
		Cash −700				B. Cordova, Drawings (+D) −700

2. Record	dr B. Cordova, Drawings (+D, −OE)........................ 700
	cr Cash (−A) 700

Note: At December 31, 2009, after the last withdrawal, the drawings account will reflect a debit balance of $8,400 ($700 x 12).

The usual journal entries for the year, including adjusting and closing entries for the revenue and expense accounts, resulted in $10,000 net income, which was closed to the capital account as follows:

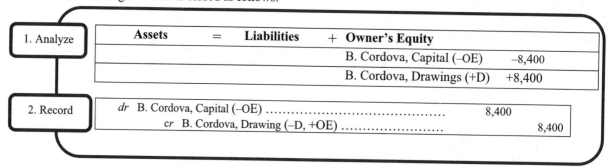

1. Analyze	Assets	=	Liabilities	+	Owner's Equity
					Revenues (−R) −35,000
					Expenses (−E) +25,000
					B. Cordova, Capital +10,000

2. Record	dr Individual Revenue Accounts (−R)........................ 35,000
	cr Individual Expense Accounts (−E) 25,000
	cr B. Cordova, Capital (+OE) 10,000

The drawings account is closed as follows:

1. Analyze	Assets	=	Liabilities	+	Owner's Equity
					B. Cordova, Capital (−OE) −8,400
					B. Cordova, Drawings (+D) +8,400

2. Record	dr B. Cordova, Capital (−OE) 8,400
	cr B. Cordova, Drawing (−D, +OE) 8,400

Balance Sheet (partial)

Owner's equity:

B. Cordova, capital, January 1, 2009	$100,000
Add: Net income for 2009	10,000
Total	110,000
Less: Withdrawals for 2009	(8,400)
B. Cordova, capital, December 31, 2009	$101,600

Any income earned from a sole proprietorship is taxed on the individual's personal income tax return. The monthly 'salary' of the owner is not recorded as expense, because an owner cannot be their own employee. Instead, this 'salary' is treated as a distribution of profits – a withdrawal – instead of salary expense.

Accounting for Partnership Equity

The Uniform Partnership Act (adopted by most states) defines a partnership as "an association of two or more persons to carry on as co-owners of a business for profit." The agreement between the partners is considered the 'partnership contract.' The agreement should indicate (1) how income is split among partners, (2) the management responsibilities of each individual partner, (3) how a transfer or sale of partnership interests is to be handled, (4) how to dispose of any remaining assets among the partners in the event of liquidation of the partnership, and (5) what should be done in the event of the death of a partner. Any of these items not addressed in the agreement will be handled according to the resident state law.

Advantages of partnerships are: (1) ease of formation; (2) partners have complete control of the business; and (3) there is no income tax on the business itself. The biggest drawback is the unlimited liability of each partner for the debts of the partnership. The personal assets of each partner can be seized to satisfy claims of creditors in the event the partnership is unable to pay.

Partnership accounting is very similar to that of a sole proprietorship. The only difference is that *each individual* partner has his own capital account and drawings account, and any income is distributed to each partner according to the partnership agreement.

C. Cage and D. Donut organized CD Partnership. Cage contributed $80,000 and Baker $20,000 cash to the partnership and agreed to divide net income (and net loss) 80% and 20%, respectively. The journal entry for the business to record the investment was as follows:

1. Analyze

Assets	=	Liabilities	+	Owners' Equity	
Cash +100,000				C. Cage, Capital (+OE)	+80,000
				D. Donut, Drawings (+OE)	+20,000

2. Record

dr Cash (+A)	100,000
cr C. Cage, Capital (+OE)	80,000
cr D. Donut, Capital (+OE)	20,000

The partners agreed that Cage would withdraw $1,500 and Donut $400 per month in cash. Accordingly, each month the following journal entry was made:

1. Analyze

Assets	=	Liabilities	+	Owners' Equity	
Cash −1,900				C. Cage, Drawings (−OE)	−1,500
				D. Donut, Drawings (−OE)	− 400

2. Record

dr C. Cage, Drawings (−OE)	1,500
dr D. Donut, Drawings (−OE)	400
cr Cash (−A)..	1,900

Note: At December 31, 2009, after the last withdrawal, the drawings account will reflect a debit balance of $18,000 for Cage ($1,500 x 12) and $4,800 for Donut ($400 x 12).

Assume that the normal closing entries for the revenue and expense accounts resulted in a net income of $65,000. The partnership agreement specified Cage would receive 80% of earnings and Donut would get 20%. The closing entry was as follows:

1. Analyze	**Assets**	**=**	**Liabilities**	**+ Owner's Equity**	
				Revenues (–R)	–100,000
				Expenses (–E)	+35,000
				C. Cage, Capital (+OE)	+52,000
				D. Donut, Capital (+OE)	+13,000

2. Record			
	dr Individual Revenue Accounts (–R)	100,000	
	cr Individual Expense Accounts (–E)		35,000
	cr C. Cage, Capital (+OE)		52,000
	cr D. Donut, Capital (+OE)		13,000

The journal entry required to close the drawings accounts follows:

1. Analyze	**Assets**	**=**	**Liabilities**	**+ Owner's Equity**	
				C. Cage, Capital	–18,000
				D. Donut, Capital	–4,800
				C. Cage, Drawings	+18,000
				D. Donut, Drawings	+ 4,800

2. Record			
	dr C. Cage, Capital (–OE)	18,000	
	dr D. Donut, Capital (–OE)	4,800	
	cr C. Cage, Drawings (+OE)		18,000
	cr D. Donut, Drawings (+OE)		4,800

A separate statement of partners' capital, similar to the following, is customarily prepared to supplement the balance sheet:

CD PARTNERSHIP **Statement of Partners' Equity** **For the Year Ended December 31, 2009**			
	C. Cage	**D. Donut**	**Total**
Investment, January 1, 2009	$ 80,000	$ 20,000	100,000
Add: Additional Investments During the Year	0	0	0
Add: Net Income for the Year	52,000	13,000	65,000
Totals	132,000	33,000	165,000
Less: Drawings During the Year	(18,000)	(4,800)	(22,800)
Partners' Equity, December 31, 2009	$114,000	28,200	142,200

Other Business Forms

New types of business forms seem to emerge often. These new forms blend features of the standard forms described in this chapter. These hybrids such as "S Corporations," Limited Liability Partnerships (LLPs), and Limited Liability Companies (LLCs) have become very popular. The LLC combines favorable features of a corporation (limited liability and separate legal entity) with the favorable tax treatment of partnerships (taxes paid by individual partners rather than the partnership). The accounting for these entities is essentially the same as the methods described in the chapter.

The financial statements of a LLC adhere to the same format as a partnership. This differs from a corporation because (1) there is an additional section on the statements called Distribution of Net Income, (2) Owner's equity on the balance is detailed for each owner; (3) there is no income tax expense reported on the income statement since each owner is taxed individually, (4) most amounts paid to the owners are not expenses of the business, instead are treated as withdrawals of capital.

REVIEW THE CHAPTER

Chapter Summary
LO1. Explain the role of stock in financing a corporation.
- ❖ The law recognizes corporations as *separate legal entities*
  - o Owners invest in a corporation and receive capital stock that can be bought from and sold to other investors.
  - o Stock provides a number of rights to its owners, including the rights to
    - ▪ Vote
    - ▪ Receive dividends, and
    - ▪ Share in residual assets at liquidation

LO2. Explain and analyze common stock transactions.
- ❖ A number of key transactions involve capital stock:
  - o Initial issuance of stock
  - o Repurchase of stock into treasury
  - o Reissuance of treasure stock
- ❖ Note that these transactions only affect the balance sheet
- ❖ Corporations do not report income arising from gains or losses on transactions involving their own stock

LO3. Explain and analyze cash dividends, stock dividends, and stock split transactions.
- ❖ Cash dividends:
  - o Reduce stockholders' equity (retained earnings), and
  - o Create a liability (dividends payable)
  - o When they are declared by the board of directors (on the date of declaration.)
  - o The liability is reduced when the dividends are paid (on the date of payment)
- ❖ Stock dividends:
  - o Are pro rata distributions of a company's stock to existing owners.
  - o The transaction typically is accounted for by:
    - ▪ Transferring an amount out of retained earnings , and
    - ▪ Into contributed capital accounts.
- ❖ Stock splits:
  - o Also involve the distributions of additional shares to owners, but
    - ▪ No additional amount is transferred into the common stock account
    - ▪ Instead, the par value of each share of stock is reduced.

LO4. Describe the characteristics of preferred stock and analyze transactions affecting preferred stock.
- ❖ Preferred stock provides investors certain advantages including:
  - o Current dividend preferences, and
  - o A preference on asset distribution in the event the corporation is liquidated.
- ❖ If Preferred stock carries Cumulative Dividend Rights, then:
  - o Any part of a current dividend that is not paid (called dividends in arrears) must be paid in full before any additional dividends can be paid to Common Stockholders

LO5. Analyze the earnings per share (EPS), return on equity (ROE), and price/earnings (P/E) ratios.

❖ The Earnings per share (EPS) ratio
- o Is calculated by dividing net income by the average number of shares of common stock outstanding during the year
- o It makes it easy to compare a company's earnings over time, but
- o Does not allow reliable comparisons across companies because:
  - ▪ it does not adjust for likely differences in the number of shares that each company has outstanding
❖ The Return on Equity (ROE) ratio relates earnings to each dollar contributed and retained by the company
- o Since it is calculated using dollar amounts contributed to and retained by a company, it allows comparisons to be made across companies
❖ The Price/Earnings (P/E) Ratio relates the company's current stock price to its most recent annual earnings per share, indicating the value investor's place on the company's stock.

READ AND RECALL QUESTIONS

After you read each section of the chapter, answer the related Read and Recall Questions below.

LEARNING OBJECTIVE
After studying the section of the chapter, you should be able to:
1. Explain the role of stock in financing a corporation

Corporate Ownership
List three reasons why the investors can easily participate in a corporation's ownership. Briefly describe each.

What types of characteristics are shared by *separate legal entities*?

List the four benefits of stock ownership. Briefly define each.

What are the advantages of equity financing? What are the disadvantages of equity financing?

LEARNING OBJECTIVE
After studying the section of the chapter, you should be able to:
2. Explain and analyze common stock transactions

Common Stock Transactions
What is *treasury stock*?

Define the terms (1) authorized, (2) issued, and (3) outstanding.

Define *Common Stock*. Distinguish between *par value* and *no-par value* common stock.

Contrast an *IPO* from a *seasoned new issue.*

Assume a company issues 10,000 shares of $5 par value stock for $20 per share. How much will be credited to the Common Stock Account? How much will be credited to the Additional Paid-in Capital account?

Why might a company repurchase its own previously issued stock? What is this type of stock called? What type of an account does it create?

When a company reissues treasury stock for an amount higher than the company paid for the treasury stock, how is the difference in price accounted for? How would the accounting change if the company received less than the price paid for the treasury stock? Why?

LEARNING OBJECTIVE
After studying the section of the chapter, you should be able to:
3. Explain and analyze cash dividends, stock dividends, and stock split transactions

Dividends on Common Stock
Explain the difference between a 'growth' investment and an 'income' investment. Which is preferable? Why?

Define the following terms related to dividends: (1) declaration date; (2) record date; and (3) payment date. On which date is a legal liability incurred by the corporation?

What two key financial requirements are necessary for declaring a cash dividend? Why is each necessary?

Stock Dividends and Splits
What is a *stock dividend?* Give two reasons why a corporation would issue them. Do stockholders 'pay' for them? Explain.

Explain the difference between a *small stock dividend* and a *large stock dividend.* How does the accounting differ for each? What is the reasoning behind this difference in treatment?

What is a *stock split?* How does it differ from a stock dividend? What type of journal entry is made for a stock split? Why?

LEARNING OBJECTIVE
After studying the section of the chapter, you should be able to:
4. Describe the characteristics of preferred stock and analyze transactions affecting preferred stock

Preferred Stock
List three ways that *preferred stock* differs from common stock. Why are preferences given to preferred stock?

What are the two most common dividend preferences? Briefly describe each.

What are *dividends in arrears?* Are they reported on the balance sheet? Why or why not?

What is Retained Earnings?

When Retained Earnings is negative, what are three things to keep in mind?

LEARNING OBJECTIVE
After studying the section of the chapter, you should be able to:
5. Analyze the earnings per share (EPS) return on equity (ROE), and price/earnings (P/E) ratios

Earnings Per Share (EPS)
How is *earnings per share* calculated? Why is this ratio so important to investors?

When would the EPS calculation be inappropriate? Why?

Return on Equity (ROE)
How is *return on equity* calculated? What does this ratio measure? From whose point of view? Why is this significant?

Price/Earnings Ratio

What kind of evaluation can be derived from a Price/Earnings Ratio that cannot be derived with EPS or ROE?

FINANCIAL ANALYSIS TOOLS

1. Earnings Per Share – to determine the amount of income generated for each share of common stock. A higher ratio means greater profitability.

$$\text{Earnings Per Share } = \frac{\text{Net Income}}{\text{Average Number of Common Shares Outstanding}}$$

2. Return on Equity – To determine the amount of income generated for each dollar contributed to and retained by a company. A higher ratio means stockholders are likely to enjoy greater returns.

$$\text{Return on Equity } = \frac{\text{Net Income}}{\text{Average Stockholders' Equity}}$$

3. Price/Earnings Ratio – To determine the value investors place on a company's common stock. A higher number means investors anticipate an improvement in the company's future results.

$$\text{Price Earnings Ratio } = \frac{\text{Current Stock Price (per share)}}{\text{Earnings Per Share (annual)}}$$

HELPFUL STUDY TIP

It can be very difficult to account for treasury stock transactions. This is primarily due to the fact that 'regular' stock issuances are based on the *par value* of the stock. However, every treasury stock transaction is based on the *amount paid by the corporation when the treasury stock was purchased (under the cost method)*. If you think of Treasury Stock as your TREASURE, and anytime someone talks about a treasure, they say things like: "That *cost* me a fortune!" Whoever heard of someone saying: "That *parred* me a fortune!" So, just remember Treasury Stock is based on COST, not par. If you keep this one basic fact in mind for every transaction related to treasury stock, it will be much, much easier. Let's briefly illustrate:

1. *Purchase of the treasury stock.* When a company purchases its own previously issued shares the following journal entry is made: (assume the company purchases 4,000 of its own stock for $40 per share.) Note that the par value of the stock is a completely irrelevant number under the cost method. The only thing that matters is the COST of the treasury stock.

1. Analyze	**Assets**	=	**Liabilities**	+ **Stockholders' Equity**
	Cash +160,000			Treasury Stock (+xSE, –SE) +160,000

2. Record	dr Treasury Stock (+xSE, –SE)	160,000	
	cr Cash (–A) (4,000 * $40).....................		160,000

2. *Reissuance of the treasury stock for an amount higher than it cost.* A company can *never* report a gain or loss on its *own* stock. Therefore, a reissuance of treasury stock can only result in (1) more contributed capital— when the stock is reissued for a higher price than it cost the company or (2) less contributed capital—when the stock is reissued for a smaller price than it cost the company. If we assume that the company reissued 1,000 of the shares at $43 per share, the following entry is made:

	1. Analyze	Assets	=	Liabilities	+	Stockholders' Equity	
		Cash +43,000				Treasury Stock (–xSE) +40,000	
						Additional paid-in capital +2,000	

2. Record			
dr Cash (+A) (1,000 * $43)...		43,000	
cr Treasury Stock (–xSE, +SE) (1,000 * $4)............			40,000
cr Additional Paid-in Capital (+SE) [1,000 * ($43 - $40)]......			3,000

Notice that the treasury stock account is credited for the COST of the treasury stock and that the amount of the cash receipt that is in excess of this cost in placed into Additional paid-in capital (a *stockholders' equity* – balance sheet) account. This amount received in excess of cost is NOT a gain (income statement). The $3,000 received over and above the cost of the shares represents an additional amount paid *by owners* for the purchase of our stock and, therefore, is reported as additional capital paid into the corporation.

3. *Reissuance of the treasury stock for an amount less than it cost.* Like the situation just described, amounts received upon reissuance of treasury stock that are less than the amount the treasury stock cost the company cannot be reported as losses because the transaction involves the company's own stock. Assume the corporation reissues 500 shares of Treasury Stock for $38 per share. The entry made when the reissue price is less than the amount paid by the corporation for the stock is:

	1. Analyze	Assets	=	Liabilities	+	Stockholders' Equity	
		Cash +19,000				Treasury Stock (–xSE) +20,000	
						Additional paid-in capital (–SE) –1,000	

2. Record			
dr Cash (+A) (500 * $38)...		19,000	
dr Additional Paid-in Capital (–SE) [500 * ($40 - $38)]............		1,000	
cr Treasury Stock (–xSE, +SE) (500 * $40)			20,000

Once again, note that the Treasury Stock account is credited for the COST of the treasury stock and that since the amount received upon reissue is less than this cost, is taken out of the Additional Paid-in capital account. The $1,000 is basically a reduction in the amount of contributions from owners to the corporation. As such, it is recorded as a decrease in the Additional Paid-in capital account.

SELF-TEST QUESTIONS AND EXERCISES

MATCHING
1. *Match each of the key terms listed below with the appropriate textbook definition on the following page.*

_____ Authorized Number of Shares	_____ Outstanding Shares
_____ Common Stock	_____ Par Value
_____ Cumulative Dividend Preference	_____ Payment Date
_____ Current Dividend Preference	_____ Preferred Stock
_____ Declaration Date	_____ Record Date
_____ Dividends in Arrears	_____ Stock Dividend
_____ Issued Shares	_____ Stock Split
_____ No-Par Value Stock	_____ Treasury Stock

A. The date on which cash dividends are paid to the stockholders of record.
B. Capital stock that has no par value specified in the corporate charter.
C. Issued shares that are currently held by stockholders other than the corporation itself.
D. The feature of preferred stock that requires current dividends that are not paid in full to accumulate for every year in which they are not paid. These must be paid before any common dividends can be paid.
E. The basic voting stock issued by a corporation to stockholders.
F. Stock that has specific rights over common stock.
G. A distribution of additional shares of a corporation's own stock.
H. The feature of preferred stock that grants priority on preferred dividends over common dividends.
I. The maximum number of shares of capital stock of a corporation that can be issued, as specified in the charter.
J. Cumulative unpaid preferred dividends that must be paid before common shareholders receive a dividend.
K. An insignificant value per share of capital stock specified in the charter; serves as the basis for legal capital.
L. An increase in the total number of authorized shares by a specified ratio that does not decrease retained earnings.
M. The date on which the board of directors officially approves a dividend.
N. Represent the total number of shares that have been sold.
O. The date on which the corporation prepares a list of current stockholders as shown on its records; dividends can be paid only to the stockholders who own stock on that date.
P. Issued shares that have been bought back by the company.

TRUE-FALSE QUESTIONS
For each of the following, enter a T or F in the blank to indicate whether the statement is true or false.

_____1. (LO1) Corporations have the huge advantage of being able to raise large amounts of money because investors can easily participate in a corporation's ownership.

_____2. (LO1) A corporation is created by submitting an application to the federal government..

_____3. (LO1) Issued shares represent the maximum number of shares of capital stock of a corporation that can be sold, as specified in the charter.

_____4. (LO1) Treasury stock is outstanding stock.

_____5. (LO2) Seasoned new issues of stock involve the very first sale of a company's stock to the public.

_____6. (LO2) Stock options can potentially motivate employees to improve the company's financial performance, which can increase stock prices and lead to increases in investor wealth.

_____7. (LO2) Treasury stock is an asset account and has a normal debit balance.

_____8. (LO2) An investor may want an immediate return on stock (through dividends) or they might prefer long-term returns (through higher stock prices).

_____9. (LO2) Because Treasury stock is an investment in a company's own stock, a gain or loss on sale of investment is recorded upon the reissuance of treasury stock.

_____10. (LO3) Corporations do not have a legal obligation to pay dividends.

_____11. (LO3) The date of record is the date a legal liability is created for dividends.

_____12. (LO3) In order to declare dividends a corporation must have sufficient common stock and sufficient cash.

_____13. (LO3) Large stock dividends issued to reduce the market price of the stock are recorded at the Market Value of the stock since the purpose is to reduce the market price.

_____14. (LO3) A 100% stock dividend, (stock split effected as a stock dividend) is not the same thing as a 2 for 1 stock split.

_____15. (LO4) Preferred stock typically has a fixed dividend rate.

_____16. (LO4) When a current dividend preference is not paid in full, the unpaid amount is called dividends in arrears and must be reported in the notes to the financial statements.

_____17. (LO5) Earnings per share (EPS) is not appropriate for comparing across companies.

_____18. (LO5) In the long-run, companies with higher ROE are likely to have higher stock prices than companies with lower ROE.

_____19. (LO5) EPS is calculated from the company's point of view, using the dollar amount contributed to or reinvested in the company.

_____20. (LO5) The Price/Earnings Ratio tells you how many times more than the current year's earnings investors are willing to pay for a company's common stock.

MULTIPLE CHOICE QUESTIONS
Choose the best answer or response by placing the identifying letter in the space provided.

_____1. (LO1) Which of the following is *not* a reason for the popularity of the corporate form?
   a. stockholders are liable for the corporation's debt
   b. ownership interests are transferable
   c. shares of stock can be purchased in small amounts
   d. all of these are reasons for the popularity of the corporate form

_____2. (LO5) Which of the following are Advantages of Equity Financing?
   a. dividends are optional
   b. new shares create a dilution of existing stockholders' control
   c. equity has to be repaid
   d. dividends are tax deductible

_____3. (LO1) Which of the following accounts is *not* found in the stockholders' equity section of the balance sheet?
   a. treasury stock
   b. additional paid-in capital
   c. dividends in arrears
   d. preferred stock

_____4. (LO1) Which of the following is *not* a benefit of stock ownership?
   a. dividends
   b. residual claim
   c. voting rights
   d. legal capital

_____5. (LO1) Which of the following is *not* used on the balance sheet to describe shares of stock?
   a. outstanding
   b. split
   c. authorized
   d. issued

_____ 6. (LO2) Which of the following is *not* a true statement about Common Stock?
   a. common stockholders have the right to vote on important decisions of the corporation and to share in its profitability
   b. par value is closely related to market value of the stock
   c. companies account for IPOs and seasoned new issues in the same way
   d. a company does not account for the sale of stock from one stockholder to another

_____ 7. (LO2) A corporation issues 20,000 shares of $5 par value common stock for $15 per share. How much will be credited to the Common Stock account for this transaction?
   a. $100,000
   b. $200,000
   c. $300,000
   d. $0. This account should be debited

_____ 8. (LO2) Assuming treasury stock costing $55,000 was reissued for $60,000, the journal entry to record this transaction includes:
   a. a debit to treasury stock for $55,000
   b. a credit to Gain on Sale of Investment for $5,000
   c. a credit to Cash for $60,000
   d. a credit to Additional Paid-in Capital for $5,000

_____ 9. (LO3) Which of the following dates is *not* related to cash dividends?
   a. date of payment
   b. date of issuance
   c. date of declaration
   d. date of record

_____ 10. (LO3) Assuming a 10-cent per share dividend was approved by a corporation the number of outstanding shares is 200,000; market price is $100; and par value is $10. How much will be paid to shareholders on the date of record?
   a. $0
   b. $20,000
   c. $200,000
   d. $2,000,000

_____ 11. (LO3) Which of the following statements is *not* true regarding Stock Dividends?
   a. small stock dividends are accounted for at the market value of the stock
   b. a company must have positive balances in both Retained Earnings and Cash to declare a stock dividend
   c. a stock dividend by itself has no economic value
   d. each stockholder receives additional shares of stock equal to the percentage of shares held

_____ 12. (LO3) Which of the following is a true statement regarding stock splits?
   a. market value per share increases
   b. par value per share changes
   c. the number of shares outstanding decreases
   d. a journal entry is made to record the changes made to stockholders' equity

_____13. (LO4) Dividends on preferred stock:
   a. cannot be paid until common shareholders are paid
   b. are based on the percentage of shares owned; a 6% dividend is paid to the owner of 6% of the preferred stock
   c. are a legal liability if not currently paid in full on a cumulative dividend preference
   d. can contain a current dividend preference or a cumulative dividend preference

_____14. (LO4) The journal entry to record the issuance of preferred stock for an amount over par value contains:
   a. a debit to Treasury Stock
   b. a credit to Cash
   c. a credit to Additional Paid-in Capital
   d. none of the above are part of the journal entry to record the issuance of preferred stock

Use the following information to answer questions 15 and 16.	
Annual Preferred Dividends	$100,000
Total Dividend Declaration-Year 1	80,000
Total Dividend Declaration-Year 2	300,000

_____15. (LO4) Assuming the preferred stock has a current dividend preference, how much will be paid to common shareholders in year 2?
   a. $0
   b. $20,000
   c. $180,000
   d. $200,000

_____16. (LO4) Assuming the preferred stock has a cumulative dividend preference, how much will be paid to the common shareholders in year 2?
   a. $0
   b. $20,000
   c. $180,000
   d. $280,000

Use the following information to answer questions 17, 18, and 19.	
Traner, Inc. had the following on its financial statements for 2006:	
Net Income	$215,000
Average Inventory	65,000
Average Stockholders' Equity	810,000
Average Common Shares Outstanding	200,000
Selling Price per share of common stock	$22.00

_____17. (LO5) Calculate the earnings per share for Traner, Inc. for 2006
   a. $1.075
   b. $2.654
   c. $37.674
   d. $93.023

_____18. (LO5) Calculate the Return on Equity for Traner, Inc. for 2006
   a. 10.75 %
   b. 26.54 %
   c. 37.67 %
   d. 93.02 %

_____19. (LO5) Calculate Price/Earnings Ratio for Traner, Inc. for 2006
   a.   9.77
   b.   20.5
   c.   36.8
   d.   48.9

_____20. (Sup) Which of the following equity accounts is *not* needed for a sole proprietorship?
   a.   Retained Earnings
   b.   A drawing account for the proprietor
   c.   A capital account for the proprietor
   d.   All of these are equity accounts needed for a sole proprietorship.

EXERCISES
Record your answer to each exercise in the space provided. Show your work.

Exercise 11-1. Computing Shares Outstanding and Unissued (LO1)
A company reports that 5,000,000 shares of common stock have been authorized. At the end of 2006, 4,269,854 had been issued and there were 247,522 shares of treasury stock. During 2006, no additional shares of treasury stock were purchased nor reissued.
Required:
1. Determine the number of shares outstanding at the end of 2006.

2. Determine the maximum number of new shares that this company could issue.

Exercise 11-2. Recording and Reporting Stockholders' Equity Transactions (LO2, 4)
Leather Corporation obtained a charter at the beginning of 2006 that authorized the following capital stock:
   Common Stock, $2 par, 500,000 shares
   Preferred Stock, 8 percent, $50 par value, 100,000 shares

During 2006, the following selected transactions occurred:
   a. Sold and issued 100,000 shares of the common stock for $16 per share.
   b. Sold and issued 5,000 shares of the preferred stock at $60 per share.
   c. Purchased 1,000 shares of the common stock for $12 per share as treasury stock.

Required:
1.   Give the journal entries indicated for each transaction.
   a.   *dr*   _____   _____
            cr   _____   _____
            cr   _____   _____

   b.   *dr*   _____   _____
            cr   _____   _____
            cr   _____   _____

   c.   *dr*   _____   _____
            cr   _____   _____

2.   Prepare the stockholders' equity section of the balance sheet at December 31, 2006. At the end of 2006, the company had Net Income of $42,000

Exercise 11-3. Recording Treasury Stock Transactions and Analyzing their Impact. (LO2)

During 2006 the following selected transactions affecting stockholders' equity occurred for Spain Corporation.

a. Mar 1   Purchased 600 shares of the company's own common stock at $32 per share.
b. Aug 15 Sold 200 of the shares purchased on March 1, 2006 for $37 per share.
c. Oct 1   Sold 100 more of the shares purchased on March 1, for $28 per share.

Required:
1. Give the indicated journal entries for each of the three transactions.

Mar 1   dr   _____   _____
                cr _____   _____

Aug 15   dr   _____   _____
                cr _____   _____
                cr _____   _____

Oct 1   dr   _____   _____
                dr _____   _____
                cr _____   _____

2. What impact does the purchase of treasury stock have on dividends paid?

3. What impact does the sale of treasury stock for an amount higher than the purchase price have on net income?

Exercise 11-4. Recording Dividends. (LO3)

Green & Porcher put out the following press release on July 20, 2006.

> The Green & Porcher Corporation announced today that its Board of Directors declared a quarterly cash dividend of $0.14 per share of the company's outstanding common stock payable September 27, 2006, to stockholders of record at the close of business on August 10, 2006.

At the time of the press release, Green & Porcher had 650,000 shares authorized and 250,800 issued and outstanding. The par value of the company's stock is $1 per share.

Required:
Prepare journal entries as appropriate for each of the three dates mentioned above.

Jul 20   dr   _____   _____
                cr _____   _____

Aug 10   _____

Sep 27   dr   _____   _____
                cr _____   _____

Exercise 11-5. Comparing Stock Dividends and Splits. (LO3)

On September 1, 2006 Legstrong Corporation had the following capital structure:

Common Stock (par $4, issued shares)	$300,000
Additional Paid-In Capital	750,000
Retained Earnings	325,000
Treasury Stock	None

Complete the following table based on three independent cases involving stock transactions:

Case (a) the board of directors declared and issued a 10 percent stock dividend when the stock was selling at $7 per share.

Case (b) the board of directors declared and issued a 100 percent stock dividend when the stock was selling at $7 per share.

Case (c) the board of directors voted a 3-for-1 stock split. The market price prior to the split was $7 per share.

	Before Stock Transactions	(a) After 10% Stock Dividend	(b) After 100% Stock Dividend	(c) After 4 for 1 Stock Split
Number of shares outstanding				
Par value per share	$4			
Common Stock Account	$300,000			
Additional Paid-In Capital	$750,000			
Retained Earnings	$325,000			
Total Stockholders' Equity				

Exercise 11-6. Calculating Cash Dividends (LO4)

Garbage Disposer, Inc. had the following stock outstanding and retained earnings at December 31, 2007.

Common Stock (par $12; outstanding 75,000 shares)	$900,000
Preferred stock, 6% (par $40; outstanding 10,000 shares)	$400,000
Retained Earnings	$125,000

The board of directors is considering the distribution of a cash dividend to the common and preferred stockholders. No dividends were declared during 2005 or 2006. Three independent cases are assumed:

Case A: The preferred stock is non-cumulative, the total amount of dividends is $50,000

Case B: The preferred stock is cumulative, the total amount of dividends is $72,000

Case C: Same as Case B, except the amount is $100,000

Required:
Compute the amount of dividends in total and per share that would be payable to each class of stock holders for each case and complete the following table.. Show Computations.

	Amt to Distrib.	Total Dividend Amount		Shares Outstanding		Dividend amount per share	
		Preferred	Common	Preferred	Common	Preferred	Common
Case A	$50,000			10,000	75,000		
Case B	$72,000			10,000	75,000		
Case C	$100,000			10,000	75,000		

Computations:

Exercise 11-7. Determining the Impact of Transactions on Earnings Per Share (EPS) and Return on Equity (ROE) (LO6)

Tune Sez Boating Academy reported the following amounts in its financial statements:

	2006	2005
Number of common shares	250,000	250,000
Net income	$64,000	$58,000
Cash dividends paid on common stock	$10,000	$10,000
Total stockholders' equity	$650,000	$600,000

Calculate the 2006 Earnings Per Share (EPS) and Return on Equity (ROE). Another boating school in the same city reported a higher net income ($75,000) in 2006, yet its EPS and ROE ratios were lower than those for Tune Sez Boating Academy. Explain how this apparent inconsistency could occur.

SOLUTIONS TO SELF-TEST QUESTIONS AND EXERCISES

MATCHING
1.

I	Authorized Number of Shares	C	Outstanding Shares
E	Common Stock	K	Par Value
D	Cumulative Dividend Preference	A	Payment Date
H	Current Dividend Preference	F	Preferred Stock
M	Declaration Date	O	Record Date
J	Dividends in Arrears	G	Stock Dividend
N	Issued Shares	L	Stock Split
B	No-Par Value Stock	P	Treasury Stock

TRUE-FALSE QUESTIONS
1. T
2. F – The application is submitted to a state government.
3. F – Issued shares represent the total number of shares of stock that have been sold..
4. F – Outstanding shares consist of issued shares that are *not held* by the corporation itself. Treasury shares are held by the corporation.
5. F – A seasoned new issue of stock occurs after a company's stock has been traded on established markets. New issuances following the first issuance are called seasoned new issues.
6. T
7. F – Treasury stock is a contra-equity account (it is subtracted from total stockholders' equity) and has a debit balance.
8. T
9. F – GAAP requires that a company not report an accounting profit or loss from investments in its own stock because transactions with owners are not considered 'profit-making' activities.
10. T
11. F – The date of declaration is the date a legal liability is created for dividends.
12. F – The corporation must have sufficient Retained Earnings and sufficient cash.
13. F – These 'large' stock dividends have a significant effect on stock price, so they are accounted for at par value rather than market value.
14. T
15. T

16. F – Dividends in arrears are created from a cumulative dividend preference, not a current dividend preference.
17. T
18. T
19. F – This is how ROE is calculated, not EPS.
20. T

MULTIPLE CHOICE QUESTIONS

1. A	6. B	11. B	16. C
2. A	7. A	12. B	17. A
3. C	8. D	13. D	18. B
4. D	9. B	14. C	19. B
5. B	10. A	15. D	20. A

EXERCISES

Exercise 11-1. Computing Shares Outstanding and Unissued (LO1)

1. Outstanding shares are issued shares that have not been repurchased by the corporation. Therefore, the number of outstanding shares for this company is: 4,022,332 (4,269,854 – 247,522)

2. The maximum number of new shares that may be issued by this company is the difference between the number of shares authorized and the number of shares issued: 730,146 (5,000,000 – 4,269,854)

Exercise 11-2. Recording and Reporting Stockholders' Equity Transactions (LO2, 4)

1. Give the journal entries indicated for each transaction.

a.	dr	Cash (+A) (100,000 x 16)	1,600,000	
	cr	Common Stock (+SE) (100,000 x $2)		200,000
	cr	Additional Paid-in Capital (+SE)		1,400,000
b.	dr	Cash (+A) (5,000 x $60)	300,000	
	cr	Preferred Stock (+SE) (5,000 x $50)		250,000
	cr	Additional Paid-in Capital, Preferred Stock (+SE)		50,000
c.	dr	Treasury Stock (+xSE, -SE) (1,000 x $12)	12,000	
	cr	Cash (-A) (1,000 x $12)		12,000

2. Prepare the stockholders' equity section of the balance sheet at December 31, 2006. At the end of 2006, the company had Net Income of $42,000

LEATHER CORPORATION
Balance Sheet
At December 31, 2006

Stockholders' Equity

Contributed capital

Preferred stock, 8% (par value $50; 100,000 authorized shares, 5,000 issued and outstanding shares)	$250,000	
Additional paid-in capital, preferred stock	50,000	
Common stock ($2 par value; authorized 500,000 shares, issued 100,000 shares of which 1,000 shares are held as treasury stock)	200,000	
Additional paid-in capital, common stock	1,400,000	
Total contributed capital		$1,900,000
Retained earnings		42,000
Less: cost of common stock held in treasury (370 shares)		(12,000)
Total stockholders' equity		$ 1,930,000

Exercise 11-3. Recording Treasury Stock Transactions and Analyzing their Impact. (LO2)

1. Give the indicated journal entries for each of the three transactions.

Mar 1	dr	Treasury Stock (+xSE, -SE) (600 x $32)	19,200
	cr	Cash		19,200

Aug 15	dr	Cash (+A) (200 x $37)	7,400
	cr	Treasury stock (−xSE, +SE) (200 x $32)		6,400
	cr	Additional paid-in capital (+SE) (200 x ($37-32))		1,000

Oct 1	dr	Cash (+A) (100 x $28)	2,800
	dr	Additional paid-in capital (+SE) (00 x ($32-28))	400
	cr	Treasury stock (−xSE, +SE) (100 x $32)		3,200

2. What impact does the purchase of treasury stock have on dividends paid?
Should dividends be declared, the treasury shares (600 – 200 – 100 = 300) are not entitled to receive them. Only issued shares that are outstanding are entitled to receive dividends. Therefore, the amount paid for dividends would be less than the amount paid if all issued shares were outstanding.

3. What impact does the sale of treasury stock for an amount higher than the purchase price have on net income?
The sale of treasury stock for an amount higher than the purchase price has *no effect on net income*. Treasury stock reissuances do not result in gains or losses, instead they increase or decrease additional paid-in capital.

Exercise 11-4. Recording Dividends. (LO3)

Jul 20	dr	Dividends Declared (+D, -SE) (250,800 x .14)	35,112
	cr	Dividends Payable (+L)		35,112

Aug 10		No journal entry on date of record

Sep 27	dr	Dividends Payable (-L)	35,112
	cr	Cash (-A)		35,112

Exercise 11-5. Comparing Stock Dividends and Splits. (LO3)

	Before Stock Transactions	(a) After 10% Stock Dividend	(b) After 100% Stock Dividend	(c) After 4 for 1 Stock Split
Number of shares outstanding	75,000	82,500	150,000	300,000
Par value per share	$4	$4	$4	$1
Common Stock Account	$300,000	$330,000	$600,000	$300,000
Additional Paid-In Capital	750,000	772,500	750,000	750,000
Retained Earnings	325,000	272,500	25,000	325,000
Total Stockholders' Equity	$1,375,000	$1,375,000	$1,375,000	$1,375,000

Before. $300,000 / $4 = 75,000 shares; 75,000 x $4 = $300,000; $300,000 + $750,000 + $325,000 = $1,375000

(a) 75,000 + (75,000 x 10%) = $82,500; $300,000 + (75,000 x 10% x $4) = $330,000;
$750,000 + (75,000 x 10% ($7 - $4)) = $772,500; $325,000 – (75,000 x 10% x $7) = $272,500;
$330,000 + $772,500 + $272,500 = $1,375,000

(b) 75,000 x 2 = 150,000; $300,000 + (75,000 x $4) = $600,000; $325,000 – (75,000 x $4) = $25,000;
$600,000 + $750,000 + $25,000 = $1 375,000

(c) 75,000 x 4 = 300,000; $4 / 4 = $1; 300,000 x $1 = $300,000

Exercise 11-6. Calculating Cash Dividends (LO4)

Compute the amount of dividends in total and per share that would be payable to each class of stock holders for each case and complete the following table. Show Computations.

	Amt to Distrib.	Total Dividend Amount		Shares Outstanding		Dividend amount per share	
		Preferred	Common	Preferred	Common	Preferred	Common
Case A	$50,000	$24,000	$26,000	10,000	75,000	$2.40	$0.35
Case B	$72,000	$72,000	0	10,000	75,000	$7.20	0.00
Case C	$100,000	$72,000	$28,000	10,000	75,000	$7.20	$0.37

Computations:

Case A: Preferred: (10,000 x $40 x 6%) = $24,000; Common: $50,000 – 24,000 = $26,000
$24,000 / 10,000 = $2.40; $26,000 / 75,000 = .346666

Case B: Preferred: 2005 preference: $24,000   Common: $72,000 – 72,000 = 0
2006 preference: 24,000
2007 preference: 24,000
Total preferred :   72,000 / 10,000 = $7.20

Case C: Preferred: 2005 preference: $24,000   Common: $100,000 – 72,000 = $28,000
2006 preference: 24,000 $28,000 / 75,000 = .373333
2007 preference: 24,000
Total preferred :   72,000 / 10,000 = $7.20

Exercise 11-7. Determining the Impact of Transactions on Earnings Per Share (EPS) and Return on Equity (ROE) (LO6)

Part A.
EPS: $64,000 / [(250,000 + 250,000) /2] = $64,000 / 250,000 = $0.256
ROE: $64,000 / [(650,000 +600,000) /2] = $64,000 / 625,000 = 10.24%

A lower EPS may be the result if the other school had more average shares of common stock outstanding. That is, if the other company had Net Income of $75,000, but average common shares outstanding were 400,000, the other company would have a lower EPS .1875 (75,000 / 400,000) even though income is higher, the other company has more stock to spread the income over.

A lower ROE could result if average stockholders' equity were higher for the other school. Assuming the same net income ($75,000), but an average stockholders' equity of $800,000, the other school has an ROE of 9.375% which is lower than Tune Sez even though income is higher for the other school.

ORGANIZATION OF THE CHAPTER

Understand the business	Study the accounting methods	Evaluate the results	Review the chapter
- Business activities and cash flows - Classifying cash flows	- Relationship with other financial statements - Preparing the statement of Cash flows	- Quality of income ratio - Capital acquisitions Ratio - Cash coverage ratio	- Demonstration case -Chapter summary - Key terms - Practice material

CHAPTER FOCUS SUGGESTIONS

Review
We're almost through! Hang in there! We can see the light at the end of the tunnel and have come through unscathed (almost.) We've covered the accounting cycle and how financial statements are prepared after adjustments have been made. Then we focused on each balance sheet account – in depth. Now, only two things remain: one more financial statement and a few more analytical tools, and we're through!

Introduction
There's a reason we waited until now to tackle this final financial statement – the Statement of Cash Flows. The reason is that a strong background in everything we've covered thus far is necessary to fully understand and prepare this statement. It draws on everything you've learned in this course.

How a company gets and uses its cash is critical to its survival. In this chapter you learn what a Statement of Cash Flows reports, how to prepare a Statement of Cash Flows, how the information it contains can be utilized by users, and how to evaluate the contents of the statement of cash flows together with other financial statements.

UNDERSTAND THE BUSINESS

Learning Objective 1
Identify cash flows arising from operating, investing, and financing activities.

Business Activities and Cash Flows
A business can be very *profitable*, yet be unable to pay its weekly payroll. This is because the income statement measures accrual-basis *profit and loss,* not cash inflows and outflows. A business can have millions of dollars in Net Income….yet be unable to pay the utility bill. The balance sheet informs users of the current balance in the Cash account….but, it doesn't show users where the company's cash came from or where it is being spent. We use the statement of cash flows (SCF) to help detect potential money problems before they become critical. Because there can be major differences between net income and cash flows, GAAP require that a statement of cash flows be presented by every company.

The purpose of a statement of cash flows is to show how each major type of business activity caused a company's cash balance to increase or decrease during the accounting period. "Cash" includes Cash and Cash Equivalents. Cash equivalents are short-term, highly liquid investments that are *both*:

(1) readily convertible into known amounts of cash, and
(2) so near to maturity that there is little risk their value will change before they mature.

We use the term "Cash" in this chapter with the understanding that it includes both Cash and Cash Equivalents.

Classifying Cash Flows
In a nutshell, the SCF details what occurred in the business to cause the cash balance at the beginning of the period to become the cash balance at the end of the period.

The statement of cash flows contains three major categories: (1) operating activities, (2) investing activities, and (3) financing activities. The net cash increase or decrease from each if these categories is combined into one large net increase or decrease to the cash account. This single increase or decrease is combined with the beginning cash balance, resulting in the ending cash balance.

For example, let's pretend that I am a small business and I need a loan. My net income is $6,000 this month and my comparative balance sheets show that my beginning Cash balance was $600 and my ending Cash balance is $500. Doesn't sound so bad, right? But, you think maybe asking me for a Statement of Cash Flows would be a good idea. So, I prepare the following statement of cash flows (summarized) for you:

Net Cash Provided by (used for) operating activities	$ (500)
+ (−) Net cash provided by (used for) investing activities	100
+ (−) Net cash provided by (used for) financing activities	300
Net increase (decrease) in cash	(100)
Cash and cash equivalents at beginning of period	600
Cash and cash equivalents at end of period	$ 500

Even though you know nothing about me, you can figure out the following about my spending habits:
- The money coming into my business from Sales wasn't enough this month to cover the payments my business made for inventory, utilities, etc. because my Net Cash Used for Operating Activities (day-to-day operations) was ($500).
- I must have sold some investments, furniture, or some other long-term asset and got $100 for it.
- I borrowed $300 from the bank or someplace else.
- I used up a bunch of the cash that I had when I started the month.

That's quite a bit of information from a few lines of a report. You also know one more thing – there's probably no way in the WORLD that you are going to lend me a dime!! I can't even pay the bills I have now, so you're thinking, if I lend this lady any money, I won't see a dime of it....and, next thing you know, we're meeting with Judge Judy on the People's Court!!! Hmmmm.....maybe this statement is kind of useful after all! The net income and cash balances didn't give you any clues about the 'real' situation of my cash. Let's look a little more closely as this statement.

1. Operating Activities
Cash flows from operating activities (or cash flows from operations) are the cash inflows and outflows that relate directly to the operating revenues and expenses reported on the income statement. They involve the day-to-day business activities with customers, suppliers, employees, landlords, etc. Examples of inflows and outflows from operating activities are:

Cash Inflows	Cash Outflows
Cash provided by:	*Cash used for:*
Customers	Purchase of goods for resale and services (electricity, etc.)
Dividends and interest on investments	Salaries and wages
	Income taxes
	Interest on obligations

The difference between these inflows and outflows is called *Net cash provided by (used for) operating activities.*

2. Investing Activities
Cash flows from investing activities are cash inflows and outflows related to the purchase and disposal of long-lived assets, including:

Cash Inflows	Cash Outflows
Cash provided by:	*Cash used for:*
Sale or disposal of property, plant, and equipment	Purchase of property, plant, and equipment
Sale or maturity of investment in securities	Purchase of investment and securities

The difference between these inflows and outflows is called *Net cash provided by (used for) investing activities.*

3. Financing Activities

Cash flows from financing activities include exchanges of cash with stockholders and cash exchanges with lenders (for principal on loans) including:

Cash Inflows	Cash Outflows
Cash provided by:	*Cash used for:*
Borrowing from lenders through formal debt contracts	Repaying principal to lenders
Issuing stock to owners	Repurchasing stock from owners (Treasury Stock)
Reissuing stock to owners (reissue Treasury Stock)	Paying dividends to owners

The difference between these inflows and outflows is called *Net cash provided by (used for) financing activities.*

Though there are exceptions, as a general rule, when you classify cash flows:

- Operating cash flows cause changes in current asset and current liability accounts
- Investing cash flows cause changes in noncurrent asset accounts
- Financing cash flows cause changes in
  - o noncurrent liability accounts
  - o stockholder equity accounts

STUDY THE ACCOUNTING METHODS

Relationship with Other Financial Statements

The statement of cash flows is prepared by converting information on the income statement and balance sheet from an accrual-basis to a cash-basis. This conversion is accomplished by analyzing the income statement and the changes in balance sheet accounts, and relating these changes to the three sections of the cash flow statement. So, to prepare a statement of cash flows, you'll need:

1. **Comparative balance sheets** – showing beginning and ending balances. They'll be used to calculate the cash flows from *all* activities (operating, investing, and financing.)
2. **Complete Income Statement** – mostly used to calculate cash flows from operating activities.
3. **Additional details** – about selected accounts that increase/decrease because of investing and/or financing activities.

It might seem like the Cash account would be the logical place to figure out what happened to Cash! Logically, that does make sense. However, in reality, it is very difficult to figure out everything that happened in Cash…by analyzing the Cash account. Here's why. Remember when you first started this class and were posting transactions into T-accounts? Which T-account had MORE TRANSACTIONS posted to it than any other T-account? RIGHT!!! Cash. More transactions involve cash than any other account. Therefore, an analysis of this account would take considerable time, man-power, and money.

A better approach is that, since we know that nearly every transaction affects cash….why don't we just figure out what happened in all those *other* T-accounts, and they will ultimately have some affect on cash. In other words, all changes in cash must be accompanied by and can be explained by changes in liabilities, stockholders' equity, and noncash assets. Here are some examples:

Category	Transaction	Cash Effect	Other Account Affected
Operating	Collect accounts receivable	+Cash	−Accounts Receivable (A)
	Pay accounts payable	−Cash	−Accounts Payable (L)
	Prepay rent	−Cash	+Prepaid Rent (A)
	Pay interest	−Cash	−Retained Earnings (SE)
	Sell goods/services for cash	+Cash	+Retained Earnings (SE)
Investing	Purchase equipment for cash	−Cash	+Equipment (A)
	Sell investment securities for cash	+Cash	−Investments (A)
Financing	Pay back debt to bank	−Cash	− Bank Loan Payable (L)
	Issue stock for cash	+Cash	+Contributed Capital (SE)

Reporting Operating Cash Flows

We start off with the most important section on the statement of cash flows – Cash flows from Operating Activities. There are two alternative methods for preparing the operating activities section of the SCF and each will be covered separately. Part A covers the Indirect method and Part B covers the Direct Method. Just keep in mind that, it doesn't matter which method you use, it is simply two different ways of arriving at the same number – Net cash flows from operating activities. The only difference will be HOW you get that amount.

1. **Direct Method:** This method reports the total cash inflow or outflow from each main type of transaction. The difference between these cash inflows and outflows is the Net cash provided by (used for) operating activities.
2. **Indirect Method:** This method starts with net income and then adjusts it by removing items that do not involve cash but were included in net income, and by adding items that involved cash but were not yet included in income. In doing this, you will also calculate the Net cash provided by (used for) operating activities.

There are two things to keep in mind here:
- It doesn't matter which method is used, they will both provide the same amount – Net Cash Flows from Operating Activities
- The choice between the direct and indirect methods affects only the operating activities section of the statement of cash flows, not the investing and financing sections.
- The FASB says it prefers the direct method and has considered requiring this method be used by everyone, but for now each company is allowed to select the method they wish to use.
- 99% of all companies use the indirect method, so we cover it first.

(NOTE: Check with your instructor to determine whether you are required to cover both methods or only one.)

Part A: Indirect Method

Learning Objective 2a
Report cash flows from operating activities using the indirect method.

The income statement and comparative balance sheets for Skylyne, Inc. (a fictitious company) are presented below to illustrate the preparation of the SCF.

Balance Sheet at December 31	2009	2008	Step 1		
Cash	$ 50,000	$ 72,000	Δ in cash		–22,000
Accounts Receivable	68,500	45,500	O	+23,000
Merchandise Inventory	60,000	31,000	O	+29,000
Prepaid Expenses	9,000	11,000	O	–2,000
Property, Plant, and Equipment	199,500	169,000	I	30,500
Less: Accumulated Depreciation	(80,000)	(61,000)	O	+19,000
Investments	5,000	8,000	I	–3,000
Total Assets	$ 312,000	$ 275,500		
Accounts Payable	23,500	21,000	O	+2,500
Wages Payable	18,200	18,500	O	–300
Accrued Liabilities	10,000	8,000	O	+2,000
Notes Payable, long-term	103,000	78,000	F	+25,000
Contributed Capital	131,000	116,000	F	+15,000
Retained Earnings	26,300	34,000	O, F	–7,700
Total Liabilities and Stockholders' Equity	$ 312,000	$ 275,500		

Income Statement for 2009	
Sales	$ 190,000
Cost of Goods Sold	125,000
Gross Profit	65,000
Operating Expenses	49,500
Operating Income	15,500
Interest Expense	8,000
Income before taxes	7,500
Income Tax Expense	2,000
Net Income	$ 5,500

Under the indirect method, there are three steps necessary to determine Cash flows from operating activities, using the income statement and comparative balance sheets. They are:

> Step 1 – Identify balance sheet accounts related to operating activities
> Step 2 – Create a schedule of operating activities which begins by assuming net income is a cash inflow
> Step 3 – Remove the effects of accrual accounting adjustment included in net income, using changes in balance sheet accounts that relate to operations.

Step 1.
For each balance sheet account, subtract the prior year balance from the current year balance and mark an "O" beside the account if it is an account that relates to operating activities. Operating activity items usually affect:

- ✓ ***Current assets*** – that are used up or converted into cash from the company's normal operating activities. For example, prepaid insurance is expensed with the usage of the insurance over time, but the purchase of the policy was a use of cash. Don't label the Cash account with an "O", since the change in this account we're trying to figure out with the statement of cash flows. Note that we've marked Accounts Receivable, Merchandise Inventory, and Pre paid expenses with an "O".

- ✓ ***Current liabilities*** – that arise from buying goods or services used for the company's operations. We've marked Accounts Payable, Wages Payable, and Accrued Liabilities with an "O".

- ✓ ***Accumulated depreciation*** – This account is increased by depreciation expense and since depreciation expense affects net income this account affects operating activities. It may seem a bit odd, but remember that depreciation expense is subtracted in arriving at current year net income and the indirect method *starts with net income*. So, it is *very* relevant in determining operating cash flows.

- ✓ ***Retained earnings*** – This account impacts both operating activities (again, because of net income which is closed to retained earnings and used in the indirect method) and financing activities because of dividends which are subtracted from retained earnings. So, mark this accounts with "O" and "F" (financing) to cover both activities.

- ✓ While you're busy "O"ing everything, you might as well label the investing and financing activities ("I" and "F") as well. For example, any property, plant and equipment accounts involve investing activities "I", while the Bonds Payable account is an "F" activity. You'll have to do it for those categories eventually anyway, so let's get it out of the way.

Step 1 has been completed for Skylyne in the column on the far right on its financial statements. Be sure to see what was done so you will understand how to do it yourself.

Step 2.
By starting this schedule with net income, we *initially* assume that *all* revenues were cash inflows and *all* expenses were cash outflows. Of course, we know this isn't true, but it's a great starting point and Step 3 finishes the job. Look at the schedule provided under Step 3b to see this step.

Step 3.
Now, using the "O" accounts identified in Step 1, we adjust the net income figure to 'get rid' of those revenue and/or expense items on the income statement that *did not involve cash*. Use the tables presented here to calculate

Income Statement Amounts or Balance Sheet Changes	Impact on the SCF
Net Income	Starting point
Depreciation expense included in accumulated depreciation	Added
Decreases in current assets	Added
Increases in current liabilities	Added
Increases in current assets	Subtracted
Decreases in current liabilities	Subtracted

the adjustments. This table contains fairly detailed information for determining the impact of various items on Net Income, when determining the Cash Flows from Operating Activities using the indirect method.

Quick and Easy Rule		
	Current Assets	Current Liabilities
Increase	–	+
Decrease	+	–

The table on the left provide and quick and easy method for adjusting Net Income for various changes in account balance when using the indirect method. The column headings indicate the type of account that will be affected (current assets or current liabilities). The row headings refer to whether the balance in the account type shown increased or decreased. For instance, if Accounts Receivable decreased, you would look under the column Current Asset and since it decreased use the second row. So, this decrease in accounts receivable would be added to net income , because of the + sign.

Before moving on to Step 3, you will need this additional information about Skylyne's Other Expenses shown on the Income Statement.

The Other expenses on Skylyne's income statement consists of: Depreciation, $19,000; wages, $20,000; other, $10,500.

Now, Step 3 is really accomplished in two parts:

Step 3a.
First, adjust net income for depreciation expense. It was subtracted on the income statement in determining net income, but this expense did not result in a corresponding *subtraction to cash*. Remember, our starting point is net income and we're trying to convert net income into 'cash' transactions only, so we have to *add back* depreciation expense. Per the additional information just provided, the depreciation expense for Skylyne is $19,000. This addition to net income is shown in Step 3b.

Step 3b.
Adjust net income for changes in current assets and current liabilities. Any change in these short-term asset and liability accounts also creates differences between net income and cash. So, we need to eliminate these differences. Here's a little hint….since you've already identified the affected accounts in this step, simply write down each of the account names that you designated with an "O" in your 'listing' under Step 1as shown below.

Now, you can use the Quick and Easy box presented at the beginning of Step 3 to determine which amounts are added and which are subtracted from net income.

Cash Flows from Operating Activities		
Net Income		$ 5,500
Adjustments to reconcile net income to net cash provided by operating activities:		
Depreciation		19,000
Changes in current assets and current liabilities		
Accounts Receivable		
Merchandise Inventory		
Prepaids		
Accounts Payable		
Accrued Liabilities		

NOTE: Each adjustment to net income for Skylyne is explained in detail here. Once you understand the concept, you will just need to know the calculation. Therefore, the calculation is shown at the end of each explanation inside of a thick black circle. So, you can skip the explanations (once you understand them) and go immediately to the calculation.

✓ *Change in Accounts Receivable* – The goal here to adjust the ***sale revenue*** amount (used in determining net income) into ***cash collected from customers***. Basically, if *all* sales for Skylyne were cash sales there would be *no accounts receivable!* That would mean all sales were collected in cash. Unfortunately, this is rarely the case because nearly all businesses sell on account.

So, if the accounts receivable go up during the year (say it started with $1,000 and ended with $5,000 – an increase of $4,000), it means the following: Some of the current year sales were *not collected in cash* because they are still in accounts receivable. So, $4,000 of the sales reported this year were never received in cash, and need to be 'removed from sales' in determining cash collections. So, cash collected from customers is $96,000 ($100,000 - $4,000.)

Similarly, if accounts receivable decreased, that means not only were *all* sales for the current period collected in cash, but *some beginning accounts receivable* were also collected in addition to these sales. Assume ending accounts receivable was $0 instead of $5,000 in the previous example. In this case, the entire $100,000 must have been collected in cash *and all of the beginning account receivable of $1,000!* Therefore, cash collected from customers must be $101,000 ($100,000 + $1,000.)

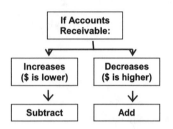

The adjustment to the SCF is not the amount of the cash collections. It is actually just the *difference between beginning and ending accounts receivable.* If you're like most people, your head really hurts and you are ready to throw your book against the wall. It's ok. This is a normal reaction to preparing a statement of cash flows (see why they saved it till the end of the book?) So, follow the simple rule on the illustrated on the left.

> Skylyne's accounts receivable increased $23,000 (as determined in Step 1). Increases in debit balance accounts are subtracted from net income. This is illustrated immediately following the completion of Step 3b

✓ *Change in Inventory* – Inventory is increased by Inventory Purchases and decreased by Cost of Goods Sold. Since Cost of Goods Sold is subtracted on the income statement in determining net income, the goal with inventory is to adjust the ***cost of goods sold*** amount to cash paid for inventory purchases. Using the beginning and ending inventory amounts, an increase in inventory means that *more inventory was purchased than was sold.*

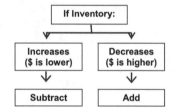

So, to adjust COGS (Cost of Goods old) to the amount *spent* on inventory purchases, we need to *subtract the extra money spent on purchases.* (If inventory had decreased, the decrease would be added on the SCF.) Once again, to make it easy, just follow the rule to the right:

> Skylyne's Merchandise Inventory increased $29,000 (refer back to the statement presented before Step 1. According to the rule, Increases in debit balance accounts are subtracted from net income. This is illustrated immediately following the completion of Step 3b.

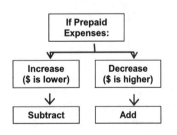

✓ *Change in Prepaid Expenses* – The income statements show expenses *incurred* for operating activities and the SCF must show amounts *paid* for these expenses. Prepaid expenses are increased by cash prepayments and decreased when prepaid expenses are 'used' and expensed on the income statement. So, an increase in prepaids indicates that more cash was spent than was expensed on the income statement. Likewise, a decrease in prepaids indicates that some prepaids have been 'used-up' and expensed but didn't involve payment of cash in the current period. Follow the rule to the left for changes in prepaids.

> Skylyne's accounts receivable decreased $2,000 (refer back to the statement presented before Step 1. According to the rule, decreases in debit balance accounts are added to net income. This is illustrated immediately following the completion of Step 3b.

Study Guide, Chapter 12

✓ *Change in Accounts Payable* – Purchases on account increase accounts payable while payments made to suppliers on account decrease accounts payable. So, if accounts payable decreased, cash paid to suppliers must be higher than the amount of purchases requiring a subtraction to the SCF. Whereas, if accounts payable increased, some current period purchases were made without the use of cash and must be subtracted from the SCF. Follow the rule to the right for changes in accounts payable.

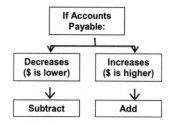

Skylyne's accounts payable increased $2,500 (refer back to the statement presented before Step 1. According to the rule, increases in credit balance accounts are added to net income. This is illustrated immediately following the completion of Step 3b.

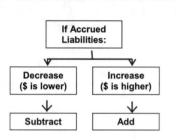

✓ *Change in Accrued Liabilities* – When expenses like salaries, sales taxes, income taxes, etc. are accrued they do not use up any cash even though they are expensed on the income statement. So, an increase in accrued liabilities represents expenses on the income statement that did not involve any payment of cash. Therefore, the increase must be added back on the SCF. Similarly, a decrease in accrued liabilities indicates the payment of some accrued expenses and these must be subtracted from the SCF to determine the cash paid. Follow the rule to the left for changes in accrued liabilities.

Skylyne's accrued wages decreased $300 and its other accrued liabilities increased $2,000 (refer back to the statement presented before Step 1. Decreases in credit balance accounts are subtracted from net income and increases in credit balance accounts are added to net income as shown in the illustration below:

Cash Flows from Operating Activities	
Net Income	$ 5,500
Adjustments to reconcile net income to net cash provided by operating activities:	
Depreciation	19,000
Changes in current assets and current liabilities	
Accounts Receivable	(23,000)
Merchandise Inventory	(29,000)
Prepaid Expenses	+2,000
Accounts Payable	+2,500
Wages Payable	(300)
Accrued Liabilities	+2,000
Net Cash Provided by (used in) Operating Activities	(21,300)

Summary
All of the typical additions/subtractions from the SCF using the indirect method can be summarized as follows:

| Item | Additions and Subtractions to Reconcile Net Income to Cash Flow from Operating Activities | |
	When Item Increases	When Item Decreases
Depreciation (and accumulated depreciation)	+	
Accounts receivable	−	+
Inventory	−	+
Prepaid expenses	−	+
Accounts payable	+	−
Accrued expense liabilities	+	−

If your instructor has only assigned the indirect method, you should skip the next section and move on to the discussion of Reporting Cash Flows from Investing and Financing Activities.

Part B: Reporting Cash Flows from Operating Activities – Direct Method

The direct method summarizes all operating transactions that created a debit or a credit to the cash account. Each unique revenue and expense item on the income statement is adjusted to convert net income into cash flows. The starting point is Sales Revenues.

Learning Objective 2b
Report cash flows from operating activities using the direct method.

✓ ***Converting Sales Revenues to Cash Inflows***

Accounts receivable is increased by Sales and decreased by customer collections. So, the following formula will convert accrual basis Sales Revenue into cash collections.

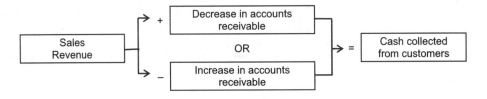

Per the income statement presented before Step 1, Skylyne's Sales Revenue is $190,000 and receivables increased by $23,000. Therefore, according to this formula, $190,000 – $23,000 = $167,000 Cash Collected from Customers.

✓ ***Converting Cost of Goods Sold to Cash Paid to Suppliers***

Cost of goods sold may be more than the amount paid for inventories or less than the amount paid for inventories, depending on the increase or decrease in inventory and the increase or decrease in accounts payable. If inventories increased, then the company bought some merchandise that it wasn't able to sell this period. Similarly, if inventories decreased, the company sold more inventories than it purchased this period. So, to convert the cost of goods sold to cash paid, *increases* in inventory must be *added to* cost of goods sold and *decreases* must be subtracted from cost of goods sold. But, that's only half of the picture, these inventory items have to be paid for, right? Purchases of inventories are typically purchased on account. So, if accounts payable increased it indicates that some of the inventory purchases have not yet been paid for. If accounts payable decreased it means that all purchases from this period were paid for *as well as some accounts payable owed at the beginning of the period.* This is depicted in the following illustration:

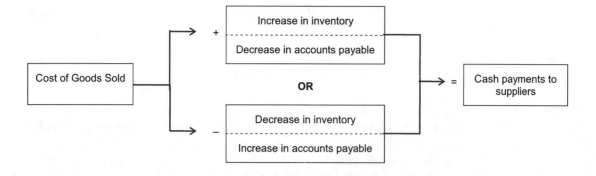

Skylyne's cost of goods sold is $125,000, inventory increased $29,000 and Accounts Payable increased $2,500. Therefore, using the above formula, $125,000 +$29,000 – 2,500 = $151,500 Cash Payments to Suppliers.

✓ **_Converting Operating Expenses to a Cash Outflow_**

Expenses reported on the income statement rarely reflect actual cash payments associated with operations. Some expenses may be the result of 'using up' a prepaid expense. Others may be expenses that were accrued, and thus not yet paid.

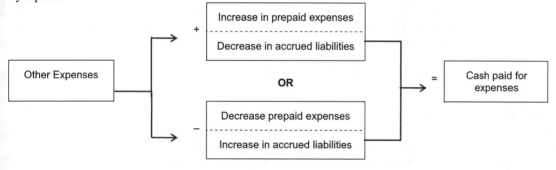

Skylyne's Operating expenses (excluding depreciation, but including interest expense, and tax expense) are $40,500 ($49,500 – $19,000 + $8,000 + $2,000); prepaid expenses decreased $2,000 and accrued liabilities decreased $300 and increased $2,000. Therefore, using the above formula: $40,500 – $2,000 +$300 –$2,000 = $36,800 Cash Paid for Expenses

Notice that we didn't include depreciation in the operating expense amount. That's because no cash is EVER paid for depreciation shown on the income statement. It's easy to convert depreciation expense on the income statement into cash paid because *no cash is paid for depreciation!* So, we simply *omit depreciation expense on the SCF.*

Now, for the important part! We should be able to use the figures we've calculated here to determine cash flows from operating activities using the direct method. Plus, we have a check figure!!!! It should be the same amount we got when we calculated it for the indirect method. If you flip back there you'll see the number was ($21,300). Let's see how we did!!! All numbers shown here were calculated in this section in case you wish to refer back to them.

Cash Flows from Operating Activities	
Cash Collections from Customers	$ 167,000
Cash Payments to Suppliers	(151,500)
Cash Paid for Expenses	(36,800)
Net Cash Provided by (used in) Operating Activities	($21,300)

TA DUM!!!!!!!!!!!!!! Both figures calculated (in very different ways) resulted in the same figure for Net Cash used in Operating Activities ($21,300)

Notice that the net cash inflow or outflow is the same regardless of the method used (indirect or direct). They simply represent two different ways of approaching the same problem.

Here is a summary of 'rules' for the direct method:

Income Statement Account	+/– Change in Balance Sheet Account(S)	= Operating Cash Flow
Sales Revenue	+Decrease in Accounts Receivable (A) –Increase in Accounts Receivable (A)	= Collections from customers
Cost of Goods Sold	+Increase in Inventory (A) –Decrease in Inventory (A) –Increase in Accounts Payable (L) +Decrease in Accounts Payable (L)	= Payments to suppliers of inventory
Other Expenses	+Increase in Prepaid Expenses (A) –Decrease in Prepaid Expenses (A) –Increase in Accrued Expenses (L) +Decrease in Accrued Expenses (L)	= Payments to suppliers of services (e.g., rent, utilities, wages, interest)
Interest Expense	–Increase in Interest Payable (L) +Decrease in Interest Payable (L)	= Payments of interest
Income Tax Expense	+Increase in Prepaid Income Taxes (Deferred Taxes) (A) –Decrease in Prepaid Income Taxes (Deferred Taxes) (A) –Increase in Income Taxes Payable (Deferred Taxes) (L) +Decrease in Income Taxes Payable (Deferred Taxes) (L)	= Payments of income taxes

Reporting Cash Flows from Investing Activities

Learning Objective 3
Report cash flows from investing activities.

When we performed the analysis of cash flows from operating activities, we only needed to know the net changes in certain balance sheet accounts. However, when you perform an analysis of the accounts involved in investing (as well as financing) activities, you need to determine what caused both the increases and the decreases to the accounts involved. Here are the most common accounts that need to be analyzed:

Related Balance Sheet Account(s)	Investing Activity	Cash Flow Effect
Investments	Purchase of investment securities for cash	Outflow
	Sale (maturity) of investment securities for cash	Inflow
Property, plant, and equipment	Purchase of property, plant, and equipment for cash	Outflow
	Sale of property, plant, and equipment for cash	Inflow

Investments

Additional information is needed to analyze this account. It must be determined whether any investments were purchased or sold. If so, the dollar amount of the purchase or sale is needed. This will normally be provided as additional information. In our example, the investments account looks like this:

dr– Investments cr +			
Beg. bal.	8,000		
		Sold	3,000
End. bal.	5,000		

Management informs us that investments were sold for book value, with no gain or loss. The $3,000 of cash received from the sale is an investing activity cash inflow. Presentation of cash flows from investing activities on the statement of cash flows follows the discussion of investments and financing.

Equipment

Like investments, additional information is needed to analyze the events in this account. It must be determined whether any equipment was purchased or sold and the dollar amount of the purchase or sale. Again, this will normally be provided as additional information. Skylyne had the following account balances related to Property, Plant, & Equipment. Management informs us that Skylyne purchased $30,500 of equipment during the year. Entering this amount allows us to completely explain the changes that occurred in the Property, Plant, and Equipment account.

dr + Property, Plant, and Equipment cr-		dr– Accumulated Depreciation cr +	
Beg. bal. 169,000			Beg. Bal. 61,000
Purch. 30,500			Deprec. 19,000
End. bal. 199,500			End. bal. 80,000

We already know from the income statement that depreciation expense of $19,000 was also recorded. That amount has been entered in Accumulated Depreciation. Changes in accumulated depreciation have also been completely explained because the depreciation expense provides us with the ending balance in the account. Presentation of this on the statement of cash flows follows the discussion of investments and financing.

Reporting Cash Flows from Financing Activities

This section includes long-term liabilities, stockholders equity, current liabilities owed to owners (dividends payable), and current liabilities owed to financial institutions (bank loans payable, short-term notes payable, current portion of long-term debt, etc.) The following table provides you with the most common:

> **Learning Objective 4**
> Report cash flows from financing activities.

Related Balance Sheet Account(s)	Financing Activity	Cash Flow Effect
Notes payable	Borrowing cash from bank or other financial institutions	Inflow
	Repayment of loan principal	Outflow
Long-term debt	Issuance of bonds for cash	Inflow
	Repayment of bond principal	Outflow
Contributed capital	Issuance of stock for cash	Inflow
	Repurchase of stock with cash	Outflow
Retained earnings	Payment of cash dividends	Outflow

To compute cash flows from financing activities, you should review changes in all debt and stockholders' equity accounts.

Long-term Debt

The key to this section is to determine any additional long-term borrowings and/or principal repayments that occurred during the period. This information will be provided as additional information. Management of Skylyne informs us that $5,000 of existing debt was repaid and an additional $30,000 was borrowed during the year. Presentation of cash flows from financing activities follows this discussion of financing activities.

dr– Notes Payable cr +	
	Beg. Bal. 78,000
Repaid 5,000	Borrowed 30,000
	End. bal. 103,000

Contributed Capital

Changes in contributed capital could be additional issuances of stock or repurchases/retirement of stock. Skylyne management informs us that an additional $15,000 was received from the issuance of stock. Presentation of cash flows from financing activities follows this discussion of financing activities.

dr– Contributed Capital cr +	
	Beg. Bal. 116,000
	Issued stk. 15,000
	End. bal. 131,000

Retained Earnings

The analysis of the account includes Net Income (or Net Loss), and any dividends declared on stock. Management informs us that net income and dividend payments were the only effects on retained earnings this year. Since we know Net Income from the income statement, we can determine dividends as $13,200 ($34,000 +$5,500 – $26,300)

dr– Retained Earnings cr +		
		Beg. Bal. 34,000
Divid.	13,200	Net Inc. 5,500
		End. bal. 26,300

Format for the Statement of Cash Flows

Now, that you've determined all of the cash provided or used from operating, investing, and financing activities, you're ready to prepare the SCF! This SCF was prepared for Skylyne, Inc. using the indirect method..

SkyLyne, Inc.
Statement of Cash Flows
For the Year Ended December 31, 2009

Cash Flows from Operating Activities		
Net Income		$ 5,500
Adjustments to reconcile net income to net cash provided by operating activities:		
Depreciation		19,000
Changes in current assets and current liabilities		
Accounts Receivable		(23,000)
Merchandise Inventory		(29,000)
Prepaid Expenses		+2,000
Accounts Payable		+2,500
Wages Payable		(300)
Accrued Liabilities		+2,000
Net Cash Provided by (used in) Operating Activities		(21,300)
Cash Flows from Investing Activities		
Proceeds from Sale of Investments	3,000	
Purchase of Equipment	(30,500)	
Net Cash provided (used in) Investing Activities		(27,500)
Cash Flows from Financing Activities		
Additional borrowings of long-term debt	30,000	
Payments of long-term debt	(5,000)	
Additional Issuances of stock	15,000	
Cash dividends paid	(13,200)	
Net cash Provided by (used in) Financing Activities		26,800
Net increase (decrease) in cash		(22,000)
Cash at beginning of period		72,000
Cash at end of period		$ 50,000

Had the SCF been prepared using the direct method, the following format would be used for operating activities (in place of the section above that is circled), and the rest of the statement would be identical to the one just presented.

Cash Flows from Operating Activities	
Cash Collections from Customers	$ 167,000
Cash Payments to Suppliers	(151,500)
Cash Paid for Expenses	(36,800)
Net Cash Provided by (used in) Operating Activities	($21,300)

Noncash Investing and Financing Activities

Thought you were all through, huh? Well, there's one more bit of information that must be reported as a supplemental schedule to the SCF. This schedule includes important investing and financing activities that *did not affect the SCF*. It is called the Schedule of Noncash Investing and Financing Activities. THIs reports material investing and financing transactions that did not have cash flow effects, but were material. They typically involve items that would have involved cash, but were 'traded' instead. For example, a purchase of a $40,000 piece of equipment entirely with a note payable. No cash – just an exchange of equipment for a note. Supplementary information must also report the amount of cash paid for interest and income taxes (for companies using the indirect method).

EVALUATE THE FINANCIAL RESULTS REPORTED IN A STATEMENT OF CASH FLOWS

> **Learning Objective 5**
> Interpret cash flows from operating, investing, and financing activities.

When evaluating the results shown on a SCF, starting with the subtotals of each section of the statement is a logical place to start. Look for patterns among the three sections to determine how well-established the company is. An established, healthy company will show positive cash flows from operations, and have a little extra that can be used for (1) purchasing additional investments thus expanding the business, (2) paying off some debt, paying extra dividends, etc. or (3) it can be used just to keep a nice little cushion of cash! This additional cash is called free cash flow. Let's look at each section individually using Skylyne's statement of cash flows.

Interpreting Cash Flows from Operating Activities

Most analysts believe this is the most important section of the SCF. That's because, in the long-run, a company's operations are its only continuing source of cash. It is an indicator of a company's ability to generate cash from its own operations, as well as how well it manages it current assets and current liabilities. Investors need to see that a company has the ability to pay dividends while creditors are most interested in a company's ability to pay debts.

The most important aspects of the operating activities section of the SCF are: whether the net cash flow is positive or negative, and any trends that may be developing from one period to the next. All companies will have fluctuations in cash, but it is the overall trend that is critical.

Skylyne, has a negative cash flow from operating activities – an alarmingly large one for a company so small. This ($21,300) negative cash flow tells potential investors and creditors that Skylyne's normal operations aren't sufficient to support its operating costs. There seems to be huge amounts of money tied up in receivable and inventory. Is Skylyne having trouble collecting from customers? Are inventories salable? Maybe customers are refusing to pay for shoddy inventory. These are just things to think about. It doesn't mean that this is the case for this company, but you need to question things and start looking a little deeper.

With these questions in mind, let's look at a tool to help us determine the quality of income...called the Quality of Income Ratio. This measures the portion of income that was generated in cash. A ratio near 1.0 indicates a high likelihood that revenues are realized in cash and that expenses are associated with cash outflows. It is most useful when compared to industry competitors or prior periods. Major deviations (those greater than 1.5 or less than .5) should be investigated further. Four potential reasons for deviations include:

1. Seasonality. Season variations in sales and inventory levels can cause the ratio to fluctuate.
2. The corporate life cycle (growth in sales). New companies often experience rapid sales growth. This causes an increase in Accounts Receivable and Inventory at a faster rate than receivable collection.
3. Changes in management of operating activities. If operating assets grow out of control, operating cash flows and the quality of income ratio will decrease. Efficient management results in the opposite effect.
4. Changes in revenue and expense recognition. Fraudulent financial reporting involves aggressive revenue recognition or delay expense recognition. Both will cause net income to increase in the current period. However, neither affects cash flow. So, this will cause the quality of income ratio to drop...a clue that there are errors or fraudulent reporting in the financials.

The Quality of Income Ratio is calculated as:

Quality of Income Ratio	=	Net Cash Flows from Operating Activities
		Net Income

$$\frac{(21,300)}{5,500} = -3.87$$

Since Skylyne's Quality of Income Ratio is way below the .50 deviation rule, this area needs to be looked at more closely. Is it a one-time thing? Is this a trend? We need previous financials to determine this.

Interpreting Investing Activities Cash Flows

Businesses must replace equipment as it deteriorates in order to keep operating cash levels consistent. One way to measure a company's ability to replace long-term assets using cash generated from its operations is the:

Capital Acquisitions Ratio	=	Net Cash Flows from Operating Activities
		Cash paid for property, plant, and equipment

$$\frac{(21,300)}{30,500} = -.70$$

This ratio measures the ratio of long-term assets financed from operating activities without the need to finance externally through additional stock issuances or incurring additional debt. A ratio in excess of 1.0 indicates that additional financing was unnecessary in the current period. The higher the ratio the less likely a company will require outside financing for expansion.

Capital expenditure requirements vary widely among industries. So, this ratio is best used in comparing a company's own performance over time rather than comparing/contrasting it with other companies or industries. A high ratio can be misleading because it may indicate a lack of updating long-lived assets rather than indicating a strong cash position. Essentially, this ratio must be interpreted based on the company's business strategy and ongoing activities.

It's safe to say that Skylyne likely had to obtain some kind of financing in order to purchase this equipment since it had negative cash flows from operations.

Interpreting Financing Cash Flows

Financing can be obtained from internally generated funds (cash from operating activities), issuing additional stock (equity financing), or long-term borrowing (debt financing.). Because interest *must* be paid on debt, and the debt itself *must* also be repaid, debt financing represents the highest risk to the company.

On the other hand, dividends do not *have* to be paid nor does stock have to be *repaid*. Therefore, equity financing represents the least risk to the company. Within the financing activities section, a company that obtains additional debt (a *plus* to cash) takes on a greater risk than a company that is paying off its debt (a *minus* from cash.) To determine whether a company has been able to pay its interest charges on debt using its cash from its operating activities, calculate a Cash Coverage Ratio:

	Net Cash Flows from Operating Activities +	
Cash	Interest Paid + Income taxes Paid	
Coverage		= −3.87
Ratio	Interest paid	

$$\frac{(21,300) + 8,000 + 2,000}{8,000} = -1.41$$

Since both Interest and income taxes are used in determining operating cash flows, we add them back to calculate the ratio. This is a very troublesome ratio for Skylyne. They have a negative ratio…indicating they couldn't even cover one interest payment from their operating cash flows. A business can't last long with a ratio like this unless something changes. This would indicate that they have to borrow or raise funds just to pay interest charges on loans.

SUPPLEMENT A – REPORTING SALES OF PROPERTY, PLANT, AND EQUIPMENT – INDIRECT METHOD

When a company sells a piece of property, plant, and equipment (PPE), three things must be recorded: (1) removal of the book value of the asset sold in the PPE account, (2) cash receipts for the amount received for the item sold, and (3) any gain or loss on the sale of the asset. A gain occurs when the cash received on the sale is greater than the book value of the asset. A loss occurs when the cash received on the sale is less than the book value of the asset. The only part of this transaction that is reported on the SCF is the cash received on the sale.

This seems easy enough. But, here's the rub. The gain or loss resulting from the sale is *included in net income!* Because the indirect method calculates net cash flows from operating activities beginning with *net income,* any gains or losses need to be 'removed' from net income. The result is that: losses need to be added back to net income and gains need to be subtracted from net income. Assume a company sold a forklift for $12,000 cash. The original cost of the forklift was $75,000 and accumulated depreciation through the date of sale was $60,000. The journal entry is:

	Assets		= Liabilities	+ Stockholders' Equity
Cash	+12,000			Loss on Disposal (+E, −3,000
Accumulated depreciation (−xA,)+60,000				
Property, plant, & equipment	−75,000			

1. Analyze

2. Record

dr Cash (+AR) ………		12,000
dr Accumulated Depreciation (−xA, +A)		60,000
dr Loss on Disposal (+E, −SE)		3,000
cr Property, Plant, and equipment (−A)		75,000

The $12,000 cash receipt will be reported as a cash inflow from investing activities. Since the $3,000 loss was included in determining net income, it must be removed (added back) in the operating activities section of the SCF.

SUPPLEMENT B – SPREADSHEET APPROACH – INDIRECT METHOD

Many businesses have complexities that require a bit more analysis than we've discussed in this chapter. In practice, most companies use a 'spreadsheet' approach in preparing the SCF. It is a more systematic way to keep track of all of the information.

Basically, the spreadsheet is developed as follows:
1. Make four columns to record dollar amounts.
    ➢ The first column should contain the beginning balances for all balance sheet accounts.
    ➢ The next two columns are to 'record' summary debit and credit transactions that must have occurred in the accounts to 'explain' how each got from the beginning balance to the ending balance.
    ➢ The last column should contain the ending balances for all balance sheet accounts.
2. Enter each account name from the balance sheet in the far left of the top half of the spreadsheet.
3. As you analyze changes in each balance sheet account, enter the name of each item to be reported on the SCF in the far left of the bottom half of the spreadsheet.
    ➢ When the debit and credit summary transactions are determined, the changes to all balance sheet accounts (except cash) are recorded in the top half of the spreadsheet. Any changes to cash are made on the bottom half of the spreadsheet.
For step-by-step instructions on how to create the spreadsheet, refer to Supplement B in Chapter 12 of your text.

REVIEW THE CHAPTER

Chapter Summary
LO1. Identify cash flows arising from operating, investing, and financing activities
*   ❖ The statement has three main sections:
    *   o Cash Flows from Operating Activities – related to earning income from normal operations
    *   o Cash Flows from Investing Activities – related to the acquisition and sale of productive assets
    *   o Cash Flows from Financing Activities – related to external financing of the enterprise
*   ❖ The net cash inflow or outflow for the period is the same amount as the increase or decrease in cash and cash equivalents for the period on the balance sheet
*   ❖ Cash equivalents are highly liquid investments purchased within three months of maturity

LO2a. Report cash flows from operating activities using the Indirect method
*   ❖ The indirect method for reporting cash flows from operating activities reports a conversion of net income to net cash flow from operating activities
*   ❖ The conversion involves additions and subtractions for the following:
    *   o Noncurrent accruals, including:
        *   ▪ Expenses (such as depreciation expense)
        *   ▪ Revenues (which do not affect current assets or current liabilities)
    *   o Changes in each of the following individual accounts
        *   ▪ Current assets, other than
            *   ✓ Cash, and
        *   ▪ Current liabilities, other than
            *   ✓ debt to financial institutions (a financing activity)

LO2b. Report cash flows from operating activities using the Direct method
*   ❖ The direct method for reporting cash flows from operating activities accumulates the operating activities into categories
    *   o All of the operating transactions that result in either a debit or a credit to cash
*   ❖ The most common inflows are cash received from:
    *   o Customers, and
    *   o Dividends and interest on investments
*   ❖ The most common outflows are cash paid for:
    *   o Purchases of services and goods for resale
    *   o Salaries and wages

- o Income taxes
- o Interest on liabilities
- ❖ It is prepared by adjusting each item on the income statement from an accrual basis to a cash basis

LO3. Report cash flows from investing activities
- ❖ Investing activities reported on the cash flow statement include:
  - o Cash payments to acquire
    - ▪ Fixed assets, and
    - ▪ investments
  - o Cash proceeds from the sale of:
    - ▪ Fixed assets, and
    - ▪ investments

LO4. Report cash flows from financing activities
- ❖ Cash inflows from financing activities include:
  - o Cash proceeds from issuance of:
    - ▪ Debt, and
    - ▪ Common stock
- ❖ Cash outflows from financing activities include:
  - o Cash principal payments on debt
  - o Cash paid for the repurchase of the company's stock (Treasury Stock)
  - o Cash dividend payments
- ❖ Cash payments associated with interest are a cash flow from operating activities

LO5. Interpret Cash flows from operating, investing, and financing activities
- ❖ A healthy company will generate positive cash flows from operations
  - o Some of which will be used to pay for purchases of property, plant, and equipment
- ❖ Any additional cash (called free-cash flow) can be:
  - o Used to further expand the business
  - o Used to pay down some of the company's debt, or
  - o Returned to stockholders
- ❖ A company is in trouble if
  - o It is unable to generate positive cash flows from operations in the long-run because eventually:
    - ▪ Creditors will stop lending to the company, and
    - ▪ Stockholders will stop investing in the company
- ❖ Three common ratios for assessing operating, investing, and financing cash flows are:
  - o Quality of income ratio
  - o Capital acquisitions ratio
  - o Cash Coverage Ratio

READ AND RECALL QUESTIONS
After you read each section of the chapter, answer the related Read and Recall Questions below.

LEARNING OBJECTIVE
After studying the section of the chapter, you should be able to:
1. Identify cash flows arising from operating, investing, and financing activities

Business Activities and Cash Flows
Why do GAAP require that a statement of cash flows be presented by every company? What is its purpose?

Classifying Cash Flows

What are the three major categories of cash inflows and outflows reported on the SCF. Briefly define each.

What are the two methods for presenting the operating activities section of the SCF? Briefly define each method. Which is preferred by GAAP?

Define cash flows from operating activities. List at least one cash inflow and two cash outflows from operating activities.

Define cash flows from investing activities. List at least one cash inflow and one cash outflow from investing activities.

Define cash flows from financing activities. List at least one cash inflow and one cash outflow from financcnig activities.

What are the three general rules for classifying cash flows?

LEARNING OBJECTIVE
After studying the section of the chapter, you should be able to:
2a. Report cash flows from operating activities using the indirect method

Relationship with Other Financial Statements

List the three things that are needed to prepare a statement of cash flows (i.e. to convert information from accrual to cash)

Reporting Operating Cash Flows

What are the two alternative methods that can be used for preparing the operating activities section of the SCF?

Briefly explain direct method.

Briefly explain the indirect method.

PART A: *Indirect Method*
What are the three steps required for calculating cash flows from operating activities using the indirect method?

What four items usually affect operating activities?

What is the starting point for calculating Net cash flows from operating activities using the indirect method? Why?

Fill in the missing items on the following Quick and Easy table:

	Current Assets	Current Liabilities
Increase		
Decrease		

How is depreciation expense treated on the SCF calculating cash flows from operating activities using the indirect method? Why?

Circle the correct answers in the following statements regarding current assets and current liabilities regarding the indirect method:

Add the change when a current asset (increases, decreases) or current liability (increases, decreases).
Subtract the change when a current asset (increases, decreases) or current liability (increases, decreases).

Would an increase in accounts receivable result in an increase or decrease in cash collections for the period? Why?

How is Net Income adjusted under the indirect method for the amount spent on inventory purchases? What income statement account is actually being adjusted? Explain.

What increases a prepaid account? What decreases it? How is each dealt with on the SCF using the indirect method?

Are changes in accounts payable and accrued liabilities are treated in the same manner on the SCF using the indirect method? Why or why not?

LEARNING OBJECTIVE
After studying the section of the chapter, you should be able to:
2b. Report cash flows from operating activities using the direct method

---

Complete the following: The direct method is prepared by adjusting each _____ and _____ account on the _____ from the _____ basis to the _____ basis.

What is the calculation for converting Sales Revenues to cash inflows using the direct method?

Which two balance sheet accounts are needed to convert Cost of Goods Sold to Cash Paid to Suppliers using the direct method? Why? What is the calculation?

Which two balance sheet accounts are needed to convert Operating Expenses to a cash outflow? Why? What is the calculation?

How is depreciation expense dealt with under the direct method? Why?

Assuming no income tax payable or interest payable accounts exist on the balance sheet, how are Income Tax Expense and Interest Expense converted to cash payments? Why?

LEARNING OBJECTIVE
After studying the section of the chapter, you should be able to:
3. Report cash flows from investing activities

Reporting Cash Flows from Investing Activities
Which two balance sheet accounts are analyzed to determine cash inflow or outflow from investing activities?

List one transaction that create cash inflows from investing activities. List one transaction that create cash outflows from investing activities.

LEARNING OBJECTIVE
After studying the section of the chapter, you should be able to:
4. Report cash flows from financing activities

Reporting Cash Flows from Financing Activities
Which four balance sheet accounts are analyzed to determine cash inflow or outflow from financing activities?

List three transactions that create cash inflows from financing activities. List four transactions that create cash outflows from financing activities.

How is net income in the retained earnings account dealt with? Explain.

Format for the Statement of Cash Flows
Complete the following:

Under either method, the statement of cash flows combines cash flows from _____, _____, and _____ activities to produce an overall net _____ (or _____) in cash. This net change is _____ to the _____ cash balance to arrive at the _____ cash balance, which is the same cash balance as reported on the balance sheet.

Noncash Investing and Financing Activities
What are *noncash investing and financing activities*? Why is this information included with the SCF? How can it be presented?

What other supplementary information must also be reported for companies using the indirect method?

LEARNING OBJECTIVE
After studying the section of the chapter, you should be able to:
5. Interpret cash flows from operating, investing, and financing activities

Interpreting Operating Cash Flows

What is *free cash* flow? Why is it important? What three things can it be used for?

What does the operating activities section of the SCF tell investors? Creditors?

What is measured by the *Quality of Income Ratio*? How is it calculated? Why is it useful for evaluating whether managers are overstating a company's net income? Explain.

What are four potential causes of deviations in the Quality of Income ratio? Briefly describe each.

Interpreting Investing Cash Flows

What does the *Capital Acquisitions Ratio* measure? How is it calculated?

Is this ratio appropriate for evaluating different companies? Why or why not?

Interpreting Financing Cash Flows

What are the three ways long-term growth of a company be financed? Which is the most risky? Why?

What is the *Cash Coverage Ratio*? How is it calculated? Why is it superior to the *Times Interest Earned Ratio* (discussed in Chapter 10) for determining the ability to pay interest charges?

FINANCIAL ANALYSIS TOOLS

1. Quality of Income Ratio – To determine the extent to which net income and operating cash flows are in sync. A ratio near 1.0 means operating cash flows and net income are in sync:

Quality of Income Ratio	=	$\dfrac{\text{Net Cash Flows from Operating Activities}}{\text{Net Income}}$

2. Capital Acquisitions Ratio – To determine whether a company's cash flows are sufficient to pay for PPE purchases. A higher ratio means less need for external financing.

Capital Acquisitions Ratio	=	$\dfrac{\text{Net Cash Flows from Operating Activities}}{\text{Cash paid for property, plant, and equipment}}$

3. Cash Coverage Ratio – To determine whether operating cash flows (before financing and tax payments) are sufficient to cover interest payments. A ratio greater than 1.0 means operating cash flows are sufficient.

Cash Coverage Ratio	$\dfrac{\text{Net Cash Flows from Operating Activities} + \text{Interest Paid} + \text{Income taxes Paid}}{\text{Interest paid}}$	=	− 3.87

HELPFUL STUDY TIP

1. OK, so here's the deal. There's no helpful study hint to get you through the SCF. Instead, let's just work one entire problem all the way through from beginning to end (including the direct method!) The SCF is the most difficult financial statement to prepare in accounting, and the only way to learn it is to do it…over and over and over again until patterns start to emerge.

   A thorough understanding of the financial statements, how they relate to one another, and their impact on every account is an absolute necessity in *understanding* the SCF. It has been my experience that most students in introductory classes *don't understand* all of the ins and outs of accounting (and, quite frankly, could care less), so just being able to *prepare the horrid thing* is an achievement…never mind understanding it. So, I'm just going to show you *how* to prepare the statement and, in time, the understanding will come.

   The following page contains the (1) comparative balance sheet for 2009 and 2008, (2) complete income statement for 2009, and (3) additional details for selected accounts involving investing and/or financing activities for Douglas, Inc.

	2009	2008	
Balance sheet at December 31			
Cash	$ 27,000	$ 26,000	
Accounts receivable	43,500	38,000	✓
Merchandise inventory	54,000	32,000	✓
Property and equipment	153,000	144,000	
Less: Accumulated depreciation	(45,000)	(40,000)	✓
	$232,500	$200,000	
Accounts payable	$ 33,000	$ 39,000	✓
Wages payable	1,500	1,000	✓
Note payable, long-term	72,000	50,000	
Contributed capital	90,000	83,000	
Retained earnings	36,000	27,000	
	$232,500	$200,000	
Income statement for 2004			
Sales	$125,000		
Cost of goods sold	75,000		
Other expenses	36,000		
Net income	$ 14,000		

Additional Data:

a. Bought equipment for cash, $9,000.

b. Received $32,000 on a long-term note payable.

c. Paid $10,000 on a long-term note payable.

d. Issued new shares of stock for $7,000 cash.

e. Declared and paid a $5,000 cash dividend.

f. Other expenses included depreciation, $5,000; wages, $12,000; taxes, $3,000; interest $7,000; other, $9,000.

g. Accounts payable includes only inventory purchases made on credit. Because there are no liability accounts relating to taxes or other expenses, assume that these expenses were fully paid in cash.

First, we'll prepare the full-blown SCF for Douglas Company for 2009 using the indirect method for operating activities. Then we'll rework the operating activities section using the direct method. Ready? Let's go!

1. Prepare the statement of cash flows for the year ended December 31, 2009, using the indirect method. The indirect method begins with accrual-basis net income. This figure is 'converted to' cash receipts and payments by taking the changes in current asset (excluding investment accounts) and current liability accounts and 'adding' or 'subtracting' these changes to the net income figure. The result is net cash inflow (outflow) from operating activities. I guess I lied a bit earlier when I indicated there were no helpful hints for this chapter. There are two steps here: (1) Add back any depreciation to net income, and (2) adjust net income for changes in current asset/liability accounts based on the '**rule.**' Here's the rule, _**for the indirect method only**_,

Account	Change in the Account from last year to this year	Treatment on SCF in Determining Net Cash Flows from Operating Activities
If a **Current Asset** account balance	⬆ (increases), then	⬇ (subtract) the 'change' from net income
	⬇ (decreases), then	⬆ (add) the 'change' to net income
If a **Current Liability** account balance	⬆ (increases), then	⬆ (add) the 'change' to net income
	⬇ (decreases), then	⬇ (subtract) the 'change' from net income

Ready to start? Ok! Here we go!

(a) Begin with a 'blank' paper for your 'SCF'. After heading it up appropriately, write **Operating Activities** on the first line and **Net Income** on the second line. In our example, Douglas Company had net income of $14,000 for 2009. (Note: for each step we do, refer to the completed SCF at the end of this Helpful Study Hint.)

(b) Step 1 in the preparation is to ***always add back depreciation expense to net income.*** Current year depreciation is $5,000 (see letter f. of the ***Additional data*** for this problem). So, we add this amount to net income.

(c) Using the table provided earlier, add or subtract any changes in current asset and current liability accounts. The following table shows all of these changes and the proper treatment of each on the SCF using the rule:

Current Assets		
Accounts Receivable (43,500 – 38,000)	⬆ (increase) of 5,500 so	⬇ (subtract) 5,500 from net income
Merchandise Inventory (54,000 – 32,000)	⬆ (increase) of 22,000 so	⬇ (subtract) 22,000 from net income
Current Liability		
Accounts Payable (39,00 – 33,000)	⬇ (decrease) of 6,000 so	⬇ (subtract) 6,000 from net income
Wages Payable (1,500 – 1,000)	⬆ (increase) of 500 so	⬆ (add) 500 to net income

(d) Now, just add and subtract these amounts from net income, ***exactly as shown on the SCF.*** If the ending number is positive (+), there is a net cash *inflow* from operating activities and if the figure is negative (–), then there is a net cash *outflow* from operating activities. In our example, there was a net cash outflow of $14,000. (Note that the fact that this number is the same as the Net Income figure is purely a coincidence.)

Now, remember this amount, because when rework this part of the problem using the direct method, we must get the *same amount of net cash outflows for operating activities!* Here's another little hint, as you *completely explain* (on the SCF) the changes in each balance sheet account, place a little check mark (✓) next to the account. When every account on the balance sheet (except cash, remember that's the one we're trying to figure out) has a check mark next to it, **all changes in cash should be accounted for!** So, at this point, the following accounts should be check marked: Accounts Receivable, Merchandise Inventory, Accounts Payable, Wages Payable, and Accumulated Depreciation…huh? Yep! When we added back depreciation expense to net income that completely explained how the accumulated depreciation account increased from $40,000 to $45,000.

(e) Take a quick peek at the items that *have not* yet been check marked: Property and Equipment, Note payable, long-term, Contributed capital, and Retained Earnings. It's no coincidence that these accounts represent investing and financing activities…those are the only parts of the SCF remaining! In order to prepare the investing and financing portions of the SCF, we usually need to have additional information to explain what caused the increases/decreases in these accounts.

So, we begin by going down the balance sheet until we find an item that is *not* check marked and we find Property and Equipment. How convenient! This is an investing activity account, and we've come to the investing activities section of the SCF! This is also where we start hunting for additional information regarding Property and Equipment. Sure enough, letter *a.* informs us that equipment of $9,000 was purchased for cash. Does this completely explain the change in Property and Equipment? Yup! The account increased $9,000 ($153,000 – $144,000.) We can check mark that baby off! By the way, you should also be check marking the additional information as it is used, to make sure you don't do anything twice or miss anything either. Since this is the only account relating to investing activities, we've can complete that section of the SCF. Put "Investing Activities" on the next blank line. What happened to cause the increase? The "Additions of Property and Equipment." List that and put the amount. Since nothing else 'investing' occurred, we can complete this section of the SCF. You have to 'calculate' net cash flows from investing activities (even though there's only one), because it is a critical piece of the SCF.

(f) Now, we continue down the balance sheet until we come to the next 'unchecked' item: Note payable, long-term. Again, we find any additional information related to this account and we actually find two of them (letters *b.* and *c.*). This tells us that the company borrowed $32,000 *and* paid $10,000 (presumably on the pre-existing balance.) This resulted in cash inflows ($32,000) and outflows ($10,000), a net inflow of $22,000 ($32,000 – $10,000.) Does this net $22,000 completely explain the change in notes payable, long-term? Yup! It increased $22,000 ($72,000 – $50,000.) So, put "Financing Activities" on the next blank line and list *each of these items separately*. Label the first, "Proceeds from Notes Payable" and the second as "Principle payment on Long-term debt" (or similar descriptions.) We can now check Notes Payable, long-term off on the balance sheet.

(g) The next unchecked account is Contributed capital. Letter *d.* of the additional information indicates that $7,000 of common stock was issued for cash. This completely explains the $7,000 increase in contributed capital ($90,000 - $83,000.) List this item on our SCF as "Issuance of Common Stock", and we're ready to tackle the last balance sheet account that is unmarked!

(h) Whoo hoo! We're almost done! The last account we have to explain is retained earnings. You may not realize it, but we've already explained a portion of the change—Net Income! Yup! The very first thing we put on the SCF explains at least *some* of the reason this account changed. If you remember the calculation for the Statement of Retained Earnings, you know that there's only one thing missing—Dividends! How convenient that letter *e.* of the additional information informs us that $5,000 of dividends were declared and paid. Do these two things completely explain the changes in Retained Earnings? Yup! Retained earnings increased by $9,000 the exact difference between net income and dividends paid ($14,000 - $5,000). Since we've already dealt with the net income, the only one we need to list as a financing outflow is dividends.

(i) Total up (exactly as listed on the SCF) the net cash flow from financing activities. A positive number indicates a net cash *inflow,* while a negative number indicates a net cash *outflow.* Douglas Company had a net cash inflow of $24,000 from financing activities.

(j) Now combine the net cash flows from operating, investing, and financing activities (exactly as listed on the SCF.) The result is the Net cash inflow (outflow). This figure should completely explain how the amount of cash at the beginning of the period became the amount of cash reported at the end of the period. So, let's give a whirl! The net cash flows from operating, investing, and financing activities were: ($14,000), ($9,000), and +$24,000. These three amounts combined result in a $1,000 net cash inflow (–$14,000 – $9,000 + $24,000.) List this figure as "Increase (decrease) in Cash."

(k) This is the last (and easiest) step. Find beginning cash on the comparative balance sheet (remember that ending balances in 2004 become beginning balances in 2005.) So, we see that beginning cash is $26,000 and we put it on the SCF with an appropriate heading. Net the "Increase (decrease) in Cash" with the beginning balance…and (hopefully) the combined result is the ***ending balance in cash!*** Always verify that this is true by comparing the ending figure on the SCF with the ending cash amount on the comparative balance sheet. Hooray! The $27,000 figure on the SCF we just prepared does, in fact, match the ending balance shown on the comparative balance sheet.

DOUGLAS COMPANY
Statement of Cash Flows
For the Year Ended December 31, 2009 ⎫ (a)

Operating activities		
Net Income	$14,000	
Depreciation Expense	5,000	(b)
Increase in Accounts Receivable	(5,500)	
Increase in Inventory	(22,000)	(c)
Decrease in Accounts Payable	(6,000)	
Increase in Wages Payable	500	
Net cash flow from operating activities	(14,000)	(d)
Investing activities		
Additions to property, plant, and equipment	(9,000)	(e)
Net cash flow from (used for) investing activities	(9,000)	(e)
Financing activities		
Proceeds from Notes Payable	32,000	(f)
Principal payments on long-term debt	(10,000)	(f)
Issued Common Stock	7,000	(g)
Cash paid for other dividends	(5,000)	(h)
Net cash flow from financing activities	24,000	(i)
Increase (decrease) in cash	1,000	(j)
Cash and cash equivalents, January 1	26,000	(k)
Cash and cash equivalents, December 31	$27,000	(k)

2. Close, but no cigar. We're not completely through yet! We need to rework the operating activities section of the SCF using the direct method. We don't need to be nearly as 'formal' now because we've already prepared the statement. If the direct method had been used rather than the indirect method, in the original problem, this section would be substituted for the operating activities section in the SCF we just prepared. So, here goes!

Rather than start with net income, we adjust each *category on the income statement individually.* The formulas will not be duplicated here because they were already presented earlier in this chapter.

    a.   Look at the income statement and simply start with the first item on it—Sales. The Sales account is adjusted to *cash collections from customers* using the formula presented earlier. Refer back to these formulas as needed.

Cash collected from customers (125,000 – 5,500)   **119,500**

    b.   The next income statement item is Cost of goods Sold. We adjust this figure for both changes in merchandise inventory and accounts payable to determine "Cash paid to Suppliers."

Cash paid to suppliers (75,000 + 22,000 + 6,000)   **(103,000)**

    c.   Finally, we come to Other Expenses on the income statement. The tricky thing to remember here is that *depreciation expense must be* <u>*ignored*</u> *when determining cash outflows because the recording of depreciation* <u>*does not use any cash.*</u> If depreciation had been listed as a separate line item on the income statement, we would simply ignore it. However, since it is *included in the $36,000,* amount reported for Other expenses (see letter *f.* of the additional information), it must be *removed from that figure.* This 'subtraction' of depreciation from expenses is <u>*only necessary if depreciation expense is not listed as a line-item on the income statement!*</u>

Cash paid for operating expenses (36,000 -5,000 - 500)   **(30,500)**

Now we combine them all *exactly as reported on the SCF* and we <u>***must***</u> get the same amount as we did under the indirect method, or something was done incorrectly.

Cash collected from customers (125,000 – 5,500)	$119,500
Cash paid to suppliers (75,000 + 22,000 + 6,000)	(103,000)
Cash paid for operating expenses (36,000 -5,000 - 500)	(30,500)
Net cash flow from operating activities	($14,000)

Since, we got the same result for cash flows from operating activities as we did using the indirect method, we can rest assured!

SELF-TEST QUESTIONS AND EXERCISES

MATCHING
1. *Match each of the key terms listed below with the appropriate textbook definition on the following page.*

_____	Capital Acquisitions Ratio	_____	Direct Method
_____	Cash Coverage Ratio	_____	Free Cash Flow
_____	Cash Equivalent	_____	Indirect Method
_____	Cash Flows from Financing Activities	_____	Noncash Investing and Financing Activities
_____	Cash Flows from Investing Activities	_____	Quality of Income Ratio
_____	Cash Flows from Operating Activities		

A. Reports the components of cash flows from operating activities as gross receipts and gross payments.
B. Compares cash flows generated from the company's operations to cash paid for interest.
C. Cash inflows and outflows related to financing sources external to the company (owners and lenders.)
D. Adjusts net income to compute cash flows from operating activities.
E. Cash inflows and outflows related to components of net income.
F. Measures whether a company is generating enough cash internally to purchase new long-term assets like equipment.
G. Positive cash flow from operations that can be used to replace company long-term investments, for various financing activities, or simply to build up the company's cash balance.
H. A short-term, highly liquid investment with an original maturity of less than three months.
I. Material investing and financing activities that did not have cash flow effects.
J. Measures the portion of net income that was generated in cash.
K. Cash inflows and outflows related to the sale or purchase of investments and long-term assets.

TRUE-FALSE QUESTIONS
For each of the following, enter a T or F in the blank to indicate whether the statement is true or false.

_____ 1. (LO1) A company cannot have high profits accompanied by negative net cash outflows.

_____ 2. (LO1) Cash equivalents are short-term, highly liquid investments that are either readily convertible into know amounts or cash, or so near to maturity that there is little risk their value will change.

_____ 3. (LO2) There are two methods for determining cash flows from financing activities: direct and indirect.

_____ 4. (LO2) Most companies use the direct method for determining cash flows from operating activities because it is preferred by GAAP.

_____ 5. (LO2) Investing and financing sections of the SCF are always presented in the same manner, regardless of the format of the operating section.

_____6. (LO2a) Accumulated depreciation is largely ignored when preparing cash flows from operating activities under the indirect method because it involves long-lived assets.

_____7. (LO2a) An increase in accrued liabilities is added to net income in determining cash flows from operating activities under the indirect method.

_____8. (LO2b) The direct method presents a summary of all operating transactions that result in either a debit or a credit to cash.

_____9. (LO2b) Cost of goods sold is adjusted for changes in inventory and prepaid expenses under the direct method in determining payments to suppliers of inventory.

_____10. (LO3) In reporting cash flows from investing activities, investments are ignored because they are considered cash equivalents.

_____11. (LO4) Cash flows from investing activities include changes in contributed capital or retained earnings because they are related to investments by the owners and reinvestment of earnings in the company.

_____12. (LO4) A schedule of noncash investing and financing activities is optional at the discretion of management.

_____13. (LO5) Most analysts believe that the operating activities section is the most important section of the SCF.

_____14. (LO5) Most companies have ups and downs in operating cash flows, especially if they run a seasonal business.

_____15. (LO8) The quality of income ratio measures the portion of income that was generated in cash.

_____16. (LO8) Seasonal variations in sales and inventory production can cause the quality of income ratio to fluctuate and these deviations should be considered extremely serious.

_____17. (LO6) Usually, the amount of cash paid for property, plant, and equipment (from the bottom part of the Capital Acquisitions Ratio) is reported in the SCF financing activities section.

_____18. (LO6) The Capital Acquisitions Ratio is an excellent tool for comparing companies in varying industries because of its consistency.

_____19. (LO7) Equity financing is the riskiest type of external financing because stockholders demand dividends and tend to bail out when too much stock is issued.

_____20. (LO7) The cash coverage ratio is not as relevant as the times interest earned ratio because financial statement users already know the cash paid for interest.

MULTIPLE CHOICE QUESTIONS
Choose the best answer or response by placing the identifying letter in the space provided.

_____1. (LO1) Which of the following is *not* true regarding the SCF?
   a. Most companies experience different cash flow patterns as they develop and mature
   b. In general, investing cash flows affect noncurrent liabilities or stockholders' equity accounts
   c. The amount of cash generated through daily operating activities has to exceed the amount spent of them in order to a company to survive in the long run
   d. All of the above are true statements regarding the SCF

_____2. (LO1) Which of the following is *not* considered cash or a cash equivalent?
   a. cash deposited in banks
   b. highly liquid investments purchased within three months of maturity
   c. investments
   d. cash on hand

_____3. (LO1) Cash flows from operating activities include all of the following *except*:
   a. cash provided by dividends and interest on investments
   b. cash used for paying dividends to owners
   c. cash used for interest on liabilities
   d. cash used for income taxes

_____4. (LO1) Cash flows from financing activities include:
   a. cash provided by sale or disposal of property, plant and equipment
   b. cash used for payment of rent
   c. depreciation expense
   d. repurchasing stock from owners

_____5. (LO2) Which of the following is *not* required to prepare the statement of cash flows?
   a. a complete income statement
   b. additional detail about selected accounts that increase or decrease because of investing and/or financing activities
   c. comparative balance sheets
   d. bank Reconciliation

_____6. (LO2a,b) Which of the following is a true statement about the operating activities section of the SCF?
   a. depreciation expense is an addition to the SCF under both the direct and indirect methods in determining cash flows from operating activities
   b. cash flows from operating activities is always the same regardless of whether it is computed using the direct or indirect method
   c. net income is the starting point for the operating activities section of the SCF regardless of whether the direct or indirect method is used
   d. GAAP requires that the indirect method be used unless there is a good and sufficient business reason for using the direct method when calculating the operating activities section of the SCF

_____7. (LO2a) Determine net cash flows from operating activities (using the indirect method) under the following assumptions:

➢ Net Income	$54,000
➢ Accounts Payable decreased	$3,000
➢ Inventory decreased	$6,000
➢ Depreciation expense	$9,000
➢ Accounts receivable increased	$15,000

   a. $ 51,000
   b. $ 57,000
   c. $ 81,000
   d. $ 87,000

_____8. (LO2a) Which of the following is *subtracted from* net income when reconciling net income to cash flows from operating activities under the indirect method?
   a. increase in accounts payable
   b. increase in prepaid expenses
   c. depreciation expense
   d. all of the above are subtracted from net income under the direct method

_____9. (LO2b) What is cash collected from customers (using the direct method) under the following assumptions?

➤ Sales Revenues	$36,000
➤ accounts receivable increased	$ 8,000
➤ Inventory decreased	$ 4,000

a. $ 24,000
b. $ 28,000
c. $ 40,000
d. $ 48,000

_____10. (LO2b) What are cash payments to suppliers assuming the following information:

➤ Cost of Goods Sold	$87,500
➤ Decrease in Inventory	$11,000
➤ Decrease in Accounts Payable	$ 6,500

a. $ 105,000
b. $ 92,000
c. $ 83,000
d. $ 70,000

_____11. (LO2b) Calculate cash paid for expenses assuming the following:

➤ Other Operating Expenses	$52,000
➤ Decrease in Prepaid Expenses	$ 4,000
➤ Increase in Accrued Liabilities	$ 8,500

a. $ 39,500
b. $ 47,500
c. $ 56,500
d. $ 64,500

_____12. (LO3) Calculate net cash flows from investing activities under the following assumptions:
➤ All changes in investments and Property, Plant and Equipment were the result of cash transactions
➤ Beginning investments $100,000
➤ Ending investments $35,000
➤ Beginning Property, Plant, and Equipment $240,000
➤ Ending Property, Plant, and Equipment $300,000

a. $5,000 increase
b. $5,000 decrease
c. $125,000 increase
d. $125,000 decrease

_____13. (LO4) Given the following information, determine net cash flows from financing activities:
➤ Bonds were issued for $200,000
➤ Dividends paid were $20,000
➤ Stock issued $100,000
➤ Treasury stock purchased $16,000

a. $136,000 net cash outflow
b. $136,000 net cash inflow
c. $264000 net cash outflow
d. $264,000 net cash inflow

Use the following information for *Innajem Corp.* to answer questions 14 and 15:

Net cash provided by Investing Activities	$120,000
Cash and cash equivalents at beginning of period	32,000
Net cash provided by financing activities	222,000
Cash and cash equivalents at end of period	56,000

_____14. (LO4) What is the net cash provided by or used for operating activities for Innajem Corp.?
    a. $24,000 net cash provided from operating activities
    b. $24,000 net cash used for operating activities
    c. $318,000 net cash provided from operating activities
    d. $318,000 net cash used for operating activities

_____15. (LO5) If you were a potential investor in Innajem Corp., would you have any concerns about its performance?
    a.   No, because it has a large amount of free cash flow
    b.   No, because it appears to be a growing company with many financing opportunities
    c.   Yes, because it had to borrow funds and sell off investments in an effort to cover its operating costs
    d.   Cannot be determined from the information provided

_____16. (LO8) Assuming the following information, calculate the quality of income ratio:
    ➤ Net cash inflow from investing activities $65,000
    ➤ Net cash inflow from operating activities $125,000
    ➤ Net cash outflow from financing activities $41,000
    ➤ Net Income $284,000

    a.   2.272
    b.   4.369
    c.   6.927
    d.   None of these is the correct amount for the quality of income ratio

_____17. (LO8) Which of the following is a deviation that could be a sign of big problems to come when the quality of income ratio declines?
    a.   Corporate life cycle (growth in sales)
    b.   Changes in revenue and expense recognition
    c.   Seasonality
    d.   all of the above are considered deviations that should be of concern to investors

_____18. (LO6) Calculate the Capital Acquisitions Ratio, given the following assumptions:
    ➤ Net cash used for Investing activities $115,000
    ➤ Net cash provided from operating activities $335,000
    ➤ Cash Paid for Property, Plant, and Equipment $225,000

    a.   1.17
    b.   1.49
    c.   3.43
    d.   6.72

_____19. (LO7) Which of the following items are *not* included in the top portion of the formula when calculating the cash coverage ratio?
    a.   Interest paid
    b.   Net cash flow from operating activities
    c.   Income taxes paid
    d.   Interest received

_____ 20. (LO7) Long-term growth of a company can be financed in each of the following ways *except*:
  a. Money borrowed on a long-term basis
  b. Issuance of common stock
  c. Sale of long-term investments
  d. Internally generated funds from operating activities

EXERCISES

Record your answer to each exercise in the space provided. Show your work.

Exercise 12-1. Matching Items Reported to SCF Categories and Determine the Effect on the SCF (Indirect Method) (LO2a)

Clamsal Inc., uses the indirect method to prepare the SCF. Indicate whether the following items should be disclosed in the Operating Activities (O), Investing Activities (I), or Financing Activities (F) section of the SCF or (NA) if the item does not appear on the SCF. Also, for those appearing on the SCF, indicate whether the item should be added (+) or subtracted (–). The first one has been done for you.

__+O__ 1. Decrease in Accounts Payable	_____	9. Purchase of Treasury Stock
_____ 2. Proceeds from long-term notes payable	_____	10. Increase in inventories
_____ 3. Payment for purchase of equipment	_____	11. Decrease in Accounts Receivable
_____ 4. Depreciation expense	_____	12. Increase in Prepaid expenses
_____ 5. Decrease in Unearned Revenues	_____	13. Proceeds from issuance of Stock
_____ 6. Purchase of investments	_____	14. Proceeds from sale of land
_____ 7. Increase in Accrued Liabilities	_____	15. Increase in Cost of Goods Sold
_____ 8. Payment of cash dividends	_____	16. Net Income

Exercise 12-2. Matching items Reported to Cash Flow Statement Categories (Direct Method) (LO 2b)

Lobesal Inc., uses the direct method to prepare the SCF. Indicate whether the following items should be disclosed in the Operating Activities (O), Investing Activities (I), or Financing Activities (F) section of the SCF or (NA) if the item does not appear on the SCF. Also, for those appearing on the SCF, indicate whether the item should be added (+) or subtracted (–). The first one has been done for you.

__+F__ 1. Proceeds from bond issuance	_____	8. Cash collections from customers
_____ 2. Net Income	_____	9. Cash receipts for interest
_____ 3. Payment for purchase of land	_____	10. Cash payments for inventory
_____ 4. Depreciation expense	_____	11. Cash payments for bank loan
_____ 5. Payment of cash dividends	_____	12. Proceeds from issuance of Stock
_____ 6. Cash paid for other expenses	_____	13. Cash payments for income taxes
_____ 7. Cash paid for interest	_____	14. Proceeds from sale of investments

Study Guide, Chapter 12

Page 411

Exercise 12-3. Computing Cash Flows from Operating Activities (Indirect Method). (LO2a)

For each of the following independent cases, compute cash flows from operating activities. Assume the following list includes all balance sheet accounts related to operating activities.

	Case A	Case B	Case C
Net Income	$4,000	$35,000	$91,000
Depreciation expense	3,000	14,000	21,000
Accounts receivable increase (decrease)	(6,000)	15,000	(5,000)
Inventory increase (decrease)	2,000	11,000	(20,000)
Accounts payable increase (decrease)	(7,000)	(24,000)	14,000
Accrued liabilities increase (decrease)	(8,000)	(14,000)	21,000
Prepaid expenses increase (decrease)	(4,000)	6,000	(17,000)

Calculations:

Exercise 12-4. Computing Cash Flows from Operating Activities (Direct Method). (LO2b)

For each of the following independent cases, compute cash flows from operating activities. Assume the list below includes all balance sheet accounts related to operating activities.

	Case A	Case B	Case C
Sales Revenues	$30,000	$160,000	$510,000
Cost of Goods Sold	18,000	80,000	275,000
Depreciation expense	3,000	14,000	21,000
Other operating expenses	5,000	31,000	123,000
Net Income	$4,000	$35,000	$91,000
Accounts Receivable increase (decrease)	(6,000)	15,000	(5,000)
Inventory increase (decrease)	2,000	11,000	(20,000)
Accounts payable increase (decrease)	(7,000)	(24,000)	14,000
Accrued liabilities increase (decrease)	(8,000)	(14,000)	21,000
Prepaid expenses increase (decrease)	(4,000)	6,000	(17,000)

Calculations:

Exercise 12-5. Computing Cash Flows from Investing and Financing Activities and Reporting Noncash Investing and Financing Activities. (LO3, 4)

Part A. Based on the following information, compute: (1) cash flows from investing activities, and (2) cash flows from financing activities.

Short-term borrowing from bank	$35,000	Dividends paid	$67,000
Cash collections from customers	$84,000	Interest Paid	$23,000
Depreciation Expense	$27,000	Purchase of equipment	$97,000
Sale of investments	$54,000		

Calculations:

Part B. For each of the following, indicate (Y) if the item would be considered a noncash investing and financing activity and (N) if it would not.

_____ An owner contributes land to the business in exchange for shares of stock.
_____ Company pays dividends
_____ A building is purchased with short-term investments
_____ Treasury stock is purchased

Exercise 12-6. Preparing a Statement of Cash Flows (indirect method) (LO2a)
Douglas Company is developing its annual financial statements at December 31, 2006. The statements are complete except for the statement of cash flows. The completed comparative balance sheets and income statement are summarized:

	2006	2005
Balance sheet at December 31		
Cash	$ 66,000	$ 27,000
Accounts receivable	40,500	43,500
Merchandise inventory	45,000	54,000
Property and equipment	166,500	153,000
Less: Accumulated depreciation	(54,000)	(45,000)
	$264,000	$232,500
Accounts payable	$ 37,500	$ 33,000
Wages payable	1,200	1,500
Note payable, long-term	57,000	72,000
Contributed capital	120,000	90,000
Retained earnings	48,300	36,000
	$264,000	$232,500

Income statement for 2006

Sales	$150,000
Cost of goods sold	91,500
Other expenses	40,500
Net income	$ 18,000

Additional Data:

a. Bought equipment for cash, $13,500.

b. Paid $15,000 on the long-term note payable.

c. Issued new shares of stock for $30,000 cash.

d. Declared and paid a $5,700 cash dividend.

e. Other expenses included depreciation, $9,000; wages, $15,000; taxes, $4,500; interest $5,000; other, $7,000.

f. Accounts payable includes only inventory purchases made on credit. Because there are no liability accounts relating to taxes or other expenses, assume that these expenses were fully paid in cash.

Required:

1. Prepare the statement of cash flows for the year ended December 31, 2006, using the indirect method.

DOUGLAS COMPANY
Statement of Cash Flows
For the Year Ended December 31, 2006

Operating activities	
Net Income	$
Depreciation Expense	
Decrease in Accounts Receivable	
Decrease in Inventory	
Increase in Accounts Payable	
Decrease in Wages Payable	
Net cash flow from operating activities	_____
Investing activities	
Additions to property, plant, and equipment	_____
Net cash flow from (used for) investing activities	_____
Financing activities	
Proceeds from issuance of stock	
Repaid principal owed on long-term debt	
Cash paid for other dividends	_____
Net cash flow from financing activities	_____
Increase (decrease) in cash and cash equivalents	
Cash and cash equivalents, December 1	_____
Cash and cash equivalents, December 31	$_____

2. Use the statement of cash flows to evaluate Douglas' cash flows.

Exercise 12-7. Computing Cash Flows from Operating Activities (Direct Method) (LO2b)

Using the information presented in **Exercise 12-6** for Douglas Company, calculate the net cash provided (used) by Douglas Company for 2006, using the direct method.

Exercise 12-8. Calculating and Interpreting the Capital Acquisitions Ratio, Cash Coverage Ratio, and Quality of Income Ratio (LO6, 7, 8)

Butterfly Bowling Equipment, Inc. reported the following information in its SCF:

	2005	2004	2003
Net cash flow from operating activities	$ 27,000	$ 23,000	$ 18,000
Interest Paid	15,000	11,000	8,000
Income taxes paid	27,000	25,000	21,000
Purchases of Property, Plant, and Equipment	85,000	50,000	40,000
Net Income	81,000	76,000	65,000
Depreciation Expense	41,000	35,000	20,000

Required:
1. a. Calculate the average capital acquisitions ratio for the period covering 2003 – 2005.

   b. What does the ratio tell you about the company's need for using external financing to replace property, plant, and equipment?

2. a. Calculate the cash coverage ratio for Butterfly Bowling Equipment for each of the three years.

   b. What do these ratios tell you about the company's ability to pay its interest costs?

3. a. Compute the quality of income ratio.

b. What does the ratio tell you about the company's accrual of revenues and/or deferral of expenses?

SOLUTIONS TO SELF-TEST QUESTIONS AND EXERCISES

MATCHING
1.

F	Capital Acquisitions Ratio	A	Direct Method
B	Cash Coverage Ratio	G	Free Cash Flow
H	Cash Equivalent	D	Indirect Method
C	Cash Flows from Financing Activities	I	Noncash Investing and Financing Activities
K	Cash Flows from Investing Activities	J	Quality of Income Ratio
E	Cash Flows from Operating Activities		

TRUE-FALSE QUESTIONS
1. F – Because of seasonal fluctuations of businesses, this situation is not unusual.
2. F – A cash equivalent must meet *both* of these definitions in order to be consider a cash equivalent.
3. F – There are two methods of determining cash flows from operating activities.
4. F – While the direct method is preferred by GAAP, 99% of large companies use the indirect method for determining cash flows from operating activities.
5. T
6. F – Accumulated depreciation is needed to determine the amount of depreciation expense taken in the current period to add back to net income under the indirect method.
7. T
8. T
9. F – Cost of goods sold under the direct method is adjusted for changes in inventory and accounts payable.
10. F – Unless they meet the definition of a cash equivalent, investments are *not* considered part of cash on the SCF.
11. F – Owner investments are considered an outside source of financing and any dealings with the owners are considered financing activities including dividends and stock issuances/repurchases.
12. F – This schedule is required for material investing and financing decisions that did not have cash flow effects. It can be presented as a supplementary schedule to the SCF or in the financial statement notes.
13. T
14. T
15. T
16. F – Usually, this isn't a cause for alarm and shouldn't be considered extremely serious since this can be caused by seasonal fluctuations.
17. F – These would be reported in the investing activities section of the SCF, not the financing section.
18. F – Needs for investment in plant and equipment differ dramatically across industries so this should only be compared with prior year figures or with companies in the same industry.
19. F – Debt financing is the riskiest form of financing.
20. F – The Times Interest Earned ratio compares interest charges to *accrual-based net income* which doesn't reflect the amount of *cash available to pay interest.* Therefore, the cash coverage ratio is a better measure of the ability of the company to generate enough *cash* to pay the interest charges.

MULTIPLE CHOICE QUESTIONS

1. B	6. B	11. A	16. D
2. C	7. A	12. A	17. D
3. B	8. B	13. D	18. B
4. D	9. B	14. D	19. D
5. D	10. C	15. C	20. C

EXERCISES

Exercise 12-1. Matching Items Reported to SCF Categories and Determine the Effect on the SCF (Indirect Method) (LO2a)

+O	1. Decrease in Accounts Payable		-F	9. Purchase of Treasury Stock
+F	2. Proceeds from long-term notes payable		-O	10. Increase in inventories
-I	3. Payment for purchase of equipment		+O	11. Decrease in Accounts Receivable
+O	4. Depreciation expense		-O	12. Increase in Prepaid expenses
-O	5. Decrease in Unearned Revenues		+F	13. Proceeds from issuance of Stock
-I	6. Purchase of investments		+I	14. Proceeds from sale of land
+O	7. Increase in Accrued Liabilities		NA	15. Increase in Cost of Goods Sold
-F	8. Payment of cash dividends		+O	16. Net Income

Exercise 12-2. Matching items Reported to Cash Flow Statement Categories (Direct Method) (LO 2b)

+F	1. Proceeds from bond issuance		+O	8. Cash collections from customers
NA	2. Net Income		+O	9. Cash receipts for interest
-I	3. Payment for purchase of land		-O	10. Cash payments for inventory
NA	4. Depreciation expense		-F	11. Cash payments for bank loan
-F	5. Payment of cash dividends		+F	12. Proceeds from issuance of Stock
-O	6. Cash paid for other expenses		-O	13. Cash payments for income taxes
-O	7. Cash paid for interest		+I	14. Proceeds from sale of investments

Exercise 12-3. Computing Cash Flows from Operating Activities (Indirect Method). (LO2a)

Case A: Net cash flows from operating activities = $0 (4,000 + 3,000 +6,000 -2,000 -7,000 -8,000 +4,000)

Case B: Net cash flows from operating activities = ($21,000) (35,000 + 14,000 – 15,000 – 11,000 – 24.000 – 14,000 – 6,000)

Case C: Net cash flows from operating activities = $189,000 (91,000 + 21,000 + 5,000 + 20,000 +14,000 + 21,000 +17,000)

Exercise 12-4. Computing Cash Flows from Operating Activities (Direct Method). (LO2b)

Case A: Cash flows from operating activities: $0

Sales (30,000 + 6,000)	$36,000
Cost of Goods Sold (18,000 +2,000 +7,000)	(27,000)
Other expenses (5,000 – 4,000 + 8,000)	(9,000)
Net cash flows	0

Case B: Cash flows from operating activities: ($21,000)

Sales (160,000 – 15,000)	$145,000
Cost of Goods Sold (80,000 +11,000 + 24,000)	(115,000)
Other expenses (31,000 + 6,000 + 14,000)	(51,000)
Net cash flows	($21,000)

Case C: Cash flows from operating activities: $189,000

Sales (510,000 + 5,000)	$515,000
Cost of Goods Sold (275,000 – 20,000 – 14,000)	(241,000)
Other expenses (123,000 – 17,000 – 21,000)	(85,000)
Net cash flows	$189,000

Exercise 12-5. Computing Cash Flows from Investing and Financing Activities. (LO3, 4)
Part A.

Cash Flows from Investing Activities:		Cash flows from Financing Activities:	
Sales of investments	$54,000	Short-term borrowing from bank	$35,000
Purchase of equipment	(97,000)	Dividends paid	(67,000)
Net Cash flow	(43,000)	Net Cash flow	(32,000)

Note: Cash collections from customers, interest paid, and depreciation expense (indirect method) are operating activity items.

Part B.

  Y   An owner contributes land to the business in exchange for shares of stock.
  N   Company pays dividends
  Y   A building is purchased with short-term investments
  N   Treasury stock is purchased

Exercise 12-6. Preparing a Statement of Cash Flows (indirect method) (LO2a)

1. Prepare the statement of cash flows for the year ended December 31, 2006, using the indirect method.

DOUGLAS COMPANY
Statement of Cash Flows
For the Year Ended December 31, 2006

Operating activities	
Net Income	$ 18,000
Depreciation Expense	9,000
Decrease in Accounts Receivable (43,500 – 40,500)	3,000
Decrease in Inventory (54,000 – 45,000)	9,000
Increase in Accounts Payable (37,500 – 33,000)	4,500
Decrease in Wages Payable (1,500 – 1,200)	(300)
Net cash flow from operating activities	43,200
Investing activities	
Additions to property, plant, and equipment	(13,500)
Net cash flow from (used for) investing activities	(13,500)
Financing activities	
Proceeds from issuance of stock	30,000
Repaid principal owed on long-term debt	(15,000)
Cash paid for other dividends	(5,700)
Net cash flow from financing activities	9,300
Increase (decrease) in cash and cash equivalents	39,000
Cash and cash equivalents, December 1	27,000
Cash and cash equivalents, December 31	$66,000

2. Use the statement of cash flows to evaluate Douglas' cash flows.

Douglas appears to be doing quite well. The vast majority of its cash is provided from operating activities. Some cash was obtained by issuing more stock. However, with these sources of cash they were able to purchase additional property, plant, and equipment, pay dividends, and (more importantly) pay down current debt.

Exercise 12-7. Computing Cash Flows from Operating Activities (Direct Method) (LO2b)

Cash collected from customers ($150,000 + $3,000)	$153,000
Cash paid to suppliers ($91,500 – $9,000 – $4,500)	(78,000)
Cash paid for operating expenses ($40,500 – $9,000 + $300)	(31,800)
Net cash flow from operating activities	$ 43,200

Exercise 12-8. Calculating and Interpreting the Capital Acquisitions Ratio, Cash Coverage Ratio, and Quality of Income Ratio (LO6, 7, 8)

1. a. Calculate the average capital acquisitions ratio for the period covering 2003 – 2005.

   Cash flow from operating activities (27,000 + 23,000 + 18,000) = 68,000
   Purchases of Property, Plant, and Equipment (85,000 +50,000 +40,000) = 175,000
   68,000 / 175,000 = .389

   b. What does the ratio tell you about the company's need for using external financing to replace property, plant, and equipment?

   This indicates that the company probably had to seek outside sources of financing in order to purchase long-term assets.

2. a. Calculate the cash coverage ratio for Butterfly Bowling Equipment for each of the three years.

   2005: (27,000 + 15,000 + 27,000) / 15,000 = 4.600
   2004: (23,000 + 11,000 + 25,000) / 11,000 = 5.364
   2003: (18,000 + 8,000 + 21,000) / 8,000 = 5.875

   b. What do these ratios tell you about the company's ability to pay its interest costs?

   The company's ability to cover interest costs has been decreasing. The company has invested in equipment heavily and has apparently financed most of it by incurring additional debt rather than issuing stock. If things don't pick up, this could be a tricky situation for Butterfly.

3. a. Compute the quality of income ratio for each of the three years:

   2005: 27,000 / 81,000 = .333
   2004: 23,000 / 76,000 = .303
   2003: 18,000 / 65,000 = .277

   b. What does the ratio tell you about the company's accrual of revenues and/or deferral of expenses?

   It appears as if the company is attempting to fudge net income because income is steadily increasing over time, but the quality of income ratio is declining steadily. If expense payments and cash receipts were in line with revenue and expense reported on the income statement, these numbers would remain consistent.

ORGANIZATION OF THE CHAPTER

Understand the business	**Study the accounting methods**	**Evaluate the results**	**Review the chapter**
- Trend and ratio analysis	- Calculating trends - Calculating ratios	- Interpreting trends and ratios - Underlying accounting Decisions and concepts	- Demonstration case -Chapter summary - Key terms - Practice material

CHAPTER FOCUS SUGGESTIONS

Review
Well, we're down to the home stretch! You've just crammed tons of accounting information into your brain from Chapters 1 – 12, and I'll bet you can hardly *wait* until you're through. It's been a challenging and, at times, amusing journey. Now we're ready to pull everything together!

Introduction
This chapter essentially reviews all of the ratios, principles, assumptions, and constraints you've learned throughout the text. We're now ready to measure and evaluate the financial performance of a company using all the tools we've learned to this point.

You need to know three things before you can properly evaluate a business: (1) the general *categories* used to evaluate the company, (2) the particular *elements* to consider within each category, and (3) how performance for each element is measured. The financial *categories* measure profitability, liquidity, and solvency. The *elements* of these categories come from information contained in the financial statements, and they are typically *measured* with ratios calculated from information contained in the financial statements.

Once these tools for measuring and evaluating a company are presented to you, a framework for organizing all of the ratios you've learned throughout this course will be presented. Finally, we'll see how financial results of a business relate to its stock prices, and we'll review key accounting concepts useful for evaluating a company and predicting its future financial performance.

UNDERSTAND THE BUSINESS

> **Learning Objective 1**
> Describe the purposes and uses of trend and ratio analyses.

Trend and Ratio Analysis
The two techniques that will be used to evaluate financial performance are (1) trend analysis, and (2) ratio analysis. Trend analysis compares individual financial statement line-items over time, with the general goal of identifying significant, sustained changes (trends). They are described in dollar amounts as well as year-over-year percentages.

The second technique is ratio analysis. This involves comparing amounts for one or more financial statement items to amounts for other items within the same year. This type of analysis considers differences in the amounts being compared so that you can evaluate how well a company has performed *given the current level of other company resources.*

Most analysts classify ratios into three categories of performance:
(1) Profitability – evaluates performance in the *current period,* especially its ability to generate income during the period.
(2) Liquidity – evaluates the company's ability to survive in the *short-term.* Emphasis is on the company's ability to use current assets to repay liabilities as they become due in the short-term.
(3) Solvency – evaluates the company's ability to survive in the *long*-run. The focus is on whether the company can repay lender when debt matures, and make interest payments on the debt prior to maturity.

None of these analyses or ratios mean anything unless the user can interpret the information in a way that allows them to understand and evaluate a company's financial results. To that end, we will be categorizing the ratios as either profitability, liquidity, or solvency.

STUDY THE ACCOUNTING METHODS

Calculating Trends

Trend analysis involves examining changes in each line of the financial statements over time. It is also known as **horizontal analysis** (because it compares horizontally across each financial statement line item) or **time-series analysis** (because it does the comparison over a series of time periods.) Either way, it is usually calculated in terms of year-over-year percentage changes. A year-over-year percentage change simply shows the dollar change of the current year as a percentage of the previous year's total. It is calculated like this:

$$\text{Year-over-year Change (\%)} = \frac{\text{Change this year}}{\text{Prior years' total}} \times 100 = \frac{(\text{Current year's total} - \text{prior year's total})}{\text{Prior year's total}} \times 100$$

For example, assume sales for this year are $130,000 and they were $100,000 in the prior year. The $30,000 increase ($130,000 − $100,000) could be described as a year-over-year increase of 30% ($30,000 / $100,000) X 100

Using the financial statements for Douglas Company, below, horizontal analysis has been performed for the year 2009. The two right-hand columns provide the dollar amount of the change and the percentage change for each item on both the income statement and the balance sheet.

	2010	2009	2008	2010 Amount	2010 Amount
Balance sheet at December 31					
Cash	$ 66,000	$ 27,000	$ 26,000	+39,000	+144.4%
Accounts receivable	40,500	43,500	38,000	–3,000	–6.9%
Merchandise inventory	45,000	54,000	32,000	–9,000	–16.7%
Total Current Assets	151,500	124,500	96,000	+27,000	+21.7%
Property and equipment	166,500	153,000	144,000	+13,500	+8.8%
Less: Accumulated depreciation	(54,000)	(45,000)	(40,000)	+9,000	+20.0%
	$264,000	$232,500	$ 200,000	+31,500	+13.5%
Accounts payable	$ 37,500	$ 33,000	$ 39,000	+4,500	+13.6%
Wages payable	1,200	1,500	1,000	–300	–20.0%
Current Liabilities	38,700	34,500	40,000	+4,200	+12.2%
Note payable, long-term	57,000	72,000	50,000	–15,000	–20.8%
Contributed capital	120,000	90,000	83,000	+30,000	+33.3%
Retained earnings	48,300	36,000	27,000	+12,300	+34.2%
	$264,000	$232,500	$ 200,000	+31,500	+13.5%
Income statement for the Year Ended December 31					
Sales	$150,000	$ 125,000	$100,000	+25,000	+20.0%
Cost of goods sold	91,500	75,000	58,000	+16,500	+22.0%
Gross Profit	58,500	50,000	42,000	+8,500	+17.0%
Interest Expense	5,000	7,000	4,500	–2,000	–28.6%
Other expenses	31,000	26,000	21,000	+5,000	+19.2%
Income tax expense	4,500	3,000	2,900	+1,500	+50.0%
Net income	$ 18,000	$ 14,000	$ 13,600	+4,000	+28.6%

Using the formula for the year-over-year change (%), the calculations for cash and accounts receivable are: (the remaining calculations are performed in the same manner.)

Cash:
2010 Amount = $66,000 – $27,000 = 39,000 increase over the previous year.
2010 Percent = +$39,000 / $27,000 * 100 = +144.4% (all percentages are rounded to the nearest tenth of a percent.)

Accounts Receivable:
2010 Amount = $40,500 – $43,500= $3,000 decrease over the previous year.
2010 Percent = ‾$3,000 / $43,500 * 100 = ‾6.9%

Overall, there has been an increase in net assets, the bulk of it coming from an increase in inventories. It appears as if most of the company's with additional long-term debt.

Calculating Ratios

A number of ratios were presented in previous chapters. Here we will be reviewing them, grouping them into the appropriate category (profitability, liquidity, or solvency), and analyzing each, using the financial statements of Douglas company that were used in the demonstration of horizontal analysis. In addition, the statement of cash flows for Douglas Company is presented here because of additional ratios that will use its information.

DOUGLAS COMPANY
Statement of Cash Flows
For the Year Ended December 31

	2010	2009	2008
Operating activities			
Net Income	$ 18,000	$ 14,000	$13,600
Depreciation Expense	9,000	5,000	7,000
Increase/Decrease in Accts. Receivable	3,000	(5,500)	(4,000)
Increase/Decrease in Inventory	9,000	(22,000)	(12,000)
Increase/Decrease in Accounts Payable	4,500	(6,000)	4,000
Increase/Decrease in Wages Payable	(300)	500	(500)
Net cash flow from operating activities	43,200	(14,000)	8,100
Investing activities			
Additions to PPE	(13,500)	(9,000)	(3,000)
Net cash flow from investing activities	(13,500)	(9,000)	(3,000)
Financing activities			
Proceeds from issuance of stock	30,000	7,000	0
Proceeds from long-term debt	0	32,000	20,000
Principal paid on long-term debt	(15,000)	(10,000)	(8,000)
Cash paid for dividends	(5,700)	(5,000)	(4,000)
Net cash flow from financing activities	9,300	24,000	8,000
Increase (decrease) in cash	39,000	1,000	13,100
Cash, December 1	27,000	26,000	12,900
Cash, December 31	$66,000	$ 27,000	$26,000

Note that horizontal analysis has not been provided for the Statement of Cash flows, but the ratios could be derived using the year-over-year formula.

Some of the ratios we will be presenting compare one amount to another larger amount on the same financial statement. These are 'standard' ratios because they frequently reveal important observations about each financial statement. However, other important relationships can be drawn from this type of comparison. Analysts refer to this type of comparison as **vertical analysis.** This analysis expresses each financial statement amount as a percentage of another amount on that financial statement. Vertical analysis of Douglas Company's income statement for 2009 and 2010 are shown here as an example.

	2010	2009	2008	2010 %	2009 %
Income statement for the Year Ended December 31					
Sales	$150,000	$125,000	$100,000	100.0%	100.0%
Cost of goods sold	91,500	75,000	58,000	61.0%	60.0%
Gross Profit	58,500	50,000	42,000	39.0%	40.0%
Interest Expense	5,000	7,000	4,500	3.3%	5.6%
Other expenses	31,000	26,000	21,000	20.7%	20.8%
Income tax expense	4,500	3,000	2,900	3.0%	2.4%
Net income	$ 18,000	$ 14,000	$ 13,600	12.0%	11.2%

All income statement ratios are calculated with net sales as the bottom figure in the calculation, and the number being compared to net sales as the top figure in the calculation. The calculations for Cost of Goods Sold and Gross Profit for each year are presented here. The other figures can be calculated in the same manner.

Cost of Goods Sold:
2010 Percent = $91,500 / $150,000 * 100 = 61.0% of net sales for 2010
2009 Percent = $75,000 / $125,000 * 100 = 60.0% of net sales for 2009

Gross Profit:
2010 Percent = $58,500 / $150,000 * 100 = 39.0% of net sales for 2010
2009 Percent = $50,000 / $125,000 * 100 = 40.0% of net sales for 2009

Ratios can be used a couple of ways: (1) they can be calculated each year and them compared *across* years to identify trends that may not have been revealed analyzing the line-items on the financial statements, or (2) they can be compared to other close competitors or to the industry as a whole. Your text focuses primarily on comparisons to close competitors. Industry averages include all shapes, sizes, and types of businesses within the industry, so they may not be useful for our purposes.

EVALUATE THE RESULTS

Interpreting Trends and Ratios
Trends Revealed in Horizontal Analysis

> **Learning Objective 3**
> Interpret the results of trend and ratio analyses.

Douglas Company appears to have grown significantly from 2008 to 2009. At the same time short-term liabilities have increased, indicating some difficulty paying off current liabilities as it grows. This is not unusual for a growing company. While some of the growth has been internally generated (via increased retained earnings) and stockholder investments, the bulk of the increase has been financed with long-term debt. While net income has increased, it hasn't increased nearly as much as sales and cost of goods sold. This is something that should be watched carefully as the company continues to grow.

Note: For each ratio presented, the calculation for 2010 will be presented. See if you can determine how the ratios were calculated for 2009, and 2008.

1. *Profitability Ratios*
Follow these steps for every transaction you analyze:

a) *Net Profit Margin* – This measures the percentage of sales revenue that becomes net income.

Year Ended December 31		2010	2009	2008
Net Profit Margin =	$\dfrac{\text{Net Income}}{\text{Net Sales}}$	12.0% *	11.2%	13.6%

* $18,000 / $150,000 x 100 = 12.0%

While a 12% profit margin is certainly nothing to sneeze at, Douglas has experienced a steady decline in profit margin since 2008 when it boasted a 13.6% profit margin. At this point, we only know the margin has declined, but have no solid reasons as to why it has declined. For further enlightenment, let's look at the next ratio.

b) **Gross Profit Percentage** – This measures how much profit is made on sales *after* deducting cost of goods sold, but *before* deducting any other expenses.

Year Ended December 31		2010	2009	2008
Gross Profit Percentage =	$\dfrac{\text{Net sales} - \text{Cost of goods sold}}{\text{Net Sales}}$	39.0% *	40.0%	42.0%

* $58,500 / $150,000 x 100% = 39.0%

Ah, yes! Things are a bit clearer now. Nearly the entire decline in net income can be explained by the nearly identical percentage decline shown in the gross profit percentage. We know that three types of expenses are subtracted from revenues in determining net income: Cost of goods sold, Operating Expenses, and 'Other' Expenses. Since gross profit is the result of net sales less cost of goods sold (the first expense type mentioned), it seems clear that the bulk of the decline in net income is a direct result of increases in cost of goods sold.

c) **Asset Turnover** – This ratio indicates the amount of sales revenue generated for each dollar invested in assets.

Year Ended December 31		2010	2009	2008
Asset Turnover =	$\dfrac{\text{Net sales}}{\text{Average total assets}}$	0.60 *	0.58	0.67**

*$150,000 / [($264,000 + $232,500)/2].
**   Assume net fixed assets of $100,000 for 2007

Douglas shows an inefficient use of assets in generating sales. It declined in 2009 and only increased a small amount in 2010. This indicates that assets aren't working very well at producing revenues. Perhaps Douglas purchased additional assets in anticipation of increased sales or maybe they purchased too many assets for the market.

d) **Fixed Asset Turnover** – This ratio shows how much the company generates in sales for each dollar invested in fixed assets.

Year Ended December 31		2010	2009	2008
Fixed Asset Turnover =	$\dfrac{\text{Net sales}}{\text{Average net fixed assets}}$	1.36 *	1.18	0.98**

*$150,000 / [($112,500 + $108,000)/2]. "Net fixed assets" refers to Property, Plant, and Equipment less Accumulated depreciation
**   Assume total assets of $170,000 for 2007

This ratio has fluctuated a bit since 2008. But, it makes sense if we assume Douglas anticipated the growth in sales and began building up its fixed assets in order to accommodate this growth. The ratio was very low in 2008 (before the growth spurt) and higher in 2009 when the anticipated sales increases began to occur. In 2010, the fixed assets turnover ratio is even higher indicating that continued growth may be anticipated.

e) **Return on Equity (ROE)** – This ratio compares the amount of net income to average stockholders' equity. It presents the net amount earned this period as a percentage of each dollar contributed (by stockholders) and retained in the business.

Year Ended December 31		2010	2009	2008
Return on equity =	$\dfrac{\text{Net income}}{\text{Average stockholders' equity}}$	12.23% *	11.86%	12.95% **

* 18,000 / [(168,300 + 126,000)/2].   ** Assume stockholders equity of $100,000 for 2007

ROE is steadily decreasing. This is the result of two things: (1) net income has declined so there is less income available to 'retain' in the business via retained earnings. The company has increased its dividend payment every year, thus keeping a smaller amount of net income in the business for growth purposes. (2)

There are a larger number of shares outstanding than there were in 2008. So, the return on each share of stock is less than it would have been if more shares had not been issued.

f) **Earnings Per Share (EPS)** – This indicates the amount of earnings generated for each share of common stock. (Note: Assume all common stock has a par value of $1 and that there was no additional paid-in capital.)

Year Ended December 31		2010	2009	2008
Earnings per share =	$\dfrac{\text{Net Income}}{\text{Average \# of shrs outstanding}}$	.1714 *	.1618	.1639**

* 18,000 / [(120,000 + 90,000)/2].   ** Assume any new shares were issued on January 1 and no new shares issued in 2007

The ROE shown previously was showing a steady decline. This may seem odd, but ROE is based on *total* stockholders' equity, and EPS focuses on the earnings of *each individual share of stock*. The bulk of the increase in stockholders' equity was net income ($13,600; $14,000; and $18,000) in 2008, 2009, and 2010 respectively. Whereas, very little common stock was issued until 2006, when 30,000 shares were issued. Even with the increased number of shares, there's been no dilution in earnings because profits increased enough to maintain (an even exceed) EPS in previous years. If Douglas can keep this up, they'll have some very happy stockholders!

g) **Quality of Income** – This shows how well operating cash flows (from the SCF) relates to net income.

Year Ended December 31		2010	2009	2008
Quality of Income =	$\dfrac{\text{Net cash from operations}}{\text{Net Income}}$	2.40 *	(1.00)	.60

* 43,200/18,000

On paper this company looks great! But, when the discussion turns to actual cash flows, there appears to be a completely different story! Notice that the ratio is wildly inconsistent over the three year period. This starkly contrasts with the ratios calculated thus far. Every profitability ratio calculated looks fabulous and investors and creditors are gleefully ready to jump in! But, if this ratio were calculated, the picture might not look so rosy.

Recall from Chapter 12, when this ratio was introduced, that some managers manipulate the timing of revenue and expense recognition to boost income figures. All other things equal, a higher quality of income ratio indicates a higher likelihood that revenues are being realized in cash and that expenses are associated with cash outflows. Major deviations should be investigated. Now, this doesn't mean that Douglas is doing any hanky-panky. There were four reasons offered in Chapter 12 that could explain deviations: (1) Seasonality—probably not a concern; (2) The corporate life cycle (growth in sales)—probably not a concern; (3) Changes in management of operating activities—maybe/maybe not a concern, and (4) Changes in revenue and expense recognition—a big concern.

h) **Price/Earnings (P/E) Ratio** – This ratio relates the company's stock price to EPS.

Year Ended December 31		2010	2009	2008
Price/Earnings =	$\dfrac{\text{Stock Price}}{\text{EPS}}$	70.01 *	61.80	48.81

* 12/.1714 Assume stock prices per share in 2008, 2009, and 2010 were $12, $10, and $8, respectively.

On paper this company looks great! But, when the discussion turns to actual cash flows, there appears to be a completely different story! Notice that the ratio is wildly inconsistent over the three year period. This starkly contrasts with the ratios calculated thus far. Every profitability ratio calculated looks fabulous and investors and creditors are gleefully ready to jump in! But, if this ratio were calculated, the picture might not look so rosy.

Without additional information about our fictitious company, it is difficult to determine anything. However, if this were a company in the middle of a huge growth period, this is probably not a big deal.

The big concern is: *Is management manipulating income?* Let's save discussion on that until we've done a bit more analysis.

2. *Liquidity Ratios*
This section focuses on the ability of the company to survive in the short-term.

i) **Receivables Turnover** – Measures the number of time (on average) the process of selling and collecting on sales is repeated. The higher the ratio, the faster the collection of receivables.

Year Ended December 31	2010	2009	2008
Receivables Turnover = $\dfrac{\text{Net sales}}{\text{Average net receivables}}$	3.57 *	3.07	2.56 **

* 150,000 / [(40,500 + 43,500)/2]   ** Assume net receivables for 2007 are $40,000

This is a little easier to evaluate if we convert it into Days to Collect (365 / receivables turnover.) This shows us the following for 2008, 2009, and 2010 respectively: 142.57 days, 118.89 days, and 102.24 days. Hmmm. Now it looks like (1) either Douglas Company has no control over receivables, (2) it is fraudulently generating fictitious sales, or (3) it operates a seasonal business. A huge clue that would help tremendously in our evaluation is: what sales terms does this company offer? If the terms are 2/10, n/30. Boy, are they in trouble! But, if this is a seasonal business, it may offer its customer extremely liberal terms, allowing payment within three to six months. If this is the case, there's probably not a problem. Let's keep going before we analyze any more. But, your radar should be humming right now! Eyebrows should be raised, questions being asked, and big decisions may come to bear…soon!

j) **Inventory Turnover** – This measures how frequently inventory is bought and sold during the year. A higher turnover indicates that inventory moves more quickly from purchase to the ultimate customer.

Year Ended December 31	2010	2009	2008
Inventory turnover = $\dfrac{\text{Cost of goods sold}}{\text{Average inventory}}$	1.85 *	1.74	1.71 **

* 91,500 / [(45,000 + 54,000)/2]   ** Assume inventory for 2007 is $36,000

Like the receivables turnover, let's convert this ratio into Days to Sell (365 / inventory turnover). For 2008, 2009, and 2010, respectively, the days to sell are: 213.45 days; 209.77 days; 197.30 days. Boy, these numbers don't look so great. Either these guys have tons of 'pet rocks' and 'cabbage patch dolls' gathering dust in inventory, or they sell something that remains in inventory for an incredibly long time. Maybe they sell 40-foot yachts in the desert or something…hey, it could happen!

k) **Current Ratio** – Measures whether a company has enough current assts to pay what it currently owes.

Year Ended December 31	2010	2009	2008
Current ratio = $\dfrac{\text{Current assets}}{\text{Current liabilities}}$	3.91 *	3.61	2.40

* 151,500/38,700

At first glance, the current ratios for 2008, 2009, and 2010 look fabulous! But, remember that this is a potentially misleading measure of liquidity if significant funds are tied up in assets that are not easily converted into cash. This company appears to have a large amount of slow-moving inventory. Inventory represents 30% – 40% of this company's current assets. That's a pretty significant chunk! We've already indicated earlier that there might be a problem in collecting receivables too slowly as well. Two major components of current assets *may be* a concern here, especially since together, they represent over 70% of current assets in 2008 and 2009, and approximately 56% in 2010! This is something that really needs to be closely scrutinized. Let's move on to the solvency ratios.

3. *Solvency Ratios*
This section covers how well the company is positioned for long-term survival, by analyzing its ability to repay debts when they come due, pay interest on that date until it *does* mature, and to finance the purchase or replacement of long-lived assets.

l) ***Debt-to-Assets*** – This shows what proportion of total assets are financed by creditors (debt.) As indicated earlier, *debt must be repaid* regardless of how the company fares performance-wise.

Year Ended December 31		2010	2009	2008
Debt-to-assets =	Total liabilities / Total assets	36.25% *	45.81%	45.00%

* 95,700/264,000

Since 2008, total assets financed by debt has actually decreased nearly 10% (from 45.00% to 36.25%.) This indicates that by 2010, the majority of assets were financed through stockholders' equity (63.75%) rather than debt (36.25%.) This looks promising for Douglas Company. Not only has it expanded over the past three years, but it has financed the majority of its assets using internally generated funds or by issuing stock.

m) ***Times Interest Earned*** – This indicates how many times interest is covered by accrual basis operating results.

Year Ended December 31		2010	2009	2008
Times interest earned =	Net Income + interest expense + income tax expense / Interest expense	5.50 *	3.43	4.67

* (18,000 + 5,000 + 4,500) / 5,000

While this ratio has fluctuated a bit, it shows a consistent ability to easily cover its interest charges. This is especially great news considering that it borrowed additional funds in two of the three years presented, so interest charges have certainly increased. In 2010, it rated its highest ratio of the three year period, indicating that the company appears to have no problem generating enough income to cover its future interest charges.

n) ***Cash Coverage Ratio*** – This ratio also indicates how many times interest is covered by operating results. However, this ratio compares the *cash generated* from the company's operating activities, to its *cash payments* for interest. It should be noted that Interest paid = Interest expense and Income Taxes paid = Income Tax expense. This is due to the fact that there are no beginning/ending interest payables or income taxes payable. Therefore, all interest and income taxes incurred this period must have also been paid this period.

Year Ended December 31		2010	2009	2008
Cash coverage ratio =	Net cash from operations + interest paid + income taxes paid / Interest paid	10.54 *	(.57)	3.44

* (43,200 + 5,000 + 4,500) / 5,000

Once again, where Cash is concerned, this company is all over the place! 2008 shows a respectable 3.44 ratio. But, 2009 showed a negative .57; then a huge increase again in 2010. Assuming this yo-yo effect was a one-time blip, there's probably no problem. It could be the company is just starting out and needs to infuse itself with cash to get rolling. That isn't unusual for a company trying to get on its feet. However, it could be a signal that the company that can't properly control cash inflows and outflows and must constantly obtain cash from outside sources (debt and equity financing) to keep itself afloat. Without more information, it is difficult to tell which scenario this company fits.

o) ***Capital Acquisitions Ratio*** – This measures the extent to which purchases of PPE are financed from operating activities (without the need for external financing.)

Year Ended December 31		2010	2009	2008
Capital acquisitions ratio =	Net cash from operations / Cash paid for PPE	3.20 *	(1.56)	2.70

* 43,200 / 13,500

Seems this is just the ratio we needed to verify or disprove the assumptions we made with the cash coverage ratio. Again, the yo-yo effect should make you a bit leery about what's happening in this company. Some companies have a tendency to get caught up in whirlwind growth and don't realize they've grown beyond their means until it's too late. Whether this is what is occurring with the company is not immediately known. But, I'd hold off and watch this company for another year or two and see how things develop.

Underlying Accounting Decisions and Concepts

Consideration must be given, not only to *accounting* issues but, to differences in business strategy and business operations. In comparing ratios with another company, it is also important to consider: (1) are their accounting policies similar?

> **Learning Objective 4**
> Describe how trend and ratio analysis depend on key accounting decisions and concepts.

The notes to the financial statements are a veritable gold mine of information for this type of analysis. This is where you look to find significant accounting policies such as the: inventory costing methods used, depreciation methods used, etc. Unless inventory is a huge part of total assets, inventory costing methods are probably not going to cause significant differences in operating results. Depreciation methods can have a big impact on financial statements if useful lives are short, depreciation is a significant expense on the income statements, or depreciable assets are major portion of a company's assets (i.e. high-tech equipment, etc.)

An important aspect of all this analysis is that: *analyzing financial statements* and *predicting stock prices* are two completely different things. The information in this chapter simply provides users with analytical tools to help them *evaluate* management's effectiveness. Predicting stock prices represents an effort to put a dollar *value* on the overall company. This requires a whole new set of tools, and another level of skill!

Accounting Concepts

Remember way back, at the beginning of the book, you learned that financial statements should be *useful for evaluating performance and predicting the future performance of a company*. It was with this goal in mind that a *conceptual framework* for accounting was developed. The following table lists the conceptual framework for accounting.

Objective:	To provide useful financial information to external users for decision-making	
Characteristics of Useful financial information:	–Relevance	–Comparability
	–Reliability	–Consistency
Elements:	Assets, liabilities, Stockholders' Equity, Revenues, Expenses	
Principles:	Cost, Revenue Recognition, Matching, Full Disclosure	
Constraints:	Cost-benefit, Materiality, Industry practices, Conservatism	

The primary objective of financial accounting is to provide useful financial information for people external to a company to use in making decisions about a company. To be useful information must be:

- Relevant – the information matters for making the decision at-hand.
- Reliable – the information can be trusted.
- Comparable – everyone is following the same rules so we can compare them to one another.
- Consistent – the rules don't change from one period to the next.

There are four concepts that have not yet been introduced in the text. So, let's take a couple of minutes to briefly introduce each.

- ***Going-concern assumption*** – (also called the continuity assumption) assumes that a business will be capable of continuing its operations long enough to realize its recorded assets and meet its obligations in the normal course of business. Basically, this just means that the business will not be declaring bankruptcy any time soon. Here are some of the factors that contribute to going-concern problems:

Revealed by Financial Analyses	Revealed by Other Analyses
▪ Declining sales	▪ Overdependence on one customer
▪ Declining gross margin	▪ Insufficient product innovation/quality
▪ Significant on-time expenses	▪ Significant barriers to expansion
▪ Fluctuating net income	▪ Loss of key personnel without replacement
▪ Insufficient current assets	▪ Inability to negotiate favorable purchases
▪ Excessive reliance on debt financing	▪ Inadequate maintenance of long-lived assets
▪ Adverse financial commitments	▪ Loss of a key patent

- *Full Disclosure* – states that the financial statements should present information needed to understand the financial results of the company's activities. Though it doesn't mean that every transaction needs to be explained, it does require that adequate information be presented to allow financial statement users to interpret the reports fairly.
- *Industry Practices* – This recognizes that some industries have such special circumstances that they need to use accounting rules that differ from what most companies use (e.g. financial services, oil and gas, etc.)
- *Cost-Benefit* – This recognizes that obtaining accurate, up-to-date information for a business is expensive. The rules set forth by GAAP, therefore, should only be implemented to the extent that the benefits outweigh the costs of following such rules. For example, if your cash account is off by $2.00 and it would cost you $25.00 to pay your accountant to fine the discrepancy, it is not worth the cost of being that accurate. This is especially true considering that whether this error is corrected or not, it would not impact the decisions made by financial statement users.

SUPPLEMENT A – NON-RECURRING AND OTHER SPECIAL ITEMS

Non-Recurring Items
Recently, new accounting standards have nearly eliminated income statement reporting requirements that had been in place for many, many years. Items referred to as *extraordinary items* and *cumulative effect of the change* are no longer reported in the same manner they once were. The definition of extraordinary items has become so restricted that few events qualify as extraordinary. Cumulative effect of the change is now reported as an adjustment to Retained Earnings. However, the following items are still reported on the income statement.

Discontinued Operations
Discontinued Operations occur when a company abandons or sells a major component of its business resulting in a Gain or Loss on Disposal of the discontinued operation, as well as any operating income (or loss) generated during the current year prior to its disposal. These items are shown *after or below income tax expense on the income statement*, so the income (or loss) from this component of the business and its resulting gain or loss on disposal must be shown on the income statement *net of any corresponding tax effects*.

Other Special Items
Comprehensive Income represents gains or losses from changes in the value of certain balance sheet accounts. These include gains/losses from changes in foreign currency exchange rates, and certain investment valuations. These gains/losses have not 'really' occurred yet, so the effects may be here today-gone tomorrow. Because they haven't actually occurred, these items are often omitted when calculating profitability ratios. Because of the complexity of this topic, further discussion is deferred to an Intermediate Accounting course.

REVIEW THE CHAPTER

Chapter Summary
LO1. Describe the purposes and uses of trend and ratio analyses
- ❖ Trend analyses compare financial statement items to comparable amount in prior periods
  - o The goal is to identify sustained changes ("trends")
- ❖ Ratio analyses compare one or more financial statement items to an amount for other items for the same year

- o Ratios take into account differences in the size of amounts to allow for evaluations of performance given the existing levels of other company resources
- ❖ When comparing over time and across companies, watch for possible differences in the following items which can affect reported financial results:
  - o Business Strategy
  - o Operations
  - o Accounting policies
  - o Non-recurring events

LO2. Calculate financial trends and ratios
- ❖ Trend analyses (also called horizontal analyses) involve
  - o Computing the dollar amount by which each account changes from one period to the next, and
  - o Expressing that change as a percentage of the balance for the prior year
- ❖ Financial ratios are commonly classified as relating to profitability, liquidity, or solvency.
  - o Profitability ratios focus on measuring the adequacy of income by comparing it to other items reported on the financial statements
  - o Liquidity ratios measure a company's ability to meet its current maturing debt
  - o Solvency ratios measure a company's ability to meet its long-term obligations
- ❖ A list of these ratios and how to compute them is contained in the Financial Analysis Tools section of this Study Guide
- ❖ Financial ratios also include vertical analysis (also called common size)which
  - o Expresses each line of
    - ▪ The income statement as a percentage of net sales
    - ▪ The balance sheet as a percentage of total assets

LO3. Interpret the results of trend and ratio analyses.
- ❖ Trend and ratio analyses are not complete unless they lead to an interpretation that helps financial statement users understand and evaluate a company's financial results.
- ❖ An understanding of whether a business is successful emerges only after you have learned to combine trend and ratio analyses into a complete picture or story that depicts the company's performance.
- ❖ To assist in developing this picture or story, most analysts compare to benchmarks such as
  - o The company's performance in prior years or
  - o To competitors' performance in the current year

LO4. Describe how trend and ratio analyses depend on key accounting decisions and concepts.
- ❖ Before comparing across companies or time periods, users should determine the extent to which difference in accounting decisions might reduce comparability or consistency of the financial information being compared.
  - o Accounting decisions in this context refers to the methods used to account for:
    - ▪ Inventory costing
    - ▪ Fixed asset depreciation
    - ▪ Contingent liabilities
    - ▪ Etc.
- ❖ Many accounting concepts were presented throughout earlier chapters, all of which aim to make accounting information more useful to creditors and investors. Four new concepts were explained in this chapter:
  - o Going concern (continuity) assumption – it is assumed that a business will continue to operate into the foreseeable future
  - o Full disclosure principle—a company's financial statements should provide all information that is important to users' decisions
  - o Industry practices constraint—general purpose accounting rules may not apply equally to all industries, recognizing that some industries may use industry-specific measurements and reporting practices
  - o Cost benefit constraint—accounting rules should be followed to the extent that the benefits to users outweigh the costs of providing the required information

READ AND RECALL QUESTIONS

After you read each section of the chapter, answer the related Read and Recall Questions below.

INTRODUCTION
What three things do you need to know in order to properly measure and evaluate the financial performance of a company?

LEARNING OBJECTIVE
After studying the section of the chapter, you should be able to:
1. Describe the purposes and uses of trend and ratio analyses

Trend and Ratio Analysis
What are the two analytical techniques discussed in this chapter?

What are the three categories of performance that most analysts use to classify ratios? Briefly describe each.

LEARNING OBJECTIVE
After studying the section of the chapter, you should be able to:
2. Calculate the financial trends and ratios

Calculating Trends
Describe the purpose of year-over-year analysis. How is it calculated? What other names is it given?

Calculating Ratios
Briefly define ratio analysis. What are the two primary ways in which ratio analysis is incorporated into financial analysis?

What are the two ways that ratios can be used for evaluation purposes?

LEARNING OBJECTIVE
After studying the section of the chapter, you should be able to:
3. Interpret the results of trend and ratio analyses

Interpreting Trends and Ratios
1. Profitability Ratios:
Define and provide the calculation for each of the following profitability ratios:
Net Profit Margin –

Gross profit percentage –

Asset turnover –

Fixed asset turnover –

Return on equity (ROE) –

Earnings per share –

Quality of income –

Price/Earnings (P/E) Ratio –

2. Liquidity Ratios:

Define and provide the calculation for each of the following liquidity ratios:
Receivables turnover –

Inventory turnover –

Current ratio –

3. Solvency Ratios:

Define and provide the calculation for each of the following solvency ratios:
Debt-to-assets –

Times interest earned –

Cash coverage ratio –

Capital acquisitions ratio –

LEARNING OBJECTIVE
After studying the section of the chapter, you should be able to:
4. Describe how trend and ratio analyses depend on key decisions and concepts

---

Underlying Accounting Decisions and Concepts
What other considerations (besides financial information) should a user consider when comparing companies to one another? Why? Where can some of this information be found?

Accounting Concepts
What is the primary objective of the financial accounting?

List and briefly define the elements of financial statements.
1.

2.

3.

4.

5.

Define the characteristics of *relevance* and *reliability*.

List and briefly define the four accounting principles that are part of the conceptual framework:
1.

2.

3.

4.

List and briefly describe the four constraints that are part of the conceptual framework:
1.

2.

3.

4.

FINANCIAL ANALYSIS TOOLS

1. Here is a listing of the ratios covered in this chapter, how they are calculated, and the chapter they were first introduced in the text.

Ratio		Basic Computation		Chapter
Tests of Profitability:				
a. Net Profit Margin		$\dfrac{\text{Net Income}}{\text{Net Sales Revenue}}$		5
b. Gross Profit Percentage		$\dfrac{\text{Net Sales Revenue} - \text{Cost of Goods Sold}}{\text{Net Sales Revenue}}$		6
c. Asset Turnover		$\dfrac{\text{Net Sales Revenue}}{\text{Average Total Assets}}$		9
d. Fixed Asset Turnover		$\dfrac{\text{Net Sales Revenue}}{\text{Average Net Fixed Assets}}$		11
e. Return on Equity (ROE)		$\dfrac{\text{Net Income}}{\text{Average Stockholders' Equity}}$		11
f. Earnings per Share (EPS)		$\dfrac{\text{Net Income}}{\text{Average Number of Shares of Common Stock Outstanding}}$		11
g. Quality of Income		$\dfrac{\text{Net Cash Flows From Operating Activities}}{\text{Net Income}}$		12
h. Price/Earnings Ratio (P/E)		$\dfrac{\text{Stock Price per Share}}{\text{EPS}}$		12
Test of Liquidity:				
i. Receivables Turnover		$\dfrac{\text{Net Credit Sales}}{\text{Average Net Receivables}}$		7
j. Inventory Turnover		$\dfrac{\text{Cost of Goods Sold}}{\text{Average Inventory}}$		8
k. Current Ratio		$\dfrac{\text{Current Assets}}{\text{Current Liabilities}}$		10
Tests of Solvency:				
l. Debt-to-Assets		$\dfrac{\text{Total Liabilities}}{\text{Total Assets}}$		5
m. Times Interest Earned		$\dfrac{\text{Net Income} + \text{Interest Expense} + \text{Income Tax Expense}}{\text{Interest Expense}}$		10

n. Cash Coverage Ratio	$$\frac{\text{Net Cash Flows from Operating Activities + Interest Paid}}{\text{Interest Paid}}$$	12
o. Capital Acquisitions Ratio	$$\frac{\text{Net Cash Flows from Operating Activities}}{\text{Net Cash Paid for Property, Plant, and Equipment}}$$	12

HELPFUL STUDY TIP

1. There are fifteen ratios in this chapter! That's a freaking lot of ratios to learn! So, here's the deal. Let the ratio tell you how it's calculated! That's right! With most of the ratios, *the name of the ratio is* actually its calculation. Before getting into the specifics, there are a couple of little things that need to be understood first.

   - Every ratio (without exception) is some sort of division. That is, some number is always divided by some other number. You're probably thinking, duh? Hello! Everyone knows that! However, I bring it up because it is critical to understanding the first little hint! The names of some ratios not only tell you what two numbers you need for the calculation, but they actually tell you which number goes on the top and which number goes on the bottom. There are two ratios with this distinction (both are hyphenated too!): The Debt-to-Assets Ratio and the Price-Earnings Ratio. With each of these ratios, the first 'name' is the top number in the division and the second name is the bottom number in the division. We only have to figure out the name of the other account that is affected.

     o Debt-to-Assets: Debt is the first word so "DEBT" goes on the top of the calculation. You know it must be TOTAL DEBT because it doesn't say anything in the name like "current" or "long-term". The second word is ASSETS so ASSETS goes on the bottom of the calculation. Again, it is TOTAL ASSETS because it doesn't mention any other kind. So, Total Debt / Total Assets!

     o Price-Earnings Ratio: Price is the first word, so PRICE is the top part of the calculation. Earnings is the second word, so EARNINGS goes on the bottom. This one is a bit tricky because there's LOTS of earnings stuff. BUT, the only PRICE you'll find is the market price PER SHARE of the stock. So, logically, the bottom number must also be PER SHARE...EARNINGS. So, it is simply Price Per Share / Earnings Per Share!

   - Ok. Next thing. This is mostly for profitability ratios. Certain 'words' in the ratio name are telling you that the ratio uses NET INCOME for the top number. Look for the following words in the name of the ratio (it must be the EXACT word, not a variation of it!): EARNINGS or NET PROFIT. We'll start with the ones that have 'earnings' in the name.

     o Earnings per Share: We already know that NET INCOME must be the top number because of the word 'earnings' in the name of the ratio. We just need to figure out what goes on the bottom. Per means 'each.' Like miles per gallon...how many miles do you get from *each* gallon. So, we just need to know how much earning do you get for each share. So, simply divide by all the 'eligible' common shares out there (remember treasury shares get nothing)! Net Income / Common Shares Outstanding.

     o Net Profit Margin: Again, NET INCOME is the top number. This one is a bit 'out there' because there aren't many hints about what goes on the bottom. But, all net profits (or net income) start from one huge number: Net Sales. Just try to remember: Net / Net. Net Profit / Net Sales.

       ▪ While we're on the Net Sales, I want to try to sneak another calculation in here. There's another ratio with the word PROFIT in it. Only it isn't NET profit, its GROSS profit. Since they're so similar, I wanted to cover it here. Use the exact same calculation that you did for NET PROFIT margin, just substitute GROSS PROFIT for the NET PROFIT number. It then becomes: Gross Profit / Net Sales!

   - Here's a fun one! Look for all the ratios that have the word "Turnover" in them. Anytime you see the word 'turnover' it means that the bottom number will be an average of some kind. The name always tells you the account that needs to be 'averaged' on the bottom (ALWAYS a balance sheet account), then figure out the income statement account it relates to because it goes on the top. Let's look at one and it will make more sense.

- o Receivables Turnover: Based on this name, can you see the account that will be averaged on the bottom? YUP! It's Receivables! You will normally be given beginning and ending accounts receivable, so average these two and put them on the bottom. Now what goes with receivables? SALES! So, that's what goes on the top! We get: Net Sales / Average Receivables
- o Fixed Asset Turnover: We sure know what gets averaged on the bottom here: Fixed Assets. The tricky part is to make sure it's NET fixed assets, meaning we need to subtract accumulated depreciation. The top number is the same one used for the receivables turnover: Net Sales. So, its simply: Net sales / Average NET fixed assets.
- o Inventory Turnover: Once again, the name of the ratio tells you the account we'll be averaging on the bottom: Inventory! Average it like you do for receivables. Now, what account is related to inventory? NOT SALES! Try again! Inventory is paid for…hmmm. It costs us something…Cost! Ah, it's Cost of Goods Sold! So, Cost of goods sold / Average Inventory
- o Return on Equity: This is kind of an oddball one. It doesn't have the word TURNOVER in it. But, I'm including it here because it also has an average number on the bottom that is part of its name: EQUITY. We're talking TOTAL EQUITY here. It is averaged on the bottom. But, what goes on the top? I nearly put this calculation up there with the profitability because RETURN also always means NET INCOME, so anything with the word RETURN in its name has net income on the top. But, I decided to put it down here with the AVERAGING ratios. Remember it whichever way is best for you. Anyhow, you get: Net Income/ Average Total Stockholders' Equity

- • Current Ratio. I don't quite know where to put this one because it is the easiest one. Current / Current! That's it! Yeah, but current what divided by current what? Well, A comes before L in the alphabet, so A on top and L on bottom. That gives us: Current Assets / Current Liabilities!

- • Weird Name in the Ratio. The ratios with really bizarre non-accounting type names (names you probably never saw in this accounting text until chapter 12) are ALMOST ALWAYS related to the cash flows statement, like: *Quality* of income ratio, Cash *Coverage* Ratio, and Capital *Acquisitions* Ratio. Quality, coverage, acquisitions? Here's the best part: *they all have Net Cash Flows from operating Activities as the top number!* We just need to figure out the bottom number!
  - o Quality of Income: OK. We know what goes on the top part. But what goes on the bottom? Maybe something to do with Income? Maybe NET INCOME! You got it! So, it is simply Net Cash Flows from Operating Activities / Net Income.
  - o Capital Acquisitions Ratio: Again, we know what goes on the top. But, what about the bottom? Capital is another name for Fixed Assets or Property, Plant, and Equipment (PPE). So, the bottom number is simply cash paid for the PPE. Net Cash Flows from Operating Activities / Net Cash Paid for PPE
  - o Cash Coverage Ratio: This is the weird one. The starting point for the top number is Net Cash Flows from Operating Activities. But, we add a couple of things back. Here's a weird hint: coverage means cover yourself, like an umbrella…and the letter "I" kind of looks like a little umbrella (ok it doesn't but pretend anyhow. Use your imagination!) The reason for the "I" is that you need to add back two different "I" costs: Interest Paid and Income Taxes Paid. Then, the bottom number is the Interest Paid Number. So,
  Net Cash Flows from Operating Activities + Interest Paid + Income Taxes Paid / Interest Paid

- • Times Interest Earned Ratio: This is the weirdest one of them all. The idea here is that the more often you are able to generate the interest charges from your current period net income, the more likely you'll be able to pay those charges in the future. It is a 'prediction' tool.

SELF-TEST QUESTIONS AND EXERCISES

MATCHING
1. *Match each of the key terms listed below with the appropriate textbook definition.*

_____ Cost-benefit constraint

_____ Discontinued Operations

_____ Full Disclosure Principle

_____ Going-concern Assumption

_____ Horizontal Analysis

_____ Industry Practices Constraint

_____ Liquidity

_____ Profitability

_____ Solvency

_____ Vertical Analysis

A. Expresses each financial statement amount as a percentage of another amount on the same financial statement.
B. States that the financial statements should present information needed to understand the financial results of the company's business activities.
C. Assumes that a business will be capable of continuing its operations long enough to meet its obligations.
D. The ability of a company to survive long enough to repay lenders when debt matures.
E. The extent to which a company generates income.
F. Advises that accounting rules be followed to the extent that the benefits outweigh the costs of doing so.
G. The extent to which a company is able to pay its currently maturing obligations.
H. Recognizes that companies in certain industries must following accounting rules peculiar to that industry.
I. Trend comparisons across time, often expressing changes in account balances as a percentage of prior year balances.
J. Result from the disposal of a major component of the business and are reported net of income tax effects.

TRUE-FALSE QUESTIONS
For each of the following, enter a T or F in the blank to indicate whether the statement is true or false.

_____ 1. (LO1) The two techniques used in this chapter for financial analysis are ratio analysis and price-earnings analysis.

_____ 2. (LO2) To calculate a year-over-year change, divide the change this year by this year's total.

_____ 3. (LO2) Vertical analysis expresses each financial statement amount as a percentage of another amount on that financial statement.

_____ 4. (LO3) Net profit margin indicates how much profit is made after deducting the cost of goods sold.

_____ 5. (LO3) The quality of income ratio is effective in determining how much cash flow is generated by each dollar of net income.

_____ 6. (LO3) The P/E ratio measures how many times more than current year's earnings the investors are willing to pay for a company's stock.

_____ 7. (LO3) The P/E ratio is a wonderful analytical tool because it reflects the truth of the company's situation in and of itself.

_____ 8. (LO3) The ratio that calculates the amount of earnings that is generated for each share of common stock is known as EPS.

_____ 9. (LO3) Liquidity ratios focus on the ability of the company to generate income during the period.

_____10. (LO3) Receivables turnover and inventory turnover calculate the amount of receivables and inventory that must be turned-over to creditors in the event the company declares bankruptcy.

_____11. (LO3) Landry's current ratio of .76 should be a big concern to them since it is less than 1.

_____12. (LO3) Solvency ratios measure a company's ability to solve problems.

_____13. (LO3) The times interest earned ratio measures how many times interest payments are covered by its net operating activities.

_____14. (LO3) Despite Landry's rapid growth, its profile of long-term financing risk has changed only slightly.

_____15. (LO4) Other things to consider besides financial results are a company's hiring policies and the results of recurring special items.

_____16. (LO4) Analyzing financial statements and predicting stock prices are not the same thing.

_____17. (LO4) The primary objective of financial accounting is to provide conceptual information to financial statement users.

_____18. (LO4) There are four principles of financial accounting: revenue recognition, matching, full disclosure, and conservatism.

_____19. (LO4) The four characteristics of financial information are relevance, reliability, comparability, and consistency.

_____20. (LO4) When the going-concern (continuity) assumption is no longer appropriate for a company, all its assets and liabilities are measured at their liquidation values.

MULTIPLE CHOICE QUESTIONS
Choose the best answer or response by placing the identifying letter in the space provided.

_____1. (LO2) Which of the following is *not* another name used for trend analysis?
   a. Horizontal analysis
   b. Time series analysis
   c. Vertical analysis
   d. Year-over-year analysis

_____2. (LO2) The formula for calculating the year-over-year analysis is:
   a. Prior year's total / this year's change
   b. Prior year change / this year's total
   c. This year's total / prior year's change
   d. This year's change / prior year's total

_____3. (LO3) All of the following are one of three general performance categories for ratio analysis *except*:
   a. Profitability
   b. Equity
   c. Solvency
   d. Liquidity

_____4. (LO3) Which of the following is *not* a profitability ratio?
   a. Times Interest Earned
   b. Return on Equity
   c. Quality of Income
   d. Fixed Asset Turnover

_____5.　(LO3)　One measure of liquidity is
    a.　Cash Coverage
    b.　Debt-to-Assets
    c.　Earnings per share
    d.　Inventory turnover

The following information will be used to answer questions 6, 7, 8, and 9.

Net Sales Revenue	$ 500,000
Cost of Goods Sold	300,000
Net Income	40,000
Average Net Fixed Assets	250,000
Average Stockholders Equity	175,000
Average Number of Common shares outstanding	2,000,000

_____6.　(LO3)　Calculate the Fixed Asset Turnover ratio:
    a.　0.16
    b.　2.00
    c.　5.00
    d.　1.25

_____7.　(LO3)　Calculate the Earnings Per Share:
    a.　.02
    b.　.25
    c.　4.00
    d.　50.00

_____8.　(LO3)　Calculate the Net Profit Margin
    a.　8.00%
    b.　13.33%
    c.　40.00%
    d.　60.00%

_____9.　(LO3)　Calculate the Return on Equity
    a.　43.75%
    b.　35.00%
    c.　28.60%
    d.　22.86%

_____10.　(LO3)　Which of the following statements regarding the Price-Earnings Ratio is true?
    a.　A high P/E ratio means a stock is priced too high
    b.　A high P/E ratio means investors expect the company to do better in the future and increase profits
    c.　A low P/E ratio means the company's stock is a bargain
    d.　None of the statements above are true statements

_____11.　(LO3)　Cash Coverage Ratio is calculated as:
    a.　(Net Cash Flows From Operating Activities + Interest Expense + Income Tax Expense)÷ Interest Expense
    b.　(Net Cash Flows From Operating Activities – Interest Expense – Income Tax Expense) ÷ Interest Expense
    c.　(Net Cash Flows From Operating Activities + Interest Paid + Income Taxes Paid) ÷ Interest Paid
    d.　(Net Cash Flows From Operating Activities – Interest Paid – Income Taxes Paid) ÷ Interest Paid

Net Sales Revenue	$ 800,000
Cost of Goods Sold	500,000
Average Inventory	175,000
Average Net Receivables	190,000
Current Assets	310,000
Current Liabilities	280,000

_____12. (LO3) Calculate Inventory Turnover:
  a. 1.60 times
  b. 1.77 times
  c. 2.86 times
  d. 4.57 times

_____13. (LO3) Calculate the Current Ratio:
  a. 0.90 to 1
  b. 1.11 to 1
  c. 1.61 to 1
  d. 2.58 to 1

_____14. (LO3) Calculate the Receivables Turnover:
  a. 2.38 times
  b. 2.63 times
  c. 4.21 times
  d. None of the above is the correct accounts receivable turnover

_____15. (LO3) All of the following are solvency ratios *except*:
  a. Capital Acquisitions
  b. Debt-to-Assets
  c. Fixed Asset Turnover
  d. Times Interest Earned

The following information will be used to answer questions 16, 17, and 18.

Net Sales Revenue	$ 800,000
Net income	48,000
Net Cash flow from operating activities	75,000
Interest Paid	110,000
Interest Expense	130,000
Total Assets	430,000
Total Liabilities	250,000
Income Taxes Paid	20,000
Income Tax Expense	16,000

_____16. (LO3) Calculate the Cash Coverage Ratio:
  a. 1.49
  b. 1.62
  c. 1.70
  d. 1.86

_____17. (LO3) Calculate the Debt-to-Assets Ratio:
  a. 17.20%
  b. 33.95%
  c. 58.14%
  d. none of the above is the correct Debt-to-Assets Ratio

_____18. (LO3) Calculate the Times Interest Earned Ratio:
   a. 1.49
   b. 1.62
   c. 1.70
   d. 1.86

_____19. (LO4) Constraints of accounting concepts include:
   a. Materiality
   b. Full disclosure
   c. Relevance
   d. None of the above are constraints of accounting concepts

_____20. (LO4) Which of the following is *not* a principle of accounting concepts?
   a. Cost
   b. Matching
   c. Full Disclosure
   d. all of the above are principles of accounting concepts

EXERCISES
Record your answer to each exercise in the space provided. Show your work.

Exercise 13-1. Preparing a Schedule Using Year-over-Year Percentages (LO1)
Assume the price of milk has increased $0.50 (25%) from $2.00 per gallon to $2.50 per gallon in 2008. Determine whether this change is reflected in the income statement of Cowland Dairy, for the year ended December 31, 2007.

	2008	2007	% Changes
a. Total Revenues	$ 786,600	$ 684,000	
b. Costs of Milk and milk products	512,500	410,000	
c. Other Operating Costs	180,000	196,000	
d. Income before Income Tax Expense	94,100	78,000	
e. Income Tax Expense	20,000	15,600	
f. Net Income	$ 74,100	$ 62,400	

Required:
Calculate the year-over- year changes in each line item. How did the change in milk prices compare to the changes in Cowland's total revenues and cost of milk and milk products?

Exercise 13-2. Inferring Information Using Various Ratios (LO2)
Part A. Alpha company reported revenues of $950,000. The company's gross profit percentage was 55 percent. What amount of cost of goods sold did the company report?

Part B. Beta Company reported total assets of $600,000 and noncurrent assets of $220,000. The company also reported a current ratio of .95. What amount of current liabilities did the company report?

Part C. Gamma Company reported average inventories of $925,000 and an inventory turnover of 5.30. Average total fixed assets were $1,000,000, and the fixed asset turnover was 7.80. Rounded to two decimal places, calculate the gross profit percentage for the year.

Exercise 13-3. Computing Liquidity Ratios (LO2)

Selected information from Cinco Corporation's balance sheet follows. For 2008, the company reported Sales Revenue of $1,750,000 and Cost of Goods Sold of $1,000,000.

Cinco	2008	2007
Cash	$ 15,200	$ 32,500
Accounts Receivable (less allowance of $10,000, and $4,000)	230,000	157,000
Inventories	258,000	108,000
Prepaid expenses	10,000	10,200
Other current assets	25,000	61,200
Accounts payable	72,000	85,000
Wages payable	24,000	27,000
Income taxes payable	61,000	64,000
Accrued liabilities	141,000	154,000
Long-term debt due within one year	26,000	16,800

Required:

For 2008, compute the (1) current ratio; (2) inventory turnover ratio; and (3) receivables turnover ratio (assuming 70 percent of sales were on credit.) Round each ratio to two decimal places.

Exercise 13-4. Analyzing the Impact of Selected Transactions on the Current Ratio. (LO2)

In its most recent annual report, Goatshead Ale reported current assets of $199,955 and a current ratio of 2.03. Determine the impact of the following transactions on the current ratio for Goatshead by completing the following table and recalculating the ratio after each of the transactions 1 – 5 (Round all ratios to two decimal places):

	Current Assets	Current Liab.	Current Ratio
Initial figures	$ 199,955	?	2.03
(1) Accrued wages of $25,000			
(2) Paid $10,000 on accounts payable			
(3) Purchased Equipment on a account $40,000			
(4) Paid previously declared dividends, $15,000			
(5) Paid Prepaid insurance of $7,000			
(6) Cash sale of $8,000			

Calculations:

(1)   (2)

(3)   (4)

(5)   (6)

Exercise 13-5. Computing Profitability Ratios (LO2)

Selecting information for Ocho Corporation is presented in the following table.

Ocho	2008	2007
Net Sales	$600,000	$ 500,000
Cost of goods sold	350,000	325,000
Net Income	102,000	67,000
Fixed Assets	160,000	110,000
Accumulated Depreciation – Fixed Assets	25,000	10,000
Stockholders' Equity	650,000	500,000
Number of common stock outstanding	280,000	280,000
Net cash flows from operating activities	120,000	60,000

Required:

For 2008, compute the following ratios for Ocho Corporation. (Round all ratios to two decimal places)

(1) Net profit margin:

(2) Gross profit percentage:

(3) Fixed asset turnover:

(4) Return on equity:

(5) Earnings per share:

(6) Quality of income:

Exercise 13-6. Interpreting Profitability, Liquidity, Solvency, and P/E Ratios (LO2)

Selected financial ratios for two novelty stores follow.

Ratio	Springboard Cards and Gifts	Hammock Gifts and Cards
Gross profit percentage	28.24%	31.96%
Net profit margin	9.33%	1.01%
Return on equity	16.32%	2.51%
EPS	$5.22	$0.05
Receivables turnover ratio	10.5 times	4.2 times
Inventory turnover ratio	4.85 times	1.87 times
Current ratio	2.22	1.85
Debt-to-assets	.37	.84
P/E ratio	16.3	51.0

Required:

1. Which company appears more profitable? Describe the ratio(s) that you used to reach this decision.

2. Which company appears more liquid? Describe the ratio(s) that you used to reach this decision.

3. Which company appears more solvent? Describe the ratio(s) that you used to reach this decision.

4. Are the conclusions from your analyses in requirements 1 – 3 consistent with the value of the two companies suggested by the P.E ratio of the two companies? If not, offer one explanation for any apparent inconsistency.

Exercise 13-7. Matching Conceptual Framework terms to Definitions (LO4)
1. *Match each of the key terms listed below with the appropriate textbook definition in the "Definition" column. Then in the "Framework" column, identify which portion of the Conceptual Frame it belongs to using the following numbers (The first one has been done for you)*

1. Primary Objective of External Financial Reporting	4. Assumptions
2. Elements of Financial Statement	5. Principles
3. Characteristics of Financial Information	6. Constraints

Definition	Framework		Definition	Framework	
X	2	Asset	_____	_____	Matching
_____	_____	Comparability	_____	_____	Materiality
_____	_____	Conservatism	_____	_____	Primary Objective
_____	_____	Consistency	_____	_____	Relevance
_____	_____	Cost	_____	_____	Reliability
_____	_____	Cost-Benefit	_____	_____	Revenue
_____	_____	Expense	_____	_____	Revenue Recognition
_____	_____	Full-Disclosure	_____	_____	Separate Entity
_____	_____	Going Concern	_____	_____	Stockholders' Equity
_____	_____	Industry Practices	_____	_____	Time Period
_____	_____	Liability	_____	_____	Unit of Measure

A. To provide useful economic information to external users for decision making
B. Relatively small amounts not likely to influence decisions are recorded in the most cost-beneficial way
C. Information capable of making a difference in decisions
D. Activities of the business are separate from activities of the owners
E. Probable future sacrifices of economic resources
F. Increase in assets or settlement of liabilities from ongoing operations
G. Benefits to users should outweigh costs of providing information
H. Entity will not go out of business in the near future
I. Cash equivalent price on the transaction date is used initially to measure value
J. Financing provided by owners and operations
K. Accounting measurements are in the national monetary unit
L. Information can be relied on
M. Decrease in assets or increase in liabilities from ongoing operations
N. The long life of a company can be reported over a series of shorter timer periods
O. Information can be used to evaluate one company with another company
P. Record expenses when incurred to generate revenues
Q. Industry-specific measurements and reporting deviations may be acceptable
R. Economic resources with probable future benefits
S. Information provided uses the same accounting methods year after year
T. Exercise care not to overstate assets and revenues or understate liabilities and expenses
U. Record revenue when it is earned, measurable, and realizable
V. Provides information sufficiently important to influence decisions

SOLUTIONS TO SELF-TEST QUESTIONS AND EXERCISES
MATCHING
1.

F	Cost-benefit constraint	H	Industry Practices Constraint
J	Discontinued Operations	G	Liquidity
B	Full Disclosure Principle	E	Profitability
C	Going-concern Assumption	D	Solvency
I	Horizontal Analysis	A	Vertical Analysis

TRUE-FALSE QUESTIONS
1. F – The two techniques are trend analysis and ratio analysis.
2. F – The calculation divides the change this year by the prior year's total.
3. T
4. F – Net profit margin represents the percentage of sales revenues that ultimately make it into net income after deducting all expenses.
5. T
6. T
7. F – Ratios cannot tell the whole story by themselves, rather they are useful in alerting you to the need to learn more about how the company is changing.
8. T
9. F – Liquidity ratios focus on the company's ability to use current assets to repay liabilities as they become due in the short-term.
10. F – Receivables turnover and inventory turnover are liquidity ratios used in evaluating the ability of a company to survive in the short-term.
11. F – For many companies, a current ratio like this would be devastating but it is not a problem for Landry's.
12. F – Solvency ratios focus on a company's ability to pay its debts as they mature as well as any interest associated with the debt up until it matures.
13. F – The times interest earned ratio measures how many times interest expense is covered by net income.
14. T
15. F – Other things to consider besides financial results are a company's accounting policies and any non-recurring special items.
16. T
17. F – The primary objective is to provide useful information to external users for decision making.
18. T
19. T
20. T

MULTIPLE CHOICE QUESTIONS

1. C	6. B	11. C	16. D
2. D	7. A	12. C	17. C
3. B	8. A	13. B	18. A
4. A	9. D	14. C	19. A
5. D	10. B	15. C	20. D

EXERCISES
Exercise 13-1. Preparing a Schedule Using Year-over-Year Percentages (LO1)

	2003	2002	% Changes
Total Revenues	$ 786,600	$ 684,000	15.00%
Costs of Milk and milk products	512,500	410,000	25.00%
Other Operating Costs	180,000	196,000	(8.16%)
Income before Income Tax Expense	94,100	78,000	20.64%
Income Tax Expense	20,000	15,600	28.21%
Net Income	$ 74,100	$ 62,400	18.75%

a. [(786,600 – 684,000) / 684,000] x 100% = 15.00% b. [(512,500 – 410,000) / 410,000] x 100% = 25.00%
c. [(180,000 – 196,000) / 196,000] x 100% = (8.16%) d. [(94,100 – 78,000) / 78,000] x 100% = 20.64%
e. [(20,000 – 15,600) / 15,600] x 100% = 28.21% f. [(74,100 – 62,400) / 62,400] x 100% = 18.75%

While milk prices for Cowland increased 25.00%, only 15% of the increase was passed on to consumers. However, milk prices fluctuate wildly. In 2003, milk prices for consumers were incredibly low, relative to the cost of milk to producers. This could be because milk was a loss-leader item in grocery stores or perhaps dairies were trying to drive out competition. 2003 could just be a bounce back year where dairies are trying to bring prices back up to realistic levels after an intensive year of competition. However, net sales only increased 15.00%, a smaller increase than costs rose. But, because of a tight rein on other operating costs, the dairy was able to secure a 16.35% net income increase over 2002.

Exercise 13-2. Inferring Information Using Various Ratios (LO2)
Part A. This can be calculated two ways:
Gross Profit is: ($950,000 x 55%) = $522,500. Since Sales – Cost of goods sold = Gross Profit, then Sales – Gross Profit = Cost of goods sold. So, $950,000 – $522,500 = $427,500 is Cost of goods Sold.

Alternatively, this can be calculated used the complement of 55%. If 55% of net sales is Gross Profit, then the complement of 55% is Cost of goods sold. The complement of 55% is 45% (100% - 55%). So, $950,000 x 45% = $427,500.

Part B.
Current Assets are Total Assets – Noncurrent Assets $600,000 - $220,000 = $380,000
Since Current Assets / Current Liabilities = Current Ratio, then $380,000 / Liabilities = .95
Solving for liabilities we get $380,000 / .95 = $400,000.
Also, always work a proof to verify that your calculations are correct. When this number is substituted into the original ratio calculation, the result should be .95.
$380,000 / $400,000 = .95 ✓

Part C. This is a tricky question! You have to infer both Net Sales (from the fixed asset turnover) and Cost of Goods Sold (from the inventory turnover) before you can calculate Gross Profit (Net Sales – Cost of Goods Sold).

Fixed Asset Turnover is: Net Sales / Average Fixed Assets So, Net Sales / $1,000,000 = 7.8. Solving for net sales gives: $1,000,000 x 7.8 = $7,800,000 are Net Sales. Again, always proof your work by substituting your answer into the original ratio and see if it works.
$7,800,000 / $1,000,000 = 7.8 ✓

Inventory Turnover is: Cost of Goods Sold / Average Inventory. So, Cost of Goods Sold / $925,000 = 5.30. Solving for Cost of goods sold, we get $925,000 x 5.30 = $4,902,500. Substituting for the proof we get: $4,902,500 / $925,000 = 5.30 ✓

Finally, we can calculate gross profit: $7,800,000 – $4,902,500 = $2,897,500

Exercise 13-3. Computing Liquidity Ratios (LO2)
(1) Current Ratio: Current Assets = $15,200 + $230,000 + $258,000 + $10,000 + $25,000 = $538,200
   Current liabilities = $72,000 + $24,000 + $61,000 + $141,000 + $26,000 = $324,000
   Current ratio = $538,200 / $324,000 = 1.66

(2) Inventory Turnover Ratio: Average inventories = ($258,000 + $108,000) / 2 = $183,000
   Inventory Turnover Ratio = $1,000,000 / $183,000 = 5.46 times

(3) Receivables Turnover Ratio: Average receivables = ($230,000 + $157,000) / 2 = $193,500
   Receivable turnover ratio: ($1,750,000 x 70%) / $193,500 = 6.33 times

Exercise 13-4. Analyzing the Impact of Selected Transactions on the Current Ratio. (LO2)
In its most recent annual report, Goatshead Ale reported current assets of $199,955 and a current ratio of 2.03. Determine the impact of the following transactions on the current ratio for Sunrise by completing the following table and recalculating the ratio after each of the transactions 1 – 5:

	Current Assets	Current Liab.	Current Ratio
Initial figures	$ 199,955	98,500	2.03
(1) Accrued wages of $25,000	199,955	123,500	1.62
(2) Paid $10,000 on accounts payable	189,955	113,500	1.67
(3) Purchased Equipment on account $40,000	189,955	153,500	1.24
(4) Paid previously declared dividends, $15,000	174,955	138,500	1.26
(5) Paid Prepaid insurance of $7,000	174,955	138,500	1.26
(6) Cash sale of $8,000	181,955	138,500	1.31

Calculations:
Determine Current liabilities first. $199,955 / CL = 2.03; Therefore, $199,955 / 2.03 = $98,500
(1) $199,955 / $123,500 = 1.62   (2) $189,955 / $113,500 = 1.67
(3) $189,955 / $153,500 = 1.24   (4) $174,955 / $138,500 = 1.26
(5) $174,955 / $138,500 = 1.21   (6) $181,955 / $138,500 = 1.31

Exercise 13-5. Computing Liquidity Ratios (LO2)
(1) Net profit margin: $102,000 / $600,000 = .17

(2) Gross profit percentage: ($600,000 – 350,000) / $600,000 = 41.67%

(3) Fixed asset turnover: Net fixed assets, 2005: $160,000 – $25,000) = $135,000
   Net fixed assets, 2004: $110,000 - $10,000 = $100,000
   Average net fixed assets: ($135,000 + $100,000) / 2 = $117,500
   Fixed asset turnover: $600,000 / $117,500 = 5.11 times

(4) Return on equity: Average stockholders' equity: ($650,000 + $500,000) / 2 = $575,000
   Return on equity: $102,000 / $575,000 = 17.74%

(5) Earnings per share: $102,000 / 280,000 = $0.36

(6) Quality of income: $120,000 / 102,000 = 1.18

Exercise 13-6. Interpreting Profitability, Liquidity, Solvency, and P/E Ratios (LO2)
1. Which company appears more profitable? Describe the ratio(s) that you used to reach this decision.

Springboard appears more profitable based on the first four ratios presented. While Hammock has a slightly higher gross profit percentage, this figure includes only cost of goods sold but no other expenses. Profit margin indicates that Springboard keeps about nine cents on the dollars and Hammock only keeps about one cent on the dollar. ROE is 16% for Springboard vs. 2.51% for Hammock, another indication that Springboard is outperforming Hammock. Finally, EPS is over $5 for Springboard vs. about 5 cents for Hammock.

2. Which company appears more liquid? Describe the ratio(s) that you used to reach this decision.

Again, Springboard comes out on top. The current ratio, inventory turnover, and receivables turnover are the liquidity ratios used for this decision. Receivables are collected more than two times as quickly for Springboard (10.5 times) versus Hammock (4.2 times). So, Springboard has a better handle on its collection procedures. We don't know if the terms offered by each company are similar, but the faster the money is collected, the better. Inventory also turns over more quickly for Springboard. They must sell similar items, but Springboard doesn't get stuck with unmovable inventories and doesn't over order. It seems Hammock is having difficulty moving its inventory. The current ratios indicate that Springboard is a bit better off than Hammock, but not by a huge amount. This may all be because of the slower receivables collections and slow-moving inventory of Hammock.

3. Which company appears more solvent? Describe the ratio(s) that you used to reach this decision.

There's only one solvency ratio here, but it's a doosie! Springboard has about 37% of its assets financed by debt (indicating 63% financed with equity), while Hammock has a whopping 84% of its assets financed with debt (indicating 16% financed with equity). Unless Hammock can invest idle cash and generate returns that are higher than the interest charges paid on the debt, this looks to be a scary situation. This would explain the much smaller profit margin, ROE, and EPS for Hammock. (This is due to the large interest expense charges that Hammock must have incurred in financing all of this debt.)

4. Are the conclusions from your analyses in requirements 1 – 3 consistent with the value of the two companies suggested by the P.E ratio of the two companies? If not, offer one explanation for any apparent inconsistency.

It appears to be inconsistent, because apparently Hammock investors are willing to pay 51 times its EPS. A company in this situation does not appear to be worth *nearly* that much. The only possible thing *might* be that it has recently announced a huge expansion effort that appears very, very promising to market analysts. But, I'd certainly think twice about this company if it were my money.

Exercise 13-7. Matching Conceptual Framework terms to Definitions (LO4)

Definition	Framework		Definition	Framework	
R	2	Asset	P	5	Matching
O	3	Comparability	B	6	Materiality
T	6	Conservatism	A	1	Primary Objective
S	3	Consistency	C	3	Relevance
I	5	Cost	L	3	Reliability
G	6	Cost-Benefit	F	2	Revenue
M	2	Expense	U	5	Revenue Recognition
V	5	Full-Disclosure	D	4	Separate Entity
H	4	Going Concern	J	2	Stockholders' Equity
Q	6	Industry Practices	N	4	Time Period
E	2	Liability	K	4	Unit of Measure

APPENDIX C
PRESENT AND FUTURE VALUE CONCEPTS

CHAPTER FOCUS SUGGESTIONS

Introduction
Present value (PV) and future value (FV) concepts are based on the time value of money. Simply put, if someone owes you $1,000, you'd much rather receive payment today than one year from now because the length of *time* you have to wait for the payment is worth something. It has *value.*

Sometimes, in business, you need to know what a cash flow is worth *today* that will not be received or paid until some time in the future. This is known as a **present value** problem. At other times you might want to know what a dollar amount received or paid for *today* will be worth at some point in the future. This is known as a **future value** problem. Look at the table below and find the question marks (?). They represent the amount that *you don't know* and are *trying to find out!* So, if you need to find out what an future amount is worth *now,* the question mark is under the heading 'now' and next to the Present Value row because you need to determine its *present value.* Similarly, if you need to find out what a current dollar amount will be worth in the *future,* the question mark is under the heading 'future' and next to the Future Value row because you need to determine its *future value.*

	Now	Future
Present value	?	$1,000
Future value	$1,000	?

Present/Future value problems may have two different kinds of cash flow: a single payment or an annuity. A single payment is like going into a store, buying a Boom Box and paying $215.65 for it, and walking out the door. One payment (single payment) was made to purchase the boom box. On the other hand, if you own a car, you make a $215.65 payment, then a month from now you make another payment of $215.65, then another payment of $215.65, etc. This series of the same payment over and over again is known as an *annuity.* Therefore, we need to learn four different situations when dealing with the time value of money:

1. Future value of a single payment.
2. Present value of a single payment.
3. Future value of an annuity.
4. Present value of an annuity.

You will need your textbook for the remainder of this appendix. The problems are solved using Tables C-1 through C-4 at the end of Appendix C.

COMPUTING FUTURE AND PRESENT VALUES OF A SINGLE AMOUNT

Future Value of a Single Amount
In this type of problem you will be asked to calculate how much money you will have in the *future* as the result of investing a *single* amount of money today (in the present.) Assume you have $15,000 you want to put into an investment on January 1, 2005 for three years earning 10%. To solve a FV problem, you need three items:

1. Amount to be invested
2. Interest rate (*i*) the amount will earn
3. Number of periods *(n)* the amount will earn interest.

FV computations are based on compound interest which means that interest is calculated on the amount in the account *plus* any interest that was added to the account. At the end of three years (December 31, 2007), you would have $19,965 in the investment. This problem is solved like this:

Year	Amount at Start of Year	+	Interest during the Year	=	Amount at End of Year
1	$15,000	+	$15,000 x 10% = $1,500	=	$16,500
2	16,500	+	16,500 x 10% = $1,650	=	18,150
3	18,150	+	18,150 x 10% = $1,815	=	19,965

But, there's a much easier way to solve this future value problem. Using the **Table C.1, Future Value of $1,** where $i = 10\%$, $n = 3$, we find the number 1.3310. We can calculate the FV of $15,000 by simply multiplying the dollar amount invested ($15,000) times the table number: $15,000 x 1.331 = $19,965. The difference between the FV calculated ($19,965) and the amount initially deposited ($15,000) is the interest earned on the investment: $4,965 ($19,965 - $15,000.)

Present Value of a Single Amount
The present value of a single amount is what something is worth to you *today* (the present) for an amount you will receive sometime in the future. Assume, your Great Aunt Martha has offered to give you $200,000 at the end of 10 years and you wonder what it would be worth today because you want to sell it to your Uncle Ralph and get some cash now! But, how much should you sell it for? To find the PV of a single amount, we have to discount (the opposite of compounding.) Basically, it just means that you subtract the interest from the amount (rather than add it) before calculating the next years' amount. Again, you need three items (1) the amount to discount, (2) interest rate (i), and number of periods (n). The amount is $200,000, assume a 10% interest rate, and number of periods is 3 years. Using **Table C.2, Present Value of $1**, the present value of this future cash flow is: $200,000 x .7513 = $150,260. Assuming the funds you get from Uncle Ralph could be invested at 10%, you should sell it for no less than $150,260. Essentially, you would be happy to accept either alternative. That is, you would be just as happy to receive $150,260 today as you would to receive $200,000 ten years from now. By the way, the assumption made in the entire PV/FV calculations is that you have no immediate need of the money today or ten years from now. All of this is useless of course if your Great Aunt Martha disapproves with any of this. But, don't worry! She's probably thrilled you're learning present value computations!

COMPUTING FUTURE AND PRESENT VALUES OF AN ANNUITY
Instead of a single payment, many business problems involve multiple cash payments over a number of periods. An **annuity** is a series of consecutive payments characterized by:

(1) An equal dollar amount each period
(2) Interest periods of equal length (year, half a year, quarter, or month)
(3) An equal interest rate each interest period

Future Value of an Annuity
Say you want to put away a certain amount of money every year for three years at 10% interest to save up for a vacation in Maui. The Future value of an annuity computation will tell you how much money will be in your savings account at the end of some future period. The FV of an annuity includes compound interest on each payment from the date of the payment to the end of the term of the annuity. Each new payment *accumulates* less interest than prior payments, only because the number of periods remaining in which to accumulate interest is shorter. Assume you deposit $2,000 on December 31 of 2004, 2005, and 2006. The first payment earns interest for two years (2005 and 2006—remember this payment was made at the END of the first year, so it doesn't earn any interest in the first year.) The second payment earns interest for one year (2006), and the third payment earns nothing because it was paid at the end of the third year just before you closed the account. We could go through all of the computations for each individual payment using three different numbers from Table C.1) a different table number for each of the three payments), but that's too much work! Instead we can just use **Table C.3, Future Value of an Annuity of $1.** Multiply the $2,000 times the table amount and you get the future value of the whole shebang! $2,000 x 3.3100 = $6,620.

The Power of Compounding
Compounding of interest is an incredibly powerful mechanism for building wealth because the longer the money is invested the more interest it earns. It makes sense that the sooner you start to compound, the more of a nest egg you can build. Thus, you will earn more money putting $1,000 a year for the first 10 years of your career than you would by putting $15,000 per year in the last 10 years of your career.

Present Value of an Annuity

The present value of an annuity is the value *now* of equal amounts to be received (or paid out) for some specified number of periods in the future. It is computed by discounting each of the equal periodic amounts. Assume you win the lottery and you have a choice of whether to take a series of future payments (an annuity) or a lump sum amount. To determine a lump sum amount, the lottery people will calculate the present value of the annuity. We could use table C.2 and find the present value of each individual payment, but luckily **Table C.4, Present Value of an Annuity of $1,** is available and the present value of three $100,000 payments, assuming an interest rate of 10% would be: $100,000 x 2.4869 = $248,690. .

Interest Rates and Interest Periods

Thus far, all we've dealt with are *annual compounding periods* for compounding and discounting. While interest rates are usually quoted in annual terms, many compounding/discounting periods are less than one year (monthly, quarterly, semi-annually). When compounding periods are less than one year, the i and n values must be restated to the actual length of the compounding period. For example, if $i = 12\%$ and everything is compounded monthly for 3 years, the following restatements are required:

Since interest is stated in annual terms (12%) and there are twelve months in a year, the 'true' interest rate for compounding is: 12% / 12 months = 1.0% per month. Also, since the number of periods is currently in years (3), it must also be restated to the compounding period: 3 years x 12 months = 36 months. This simply means that interest will be calculated 36 times in three years (monthly).

Had this been 10% for 5 years with quarterly compounding, the restatement would be:
10% / 4 quarters = 2.5% (divide by four because there are four quarters in a year)
5 years x 4 quarters = 20 (in five years' time interest will be calculated 20 times—once every quarter)

ACCONTING APPLICATIONS OF PRESENT VALUES

We will apply present value concepts to three common accounting situations:

Case A – Present Value of a Single Amount

On January 1, 2005, Blue Spruce bought some new equipment. The company signed a note and agreed to pay $500,000 on December 31, 2006, an amount representing the cash equivalent price of the trucks plus interest for two years. The market rate of interest for this note was 12%.

1. How should the accountant record the purchase? The cost principle states that the cost of the equipment is its cash equivalent price on January 1, 2005, not December 31, 2006 when the $500,000 is payable. Therefore, we must compute the present value of a single amount using **Table C.2, Present Value of $1,** where $i = 12\%$ and $n = 2$. The present value of the $500,000 is: $500 000 x 0.7972 = $398,600 and the journal entry is:

dr Equipment (+A)   398,600
   cr Note payable (+L)   398,600

Assets	=	Liabilities	+	Stockholders' Equity
Delivery trucks +398,600		Note payable + 398,600		

2. What journal entry should be made at the end of 2005 and 2006, to record the interest expense? Each year's interest expense is recorded as an adjusting entry like this:

dr Interest expense (+E, -SE) 47,832
   cr Note payable (+L)   47,832

*$398,600 x 12% x 12/12 = $47,832

Assets	=	Liabilities	+	Stockholders' Equity
		Note payable + 47,832		Interest expense (+E) - 47,832

At the end of year 2006, the entry would be like this:

    dr Interest expense (+E, -SE) 53,568
        cr Note payable (+L)   53,568

    *($398,600 + 47,832) x 12% x 12/12 = $53,572 – 4 (adjusted for rounding errors)

Assets	=	Liabilities	+	Stockholders' Equity
		Note payable + 53,568		Interest expense (+E) - 53,568

3. What journal entry should be made on December 31, 2006 to record payment of the debt? At the end of two years, the amount in the Note Payable account is, in fact, the amount owed—$500,000! At this point, when the payment is made, simply record the payment of the entire amount of the note, like this:

    dr Note payable (-L)   500,000
        cr Cash (-A)   500,000

Assets	=	Liabilities	+	Stockholders' Equity
Cash - 500,000		Note payable - 500,000		

Case B – Present Value of an Annuity

On January 1, 2005, Blue Spruce bought new forklifts. The company decided to finance the purchase with a note payable to paid off in three years in annual installments of $327,372. Each installment includes principle plus interest on the unpaid balance at 11% per year. The annual installments are due on December 31, 2005, 2006, and 2007.

1. What is the amount of the note? The note is equal to the present value of each installment payment, $i = 11\%$, and $n = 3$. This is an annuity payment because payment is made in three equal installments. The amount of the note is: $800,000 (rounded) = $327,372 x 2.4437 (**Table C.4**). The journal entry is:

    dr Forklifts (+A)   800,000
        cr Note payable (+L)   800,000

Assets	=	Liabilities	+	Stockholders' Equity
Delivery trucks +800,000		Note payable + 800,000		

2. What journal entries should be made at the end of 2005, 2006, and 2007, to record the payments on the note?
On December 31, 2005:

    dr Note payable (-L) ($327,372 - $88,000)   239,372
    dr Interest expense (+E, -SE) ($800,000 x 11% x 12/12) . .   88,000
        cr Cash (-A)   327,372

Assets	=	Liabilities	+	Stockholders' Equity
Cash - 327,372		Note payable -239,372		Interest Expense - 88,000

On December 31, 2006:

    dr Note payable (-L) ($327,372 - $61,669)   265,703
    dr Interest expense (+E, -SE)   61,669
        cr Cash (-A)   327,372
    * Interest expense ($800,000 – 239,372) x 11% x 12/12 (rounded)

Assets	=	Liabilities	+	Stockholders' Equity
Cash - 327,372		Note payable -265,703		Interest Expense - 61,669

On December 31, 2007

    dr Note payable (-L) ($800,000 - $239,372 - $265,703) 294,925
    dr Interest expense (+E, -SE)   32,447
        cr Cash (-A)   327,367
    * Interest expense ($800,000 – 239,372 – 265,703) x 11% x 12/12 (adjusted for rounding errors)

Assets	=	Liabilities	+	Stockholders' Equity
Cash - 327,367		Note payable -294,925		Interest Expense - 32,442

3. What journal entry should be made on December 31, 2006 to record payment of the debt?

       dr Note payable (-L)   800,000

          cr Cash (-A)   800,000

Assets	=	Liabilities	+	Stockholders' Equity
Cash - 800,000		Note payable - 800,000		

Case C – Present Value of a Single Amount and an Annuity

On January 1, 2006, Blue Spruce issued a 4-year $200,000 bond. The bond pays interest annually at a rate of 6% of face value. What would investors be willing to pay for the bond if they require an annual return of (a) 4%, (b) 6%, or (c) 8%? This requires the computation of the present value of a single amount (for the face value paid at maturity), plus the present value of an annuity (for the annual interest payments).

a. **4% Market Interest Rate:**

       The present value of the $200,000 face value is computed using **Table C.2** as follows:

           $200,000 x 0.8548 = $170,960

  The present value of the $12,000 annuity is computed using **Table C.4** as follows:

           $12,000 x 3.6299 = $43,559

       The present value of the total bond payments, computed using the discount rate of 4% is:

           $214,519 ($170,960 + $43,559)

b. **6% Market Interest Rate:**

       The present value of the $200,000 face value is computed using **Table C.2** as follows:

           $200,000 x 0.7921 = $158,420

  The present value of the $12,000 annuity is computed using **Table C.4** as follows:

           $12,000 x 3.4651 = $41,581

       The present value of the total bond payments, computed using the discount rate of 4% is:

           $200,000 ($158,420+ $41,580 rounded)

c. **8% Market Interest Rate:**

       The present value of the $200,000 face value is computed using **Table C.2** as follows:

           $200,000 x 0.7350 = $147,000

  The present value of the $12,000 annuity is computed using **Table C.4** as follows:

           $12,000 x 3.3121 = $39,745

       The present value of the total bond payments, computed using the discount rate of 4% is:

           $186,745 ($158,418 + $39,745)

READ AND RECALL QUESTIONS

After you read each section of the chapter, answer the related Read and Recall Questions below.

INTRODUCTION
Explain what is meant by the *time value of money.*

Briefly define (1) *present value,* and (2) *future value.* What two types of cash flow can be found in present and future value problems?

List the four types of situations presented in this Appendix related to the time value of money.

Future and Present Values of a Single Amount

Future Value of a Single Amount
What three items must you have in order to solve a future value problem? What concept is future value based on?

Which table is used for calculating the future value of a single amount? When the computation is complete, is the result larger or smaller than the amount you started with? Why?

Present Value of a Single Amount
Describe what is calculated in a present value problem. Why would this type of calculation be useful?

What concept is present value based on? How does it differ from compounding?

Which table is used for calculating the present value of a single amount? When the computation is complete, is the result larger or smaller than the amount you started with? Why?

Future and Present Values of an Annuity

What are the three characteristics of an annuity?   Give an example of an annuity.

What does the future value of an annuity computation tell you? Why would this be useful?

Future Value of an Annuity

What does the future value of an annuity computation tell you? Why would this be useful? Which table is used to calculate the future value of annuity?

Assuming there are three compounding periods and three deposits, in a future value of an annuity situation, how many compounding periods will each deposit earn compounded interest?

The Power of Compounding

Why is it better to save small amounts early in your career rather than saving large amounts later in your career? Why is this so?

Present Value of an Annuity

Describe what the present value of an annuity calculates. Why might this be useful? How is it computed?

Which table is used to calculate the present value of an annuity?

Interest Rates and Interest Periods

How are interest rates quoted? What must be done with the interest rate when compounding periods are less than one year? What must be done with the number of years when the compounding periods are less than one year? Why?

Accounting Applications of Present Values

Case A – Present Value of a Single Amount

Why might present value concepts be used when assets are purchased with Notes Payable requiring a lump sum payment in the future?   What accounting concept is being enforced in this situation?

At what amount would an asset purchased in the manner just described be recorded? When the note matures, what value has accumulated in the Notes Payable account? Explain.

Case B – Present Value of an Annuity

Why are present value concepts necessary when assets are purchased with a Note Payable requiring annual payments that include both principle and interest? How is the current value of the note determined?

How is the amount of each payment applied towards the principle amount of the Note Payable determined? What value has accumulated in the Notes Payable account when the note matures?

Case C – Present Value of a Single Amount and an Annuity

Why are present value concepts necessary when issuing Bonds Payable? What two amounts on the face of the bond are used for this calculation?   Why?

What two tables are used when calculating the present value of a bond? How is the final issue price of the bond determined after the calculations have been made?

What happens when the coupon rate on the bond is the same as the market rate demanded by investors? Why does this occur?

FINDING FINANCIAL INFORMATION

1. Bonds Issued at a Premium, Discount, or Face Value: a reminder:

WHAT THE BOND SAYS	WHAT IF LENDERS EXPECT ...	WHAT LENDERS THINK	WHAT LENDERS PAY
6% Stated interest rate	**4% Market interest rate**	*Wow, I'll pay extra!*	**Premium**
	6% Market interest rate	*It's just enough.*	**Face value**
	8% Market interest rate	*I'm not attracted (yet).*	**Discount**

SELF-TEST QUESTIONS AND EXERCISES

MATCHING

1. *Match each of the key terms listed below with the appropriate textbook definition.*

_____ Annuity   _____ Present Value

_____ Future Value   _____ Time Value of Money

A. A series of periodic cash receipts or payments that are equal in amount each interest period
B. The current value of an amount to be received in the future determined by discounting
C. The idea that money received today is worth more than money to be received one year from today
D. The amount to which an amount will increase as the result of compound interest

TRUE-FALSE QUESTIONS

For each of the following, enter a T or F in the blank to indicate whether the statement is true or false.

_____1.   (AC) Money to be received one year from today is worth more than money received today.

_____2.   (AC) In some business situations you will know the dollar amount of a cash flow that occurs in the future and will need to determine its value now .

_____3.   (AC) Present and future value problems may involve two types of cash flows, so you need to learn how to deal with two different situations related to the time value of money.

_____4.   (AC) It is necessary to multiply the value from the table by the amount of the payment since no fundamental differences exist for cash payments versus cash receipts.

_____5.   (AC) The future value of a single amount is defined as: the worth to you today of receiving that amount some time in the future.

_____6.   (AC) The future value computation is based on a discounting procedure.

_____7.   (AC) When calculating the present value of an amount to be received in the future, the computation results in an amount less than the original amount.

_____8.   (AC) An annuity is a series of periodic cash receipts or payments that are equal in amount each interest period.

_____9.   (AC) Although interest rates are usually quoted on an annual basis, many compounding periods in business are less than one year.

_____10. (AC) Calculating the present value of a bond requires compounding two separate cash flows: the present value of a single amount and the future value of an annuity.

MULTIPLE CHOICE QUESTIONS
Choose the best answer or response by placing the identifying letter in the space provided.

_____1. (AC) The current value of an amount to be received in the future is known as:
   a. future value
   b. annuity
   c. present value
   d. none of these

_____2. (AC) Which of the following is *not* a type of present or future value calculation discussed in this appendix?
   a. future value of a single payment
   b. present value of an annuity
   c. present value of a single payment
   d. time value of an annuity

_____3. (AC) Which of the following is *not* an item needed to solve a future value problem?
   a. number of periods in which the amount will earn interest.
   b. amount to be invested.
   c. interest rate the amount will earn.
   d. all of the above are needed to solve a future value problem.

_____4. (AC) When interest is calculated on interest it is referred to as:
   a. compounding
   b. time value of money
   c. discounting
   d. none of the above describes this concept

_____5. (AC) Which of the following is an example of a business situation requiring the computation of the present value of a single amount?
   a. determining how much will be in an investment in 10 years when money is invested today
   b. determining how much will be in an investment in 4 years when money is invested at the end of each of the four years.
   c. the opportunity to invest in a financial instrument that would pay you $6,000 in 6 years
   d. none of the above are an example of the present value of a single amount

_____6. (AC) Which of the following is *not* a characteristic of an annuity?
   a. an equal interest rate is applied each compounding period
   b. a single dollar amount is invested
   c. interest periods of equal length
   d. all of the above are characteristics of an annuity

_____7. (AC) The value now of a series of equal amounts to be received (or paid out) for some specified number of periods in the future computed by discounting each of the equal periodic amounts, is:
   a. present value of a single dollar amount
   b. present value of an annuity
   c. future value of a single dollar amount
   d. future value of an annuity

_____8. (AC) An annual interest rate of 10%, with compounding quarterly for five years will be compounded at
_____ percent for _____ periods
a.   2.5 percent; 20 periods
b.   10 percent; 5 periods
c.   3.33 percent; 15 periods
d.   2 percent; 10 periods

_____9. (AC) A truck is purchased with a Note Payable requiring payment of $40,000 at the end of two years.
The journal entry to record the purchase of the truck will include:
a.   a debit to the truck account for $40,000
b.   a debit to Interest expense for $40,000
c.   a credit to Notes Payable for $40,000
d.   none of the above is part of the journal entry to record the purchase of the truck

_____10. (AC) Which of the following tables are used to calculate the issue price of a bond payable?
a.   present value of a single $1
b.   future value of a single $1
c.   present value of a Bond
d.   future value of an annuity

EXERCISES
Record your answer to each exercise in the space provided. Show your work.

Exercise C-1. Computing Growth in a Savings Account: A Single Amount (AC)
On January 1, 2006, you deposited $9,000 in a savings account. The account will earn 12 percent annual compound interest, which will be added to the fund balance at the end of each year.

Required (round to the nearest dollar):
1. What will be the balance in the savings account at the end of 10 years?

2. What is the interest for the 10 years?

Exercise C-2. Computing Deposit Required and Accounting for a Single-Sum Savings Account (AC)
On January 1, 2006, Ben Prince decided to transfer an amount from his checking account into a savings account that later will provide $100,000 to send his daughter to college (five years from now). The savings account will earn 10 percent, which will be added to the fund each year-end.

Required (show computations and round to the nearest dollar):
1. How much must Ben deposit on January 1, 2006?

2. Give the journal entry that Ben should make on January 1, 2006 to record the transfer.

3. What is the interest for the five years?

4. Give the journal entry that Ben should make on (a) December 31, 2006, and (b) December 31, 2007.

Exercise C-3. Recording Growth in a Savings Account with Equal Periodic Payments. (AC)
On each December 31, you plan to transfer $6,000 from your checking account into a savings account. The savings account will earn 6 percent annual interest, which will be added to the savings account balance at each year-end. The first deposit will be made December 31, 2005 (at the end of the period).

Required (show computations and round to the nearest dollar):
1. Give the required journal entry on December 31, 2005.

2. What will be the balance in the savings account at the end of the 10th year (i.e., 10 deposits)?

3. What is the total amount of interest earned on the 10 deposits?

4. How much interest revenue did the fund earn in 2005? 2006?

5. Give all required journal entries at the end of 2005 and 2006.

Exercise C-4. Computing Value of an Asset Based on Present Value. (AC)
You have the chance to purchase an oil well. Your best estimate is that the oil well's net royalty income will average $40,000 per year for seven years. There will be no residual value at that time. Assume that the cash inflow occurs at each year-end and that considering the uncertainty in your estimates, you expect to earn 12 percent per year on the investment. What should you be willing to pay for this investment right now?

Exercise C-5. Computing Present Value of a Bond. (AC)
On January 1, 2007, a company issued a 4-year, $200,000 bond. The bond pays interest annually at a rate of 8% of face value. Calculate the purchase price of the bonds under each of the following circumstances:

(a) 10% Market Rate of Interest:

(b) 8% Market Rate of Interest:

(c) 6% Market Rate of Interest:

SOLUTIONS TO SELF-TEST QUESTIONS AND EXERCISES
MATCHING
1.

A	Annuity	B	Present Value
D	Future Value	C	Time Value of Money

TRUE-FALSE QUESTIONS
1. F – Money received today is worth more than money to be received one year from today.
2. T
3. F – Present and future value problems may involve two types of cash flows, so you need to learn how to deal with four different situations related to the time value of money.
4. T
5. F – The future value of a single amount calculates how much money you will have in the future as a result of investing a certain amount in the present.
6. F – The future value computation is based on compound interest.
7. T
8. T
9. T
10. F – Calculating the present value of a bond requires discounting two separate cash flows: the present value of a single amount and the present value of an annuity.

MULTIPLE CHOICE QUESTIONS
1. C   6. B
2. D   7. B
3. D   8. A
4. A   9. D
5. C   10. A

EXERCISES
Exercise C-1. Computing Growth in a Savings Account: A Single Amount (AC)
1. What will be the balance in the savings account at the end of 10 years?
    $9,000 x 3.1058 = $27,953   Table C.1 Future Value of $1

2. What is the interest for the 10 years?
    $27,952 – $9,000 = $18,952

Exercise C-2. Computing Deposit Required and Accounting for a Single-Sum Savings Account (AC)

1. How much must Ben deposit on January 1, 2006?
    $100,000 x 0.6209 = $62,090   Table C.2 Present Value of $1

2. Give the journal entry that Ben should make on January 1, 2006 to record the transfer.

    dr Savings Account (+A)   62,090
      cr Cash (- A).   62,090

3. What is the interest for the five years?
   $100,000 – $62,090 = $37,910

4. Give the journal entry that Ben should make on (a) December 31, 2006, and (b) December 31, 2007.
December 31, 2006: This can be calculated using the interest formula, $62,090 x 10% = 6,209

    dr Savings Account (+A)   6,209
      cr Interest Revenue (+R, +SE)   6,209

December 31, 2007: ($62,090 + $6,209) x 10% = $6,830

    dr Savings Account (+A)   6,830
      cr Interest Revenue (+R, +SE)   6,830

Exercise C-3. Recording Growth in a Savings Account with Equal Periodic Payments. (AC)
1. Give the required journal entry on December 31, 2005.

    dr Savings Account (+A)   6,000
      cr Cash (- A).   6,000

2. What will be the balance in the savings account at the end of the 10th year (i.e., 10 deposits)?
   $6,000 x 13.1808 = $79,085   Table C.3 Future Value of an Annuity of $1

3. What is the total amount of interest earned on the 10 deposits?
   $79,085 – ($6,000 x 10) = $19,085

4. How much interest revenue did the fund earn in 2005? 2006? 2007?
2005: No interest earned because the payment was made on the last day of the year.
2006: $6,000 x 6% = 360
2007: ($6,360 + $6,000) x 6% = $742

5. Give all required journal entries at the end of 2005, 2006, and 2007.
December 31, 2005

    dr Savings Account (+A)   6,000
      cr Cash (- A).   6,000

December 31, 2006:

    dr Savings Account (+A)   360
      cr Interest Revenue (+R, +SE)   360

    dr Savings Account (+A)   6,000
      cr Cash (- A).   6,000

December 31, 2007:

    dr Savings Account (+A)   742
      cr Interest Revenue (+R, +SE)   742

    dr Savings Account (+A)   6,000
      cr Cash (- A).   6,000

Exercise C-4. Computing Value of an Asset Based on Present Value. (AC)

$40,000 x 4.5638 = $182,552 Table C.4 Present Value of an Annuity of $1

Exercise C-5. Computing Present Value of a Bond. (AC)
 (a) 10% Market Rate of Interest:

Present Value of the $200,000 face value: ($200,000 x .6830 Table C.2) =	$136,600
Present value of the $16,000 annuity: ($16,000 x 3.1699 Table C.4) =	50,718
Present value of the total bond payments at 10% discount rate	$187,318

(b) 8% Market Rate of Interest:

Present Value of the $200,000 face value: ($200,000 x .7350 Table C.2) =	$147,000 (rounded)
Present value of the $16,000 annuity: ($16,000 x 3.3121 Table C.4) =	52,994
Present value of the total bond payments at 10% discount rate	$200,000

(c) 6% Market Rate of Interest:

Present Value of the $200,000 face value: ($200,000 x .7921 Table C.2) =	$158,420
Present value of the $16,000 annuity: ($16,000 x 3.4651 Table C.4) =	55,442
Present value of the total bond payments at 10% discount rate	$213,862

CHAPTER FOCUS SUGGESTIONS

UNDERSTAND THE BUSINESS

Why a Company Invests in Other Corporations

A company can invest in either stock or bonds issued by another corporation. We'll be focusing on stock investments. A company invests in stock issued by other corporations for one of four reasons:

1. *Take Control.* The fastest way to expand into other industries or markets is to take over control of another corporation (usually by purchasing more than 50 percent of its stock.)
2. *Exert Significant Influence.* A company may be happy just obtaining significant influence (rather than control) over the decisions of another corporation. This level of influence is usually obtained by purchasing 20 – 50 percent of the corporation's common stock.
3. *Passively Invest in Securities Available for Sale.* When a company has extra cash lying around it might invest in another corporation's stock in order to receive dividends. No active involvement in decision-making is intended. The purpose of the investment is one of obtaining the dividends so the stock can be sold any time the purchaser is in need of additional cash. These types of investments are called **securities available for sale.**
4. *Profit from Buying and Selling.* Some companies are in the business of buying and selling securities for profit. The intention is to purchase the securities when prices are low and quickly selling them when prices are higher. These types of investments are called **trading securities.**

Investments in other corporation's stock are essentially accounted for on the basis of which of these four reasons the stock was purchased. Since the intention it isn't always obvious when stock is purchased, a set of guidelines has been established to help in making this determination. It is based on the percentage of stock ownership.

STUDY THE ACCOUNTING METHODS

Consolidation Method for Investments Involving Control

When one company can control the decisions of another company (greater than 50% ownership), it is called the **parent company.** The company controlled by the parent company is called the **subsidiary.** When one company controls another company in this manner the parent company must prepare a set of **consolidated financial statements.** In essence, it combines the accounts of the parent company with the accounts of all of its subsidiary companies. Therefore, the process of consolidation *adds together the separate financial statements of two or more companies to make it appear as if only a single company exists.* While subsidiary companies exist as separate legal entities, all financial decisions are made by the parent company and, as such, the success or failure of the subsidiaries is ultimately the responsibility of the parent company. The heading on the financial statements of a parent company that controls other companies contain the word 'consolidated' to inform users of this status.

Equity Method for Investments Involving Significant Influence

When an investor can exert significant influence over a company (an assumption made if 20 – 50 percent of the stock is owned by the investor), the equity method is used to account for the investment. Since less than 51% of the stock is owned, the investor doesn't have control and, therefore, its accounts are not combined with the investor's accounts. Rather, the investment is recorded by the investor in an account called: Investments. Under the equity method, the investment is initially recorded at cost by the investor. Each year following the initial investment, the investor records its share of the investee's net income and its share of the investee's dividend distributions as follows:

- Net income of investee: The investor increases (debits) its investment account for its percentage share of the investee's net income. The credit is made to an account called *Investment Income* and is reported on the income statement under *Other Revenues and Gains,* or *Other Expenses and Losses.* The increase in the investment account is made because it is implied that the investor will receive greater dividends or its investment value will increase in the future.

- Dividends paid by investee: Any dividends paid during the year will increase the Cash of the investor and decrease (credit) the investment account. This may seem odd, but think of it like your savings account, as long as the funds are in the account, the account will increase in value over time. But, as soon as you take some of the cash out, the investment declines. You may have *personally* increased your wealth, but your investment has lost some of its wealth.

Investments (A)	
Beginning balance	
Initial investment (also credit Cash)	
Company's % share of investee's net income (also record credit to Investment Income)	Company's % share of investee's dividends declared for the period (also debit to Cash)
Ending balance	

1. *Purchase of Stock*: Assume you buy 30,000 common shares of ABC Company for $240,000. Since ABC has 100,000 common shares outstanding, you own 30% of the company and are deemed to have significant influence over its operations. You must make the following entry upon purchase of the stock:

    dr Investments (+A) 240,000
        cr Cash (-A). 240,000

Assets		=	Liabilities	+	Stockholders' Equity
Investments	+ 240,000				
Cash	-240,000				

2. *Share of Net Income Earned*: Since you have influence over the earnings of ABC Company, it is assumed you are responsible for some of its 'profits' or 'losses.' It is assumed if you own 30% of the company, you are responsible for 30% of its profits/losses. If AIBC Company reported $365,000 of net income for the year, this entry is made:

    dr Investments (+A) .(30% x $365,000). 109,500
        cr Investment income (+R, +SE) 109,500

Assets		=	Liabilities	+	Stockholders' Equity	
Investments	+109,500				Investment income (+R)	+109,500

Had ABC reported a Net Loss, the debit would be to *Investment Loss* and the credit would be to *Investments*.

3. *Dividends Received*: Dividends received are not recorded as investment income because dividends *reduce the underlying assets of ABC*. This reduces your investment in ABC (even though you receive the dividends.) Assume ABC declared a $2.50 per share dividend, you would make the following entry for the dividends you received:

    dr Cash (+A) . (30,000 x $2.50). 75,000
        cr Investments (-A) 75,000

Assets		=	Liabilities	+	Stockholders' Equity
Cash	+ 75,000				
Investments	- 75,000				

The results are summarized in the following T-accounts:

Investments (A)					Investment Income (R, SE)		
Beg. bal.	0					0	Beg. bal.
Purchase	240,000						
Share of ABC's net income	109,500	75,000	Share of ABC's dividends			109,500	Share of ABC's net income
End. bal.	274,500					109,500	End. bal.

Market Value Methods for Passive Investments

It is very rare to report assets at market value since market could be higher than historical cost (thus violating the cost principle.) But, in some cases, a 'market-to-market' approach is taken.

1. *Why are passive investments reported at fair market value on the balance sheet?* There are two major reasons:

- *Relevance.* Analysts want to know how companies can generate cash for expansion, dividend payments, or survival in tough economic times. The sale of passive investments is one potential source of cash. Market value is the best indicator of the cash that could be obtained from selling these securities.
- *Measurability.* Since securities are actively traded on stock exchanges, determining an accurate, reliable, fair value is easy. Many assets cannot be reported at a reliable value because there is no consistent, reliable method of determining value. This is not the case with actively traded stocks.

2. *When the investment account is adjusted to reflect changes in fair market value, what other account is affect when the asset account is increased or decreased?* When the investment account is adjusted to market value, some other account must also be affected. The account used is called **unrealized holding gains or losses.** These are 'unrealized' because no actual sale has occurred! Simply by holding on to the security, its value has changed. If the value of the securities was $300,000, an unrealized holding gain of $25,500 ($300,000 - $274,500) would be recorded. If the value of the securities was, instead, $250,000, an unrealized holding loss of $24,500 ($274,500 - $250,000) would have been recorded. The appropriate treatment of the holding gains/losses depends on whether the investment is classified as *securities available for sale* or *trading securities*.

Securities Available for Sale

Passive investments purchased with excess funds, with the intent of earning a return until the funds are needed for the company's operating or financing activities are called Securities Available for Sale (SAS).

1. *Purchase of Stock*: When the stock is purchased it is treated like any other investment in stock that does not give the investor control. Assume 20,000 shares of XYZ Company are purchased for $45 per share. Since XYZ Company has 400,000 shares outstanding, you own 5% of the stock (20,000 / 400,000), and is considered a passive investment in securities available for sale (SAS). The entry is recorded at cost:

> *dr* Investment in SAS (+A) 900,000
>   *cr* Cash (-A).   900,000

Assets		=	Liabilities	+	Stockholders' Equity
Investment in SAS	+ 900,000				
Cash	-900,000				

Once the stock is purchased, a return is earned through (1) dividends, and (2) stock price increases.

2. *Dividends Received*: Under the market value method, dividends are considered earnings from the investment and recorded in an account called Investment Income. If XYZ declares $1.85 per share dividend, this entry is made:

> *dr* Cash (+A) . (20,000 x $1.85). 37,000
>   *cr* Investment Income (+R, +SE)   37,000

Assets		=	Liabilities	+	Stockholders' Equity
Cash	+ 37,000				Investment Income - 37,000

3. *Price Increases*: At the end of the accounting period, passive investment are reported on the balance sheet at fair market value. So, if the value of XYZ stock was $40 per share at the end of the accounting period, a $100,000 [20,000 x ($45 - $40)] reduction in value has occurred. The market value method for SAS investments requires that all unrealized holding gains or losses should *not* be reported in the investor's net income. Since the investor intends to hold SAS investments into the future, there is a strong possibility that the value of the stock will change again before the stock is actually sold. So, rather than report any unrealized gain or loss in net income, it is recorded in a stockholders' equity account called *Unrealized gains and losses in*

equity. When securities are actually sold, those gains/losses would be included in determining net income on the income statement.

To summarize, the reporting of SAS investments at market value requires adjusting it to market value at the end of each accounting period using the account *Allowance to value SAS at Market* and a corresponding entry to *Unrealized gains and losses in equity.* A debit balance in the 'Allowance' account is added to the Investment in SAS account while a credit balance in the 'Allowance' account is subtracted from the Investment in SAS account. Similarly, if the *Unrealized gains and losses in equity* account has a credit balance, it increases stockholders' equity and if it has a debit balance it decreases stockholders' equity.

In referring back to the decrease in value of the stock by $100,000, the following entry would be made at year-end:

       dr Unrealized gains and losses in equity (-SE) 100,000
          cr Allowance to value at market—SAS (-A)   100,000

Assets		=	Liabilities	+	Stockholders' Equity	
Allowance to value					Unrealized gains and	
SAS at market	-100,000				losses in equity	-100,000

The balance in the allowance account is subtracted from the Investment in SAS account on the balance sheet. If management intends to sell these investments within a year, they would be classified as current assets. The unrealized account is reported in the stockholders' equity section of the balance sheet as a negative amount.

4. Sale of Stock

Three accounts on the balance sheet may be affected when SAS investments are sold:
(1) Investment in SAS, (2) Allowance to Value SAS at Market, (3) Unrealized Gains and Losses in Equity. Assume that you sold the XYZ stock when the price was still $40 per share. Two journal entries are required for the sale:

    (1) *dr* Cash (+A) 800,000
         dr Loss on Investment (-E, -SE) 100,000
            cr Investment in SAS (-A)   900,000
    (2) *dr* Allowance to value SAS at market (+A) 100,000
         cr Unrealized gains and losses in equity (+SE)   100,000

Assets		=	Liabilities	+	Stockholders' Equity	
(1) Cash	+800,000				Investment Loss (+E)	-100,000
Investment in SAS	- 900,000					
(2) Allowance to value					Unrealized gains and	
SAS at market	+100,000				losses in equity	+100,000

Trading Securities

Trading securities are considered passive investments because the investor does not acquire enough of the stock to significantly influence the operating or financing decision of the investee. Also, investments in trading securities are reported on the balance sheet at market value. Trading securities can earn a return from both dividends and stock price increases. In these respects, trading securities are very similar to securities available for sale. But, they differ in that trading securities are purchased with the primary purpose of the value of the stock increasing until it is sold. Since the increase in value is a primary motive, any increase or decrease in stock price is *reported as income by the investor regardless of whether they are realized unrealized at year end.* So, rather than place them in stockholders' equity, they are reported on the income statement. If the XYZ stock were considered a trading security rather than a security available for sale, the entry made at year-end would be:

       dr Loss on Investment in TS (+A)   100,000
          cr Allowance to value TS at market (+E, -SE) 100,000

Assets		=	Liabilities	+	Stockholders' Equity	
Allowance to value					Investment income (+E)	-100,000
TS at market	-100,000					

Demonstration Case A – Equity Method for Significant Influence Investments

On January 1, 2006, Clearwater Company purchased 45 percent of the outstanding voting shares of Lockness Company on the open market for $95,000 cash. Lockness declared $12,000 in cash dividends and reported net income of $80,000 for the year.

Required:
1. Prepare the journal entries for 2006.
2. What accounts and amounts were reported on Clearwater's balance sheet at the end of 2006? On Clearwater's income statement for 2006?

Suggested Solution for Case A

1. Jan. 1   *dr* Investments (+A) 95,000
            cr Cash (-A)   95,000

    Dec. 31   *dr* Cash (+A) (45% x $12,000) 5,400
                 cr Investments (+A)   5,400

    Dec. 31   *dr* Investments (+A) (45% x $80,000) .36,000
                 cr Investment income (+R, +SE)   36,000

2.

On the Balance Sheet		On the Income Statement	
Noncurrent Assets:		*Other Items:*	
Investments	$125,600	Investment income	$36,000
($95,000 - $5,400 + $36,000)			

Demonstration Case B – Market Value Method for Securities Available for Sale

Thurston Equipment Corporation sells and services a major line of bowling equipment. Both sales and service operations have been profitable. The following transactions affected the company during 2006:

a.   Jan. 1 Purchased 4,000 shares of common stock of Yak Company at $30 per share. This purchase represented 1 percent of the shares outstanding. Based on management's intent, the Yak Company shares are considered securities available for sale.
b. Dec. 28 Received $8,000 cash dividend on the Yak Company stock.
c. Dec. 31 Determined that the current market price of the Elk stock was $31.

Required:
1. Prepare the journal entry for each of these transactions.
2. What accounts and amounts will be reported on the balance sheet at the end of 2006? On the income statement for 2006?

Suggested Solution for Case B

1. *a.* Jan. 1   *dr* Investment in SAS (+A) 120,000
                cr Cash (-A) (4,000 shares x $30 per share)   120,000

  b. Dec.28 *dr* Cash (+A) 8,000
                cr Investment income (+R, +SE).   8,000

  c. Dec.31 *dr* Allowance to value SAS at market (+A). 4,000
                cr. Unrealized gains and losses in equity (+SE).   4,000

Year	Market Value	-	Cost	= Balance Needed in Valuation Allowance	-	Unadjusted Balance in Valuation Allowance	=	Adjustment to Valuation Allowance
2006	$124,000 ($31 x 4,000 shares)	-	$120,000 =	$4,000	-	$0	=	$4,000 an unrealized gain for the period

2. **On the Balance Sheet**   **On the Income Statement**

Current or Noncurrent Assets: *Other Items:*

Investment in SAS $124,000 Investment income $8,000
 ($120,000 cost + $4,000 allowance)

Stockholders' Equity:

Unrealized gains and losses in equity 4,000

Demonstration Case C – Market Value Method for Trading Securities

Assume the same facts as in Case C, except that the securities were purchased for the purpose of active trading.

Required:

1. Prepare the journal entry for each of these transactions.
2. What accounts and amounts will be reported on the balance sheet at the end of 2006? On the income statement for 2006?

Suggested Solution for Case C

1. *a.* Jan. 1 *dr* Investment in TS (+A) 120,000
     cr Cash (-A) (4,000 shares x $30)   120,000

 b. Dec. 28 *dr* Cash (+A) 8,000
     cr Investment income (+R, +SE).   8,000

 c. Dec. 31 *dr* Allowance to value TS at market (+A). 4,000
     cr Investment income (+R, +SE)   4,000

Year	Market Value	-	Cost	= Balance Needed in Valuation Allowance	-	Unadjusted Balance in Valuation Allowance	=	Adjustment to Valuation Allowance
2006	$124,000 ($31 x 4000 shares)	-	$120,000 =	$4,000	-	$0	=	$4,000 an unrealized gain for the period

2. **On the Balance Sheet**   **On the Income Statement**

Current Assets: *Other Nonoperating Items:*

Investment in TS $124,000 Investment income $12.000
 ($120,000 cost + $4,000 allowance) ($8,000 dividend + $4,000 unrealized gain)

READ AND RECALL QUESTIONS

After you read each section of the chapter, answer the related Read and Recall Questions below.

WHY DOES A COMPANY INVEST IN OTHER CORPORATIONS?
List and briefly define the four reasons a company might invest in the stock issued by other corporations.

Define the following (1) Securities Available for Sale, and (2) Trading Securities.

Consolidation Method for Investments Involving Control
What percentage of ownership is required in order for the investor to use the consolidation method? Define a parent company. Define a subsidiary company.

What are consolidated financial statements? Explain how subsidiary accounts are reported on consolidated financial statements.

Equity Method for Investments Involving Significant Influence
What percentage of ownership is required in order for the investor to use the equity method? How are transactions involving the investee recorded?

How is the net income of the investee treated by the investor? How are the dividends paid by the investee treated by the investor?

What value is used to record the initial purchase of the stock of an investee under the equity method? Why?

What accounts of the investor are affected by the investee's reported net income? How is the amount determined?

What accounts of the investor are affected by the receipt of dividends from the investee? Why?

Are market fluctuations of the investee's stock reported by the investor? Why or why not?

Securities Available for Sale

Define *securities available for sale*.   How are returns earned on these securities? How are dividends received from the investee treated?

How are market increases and decreases treated on the balance sheet? Does this conflict with any conceptual framework principles? If so, which one(s).

How are unrealized gains and losses reported on the balance sheet under the market value method for SAS investments? Why?

When SAS investment are sold, list three accounts that may be affected by the sale. How many entries are required to record the sale? Why?

Trading Securities

Define trading securities. How do they differ from Securities available for sale? Why is this important?

How does the recording of the purchase of stock and the receipt of dividends for trading investments compare to the same transactions for securities available for sale? How are unrealized gains/losses treated on the balance sheet?

FINDING FINANCIAL INFORMATION

1. Determining the appropriate accounting method based on stock ownership percentage:

Level of Involvement in Decision-Making (Percent of Ownership)	Reason for the Investment		Method of Accounting	How it works
Control (more than 50%)	• take over the company	→	Consolidation	Combine the financial statements of parent and subsidiaries
Significant Influence (20 – 50%)	• influence the company	→	Equity	Record investment at cost, add % share of net income, deduct % share of dividends
Passive (less than 20%)	• invest excess cash to earn greater return	→	Market Value for Securities Available for Sale	Report dividends and realized gains/losses investment income o the income statement report unrealized gains/losses in stockholders' equity
Passive (less than 20%)	• securities trading	→	Market Value for Trading Securities	Report dividends and all gains/losses (either realized or unrealized as investment income on the income statement

SELF-TEST QUESTIONS AND EXERCISES

MATCHING
1. *Match each of the key terms listed below with the appropriate textbook definition.*

_____ Consolidated Financial Statements   _____ Securities available for sale

_____ Equity Method   _____ Subsidiary company

_____ Market Value Method   _____ Trading securities

_____ Parent Company   _____ Unrealized holding gains and losses

A. Financial statements that combine information from both the controlled company and the company under its control to create a single set of financial statements
B. Method used for passive investments in the common stock of another company
C. The entity that controls another company .
D. Method used when investor has significant influence over the investee, but not control
E. Purchased with excess funds, with the intent of earning a return until the funds are needed for the company's operating or financing activities
F. Amounts associated with price changes of securities that are currently held
G. An entity under the control of another company
H. Purchased with the intent of selling them in the near future at a profit

TRUE-FALSE QUESTIONS
For each of the following, enter a T or F in the blank to indicate whether the statement is true or false.

_____1. (AD) Passive investments in securities are accounted for using the equity method.

_____2. (AD) A company trying to earn profits by buying securities at one price and selling them in the near future at a higher price are called securities available for sale.

_____3. (AD) When one company owns 50% of another company, it has control over that company.

_____4. (AD) Both Securities available for sale and Trading securities are accounted for with a version of the market value method.

_____5. (AD) The subsidiary company prepares a set of consolidated financial statements that combines its accounts with the accounts of the parent company.

_____6. (AD) Significant influence over a company is presumed if the investor owns between 20 and 50 percent of the investee's outstanding, voting, common stock.

_____7. (AD) The investor records a reduction in its investment account when it receives dividends from the investee under the equity method.

_____8. (AD) Passive investments are reported at fair market value on the balance sheet for the following primary reasons: relevance and measurability.

_____9. (AD) When the investment account is adjusted to reflect changes in fair market value, the unrealized holding gains or losses account is also affected.

_____10. (AD) At the end of the accounting period, passive investments are reported on the balance sheet at historical cost.

Choose the best answer or response by placing the identifying letter in the space provided.

_____1.   (AD) Which of the following is *not* a reason a company might invest in stock issued by other corporations?
a.   exert passive influence
b.   profit from buying and selling
c.   take control
d.   passively invest in securities available for sale

_____2.   (AD) Which method of accounting is used when the investor controls the investee?
a.   equity
b.   market value
c.   consolidation
d.   none of these methods are used when the investor controls the investee

_____3.   (AD) When consolidated financial statements are prepared, which company(ies) is (are) considered separate legal entities?
a.   the Parent.
b.   the Subsidiary
c.   none of the above are considered separate legal entities
d.   all of the above are considered separate legal entities

_____4.   (AD) Significant influence is presumed for what level of ownership?
a.   less than 20% and greater than 50%
b.   between 20% and 50%
c.   greater than 50%
d.   less than 20%

_____5.   (AD) Under the equity method, which of the following events are recorded in the investment account?
a.   company's percentage share of investee's dividends declared for the period
b.   initial investment
c.   company's percentage share of investee's net income
d.   all of the above are recorded in the investment account under the equity method

_____6.   (AD) If an investor owns 45% of an investee and the investee earns $120,000 and the investor receives $20,000 in dividends from the investee, how much should the investor report as investment income and reduction of the investment account, respectively?
a. $54,000 of investment income and a $9,000 reduction in the investment account
b. $54,000 of investment income and a $20,000 reduction in the investment account
c. $120,000 of investment income and a $9,000 reduction in the investment account
d. $120,000 of investment income and a $20,000 reduction in the investment account

_____7.   (AD) What are two primary reasons passive investments are reported at fair market value?
a.   relevance and reliability
b.   reliability and measurability
c.   relevance and measurability
d.   relevance and Historic cost

_____8.   (AD) When the investment account is adjusted to reflect changes in fair market value, what other account is affect when the asset account is increased or decreased?
a.   realized gains and losses
b.   cash
c.   investment income
d.   unrealized holding gains or losses

_____9. (AD) All of the following are similarities between trading securities and securities available for sale except:
   a. both are purchased with the intent to earn profits primarily from the 'buy low, sell high' philosophy
   b. both are considered passive investments
   c. both can earn a return from two sources: dividends and price increases
   d. both are reported on the balance sheet at market value

_____10. (AD) How are unrealized gains and losses in equity reported on the balance sheet for securities available for sale?
   a. they are added to or subtracted from stockholders' equity
   b. they are added to or subtracted from investment income
   c. they are added to or subtracted on the income statement as Other Revenues and Gains or Other Expenses and Losses
   d. none of the above is the proper treatment for unrealized gains and losses in equity

EXERCISES

Record your answer to each exercise in the space provided. Show your work.

Exercise D-1. Recording and Reporting Equity Method Securities Transactions (AD)

Alicia Company acquired 33,000 of the 110,000 shares of outstanding common stock of Santistevan Corporation during 2005 as a long-term investment. The annual accounting period for both companies ends December 31. The following transactions occurred during 2004:

Jan	15	Purchased 33,000 shares of Santistevan common stock at $23 per share.
Dec	31	Santistevan Corporation reported net income of $87,000.
Dec	31	Santistevan Corporation declared and paid a cash dividend of $1.02 per share.
Dec	31	Determine the market price of Santistevan stock to be $20 per share

Required:
1. What account method should Alicia Company use?

2. Give the journal entries for each of these transactions for Alicia Company. If no entry is required, explain why.

Jan 15	dr			
	cr			
Dec 31	dr			
	cr			
Dec 31	dr			
	cr			
Dec 31	dr			
	cr			

3. Show how the long-term investment and the related revenue should be reported on the 2005 financial statements of Alicia Company.

Exercise D-2. Recording and Reporting Trading Securities Transactions. (AD)
During 2005 Yaller Company acquired some of the 100,000 outstanding shares of the common stock of Croix Corporation as trading securities. The accounting period for both companies ends December 31.

Jan	4	Purchased 10,000 shares of Croix common stock at $14 per share.
Dec	18	Croix Corporation declared and paid a cash dividend of $2 per share.
Dec	31	Croix Corporation reported net income of $120,000.
Dec	31	Determine the market price of Croix stock to be $15 per share

Required:
1. What accounting method should Yaller Company use?

2. Give the journal entries for each of these transactions for Yaller Company. If no entry is required, explain why.

Jan 4	dr			
	cr			
Dec 18	dr			
	cr			
Dec 31	dr			
	cr			
Dec 31	dr			
	cr			

3. Show how the long-term investment and the related revenue should be reported on the 2005 financial statements of Yaller Company.

Year	Market Value	-	Cost	= Balance Needed in Valuation Allowance	-	Unadjusted Balance in Valuation Allowance	=	Adjustment to Valuation Allowance
2005								

Exercise D-3. Recording and Reporting Securities Available for Sale Transactions. (AD)
Using the data in Exercise D-2, assume that Yaller Company purchased the voting stock of Croix Corporation for its portfolio of securities available for sale instead of its trading securities portfolio.

Required:
1. What accounting method should Yaller Company use?

2. Give the journal entries for each of these transactions for Yaller Company. If no entry is required, explain why.

Jan 4	dr			
	cr			
Dec 18	dr			
	cr			
Dec 31	dr			
	cr			
Dec 31	dr			
	cr			

3. Show how the long-term investment and the related revenue should be reported on the 2005 financial statements of Yaller Company.

Year	Market Value	-	Cost	Balance Needed in = Valuation Allowance	-	Unadjusted Balance in Valuation Allowance	=	Adjustment to Valuation Allowance
2005								

SOLUTIONS TO SELF-TEST QUESTIONS AND EXERCISES

MATCHING
1.

A	Consolidated Financial Statements		E	Securities available for sale
D	Equity Method		G	Subsidiary company
B	Market Value Method		H	Trading securities
C	Parent Company		F	Unrealized holding gains and losses

TRUE-FALSE QUESTIONS
1. F – Passive investments in securities are accounted for using the market value method.
2. F – A company trying to earn profits by buying securities at one price and selling them in the near future at a higher price are called trading securities.
3. F – it must own more than 50% of a company in order to control it.
4. T – Though treatment of unrealized gains and losses is different, both use the market value method for reporting the investment account at market value.
5. F – The parent company prepares the consolidated financial statements.
6. T
7. T
8. T
9. T
10. F – At the end of the accounting period, passive investments are reported on the balance sheet at fair market value.

MULTIPLE CHOICE QUESTIONS
1. A   6. B
2. C   7. C
3. D   8. D
4. B   9. A
5. D   10. A

EXERCISES

Exercise D-1. Recording and Reporting Equity Method Securities Transactions (AD)

1. What accounting method should Alicia Company use?

Alicia Company should use the equity method because they are deemed to have significant influence over Santistevan Company since they own 30% (33,000 / 110,000) of the outstanding stock of the company.

2. Give the journal entries for each of these transactions. If no entry is required, explain why.

Jan 15	dr		Investments (+A) (33,000 x $23)	759,000	
	cr		Cash (– A)		759,000
Dec 31	dr		Investments (+A) ($87,000 x 30%)	26,100	
	cr		Investment Income(+R, +SE)		26,100
Dec 31	dr		Cash (+A) (33,000 x $1.02)	33,660	
	cr		Investments (– A)		33,660
Dec 31	dr		No entry is made because the equity method		
	cr		doesn't report the investment account at market value		

3. Show how the long-term investment and the related revenue should be reported on the 2005 financial statements of Alicia Company.

On the Balance Sheet		On the Income Statement	
Noncurrent Assets:		*Other Items:*	
Investments	$751,440	Investment income	$26,100
($759,000 - $33,660 + $26,100)			

Exercise D-2. Recording and Reporting Trading Securities Transactions. (AD)

1. What accounting method should Yaller Company use?
   Yaller Company should use the Market Value Method for Trading Securities because it owns less than 20% of Croix Corporation Stock (10,000 / 400,000 = 10%.)

2. Give the journal entries for each of these transactions for Yaller Company. If no entry is required, explain why.

Jan 4	dr		Investment in TS (+A)	140,000	
	cr		Cash (– A) (10,000 x $14)		140,000
Dec 18	dr		Cash (+A) (10,000 x $2)	20,000	
	cr		Investment Income (+R, +SE)		20,000
Dec 31	dr		No entry is made under this method for the investor's portion		
	cr		of the investee's net income because no significant influence exists		
Dec 31	dr		Allowance to value TS at market (+A) ($15 - $14) x 10,000	10,000	
	cr		Investment Income (+R, +SE)		10,000

Study Guide, Appendix D

3. Show how the long-term investment and the related revenue should be reported on the 2005 financial statements of Yaller Company.

Year	Market Value	-	Cost	=	Balance Needed in Valuation Allowance	-	Unadjusted Balance in Valuation Allowance	=	Adjustment to Valuation Allowance
2004	$150,000 ($15 x 10,000 shares)	-	$140,000	=	$10,000	-	$0	=	$10,000 an unrealized gain for the period

On the Balance Sheet
Current or Noncurrent Assets:
Investment in SAS $150,000
   ($140,000 cost + $10,000 allowance)

On the Income Statement
Other Items:
Investment income $30,000
   ($20,000 dividend + $10,000 unrealized gain)

Exercise D-3. Recording and Reporting Securities Available for Sale Transactions. (AD)
1. What accounting method should Yaller Company use?
   In this situation, Yaller Company should use the Market Value Method for Securities Available for Sale.

2. Give the journal entries for each of these transactions for Yaller Company. If no entry is required, explain why.

Jan 4	dr		Investment in SAS (+A)	140,000	
		cr	Cash (–A) (10,000 x $14)		140,000
Dec 18	dr		Cash (+A)	20,000	
		cr	Investment Income (+R, +SE)		20,000
Dec 31	dr		No entry is made under this method for the investor's portion		
		cr	of the investee's net income because no significant influence		
			exists		
Dec 31	dr		Allowance to value SAS at market (+A) ($15 - $14 x 10,000)	10,000	
		cr	Unrealized gains and losses in equity (+SE)		10,000

3. Show how the long-term investment and the related revenue should be reported on the 2005 financial statements of Yaller Company.

Year	Market Value	-	Cost	=	Balance Needed in Valuation Allowance	-	Unadjusted Balance in Valuation Allowance	=	Adjustment to Valuation Allowance
2004	$150,000 ($15 x 10,000 shares)	-	$140,000	=	$10,000	-	$0	=	$10,000 an unrealized gain for the period

2. On the Balance Sheet
Current Assets:
Investment in SAS $150,000
   ($140,000 cost + $10,000 allowance)
Stockholders' Equity:
Unrealized gains and losses in equity   10,000

On the Income Statement
Other Nonoperating Items:
Investment income $20,000
   ($20,000 dividend)